C000259182

STREET ATLAS
Bedfordshire
and Luton

First published in 2000 by

Philip's, a division of
Octopus Publishing Group Ltd
2–4 Heron Quays, London E14 4JP

Second edition 2003
First impression 2003

ISBN 0-540-08292-9 (spiral)

© Philip's 2003

Ordnance Survey

This product includes mapping data licensed
from Ordnance Survey® with the permission of
the Controller of Her Majesty's Stationery Office.
© Crown copyright 2003. All rights reserved.
Licence number 100011710.

Printed and bound in Spain
by Cayfosa-Quebecor

Contents

III   **Key to map symbols**

IV   **Key to map pages**

VI   **Route planning**

VIII   **Administrative and Postcode boundaries**

1   **Street maps** at 3½ inches to 1 mile

133   **Index** of towns and villages

134   **Index** of streets, hospitals, industrial estates, railway
stations, schools, shopping centres and universities
and places of interest

Digital Data

The exceptionally high-quality mapping found in this atlas is available as digital data in TIFF format,
which is easily convertible to other bitmapped (raster) image formats.

The index is also available in digital form as a standard database table. It contains all the details
found in the printed index together with the National Grid reference for the map square in which
each entry is named.

For further information and to discuss your requirements, please contact Philip's on
020 7644 6932 or james.mann@philips-maps.co.uk

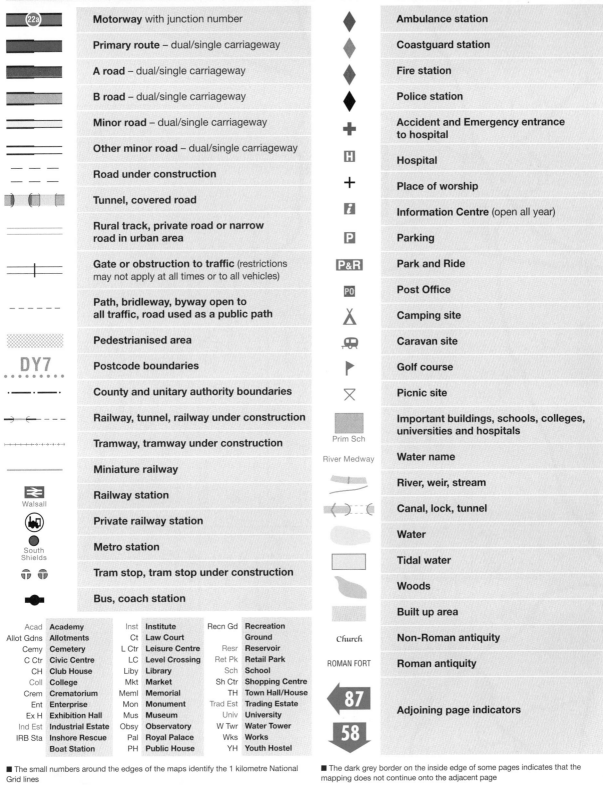

Symbol	Description
(22a)	**Motorway** with junction number
	Primary route – dual/single carriageway
	A road – dual/single carriageway
	B road – dual/single carriageway
	Minor road – dual/single carriageway
	Other minor road – dual/single carriageway
	Road under construction
	Tunnel, covered road
	Rural track, private road or narrow road in urban area
	Gate or obstruction to traffic (restrictions may not apply at all times or to all vehicles)
	Path, bridleway, byway open to all traffic, road used as a public path
	Pedestrianised area
DY7	**Postcode boundaries**
	County and unitary authority boundaries
	Railway, tunnel, railway under construction
	Tramway, tramway under construction
	Miniature railway
Walsall	**Railway station**
	Private railway station
South Shields	**Metro station**
	Tram stop, tram stop under construction
	Bus, coach station

Symbol	Description
◆	**Ambulance station**
◆	**Coastguard station**
◆	**Fire station**
◆	**Police station**
✚	**Accident and Emergency entrance to hospital**
H	**Hospital**
+	**Place of worship**
i	**Information Centre** (open all year)
P	**Parking**
P&R	**Park and Ride**
PO	**Post Office**
⋏	**Camping site**
	Caravan site
▶	**Golf course**
✕	**Picnic site**
Prim Sch	**Important buildings, schools, colleges, universities and hospitals**
River Medway	**Water name**
	River, weir, stream
	Canal, lock, tunnel
	Water
	Tidal water
	Woods
	Built up area
Church	**Non-Roman antiquity**
ROMAN FORT	**Roman antiquity**
87 / 58	**Adjoining page indicators**

Acad	Academy	Inst	Institute	Recn Gd	Recreation Ground
Allot Gdns	Allotments	Ct	Law Court		
Cemy	Cemetery	L Ctr	Leisure Centre	Resr	Reservoir
C Ctr	Civic Centre	LC	Level Crossing	Ret Pk	Retail Park
CH	Club House	Liby	Library	Sch	School
Coll	College	Mkt	Market	Sh Ctr	Shopping Centre
Crem	Crematorium	Meml	Memorial	TH	Town Hall/House
Ent	Enterprise	Mon	Monument	Trad Est	Trading Estate
Ex H	Exhibition Hall	Mus	Museum	Univ	University
Ind Est	Industrial Estate	Obsy	Observatory	W Twr	Water Tower
IRB Sta	Inshore Rescue Boat Station	Pal	Royal Palace	Wks	Works
		PH	Public House	YH	Youth Hostel

■ The small numbers around the edges of the maps identify the 1 kilometre National Grid lines

■ The dark grey border on the inside edge of some pages indicates that the mapping does not continue onto the adjacent page

The scale of the maps on the pages numbered in blue is 5.52 cm to 1 km • 3½ inches to 1 mile • 1: 18103

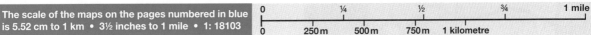

| 0 | ¼ | ½ | ¾ | 1 mile |
| 0 | 250m | 500m | 750m | 1 kilometre |

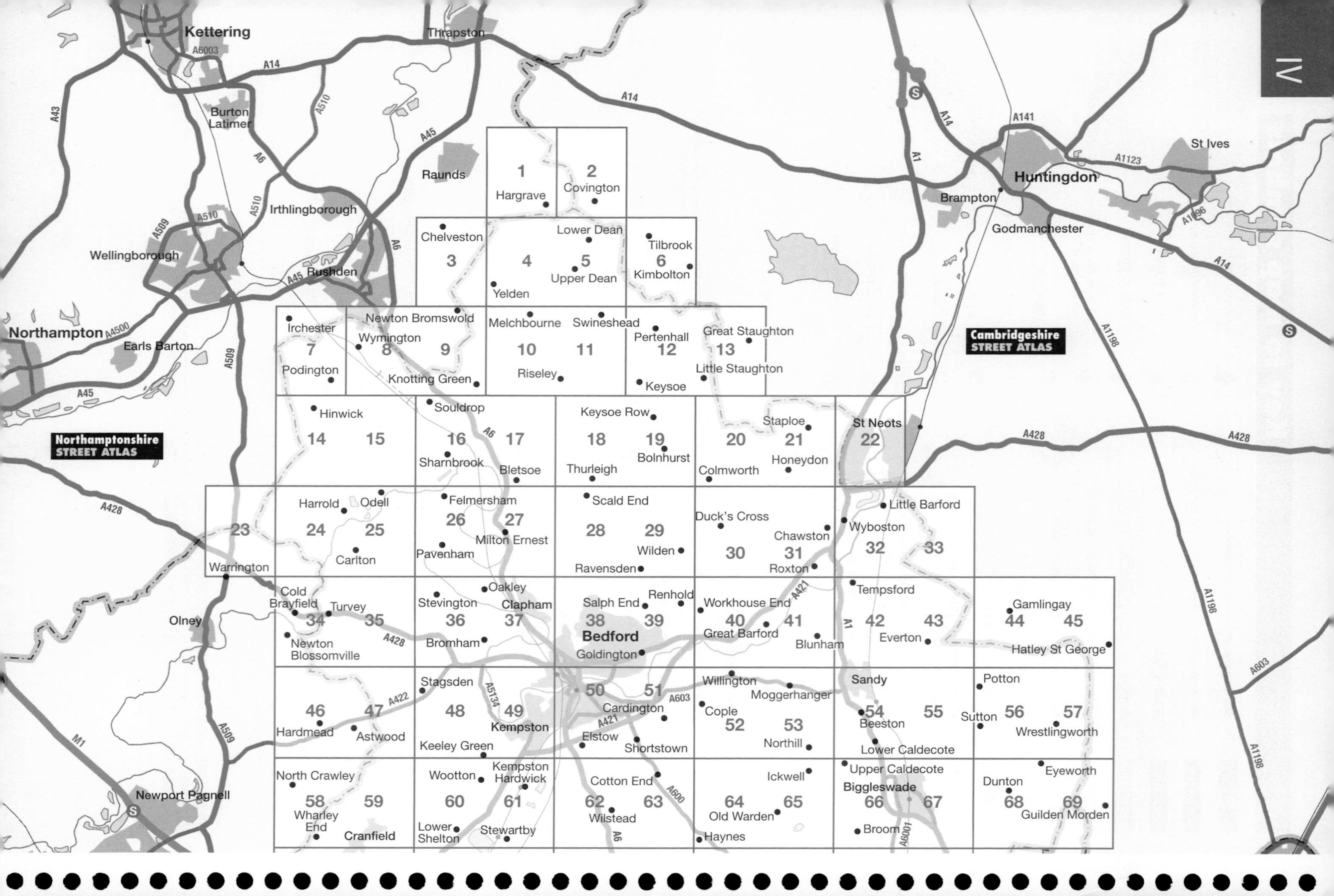
Kettering
Thrapston
Burton Latimer
Raunds
Irthlingborough
Wellingborough
Rushden
Northampton
Earls Barton
Northamptonshire STREET ATLAS
Cambridgeshire STREET ATLAS
Huntingdon
St Ives
Brampton
Godmanchester
St Neots
Olney
Newport Pagnell
Bedford
Kempston
Sandy
Biggleswade
1 Hargrave
2 Covington
3 Chelveston
4 Yelden
5 Lower Dean
Upper Dean
6 Tilbrook
Kimbolton
7 Irchester
Podington
8 Wymington
9 Newton Bromswold
Knotting Green
10 Melchbourne
Riseley
11 Swineshead
12 Pertenhall
Keysoe
13 Great Staughton
Little Staughton
14 Hinwick
15
16 Souldrop
Sharnbrook
17 Bletsoe
18 Keysoe Row
Thurleigh
19 Bolnhurst
20 Colmworth
21 Staploe
Honeydon
22
23 Warrington
24 Harrold
25 Odell
Carlton
26 Felmersham
Pavenham
27 Milton Ernest
28 Scald End
Ravensden
29 Wilden
30 Duck's Cross
31 Chawston
Roxton
32 Little Barford
Wyboston
33
34 Cold Brayfield
Turvey
Newton Blossomville
35
36 Stevington
Bromham
37 Oakley
Clapham
38 Salph End
Goldington
39 Renhold
40 Workhouse End
Great Barford
41 Blunham
42 Tempsford
43 Everton
44 Gamlingay
45 Hatley St George
46 Hardmead
47 Astwood
48 Stagsden
Keeley Green
49
50 Elstow
51 Cardington
Shortstown
52 Willington
Cople
53 Moggerhanger
Northill
54 Beeston
Lower Caldecote
55
56 Potton
Sutton
57 Wrestlingworth
58 North Crawley
Wharley End
59 Cranfield
60 Wootton
Lower Shelton
61 Kempston Hardwick
Stewartby
62 Cotton End
Wilstead
63
64 Old Warden
Haynes
65 Ickwell
66 Upper Caldecote
Broom
67
68 Dunton
69 Eyeworth
Guilden Morden
A14
A6003
A43
A510
A6
A45
A509
A4500
A428
M1
A422
A5134
A421
A603
A600
A1
A6001
A141
A1123
A1096
A1198

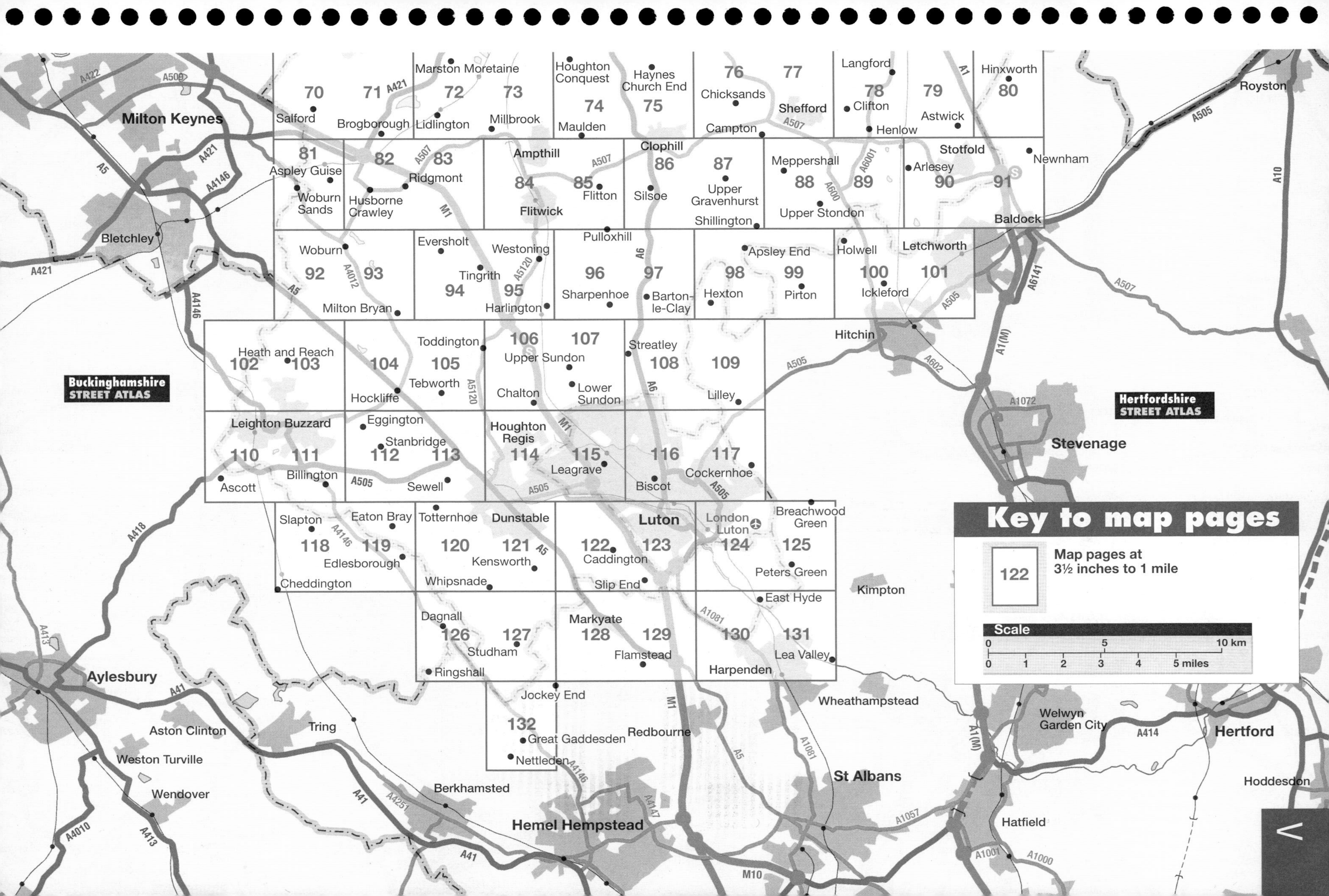

Key to map pages

Map pages at
3½ inches to 1 mile

122

Scale

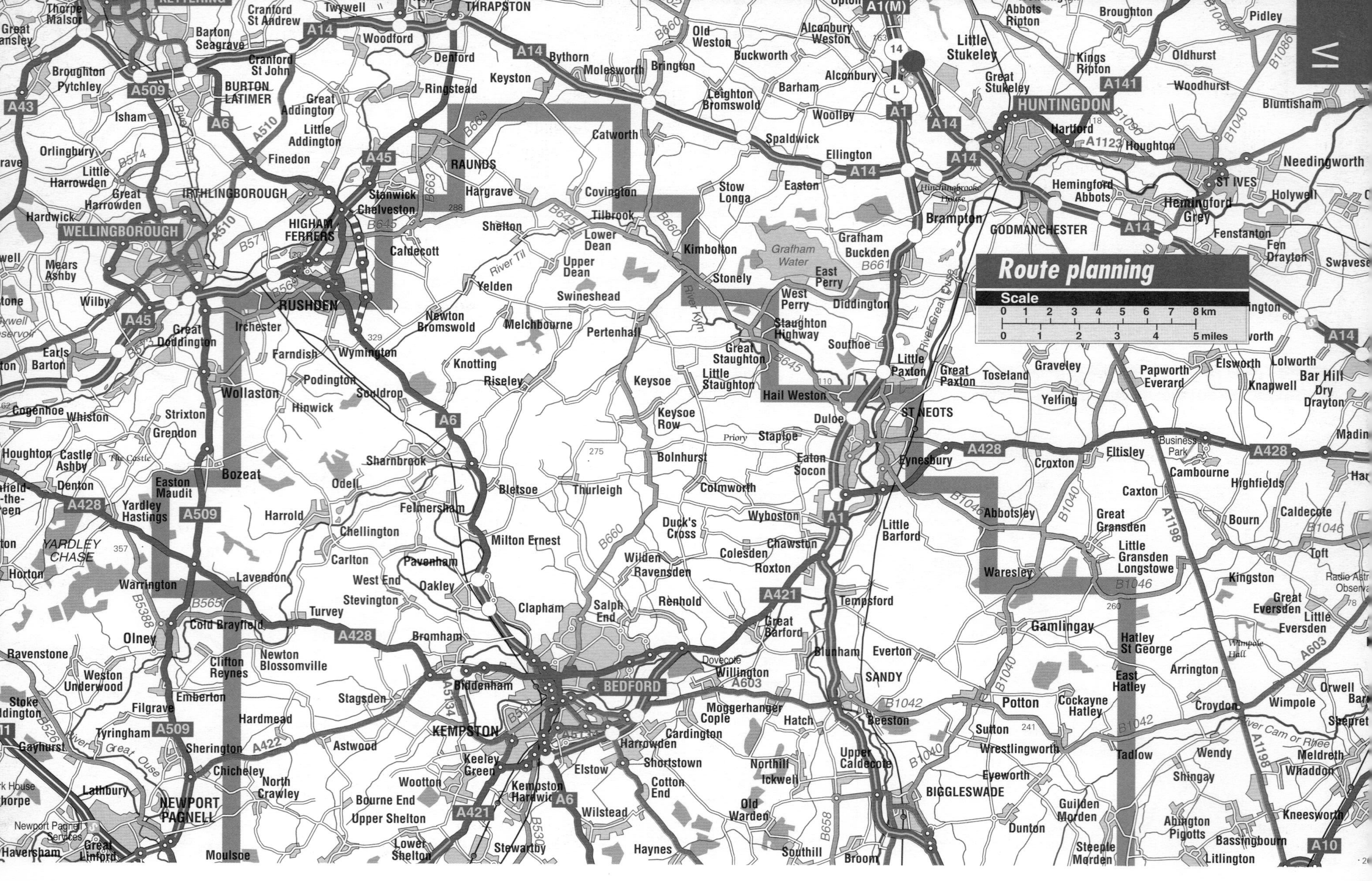
Route planning
Scale
0 1 2 3 4 5 6 7 8 km
0 1 2 3 4 5 miles
KETTERING
THRAPSTON
HUNTINGDON
GODMANCHESTER
ST IVES
ST NEOTS
SANDY
BIGGLESWADE
BEDFORD
KEMPSTON
RUSHDEN
HIGHAM FERRERS
IRTHLINGBOROUGH
WELLINGBOROUGH
BURTON LATIMER
RAUNDS
NEWPORT PAGNELL
Olney
Grafham Water
YARDLEY CHASE
River Great Ouse
River Kym
River Til
A1(M)
A1
A14
A6
A45
A421
A428
A509
A603
A1198
A141
A422
A43
A10

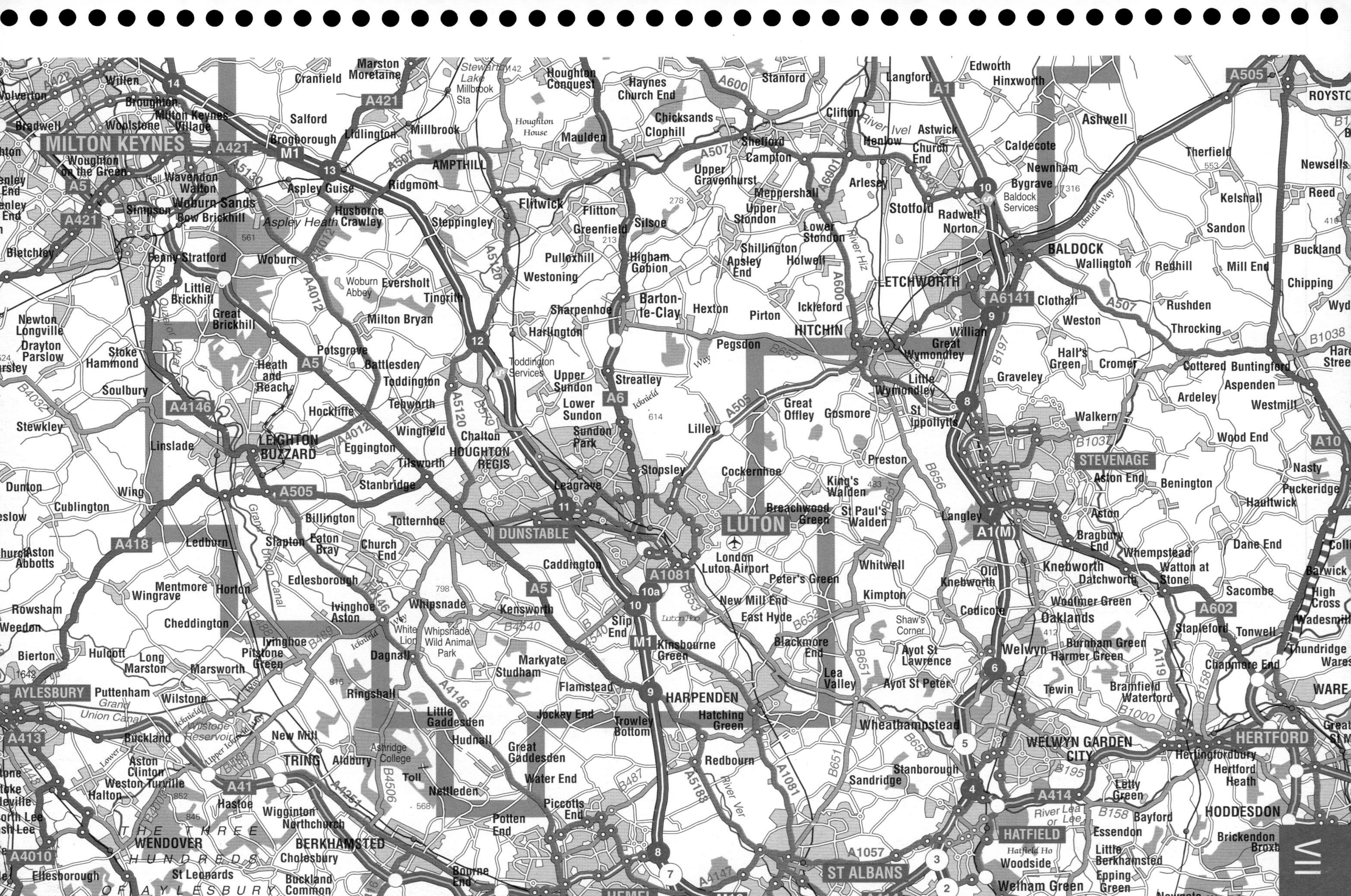

VII
MILTON KEYNES
LEIGHTON BUZZARD
DUNSTABLE
HOUGHTON REGIS
LUTON
London Luton Airport
HARPENDEN
ST ALBANS
HATFIELD
WELWYN GARDEN CITY
HERTFORD
HODDESDON
WARE
STEVENAGE
HITCHIN
LETCHWORTH
BALDOCK
AMPTHILL
AYLESBURY
TRING
BERKHAMSTED
WENDOVER
Woburn
Woburn Abbey
Flitwick
Shefford
Arlesey
Stotfold
Knebworth
Welwyn
Wheathampstead
Redbourn
Markyate
Caddington
Toddington
Ivinghoe
Whipsnade
Whipsnade Wild Animal Park
Ashridge College
Grand Union Canal
River Ivel
River Hiz
River Ver
River Lea or Lee
A1(M)
M1
M10
A5
A6
A505
A507
A600
A602
A414
A418
A421
A4146
A41
A5120
A1081
THE THREE HUNDREDS OF AYLESBURY

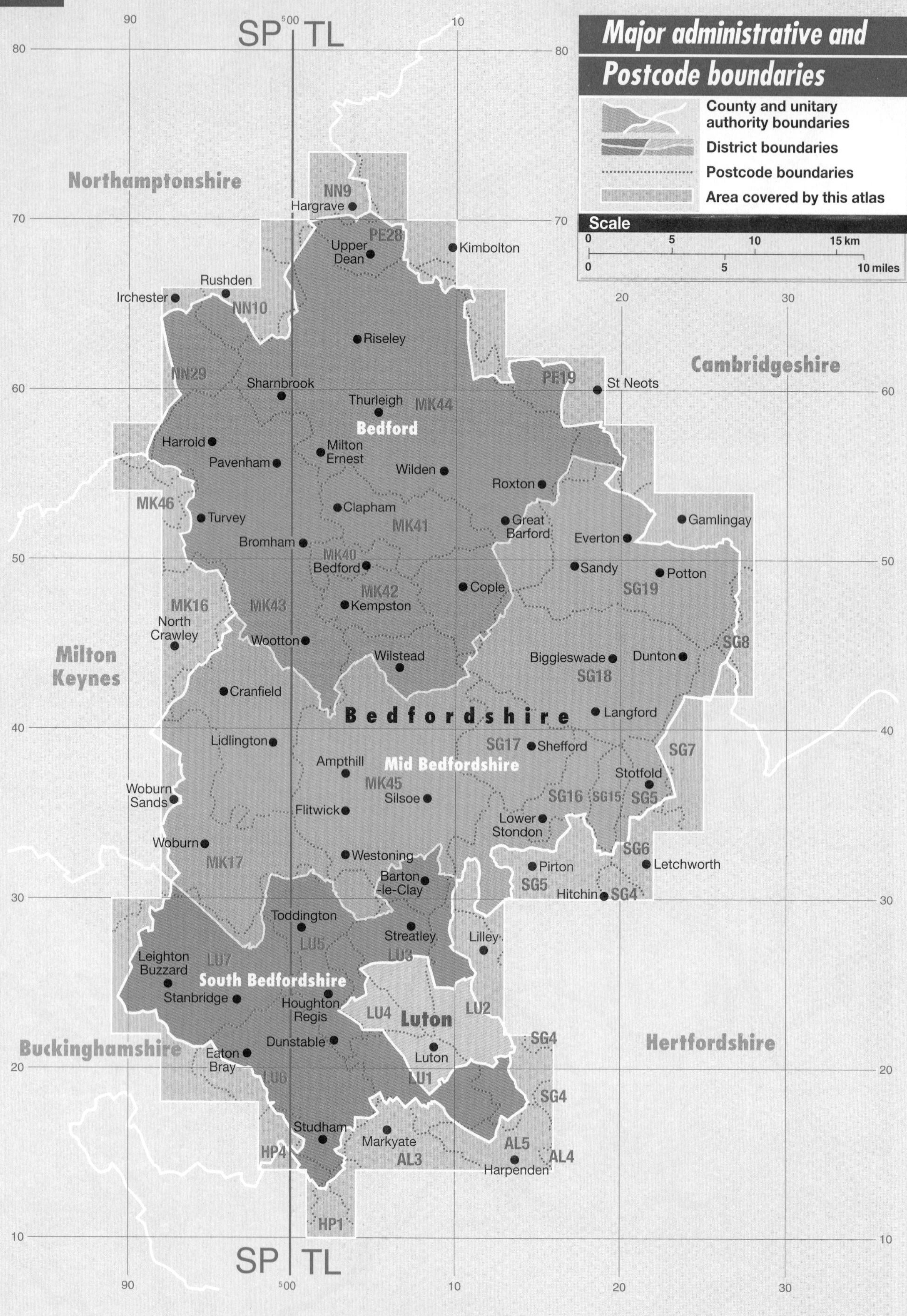

Major administrative and Postcode boundaries
County and unitary authority boundaries
District boundaries
Postcode boundaries
Area covered by this atlas
Scale
0 5 10 15 km
0 5 10 miles
SP TL
Northamptonshire
Cambridgeshire
Milton Keynes
Buckinghamshire
Hertfordshire
Bedfordshire
Bedford
Mid Bedfordshire
South Bedfordshire
Luton
NN9
Hargrave
PE28
Upper Dean
Kimbolton
Rushden
Irchester
NN10
Riseley
NN29
PE19
St Neots
Sharnbrook
Thurleigh
MK44
Harrold
Milton Ernest
Pavenham
Wilden
Roxton
MK46
Turvey
Clapham
MK41
Great Barford
Gamlingay
Everton
Bromham
MK40
Bedford
Sandy
Potton
SG19
Cople
MK42
MK16
MK43
Kempston
North Crawley
Wootton
SG8
Wilstead
Biggleswade
Dunton
SG18
Cranfield
Langford
Lidlington
SG17
Shefford
SG7
Ampthill
Stotfold
MK45
Woburn Sands
Silsoe
SG16
SG15
SG5
Flitwick
Lower Stondon
Woburn
SG6
Letchworth
MK17
Westoning
Pirton
Barton -le-Clay
SG5
Hitchin
SG4
Toddington
Streatley
Lilley
LU5
LU3
Leighton Buzzard
LU7
Stanbridge
Houghton Regis
LU4
LU2
Dunstable
Luton
SG4
Eaton Bray
LU6
LU1
SG4
Studham
Markyate
AL5
HP4
AL3
AL4
Harpenden
HP1

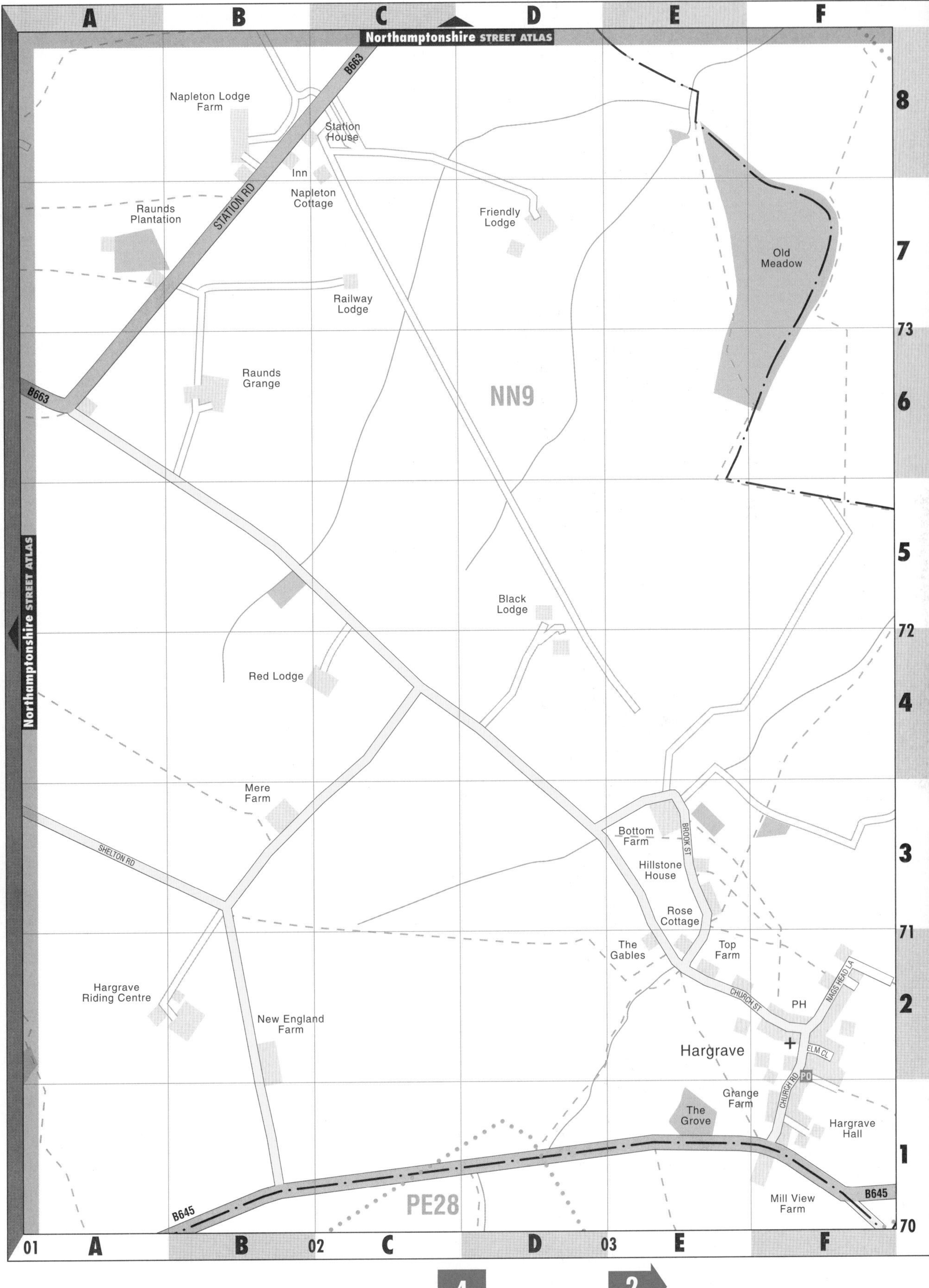

Northamptonshire STREET ATLAS

Napleton Lodge Farm

Station House

Inn

Napleton Cottage

Raunds Plantation

Friendly Lodge

Old Meadow

Railway Lodge

Raunds Grange

NN9

B663

STATION RD

B663

Red Lodge

Black Lodge

Mere Farm

Bottom Farm

BROOK ST

Hillstone House

Rose Cottage

SHELTON RD

The Gables

Top Farm

Hargrave Riding Centre

New England Farm

CHURCH ST

PH

MASSINGADL LA

ELM CL

Hargrave

PO

CHURCH RD

Grange Farm

The Grove

Hargrave Hall

PE28

B645

Mill View Farm

B645

8

7

73

6

5

72

4

3

71

2

1

70

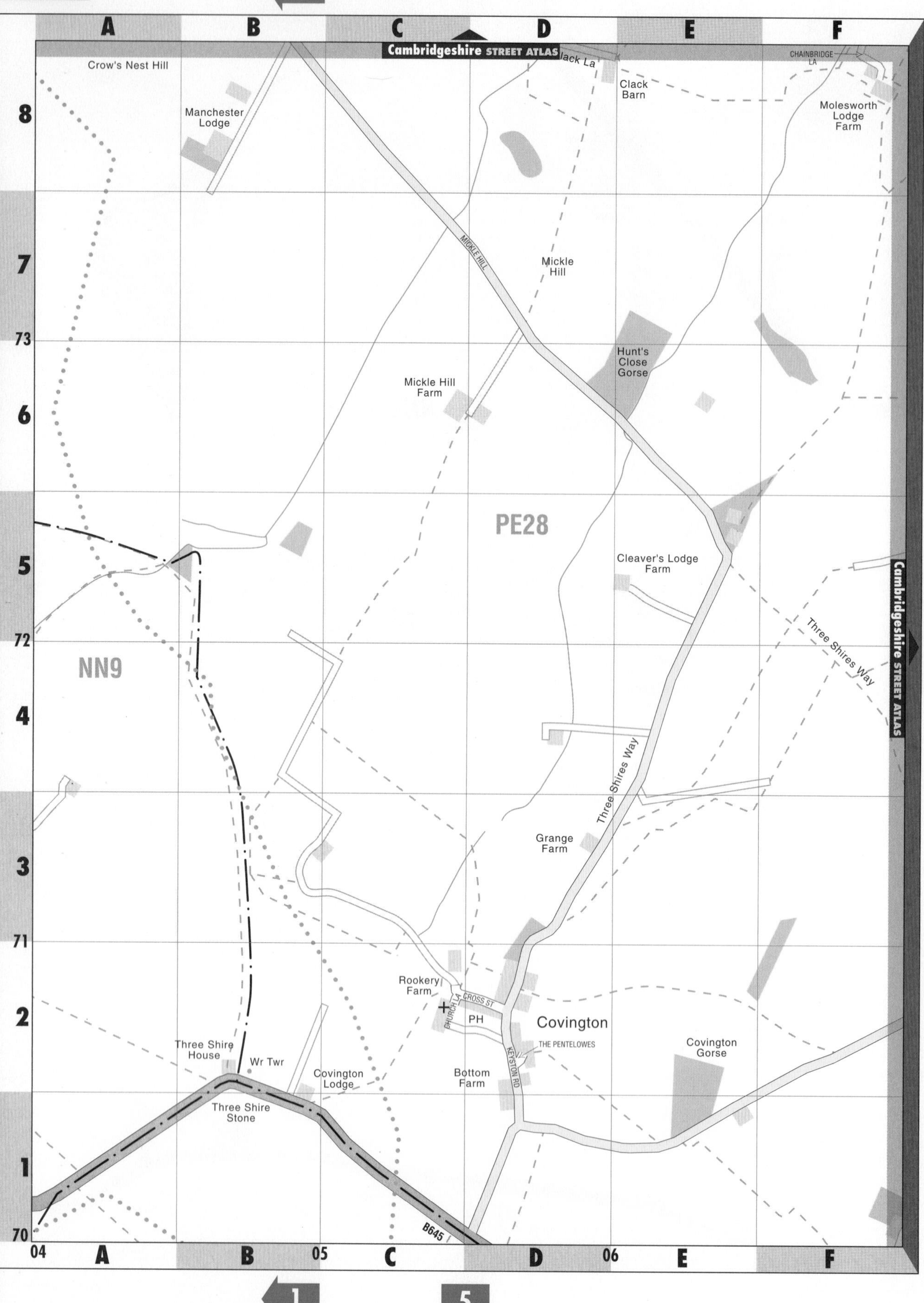

Cambridgeshire STREET ATLAS

Cambridgeshire STREET ATLAS

8

7

73

6

5

72

4

3

71

2

1

70

A   B   C   D   E   F

NN9

PE28

Crow's Nest Hill

Manchester Lodge

lack La

Clack Barn

Molesworth Lodge Farm

CHAINBRIDGE LA

MICKLE HILL

Mickle Hill

Hunt's Close Gorse

Mickle Hill Farm

Cleaver's Lodge Farm

Three Shires Way

Three Shires Way

Grange Farm

Rookery Farm

CROSS ST

CHURCH LA

PH

Covington

THE PENTELOWES

Covington Gorse

Three Shire House

Wr Twr

Covington Lodge

KEYSTON RD

Bottom Farm

Three Shire Stone

B645

04   A   B   05   C   D   06   E   F

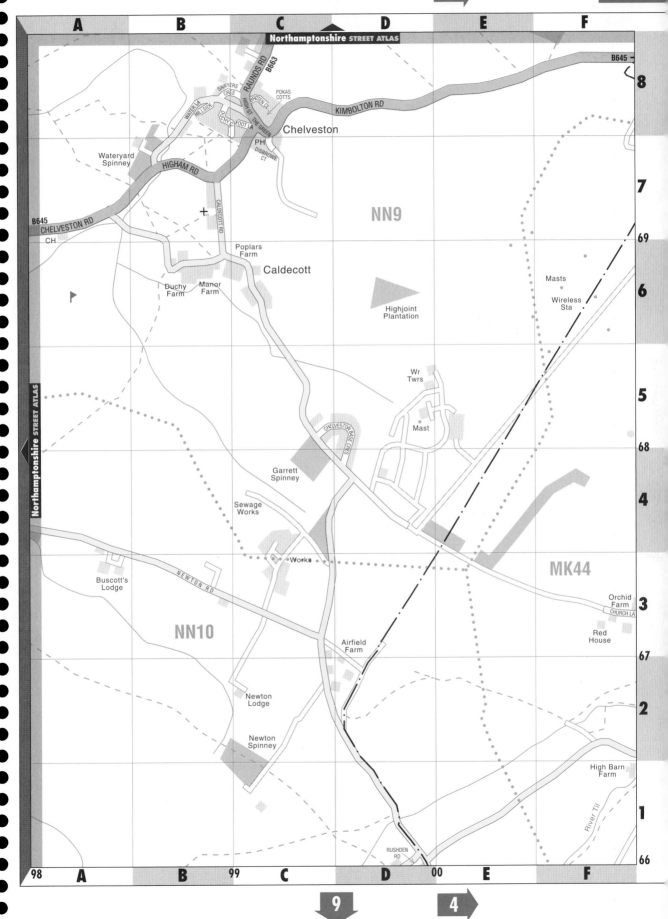

Northamptonshire STREET ATLAS

Northamptonshire STREET ATLAS

B645

B663

RAUNDS RD

SAWYERS CRES

POKAS COTTS

WATER LA

HILLSIDE

DUCHY CL

FOOT LA

HIGH ST

BRITTEN CL

THE GREEN

KIMBOLTON RD

Chelveston

PH

DISBROWE CT

Wateryard Spinney

HIGHAM RD

NN9

CALDECOTT RD

B645

CHELVESTON RD

CH

Poplars Farm

Caldecott

Duchy Farm

Manor Farm

Highjoint Plantation

Masts

Wireless Sta

Wr Twrs

Mast

CHELVESTON BASE CRES

Garrett Spinney

Sewage Works

Works

MK44

Buscott's Lodge

NEWTON RD

NN10

Orchid Farm

CHURCH LA

Red House

Airfield Farm

Newton Lodge

Newton Spinney

High Barn Farm

River Til

RUSHDEN RD

98   99   00

8 7 69 6 5 68 4 3 67 2 1 66

A B C D E F

8

7

69

6

5

68

4

3

67

2

1

66

01 A B 02 C D 03 E F

B645

NN9

NN9

Lodge Farm

The Lodge

Shelton Grange Farm

Mast

Elmsleigh

Shelton Gorse

Shelton

Mast

Shelton Hall

Manor Farm

Shelton Spinney

Mill Farm

PE28

Three Shires Way

River Til

Middle Lodge

The Manor

Bottom Farm

Dean Lodge

PHILLIPS MDWS
STANBROOK WAY
FORD GDNS
CHURCH LA
TRAILLY CL
SPRING LA

Dean Lodge Spinney

Castle Hill

MK44

Yelden

HIGH ST

PH

Grange Farm

HIGH TOP BARNS

High Top Farm

Yelden Spinney

PH

Crowfield Farm

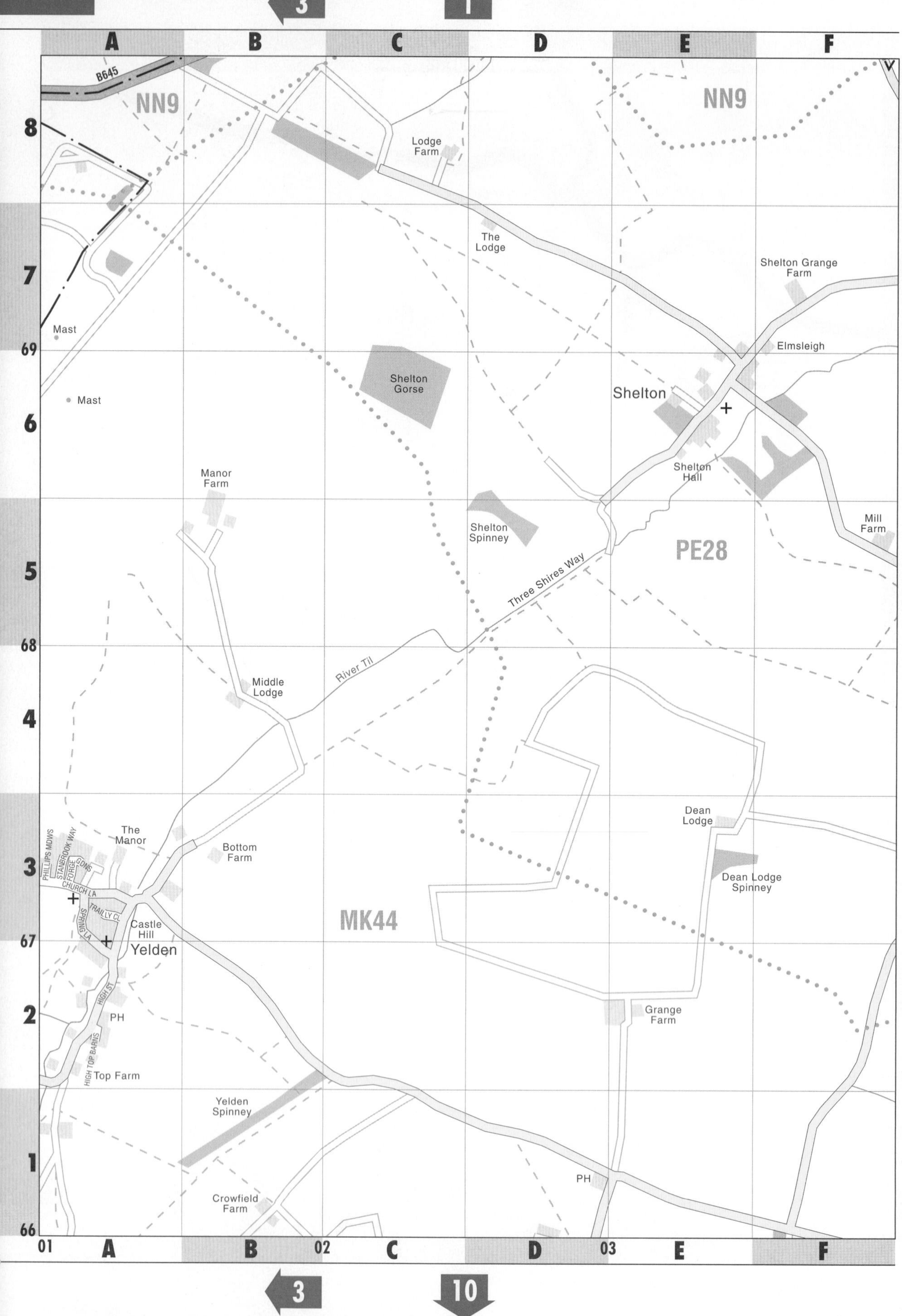

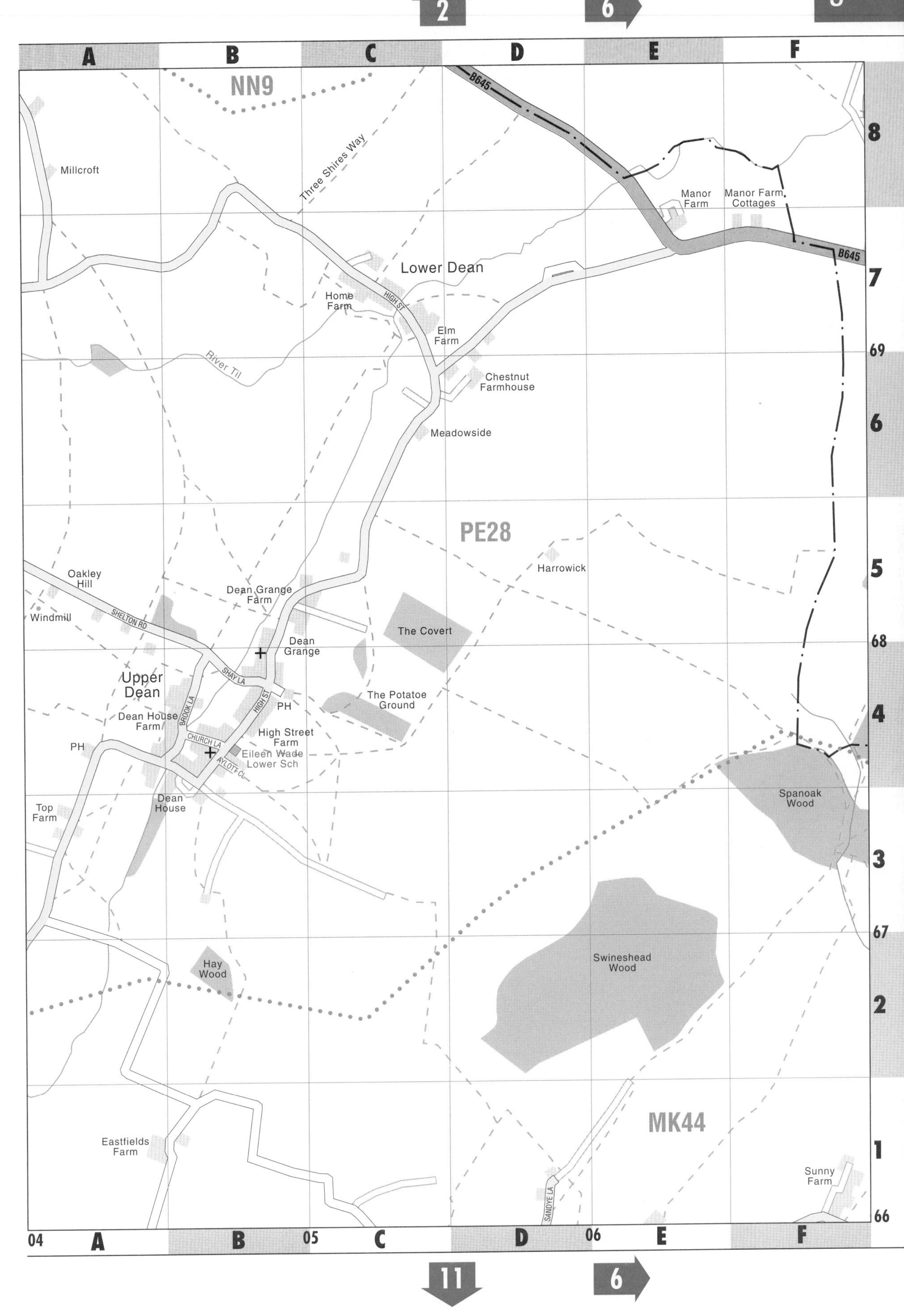

2
6
A
B
C
D
E
F
NN9
B645
Three Shires Way
8
Millcroft
Manor
Farm
Manor Farm
Cottages
B645
Lower Dean
Home
Farm
HIGH ST
7
Elm
Farm
River Til
69
Chestnut
Farmhouse
Meadowside
6
PE28
Oakley
Hill
Harrowick
5
Dean Grange
Farm
Windmill
SHELTON RD
The Covert
Dean
Grange
68
Upper
Dean
SHAY LA
The Potatoe
Ground
BROOK LA
HIGH ST
PH
4
Dean House
Farm
High Street
Farm
PH
CHURCH LA
Eileen Wade
Lower Sch
AYLOTT CL
Spanoak
Wood
Top
Farm
Dean
House
3
67
Swineshead
Wood
Hay
Wood
2
MK44
1
Eastfields
Farm
Sunny
Farm
SANDYE LA
66
04
A
B
05
C
D
06
E
F
11
6

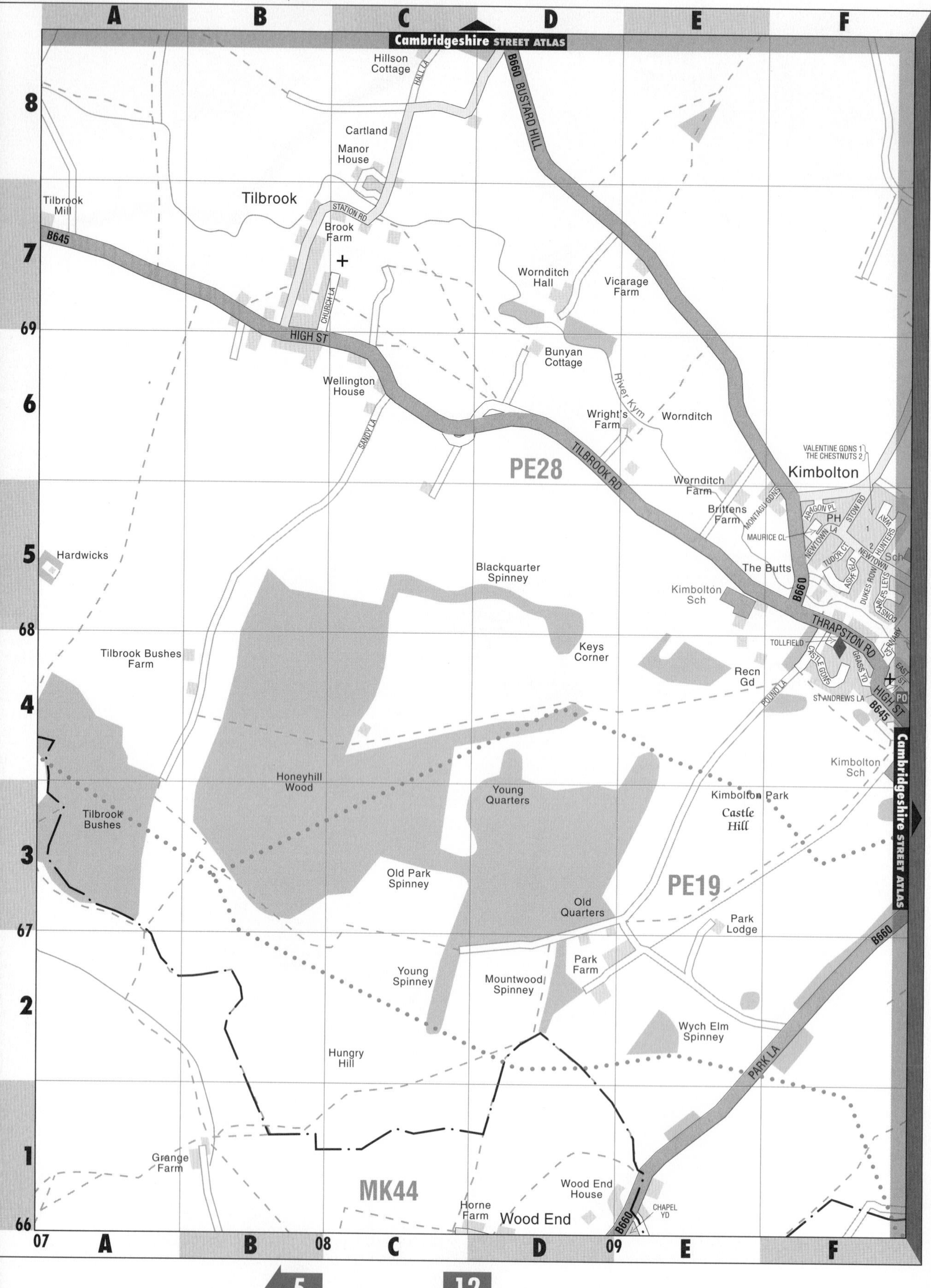

Cambridgeshire STREET ATLAS

Cambridgeshire STREET ATLAS

8 ➡

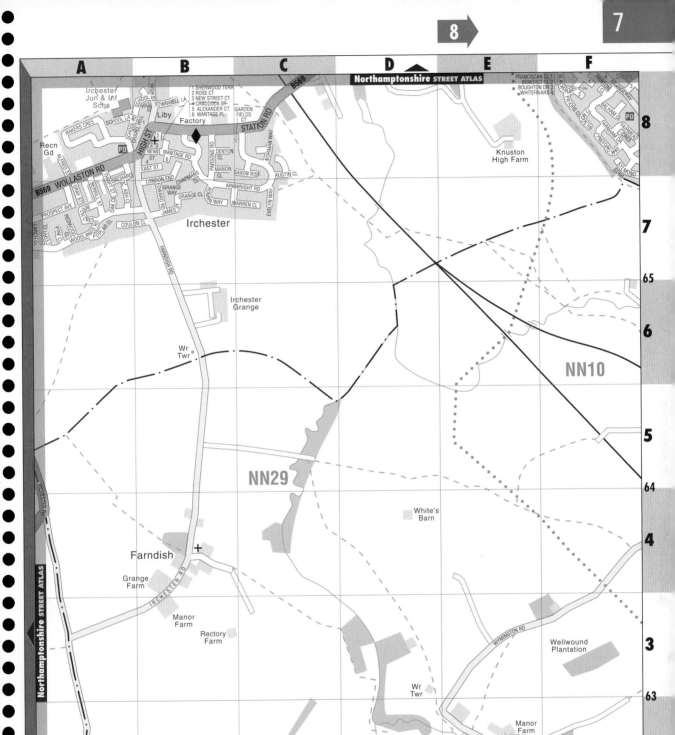

A **B** **C** **D** **E** **F**

Irchester Jun & Inf Schs

1 SHERWOOD TERR
2 ROSE CT
3 NEW STREET CT
4 CRADDOCK CT
5 ALEXANDER CT
6 WANTAGE PL

BAKERS CRES

SCHOOL LA RD

HIGH ST

CHAPEL HILL

Liby

Factory

STATION RD

B569

GARDEN FIELDS CT

FRANCISCAN CL 1
BENEDICT CL 2
BOUGHTON DR 3
WHITEFRIARS 4

BLACKFRIARS

FRINTON CL

GRANGEWAY

BLACK MARS

CROSS LA

BALHAM CL

FAIRMEAD

FARNHAM CRES

CLNEFORD WAY

ST MOND

PO

Recn Gd

ALFRED ST

THRIFT ST

NEW ST

WANTAGE RD

EAST ST

PARSONS RD

DENTON CL

MANOR CL

SAXON RISE

NORMAN WAY

AUSTIN CL

Knuston High Farm

WOLLASTON RD

B569

GRAY ST

BERRILL ST

OAK CL

ASH CL

ORCHARD

LONDON END

EDWARD RD

GRANGE WAY

CHAPMANS CL

GRANGE CL

MANOR WAY

JAMES ST

WARREN CL

ARKWRIGHT RD

EVELYN WAY

PROSPECT AVE

REDWOOD

PINE CL

WOODLANDS RD

POPLAR CL

COULON CL

LARCH CL

Irchester

8

FARNDISH RD

7

Irchester Grange

65

Wr Twr

6

NN10

5

NN29

64

White's Barn

ICHESTER RD

4

Farndish

✝

Grange Farm

Manor Farm

Rectory Farm

WYMINGTON RD

Wellwound Plantation

3

63

Wr Twr

Manor Farm

2

Long Plantation

Hall Farm

GOLD ST

HORNBEAM CL

HIGH ST

PO

Podington

Glebe Farm

HINWICK RD

CORNER CL

Podington Prim Sch

Knapwell Farm

Hall Lane Spinney

Hinwick Hall Coll of F Ed

Nursery

COUNCIL HOS

1

Southwood House

62

92 **A** **B** **93** **C** **D** **94** **E** **F**

14 ⬇

8 ➡

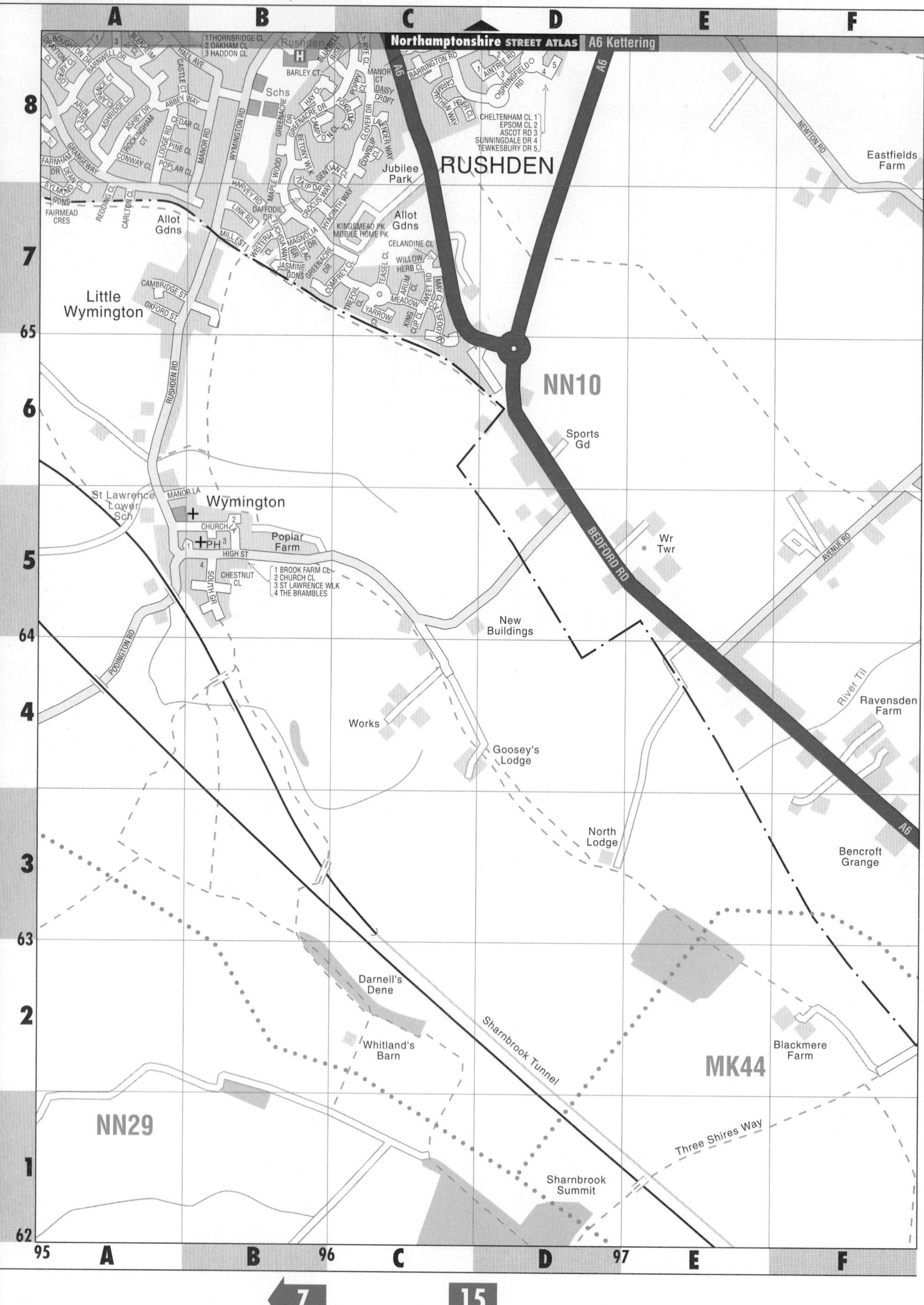

7

Northamptonshire STREET ATLAS | A6 Kettering

RUSHDEN

1 THORNBRIDGE CL
2 OAKHAM CL
3 HADDON CL

CHELTENHAM CL 1
EPSOM CL 2
ASCOT RD 3
SUNNINGDALE DR 4
TEWKESBURY DR 5

Little
Wymington

Allot
Gdns

Jubilee
Park

Allot
Gdns

NN10

Sports
Gd

St Lawrence
Lower
Sch

Wymington

Poplar
Farm

CHESTNUT
CL

1 BROOK FARM CL
2 CHURCH CL
3 ST LAWRENCE WLK
4 THE BRAMBLES

New
Buildings

Wr
Twr

Works

Goosey's
Lodge

North
Lodge

River Til

Ravensden
Farm

Bencroft
Grange

Darnell's
Dene

Sharnbrook Tunnel

MK44

Blackmere
Farm

Whitland's
Barn

NN29

Three Shires Way

Sharnbrook
Summit

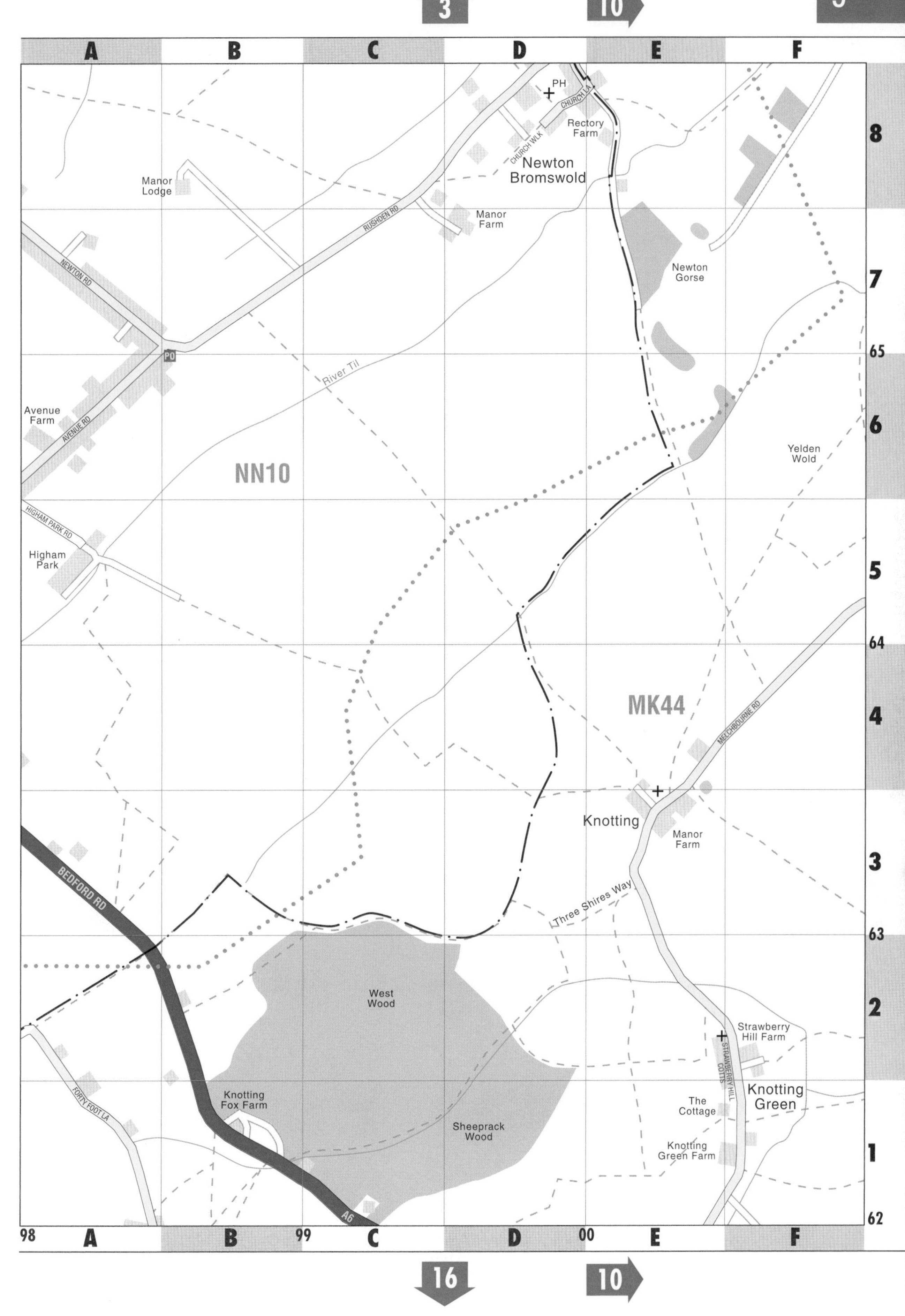
3
10
A
B
C
D
E
F
PH
CHURCH LA
Rectory Farm
CHURCH WLK
Newton Bromswold
Manor Lodge
RUSHDEN RD
Manor Farm
NEWTON RD
Newton Gorse
PO
River Til
Avenue Farm
AVENUE RD
NN10
Yelden Wold
HIGHAM PARK RD
Higham Park
MK44
MELCHBOURNE RD
Knotting
Manor Farm
BEDFORD RD
Three Shires Way
West Wood
Strawberry Hill Farm
STRAWBERRY HILL COTTS
Knotting Green
The Cottage
FORTY FOOT LA
Knotting Fox Farm
Sheeprack Wood
Knotting Green Farm
A6
8
7
65
6
5
64
4
3
63
2
1
62
98
99
00
16
10

9
4

A B C D E F

8

7

65

6

5

64

4

3

63

2

1

62

Three Shires Way

Redhill Barn

Barton's Spinney

Melchbourne

Vicarage Farm

Hall

Inn Farm

Hillands Farm

Wimsells

Hillands Plantation

Melchbourne House

Three Cornered Wimsells

KNOTTING RD

PARK RD

Woodleys

Melchbourne Park

Coppice Wood

Three Shires Way

MK44

Lady Wood

Oakley Hunt Kennels

MELCHBOURNE RD

Penn Wood

Worley's Wood

Sackville Lodge Farm

Sackville Lodge Nurseries

Haring's Farm

Lodge Farm

Kings Close La

Church La

Dag La

Riseley CE Lower Sch

Rotten Row

Gold St

The Orchard

Bourne Rd

Wells Rd

College Dr

PH

Strawberry Hill Buildings

Outdoor Activities Ctr

Shooting Range

KNOTTING LA

The Butts

Brooklands Rd

High St

London La

Town Farm

Top End

Masts

High Barn Farm

The Mallowry

5
12

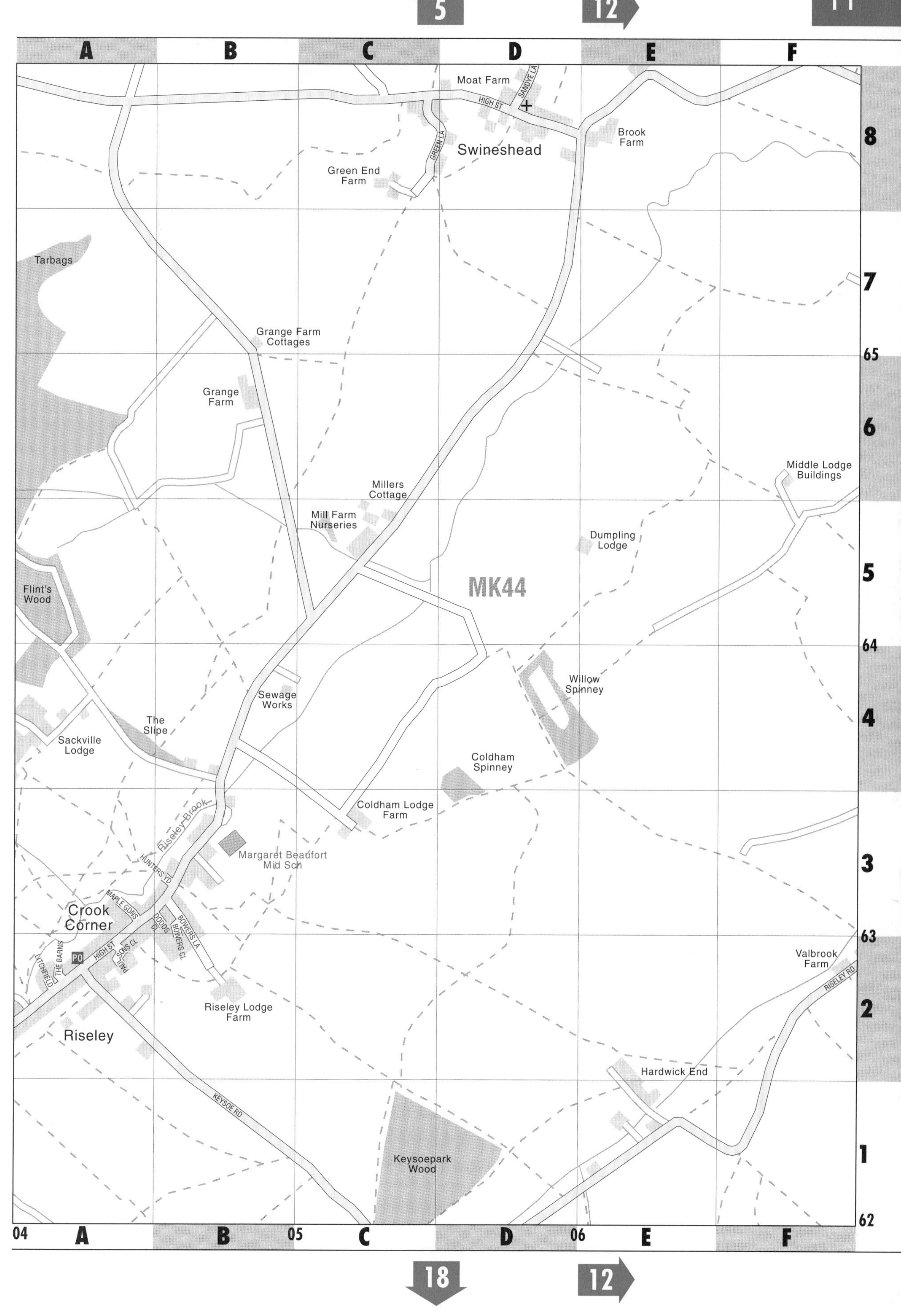
A
B
C
D
E
F
Moat Farm
HIGH ST
SANDYE LA
Brook Farm
Swineshead
GREEN LA
Green End Farm
Tarbags
Grange Farm Cottages
Grange Farm
Middle Lodge Buildings
Millers Cottage
Mill Farm Nurseries
Dumpling Lodge
Flint's Wood
MK44
Willow Spinney
Sewage Works
The Slipe
Sackville Lodge
Coldham Spinney
Coldham Lodge Farm
Risely Brook
Margaret Beaufort Mid Sch
HUNTERS YD
MAPLE GDNS
Crook Corner
DODDS CL
BOWERS LA
BOWERS CL
PAULSONS CL
HIGH ST
PO
THE BARNS
LYTCHFIELD
Valbrook Farm
RISELEY RD
Riseley Lodge Farm
Riseley
Hardwick End
KEYSOE RD
Keysoepark Wood
8
7
65
6
5
64
4
3
63
2
1
62
04
05
06

18
12

A B C D E F

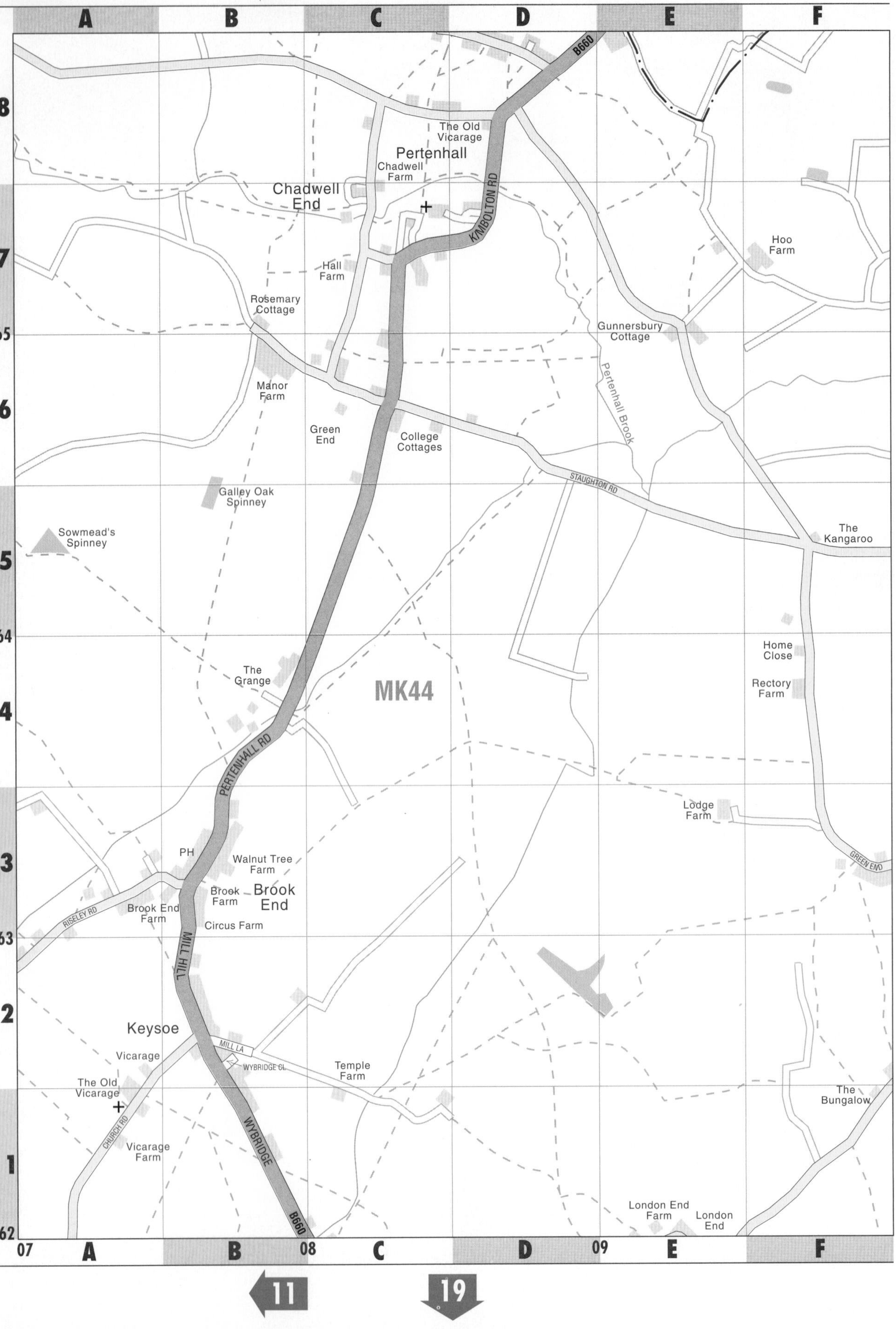

8

The Old
Vicarage
Pertenhall
Chadwell
Farm
Chadwell
End

Hall
Farm

7

KIMBOLTON RD

Hoo
Farm

Rosemary
Cottage

65

Gunnersbury
Cottage

Manor
Farm

6

Green
End

College
Cottages

Pertenhall Brook

STAUGHTON RD

Galley Oak
Spinney

Sowmead's
Spinney

The Kangaroo

5

64

Home
Close

The
Grange

MK44

Rectory
Farm

4

PERTENHALL RD

Lodge
Farm

PH

Walnut Tree
Farm

GREEN END

3

RISELEY RD

Brook
Farm

Brook
End

Brook End
Farm

Circus Farm

63

MILL HILL

2

Keysoe

MILL LA

Vicarage

Temple
Farm

WYBRIDGE CL

The Old
Vicarage

CHURCH RD

Vicarage
Farm

WYBRIDGE

The
Bungalow

1

B660

London End
Farm

London
End

62

07 A B 08 C D 09 E F

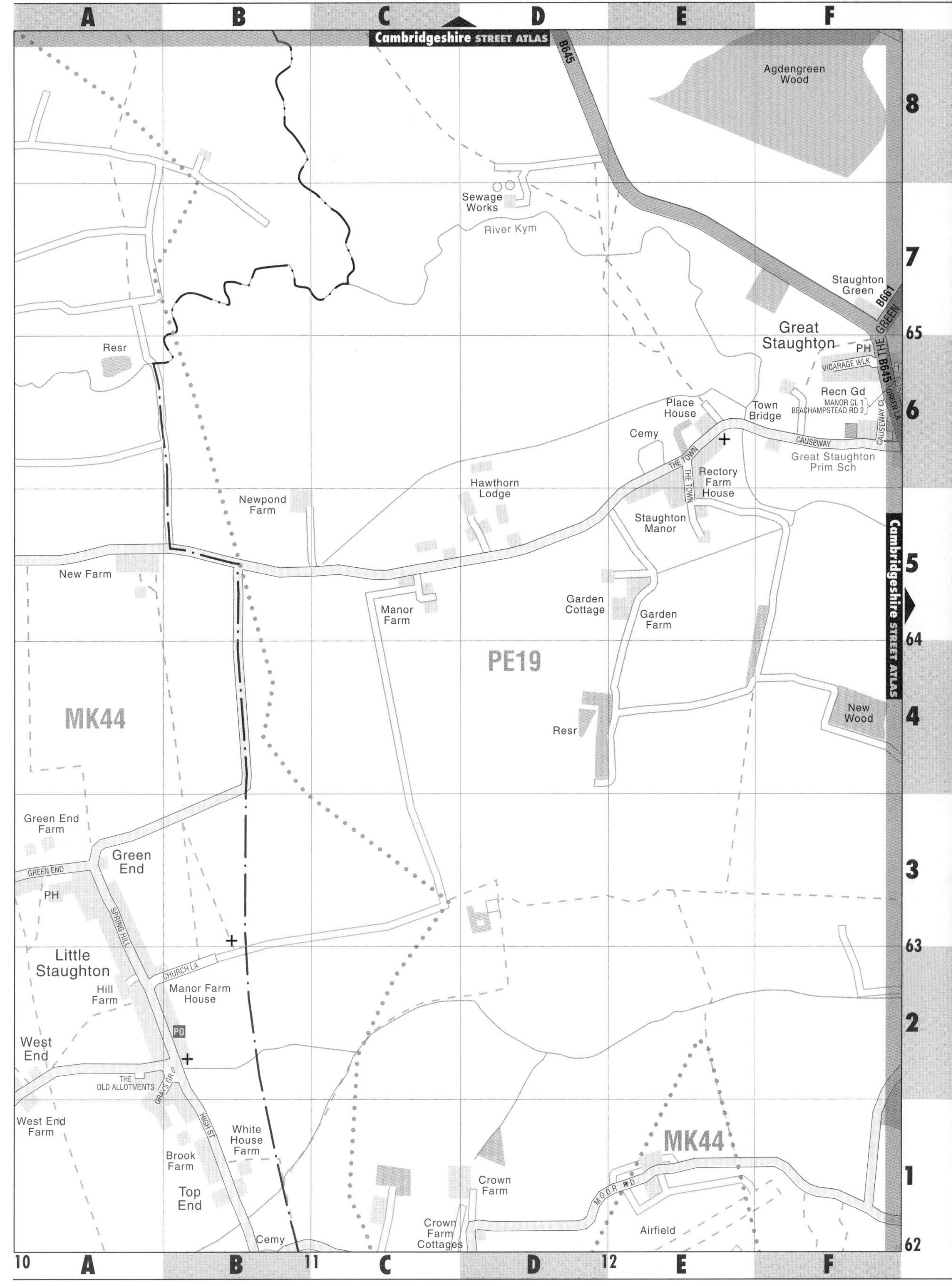

A B C D E F

Agdengreen
Wood

B645

8

Sewage
Works

River Kym

7

Staughton
Green

B661

THE GREEN

65

Great
Staughton

PH

VICARAGE WLK

Resr

GREEN LA

Recn Gd

MANOR CL 1
BEACHAMPSTEAD RD 2

CAUSEWAY CL

6

Place
House

Town
Bridge

CAUSEWAY

Cemy

Great Staughton
Prim Sch

Newpond
Farm

Hawthorn
Lodge

THE TOWN

Rectory
Farm
House

New Farm

Staughton
Manor

THE TOWN

5

Manor
Farm

Garden
Cottage

Garden
Farm

64

PE19

MK44

Resr

New
Wood

4

Green End
Farm

Green End

Green
End

3

GREEN END

PH

SPRING HILL

63

Little
Staughton

Hill
Farm

Manor Farm
House

CHURCH LA

2

PO

West
End

THE
OLD ALLOTMENTS

GRAYS CR

HIGH ST

West End
Farm

White
House
Farm

MK44

MOOR RD

1

Brook
Farm

Top
End

Crown
Farm

Cemy

Crown
Farm
Cottages

Airfield

62

10 A B 11 C D 12 E F

7

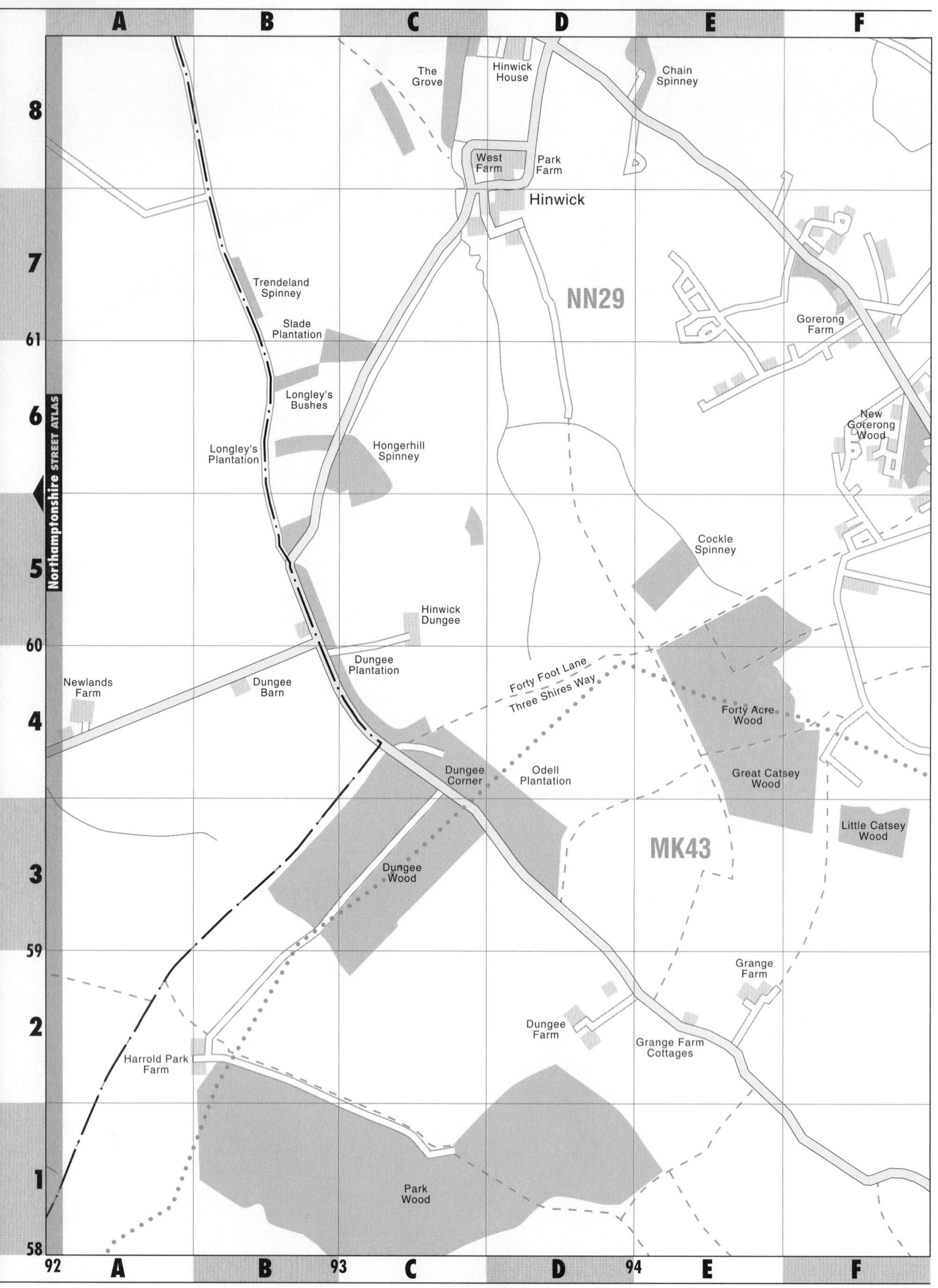
A
B
C
D
E
F
8
7
61
6
5
60
4
3
59
2
1
58
92
93
94
Northamptonshire STREET ATLAS
The Grove
Hinwick House
Chain Spinney
West Farm
Park Farm
Hinwick
Trendeland Spinney
NN29
Slade Plantation
Gorerong Farm
Longley's Bushes
New Gorerong Wood
Longley's Plantation
Hongerhill Spinney
Cockle Spinney
Hinwick Dungee
Newlands Farm
Dungee Barn
Dungee Plantation
Forty Foot Lane
Three Shires Way
Forty Acre Wood
Dungee Corner
Odell Plantation
Great Catsey Wood
Little Catsey Wood
MK43
Dungee Wood
Grange Farm
Dungee Farm
Harrold Park Farm
Grange Farm Cottages
Park Wood

24

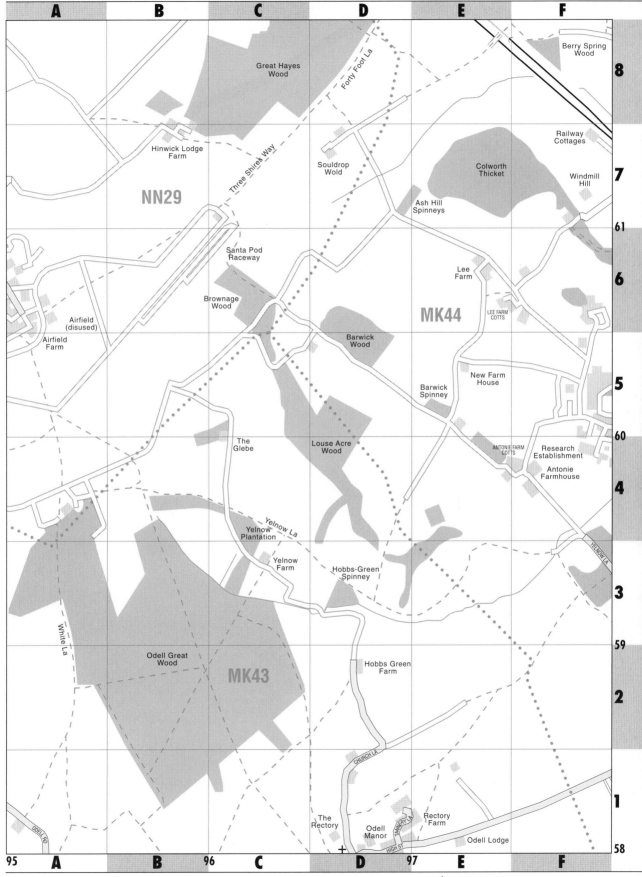
8

16

A B C D E F

Great Hayes Wood
Forty Foot La
Berry Spring Wood
8
Hinwick Lodge Farm
Three Shires Way
Souldrop Wold
Railway Cottages
Colworth Thicket
Windmill Hill
7
NN29
Ash Hill Spinneys
61
Santa Pod Raceway
Lee Farm
6
Browntage Wood
MK44
LEE FARM COTTS
Airfield (disused)
Airfield Farm
Barwick Wood
New Farm House
5
Barwick Spinney
60
The Glebe
Louse Acre Wood
ANTONIE FARM COTTS
Research Establishment
Antonie Farmhouse
4
Yelnow La
Yelnow Plantation
YELNOW LA
Yelnow Farm
Hobbs-Green Spinney
3
White La
59
Odell Great Wood
MK43
Hobbs Green Farm
2
CHURCH LA
1
The Rectory
TANNERY LA
Rectory Farm
Odell Manor
ODELL RD
HIGH ST
Odell Lodge
58

95 A B 96 C D 97 E F

25

16

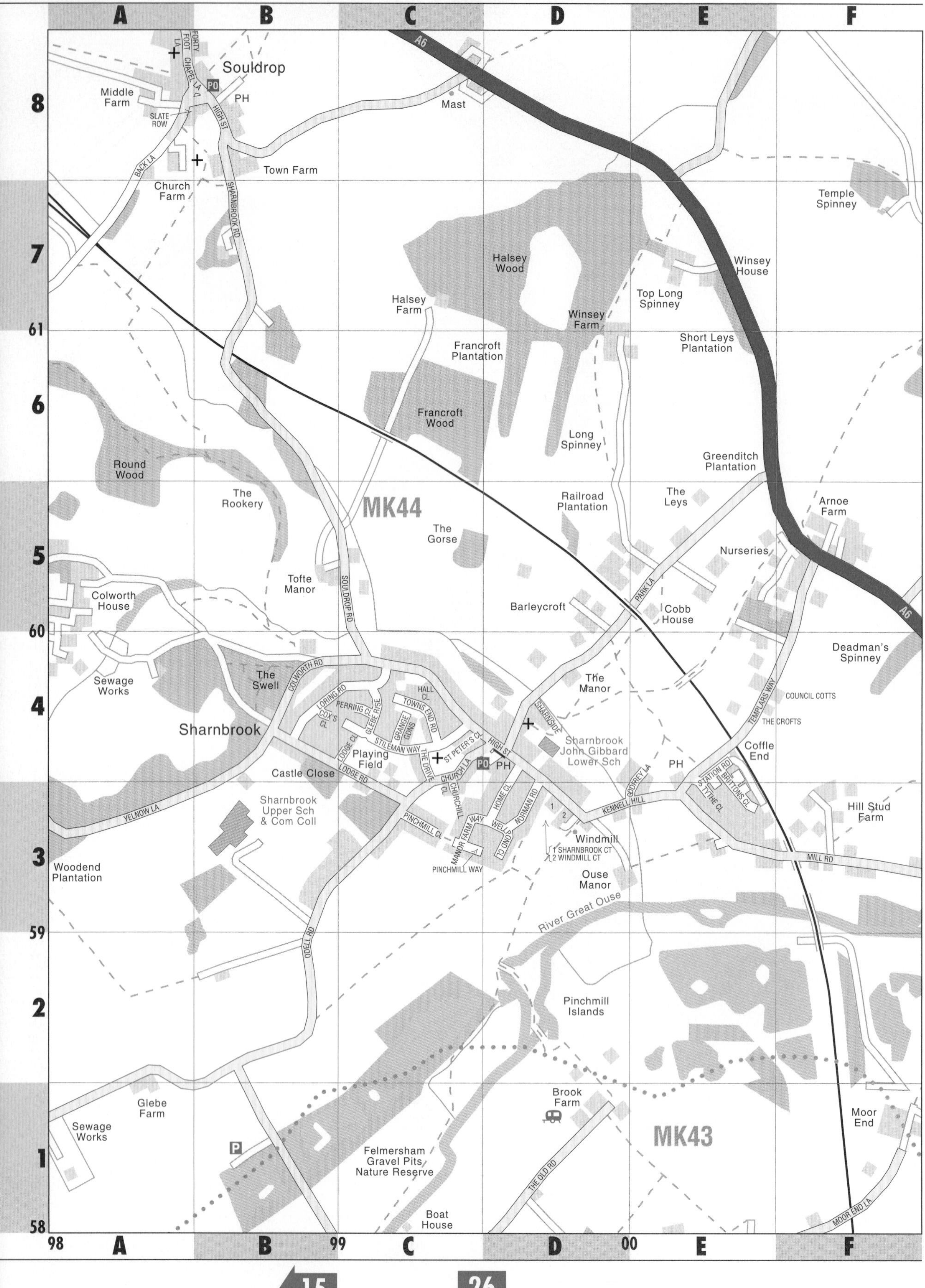

A | B | C | D | E | F

Souldrop
Middle Farm
PH
Mast
SLATE ROW
Town Farm
Church Farm
Temple Spinney

8

Halsey Wood
Winsey House

7

Halsey Farm
Winsey Farm
Top Long Spinney
Short Leys Plantation

61

Francroft Plantation

Francroft Wood
Long Spinney
Greenditch Plantation

6

Round Wood

The Rookery
MK44
Railroad Plantation
The Leys
Arnoe Farm

5

The Gorse
Nurseries

Colworth House
Tofte Manor
Barleycroft
Cobb House
Deadman's Spinney

60

The Swell
The Manor
COUNCIL COTTS
THE CROFTS

Sewage Works

4

Sharnbrook
Playing Field
Sharnbrook John Gibbard Lower Sch
PH
Coffle End

Castle Close
PH
Hill Stud Farm

YELNOW LA
Sharnbrook Upper Sch & Com Coll
PINCHMILL CL
Kennell Hill
MILL RD

3

Woodend Plantation
Windmill
1 SHARNBROOK CT
2 WINDMILL CT
Ouse Manor

PINCHMILL WAY
River Great Ouse

59

ODELL RD

2

Pinchmill Islands

Glebe Farm
Brook Farm
MK43
Moor End

Sewage Works
P
Felmersham Gravel Pits Nature Reserve

1

Boat House
THE OLD RD
MOOR END LA

58

10
18

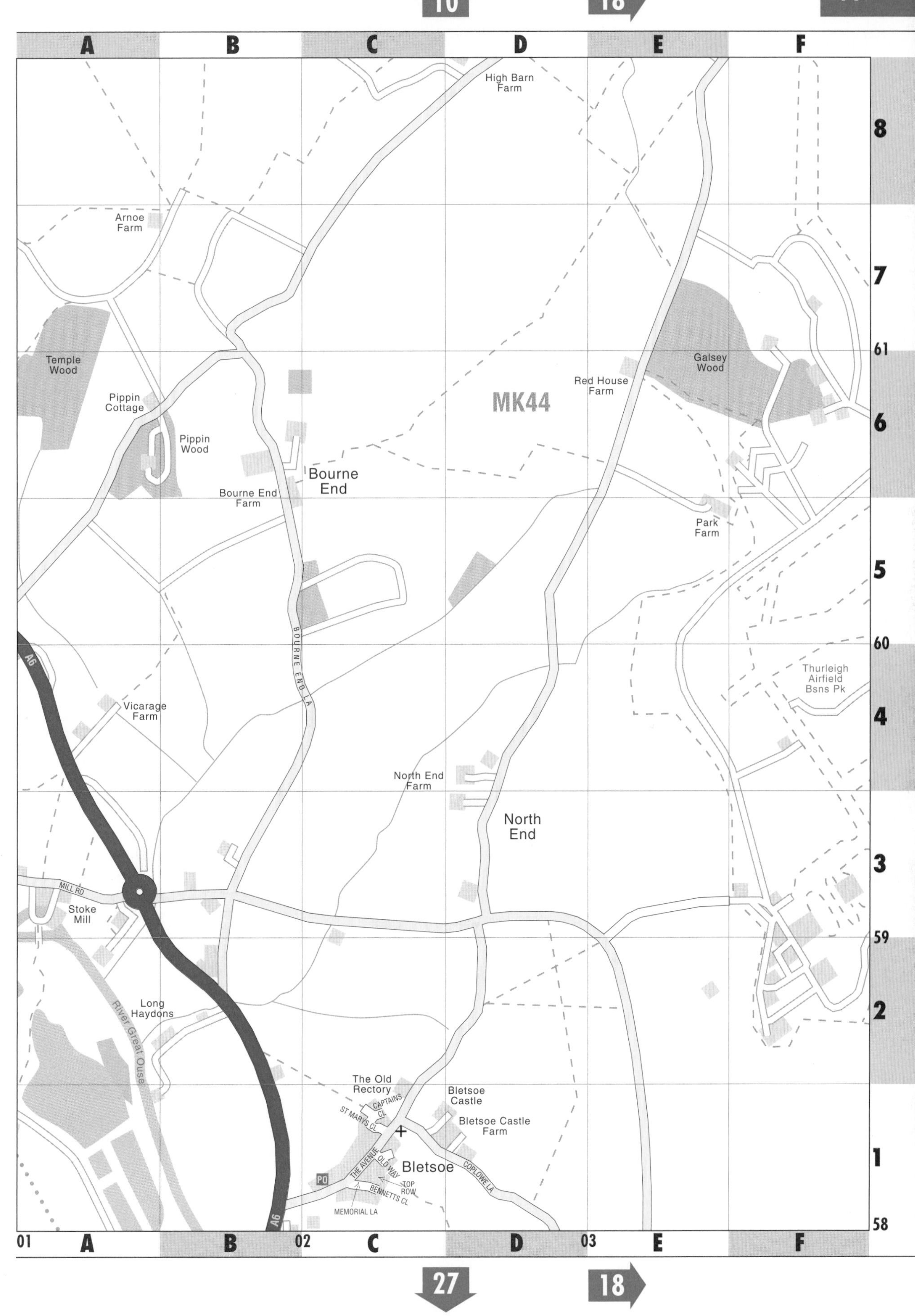
A
B
C
D
E
F
8
7
61
6
5
60
4
3
59
2
1
58
01
02
03
High Barn Farm
Arnoe Farm
Temple Wood
Pippin Cottage
Pippin Wood
Bourne End Farm
Bourne End
MK44
Red House Farm
Galsey Wood
Park Farm
Thurleigh Airfield Bsns Pk
Vicarage Farm
BOURNE END LA
A6
North End Farm
North End
MILL RD
Stoke Mill
Long Haydons
River Great Ouse
The Old Rectory
CAPTAINS CL
ST MARYS CL
Bletsoe Castle
Bletsoe Castle Farm
THE AVENUE
OLD WAY
Bletsoe
TOP ROW
BENNETTS CL
COPLOWE LA
PO
MEMORIAL LA

27
18

17
11

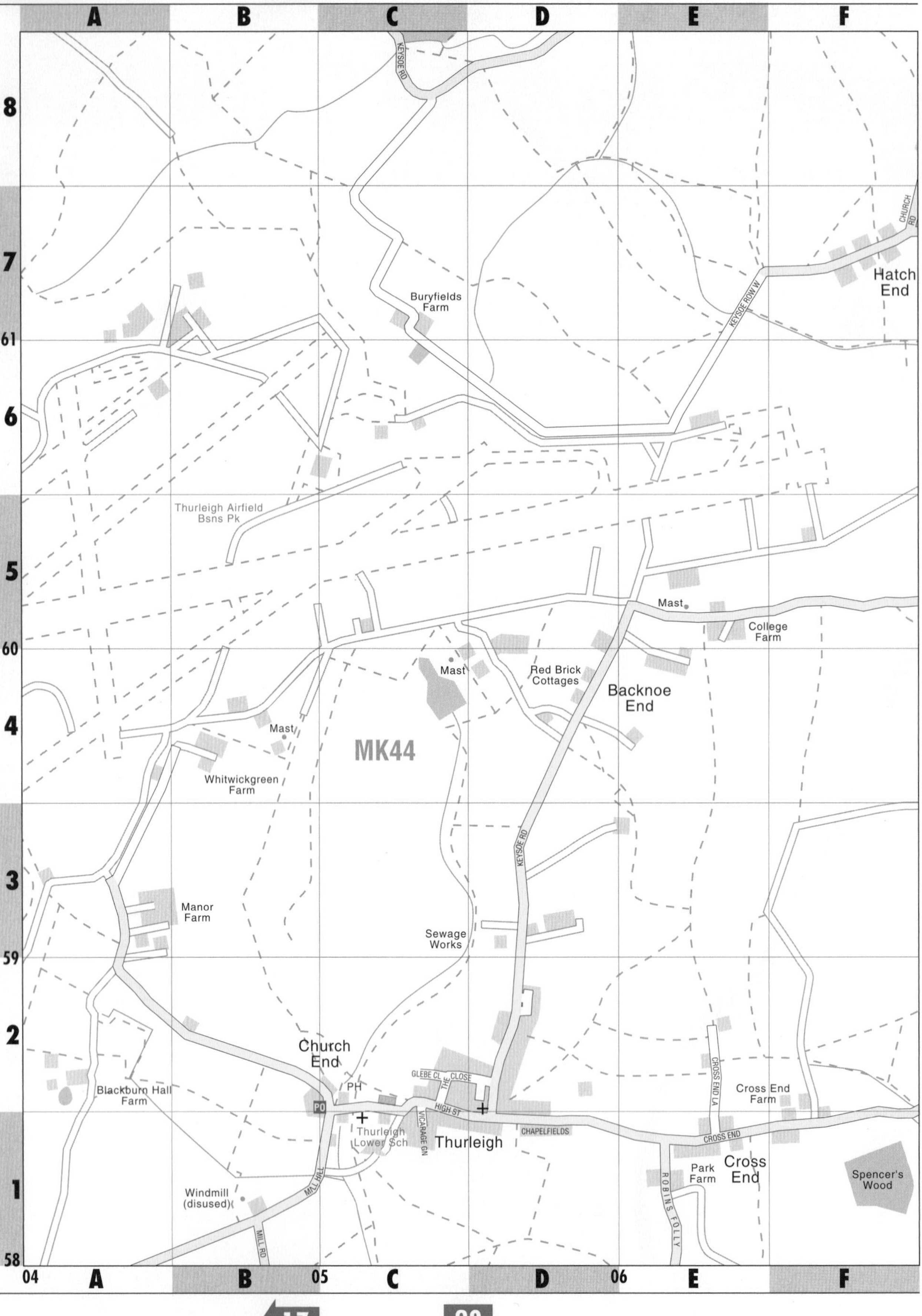

A   B   C   D   E   F

8

7

61

6

Thurleigh Airfield
Bsns Pk

5

60

4

MK44

3

59

2

1

58

04   A   B   05   C   D   06   E   F

KEYSOE RD

Buryfields
Farm

KEYSOE ROW W

CHURCH RD

Hatch
End

Mast

College
Farm

Mast

Red Brick
Cottages

Backnoe
End

KEYSOE RD

Mast

Whitwickgreen
Farm

Manor
Farm

Sewage
Works

Church
End

Blackburn Hall
Farm

PH

PO

Thurleigh
Lower Sch

GLEBE CL

THE CLOSE

HIGH ST

VICARAGE GN

Thurleigh

CHAPELFIELDS

CROSS END LA

Cross End
Farm

CROSS END

ROBINS FOLLY

Park
Farm

Cross
End

Spencer's
Wood

Windmill
(disused)

MILL RD

MILL RD

17
28

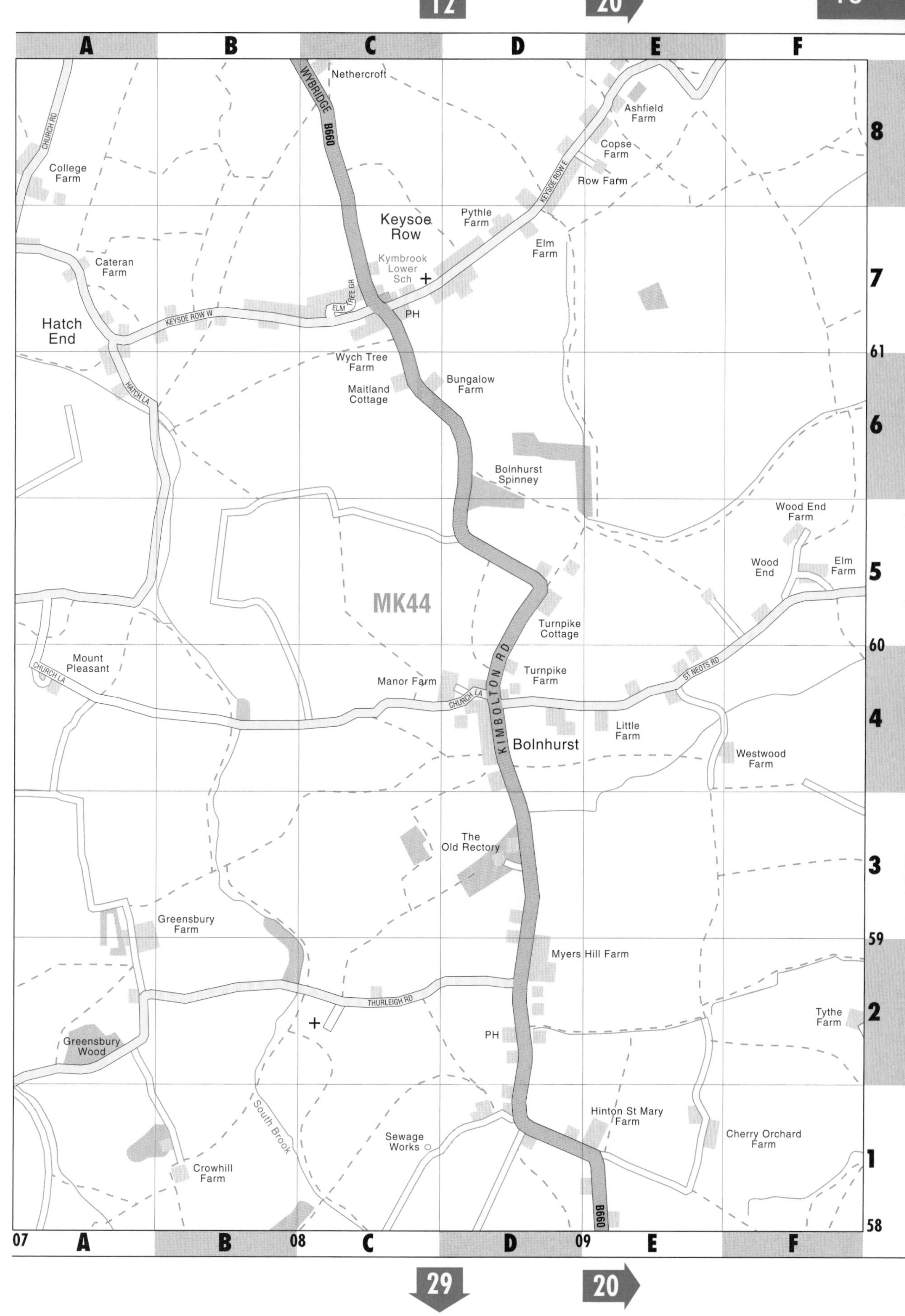

A B C D E F

8
7
61
6
5
60
4
3
59
2
1
58

Nethercroft

WYBRIDGE

B660

College Farm

CHURCH RD

Ashfield Farm

Copse Farm

Row Farm

Keysoe Row

Pythle Farm

KEYSOE ROW E

Elm Farm

Cateran Farm

Kymbrook Lower Sch

Hatch End

KEYSOE ROW W

ELM TREE GR

PH

Wych Tree Farm

HATCH LA

Maitland Cottage

Bungalow Farm

Bolnhurst Spinney

Wood End Farm

Wood End

Elm Farm

MK44

Turnpike Cottage

Mount Pleasant

CHURCH LA

Manor Farm

KIMBOLTON RD

CHURCH LA

Turnpike Farm

ST NEOTS RD

Bolnhurst

Little Farm

Westwood Farm

The Old Rectory

Greensbury Farm

Myers Hill Farm

THURLEIGH RD

PH

Tythe Farm

Greensbury Wood

South Brook

Sewage Works

Hinton St Mary Farm

Cherry Orchard Farm

Crowhill Farm

B660

19
13

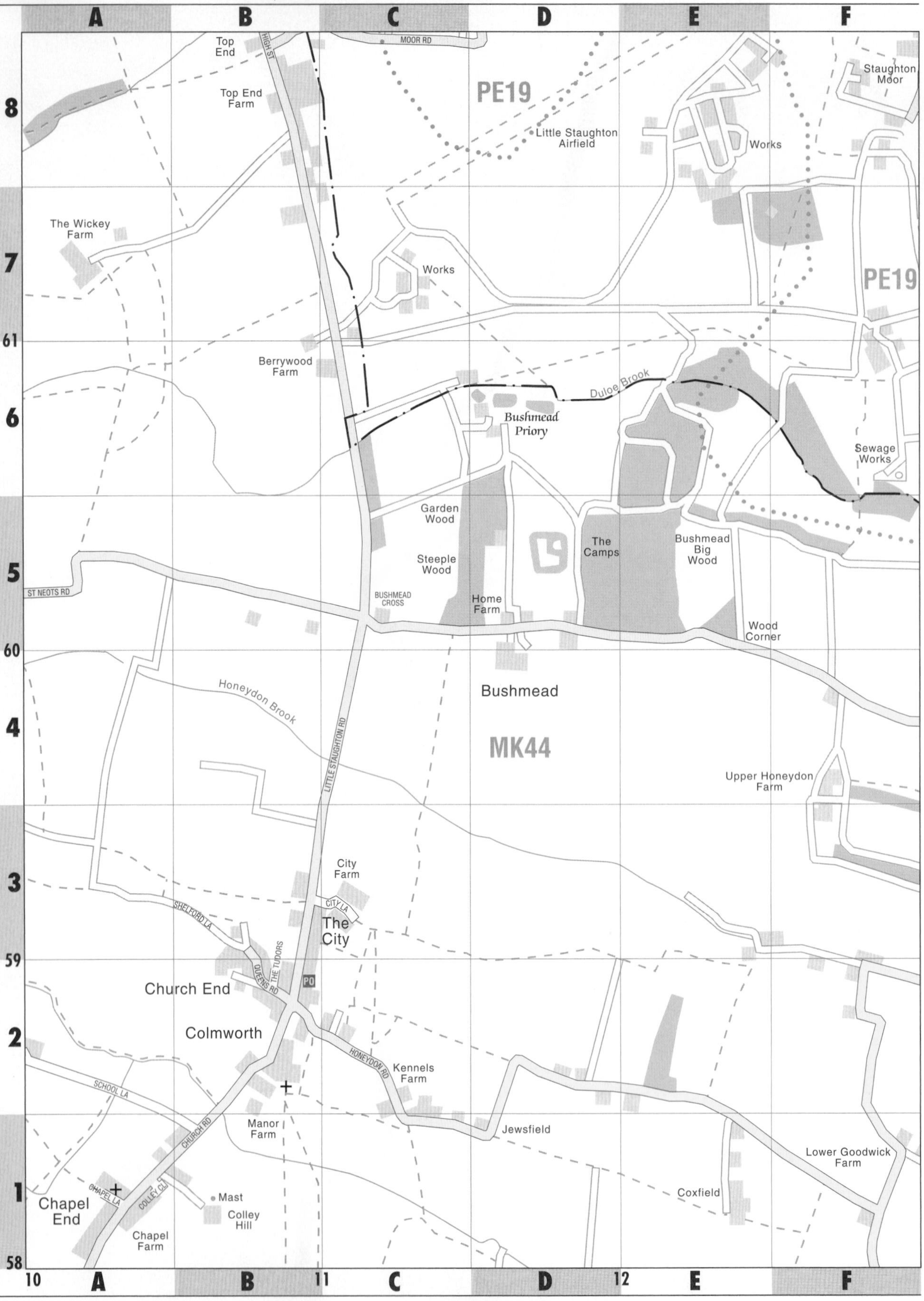

A B C D E F

8

PE19

Top End

Top End
Farm

Staughton
Moor

Little Staughton
Airfield

Works

7

The Wickey
Farm

Works

PE19

61

Berrywood
Farm

Duloe Brook

6

Bushmead
Priory

Sewage
Works

Garden
Wood

The
Camps

Bushmead
Big Wood

5

ST NEOTS RD

Steeple
Wood

Home
Farm

Wood
Corner

BUSHMEAD
CROSS

60

Honeydon Brook

Bushmead

4

MK44

LITTLE STAUGHTON RD

Upper Honeydon
Farm

3

City
Farm

CITY LA

SHELFORD LA

The
City

59

THE TUDORS

QUEENS RD

PO

Church End

2

Colmworth

HONEYDON RD

Kennels
Farm

SCHOOL LA

Jewsfield

CHURCH RD

Manor
Farm

Lower Goodwick
Farm

1

CHAPEL LA

COLLEY CL

Mast

Chapel
End

Colley
Hill

Coxfield

Chapel
Farm

58

10 A B 11 C D 12 E F

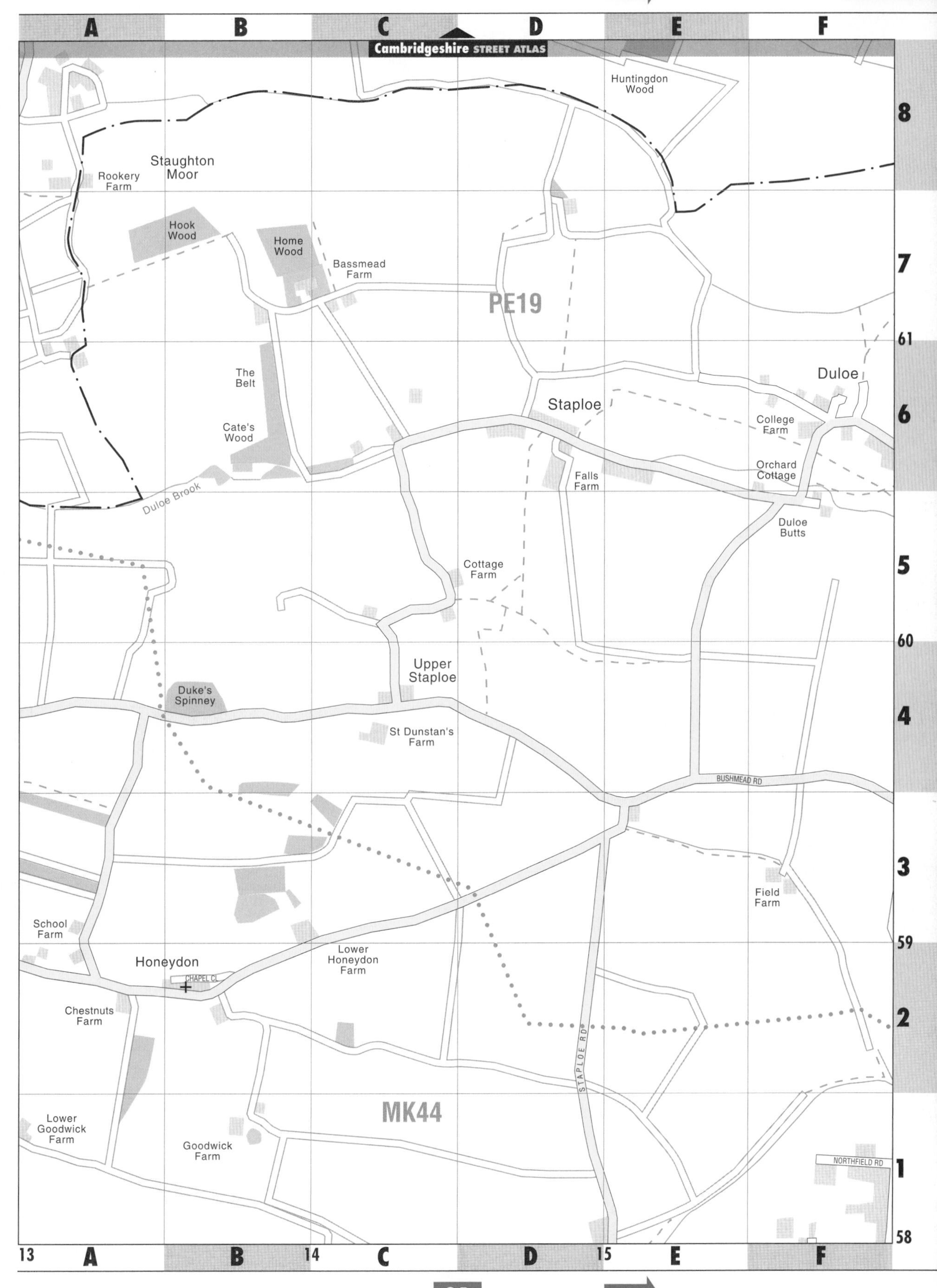

Cambridgeshire STREET ATLAS

Huntingdon Wood

Staughton Moor

Rookery Farm

Hook Wood

Home Wood

Bassmead Farm

PE19

The Belt

Cate's Wood

Staploe

Duloe

College Farm

Orchard Cottage

Falls Farm

Duloe Brook

Duloe Butts

Cottage Farm

Upper Staploe

Duke's Spinney

St Dunstan's Farm

BUSHMEAD RD

Field Farm

School Farm

Honeydon

CHAPEL CL

Lower Honeydon Farm

Chestnuts Farm

STAPLOE RD

MK44

Lower Goodwick Farm

Goodwick Farm

NORTHFIELD RD

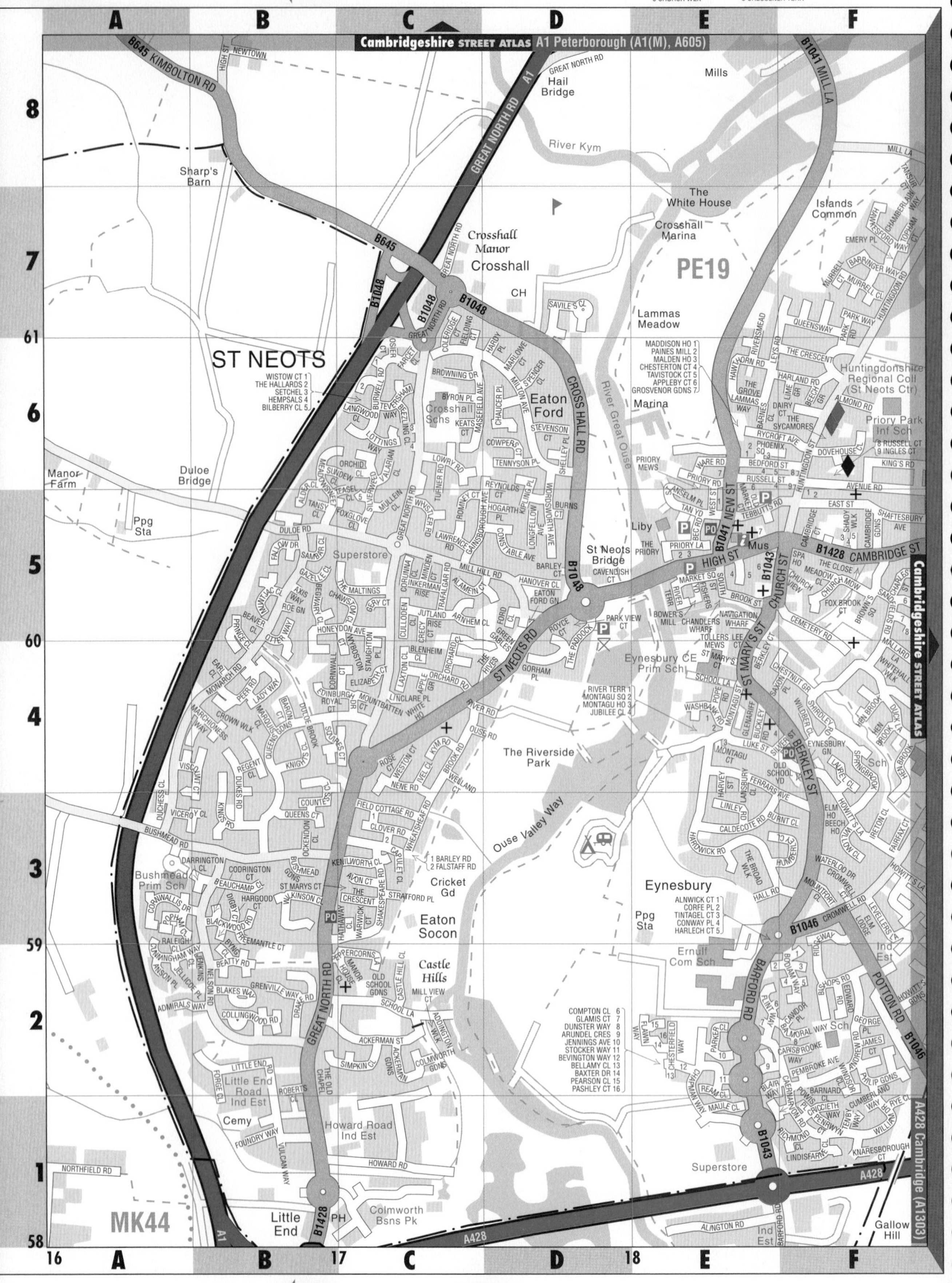

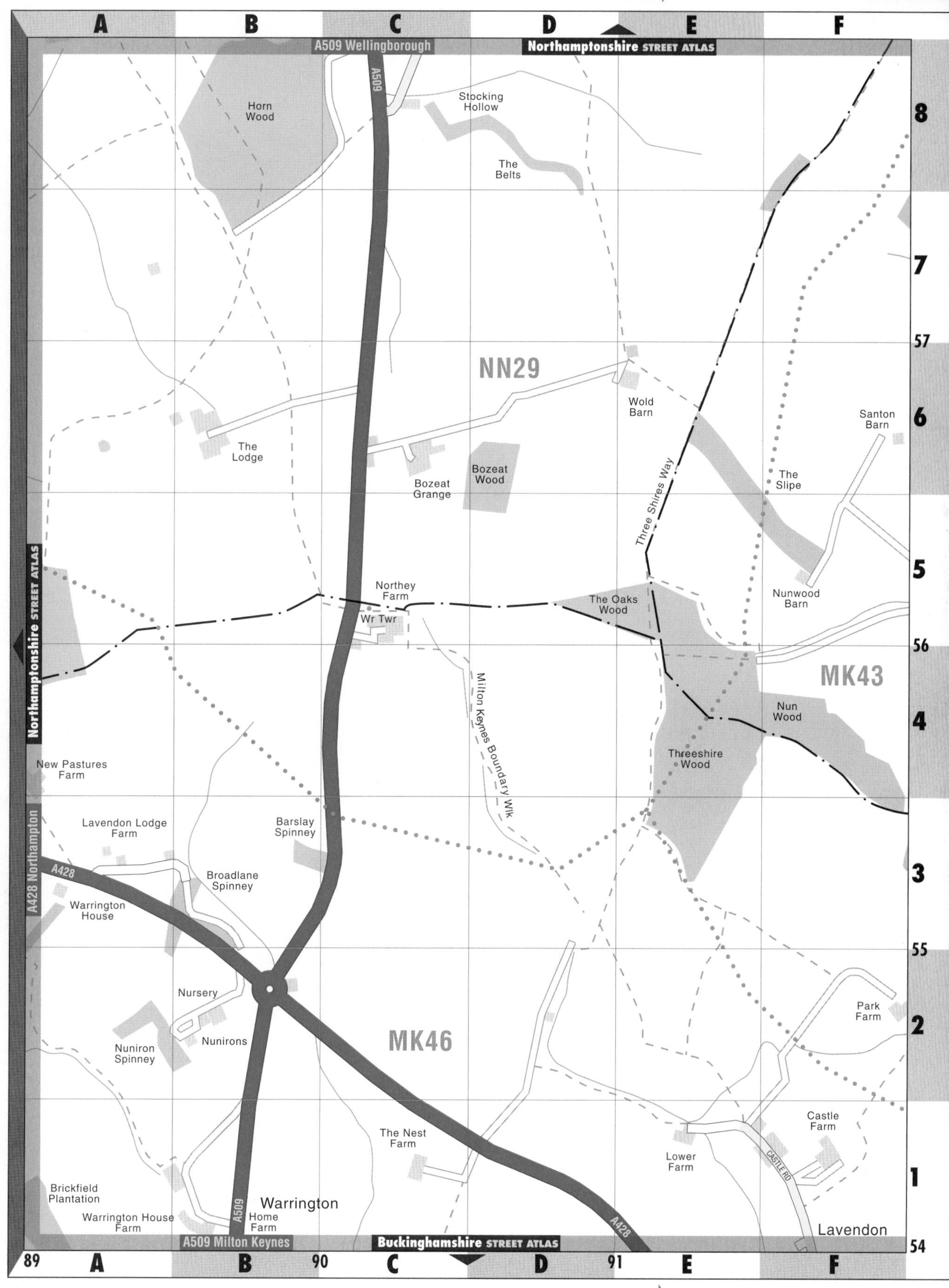

Horn Wood

Stocking Hollow

The Belts

8

7

57

NN29

Wold Barn

Santon Barn

6

The Lodge

Bozeat Grange

Bozeat Wood

Three Shires Way

The Slip

Nunwood Barn

5

Northey Farm

Wr Twr

The Oaks Wood

MK43

56

Milton Keynes Boundary Wlk

Nun Wood

4

New Pastures Farm

Lavendon Lodge Farm

Barslay Spinney

Threeshire Wood

Broadlane Spinney

3

Warrington House

55

Nursery

Park Farm

Nuniron Spinney

Nunirons

MK46

2

The Nest Farm

Castle Farm

Brickfield Plantation

Lower Farm

CASTLE RD

1

Warrington House Farm

Warrington Home Farm

Lavendon

54

A428 Northampton

A509

A428

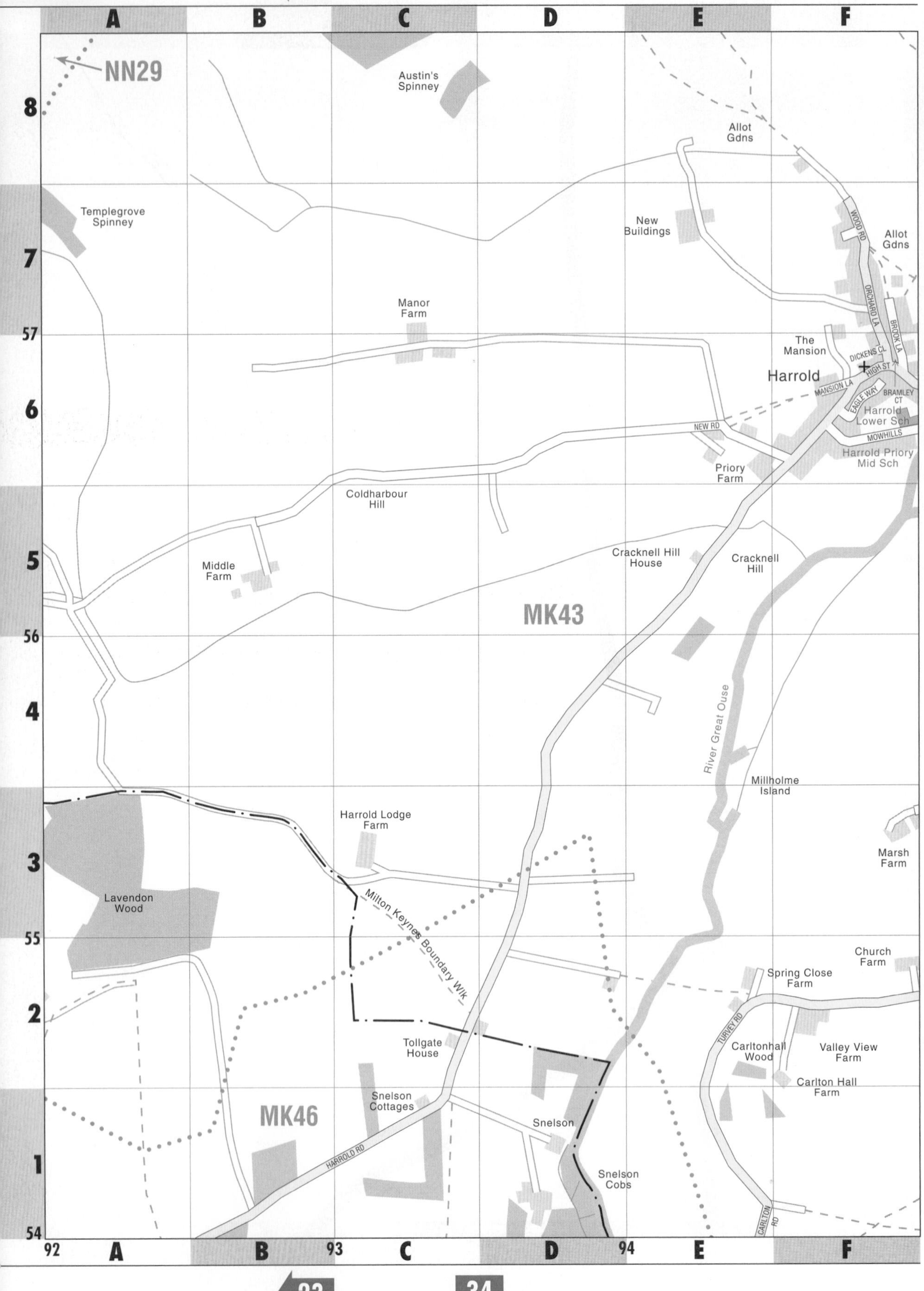

A B C D E F

8

NN29

Austin's
Spinney

Allot
Gdns

Templegrove
Spinney

New
Buildings

Allot
Gdns

7

Manor
Farm

57

The
Mansion

Harrold

6

NEW RD

Harrold
Lower Sch

Priory
Farm

Harrold Priory
Mid Sch

Coldharbour
Hill

Cracknell Hill
House

Cracknell
Hill

5

Middle
Farm

MK43

56

4

River Great Ouse

Millholme
Island

Marsh
Farm

Harrold Lodge
Farm

3

Lavendon
Wood

Milton Keynes Boundary Wlk

Church
Farm

55

Spring Close
Farm

2

Tollgate
House

Carltonhall
Wood

Valley View
Farm

Carlton Hall
Farm

MK46

Snelson
Cottages

Snelson

HARROLD RD

1

Snelson
Cobs

TURVEY RD

CARLTON RD

54

92 A B 93 C D 94 E F

A   B   C   D   E   F

Odell

8

Works

Folly

Southend
Farm

Little
Odell

ODELL RD

High St

Haswell Hall
Farm

MILL LA

HORSEFAIR LA

PH

7

Daisy
Bank

P

CARLTON RD

MEADWAY

PEACHS CL

Harrold Odell
Country Park

River Great Ouse

Woodside
House

Prigmoor
Bushes

57

DOVE LA

HIGH ST

THE GREEN

PO

PH

Hardwick
Farm

6

MOY'HULLS
Sch

PRIORY CT

CHURCH WLK

HALL CL

Visitor
Ctr

P

CARLTON RD

Harold
Bridge

Sewage
Works

FELMERSHAM RD

Hill
Farm

Lodge
Farm

5

Freer's Wood
Farm

56

Victoria
Farm

BRIDGE END

PH

PO

Freer's
Wood

4

Allot
Gdns

THE MOOR

CARRIERS WAY

Chellington

MK43

Monks
Wood

RECTORY CL

Carlton
Lower Sch

THE CAUSEWAY

Carlton

PAVENHAM RD

Westend
Farm

THE MARSH

STREET CL

HIGH ST

BEERY WAY

PH

MANOR CL

Braehead

HIGH ST

3

Nicholas
Farm

Piper's Highway

New Barns
Farm House

55

The
Spinney

EDENS LA

Wykes
Farm

Fishers
Farm

2

SCHOOL LA

Tankards

New Barns
Farm

HIGH ELMS

1

Northey
Farm

Blackwell
Spinney

54

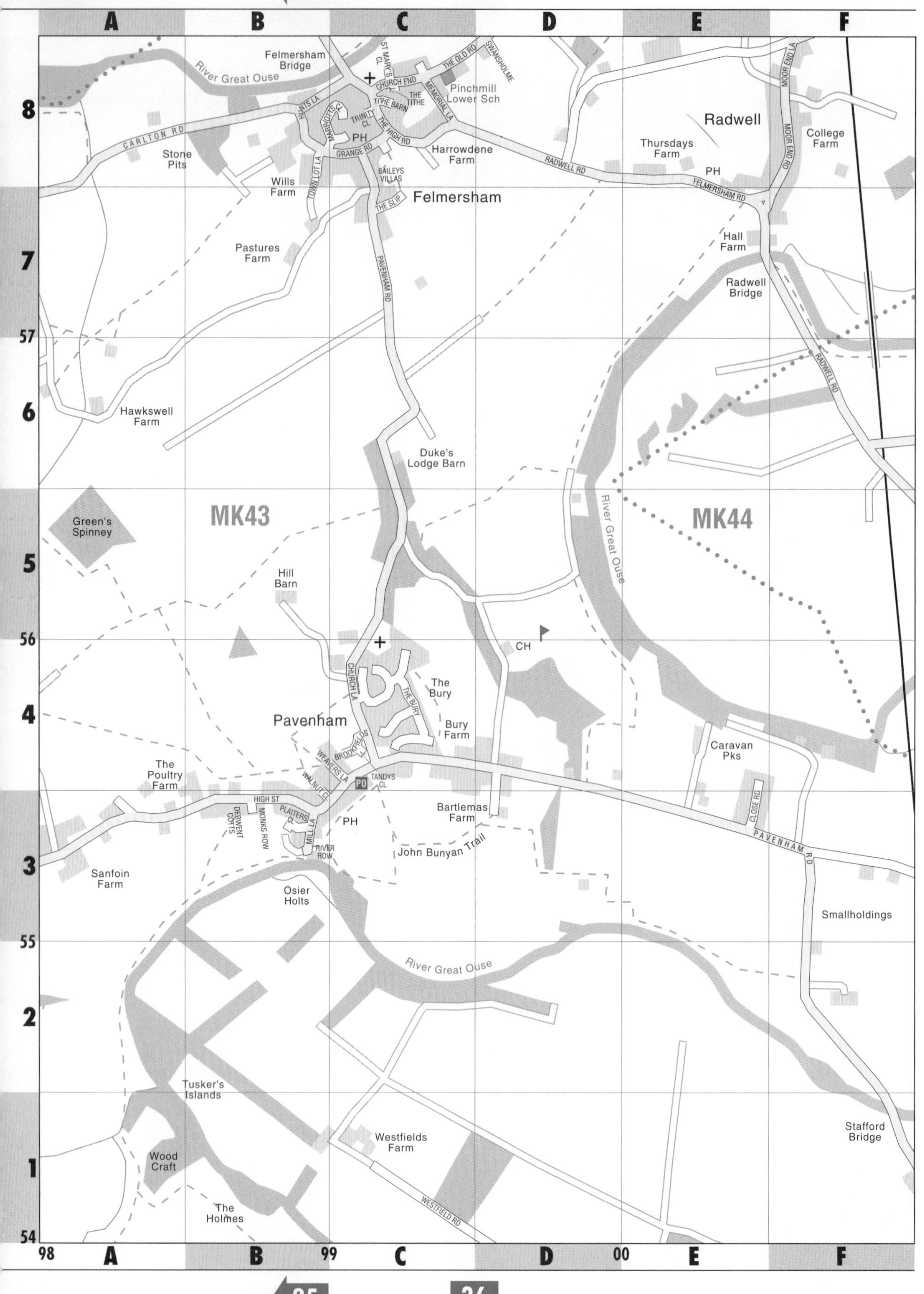

A B C D E F

8

Felmersham Bridge

River Great Ouse

St Mary's Cl

CHURCH END

THE OLD RD

SWANSHOLME

Pinchmill Lower Sch

Radwell

CARLTON RD

NUTS LA

MANOR CL

THE TITHE

TITHE BARN

THE HIGH RD

MEMORIAL LA

Thursdays Farm

PH

College Farm

MOOR END RD

MOOR END LA

Stone Pits

TRINITY CL

PH

GRANGE RD

Harrowdene Farm

RADWELL RD

FELMERSHAM RD

Wills Farm

TOWN LOT LA

BAILEYS VILLAS

Felmersham

THE SLIP

Hall Farm

7

Pastures Farm

PAVENHAM RD

Radwell Bridge

RADWELL RD

57

6

Hawkswell Farm

Duke's Lodge Barn

River Great Ouse

MK43

MK44

Green's Spinney

5

Hill Barn

CH

56

CHURCH LA

THE BURY

The Bury

Pavenham

Bury Farm

4

BROOKFIELDS LA

Bury Farm

Caravan Pks

CLOSE RD

The Poultry Farm

WEAVERS LA

WALNUT CL

PO

TANDYS CL

HIGH ST

MONKS ROW

PLAITERS CL

PH

Bartlemas Farm

PAVENHAM RD

Sanfoin Farm

DERWENT COTTS

MILL LA

RIVER ROW

John Bunyan Trail

3

Osier Holts

Smallholdings

55

River Great Ouse

Tusker's Islands

2

Westfields Farm

Wood Craft

Stafford Bridge

1

The Holmes

WESTFIELD RD

54

98 A B 99 C D 00 E F

17
28

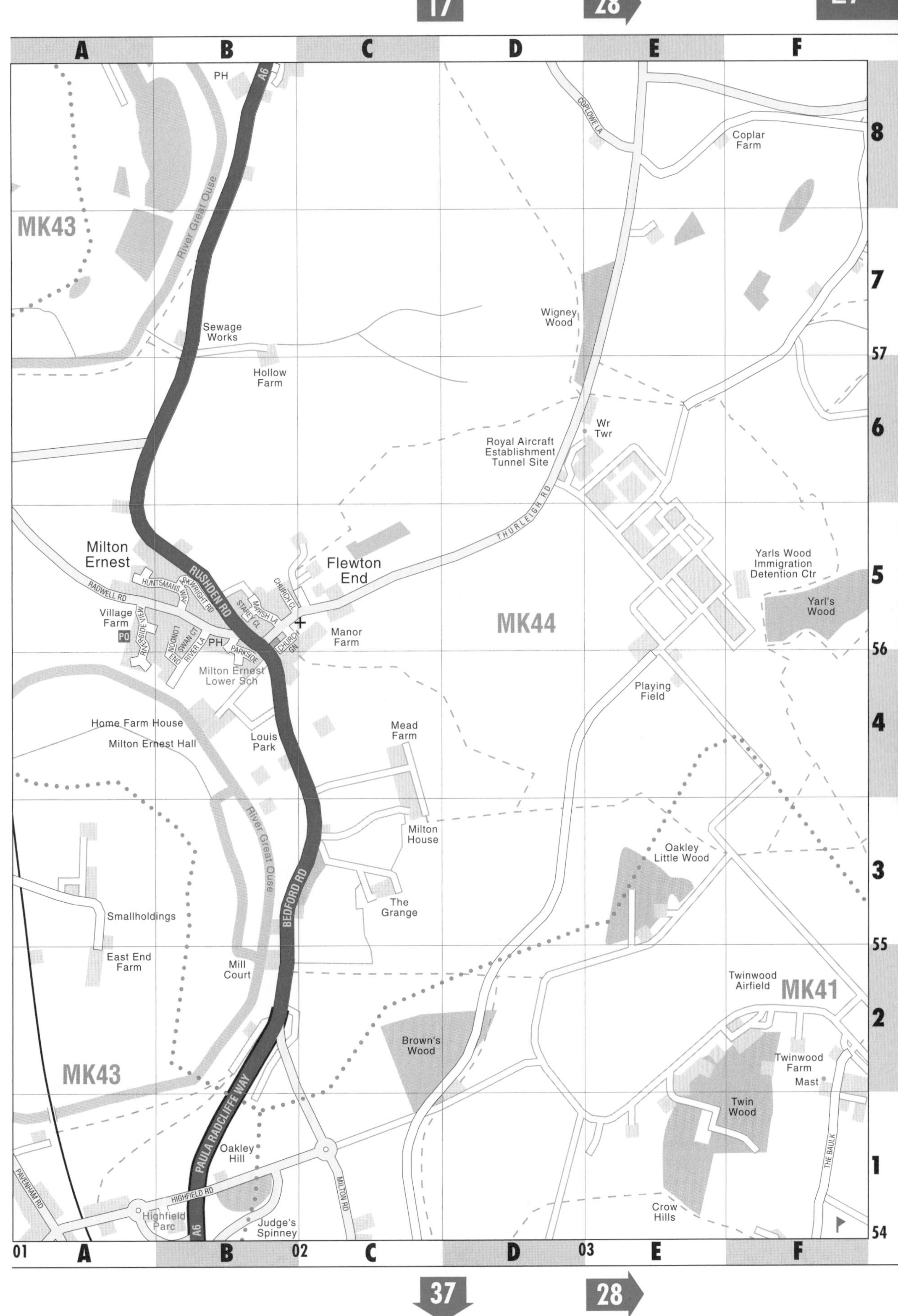
A
B
C
D
E
F
8
7
57
6
5
56
4
3
55
2
1
54
01
02
03
MK43
MK44
MK41
PH
A6
River Great Ouse
Sewage Works
Hollow Farm
COPLOWE LA
Coplar Farm
Wigney Wood
Wr Twr
Royal Aircraft Establishment Tunnel Site
THURLEIGH RD
Milton Ernest
Flewton End
RUSHDEN RD
HUNTSMANS WAY
RADWELL RD
Village Farm
PO
RIVERSIDE VIEW
LONDON END
SWAN CT
RIVER LA
PARKSIDE
STAREY CL
MARSH LA
CHURCH CL
CHURCH GN
Manor Farm
Milton Ernest Lower Sch
Yarls Wood Immigration Detention Ctr
Yarl's Wood
Playing Field
Home Farm House
Milton Ernest Hall
Louis Park
Mead Farm
Milton House
Oakley Little Wood
BEDFORD RD
The Grange
Smallholdings
East End Farm
Mill Court
Twinwood Airfield
Brown's Wood
Twinwood Farm
Mast
Twin Wood
PAULA RADCLIFFE WAY
Oakley Hill
PAVENHAM RD
HIGHFIELD RD
Highfield Parc
Judge's Spinney
MILTON RD
THE BAULK
Crow Hills

37
28

27
18

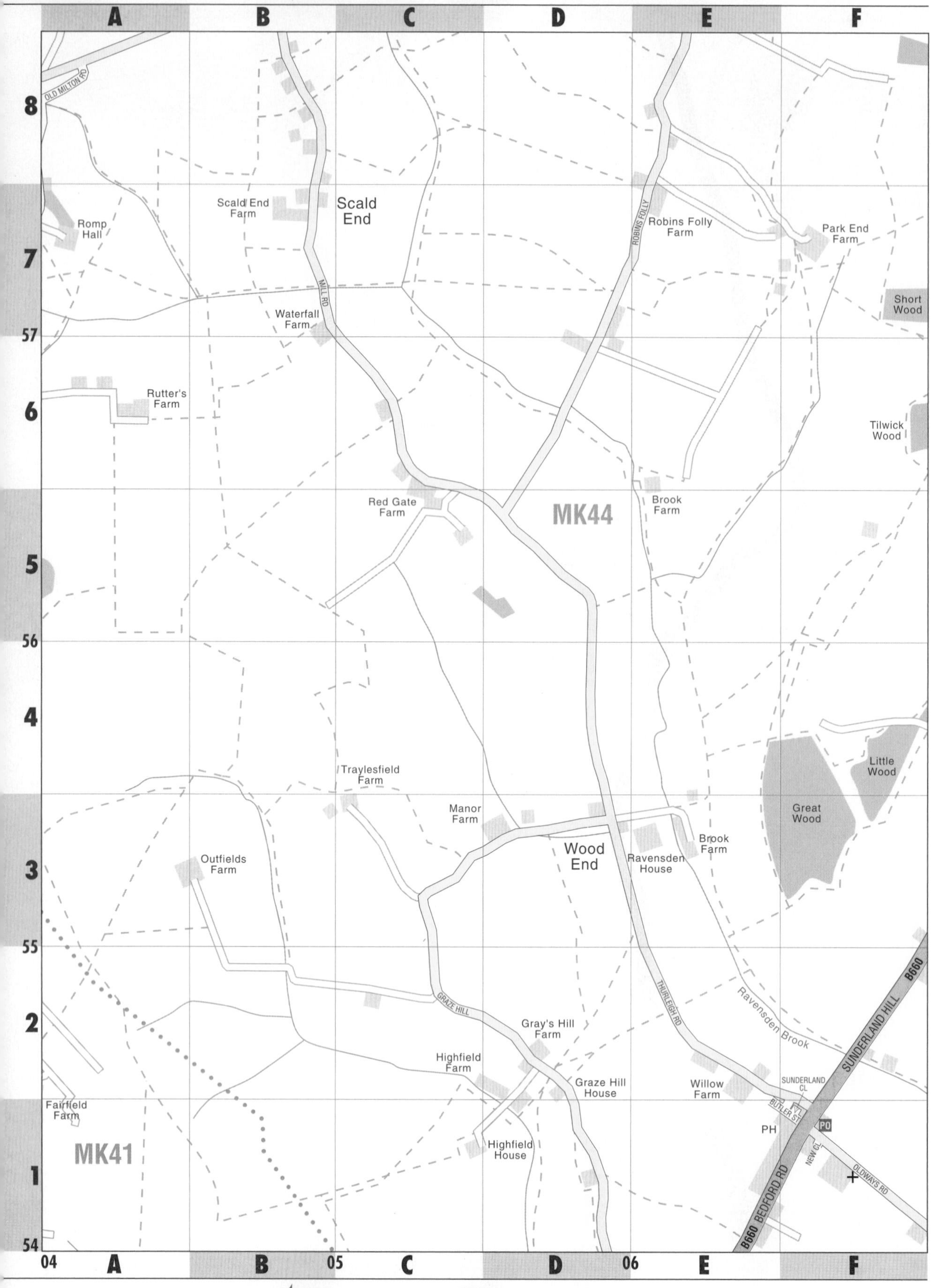

A B C D E F

8

Scald End
Farm

Scald
End

Romp
Hall

Robins Folly
Farm

Park End
Farm

7

Short
Wood

57

Waterfall
Farm

OLD MILTON RD

MILL RD

ROBINS FOLLY

Rutter's
Farm

6

Tilwick
Wood

Red Gate
Farm

MK44

Brook
Farm

5

56

4

Little
Wood

Traylesfield
Farm

Manor
Farm

Great
Wood

Outfields
Farm

Wood
End

Ravensden
House

Brook
Farm

3

55

GRAZE HILL

Gray's Hill
Farm

Ravensden Brook

SUNDERLAND HILL

B560

THURLEIGH RD

2

Highfield
Farm

Graze Hill
House

Willow
Farm

SUNDERLAND
CL

BUTLER ST

PO

Fairfield
Farm

MK41

Highfield
House

PH

NEW CL

OLDWAYS RD

B560 BEDFORD RD

1

54

04 A B 05 C D 06 E F

19
30
A
B
C
D
E
F
8
7
57
6
5
56
4
3
55
2
1
54
07
08
09
Brook Farm
B660
Mavourn Farm
Southfields Farm
New Road Farm
NEW RD
PH
Wheatsheaf Farm
KIMBOLTON RD
Smartwick Cottage Farm
CH
Blacklands
Tilwick Farm
Hook Spinneys
Smartwick Farm
MK44
CHEQUERS HILL
Rectory Farm
Shrubbery Farm
Top Farm
SHRUBBERY LA
Cricket Ground
Wr Twr
SUNDERLAND HILL
Redbrick Cottages
Manor Farm
Church End Farm
Wilden CE Lower Sch
Wilden
PH
Elm Cottages
RAVENSDEN RD
MANOR CL
Brook Farm
HIGH ST
HOLLIS LA
MAYES CL
Grange Farm
Glebe Farm
Crow Hill Farm
Green La
Church End
Poplar Farm
Sevick End
Newlands Farm
Avenue Farm
Bedford Butterfly Park
CHURCH END
VICARAGE CL
RENHOLD RD
Ravensden CE Lower Sch
Ravensden
High Farm
Sevick End Farm
PH
MK41
OLDWAYS RD
39
30

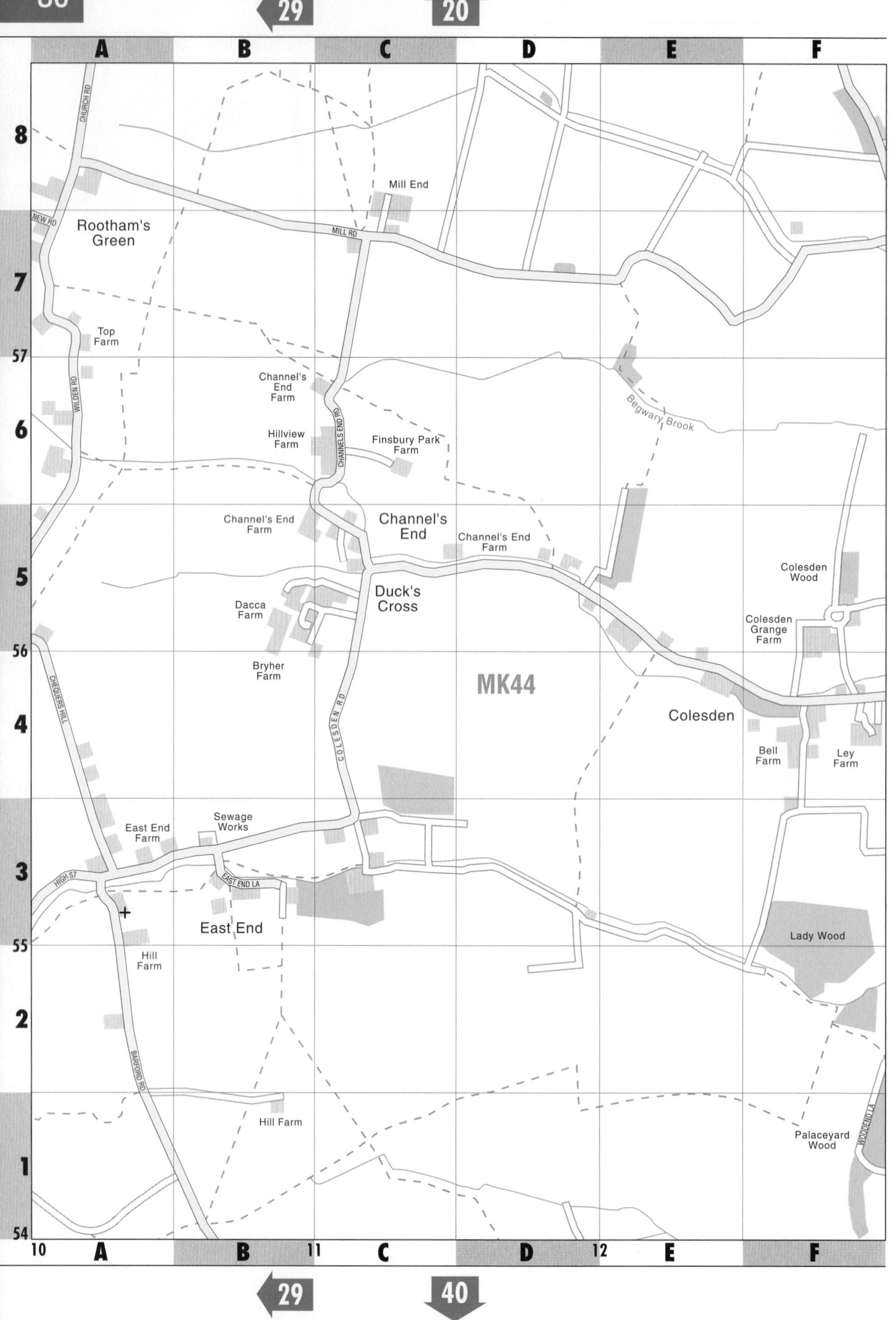

A **B** **C** **D** **E** **F**

8

Mill End

CHURCH RD

NEW RD

Rootham's
Green

MILL RD

7

Top
Farm

WILDEN RD

57

Channel's
End
Farm

CHANNELS END RD

6

Hillview
Farm

Finsbury Park
Farm

Begwary Brook

Channel's End
Farm

Channel's
End

Channel's End
Farm

Colesden
Wood

5

Dacca
Farm

Duck's
Cross

Colesden
Grange
Farm

COLESDEN RD

56

Bryher
Farm

MK44

Colesden

4

Bell
Farm

Ley
Farm

CHEQUERS HILL

Sewage
Works

East End
Farm

3

HIGH ST

EAST END LA

East End

Lady Wood

55

Hill
Farm

BARFORD RD

2

Hill Farm

Palaceyard
Wood

WOODEND LA

1

54

10 **A** **B** **11** **C** **D** **12** **E** **F**

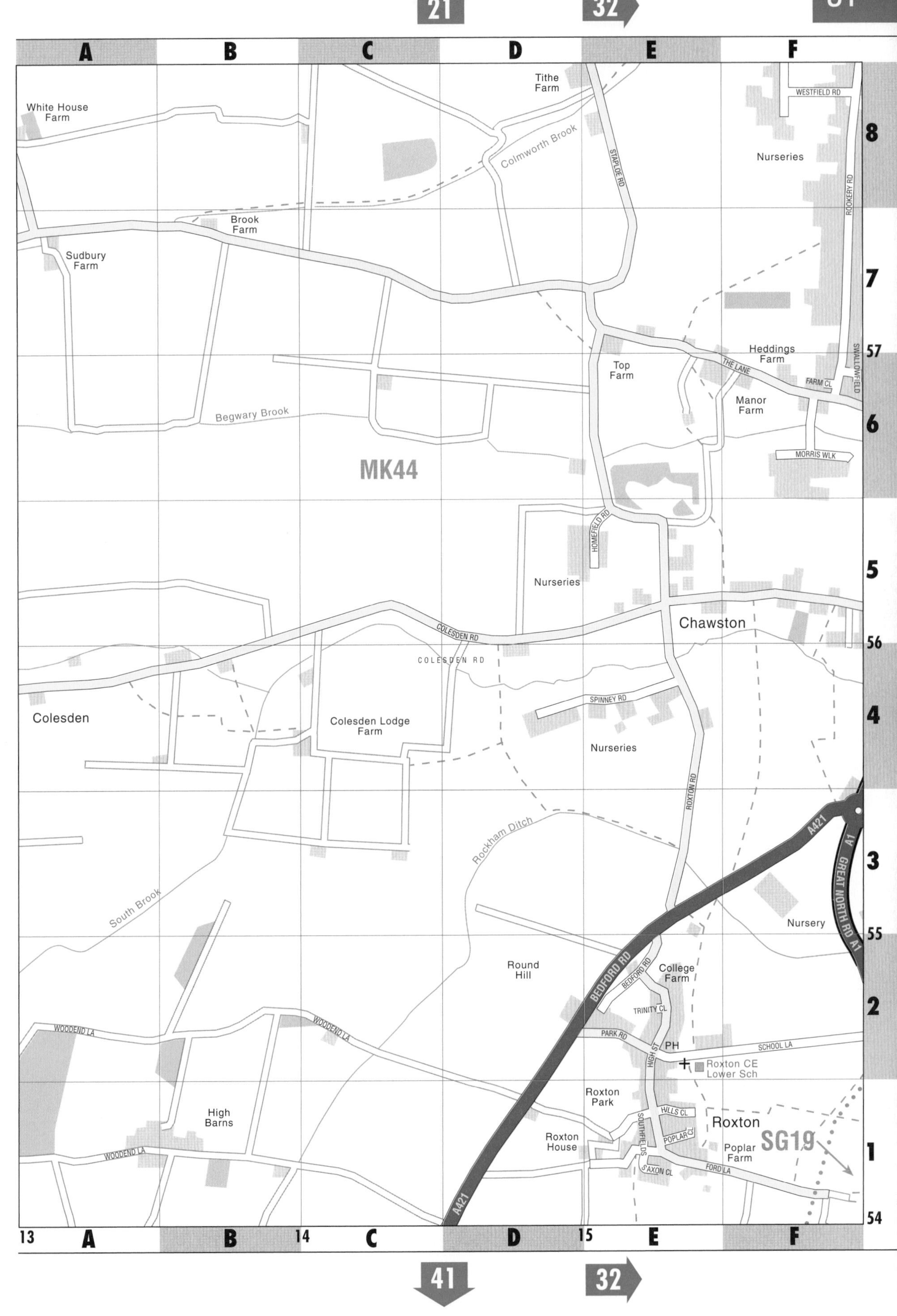
21
32
A
B
C
D
E
F
Tithe Farm
WESTFIELD RD
White House Farm
Colmworth Brook
STAPLOE RD
8
Nurseries
ROOKERY RD
Brook Farm
Sudbury Farm
7
57
Heddings Farm
THE LANE
SWALLOWFIELD
Top Farm
FARM CL
Manor Farm
Begwary Brook
6
MORRIS WLK
MK44
HOMEFIELD RD
5
Nurseries
Chawston
56
COLESDEN RD
SPINNEY RD
4
Colesden
Colesden Lodge Farm
Nurseries
ROXTON RD
A421
A1
Rockham Ditch
3
GREAT NORTH RD
South Brook
Nursery
55
BEDFORD RD
Round Hill
College Farm
2
TRINITY CL
WOODEND LA
PARK RD
PH
SCHOOL LA
HIGH ST
Roxton CE Lower Sch
Roxton Park
High Barns
HILLS CL
Roxton
SOUTHFIELDS
Roxton House
POPLAR CL
SG19
1
Poplar Farm
SAXON CL
FORD LA
54
13
14
15
41
32

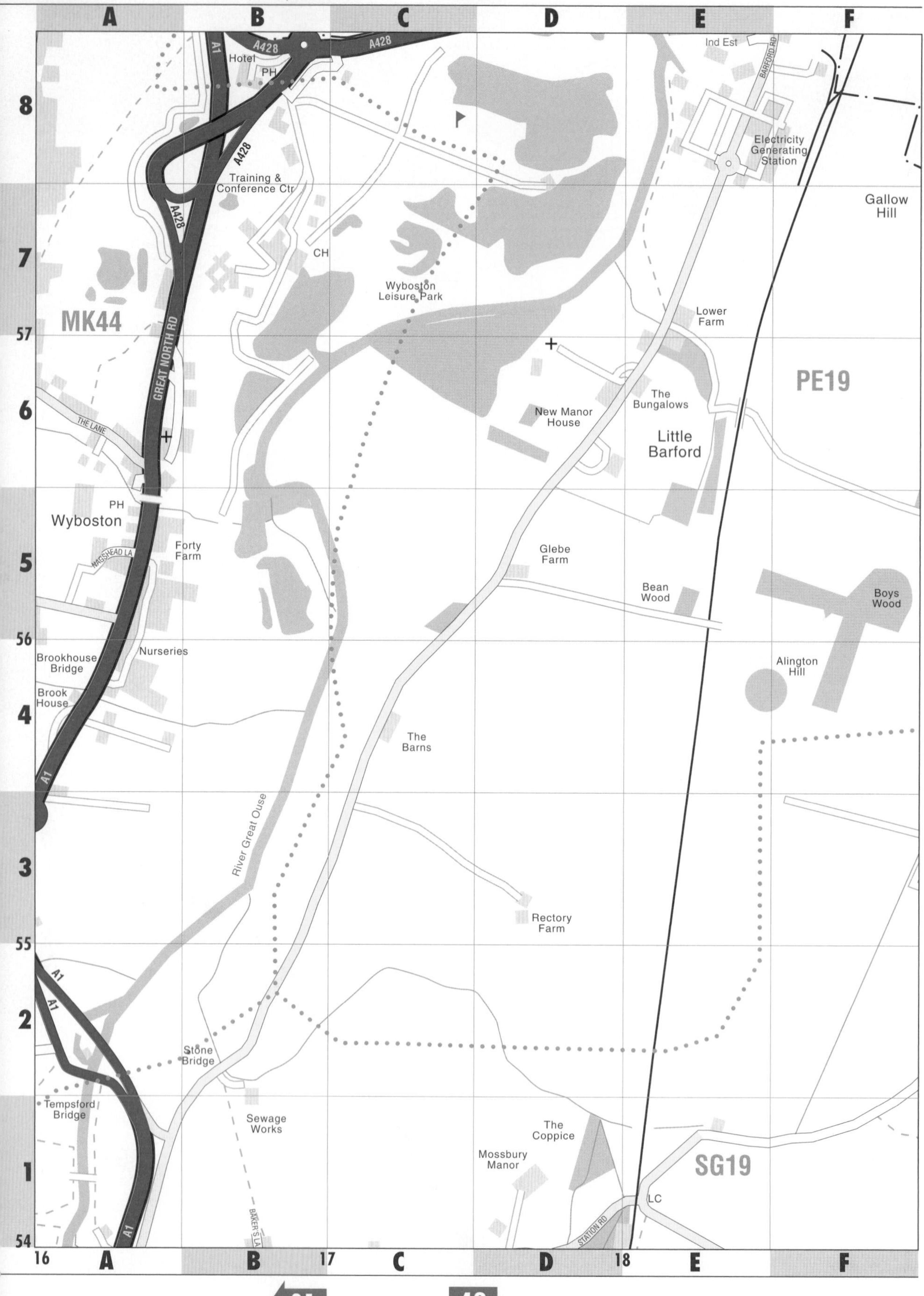

A   B   C   D   E   F

Ind Est

Hotel

PH

8

A428

Training &
Conference Ctr

Electricity
Generating
Station

Gallow
Hill

CH

7

Wyboston
Leisure Park

Lower
Farm

57

PE19

MK44

6

New Manor
House

The
Bungalows

Little
Barford

THE LANE

PH

Wyboston

Forty
Farm

Glebe
Farm

Bean
Wood

Boys
Wood

5

NAGSHEAD LA

56

Nurseries

Brookhouse
Bridge

Alington
Hill

Brook
House

4

The
Barns

River Great Ouse

GREAT NORTH RD

A1

3

Rectory
Farm

55

A1

2

Stone
Bridge

Tempsford
Bridge

Sewage
Works

The
Coppice

SG19

BAKER'S LA

Mossbury
Manor

1

LC

A1

STATION RD

54

16   A   B   17   C   D   18   E   F

Cambridgeshire STREET ATLAS

A B C D E F

8
7
57
6
5
56
4
3
55
2
1
54

Rectory Farm

Parker's Farm

Lansbury Farm

Round Spinney

Hail La

Hail Lane Plantation

ST NEOTS RD

B1046

B1046

CH

St Neots L Ctr

Hardwicke Spinneys

Long Plantation

Top Farm

Hotel

CH

Pear Tree Spinney

PE19

Abbotsley Downs

Gipsy Corner

Highbarns

Downs Plantation

Highfield Kennels

Southwood Farm

Highfield Spinney

DREWELS LA

PITSDEAN RD

Bushy Common Plantation

Sir John's Wood

Highfield Farm

Crane Hill

Highfield Cottages

Crab Tree Spinney

Hill's Farm

The Decoy

Stone Hill Farm

Ash Plantation

New Farm

SG19

Cold Arbour

Kims Spinney

SG19

Cambridgeshire STREET ATLAS

19 A B 20 C D 21 E F

24

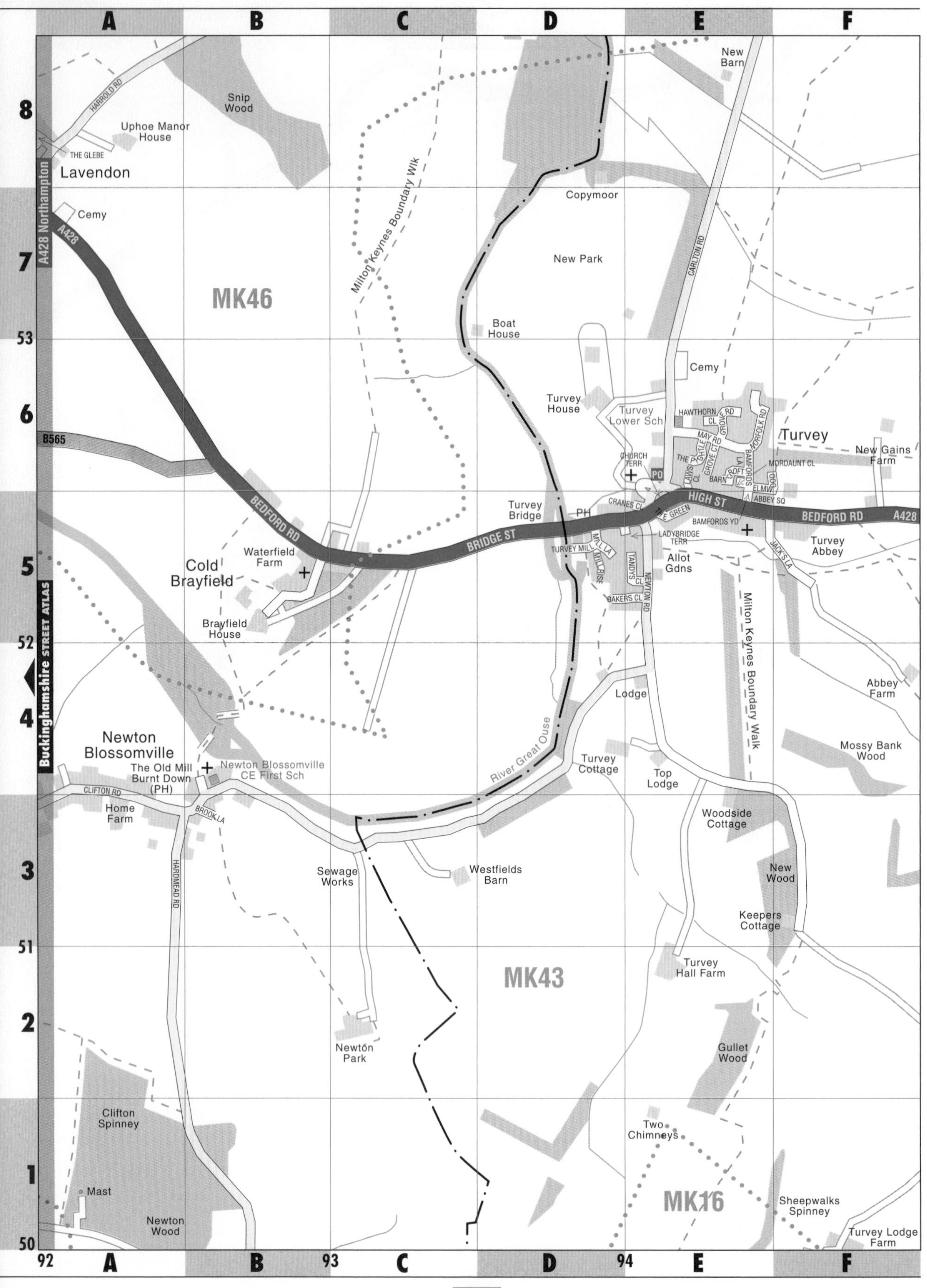

A
B
C
D
E
F
8
7
53
6
5
52
4
3
51
2
1
50
92
93
94
Snip Wood
Uphoe Manor House
New Barn
THE GLEBE
Lavendon
HARROLD RD
Cemy
A428 Northampton
A428
MK46
Milton Keynes Boundary Wlk
Copymoor
New Park
CARLTON RD
Boat House
Cemy
Turvey House
Turvey Lower Sch
HAWTHORN RD
Turvey
New Gains Farm
B565
CHURCH TERR
PO
MORDAUNT CL
HIGH ST
ABBEY SQ
Turvey Bridge
PH
CRANES CL
THE GREEN
BAMFORDS YD
BEDFORD RD
A428
BEDFORD RD
BRIDGE ST
LADYBRIDGE TERR
Waterfield Farm
Cold Brayfield
TURVEY MILL
MILL LA
MILL RISE
TANDYS CL
NEWTON RD
BAKERS CL
Allot Gdns
JACK'S LA
Turvey Abbey
Milton Keynes Boundary Walk
Brayfield House
Abbey Farm
Lodge
Newton Blossomville
Buckinghamshire STREET ATLAS
River Great Ouse
Mossy Bank Wood
The Old Mill Burnt Down (PH)
Newton Blossomville CE First Sch
Turvey Cottage
Top Lodge
CLIFTON RD
BROOK LA
Home Farm
Woodside Cottage
Sewage Works
Westfields Barn
New Wood
HARDMEAD RD
Keepers Cottage
Turvey Hall Farm
MK43
Newton Park
Gullet Wood
Clifton Spinney
Two Chimneys
Mast
MK16
Sheepwalks Spinney
Newton Wood
Turvey Lodge Farm

46

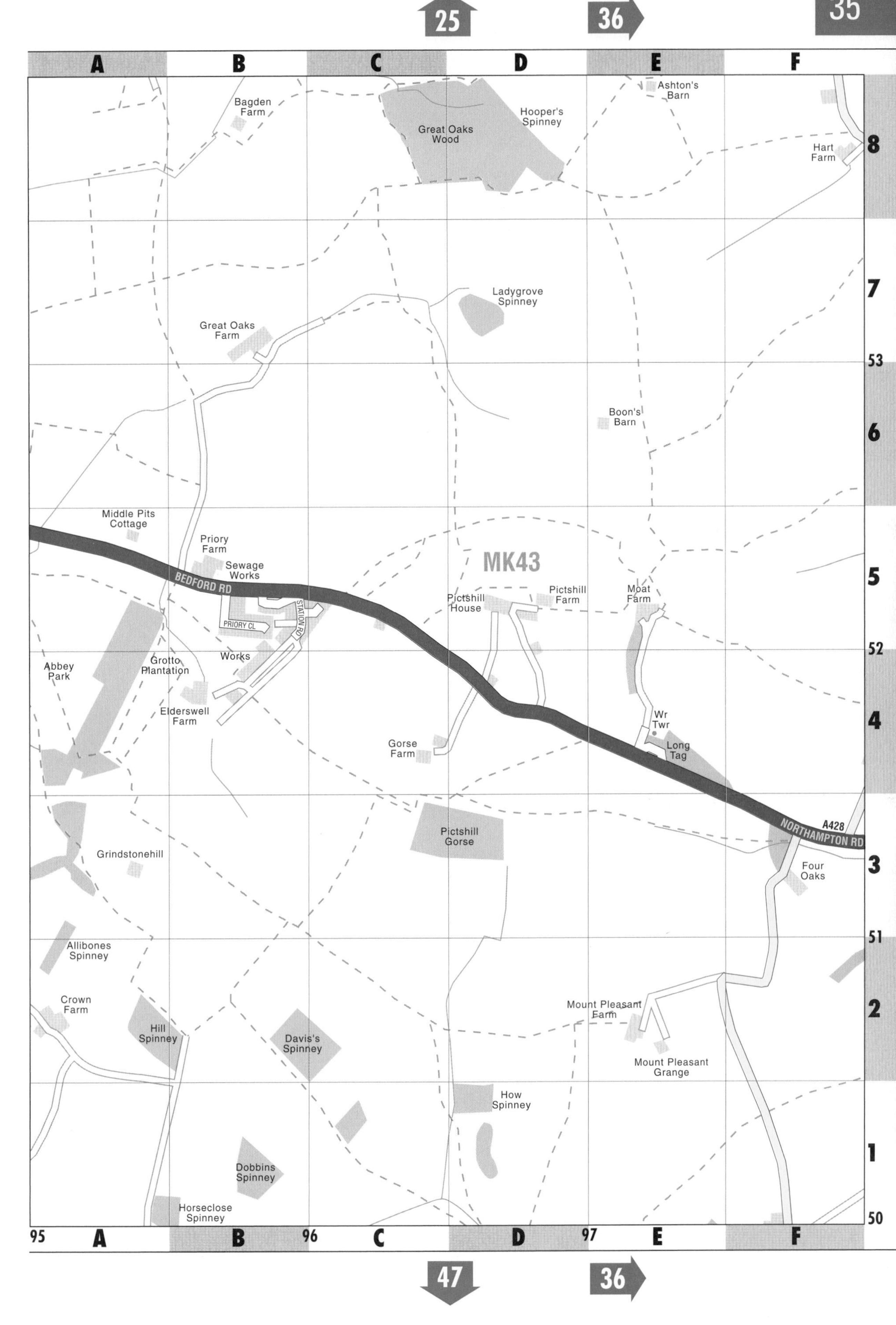

A   B   C   D   E   F

Bagden
Farm

Great Oaks
Wood

Hooper's
Spinney

Ashton's
Barn

8

Hart
Farm

Ladygrove
Spinney

7

53

Great Oaks
Farm

Boon's
Barn

6

Middle Pits
Cottage

MK43

5

Priory
Farm

Sewage
Works

BEDFORD RD

Pictshill
Farm

Moat
Farm

Pictshill
House

STATION RD

PRIORY CL

52

Works

Abbey
Park

Grotto
Plantation

Elderswell
Farm

Gorse
Farm

Wr
Twr

Long
Tag

4

NORTHAMPTON RD

A428

Pictshill
Gorse

Grindstonehill

Four
Oaks

3

51

Allibones
Spinney

Mount Pleasant
Farm

2

Crown
Farm

Hill
Spinney

Davis's
Spinney

Mount Pleasant
Grange

How
Spinney

1

Dobbins
Spinney

Horseclose
Spinney

50

95   A   B   96   C   D   97   E   F

A B C D E F

8 7 53 6 5 52 4 3 51 2 1 50

West End
Meeting Farm
Westend Farm
Langcroft Farm
Manor Farm
Church End
Stevington
Duck End Farm
Duck End
Park End
Mill Farm
Stevington Windmill
Park Farm
Stevington Belt
River Great Ouse
Fox Covert
Town Farm
Oakley House
Oakley Bridge
Bromham Plantation
Mushroom Hill
Skylark Cottage
MK43
John Bunyan Trail
Tithe Farm
Molliver's Wood
Salem Thrift
Wr Twr
West Lodge
London Barn Farm
Rainbow Sch
East Lodge
Salem Cottages
Bowels Wood
Bromham
Bromham CE Lower Sch
Liby
Burdelys Manor
White's Wood
Bury End
Kinsbourne Farm
Brookside Caravan Park
Bridge End
How Wood
Becks Ash Spinney
Wick End Farm
Dropshort Farm

WEST END, COURT LA, CHURCH RD, SILVER ST, THE BAKERY, FARLEY WAY, BURRIDGE'S CL, FOXBROOK, PARK RD, WESTFIELD RD, FARSANDS, QUEENS CL, HIGH ST, REYNES DR, GRENIDGE WAY, DEWLANDS, THE DRIVE, CHURCH LA, RUFFS FURZE, OAKLEY RD, WOODLAND DR, WINGFIELD RD, ORCHARD CL, AVOCA HO, MOLIVERS LA, WILLOW CL, THE GREEN, TUDOR CL, MOWBRAY CL, CORNWALLIS CL, SPRINGFIELD DR, GRANGE LA, VILLAGE RD, NORTHAMPTON RD, GRANGE CT, NEVILLE CL, NEVILLE CRES, GODWIN CL, GODWIN WAY, RANDALLS CL, TREVOR DR, ROSEMARY DR, BROOK WAY, LEY SIDE, WEBBS CL, BUCKS CL, MILLFIELD, BERRY DR, DOVEHOUSE CL, STAGSDEN RD, BOX END RD, HERONS MEAD, THE PADDOCKS, BRETT DR, JACKMAN CL, MAYHEW CL, BATCHELOR GDNS, QUEENSBY WAY, SYMONDS CL, THISTLE LA, PINSENT AVE, CARTWRIGHT CL, NEW RD, LIME CL, TOLLGATE CL, DYNEVOR CL, PRINCESS RD, WALNUT CL, PEAR TREE CL, PARTRIDGE LA, RED CEDAR RD, CHESTNUT AVE, THE GLADE, STONE PINE RD, TULIP TREE CL, PARKLAND, NORTHAMPTON RD, NORTHAMPTON RD, BEDFORD RD

1 RED OAK CL
2 BLUE SPRUCE CL

A428, A422, A5134

PH, PO, P

98 99 00

A B C D E F

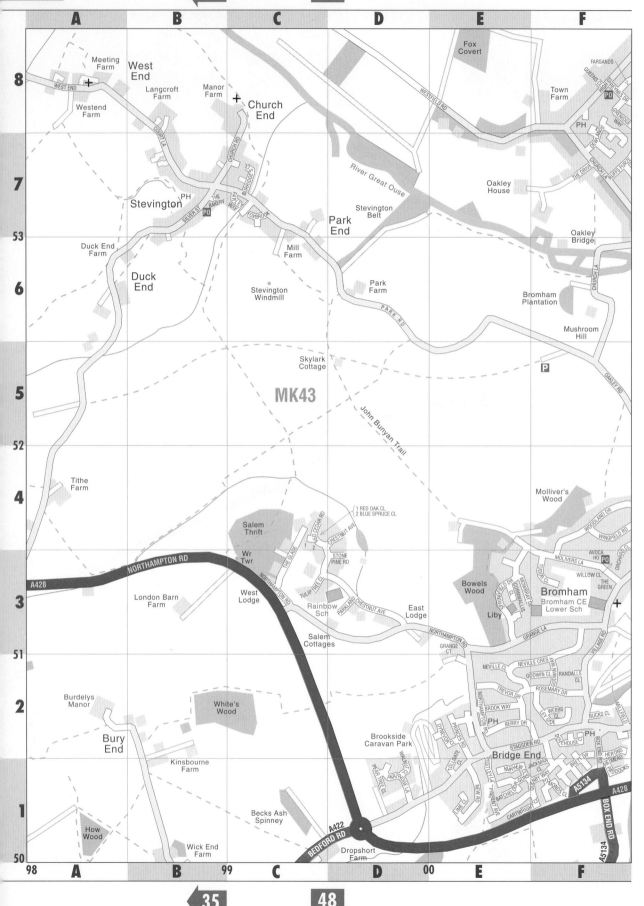

27
38

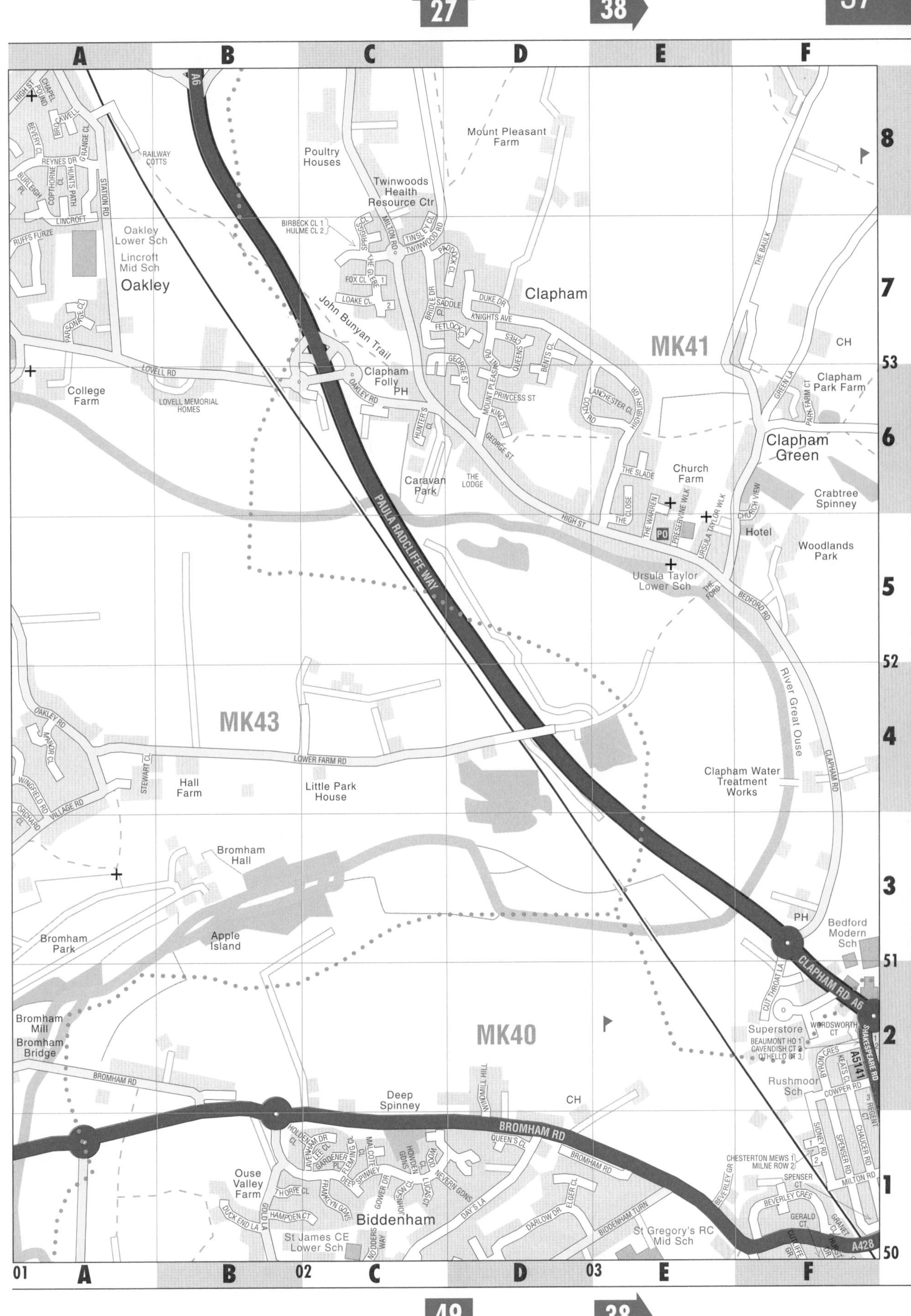
A
B
C
D
E
F
8
7
6
5
4
3
2
1
53
52
51
50
01
02
03
Oakley
Clapham
Clapham Green
Biddenham
MK41
MK43
MK40
A6
PAULA RADCLIFFE WAY
BROMHAM RD
CLAPHAM RD A6
A5141
A428
Mount Pleasant Farm
Poultry Houses
Twinwoods Health Resource Ctr
RAILWAY COTTS
Oakley Lower Sch
Lincroft Mid Sch
College Farm
LOVELL MEMORIAL HOMES
LOVELL RD
John Bunyan Trail
Clapham Folly
PH
OAKLEY RD
Caravan Park
THE LODGE
Church Farm
Hotel
CH
Clapham Park Farm
Crabtree Spinney
Woodlands Park
Ursula Taylor Lower Sch
River Great Ouse
Clapham Water Treatment Works
LOWER FARM RD
Hall Farm
Little Park House
Bromham Hall
Apple Island
Bromham Park
Bromham Mill
Bromham Bridge
BROMHAM RD
Deep Spinney
Ouse Valley Farm
St James CE Lower Sch
St Gregory's RC Mid Sch
Bedford Modern Sch
Superstore
Rushmoor Sch
HIGH ST
PO
BIRBECK CL 1
HULME CL 2
BEAUMONT HO 1
CAVENDISH CT 2
OTHELLO CT 3
CHESTERTON MEWS 1
MILNE ROW 2

49
38

MK44

MK41

MK40

Clapham Park Wood

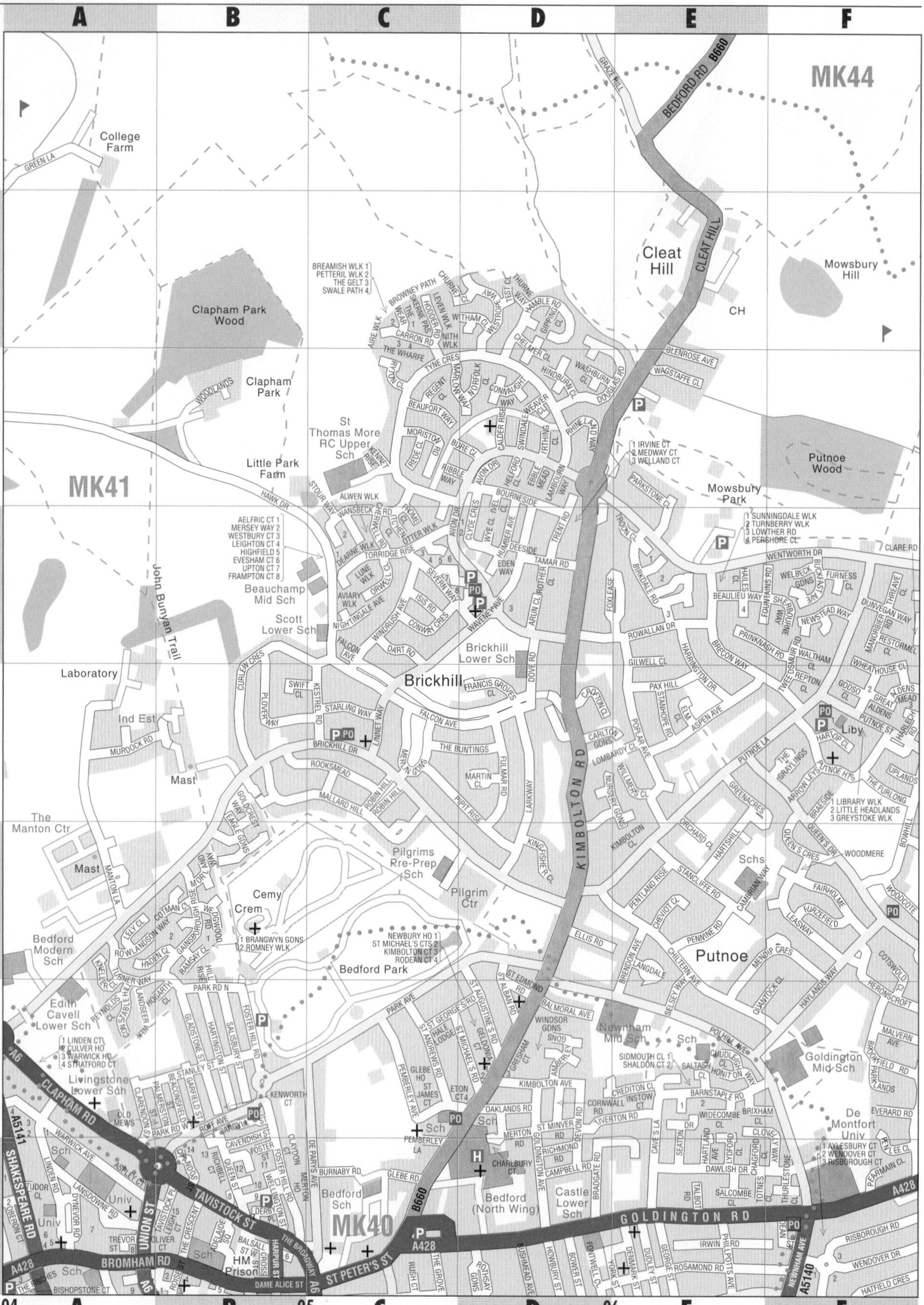

Clapham Park

Little Park Farm

College Farm

Cleat Hill

Mowsbury Hill

Putnoe Wood

Mowsbury Park

St Thomas More RC Upper Sch

Beauchamp Mid Sch

Scott Lower Sch

Brickhill Lower Sch

BRICKHILL

Laboratory

Ind Est

Mast

The Manton Ctr

Mast

Bedford Modern Sch

Cemy Crem

Pilgrims Pre-Prep Sch

Pilgrim Ctr

Bedford Park

Edith Cavell Lower Sch

Livingstone Lower Sch

Newnham Mid Sch

Goldington Mid Sch

De Montfort Univ

Putnoe

Liby

Schs

Woodmere

HM Prison

Bedford Sch

Bedford (North Wing)

Castle Lower Sch

GOLDINGTON RD

John Bunyan Trail

BREAMISH WLK 1
PETTERIL WLK 2
THE GELT 3
SWALE PATH 4

AELFRIC CT 1
MERSEY WAY 2
WESTBURY CT 3
LEIGHTON CT 4
HIGHFIELD 5
EVESHAM CT 6
UPTON CT 7
FRAMPTON CT 8

1 IRVINE CT
2 MEDWAY CT
3 WELLAND CT

1 SUNNINGDALE WLK
2 TURNBERRY WLK
3 LOWTHER RD
4 PERSHORE CL

7 CLARE RD

1 BRANGWYN GDNS
2 ROMNEY WLK

NEWBURY HO 1
ST MICHAEL'S CTS 2
KIMBOLTON CT 3
RODEN CT 4

1 LINDEN CT
2 CULVER HO
3 WARWICK HO
4 STRATFORD CT

1 LIBRARY WLK
2 LITTLE HEADLANDS
3 GREYSTOKE WLK

1 AYLESBURY CT
2 WENDOVER CT
3 RISBOROUGH CT

A1	B1	
1 REGENT CT	1 PRIORY CT	10 ALBERT ST
2 MILTON RD	2 NORTH PAR	11 COBDEN SQ
3 STOKE ALBANY MEWS	3 ROISE CT	12 QUEEN'S CT
4 PADBURY HO	4 PRIORY TERR	13 BOSWELL CT
5 BEECH CT	5 GWYN ST	14 CHANDOS CT
6 CYMBELINE CT	6 BALSALL ST E	15 ARLINGTON CT
7 LANSDOWNE TERR	7 PEEL ST	
8 SALISBURY HO	8 BOSWELL PL	
9 BEAUCHAMP CT	9 PRINCES ST	

29
40

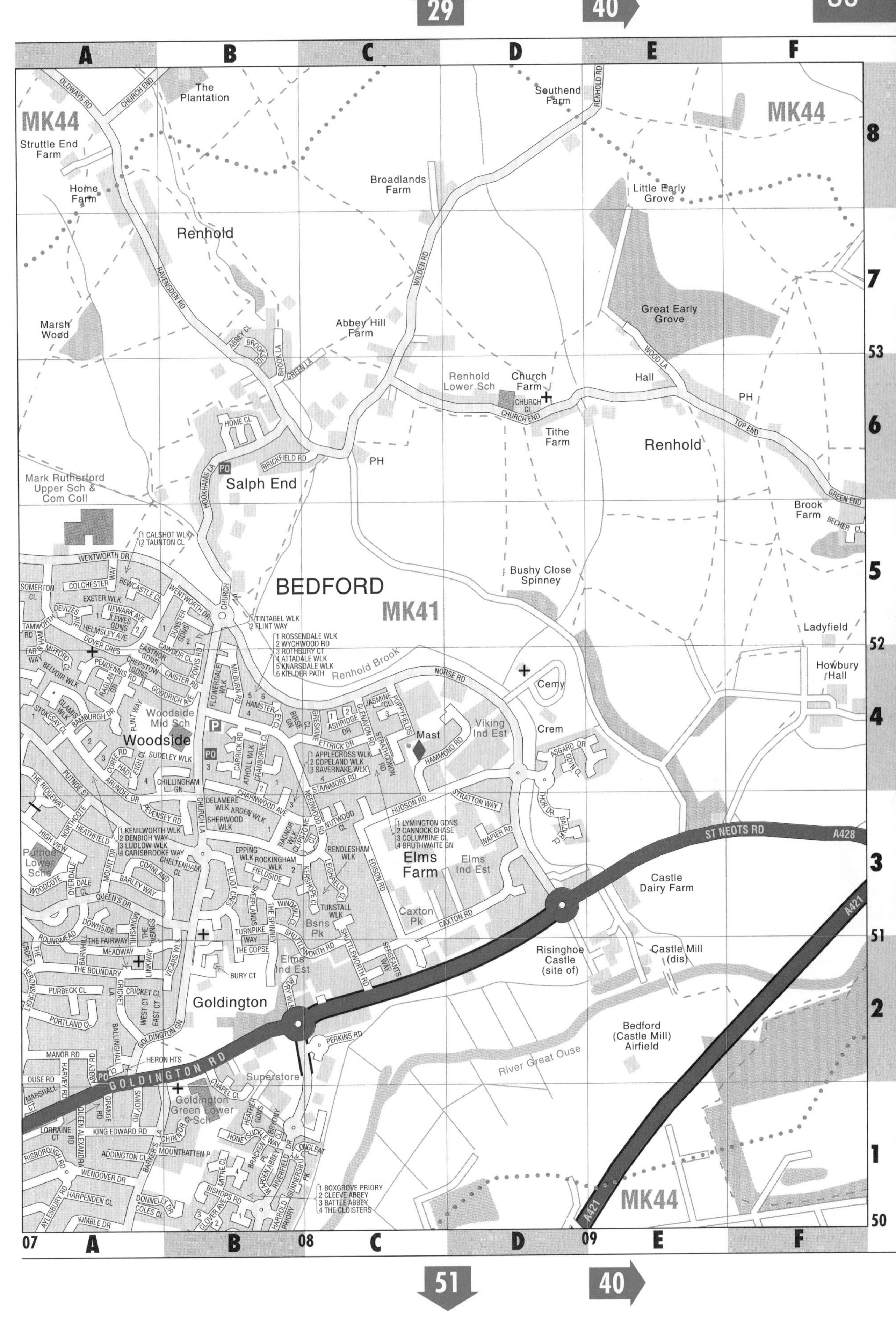
A
B
C
D
E
F
8
7
53
6
5
52
4
3
51
2
1
50
07
08
09
MK44
Struttle End Farm
The Plantation
OLDWAYS RD
CHURCH END
Southend Farm
RENHOLD RD
MK44
Home Farm
Broadlands Farm
Little Early Grove
Renhold
RAVENSDEN RD
WILDEN RD
Marsh Wood
Abbey Hill Farm
Great Early Grove
WOOD LA
ABBEY CL
BROOK LA
GREEN LA
Renhold Lower Sch
Church Farm
CHURCH CL
CHURCH END
Hall
PH
TOP END
HOME CL
Tithe Farm
Renhold
HOOKHAMS LA
PO
BRICKFIELD RD
PH
Salph End
Mark Rutherford Upper Sch & Com Coll
GREEN END
Brook Farm
BECHER CL
1 CALSHOT WLK
2 TAUNTON CL
WENTWORTH DR
BEDFORD
MK41
Bushy Close Spinney
SOMERTON CL
COLCHESTER
BEWCASTLE CL
EXETER WLK
CHURCH LA
WENTWORTH DR
1 TINTAGEL WLK
2 FLINT WAY
Ladyfield
DEVIZES AVE
NEWARK AVE
LEWES GDNS
HELMSLEY AVE
DUNSTER GDNS
1 ROSSENDALE WLK
2 WYCHWOOD RD
3 ROTHBURY CT
4 ATTADALE WLK
5 KNARSDALE WLK
6 KIELDER PATH
TAMWORTH RD
MITFORD CL
DOVER CRES
EASTNOR GDNS
CAWDOR CL
POWIS RD
Renhold Brook
NORSE RD
Howbury Hall
FAR WAY
BELVOIR WLK
PENDENNIS RD
CHEPSTOW GDNS
CAISTER RD
FLOWERDALE WLK
MILBURN RD
Cemy
RAGLAN GN
GODDRICH AVE
HAMSTER
BIRSE GN
GRESKINE CL
JASMINE CL
POPPYFIELDS
GLAMIS WLK
BAMBURGH DR
FLINT WAY
Woodside Mid Sch
ASHRIDGE DR
GLENAVON RD
Viking Ind Est
Crem
STOKESAY CL
Woodside
P
ETTRICK DR
Mast
STRATHCONON RD
HAMMOND RD
ASGARD DR
ODIN CL
CORFE RD
SUDELEY WLK
PO
CARRICK RD
ATHOLL WLK
GRAMBORNE CL
1 APPLECROSS WLK
2 COPELAND WLK
3 SAVERNAKE WLK
THE RIDGEWAY
PUTNOE ST
HADL
CHILLINGHAM GN
STAINMORE RD
ARUNDEL DR
DELAMERE WLK
ARDEN WLK
CHARNWOOD AVE
HUDSON RD
STRATTON WAY
THOR DR
BALDUR CL
NORTHCOTE
HEATHFIELD
PEVENSEY RD
SHERWOOD WLK
RADNOR WLK
CLIPSTONE CL
NEEDWOOD RD
NUTWOOD CL
1 LYMINGTON GDNS
2 CANNOCK CHASE
3 COLUMBINE CL
4 BRUTHWAITE GN
NAPIER RD
ST NEOTS RD
A428
HIGH VIEW
1 KENILWORTH WLK
2 DENBIGH WAY
3 LUDLOW WLK
4 CARISBROOKE WAY
Elms Farm
Elms Ind Est
Putnoe Lower Schs
EPPING WLK
ROCKINGHAM WLK
RENDLESHAM WLK
CHELTENHAM CL
Castle Dairy Farm
MOUNT DR
OVERDALE
CORNLAND
FIELDSIDE
LEIGHFIELD CL
EDISON RD
WOODCOTE
DALE CL
BARLEY WAY
ELLIOT CRES
KERSHOPE CL
QUEEN'S DR
WINDMILL CL
TUNSTALL WLK
Caxton Pk
CAXTON RD
A421
DOWNSIDE
SHEEPLANDS
THE SPINNEY
Bsns Pk
MONKSHILL
THE RISINGS
ROUNDMEAD
THE FAIRWAY
TURNPIKE WAY
SHUTTLEWORTH RD
Risinghoe Castle (site of)
Castle Mill (dis)
MEADWAY
LINKWAY
VICARS WLK
THE COPSE
SERGEANTS WAY
THE CROFT
BARNHILL
Elms Ind Est
HERONSCROFT
THE BOUNDARY
BURY CT
PURBECK CL
CRICKET LA
CRICKET CL
WEST CT
EAST CT
Goldington
PORTLAND CL
BALLINGHALL
GOLDINGTON GN
PERKINS RD
Bedford (Castle Mill) Airfield
MANOR RD
HERON HTS
River Great Ouse
OUSE RD
HARVEY RD
ABBEY RD
PO
GOLDINGTON RD
Superstore
MARSHALL CT
GRANGE RD
SANDY RD
CHAPEL CL
Goldington Green Lower Sch
HEATHER GDNS
BRYONY
LORRAINE CT
QUEEN ALEXANDRA RD
KING EDWARD RD
CHINVOR CL
HONEYSUCKLE WAY
BARKERS LA
RISBOROUGH RD
ADDINGTON CL
MOUNTBATTEN P
RIVERFIELD DR
DUNGLEAT
WENDOVER DR
MITRE CL
BRAKEN
WARDEN ABBEY
GUNNERSBURY PK
AYLESBURY RD
HARPENDEN CL
BISHOPS RD
1 BOXGROVE PRIORY
2 CLEEVE ABBEY
3 BATTLE ABBEY
4 THE CLOISTERS
DONNELLY DR
COLES CL
GLOVER AVE
HARROLD PRIORY
KIMBLE DR
MK44
A421
07
A
B
08
C
D
09
E
F

51
40

39
30

A B C D E F

8
7
53
6
5
52
4
3
51
2
1
50

Birchfield Farm
Little Birchfield Farm
Northfield Farm
BARFORD RD
BIRCHFIELD RD
MK44
The Creakers
Mill House
Woodfield Farm
Green End
Greenend Bridge
Hall
GREEN END RD
FISHERS CL
PEASHILL LA
PENNWRIGHTS LA
A421
FAIR WAY
WOODFIELD LA
Greenend Farm
NORMAN CL
PH
WILLOUGHBY CL
BECHER CL
Workhouse End
GREEN END
CHAPEL FIELD
PO
HIGH ST
HUNTS FIELD
DOTHANS CL
CHAPEL CL
COOPERS CL
Brewer's Hall Farm
PYMS CL
SOUTHVIEW
MK41
SHELTON CT
SILVER ST
BEREFORD CL
Great Barford Lower Sch
SILVER ST
Alban CE Mid Sch
Great Barford
WATER END
BEDFORD RD
Great Dairy Farm
A428
ST NEOTS RD
A421
Hill Farm
Dairy Farm
Cuckoo Bridge
Gadsey Brook
Bedford to Sandy Country Way
River Great Ouse
Willington Lock
Sewage Works
Mill Farm
Willington Lower Sch
CHURCH END
CHURCHILL PL
CHURCH RD
STATION RD
CHAPEL LA
MOWBRAY PL
RUSSELL DR
BARFORD RD

10 A B 11 C D 12 E F

39
52

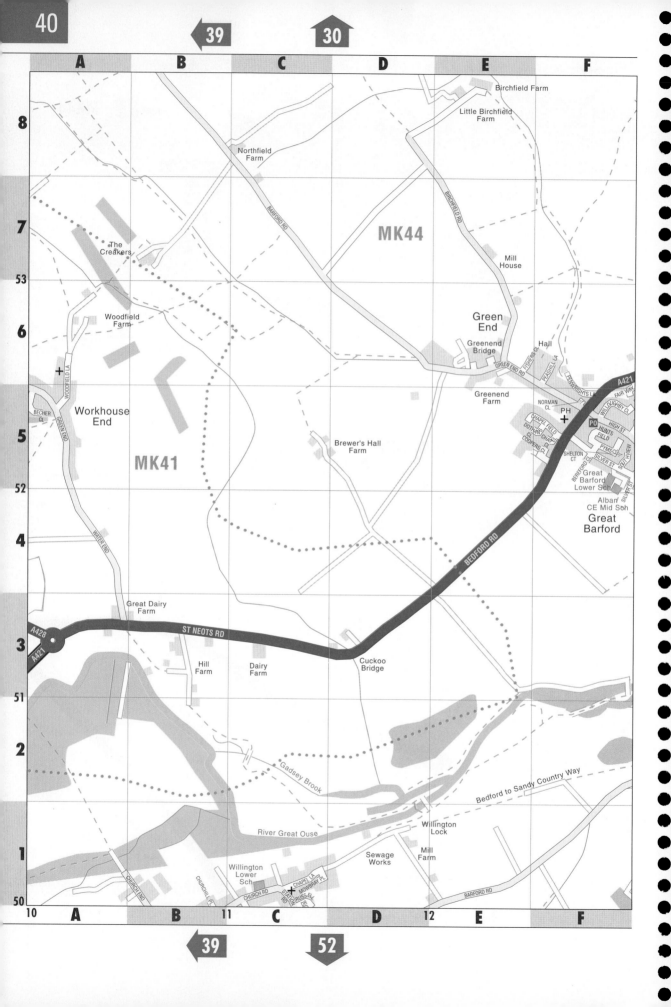

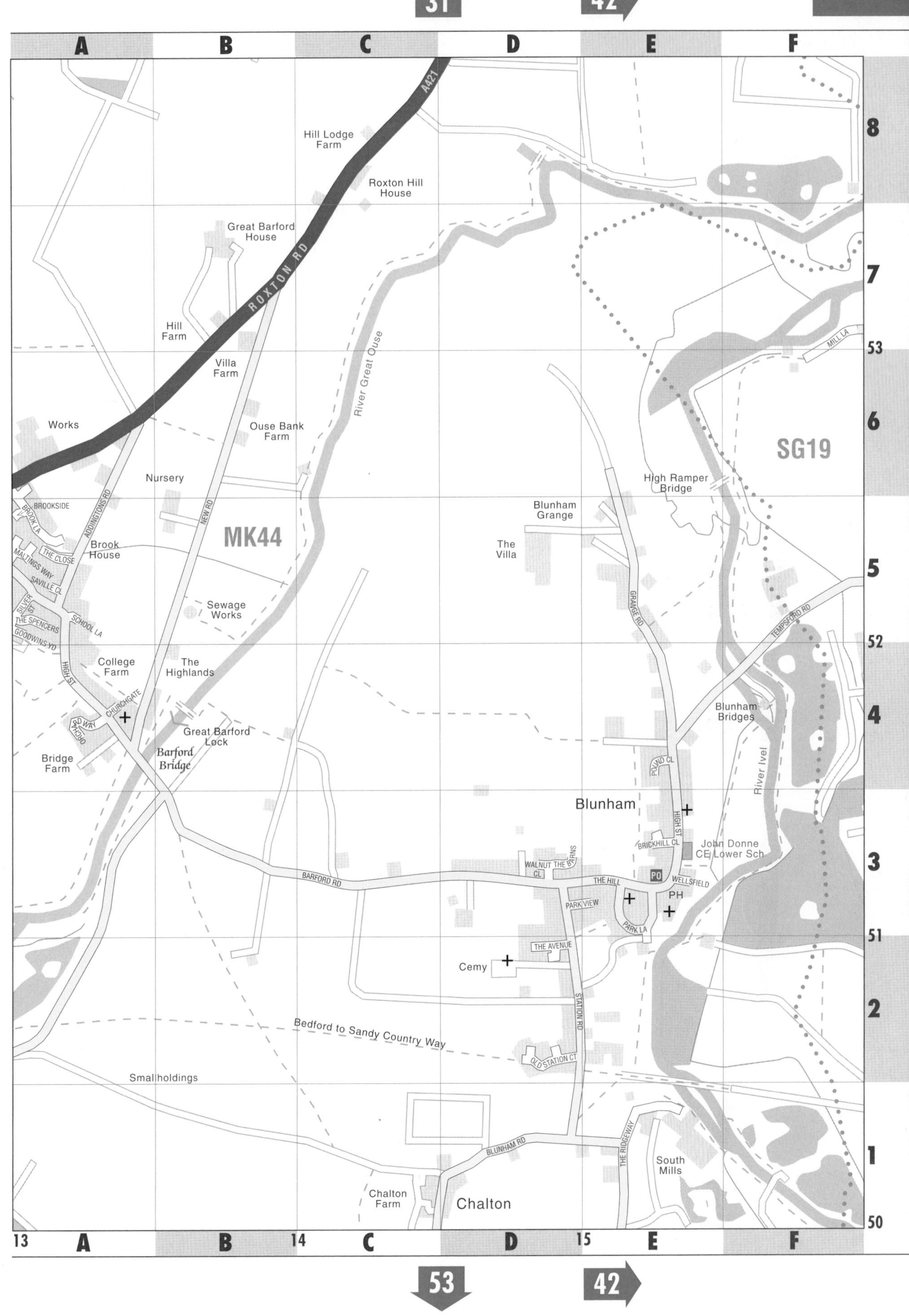

A B C D E F

8

Hill Lodge Farm

Roxton Hill House

Great Barford House

7

53

ROXTON RD

A421

River Great Ouse

Hill Farm

Villa Farm

Works

6

Ouse Bank Farm

Nursery

SG19

NEW RD

ADDINGTONS RD

BROOKSIDE

Brook House

MK44

High Ramper Bridge

Blunham Grange

The Villa

MILL LA

BROOK LA

THE CLOSE

MALTINGS WAY

SAVILLE CL

Sewage Works

5

52

GRANGE RD

TEMPSFORD RD

THE SPENCERS

SCHOOL LA

GOODWINS YD

HIGH ST

College Farm

The Highlands

Blunham Bridges

4

RD WRT

CHURCHGATE

CHD

Great Barford Lock

River Ivel

Bridge Farm

Barford Bridge

Blunham

HIGH ST

PV ND CL

BRICKHILL CL

John Donne CE Lower Sch

WALNUT CL

THE BURNS

PO

Wellsfield

BARFORD RD

PARK VIEW

The Hill

PH

3

51

THE AVENUE

Cemy

Park La

STATION RD

2

Bedford to Sandy Country Way

OLD STATION CT

Smallholdings

THE RIDGEWAY

South Mills

1

BLUNHAM RD

Chalton Farm

Chalton

50

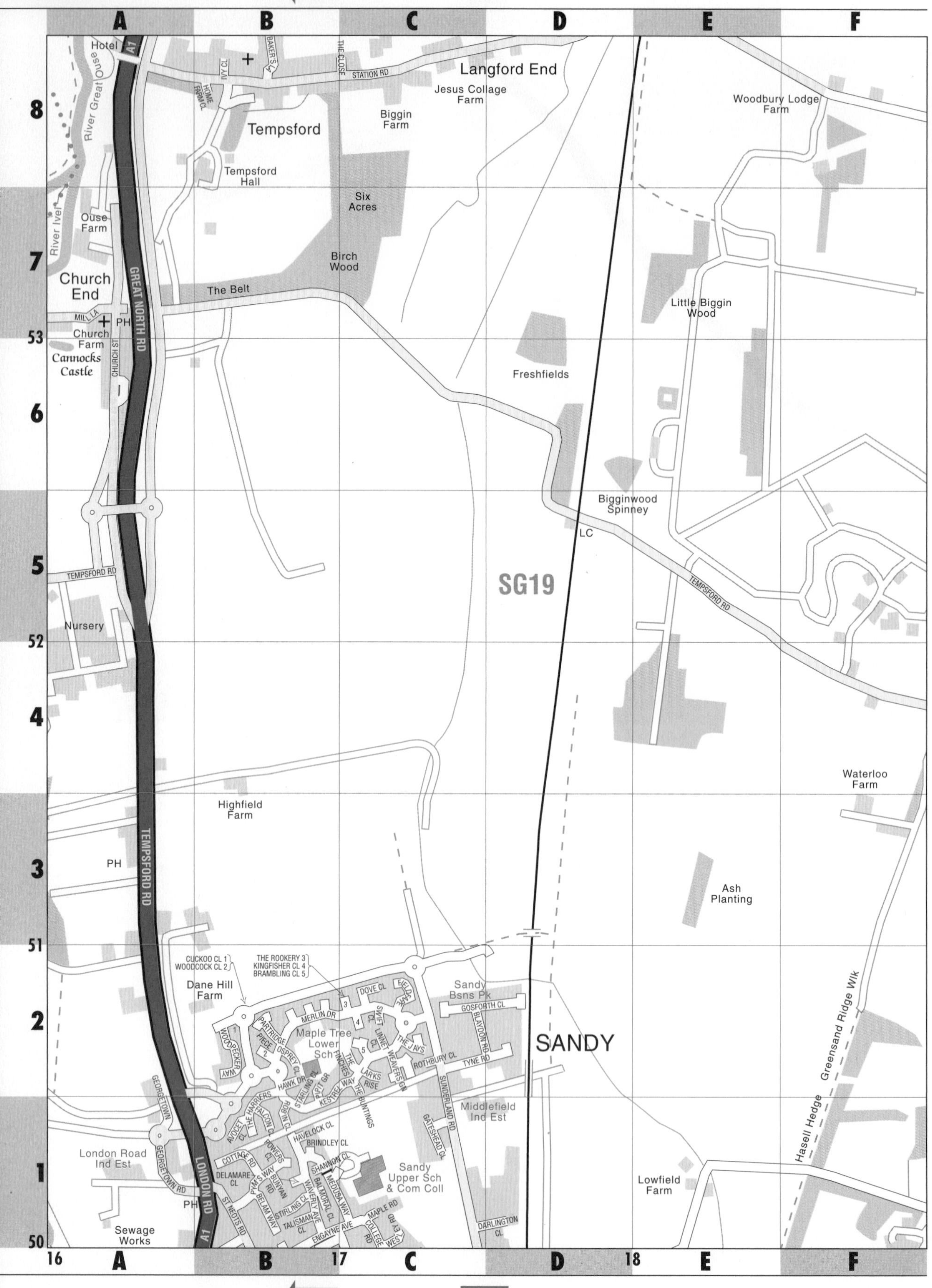

41
32

A B C D E F

8 River Great Ouse A1 Hotel
Tempsford
BAKER'S CL
THE CLOSE
STATION RD
Langford End
Jesus Collage Farm
Biggin Farm
HOME FARM CL
CLAY LA
Woodbury Lodge Farm

Tempsford Hall

Six Acres

River Ivel
Ouse Farm
7 Church End
The Belt
Birch Wood
GREAT NORTH RD
Little Biggin Wood

53 MILL LA
PH
Church Farm
Cannocks Castle
CHURCH ST
Freshfields

6

Bigginwood Spinney

5 TEMPSFORD RD
LC
TEMPSFORD RD
SG19

52 Nursery

4

Waterloo Farm

Highfield Farm
TEMPSFORD RD

3 PH
Ash Planting

51

CUCKOO CL 1
WOODCOCK CL 2
THE ROOKERY 3
KINGFISHER CL 4
BRAMBLING CL 5
Sandy Bsns Pk
GOSFORTH CL

2 Dane Hill Farm
MERLIN DR
DOVE CL
WELD
SWIFT
LINNET CL
THE JAYS
BLAXTON RD
ROTHBURY CL
TYNE RD
SANDY

Maple Tree Lower Sch
PARTRIDGE PIECE
OSPREY
THE FINCHES
WEAVERS RD
LARKS RISE
SANDERLING RD
Middlefield Ind Est

WOODCOCK WAY
HAWK DR
KESTREL WAY
GATESHEAD CL

1 London Road Ind Est
GEORGETOWN RD
AVOCET
HARRIERS CL
FALCON CL
RBS CL
STIRLING CL
HAVELOCK CL
BRINDLEY CL
Sandy Upper Sch & Com Coll

LONDON RD
COTTAGE RD
DELAMARE CL
PIXIES WAY
BRENT WAY
SHANNON CL
BALMORE CL
MEDINA WAY
MAPLE RD WEST
Lowfield Farm

PH
A1
ST NEOTS RD
TALISMAN CL
WINGATE AVE
ENGAYNE AVE
MAPLE RD
DARLINGTON CL

50 Sewage Works
16 A B 17 C D 18 E F

HASELL HEDGE
Greensand Ridge Wlk

41
54

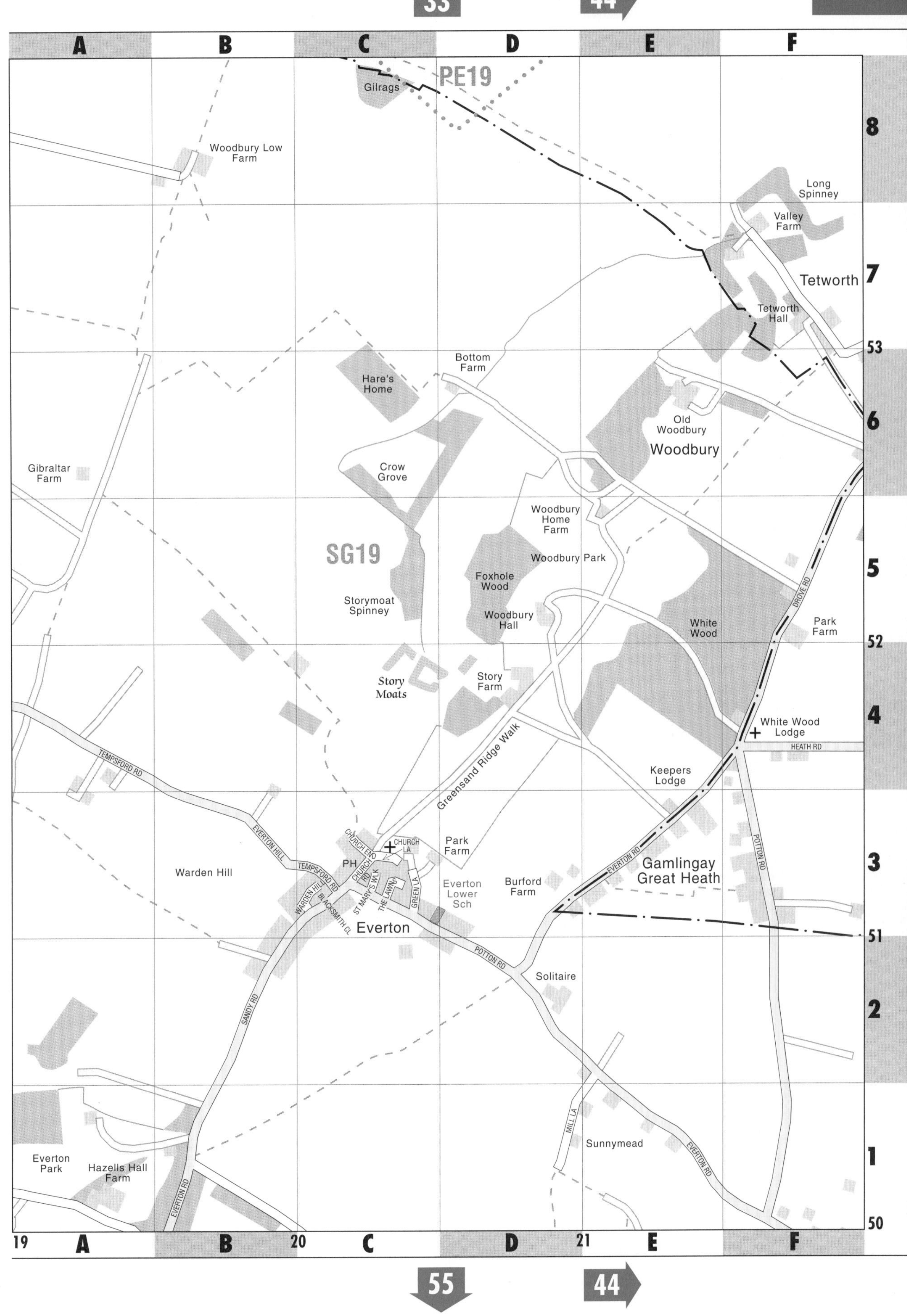
33
44
A
B
C
D
E
F
PE19
Gilrags
Woodbury Low Farm
Long Spinney
Valley Farm
Tetworth
Tetworth Hall
Bottom Farm
Hare's Home
Old Woodbury
Woodbury
Crow Grove
Gibraltar Farm
Woodbury Home Farm
SG19
Woodbury Park
Foxhole Wood
Storymoat Spinney
Woodbury Hall
White Wood
Park Farm
DROVE RD
Story Moats
Story Farm
White Wood Lodge
HEATH RD
Greensand Ridge Walk
TEMPSFORD RD
Keepers Lodge
EVERTON HILL
CHURCH END
CHURCH LA
Park Farm
PH
CHURCH RD
Warden Hill
TEMPSFORD RD
WARDEN HILL
BLACKSMITH CL
ST MARY'S WLK
THE LAWNS
GREEN LA
Everton Lower Sch
Burford Farm
EVERTON RD
Gamlingay Great Heath
POTTON RD
Everton
POTTON RD
Solitaire
SANDY RD
MILL LA
Sunnymead
EVERTON RD
Everton Park
Hazells Hall Farm
EVERTON RD
8
7
53
6
5
52
4
3
51
2
1
50
19
20
21
55
44

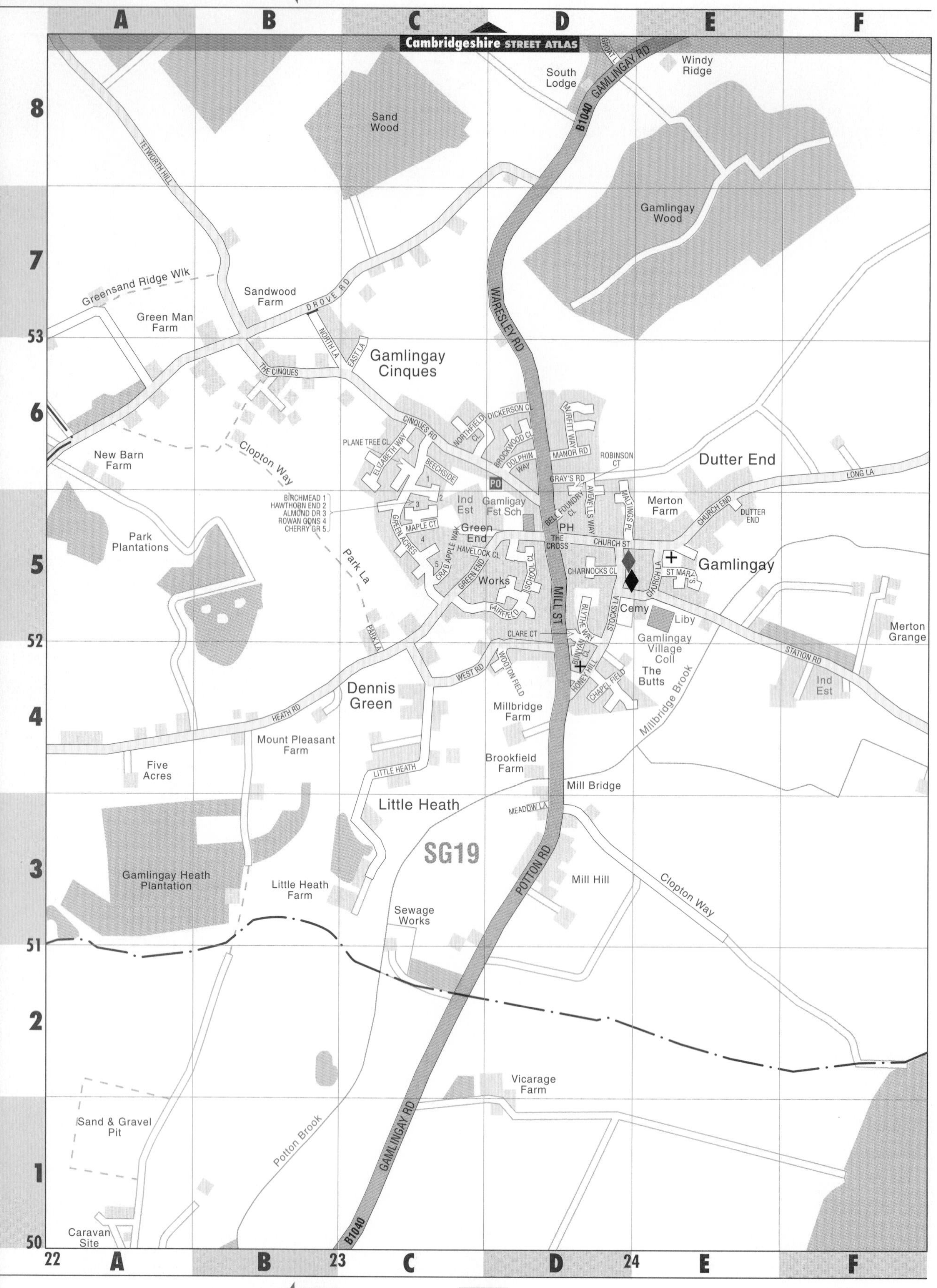

Cambridgeshire STREET ATLAS

South Lodge

Windy Ridge

B1040 GAMLINGAY RD

Sand Wood

Gamlingay Wood

TETWORTH HILL

Greensand Ridge Wlk

Sandwood Farm

DROVE RD

WARESLEY RD

Green Man Farm

NORTH LA

EAST LA

THE CINQUES

Gamlingay Cinques

New Barn Farm

Clopton Way

CINQUES RD

Plane Tree Cl

NORTHFIELD CL

DICKERSON CL

BIRCHWOOD CL

MANOR RD

Robinson CT

Dutter End

LONG LA

ELIZABETH WAY

BEECHSIDE

DOLPHIN WAY

MURITT WAY

Park Plantations

1

GRAY'S RD

ARDELLS WAY

Merton Farm

MALTINGS PL

CHURCH END

DUTTER END

BIRCHMEAD 1
HAWTHORN END 2
ALMOND DR 3
ROWAN GDNS 4
CHERRY GR 5

GREEN ACRES

MAPLE CT

3

Ind Est

Gamligay Fst Sch

PO

Green End

BELL FOUNDRY CL

PH

St MARY'S

Gamlingay

Park La

4

THE CROSS

CHURCH ST

CRAB & APPLE WAY

HAVELOCK CL

GREEN END

5

TD TOCOUT

Works

Charnocks Cl

CHARNOCKS CL

Cemy

Liby

Merton Grange

PARK LA

FAIRFIELD

MILL ST

STOCKS LA

CHURCH LA

STATION RD

CLARE CT

BLYTHE WAY

Gamlingay Village Coll

Ind Est

Dennis Green

WEST RD

WOOTTON FIELD

TD TOCOUT

HONEY HILL

CHAPEL FIELD

The Butts

Millbridge Brook

HEATH RD

Mount Pleasant Farm

Millbridge Farm

Five Acres

LITTLE HEATH

Brookfield Farm

Mill Bridge

Little Heath

MEADOW LA

SG19

Gamlingay Heath Plantation

Little Heath Farm

POTTON RD

Mill Hill

Clopton Way

Sewage Works

Potton Brook

Vicarage Farm

Sand & Gravel Pit

GAMLINGAY RD

B1040

Caravan Site

SG19

Airfield

Ash Tree Cottage

Fuller's Hill Farm

Crooked Billet Farm

LONG LA

Model Farm

B1046

B1046

Millbridge Brook

Castle Farm

HATLEY RD

Newlands Buildings

Newlands Cottages

West Lodge

North Lodge

Church Farm

ST GEORGES TOWER

Stud Bungalow

Hatley Park

Hatley St George

MAIN ST

Stud Cottage

Dower House

BAR LA

Hatley Park

Wood Farm

Cockayne Hatley Wood

Potton Wood

Pincote Barn

BUFF LA

34

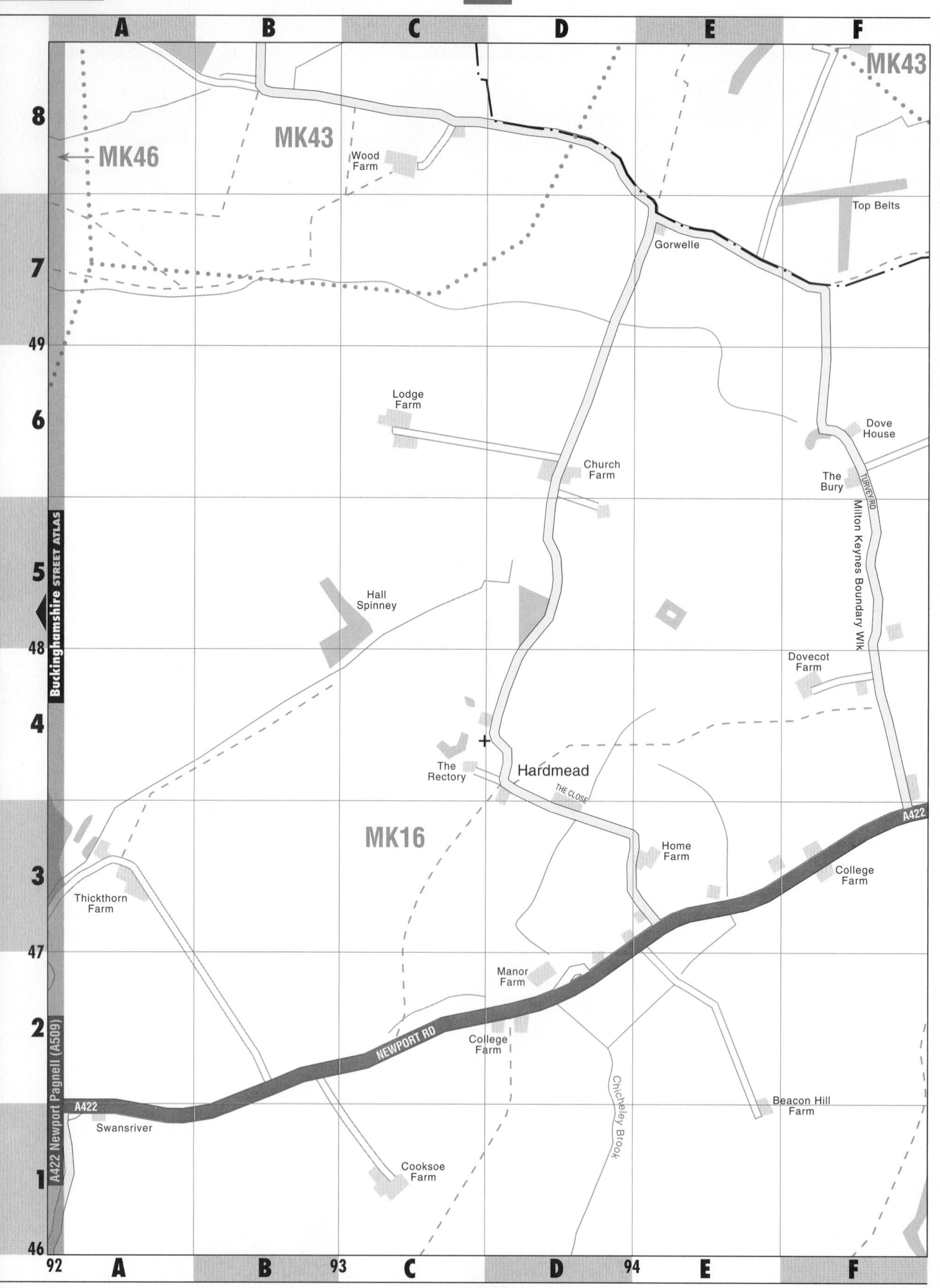

A
B
C
D
E
F
MK43
MK46
MK43
Wood Farm
Top Belts
Gorwelle
8
7
49
6
5
48
4
3
47
2
1
46
Lodge Farm
Church Farm
Dove House
The Bury
TURVEY RD
Milton Keynes Boundary Wlk
Hall Spinney
Dovecot Farm
The Rectory
Hardmead
THE CLOSE
MK16
Home Farm
A422
College Farm
Thickthorn Farm
Manor Farm
NEWPORT RD
College Farm
Chicheley Brook
Beacon Hill Farm
A422
Swansriver
Cooksoe Farm
Buckinghamshire STREET ATLAS
A422 Newport Pagnell (A509)
92
93
94

58

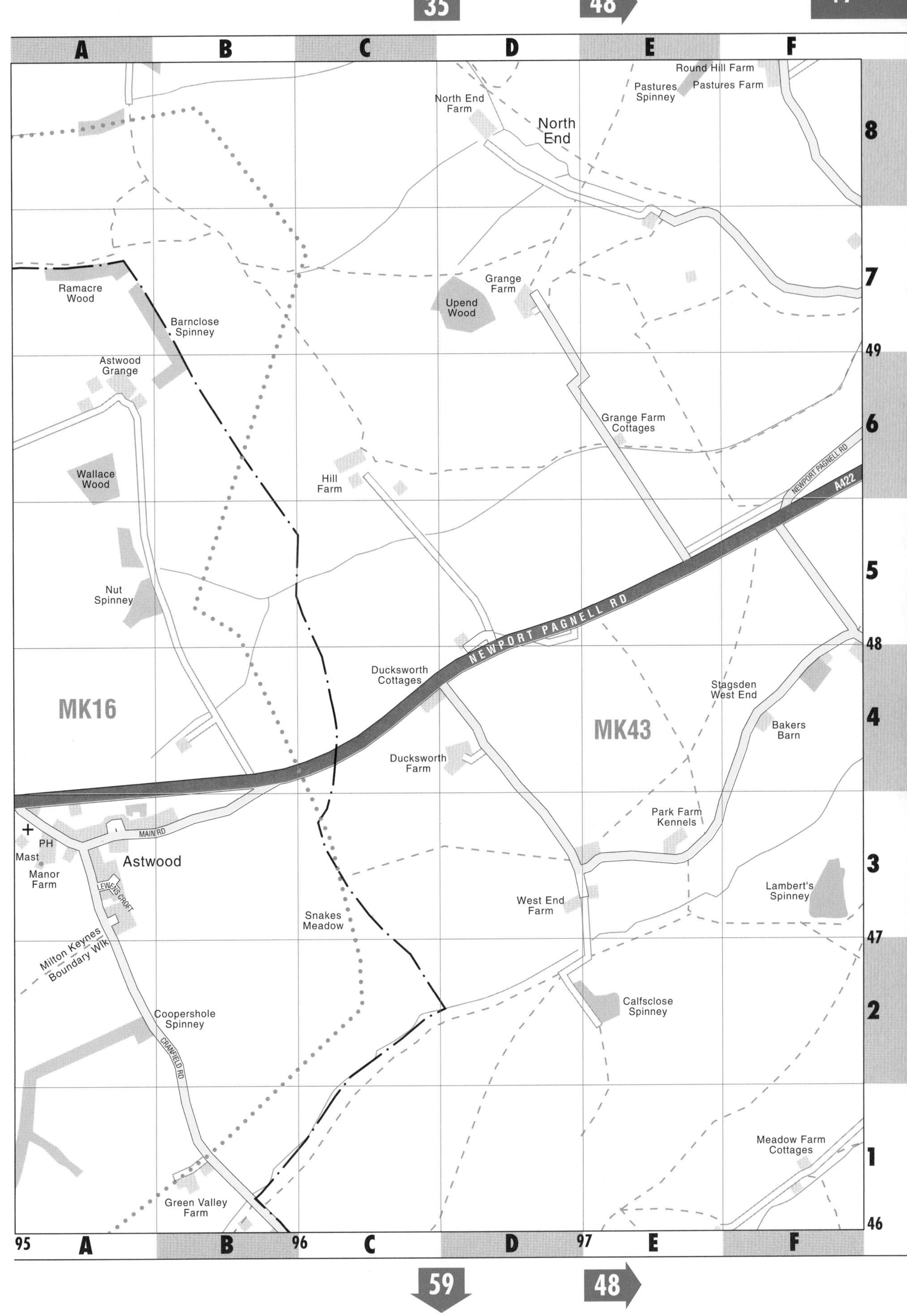

A B C D E F

8

Round Hill Farm
Pastures Farm
Pastures Spinney
North End Farm
North End

7

Ramacre Wood
Barnclose Spinney
Grange Farm
Upend Wood

Astwood Grange

49

Grange Farm Cottages

6

Wallace Wood
Hill Farm

NEWPORT PAGNELL RD
A422

5

Nut Spinney

48

Ducksworth Cottages
Stagsden West End

MK16
MK43

4

Bakers Barn

Ducksworth Farm
Park Farm Kennels

+ Mast
PH
MAIN RD

Manor Farm
Astwood

Lambert's Spinney

3

LEWIS CROFT

West End Farm

Snakes Meadow

47

Milton Keynes Boundary Wlk

Calfsclose Spinney

2

Coopershole Spinney
CRANFIELD RD

Meadow Farm Cottages

1

Green Valley Farm

46

95 A B 96 C D 97 E F

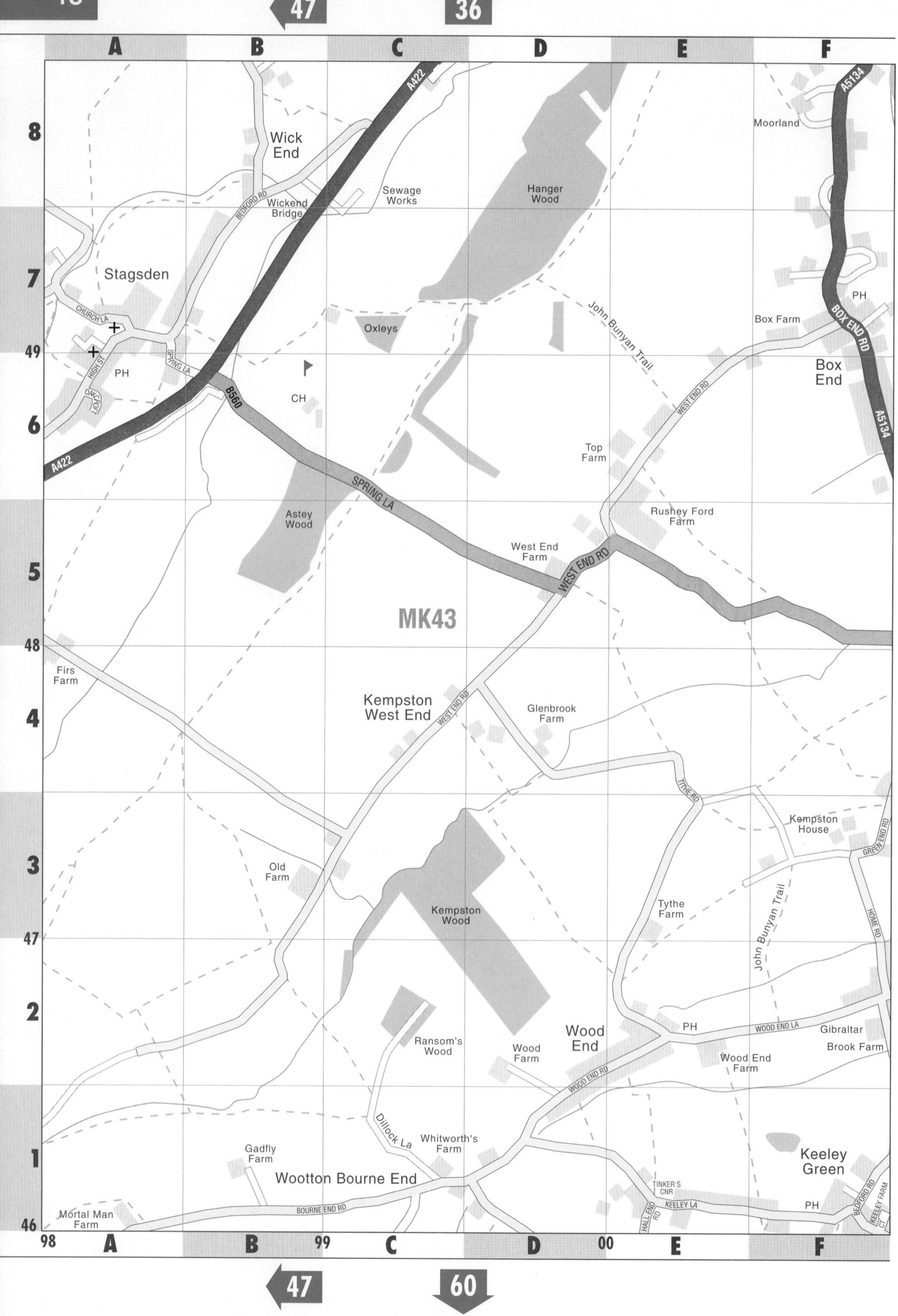
A
B
C
D
E
F
8
7
49
6
5
48
4
3
47
2
1
46
98
99
00
Wick
End
Sewage
Works
Hanger
Wood
Moorland
A5134
A422
BEDFORD RD
Wickend
Bridge
Stagsden
CHURCH LA
HIGH ST
SPRING LA
PH
OAKCROFT
Oxleys
CH
B560
John Bunyan Trail
Box Farm
PH
BOX END RD
Box
End
WEST END RD
Top
Farm
Astey
Wood
SPRING LA
Rushey Ford
Farm
West End
Farm
MK43
Firs
Farm
Kempston
West End
Glenbrook
Farm
TITHE RD
Kempston
House
GREEN END RD
Old
Farm
Kempston
Wood
Tythe
Farm
HOME RD
Wood
End
PH
WOOD END LA
Gibraltar
Brook Farm
Ransom's
Wood
Wood
Farm
Wood End
Farm
WOOD END RD
Dillock La
Whitworth's
Farm
Gadfly
Farm
Wootton Bourne End
Keeley
Green
TINKER'S
CNR
KEELEY LA
HALL END RD
PH
BEDFORD RD
KEELEY FARM CT
BOURNE END RD
Mortal Man
Farm

37
50

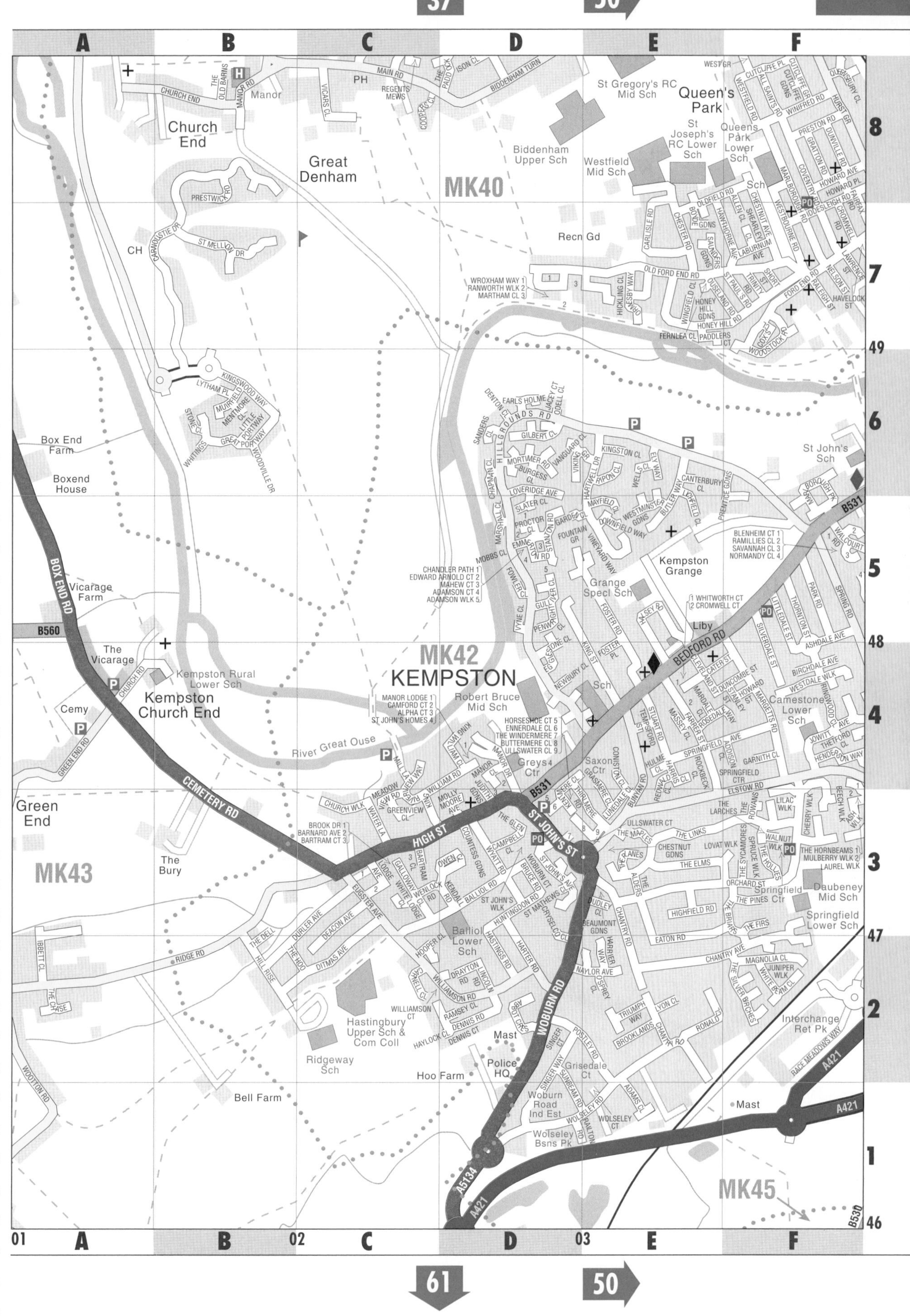
A
B
C
D
E
F
8
7
49
6
5
48
4
3
47
2
1
46
01
02
03
Church End
Manor
Great Denham
PH
MAIN RD
REGENTS MEWS
BIDDENHAM TURN
MK40
Biddenham Upper Sch
St Gregory's RC Mid Sch
Queen's Park
St Joseph's RC Lower Sch
Queens Park Lower Sch
Westfield Mid Sch
Recn Gd
PRESTWICK RD
CARNOUSTIE DR
ST MELLION DR
CH
OLD FORD END RD
FERNLEA CL
PADDLERS CT
WROXHAM WAY 1
RANWORTH WLK 2
MARTHAM CL 3
KINGSWOOD WAY
LYTHAM PL
Box End Farm
Boxend House
BOX END RD
Vicarage Farm
B560
The Vicarage
Kempston Rural Lower Sch
Kempston Church End
Cemy
GREEN END RD
Green End
MK43
CEMETERY RD
The Bury
MK42
KEMPSTON
River Great Ouse
Robert Bruce Mid Sch
MANOR LODGE 1
CAMFORD CT 2
ALPHA CT 3
ST JOHN'S HOMES 4
CHANDLER PATH 1
EDWARD ARNOLD CT 2
MAHEW CT 3
ADAMSON CT 4
ADAMSON WLK 5
HORSESHOE CT 5
ENNERDALE CL 6
THE WINDERMERE 7
BUTTERMERE CL 8
ULLSWATER CL 9
Kempston Grange
Grange Specl Sch
1 WHITWORTH CT
2 CROMWELL CT
Liby
BEDFORD RD
B531
BLENHEIM CT 1
RAMILLIES CL 2
SAVANNAH CL 3
NORMANDY CL 4
St John's Sch
Camestone Lower Sch
Greys Ctr
Saxon Ctr
Springfield Ctr
HIGH ST
ST JOHN'S ST
BROOK DR 1
BARNARD AVE 2
BARTRAM CT 3
Balliol Lower Sch
THE HORNBEAMS 1
MULBERRY WLK 2
LAUREL WLK
Daubeney Mid Sch
Springfield Lower Sch
RIDGE RD
Hastingbury Upper Sch & Com Coll
Ridgeway Sch
WOBURN RD
Mast
Police HQ
Hoo Farm
Grisedale Ct
Woburn Road Ind Est
Wolseley Bsns Pk
Bell Farm
Interchange Ret Pk
A421
A5134
MK45
B530

61
50

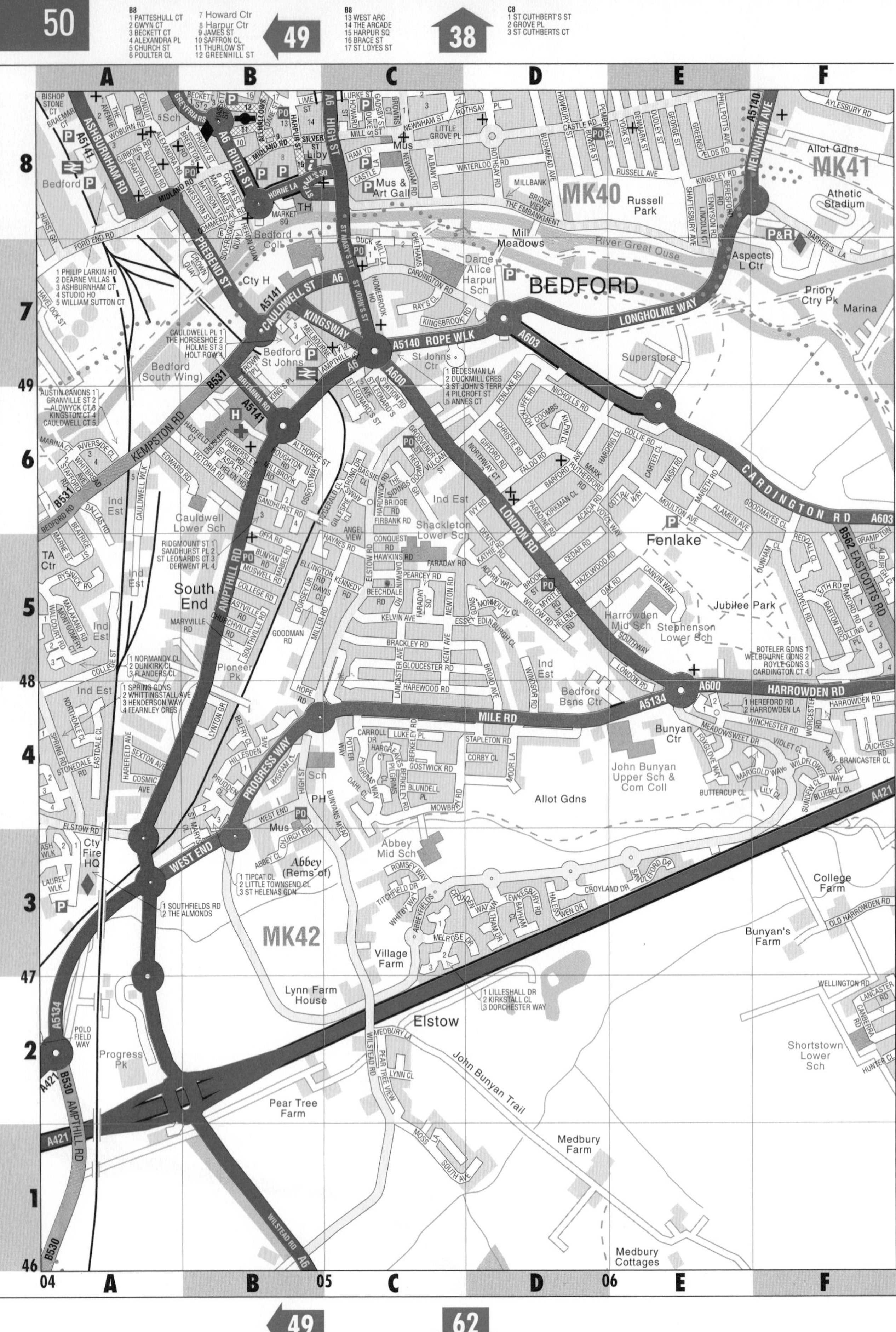

39
52

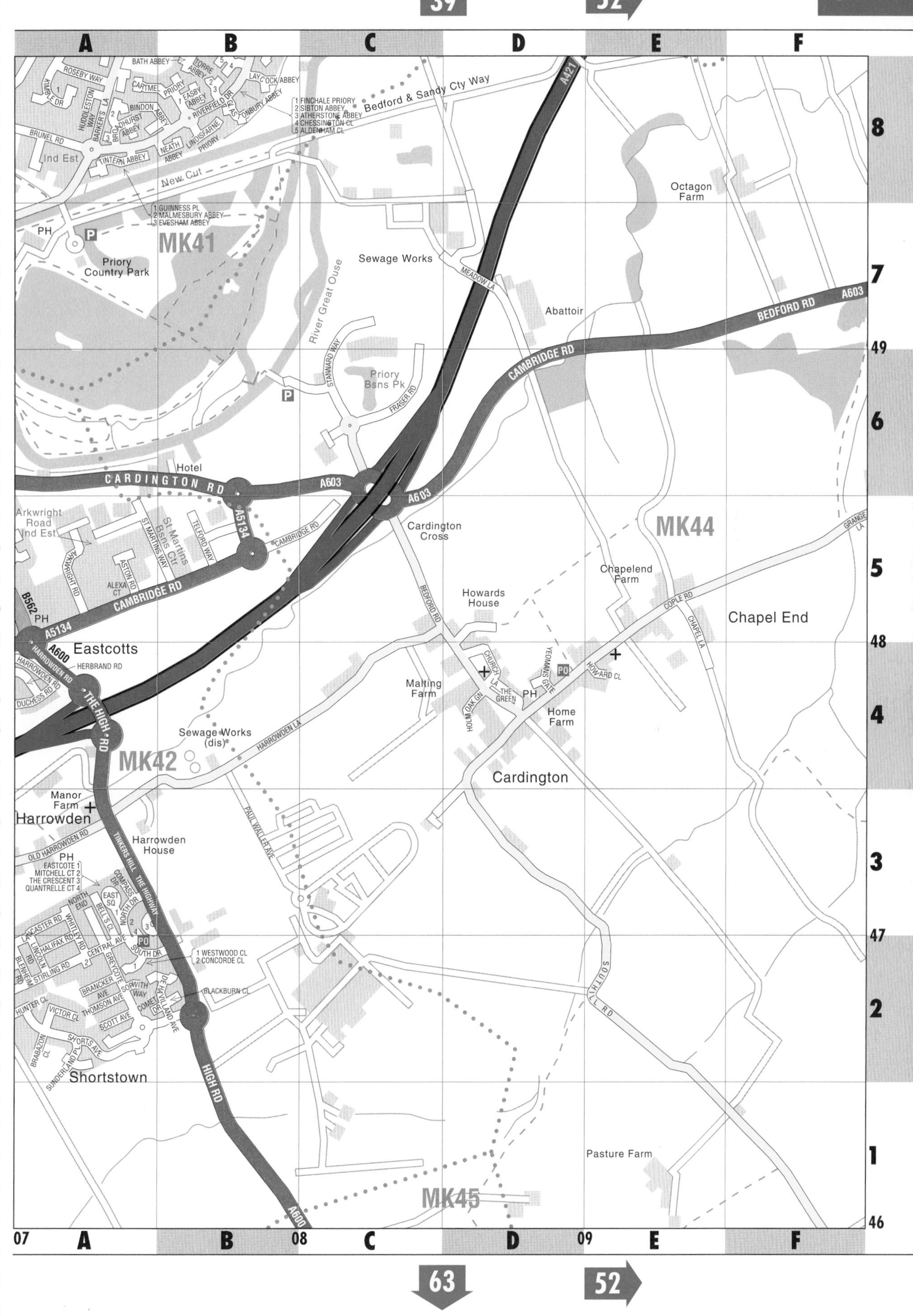
A
B
C
D
E
F
Bedford & Sandy Cty Way
New Cut
PH
MK41
Priory Country Park
Sewage Works
River Great Ouse
Octagon Farm
MEADOW LA
Abattoir
BEDFORD RD
A603
CAMBRIDGE RD
STANNARD WAY
Priory Bsns Pk
FRASER RD
Hotel
CARDINGTON RD
A603
A5134
Arkwright Road Ind Est
St Martins Bsns Ctr
TELFORD WAY
CAMBRIDGE RD
Cardington Cross
MK44
Chapelend Farm
Howards House
BEDFORD RD
Chapel End
COPLE RD
CHAPEL LA
GRANGE LA
B562
A5134
A600
Eastcotts
HERBRAND RD
HARROWDEN RD
THE HIGH RD
Malting Farm
CHURCH LA
THE GREEN
PH
YEOMANS GATE
PO
HOWARD CL
Home Farm
HOLM OAK GN
Sewage Works (dis)
HARROWDEN LA
MK42
Cardington
Manor Farm
Harrowden
Harrowden House
OLD HARROWDEN RD
PAUL WALLER AVE
TINKERS HILL
THE HIGHWAY
PH
EASTCOTE 1
MITCHELL CT 2
THE CRESCENT 3
QUANTRELLE CT 4
1 WESTWOOD CL
2 CONCORDE CL
BLACKBURN CL
SOUTHILL RD
Shortstown
HIGH RD
Pasture Farm
MK45
A600
8
7
6
5
4
3
2
1
49
48
47
46
07
08
09

63
52

51
40

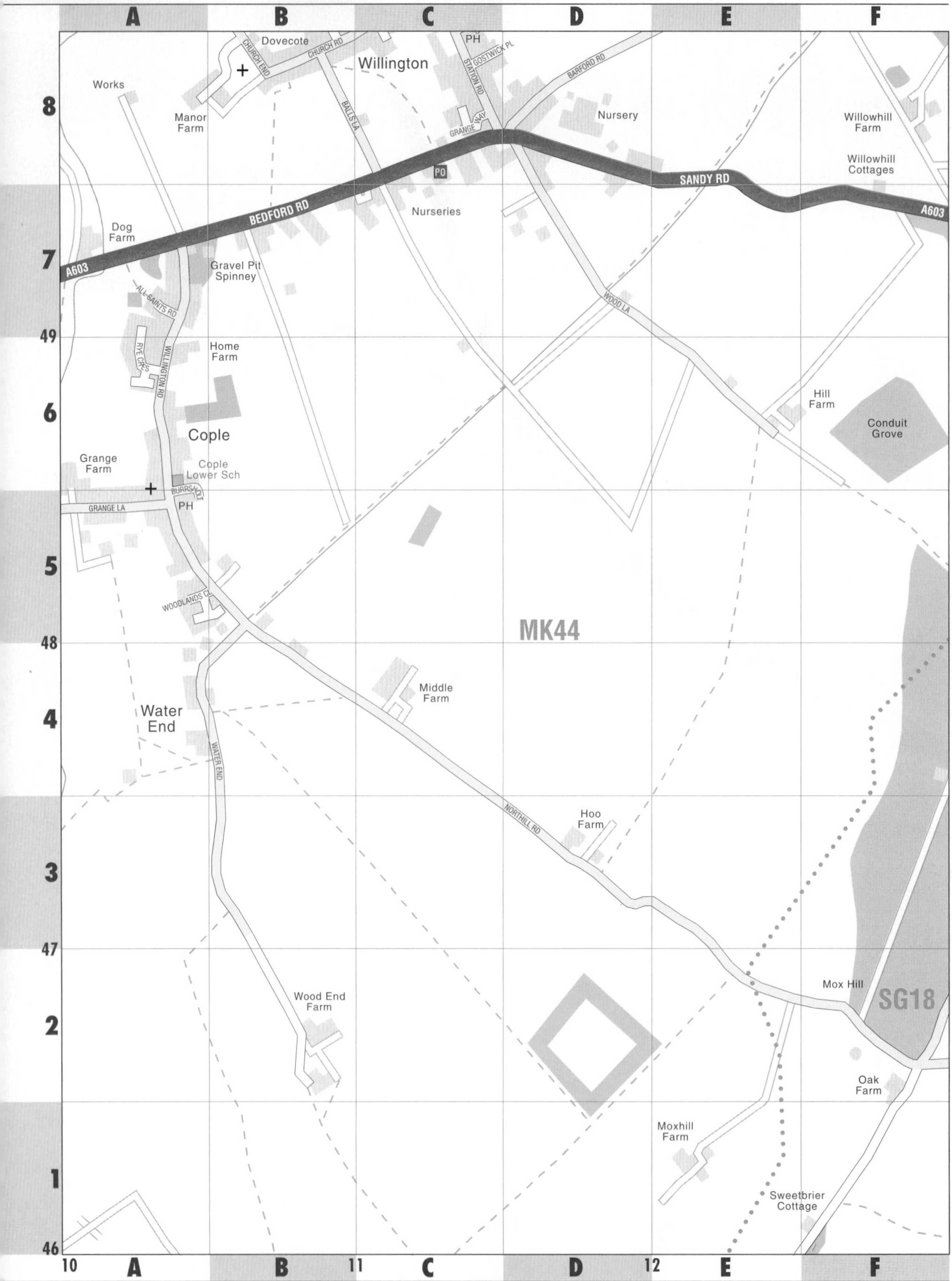

A B C D E F

8

Works

Dovecote

Willington

CHURCH RD

Manor
Farm

CHURCH END

BALLS LA

STATION RD

GOSTWICK PL

PH

Nursery

BARFORD RD

Willowhill
Farm

Willowhill
Cottages

GRANGE WAY

PO

SANDY RD

A603

Nurseries

BEDFORD RD

7

Dog
Farm

A603

Gravel Pit
Spinney

WOOD LA

ALL SAINTS RD

49

RYE CLS

Home
Farm

WILLINGTON RD

Hill
Farm

6

Cople

Conduit
Grove

Grange
Farm

Cople
Lower Sch

BURRS MT

GRANGE LA

PH

5

WOODLANDS CL

MK44

48

Middle
Farm

4

Water
End

WATER END

Hoo
Farm

NORTHILL RD

3

47

Wood End
Farm

Mox Hill

SG18

2

Moxhill
Farm

Oak
Farm

1

Sweetbrier
Cottage

46

10 A B 11 C D 12 E F

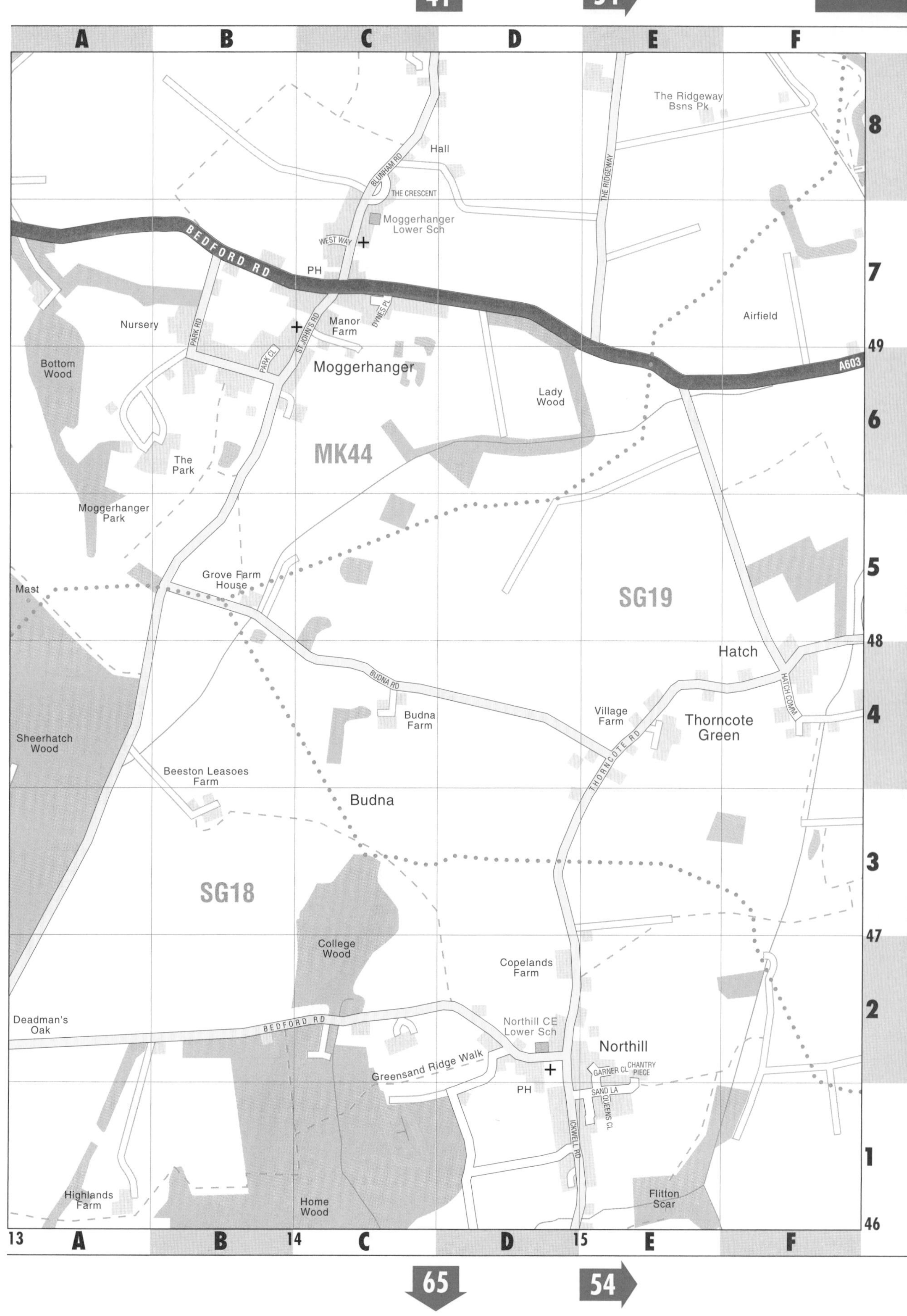
41
54
A
B
C
D
E
F
8
7
6
5
4
3
2
1
49
48
47
46
13
14
15
The Ridgeway Bsns Pk
Hall
BLUNHAM RD
THE CRESCENT
THE RIDGEWAY
Moggerhanger Lower Sch
WEST WAY
BEDFORD RD
PH
Airfield
Nursery
PARK RD
ST JOHN'S RD
Manor Farm
DYNES PL
PARK CL
Moggerhanger
A603
Bottom Wood
Lady Wood
MK44
The Park
Moggerhanger Park
Grove Farm House
Mast
SG19
Hatch
BUDNA RD
HATCH COMM
Village Farm
Thorncote Green
Budna Farm
Sheerhatch Wood
THORNCOTE RD
Beeston Leasoes Farm
Budna
SG18
College Wood
Copelands Farm
Deadman's Oak
BEDFORD RD
Northill CE Lower Sch
Northill
Greensand Ridge Walk
GARNER CL
CHANTRY PIECE
PH
SAND LA
QUEENS CL
ICKWELL RD
Highlands Farm
Home Wood
Flitton Scar
65
54

53 42

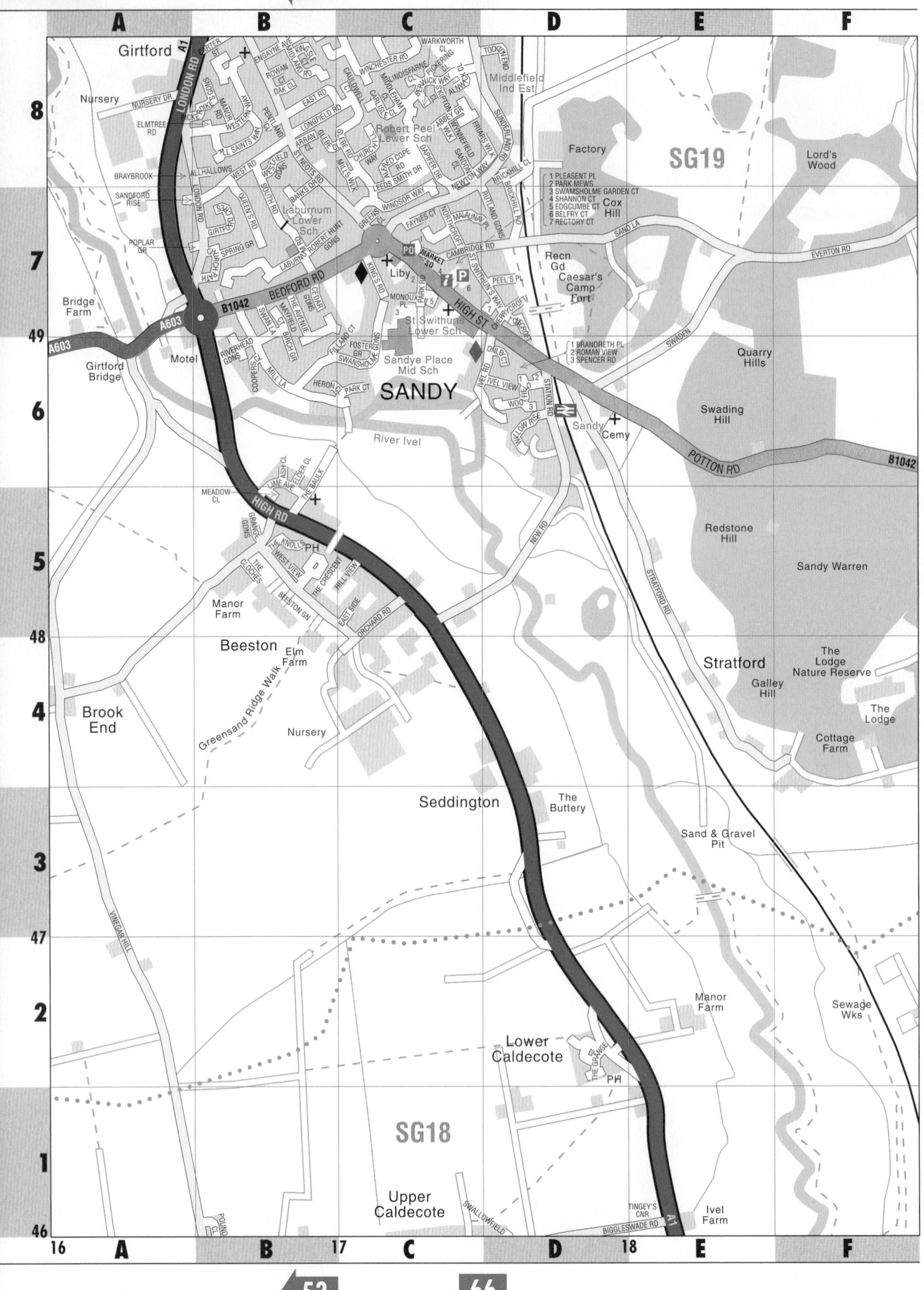

A B C D E F
8 7 6 5 4 3 2 1
49 48 47 46
16 17 18
Girtford
Nursery
NURSERY DR
ELMTREE RD
BRAYBROOK
SANDFORD RISE
POPLAR GR
Bridge Farm
Girtford Bridge
Motel
A603
A1
LONDON RD
B1042
BEDFORD RD
WEST RD
ALLHALLOWS
ALL SAINTS WAY
QUEEN'S RD
SOUTH RD
SPRING GR
CHURCH PATH
MANOR
WESTERN
PENTLAND
ARRAN CL
LONGFIELD RD
EAST RD
ROWAN CT
OAK CL
ENGAYNE AVE
MIDLAND RD
WINCHESTER RD
WARKWORTH CL
LINDISFARNE CL
PICKERING CL
BERWICK WAY
SKIPTON
ALNWICK CL
ABBEY GR
WYNNEFIELD
FRIARS WALK
CAULDWELL
MIDDLEHAM CL
CARLISLE CL
Robert Peel Lower Sch
CHURCH WAY
ALFRED COPE RD
LEEDS SMITH DR
DAPIFER DR
SANDON CL
NEWTON WAY
SUNDERLAND RD
BRICKHILL CL
BRICKHILL RD
RUTLAND GDNS
Middlefield Ind Est
TOOTING END
ST NEOTS RD
BANKS DR
MILLS WALK
GLEBE RD
WESTFIELD GDNS
Laburnum Lower Sch
ROBERT HUNT GDNS
LABURNUM RD
GREENS CL
WINDSOR WAY
FAYNES CT
NORTHCROFT
MALAUNAY PL
CAMBRIDGE RD
PO
MARKET SQ
Liby
KING'S RD
PARK RD
MONOUX PL
PEEL'S PL
ST SWITHUN'S WAY
CHERRYCROFT
SHERRYCROFT
HIGH ST
St Swithuns Lower Sch
Sandye Place Mid Sch
SANDY
SWAN LA
THE AVENUE
MAYFIELD
CEDAR GDNS
BIRCH GR
RIVERHEAD GDNS
COOPERS CL
MILL LA
FILLAND CT
FOSTER GR
SWANSHOLME GDNS
HERON CL
PARK CT
ONLEY CT
IVEL RD
IVEL VIEW
WOODFIELD
WILLOW RISE
STATION RD
Sandy
Cemy
River Ivel
1 PLEASENT PL
2 PARK MEWS
3 SWAMSHOLME GARDEN CT
4 SHANNON CT
5 EDGCUMBE CT
6 BELFRY CT
7 RECTORY CT
Cox Hill
Factory
SG19
Lord's Wood
SAND LA
EVERTON RD
Recn Gd
Caesar's Camp
Fort
1 BRANDRETH PL
2 ROMAN VIEW
3 SPENCER RD
SWADEN
Quarry Hills
Swading Hill
POTTON RD
B1042
Redstone Hill
Sandy Warren
MEADOW CL
ASH CL
ELDER CL
LIME AVE
THE BAULK
HIGH RD
GRANGE GDNS
THE KNOLLS
PH
THE WEST VIEW
THE CLOCHES
THE CRESCENT
HILL VIEW
BEESTON GN
EAST SIDE
ORCHARD RD
NEW RD
STRATFORD RD
Manor Farm
Beeston
Elm Farm
Greensand Ridge Walk
Brook End
Nursery
Stratford
Galley Hill
The Lodge Nature Reserve
The Lodge
Cottage Farm
Seddington
The Buttery
Sand & Gravel Pit
VINEGAR HILL
Manor Farm
Sewage Wks
Lower Caldecote
THE GRANGE
PH
SG18
Upper Caldecote
SWALLOWFIELD
POUND CL
TINGEY'S CNR
BIGGLESWADE RD
A1
Ivel Farm

53 66

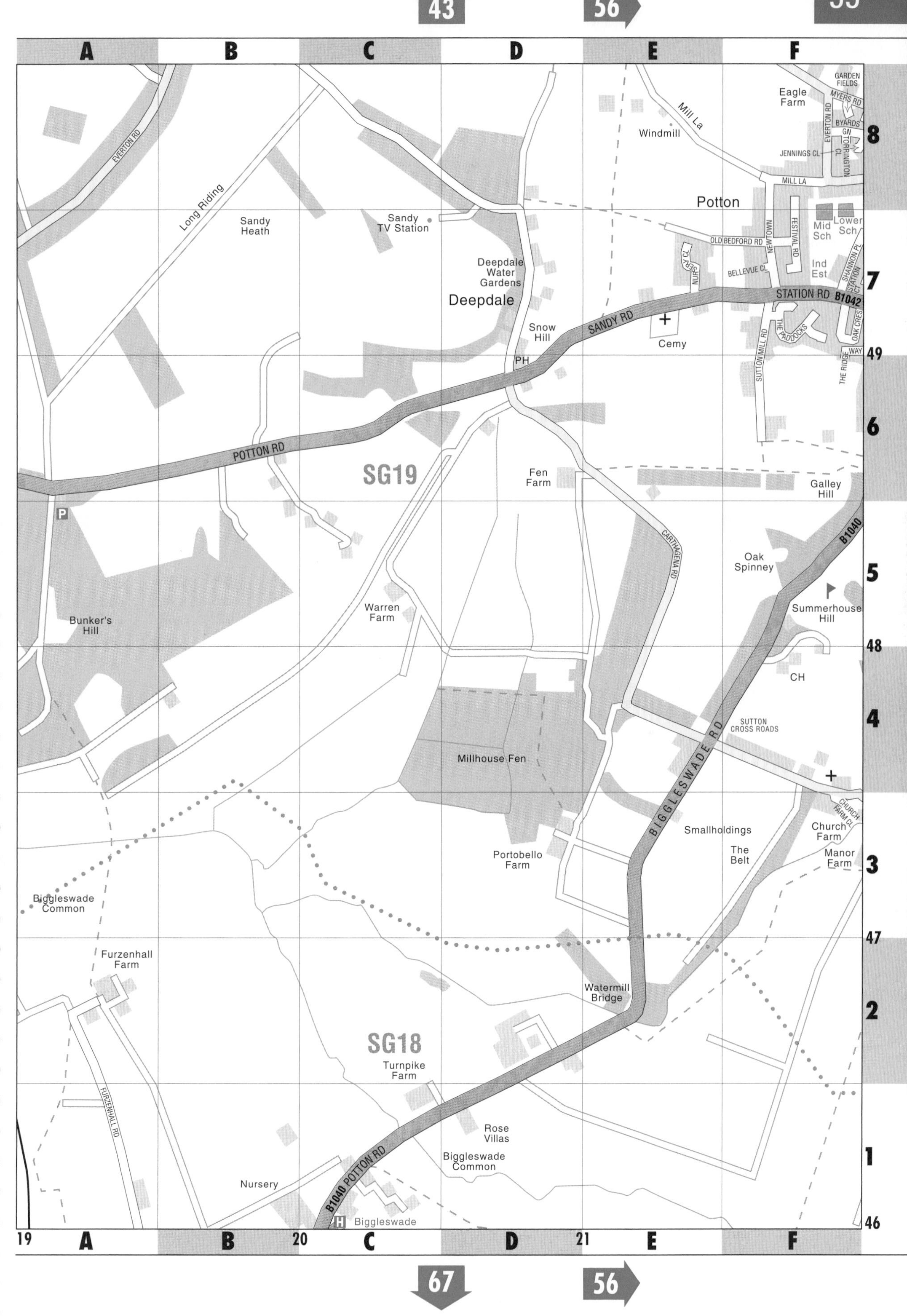
43
56
A
B
C
D
E
F
EVERTON RD
Long Riding
Sandy Heath
Sandy TV Station
Deepdale Water Gardens
Deepdale
Snow Hill
PH
SANDY RD
Windmill
Mill La
Eagle Farm
GARDEN FIELDS
MYERS RD
BYARDS GN
EVERTON RD
TORRINGTON CL
JENNINGS CL
MILL LA
Potton
Mid Sch
Lower Sch
OLD BEDFORD RD
NEWTOWN
FESTIVAL RD
BELLEVUE CL
Ind Est
SHANNON PL
STATION CT
STATION RD
B1042
THE PADDOCKS
OAK CRES
Cemy
SUTTON MILL RD
THE RIDGE
WAY
8
7
49
6
5
48
4
3
47
2
1
46
POTTON RD
SG19
Fen Farm
Galley Hill
P
CARTHAGENA RD
B1040
Oak Spinney
Summerhouse Hill
Warren Farm
Bunker's Hill
CH
SUTTON CROSS ROADS
BIGGLESWADE RD
Millhouse Fen
CHURCH FARM CL
Smallholdings
Church Farm
The Belt
Manor Farm
Portobello Farm
Biggleswade Common
Furzenhall Farm
Watermill Bridge
SG18
Turnpike Farm
FURZENHALL RD
Rose Villas
Biggleswade Common
B1040 POTTON RD
Nursery
H
Biggleswade
19
20
21
67
56

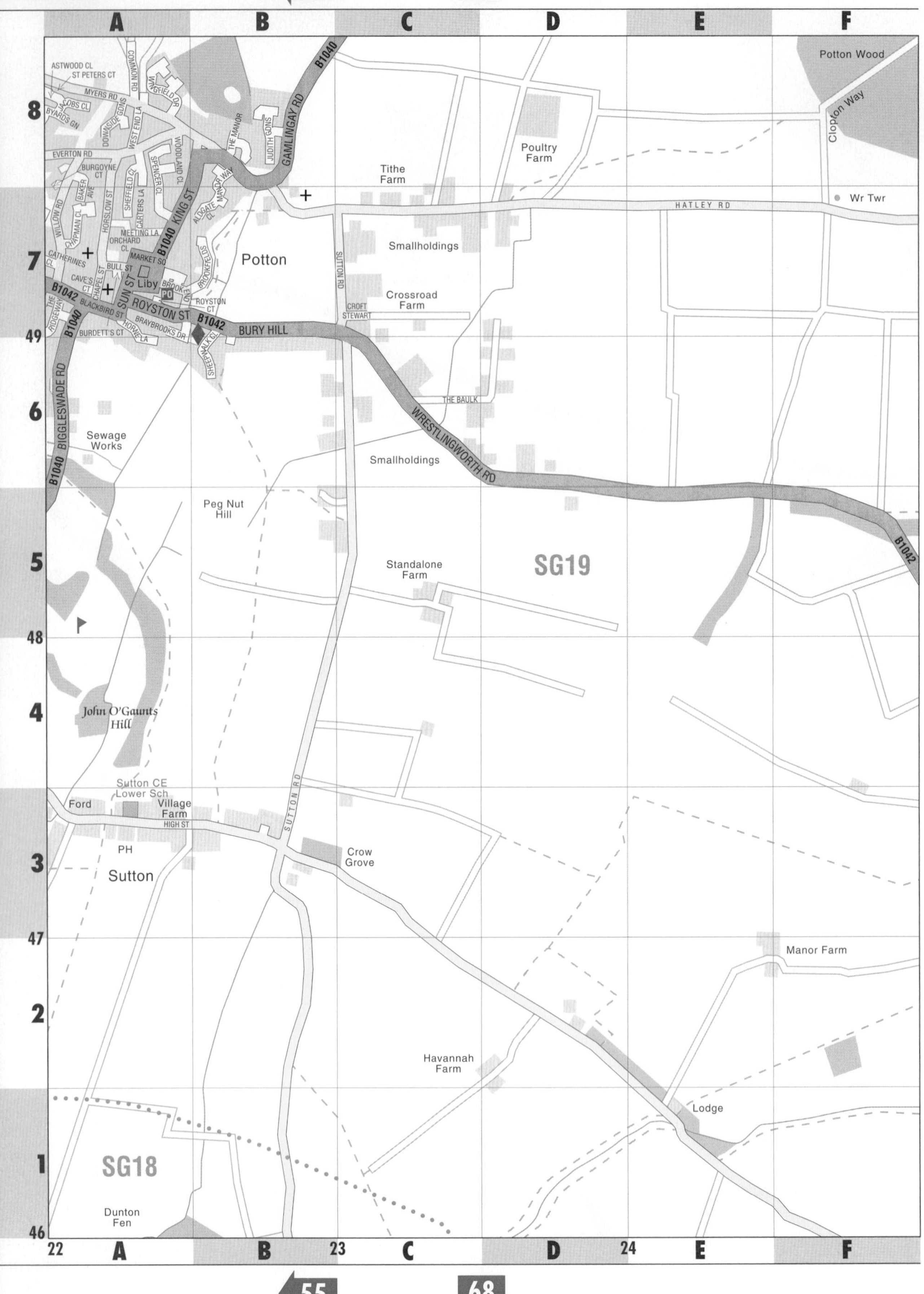

A B C D E F

8

Potton Wood

ASTWOOD CL
ST PETERS CT
MYERS RD
COBS CL
BYARDS GN

Clopton Way

Tithe
Farm

Poultry
Farm

HATLEY RD

● Wr Twr

EVERTON RD
BURGOYNE
CT

7

Smallholdings

Potton

Crossroad
Farm

CROFT
STEWART

Liby

ROYSTON ST

ROYSTON
CT

49

BURY HILL

SHEEPWALK

B1042

THE BAULK

6

WRESTLINGWORTH RD

Sewage
Works

Smallholdings

BIGGLESWADE RD

Peg Nut
Hill

B1042

5

Standalone
Farm

SG19

48

4

John O'Gaunts
Hill

Sutton CE
Lower Sch

Ford

Village
Farm

HIGH ST

SUTTON RD

Crow
Grove

3

PH

Sutton

47

Manor Farm

2

Havannah
Farm

Lodge

1

SG18

Dunton
Fen

46

22 A 23 B C 23 D 24 E F

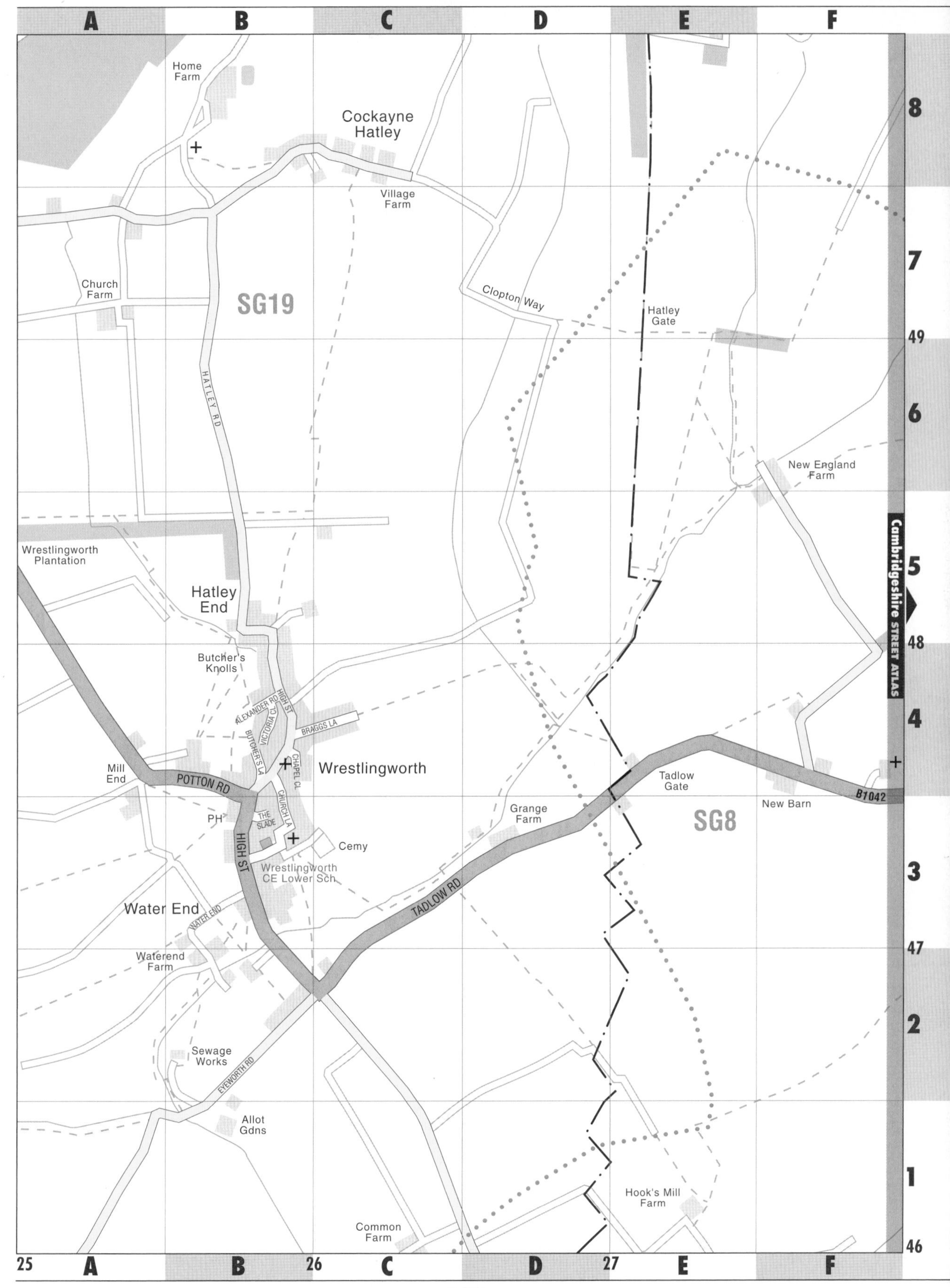

A B C D E F

8

Home
Farm

Cockayne
Hatley

Village
Farm

7

Church
Farm

SG19

Clopton Way

Hatley Gate

49

6

New England
Farm

Wrestlingworth
Plantation

Hatley
End

5

48

Cambridgeshire STREET ATLAS

Butcher's
Knolls

4

ALEXANDER RD
HIGH ST
VICTORIA RD
BRAGGS LA
BUTCHER'S LA
CHAPEL CL
Mill
End
POTTON RD

Wrestlingworth

Tadlow
Gate

New Barn
B1042

Grange
Farm

SG8

PH
THE SLADE
CHURCH LA
HIGH ST

Cemy

Wrestlingworth
CE Lower Sch

3

Water End
WATER END
TADLOW RD

47

Waterend
Farm

EYEWORTH RD

2

Sewage
Works

Allot
Gdns

1

Hook's Mill
Farm

Common
Farm

46

25 A B 26 C D 27 E F

46

A
B
C
D
E
F
8
7
45
6
5
44
4
3
43
2
1
42
92
93
94
Buckinghamshire STREET ATLAS
Little Crawley House
Little Crawley
Old Moat Farm
Gumbrills Farm
Dollars Grove Farm
Dollars Grove
CHICHELEY RD
ORCHARD WAY
HACKETT PL
BRYANS CRES
KILPIN GN
VIOLETS CL
POUND LA
Crawley Grange
Chicheley Brook
East End Farm
Quaker's House
North Crawley
HIGH ST
PH
CHEQUERS LA
CHURCH WLK
Church Farm
BROOK END
North Crawley CE Fst Sch
Broadmead House
Rookery Farm
East End
Lodge Farm
MK16
Ringtail Farm
FOLLY LA
SHIRE LA
Ring Croft Farm
Murtland's Farm
Rings Wharley Farm
Hurstend Farm
Hurst End
Sewage Works
Wharley Farm
Shire La
Milton Keynes Boundary Wlk
FEDDEN HO
ROYCE RD
THE CRESCENT
NASMYTH CL
REYNOLDS CL
HANDLEY PAGE CL
DUNCAN RD
Cranfield Conference Ctr
PRINCE PHILIP AVE
EAST RD
MITCHELL RD
STRINGFELLOW CL
MERCHANT LA
WEST RD
THE DRIVE
Wharley End
THE GREEN
COLLEGE RD
PO
LANCHESTER RD
CENTRAL AVE
Cranfield Univ
Liby
Moulsoe Old Wood
The Cottage
Chapelclose Spinney
Wharley End Farm
UNIVERSITY WAY
MK43
Cranfield Airfield

70

47
60

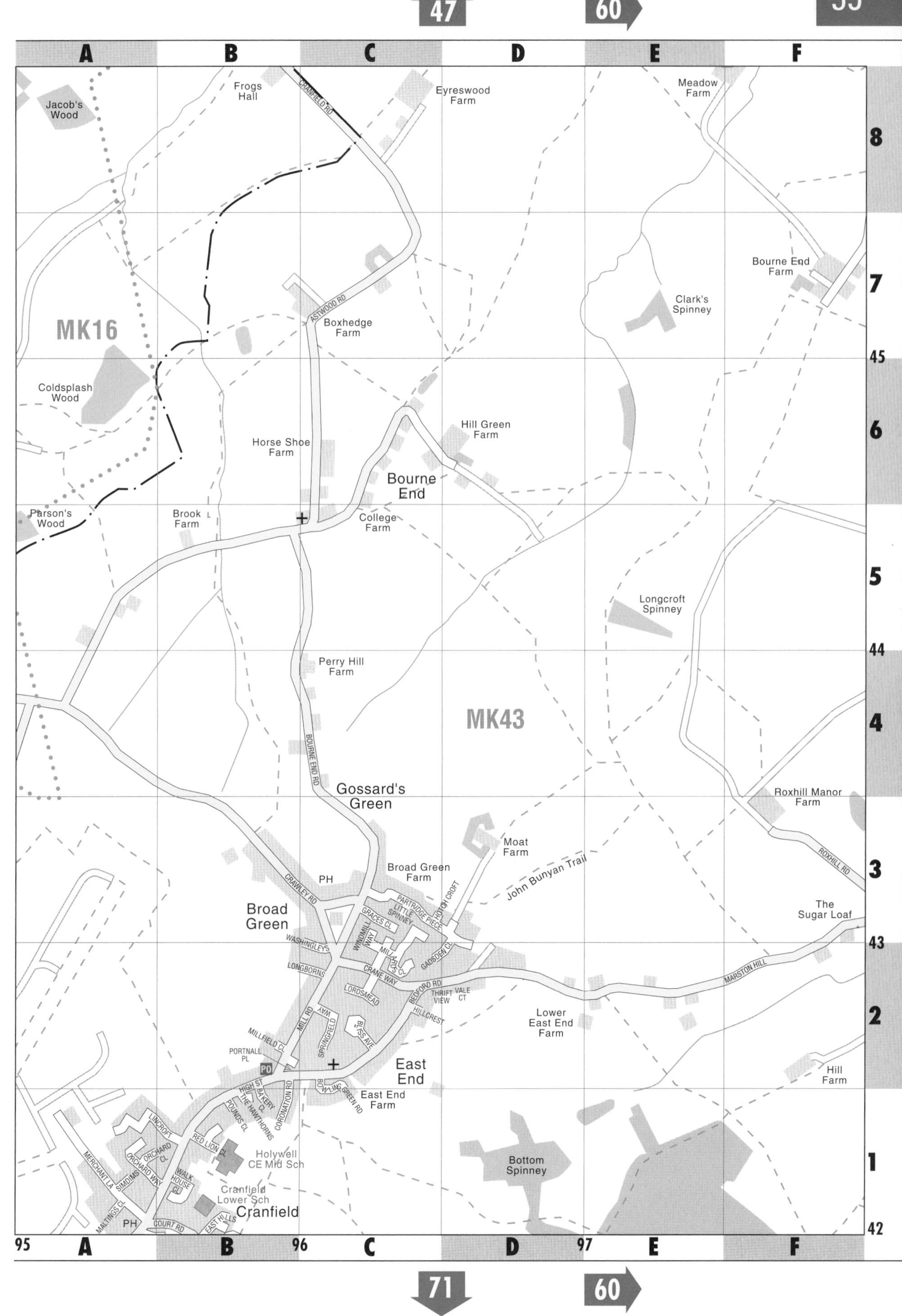
A
B
C
D
E
F
Jacob's Wood
Frogs Hall
CRANFIELD RD
Eyreswood Farm
Meadow Farm
8
Bourne End Farm
Clark's Spinney
7
ASTWOOD RD
Boxhedge Farm
MK16
45
Coldsplash Wood
Hill Green Farm
Horse Shoe Farm
6
Bourne End
Parson's Wood
Brook Farm
College Farm
5
Longcroft Spinney
44
Perry Hill Farm
MK43
4
BOURNE END RD
Gossard's Green
Roxhill Manor Farm
Moat Farm
ROXHILL RD
Broad Green Farm
3
PH
John Bunyan Trail
CRAWLEY RD
HOTCH CROFT
PARTRIDGE PIECE
LITTLE SPINNEY
GRACES CL
Broad Green
The Sugar Loaf
WINDMILL WAY
MILLARDS CL
WASHINGLEYS
GADSDEN CL
43
LONGBORNS
CRANE WAY
MARSTON HILL
BEDFORD RD
LORDSMEAD
THRIFT VIEW
VALE CT
Lower East End Farm
MILL RD
WAY
SPRINGFIELD
BLISS AVE
HILLCREST
2
MILLFIELD CL
PORTNALL PL
PO
East End
Hill Farm
HIGH ST
BAKERY CL
THE HAWTHORNS
CORONATION RD
BOWLING GREEN RD
East End Farm
POUNDS CL
LINCROFT
RED LION CL
ORCHARD CL
Holywell CE Mid Sch
Bottom Spinney
1
MERCHANT LA
SIMDIMS
ORCHARD WAY
WALK HOUSE CL
Cranfield Lower Sch
Cranfield
MALTINGS CL
PH
COURT RD
EAST HILLS
42
95
96
97

71
60

59
48

A B C D E F

8
7
45
6
5
44
4
3
43
2
1
42

Vine Cottage Farm
Hall End
PH
Wootton Bourne End
BOURNE END RD
HOD CL 1
EMERTON WAY 2
SANDERS WAY 3
HANOVER CT 4
NEALE WAY
THORPE WAY
CANONS CL
LORRAINE RD
Cemy
Liby
DIMMOCK RD
POPES WAY
CAUSE END RD
FARRE
HALL END RD
Bourne End House
STUDLEY RD
ST MARY'S RD
TITHE BARN RD
Wootton Lower Sch
John Bunyan Trail
Wootton Upper Sch
PH
GROVEBURY CT
CHURCH ROW
OLD SCHOOL GDNS
SCHOOL LA
BEDFORD RD
PAYNE RD
CHURCH RD
Church End
FIELDS RD
JEAKYN RD
RUSSELL WAY
SQUIRES RD
Playing Field
Wootton Wood
BARNES RD
SOMMERFIELD DR
BELLAMY RD
BROWNS LA
Top Farm
Ashbrook
MK43
CRANFIELD RD
Wood Farm
Wootton Green Farm
The Croft
Berry Farm
The Hoo Farm
The Hoo
PH
Wootton Green
UPPER SHELTON RD
BEDFORD RD
Walnut Tree Farm
Upper Shelton
Shelton Lower Sch
HOO LA
Hoolane Farm
A421
Shelton Farm
Lower Roxhill Farm
Shelton Manor Farm
LOWER SHELTON RD
CHEQUERS CL
STRATFORD WAY
BEDFORD RD
Lower Shelton
FRANKLIN CL
Charity Farm
ROBERTS DR
Stewartby Lake
Marston Vale Millennium Country Park
BEANCROFT RD
CAMPIN CT
HORSESHOE CL
SNAGGE CT
ALLEN CT
Saw Mill
BEDFORD RD
Caulcott
Beancroft Farm
Draper's Farm
A421
BARKERS PIECE

98 A B 99 C D 00 E F

59
72

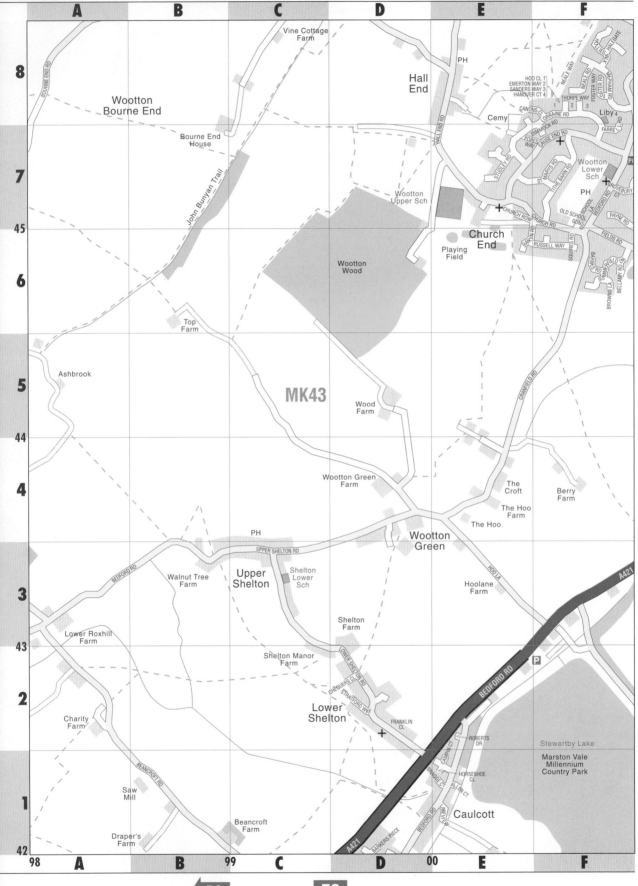

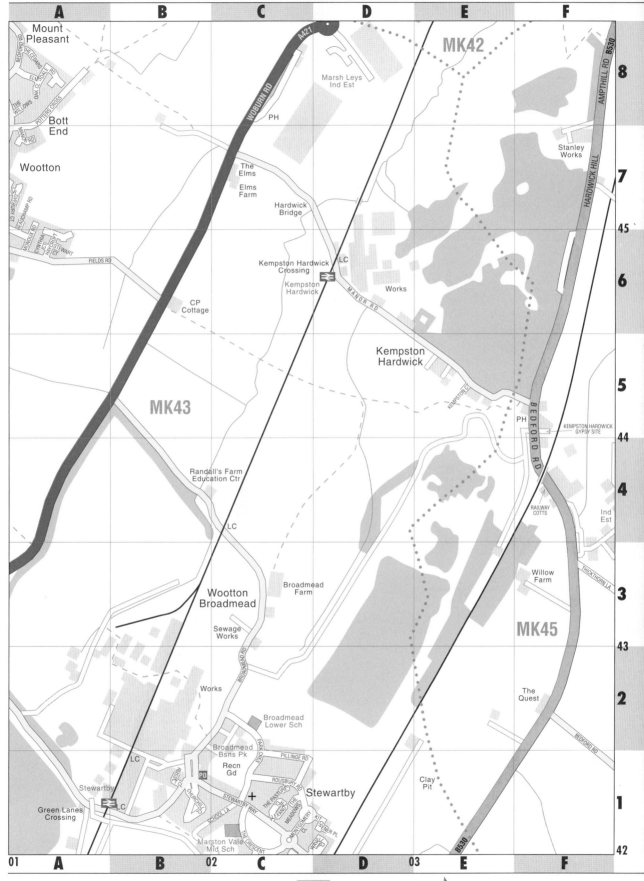

A B C D E F

Mount Pleasant
Bott End
Wootton
BEDFORD RD
THE CEDARS
DALE RD
OAK CL
ELM
THE WILLOWS
POTTERS CROSS
MANOR RD
OVERBURY CT
BEAUCHAMP RD
MONOUX RD
CYNTHIA CT
HAYCROFT
STEWART CT
FIELDS RD
A421
WOBURN RD
PH
Marsh Leys Ind Est
MK42
The Elms
Elms Farm
Hardwick Bridge
Kempston Hardwick Crossing
LC
Kempston Hardwick
MANOR RD
Works
Stanley Works
AMPTHILL RD
B530
HARDWICK HILL
CP Cottage
Kempston Hardwick
KEMPSTON CT
MK43
PH
BEDFORD RD
KEMPSTON HARDWICK GYPSY SITE
Randall's Farm Education Ctr
LC
RAILWAY COTTS
Ind Est
Willow Farm
THICKTHORN LA
Wootton Broadmead
Broadmead Farm
Sewage Works
MK45
BROADMEAD RD
Works
The Quest
Broadmead Lower Sch
BEDFORD RD
Broadmead Bsns Pk
PARK CRES
PILLINGE RD
LC
Recn Gd
PO
ROUSBURY RD
RUSSELL CL
Stewartby
CHURCHILL CL
STEWARTBY WAY
THE PASTURES
Stewartby
THE MEADOWS
ALEXANDER CL
Clay Pit
Green Lanes Crossing
LC
SCHOOL LA
MONTGOMERY CL
KITCHENER PL
THE CRESCENT
WAVELL CL
Marston Vale Mid Sch
B530

8 7 45 6 5 44 4 3 43 2 1 42

01 A B 02 C D 03 E F

61
50

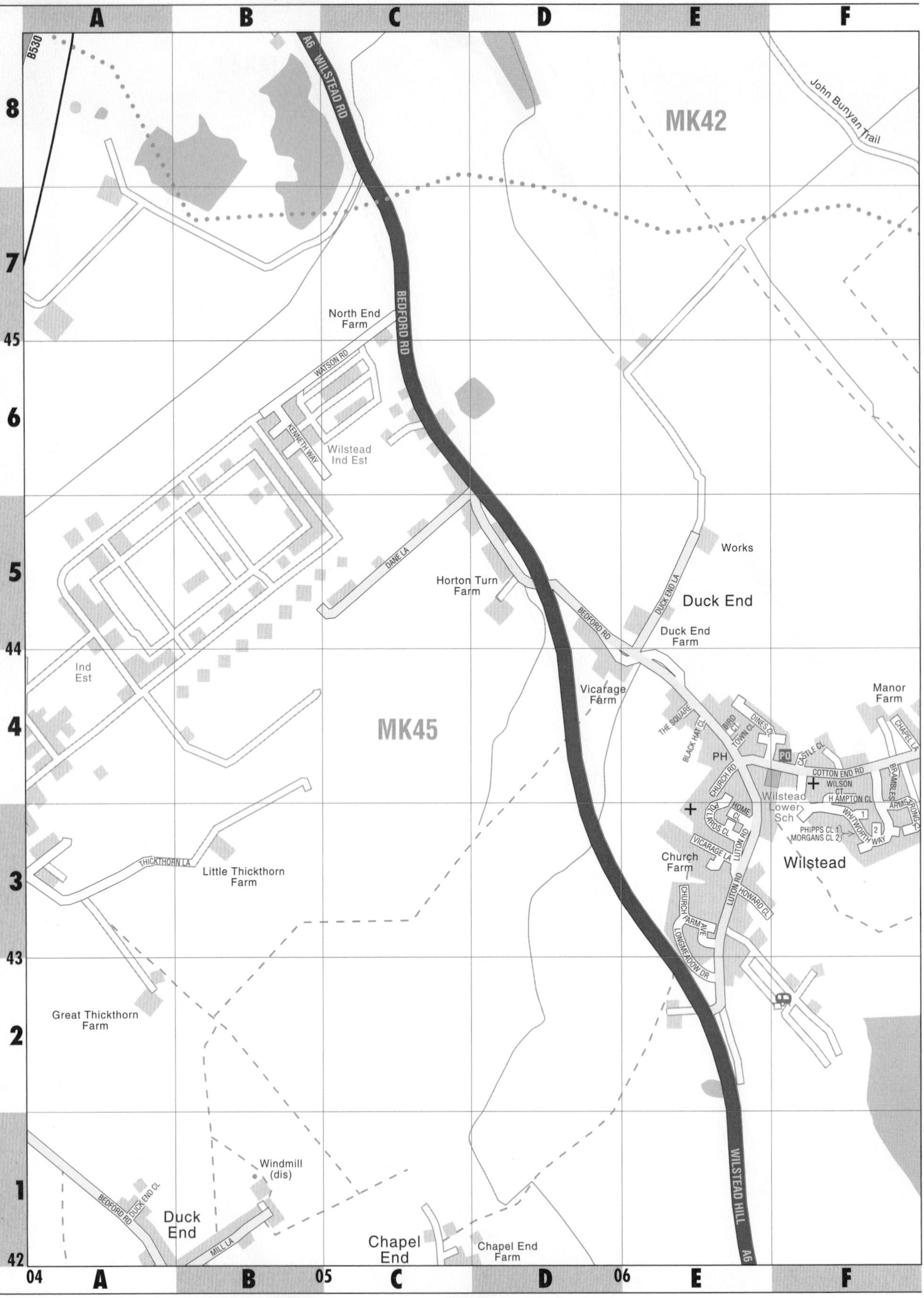

A B C D E F

8

MK42

John Bunyan Trail

7

45

North End
Farm

BEDFORD RD

A6 WILSTEAD RD

6

WATSON RD

KENNET WAY

Wilstead
Ind Est

Works

5

DANE LA

Horton Turn
Farm

Duck End

BEDFORD RD

DUCK END LA

Duck End
Farm

44

Ind
Est

Vicarage
Farm

Manor
Farm

4

MK45

THE SQUARE

BLACK HAT CL

BIRD CT

DINES CL

TOWN CL

CASTLE CL

WILSON
CT.

H. AMPTON CL

CHAPEL LA

BRAMBLES

ARMSTRONG

COTTON END RD

PH

PO

Wilstead
Lower
Sch

CHURCH RD

HOME
CL

LYARDS CL

WHITWORTH WAY

1

2

PHIPPS CL 1
MORGANS CL 2

Wilstead

3

THICKTHORN LA

Little Thickthorn
Farm

Church
Farm

VICARAGE LA

HOWARD CL

LONGMEADOW DR

CHURCH FARM AVE

LYTTON RD

43

Great Thickthorn
Farm

2

Windmill
(dis)

WILSTEAD HILL

1

BEDFORD RD

DUCK END CL

MILL LA

Duck
End

Chapel
End

Chapel End
Farm

A6

42

04 A B 05 C D 06 E F

61
74

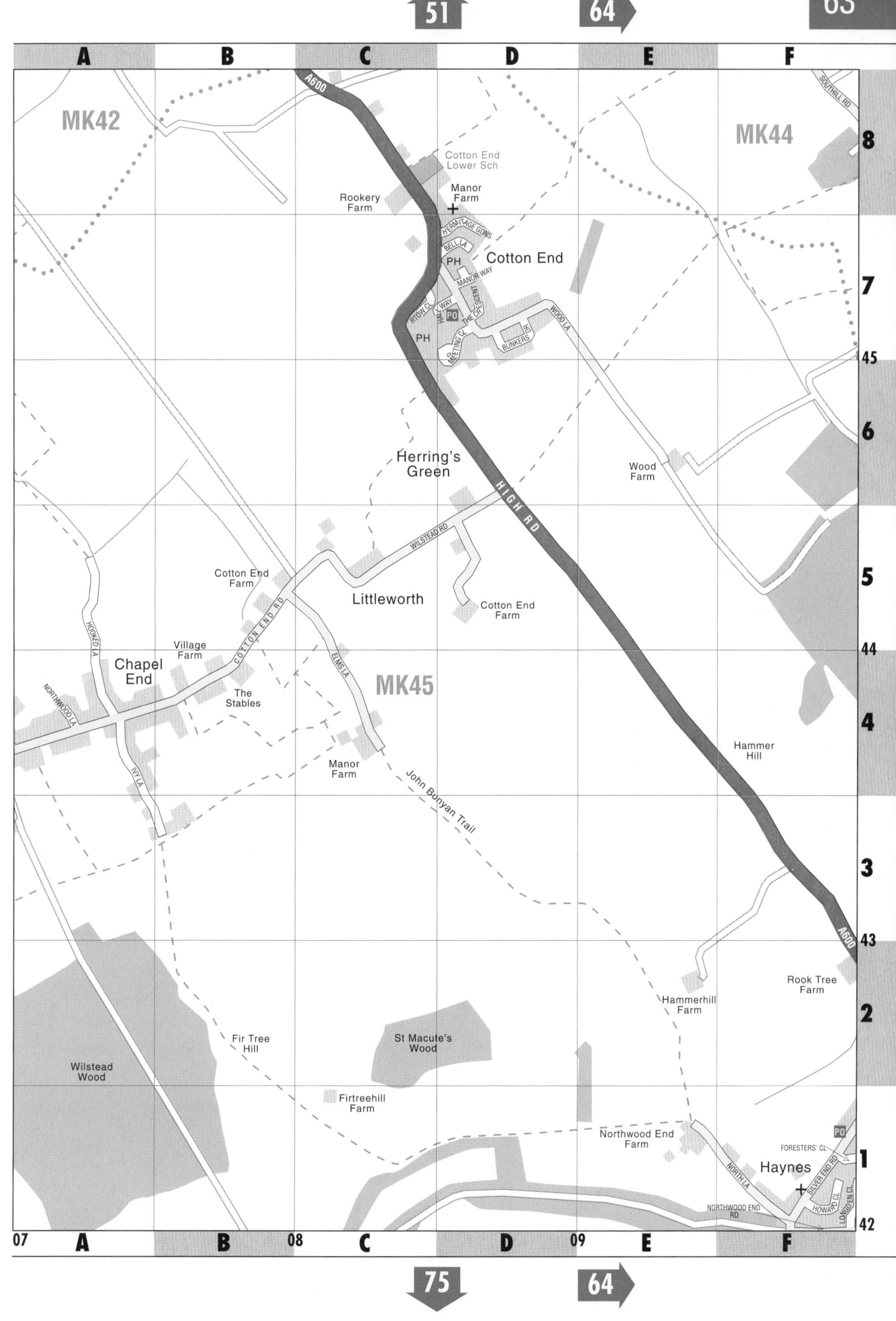

A B C D E F

MK42

A600

MK44

SOUTHILL RD

8

Cotton End
Lower Sch

Rookery
Farm

Manor
Farm

HERMITAGE GDNS

BELL LA

PH

Cotton End

MANOR WAY

7

HAYE WAY

THE CRESCENT

WOOD LA

PO

45

PH

MEETING CL

BUNKERS

6

Herring's
Green

Wood
Farm

HIGH RD

5

Cotton End
Farm

Littleworth

WILSTEAD RD

Cotton End
Farm

COTTON END RD

44

Village
Farm

HOOKED LA

Chapel
End

NORTHWOOD LA

MK45

ELMS LA

The
Stables

4

IVY LA

Manor
Farm

Hammer
Hill

John Bunyan Trail

3

A600

43

Rook Tree
Farm

Hammerhill
Farm

2

Fir Tree
Hill

St Macute's
Wood

Wilstead
Wood

Firtreehill
Farm

PO

FORESTERS' CL

Northwood End
Farm

NORTH LA

Haynes

SILVER END RD

LONDON IN CL

HOWARD CL

1

NORTHWOOD END
RD

42

07 A B 08 C D 09 E F

A B C D E F

8
7
45
6
5
44
4
3
43
2
1
42
10 A B 11 C D 12 E F

MK44

SOUTHILL RD

The Gables

Hillfoot Farm

Sweetbrier Farm

Palmers Wood

Manor Wood

BORDEN LA

Greensand Ridge Walk

Park Farm

Warden Street

Exeter Wood

BEDFORD RD

SG18

Warden Little Wood

Abbey Farm

Claypits Farm

Warden Great Wood

MK45

A600

HIGH RD

SILVER END RD

OAKTREE WAY

FORESTERS CL

Haynes

Haynes Lower Sch

LONGDEN CL

A600

SG17

Old Rowney Cottages

53
66

A
B
C
D
E
F
Highlands Ashes
Hangman's Spinney
Tabaccopipe Spinney
Wood Farm
Ickwell Park
Ickwell Bury
NORTHILL RD
TOMPIONS END
CALDECOTE RD
ICKWELL RD
Ickwell Green
Palmer's Spinney
Ickwell
COLEMOREHAM CT
WARDEN RD
P
HILL LA
Mount Pleasant Farm
Mount Pleasant House
The Shuttleworth Collection Mus
Swiss Garden
Shuttleworth (Old Warden) Airfield
Quince Hill
Church End
Old Warden Park
Home Farm
Shuttleworth College
SG18
Brickclamp Covert
PH
PO
Old Warden
Laundry Farm
RICHARD'S CRES
BEDFORD RD
Lowsiebush Covert
Warden Warren
Foxhole Covert
Gastlings
Reed Bed
Home Farm
Flannels
Round Basin
Yew Tree Farm
Southill Lower Sch
SCHOOL LA
HOWARD'S CL
Vicarage
Park Farm
Southill Park
SG17
8
7
45
6
5
44
4
3
43
2
1
42
13
14
15

77
66

65
54

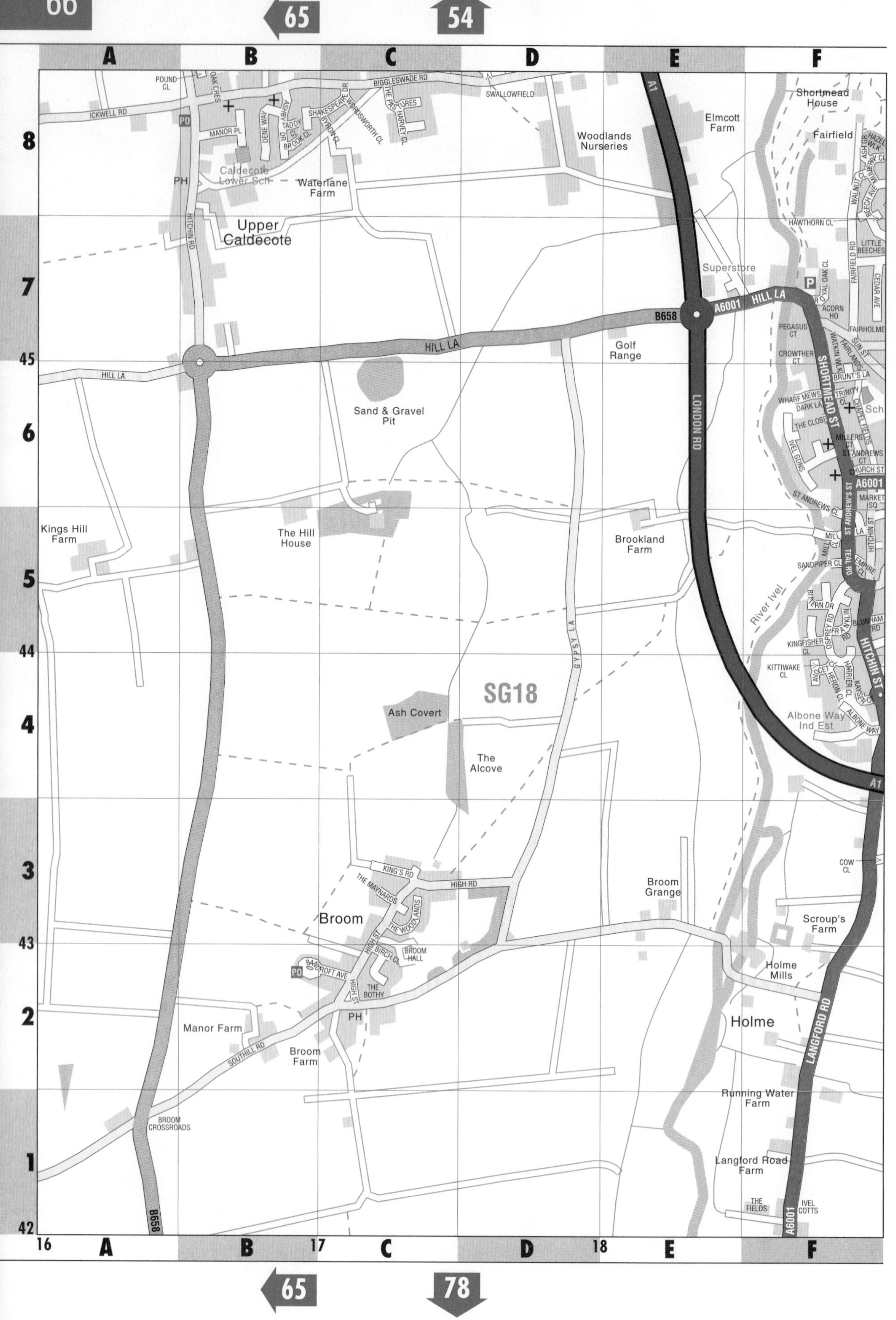
A
B
C
D
E
F
8
7
45
6
5
44
4
3
43
2
1
42
16
17
18
Upper Caldecote
Caldecote Lower Sch
Waterlane Farm
Woodlands Nurseries
Elmcott Farm
Shortmead House
Fairfield
Superstore
Golf Range
HILL LA
B658
A6001
A1
LONDON RD
Sand & Gravel Pit
The Hill House
Kings Hill Farm
Brookland Farm
River Ivel
SG18
Ash Covert
The Alcove
GYPSY LA
Albone Way Ind Est
Broom
HIGH RD
KING'S RD
THE MAYNARDS
THE WOODLANDS
BROOM HALL
Broom Grange
Scroup's Farm
Holme Mills
Holme
Manor Farm
Broom Farm
SOUTHILL RD
BROOM CROSSROADS
Running Water Farm
Langford Road Farm
LANGFORD RD
THE FIELDS
IVEL COTTS
SHORTMEAD ST
HITCHIN ST
HITCHIN RD
ICKWELL RD
BIGGLESWADE RD
SWALLOWFIELD
MANOR PL
POUND CL
OAK CRES
DENE WAY
HAWTHORN CL
CEDAR AVE
FAIRHOLME
PEGASUS CT
CROWTHER CT
WHARF MEWS
DARK LA
THE CLOSE
IVEL GDNS
ST ANDREWS CL
MARKET SQ
SANDPIPER CL
KINGFISHER CL
KITTIWAKE CL
COW CL
PH
PO
Sch

65
78

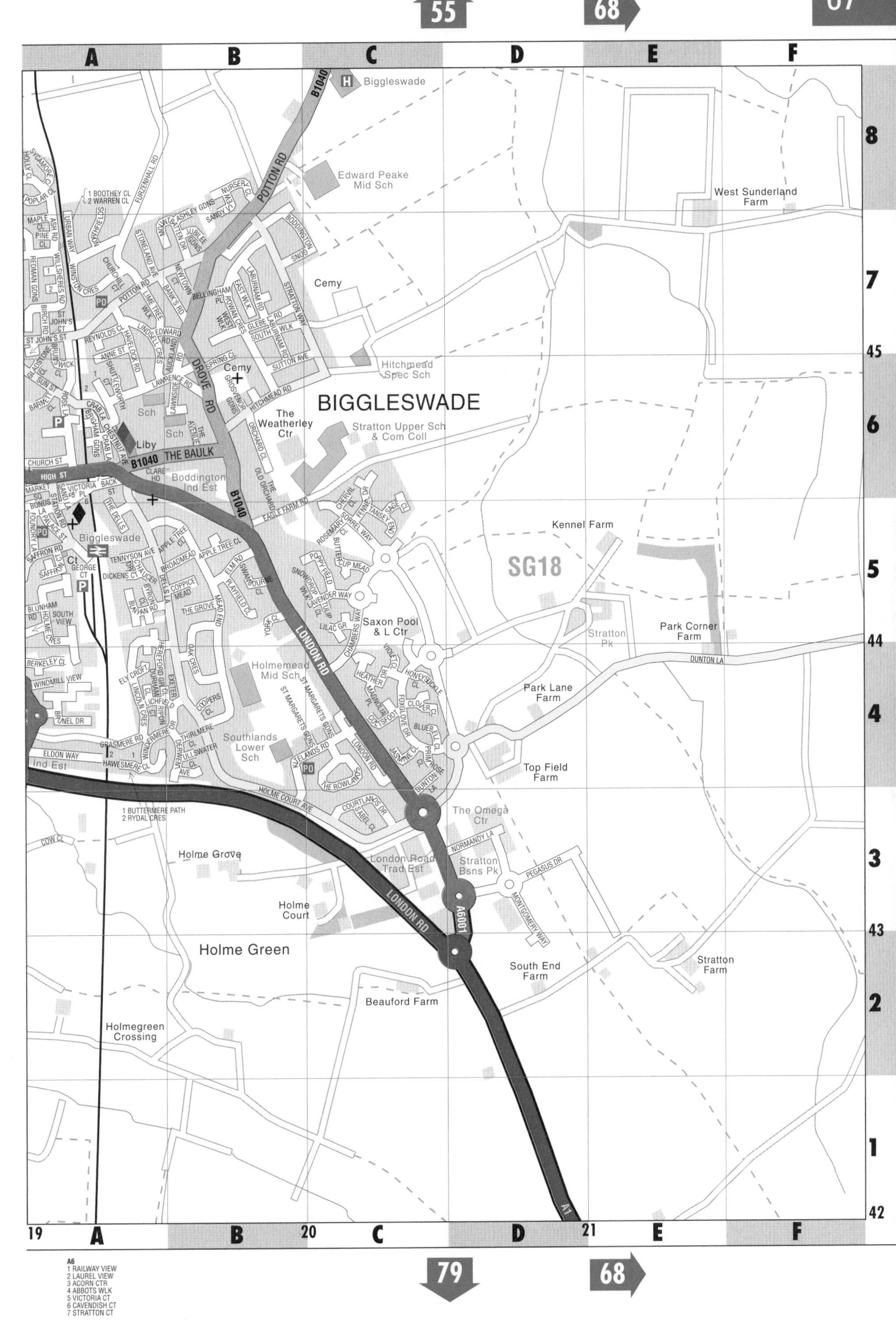

55
68
A
B
C
D
E
F
8
7
45
6
5
44
4
3
43
2
1
42
19
20
21
79
68
Biggleswade
B1040
Edward Peake
Mid Sch
West Sunderland
Farm
Cemy
Hitchmead
Spec Sch
BIGGLESWADE
The
Weatherley
Ctr
Stratton Upper Sch
& Com Coll
Sch
Liby
B1040 THE BAULK
Boddington
Ind Est
HIGH ST
Biggleswade
Kennel Farm
SG18
Saxon Pool
& L Ctr
Park Corner
Farm
Stratton
Pk
DUNTON LA
Park Lane
Farm
Holmemead
Mid Sch
Southlands
Lower
Sch
Top Field
Farm
LONDON RD
POTTON RD
DROVE RD
EAGLE FARM RD
HOLME COURT AVE
ELDON WAY
Ind Est
1 BUTTERMERE PATH
2 RYDAL CRES
The Omega
Ctr
NORMANDY LA
PEGASUS DR
London Road
Trad Est
Stratton
Bsns Pk
MONTGOMERY WAY
Holme Grove
Holme
Court
A6001
Holme Green
South End
Farm
Stratton
Farm
Beauford Farm
Holmegreen
Crossing
A1
1 BOOTHEY CL
2 WARREN CL
A6
1 RAILWAY VIEW
2 LAUREL VIEW
3 ACORN CTR
4 ABBOTS WLK
5 VICTORIA CT
6 CAVENDISH CT
7 STRATTON CT

67
56

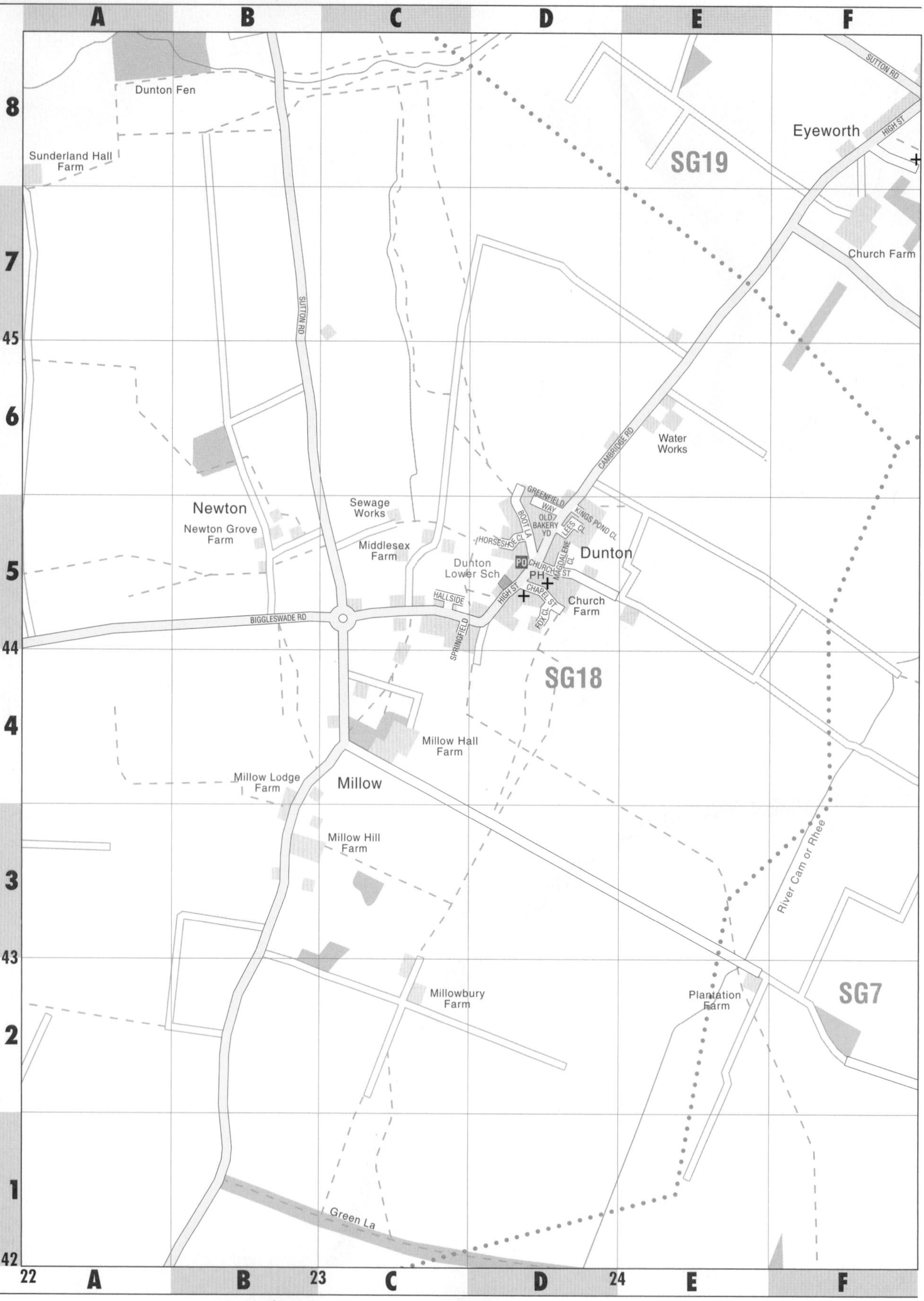

	A	B	C	D	E	F

8

Dunton Fen

Sunderland Hall Farm

Eyeworth

SUTTON RD

HIGH ST

SG19

Church Farm

7

45

SUTTON RD

6

CAMBRIDGE RD

Water Works

Newton

Sewage Works

GREENFIELD WAY

BOOT LA

KINGS POND CL

OLD BAKERY YD

Dunton

Newton Grove Farm

Middlesex Farm

HORSESH ST

HS CL

5

Dunton Lower Sch

PD
PH

CHURCH ST

MAGDALENE CL

Church Farm

HALLSIDE

CHAPEL ST

FOX CL

BIGGLESWADE RD

HIGH ST

SPRINGFIELD

44

SG18

4

Millow Hall Farm

Millow Lodge Farm

Millow

Millow Hill Farm

3

River Cam or Rhee

43

Millowbury Farm

Plantation Farm

SG7

2

1

Green La

42

22	A		B	23	C		D	24	E		F

67
80

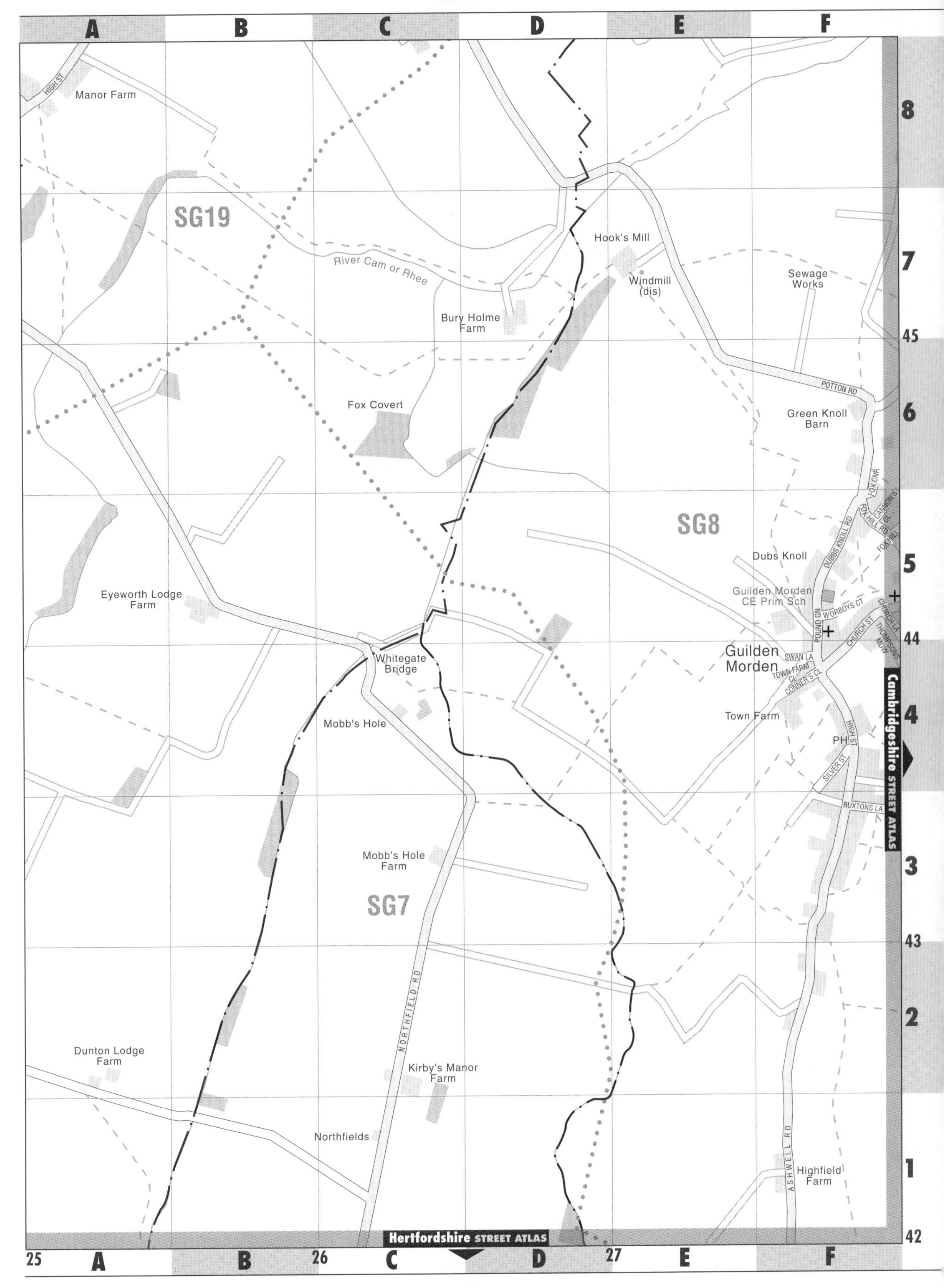

Cambridgeshire STREET ATLAS

SG19

SG8

SG7

HIGH ST

Manor Farm

River Cam or Rhee

Bury Holme Farm

Fox Covert

Hook's Mill

Windmill (dis)

Sewage Works

POTTON RD

Green Knoll Barn

Dubs Knoll

Guilden Morden CE Prim Sch

Guilden Morden

FOX CNR

DUBS KNOLL RD

FOX HILL RD

CANNONS ST

FOX HILL RD HL

POUND GN

CHURCH LA

WORBOYS CT

CHURCH ST

THOMPSONS

MEADW

SWAN LA

TOWN FARM CL

CONNER'S CL

HIGH ST

Town Farm

PH

SILVER ST

BUXTONS LA

Eyeworth Lodge Farm

Whitegate Bridge

Mobb's Hole

Mobb's Hole Farm

NORTHFIELD RD

Dunton Lodge Farm

Kirby's Manor Farm

Northfields

ASHWELL RD

Highfield Farm

58

A
B
C
D
E
F
8
7
41
6
5
40
4
3
39
2
1
38
92
93
94
Wood End Farm
Lower Wood
UNIVERSITY WAY
Cranfield Technology Pk
Stilliters Farm
West End
LODGE RD
MK43
Villa Park (Mobile Home Pk)
Leys Farm
MK16
Conn's Farm
Broughton Grounds
Salford Wood
Holcotmoors Farm
CRANFIELD RD
Holcotmoors Lodge
Milton Keynes Boundary Wlk
Whitsundoles Farm
Buckinghamshire STREET ATLAS
Salford
Rectory Farm
College Farm
Mill Farm
BROUGHTON RD
BRITTONS LA
PH
MK17
M1 Northampton (A508)
M1
MILL LA
THE COURT
MANOR CL
Rooktree Farm
Manor House
The Islands
Church House
PH
Salfordford Bridge
WAVENDON RD
Waterhall
Hulcote
Fox Covert
Byron Lodge
Water Hall Farm
Hulcot Manor
A421 Buckingham
A421
Eagle Farm
Aspley Hall
MILL LA
Wavendon Lodge
CRANFIELD RD
LOWER END RD
A421
M1

81

59
72

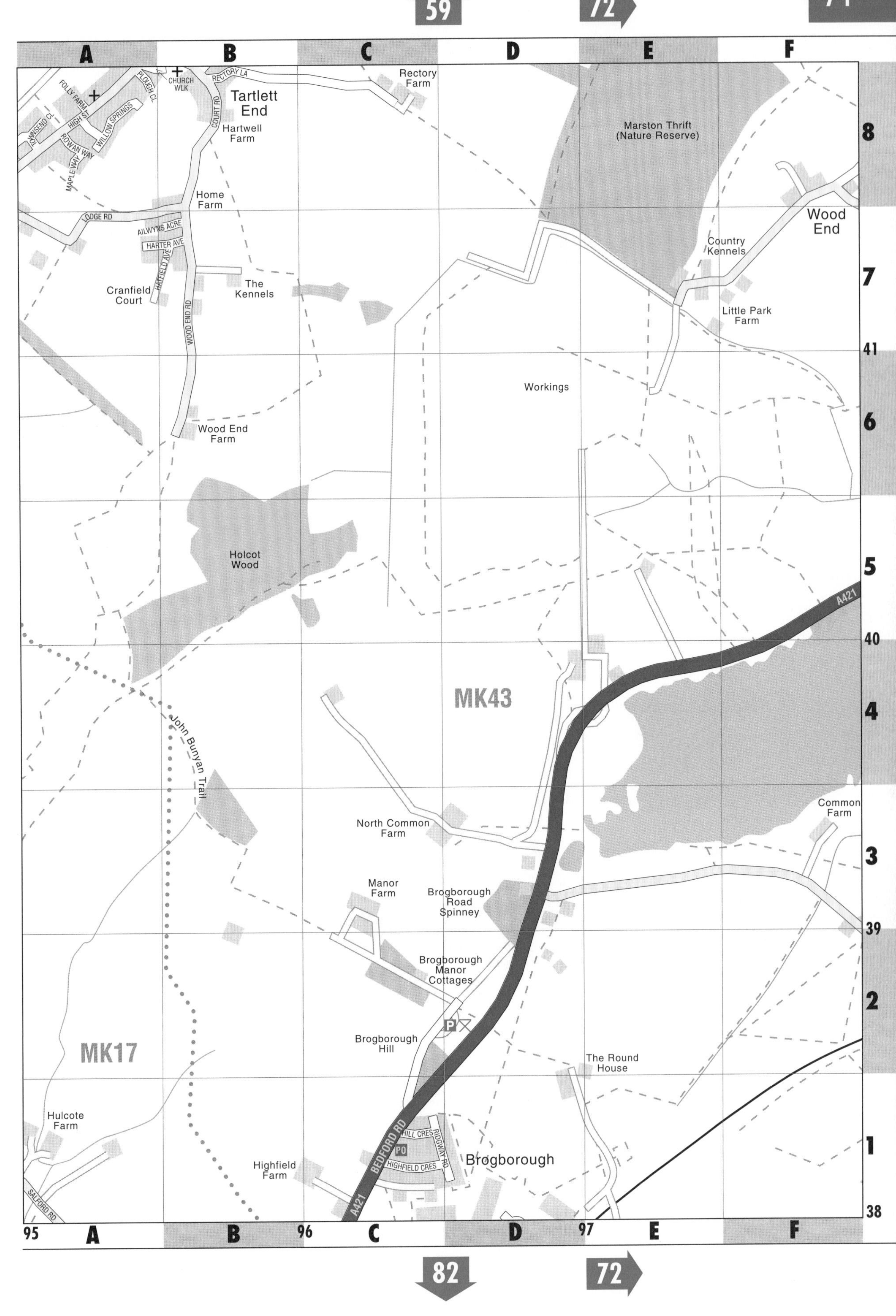

A
B
C
D
E
F
Tartlett End
Rectory Farm
Hartwell Farm
Marston Thrift (Nature Reserve)
Home Farm
Wood End
Country Kennels
Cranfield Court
The Kennels
Little Park Farm
Workings
Wood End Farm
Holcot Wood
MK43
John Bunyan Trail
North Common Farm
Common Farm
Manor Farm
Brogborough Road Spinney
Brogborough Manor Cottages
Brogborough Hill
The Round House
MK17
Hulcote Farm
Highfield Farm
Brogborough
FOLLY FARM
HIGH ST
TOWNSEND CL
ROWAN WAY
MAPLE WAY
WILLOW SPRINGS
PLOUGH CL
CHURCH WLK
RECTORY LA
COURT RD
LODGE RD
AILWYNS ACRE
HARTER AVE
HATFIELD AVE
WOOD END RD
BEDFORD RD
A421
HILL CRES
RIDGWAY RD
HIGHFIELD CRES
SALFORD RD
PO
P
8
7
41
6
5
40
4
3
39
2
1
38
95
96
97

82
72

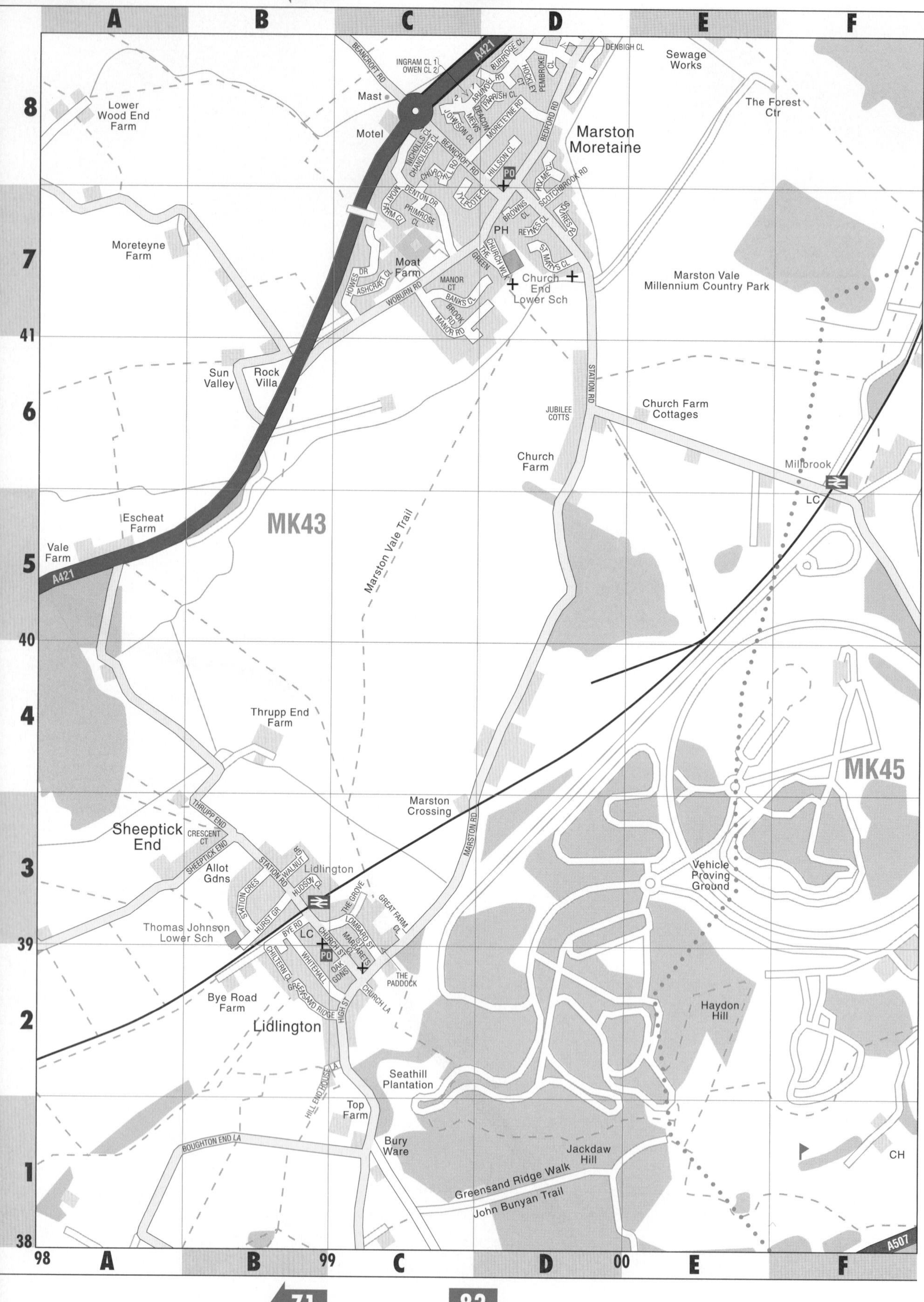

A B C D E F

8
7
41
6
5
40
4
3
39
2
1
38

Lower Wood End Farm
Moreteyne Farm
Sun Valley
Rock Villa
Escheat Farm
Vale Farm
A421
MK43
Marston Vale Trail
Thrupp End Farm
Sheeptick End
THRUPP END
CRESCENT CT
SHEEPTICK END
Allot Gdns
STATION RD
HURST GR.
WALNUT
HUDSON
Lidlington
THE GROVE
GREAT FARM CL
Marston Crossing
Thomas Johnson Lower Sch
LC
BYE RD
PO
CHILTERN CL
GREENSAND RIDGE
WHITEHALL
LOMBARDY
ST MARGARET
OAK GDNS
THE PADDOCK
CHURCH LA
HIGH ST
Bye Road Farm
Lidlington
HILL END
BOUGHTON END LA
Top Farm
Seathill Plantation
Bury Ware
Greensand Ridge Walk
John Bunyan Trail
Jackdaw Hill
Haydon Hill
MK45
Vehicle Proving Ground
CH
A507

BEANCROFT RD
INGRAM CL 1
OWEN CL 2
Mast
Motel
A421
DENBIGH CL
Sewage Works
BURROGE CL
HOCKCL
PEMBROKE CL
PARRISH CL
JOWELL RD
MEADOW
MORETEYNE RD
HILSON CL
BEDFORD RD
Marston Moretaine
The Forest Ctr
NICHOLLS CL
CHANDLERS CL
JOHNSON CL
BEANCROFT RD
CHURCH
LYDON
FARM CL
DENTON DR
PRIMROSE CL
POTFOL
BROWNS CL
PO
HOLMAN CL
HOLLY CL
SCOTCHBROOK RD
REYNES CL
ST MARYS CL
PH
PARSEY RD
Moat Farm
THE GREEN
HOWES DR
ASHCRAFT
WOBURN RD
MANOR CT
BANK'S CL
BROWN
MANOR RD
CHURCH WLK
Church End Lower Sch
Marston Vale Millennium Country Park
STATION RD
JUBILEE COTTS
Church Farm Cottages
Church Farm
Millbrook
LC

61 74

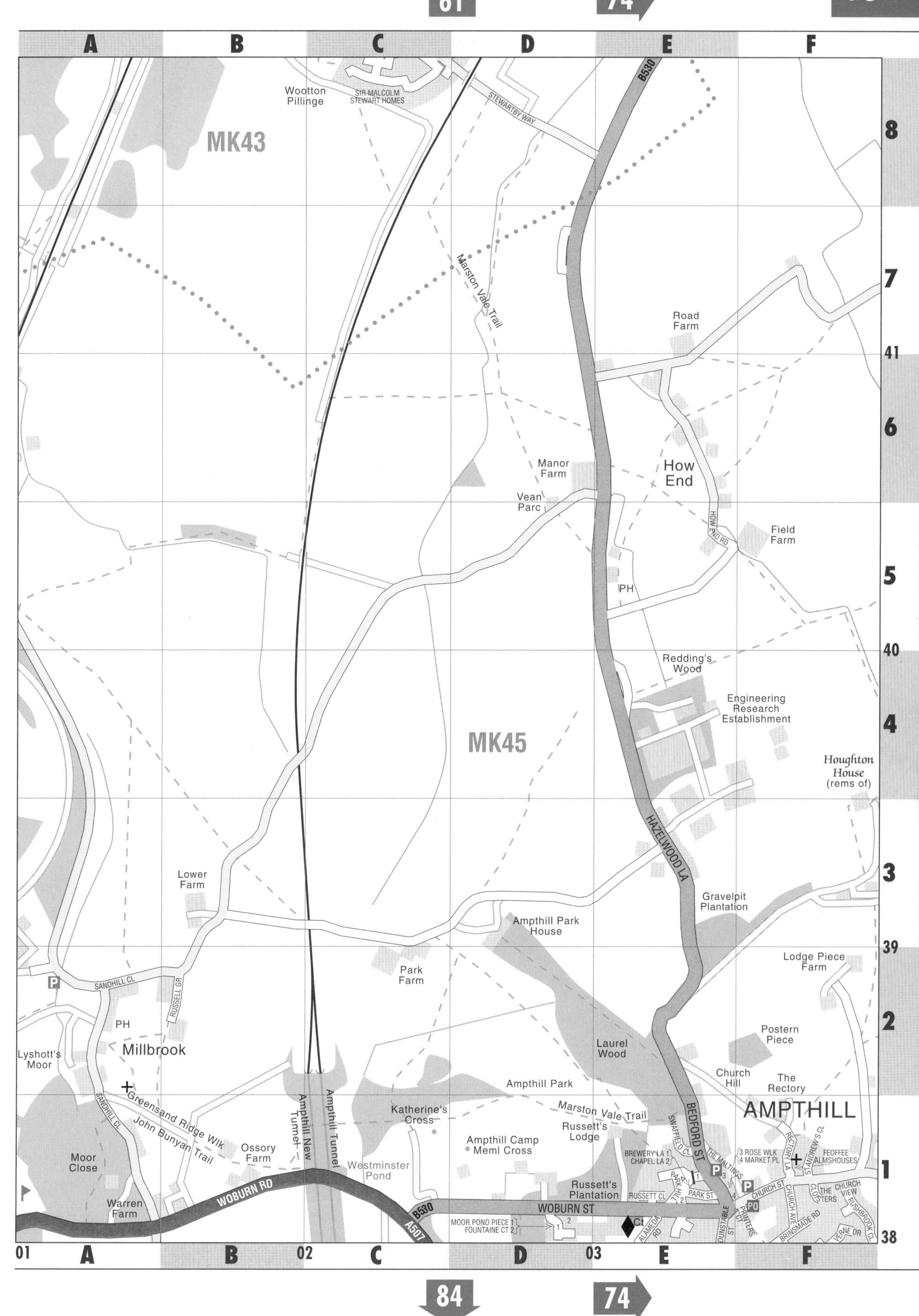

A B C D E F
8 7 41 6 5 40 4 3 39 2 1 38
01 02 03
MK43
MK45
Wootton Pillinge
SIR MALCOLM STEWART HOMES
STEWARTBY WAY
B530
Marston Vale Trail
Road Farm
Manor Farm
How End
Vean Parc
HOW END RD
Field Farm
PH
Redding's Wood
Engineering Research Establishment
Houghton House (rems of)
HAZELWOOD LA
Lower Farm
Gravelpit Plantation
Ampthill Park House
Lodge Piece Farm
SANDHILL CL
RUSSELL GR
Park Farm
PH
Millbrook
Lyshott's Moor
Laurel Wood
Postern Piece
Church Hill
The Rectory
Ampthill Park
SANDHILL CL
Greensand Ridge Wlk
John Bunyan Trail
Ampthill New Tunnel
Ampthill Tunnel
Katherine's Cross
Marston Vale Trail
Russett's Lodge
BEDFORD ST
AMPTHILL
Moor Close
Ossory Farm
Westminster Pond
Ampthill Camp Meml Cross
SWAFFIELD CL
BREWERY LA 1
CHAPEL LA 2
THE MALTINGS
3 ROSE WLK
4 MARKET PL
RECTORY LA
ST ANDREW'S CL
FEOFFEE ALMSHOUSES
WOBURN RD
Russett's Plantation
RUSSETT CL
PARK HILL
PARK ST
CHURCH ST
THE CLOISTERS
CHURCH VIEW
Warren Farm
B530
WOBURN ST
A507
MOOR POND PIECE 1
FOUNTAIN CT 2
ALAMEDA RD
DUNSTABLE ST
PRINTERS CT
CHURCH AVE
BRINSMADE RD
VERNE DR
RUSHBROOK CL

84 74

73
62

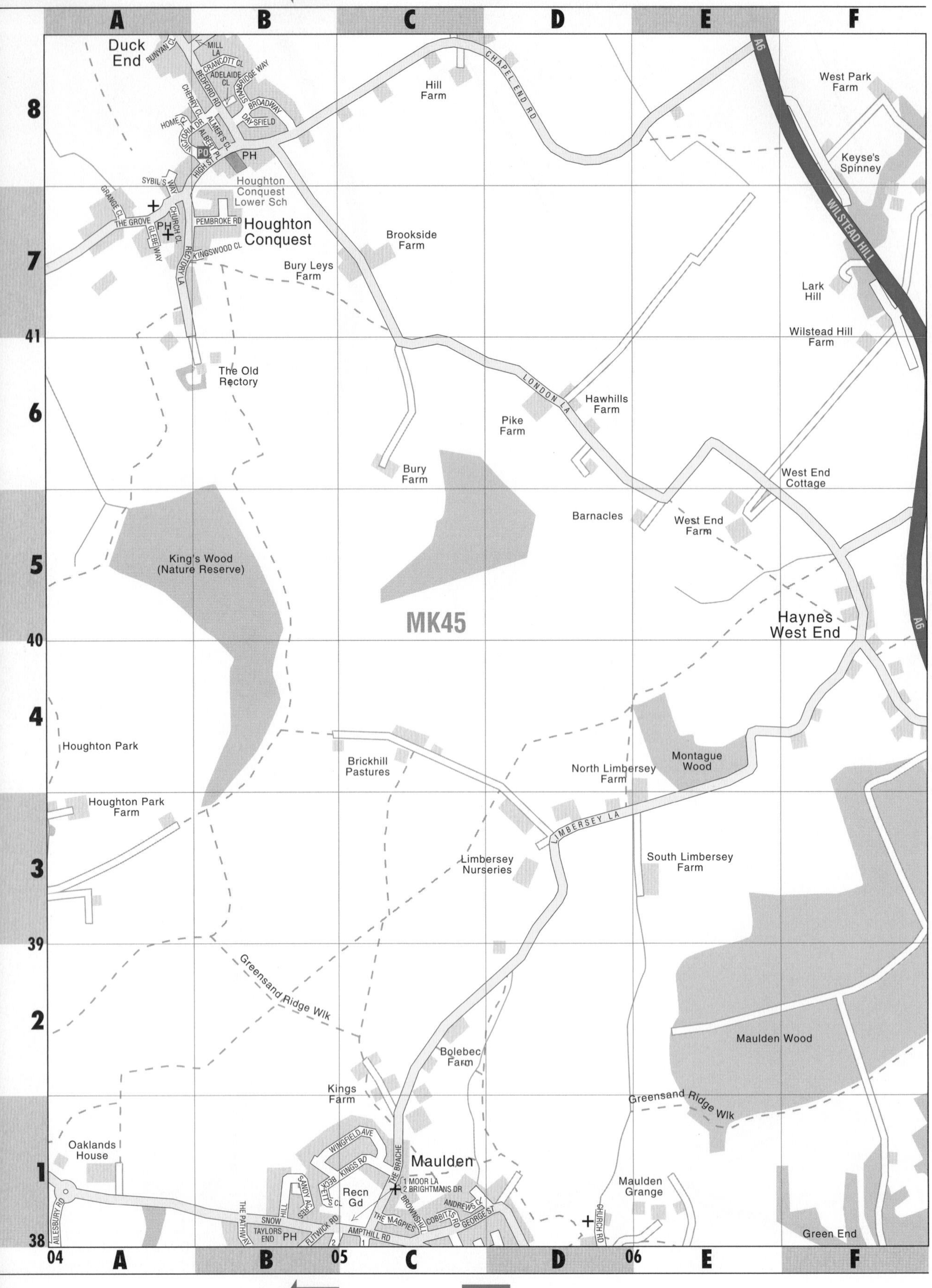
Duck End
Houghton Conquest
Houghton Conquest Lower Sch
Hill Farm
Brookside Farm
Bury Leys Farm
West Park Farm
Keyse's Spinney
Lark Hill
Wilstead Hill Farm
The Old Rectory
Hawhills Farm
Pike Farm
Bury Farm
West End Cottage
Barnacles
West End Farm
King's Wood (Nature Reserve)
MK45
Haynes West End
Houghton Park
Brickhill Pastures
Montague Wood
North Limbersey Farm
Houghton Park Farm
Limbersey Nurseries
South Limbersey Farm
Greensand Ridge Wlk
Bolebec Farm
Maulden Wood
Kings Farm
Oaklands House
Maulden
Recn Gd
Maulden Grange
Green End
CHAPEL END RD
LONDON LA
LIMBERSEY LA
WILSTEAD HILL
A6
AILESBURY RD
THE PATHWAY
SNOW HILL
TAYLORS END
FLITWICK RD
AMPTHILL RD
THE MAGPIES
BROWNSHILL
COBBITTS RD
GEORGE ST
ANDREWS CL
THE BRACHE
WINGFIELD AVE
KINGS RD
SANDY ACRES
CHURCH RD
1 MOOR LA
2 BRIGHTMANS DR
BUNYAN CL
MILL LA
CRANCOTT CL
ADELAIDE CL
BEDFORD RD
STAINSBRIDGE WAY
BROADWAY
DAYSFIELD
CHERRY CL
ALMER'S CL
HOME CL
VICTORIA DR
ALBERT PL
HIGH ST
SYBIL'S WAY
GRANGE CL
THE GROVE
CHURCH CL
GLEBE WAY
PEMBROKE RD
KINGSWOOD CL
RECTORY LA
PO
PH
A B C D E F
8 7 41 6 5 40 4 3 39 2 1 38
04 05 06

73
85

63
76

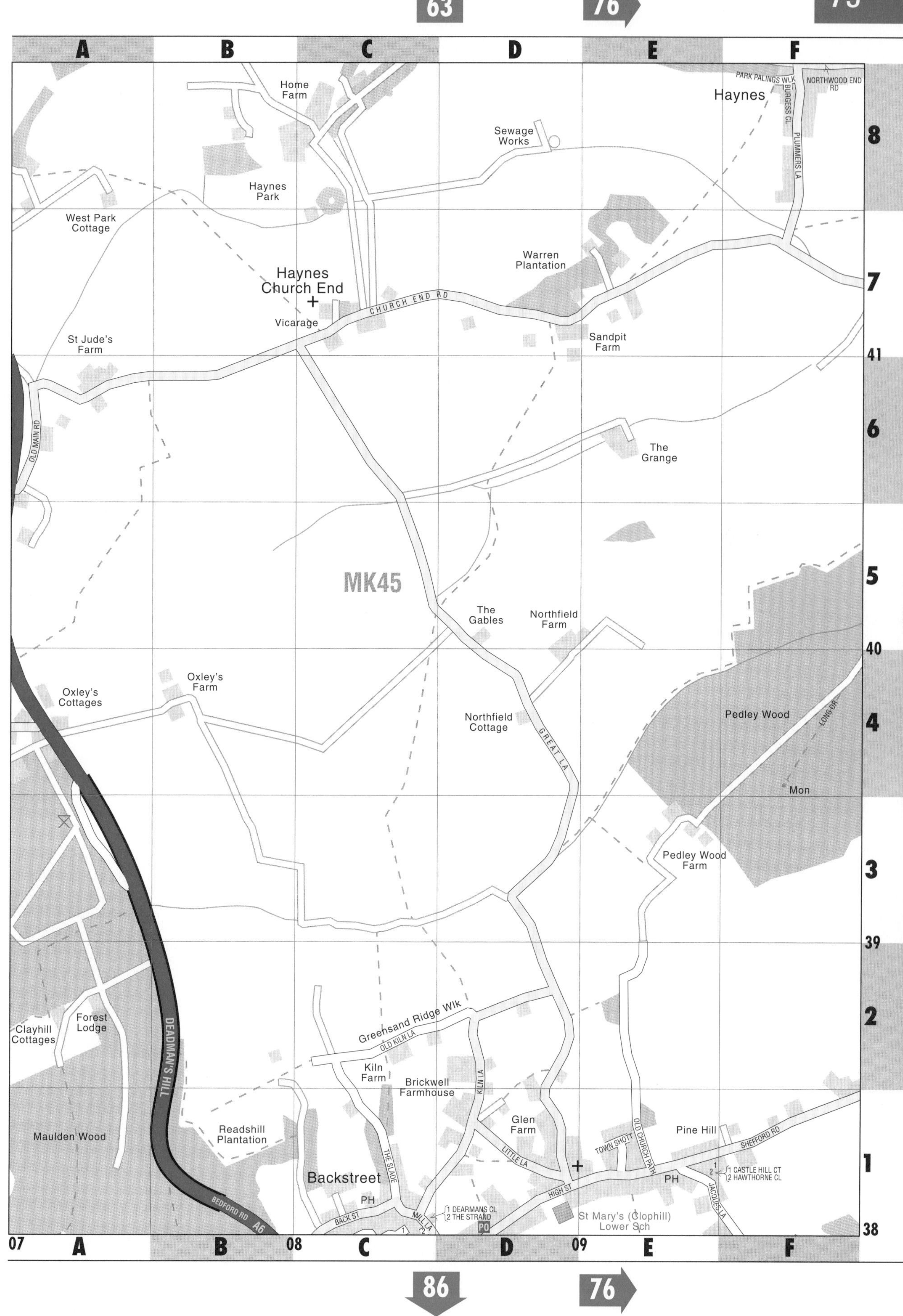
A
B
C
D
E
F
8
7
41
6
5
40
4
3
39
2
1
38
07
08
09
Home Farm
Sewage Works
Haynes
PARK PALINGS WLK
NORTHWOOD END RD
BURGESS CL
PLUMMERS LA
Haynes Park
West Park Cottage
Warren Plantation
Haynes Church End
CHURCH END RD
Vicarage
St Jude's Farm
Sandpit Farm
OLD MAIN RD
The Grange
MK45
The Gables
Northfield Farm
Oxley's Farm
Oxley's Cottages
Northfield Cottage
GREAT LA
Pedley Wood
LONG DR
Mon
Pedley Wood Farm
Greensand Ridge Wlk
OLD KILN LA
Clayhill Cottages
Forest Lodge
DEADMAN'S HILL
Kiln Farm
Brickwell Farmhouse
KILN LA
Maulden Wood
Readshill Plantation
Glen Farm
Pine Hill
TOWN SHOTT
OLD CHURCH PATH
SHEFFORD RD
LITTLE LA
Backstreet
THE SLADE
PH
1 CASTLE HILL CT
2 HAWTHORNE CL
JACQUES LA
HIGH ST
BEDFORD RD
A6
BACK ST
MILL LA
1 DEARMANS CL
2 THE STRAND
PO
St Mary's (Clophill) Lower Sch

86
76

A B C D E F

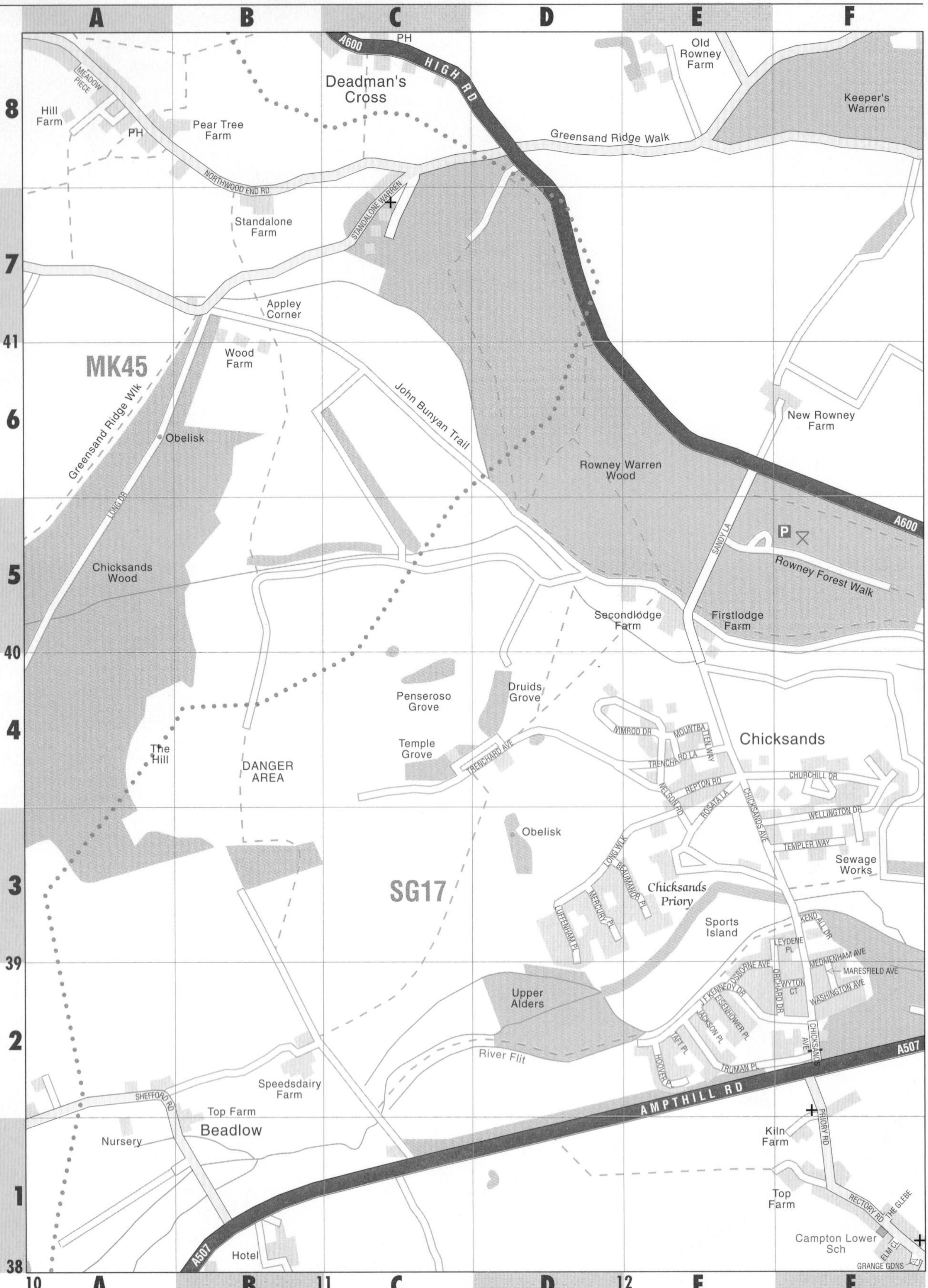

8

Hill Farm
PH
Pear Tree Farm
Deadman's Cross
A600
PH
HIGH RD
Old Rowney Farm
Keeper's Warren
Greensand Ridge Walk

MEADOW PIECE
NORTHWOOD END RD
Standalone Farm
STANDALONE WARREN

7

41

Appley Corner
Wood Farm
New Rowney Farm

MK45

Greensand Ridge Wlk
LONG DR
Obelisk
John Bunyan Trail

6

Chicksands Wood
Rowney Warren Wood
SANDY LA
A600

P
Rowney Forest Walk

5

40

Secondlodge Farm
Firstlodge Farm

The Hill
DANGER AREA
Penseroso Grove
Druids Grove
Temple Grove
NIMROD DR
MOUNTBA
TEN WAY
Chicksands
TRENCHARD AVE
TRENCH RD LA
CHURCHILL DR

4

ACLSON PD
REPTON RD
WELLINGTON DR
CHICKSANDS AVE
ROSATA LA
TEMPLER WAY
Sewage Works

3

SG17
Obelisk
LONG WLK
BEAUMANOR PL
MERCURY PL
Chicksands Priory
Sports Island
KEND AL DR
LEYDENE PL
MEDMENHAM AVE

LUFFENHAM PL
Maresfield Ave
WYTON CT
WASHINGTON AVE

39

OSBORNE DR
ORCHARD DR
F KENNEDY DR
EISENHOWER DR
Upper Alders
JACKSON PL
JET PL
HOOVER PL
TRUMAN PL
A507

2

Speedsdairy Farm
River Flit
AMPTHILL RD

SHEFFORD RD
Top Farm
Beadlow
Nursery
Kiln Farm
PRIORY RD
THE GLEBE

1

A507
Top Farm
RECTORY RD
ELM CL

Hotel
Campton Lower Sch
GRANGE GDNS

38

10 A 11 B C 12 D E F

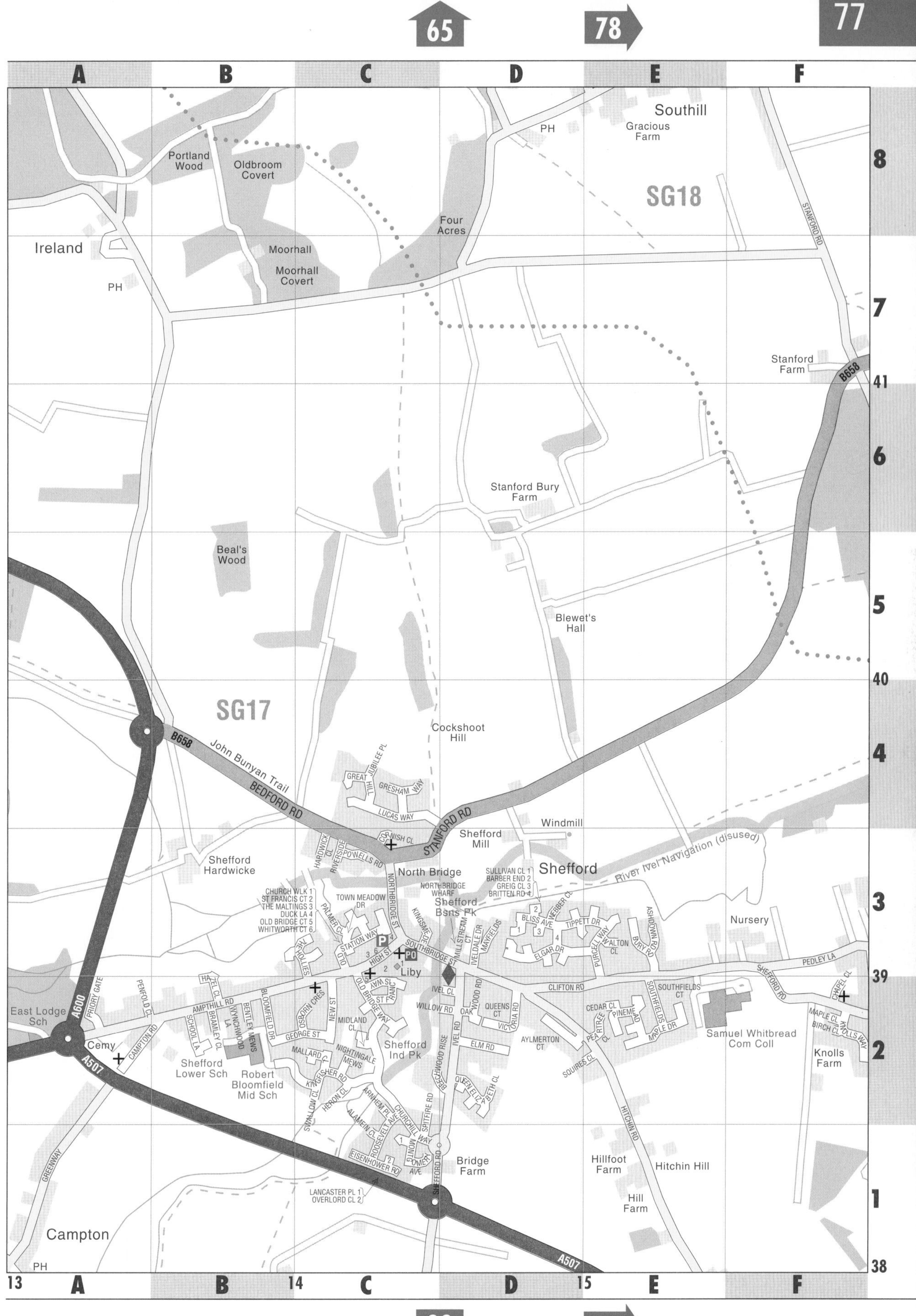

A B C D E F

8

Southill
Gracious
Farm

SG18

Portland
Wood

Oldbroom
Covert

Four
Acres

PH

7

Ireland

Moorhall

Moorhall
Covert

PH

Stanford
Farm

B658

41

6

Stanford Bury
Farm

Beal's
Wood

Blewet's
Hall

5

40

SG17

B658

John Bunyan Trail

BEDFORD RD

Cockshoot
Hill

40

4

GREAT
THE JUBILEE PL
GRESHAM WAY
LUCAS WAY

STANFORD RD

Windmill

River Ivel Navigation (disused)

SPANISH CL

Shefford
Mill

Shefford

Shefford
Hardwicke

HARDWICK
RD
RIVERSIDE
POWELLS RD

NORTHBRIDGE ST

North Bridge

NORTHBRIDGE
WHARF

SULLIVAN CL 1
BARBER END 2
GREIG CL 3
BRITTEN RD 4

CHURCH WLK 1
ST FRANCIS CT 2
THE MALTINGS 3
DUCK LA 4
OLD BRIDGE CT 5
WHITWORTH CT 6

TOWN MEADOW
DR

Shefford
Bsns Pk

BLISS AVE

WEBBER CL

TIPPETT DR

ASHDOWN RD

Nursery

3

KINGSMEAD RD

PALMERS WAY

STATION WAY

P

HIGH ST

SOUTHBRIDGE ST

HILLSTREAM DR

IVELDALE DR

MAYFIELDS

ELGAR DR

PURCELL CL

WALTON
CL

BURY RD

PEDLEY LA

PO

Liby

OLD BRIDGE WAY
AYLMER CL
ST FRANCIS

IVEL CL

WOOD RD

CLIFTON RD

SOUTHFIELDS

SHEFFORD RD

39

East Lodge
Sch

A600

PRIORY GATE

PENFOLD CL

HA

CAMPTON RD

AMPTHILL RD
BRAMLEY CL
SCHOOL LA
WYNGHWOOD

OSBORN CRES
BENTLEY DR
BLOOMFIELD DR

GEORGE ST

NEW ST

MIDLAND
CL

WILLOW RD

OAK
RD

QUEENS
CT

VICTORIA RD

ELM RD

AYLMERTON
CT

CEDAR CL

SOUTHFIELDS
CT

PINEME

PEARTREE CL

MAPLE DR

Samuel Whitbread
Com Coll

MAPLE CL

BIRCH CL

CHERRY CL

KNOLLS WAY

Knolls
Farm

2

Cemy

A507

Shefford
Lower Sch

Robert
Bloomfield
Mid Sch

MALLARD
KINGFISHER CL
HERON CL

NIGHTINGALE
MEWS

SWALLOW CL
ALAMEIN CL

ARNHEM RD

RODER CL
SETTLE
PLOVER
AVE

CHURCHILL WAY

SPITFIRE RD

SHEFFORD RD

Shefford
Ind Pk

ROCKINGHAM RISE

QUEENS CL

OAK RD

ELM CL

SQUIRES CL

HITCHIN RD

Hillfoot
Farm

Hitchin Hill

1

Campton

GREENWAY

EISENHOWER AVE

LANCASTER PL 1
OVERLORD CL 2

Bridge
Farm

Hill
Farm

PH

A507

13 A B 14 C D 15 E F 38

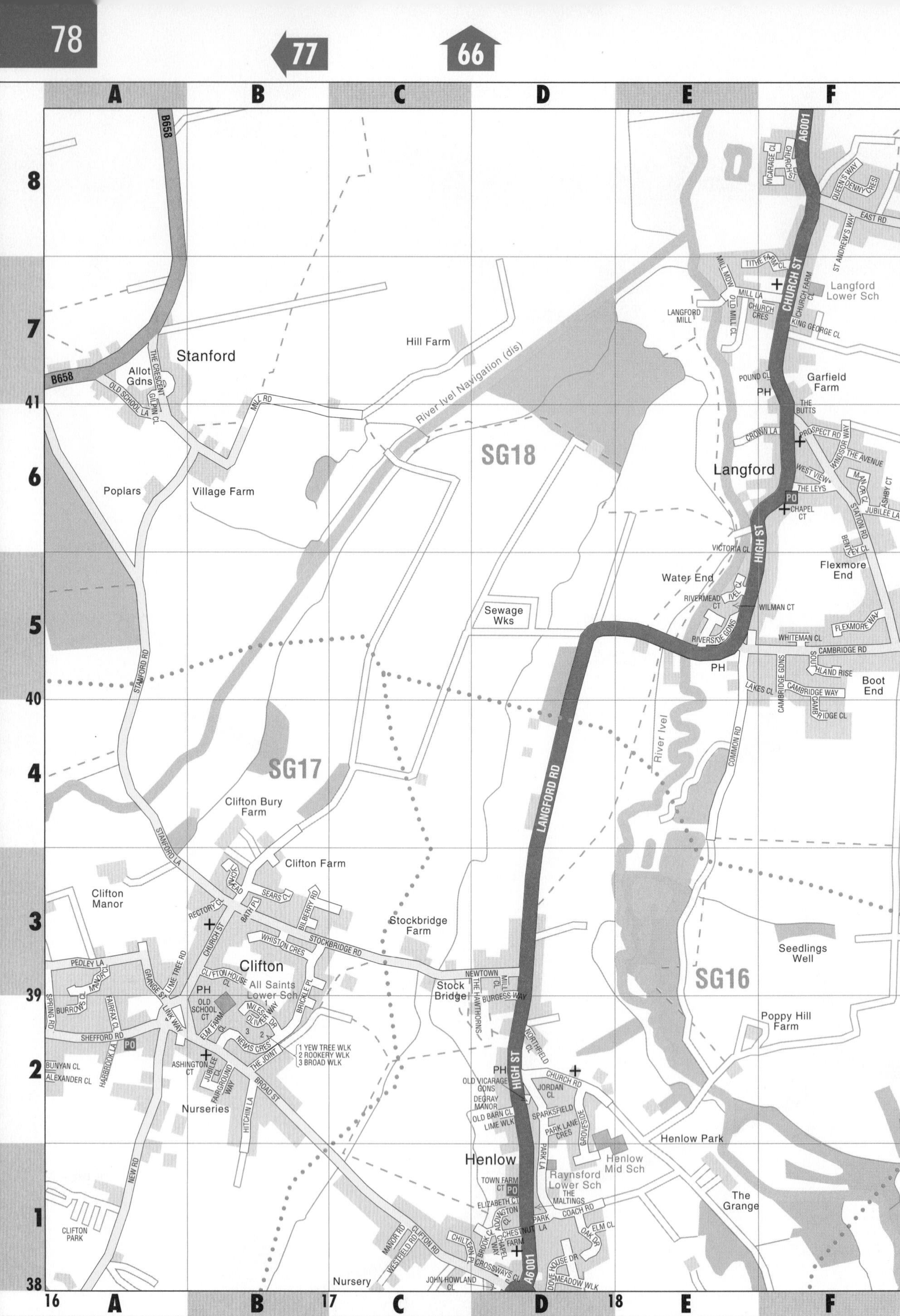
Stanford
Allot Gdns
Poplars
Village Farm
Hill Farm
River Ivel Navigation (dis)
SG18
Sewage Wks
SG17
Clifton Bury Farm
Clifton Farm
Clifton Manor
Clifton
All Saints Lower Sch
Stockbridge Farm
Stock Bridge
Nurseries
Henlow
Henlow Mid Sch
Raynsford Lower Sch
Henlow Park
The Grange
Nursery
Langford
Langford Lower Sch
Langford Mill
Garfield Farm
Water End
Flexmore End
Boot End
River Ivel
SG16
Seedlings Well
Poppy Hill Farm
Clifton Park
1 YEW TREE WLK
2 ROOKERY WLK
3 BROAD WLK
LANGFORD RD
HIGH ST
CHURCH ST
STANFORD RD
STOCKBRIDGE RD
SHEFFORD RD
BROAD ST
A6001
B658

67
80

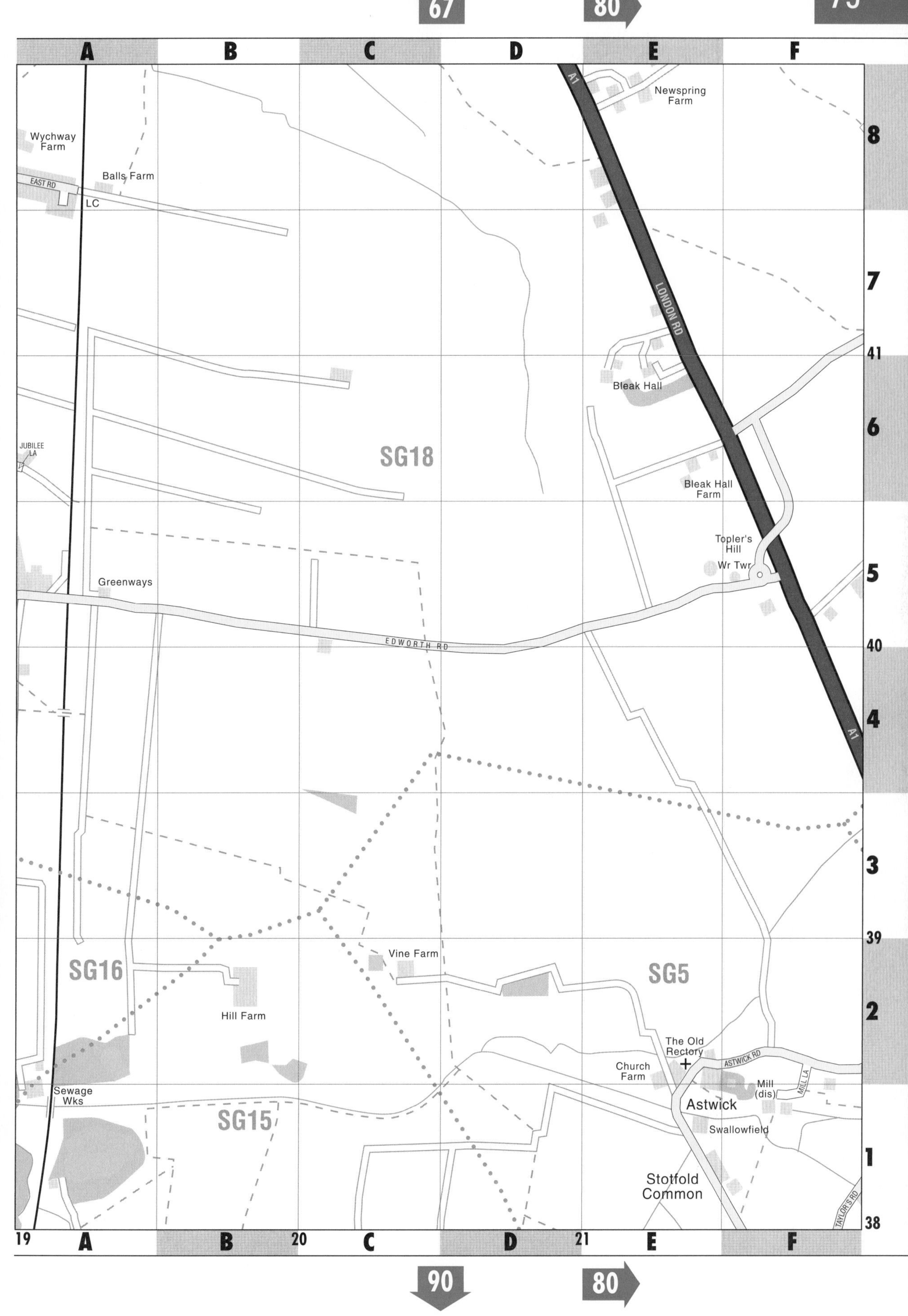
A
B
C
D
E
F
Newspring Farm
Wychway Farm
Balls Farm
EAST RD
LC
A1
LONDON RD
Bleak Hall
JUBILEE LA
SG18
Bleak Hall Farm
Topler's Hill
Wr Twr
Greenways
EDWORTH RD
Vine Farm
SG16
SG5
Hill Farm
The Old Rectory
Church Farm
ASTWICK RD
Mill (dis)
MILL LA
Sewage Wks
Astwick
SG15
Swallowfield
Stotfold Common
TAYLOR'S RD
8
7
41
6
5
40
4
3
39
2
1
38
19
20
21

90
80

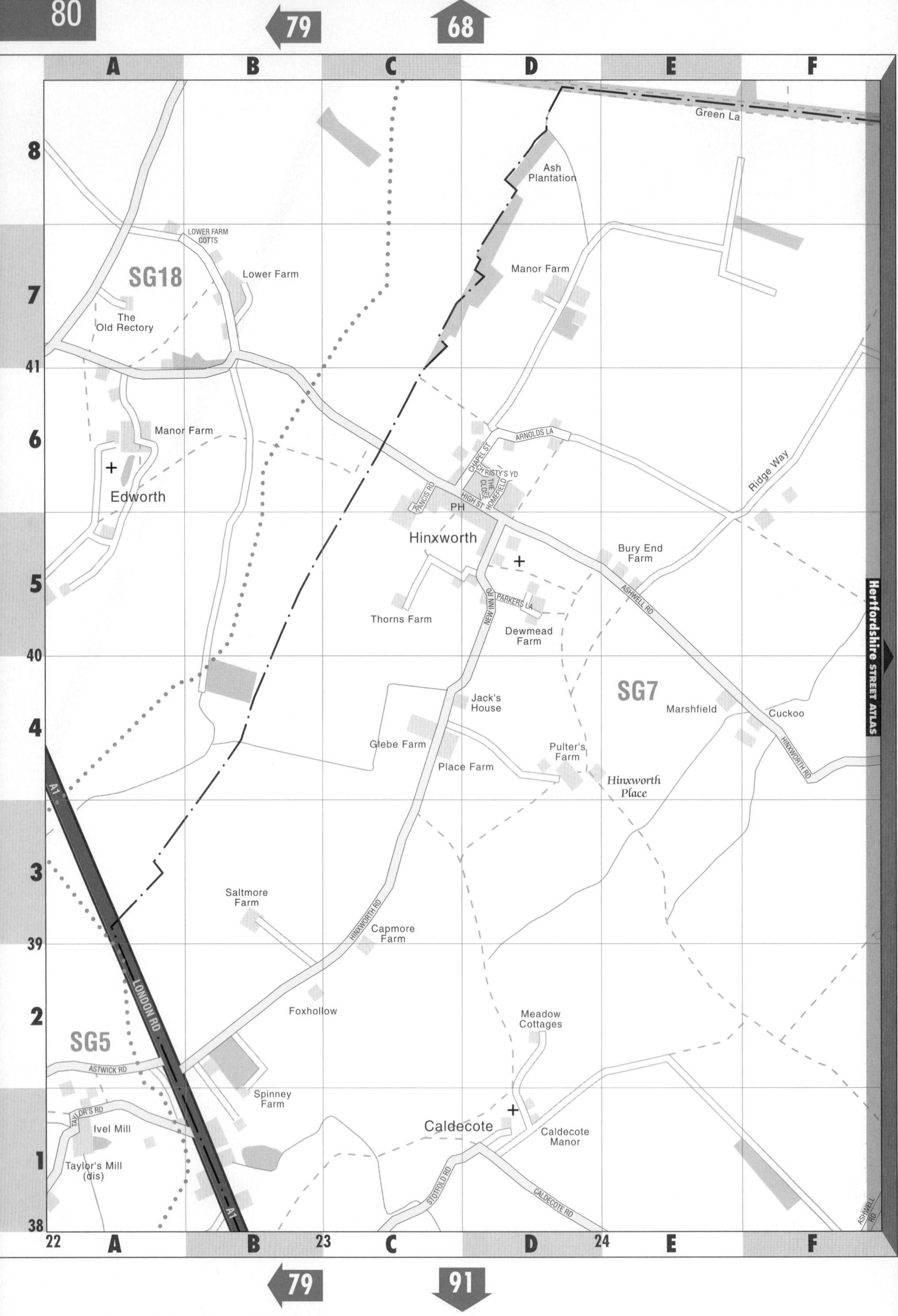

Green La

Ash
Plantation

SG18

Lower Farm

LOWER FARM
COTTS

Lower Farm

The
Old Rectory

Manor Farm

41

Manor Farm

6

ARNOLDS LA

CHAPEL ST

CHRISTY'S YD

THE CLOSE

HIGH ST

FRANCIS RD

PH

Ridge Way

+

Edworth

Hinxworth

Bury End
Farm

5

PARKERS LA

NEW INN RD

ASHWELL RD

Thorns Farm

Dewmead
Farm

40

SG7

Jack's
House

Marshfield

Cuckoo

HINXWORTH RD

4

Glebe Farm

Pulter's
Farm

Place Farm

Hinxworth
Place

A1

3

Saltmore
Farm

39

HINXWORTH RD

Capmore
Farm

2

Foxhollow

Meadow
Cottages

SG5

ASTWICK RD

Spinney
Farm

Caldecote

+

Caldecote
Manor

TAYLOR'S RD

LONDON RD

Ivel Mill

1

Taylor's Mill
(dis)

STOTFOLD RD

CALDECOTE RD

ASHWELL RD

38

22

A

B

23

C

D

24

E

F

A B C D E F

Lower End
CH
LOWER END RD
The Lodge
WAVENDON HOUSE DR
CROW LA
Crabtree
Farm
A421
M1
WAVENDON
HO
Park Farm
Hayfield
Farm
Hayfield
Farm Cottages
Milton Keynes Bdy Wlk
Wks
CRANFIELD RD
Braystone
SALFORD RD
Elm
Cottage
Nursery
Berrylane
Farm
BERRY LA
BELLWAY
PARKWAY
Deethe
Farm
Aspley Guise
LC
LC
NEWPORT RD
A5130
HILLWAY
RIDGWAY
TAVISTOCK CL
VANDYKE CL
MEADOW
VIEW
TRUNK FURLONG
EST
PANTRY CL
DEETHE CL
TURNPIKE
CT
HUTTON WAY
Mill
Farm
BROWNS WAY
MK17
Woburn Sands
Swallowfield
Lower Sch
WEATHERCOCK CL
SADLEIRS GN
MILL LA
LC
THE GROVE
STATION RD
BURROWS CL
Radwell
Pit
MILL WAY
Cemy
Wensdon
Hill
CHURCH ST
CHURCH WLK
The Old House
CRAMBER CROOK
WEST RD
SPRING GR
Fulbrook
Mid Sch
Common
Farm
THE
TERRACE
Aspley House
Guise House
THE SQUARE
BEDFORD RD
Woburn Sands
MAPLE GR
THE CLOSE
WEATHERCOCK LA
PO
PH
Aspley Guise
Lower Sch
MOUNT PLEASANT
BLACKTHORN GR
ELM GR
CH
P
THEYDON AVE
PINE GR
THE LEYS
RUSSELL ST
THE MOUNT
SPINNEY LA
GUISE CT
SAN REMO RD
LIME GR
WOOD ST
ASPLANDS CL
P
WEST HILL
Aspley Guise
BOW BRICKHILL RD
TIDBURY CL
CHAPEL ST
PO
VICARAGE ST
CONCRA PK
ST VINCENTS
DUKE ST
Allot
Gdns
THE LEYS
P
HIGH ST
DOWNHAM RD
ASPLEY HILL
WOOD LA
GREEN LA
WOBURN LA
SHELDON
PH
MENTONE AVE
HARDWICK PL
Liby
WOODLAND WAY
HARDWICK RD
DENE CL
HEATH CL
WOODSIDE
HARDWICK MEWS
PEERS DR
Edgewick
Farm
BISHOPS WLK
ASPLEY CT
GYPSY LA
CHARLEWOOD
HO
Wavendon
Wood
Milton Keynes Bdy Wlk
NARROW PATH
CHURCH RD
WERTH DR
SANDY LA
Aspley Heath
Aspley Wood
Danesborough
LA
SILVERBIRCHES
HOLLY
WLK
Mermaid's
Pond
DANESBOROUGH
DR
HEATH LA
Old Wavendon
Heath
ASPLEY LA
Birchmoor
Lodge
Fernwood
Sch
HEATH LA
WOBURN RD
DANESWOOD
THE KNOLL
Birchmoor
Farm
Shepherd's
Cottage
Fuller's Earth
Lodge
New Wavendon
Heath
A5130

8 7 37 6 5 36 4 3 35 2 1 34

92 A B 93 C D 94 E F

A5130 Milton Keynes (A509)

Buckinghamshire STREET ATLAS

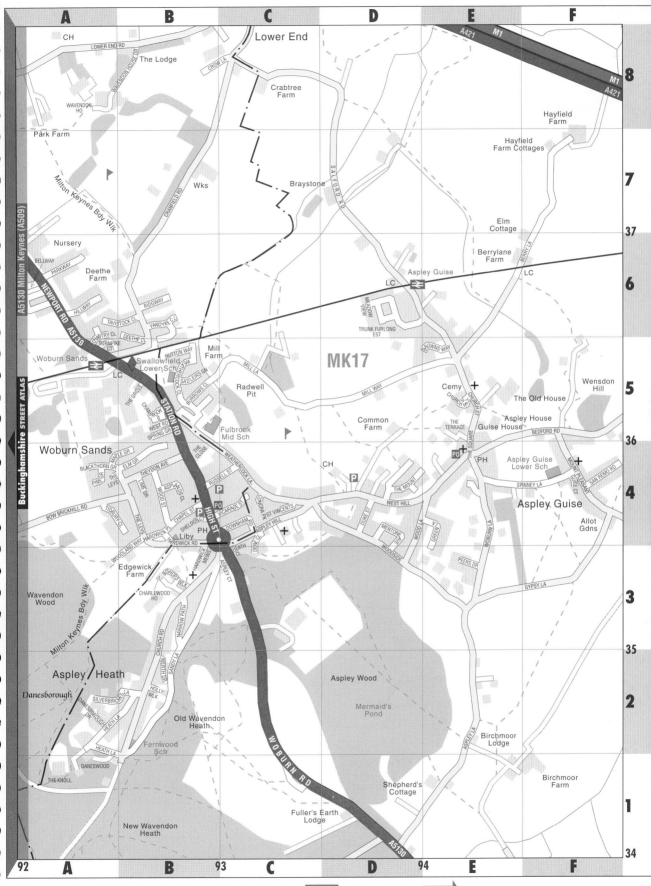

81
71

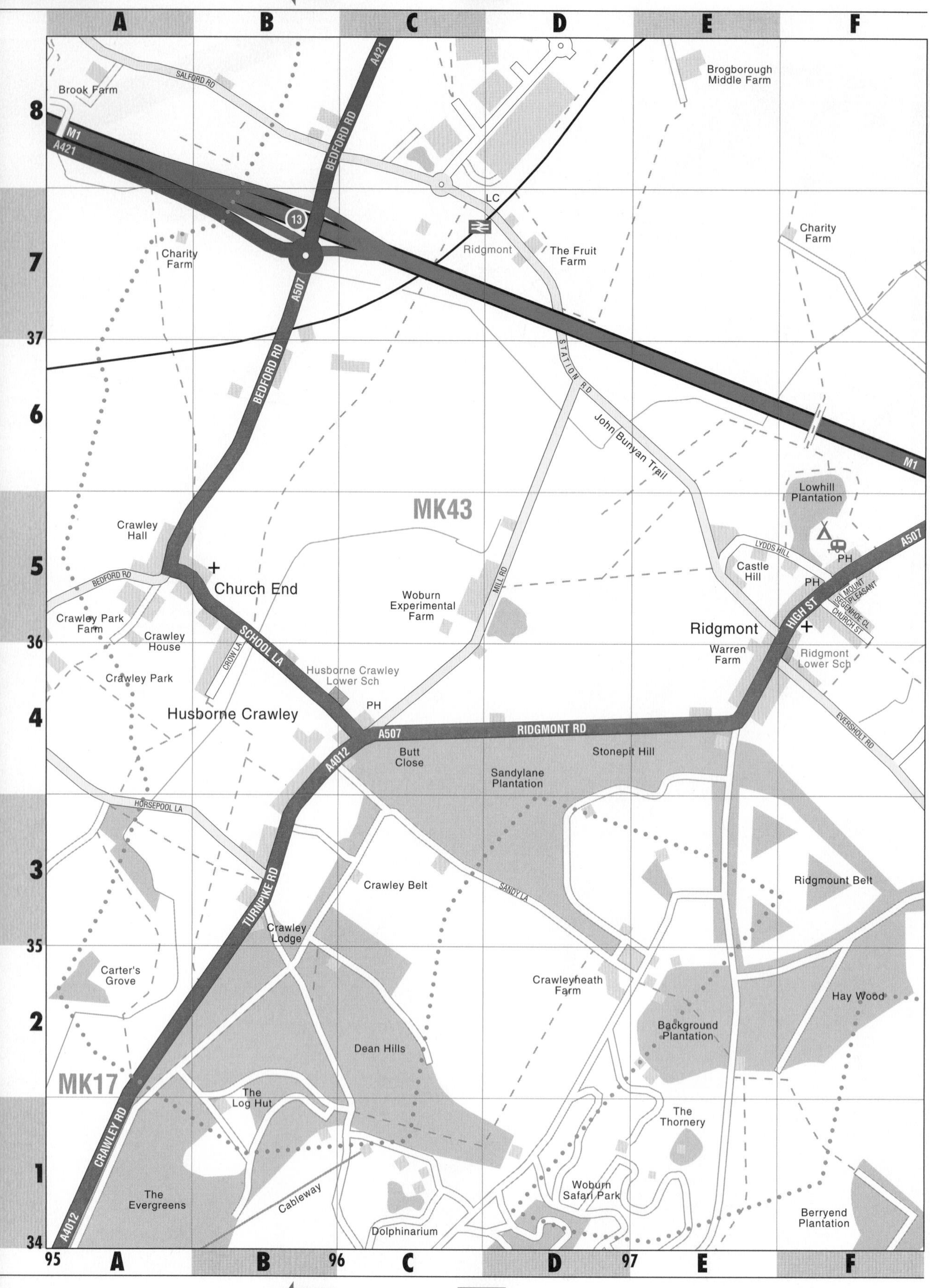
A
B
C
D
E
F
8
7
37
6
5
36
4
3
35
2
1
34
95
96
97
Brook Farm
SALFORD RD
Brogborough Middle Farm
M1
A421
A421
BEDFORD RD
LC
13
Charity Farm
Ridgmont
The Fruit Farm
Charity Farm
A507
BEDFORD RD
STATION RD
John Bunyan Trail
M1
MK43
Lowhill Plantation
Crawley Hall
Church End
LYDDS HILL
Castle Hill
PH
PH
A507
BEDFORD RD
MILL RD
Woburn Experimental Farm
MOUNT PLEASANT
SEGENHOE CL
CHURCH ST
HIGH ST
Crawley Park Farm
Crawley House
SCHOOL LA
Ridgmont
Warren Farm
Ridgmont Lower Sch
Crawley Park
CROW LA
Husborne Crawley Lower Sch
PH
EVERSHOLT RD
Husborne Crawley
A507
RIDGMONT RD
A4012
Butt Close
Stonepit Hill
Sandylane Plantation
HORSEPOOL LA
Crawley Belt
SANDY LA
Ridgmount Belt
TURNPIKE RD
Crawley Lodge
Carter's Grove
Crawleyheath Farm
Hay Wood
Background Plantation
Dean Hills
MK17
The Log Hut
The Thornery
CRAWLEY RD
The Evergreens
Cableway
Woburn Safari Park
Berryend Plantation
A4012
Dolphinarium

81
93

72
84

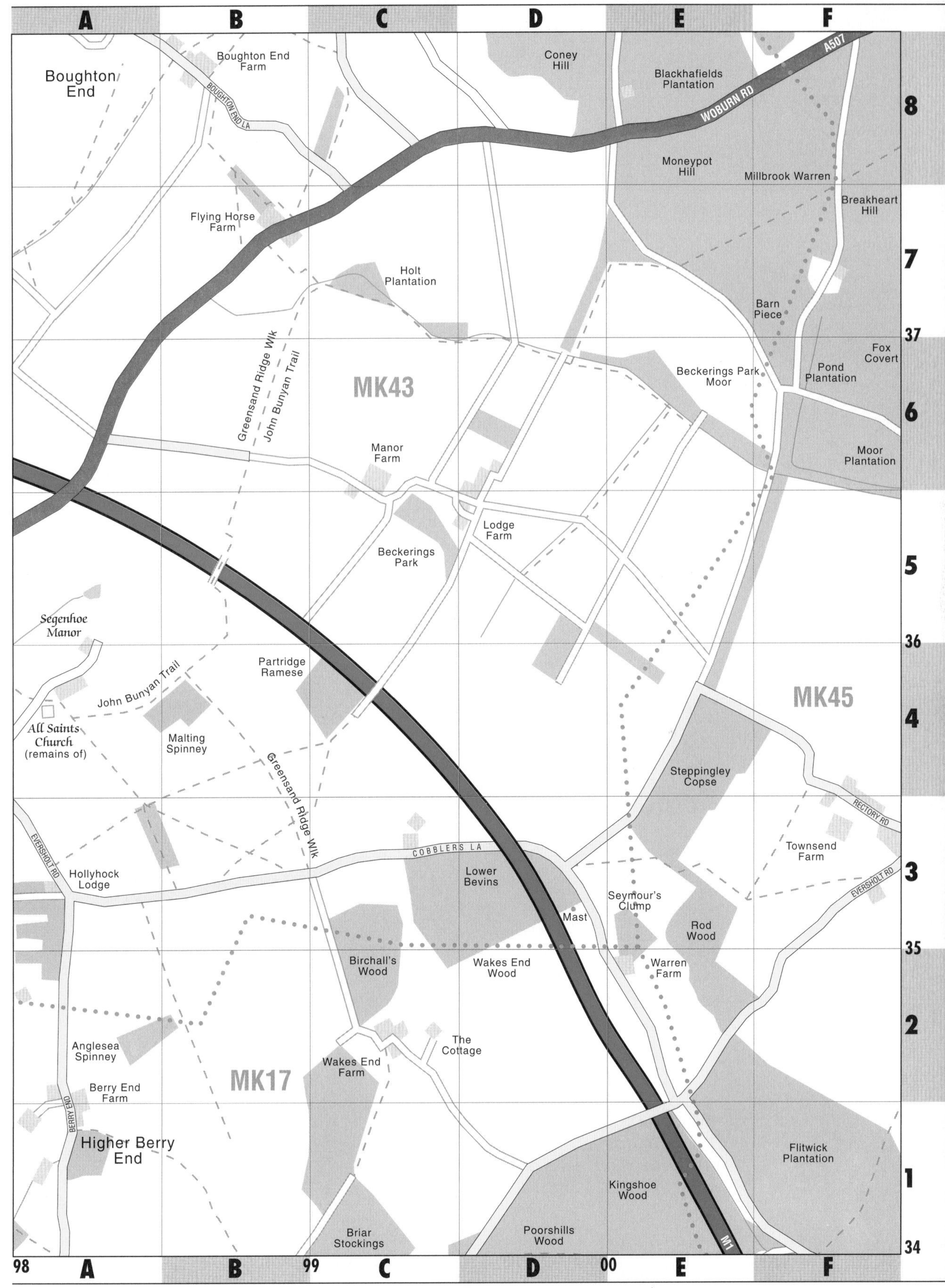
A
B
C
D
E
F
Boughton End
Boughton End Farm
BOUGHTON END LA
Coney Hill
Blackhafields Plantation
A507
WOBURN RD
Moneypot Hill
Millbrook Warren
Breakheart Hill
Flying Horse Farm
Holt Plantation
Barn Piece
Fox Covert
Pond Plantation
Beckerings Park Moor
MK43
Greensand Ridge Wlk
John Bunyan Trail
Manor Farm
Moor Plantation
Lodge Farm
Beckerings Park
Segenhoe Manor
Partridge Ramese
John Bunyan Trail
MK45
All Saints Church (remains of)
Malting Spinney
Greensand Ridge Wlk
Steppingley Copse
RECTORY RD
Townsend Farm
EVERSHOLT RD
COBBLERS LA
Hollyhock Lodge
Lower Bevins
Seymour's Clump
Mast
Rod Wood
EVERSHOLT RD
Birchall's Wood
Wakes End Wood
Warren Farm
Anglesea Spinney
The Cottage
Wakes End Farm
MK17
Berry End Farm
BERRY END
Higher Berry End
Flitwick Plantation
Kingshoe Wood
Poorshills Wood
Briar Stockings
M1
8
7
37
6
5
36
4
3
35
2
1
34
98
99
00

94
84

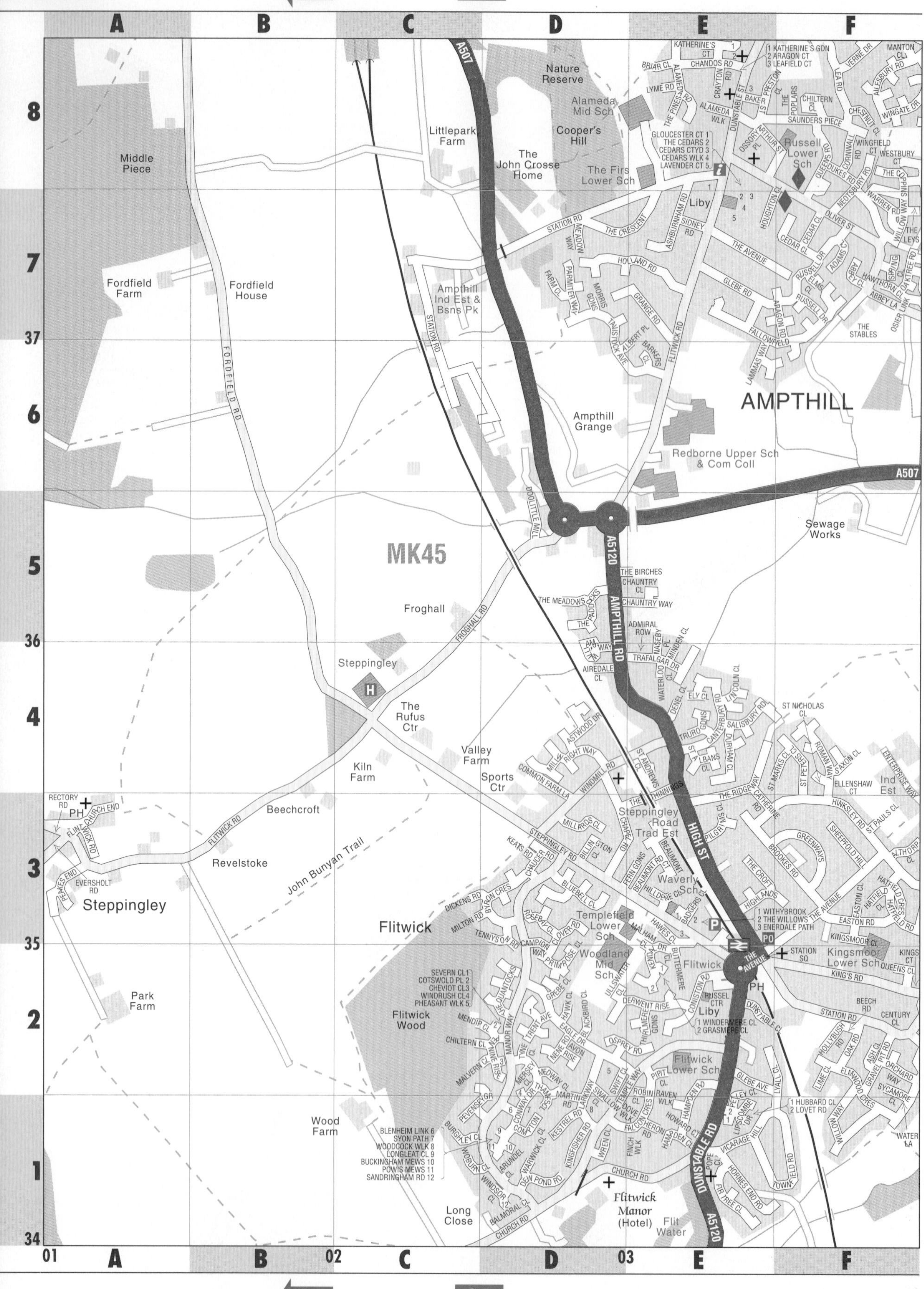

A B C D E F

8

7

37

6

Middle
Piece

Fordfield
Farm

Fordfield
House

FORDFIELD RD

Littlepark
Farm

Nature
Reserve

The John Crosse
Home

Cooper's
Hill

Alameda
Mid Sch

The Firs
Lower Sch

KATHERINE'S
CT

1 KATHERINE'S GDN
2 ARAGON CT
3 LEAFIELD CT

BRIAR CL

LYME RD

CHANDOS RD

THE PINES

1 GLOUCESTER CT
2 THE CEDARS
3 CEDARS CTYD
4 CEDARS WLK
5 LAVENDER CT

Liby

Russell
Lower Sch

MANTON

A507

Ampthill
Ind Est &
Bsns Pk

STATION RD

STATION RD

Ampthill
Grange

AMPTHILL

Redborne Upper Sch
& Com Coll

A507

A5120

Sewage
Works

5

MK45

Froghall

Steppingley

FROGHALL RD

The
Rufus
Ctr

H

THE MEADOWS

THE PADDOCKS

AMPTHILL RD

THE BIRCHES

CHAUNTRY
CL

CHAUNTRY WAY

ADMIRAL
ROW

36

4

Kiln
Farm

Valley
Farm

Sports
Ctr

Beechcroft

John Bunyan Trail

Revelstoke

FLITWICK RD

WINDMILL RD

Steppingley
Road Trad Est

HIGH ST

Ind Est

3

Steppingley

EVERSHOLT
RD

RECTORY
RD

PH

Flitwick

Dickens Rd

Templefield
Lower Sch

Woodland
Mid Sch

Waverly
Lower Sch

P

PO

Flitwick

Flitwick
Lower Sch

Liby

1 WITHYBROOK
2 THE WILLOWS
3 ENERDALE PATH

Station
Sq

Kingsmoor
Lower Sch

PH

1 WINDERMERE CL
2 GRASMERE CL

35

2

Park
Farm

Flitwick
Wood

1 SEVERN CL
2 COTSWOLD PL
3 CHEVIOT CL
4 WINDRUSH CL
5 PHEASANT WLK

DUNSTABLE RD

GLEBE AVE

1

Wood
Farm

6 BLENHEIM LINK
7 SYON PATH
8 WOODCOCK WLK
9 LONGLEAT CL
10 BUCKINGHAM MEWS
11 POWIS MEWS
12 SANDRINGHAM RD

1 HUBBARD CL
2 LOVET RD

PH

CHURCH RD

Flitwick
Manor
(Hotel)

Flit
Water

A5120

34

Long
Close

01   A   B   02   C   D   03   E   F

74
86
A
B
C
D
E
F
Duck End
Maulden Lower Sch
Old Farm
Green End Farm
Works
Allot Gdns
Coy House Farm
Hill Farm
Longview Farm
Rosedale Farm
Relley Farm
Abbey Farm
Lower Triangle
Russell Farm
Quinville House
John Bunyan Trail
Model Farm
Black Moor Farm
Hollington
Hollington Basin
Hollington Farm
Beaumont Farm
Woburn Lodge
Brookside Farm
MK45
Ruxox House
Ruxox Farm
Flitton Moor
De Grey Mausoleum
Flitton
Wardhedges
Little Farm
Folly Farm
Maulden Road Ind Est
Cemy
River Flit
The Folly
Flitwick Moor
Nature Reserve
Flitwick Mill
Poplar Tree Farm
Greenfield CE Lower Sch
Gardners Farm
Pulloxhill Bsns Pk
Greenfield
Puzzles Farm
Town Farm
Pulloxhill
College Farm
Hillside Farm
A507
FLITWICK RD
MAULDEN RD
SILSOE RD
CLOPHILL RD
WATER END RD
NEW RD
FLITTON HILL
WARDHEDGES RD
GREENFIELD RD
SAND RD
FLITTON RD
PULLOXHILL RD
HIGH ST
WESTONING RD
BARTON RD
8
7
37
6
5
36
4
3
35
2
1
34
04
05
06
96
86

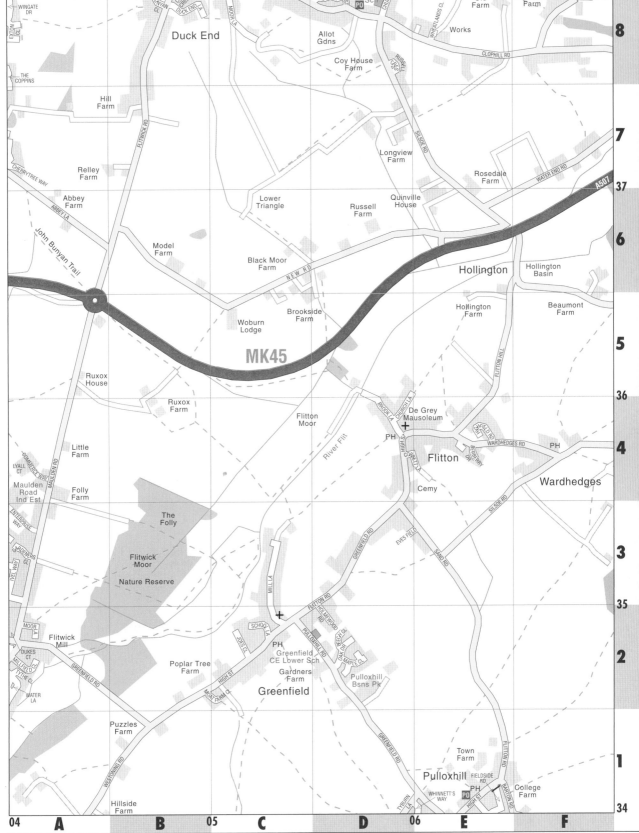

85
75

A
B
C
D
E
F
Hall End
Clophill
Water End Farm
Water End
Mill Farm
Pennyfather's Moors
Firs Farm
Simpson Hill Plantation
Warren Wood
Sewage Works
Warren Farm
Castle Hill
A507
A6
BEDFORD RD
Home Farm
Brabury Lodges
Beans Close Lodge
Road Farm
Road Houses
Newbury Farm
MK45
Silsoe
Silsoe Lower Sch
Wrest Ho
Silsoe Research Inst
Lodges
Silsoe College Farm
West End
Cranfield Univ Silsoe Coll
Wrest Park Gardens
Mon
Cain Hill
Thrift Wood
Oldpark Water
Long Canal
Broad Water
Old Park
Serpentine
Whitehall
Corn Fields
Taymer House
Buckle Grove
Terrace Plantation
Whitehall Plantation
Gagmansbury Farm
DOUG HARRIS WAY 1
INNS LA 2
BRIAN MAY GR 3
DON BUTLER CL 4
MENDHAM WAY 1
GOODHALL CR 2
HOWARDS MEWS 3
07
08
09
37
36
35
34

85
97

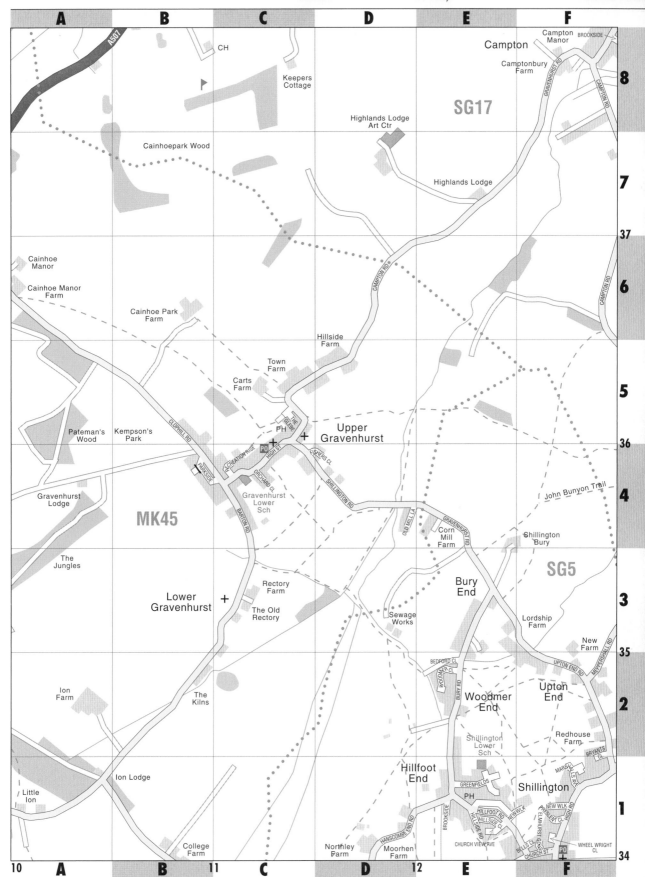

CH

Keepers
Cottage

Campton

Campton
Manor

BROOKSIDE

Camptonbury
Farm

GRAVENHURST RD

CAMPTON RD

SG17

8

Cainhoepark Wood

Highlands Lodge
Art Ctr

Highlands Lodge

7

37

CAMPTON RD

6

Cainhoe
Manor

Cainhoe Manor
Farm

Cainhoe Park
Farm

Hillside
Farm

Town
Farm

Carts
Farm

5

Pateman's
Wood

Kempson's
Park

CLOPHILL RD

PARK SIDE

SCREATION RISE

ORCHARD CL

The
GLEBE
PH
HIGH ST
PO

FISHERS CL

Upper
Gravenhurst

36

Gravenhurst
Lower
Sch

SHILLINGTON RD

John Bunyon Trail

4

MK45

BARTON RD

Gravenhurst
Lodge

OLD MILL LA

GRAVENHURST RD

Corn
Mill
Farm

Shillington
Bury

SG5

The
Jungles

Lower
Gravenhurst

Rectory
Farm

The Old
Rectory

Sewage
Works

Bury
End

Lordship
Farm

3

New
Farm

MEPPERSHALL RD

35

BEDFORD CL

WOODMER CL

BURY RD

UPTON END RD

Ion
Farm

The
Kilns

Woodmer
End

Upton
End

2

Shillington
Lower
Sch

Redhouse
Farm

BRYANTS CL

MARSOMS AVE

Ion Lodge

Hillfoot
End

GREENFIELDS
PH

Shillington

NEW WLK

ELMHURST GDNS

CRESCENT CL

HIGH ST

Little
Ion

HILLFOOT END RD

BROOKSIDE

HILLSIDE CL

HILLSIDE RD

NEW WLK

NEW WLK

BELLS CL

PO

WHEEL WRIGHT
CL

1

College
Farm

Northley
Farm

HANSCOMBE END RD

Moorhen
Farm

CHURCH VIEW AVE

CHURCH ST

34

87
77

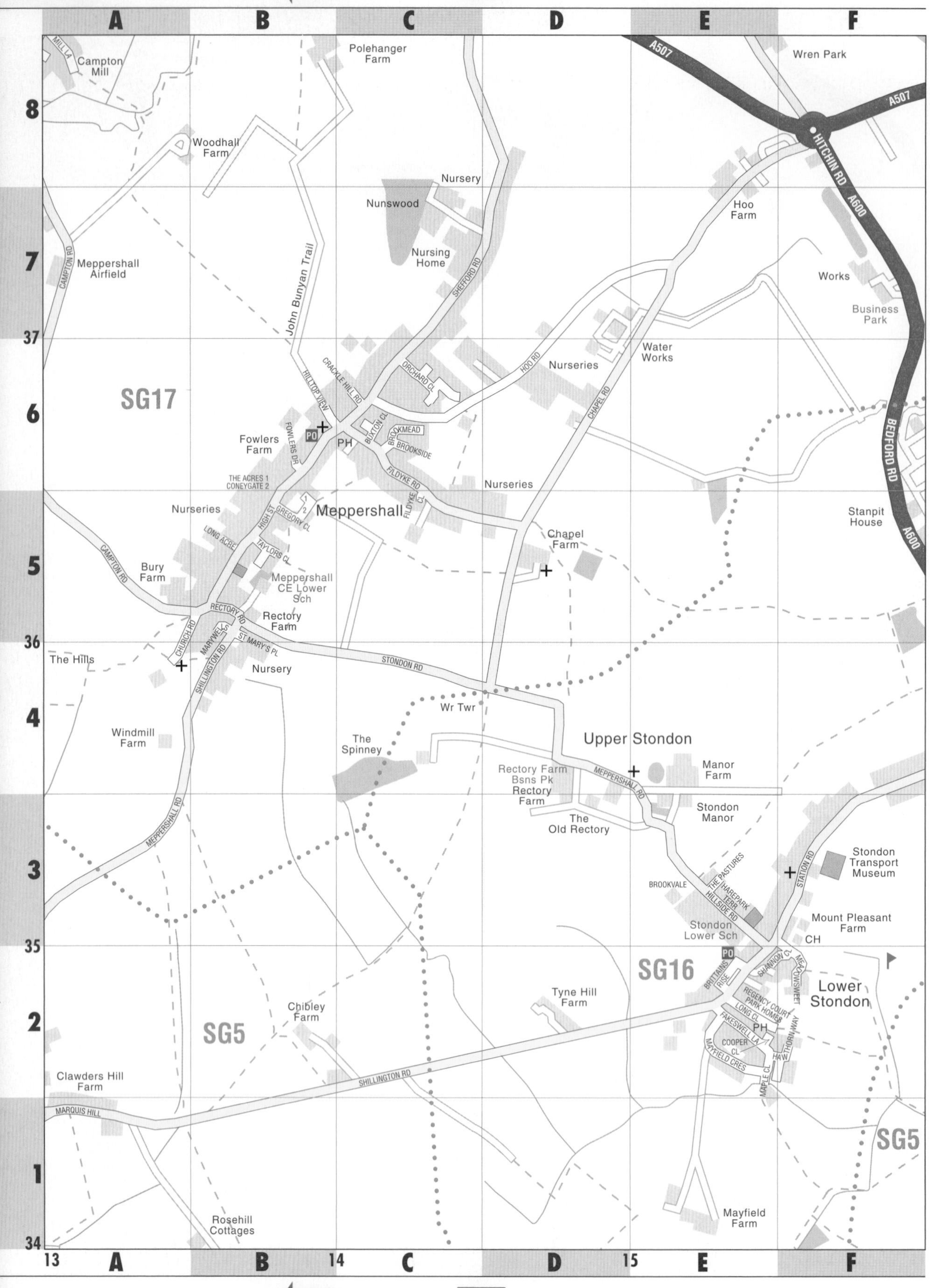
A
B
C
D
E
F
8
7
37
6
5
36
4
3
35
2
1
34
13
14
15
Campton Mill
MILL LA
Polehanger Farm
Wren Park
A507
Woodhall Farm
HITCHIN RD
A600
Nursery
Nunswood
Hoo Farm
Nursing Home
Meppershall Airfield
CAMPTON RD
John Bunyan Trail
SHEFFORD RD
Works
Business Park
Water Works
Nurseries
HOO RD
CRACKLE HILL RD
ORCHARD CL
SG17
HILLTOP VIEW
CHAPEL RD
BEDFORD RD
Fowlers Farm
FOWLERS DR
PO
PH
BUXTON CL
BROOKMEAD
BROOKSIDE
FILDYKE RD
THE ACRES 1
CONEYGATE 2
Nurseries
Meppershall
GREGORY CL
HIGH ST
FILDYKE CL
Stanpit House
LONG ACRE
TAYLORS CL
Chapel Farm
CAMPTON RD
Bury Farm
Meppershall CE Lower Sch
RECTORY RD
Rectory Farm
CHURCH RD
MARYWELL
ST MARY'S PL
STONDON RD
The Hills
SHILLINGTON RD
Nursery
Wr Twr
Upper Stondon
Windmill Farm
The Spinney
Rectory Farm Bsns Pk
Rectory Farm
MEPPERSHALL RD
Manor Farm
Stondon Manor
The Old Rectory
MEPPERSHALL RD
THE PASTURES
Stondon Transport Museum
STATION RD
BROOKVALE
HAREPARK TERR
HILLSIDE RD
Mount Pleasant Farm
Stondon Lower Sch
CH
PO
SG16
BRITTAINS RISE
SHANNON CL
MEADOWSWEET
Lower Stondon
Tyne Hill Farm
REGENCY COURT PARK HOMES
LONG CL
Chibley Farm
FAKESWELL LA
PH
SG5
COOPER CL
HAW
THORN WAY
MAYFIELD CRES
MAPLE CL
Clawders Hill Farm
SHILLINGTON RD
MARQUIS HILL
SG5
Rosehill Cottages
Mayfield Farm

87
99

78
90

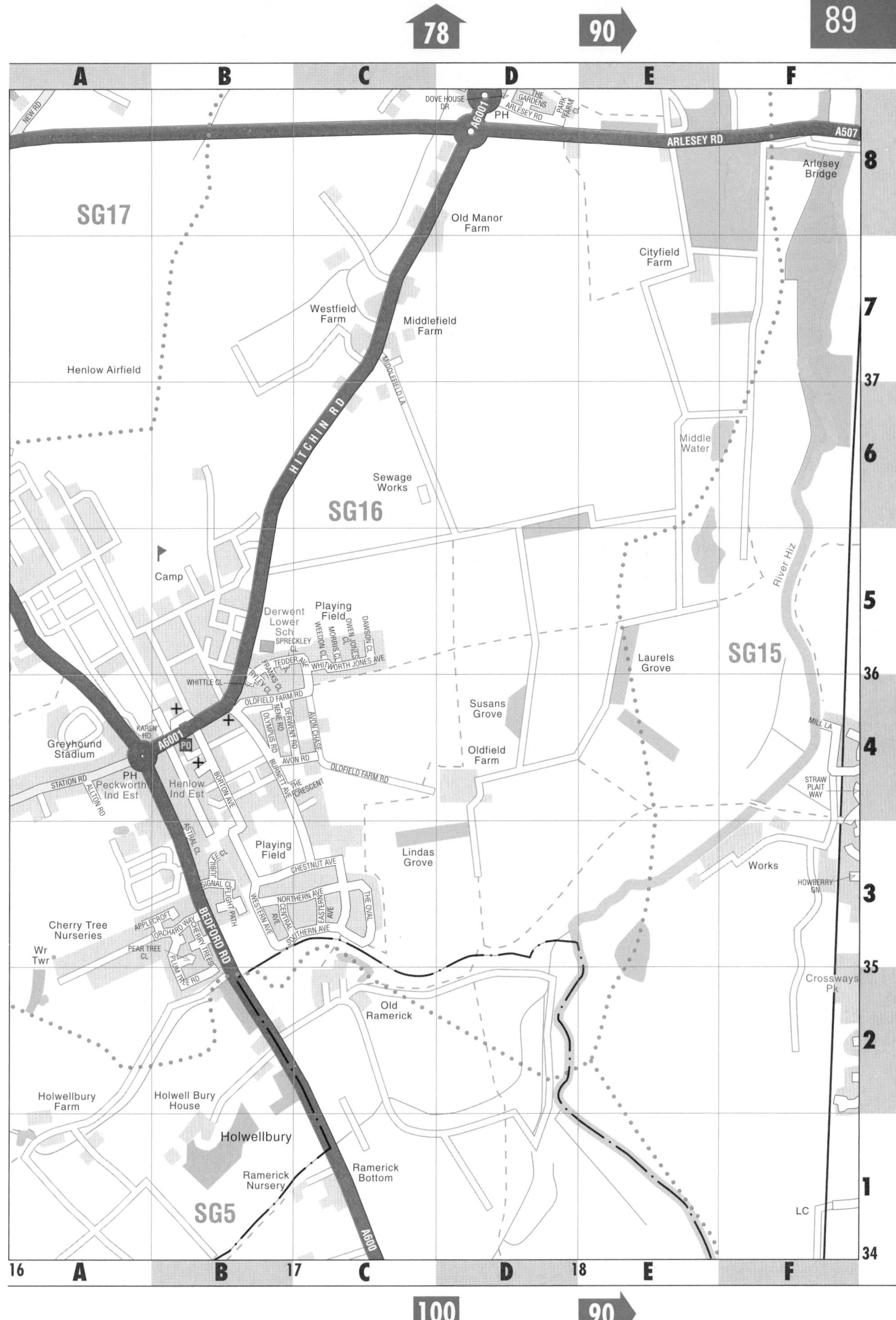
A
B
C
D
E
F
SG17
SG16
SG15
SG5
ARLESEY RD
A507
A6001
Arlesey Bridge
Old Manor Farm
Cityfield Farm
Westfield Farm
Middlefield Farm
MIDDLEFIELD LA
HITCHIN RD
Henlow Airfield
Middle Water
Sewage Works
Camp
River Hiz
Derwent Lower Sch
Playing Field
Laurels Grove
Susans Grove
Oldfield Farm
OLDFIELD FARM RD
Greyhound Stadium
STATION RD
PH
Peckworth Ind Est
Henlow Ind Est
BEDFORD RD
Playing Field
Lindas Grove
Works
MILL LA
STRAW PLAIT WAY
HOWBERRY GN
Cherry Tree Nurseries
Wr Twr
Crossways Pk
Old Ramerick
Holwellbury Farm
Holwell Bury House
Holwellbury
Ramerick Nursery
Ramerick Bottom
A600
LC
8
7
37
6
5
36
4
3
35
2
1
34
16
17
18

100
90

89 79

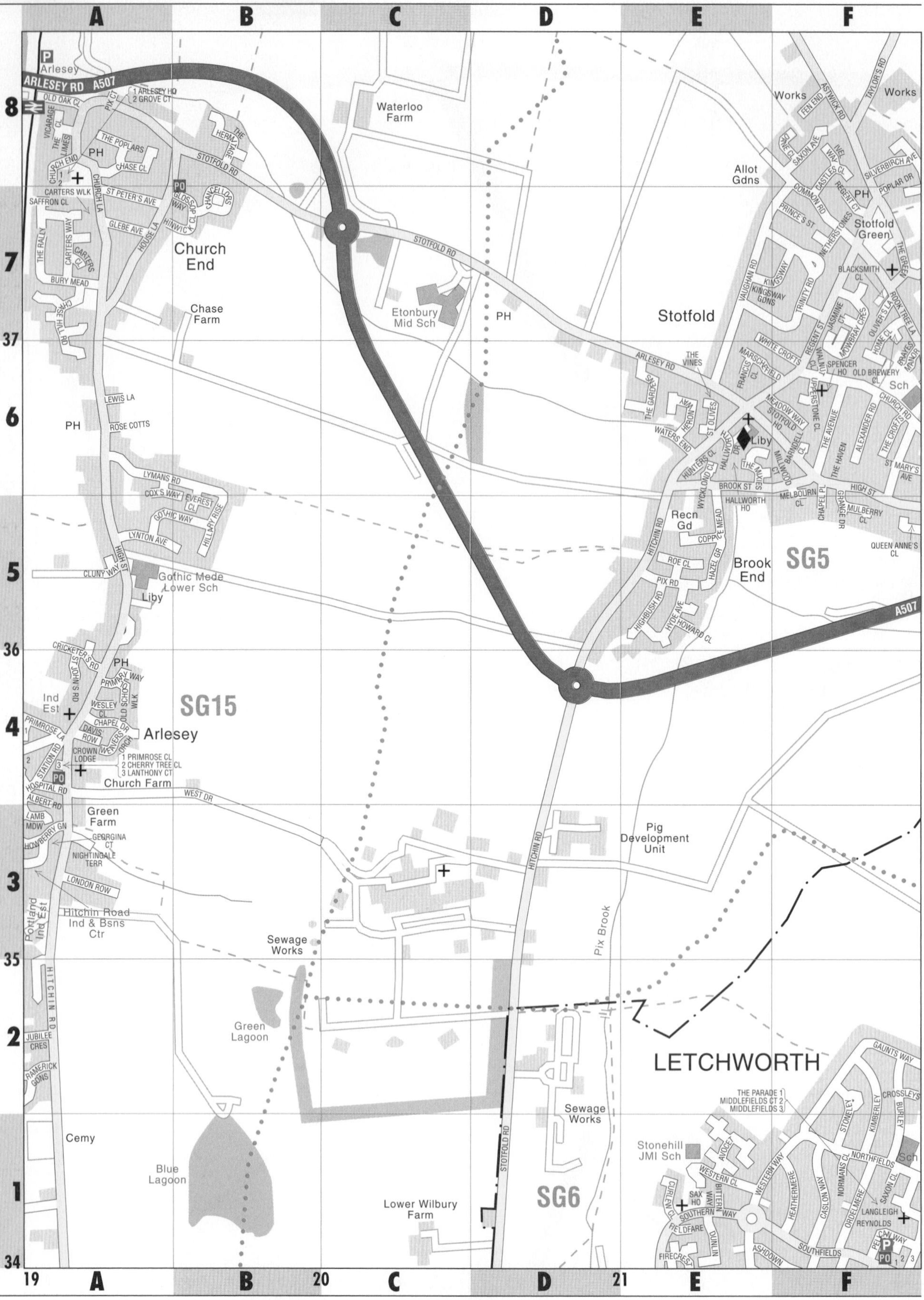

A B C D E F

8

P Arlesey
ARLESEY RD A507
OLD OAK CL
1 ARLESEY HO
2 GROVE CT
VICARAGE
THE LIMES
PIX HILL
THE HERMITAGE
THE
THE POPLARS
STOTFOLD RD
Waterloo Farm
Works
Works
FEN END
ASHWICK RD
TAYLOR'S RD
SILVER BIRCH AVE
POPLAR DR
PH

CHURCH END
PH
CARTERS WLK
ST PETER'S AVE
GLOS CP CL WAY
HINWICK
CHASE CL
CHASE CL
SAFFRON CL
CHASE HILL
CARTERS WAY
GLEBE AVE
HOUSE LA
Church End
CARTERS
BURY MEAD
Chase Farm
Stotfold Rd
Etonbury Mid Sch
PH
ARLESEY RD
THE VINES
Stotfold
PRINCE'S ST
TRINITY RD
KINGSWAY
REGENT ST
CASTLE'S CL
COMMON RD
CHURCH RD
Stotfold Green
BLACKSMITH CL
THE GREEN
Sch
Old Brewery

7

THE RALLY
LEWIS LA
PH
ROSE COTTS
LYMANS RD
COX'S WAY
EVEREST CL
GOTHIC WAY
HILL PIT RISE
LYNTON AVE
HIGH ST
CLUNY WAY
Liby
Gothic Mede Lower Sch
VAUGHAN RD
WHITE CROFTS
MARSCHEFIELD
FRANCIS HO
SPENCER
AMANDA CRES
THE GARDEN
WATERS END
HUNTERS CL
ST OLIVES
HALLWORTH
BROOK ST
MELBOURN CL
Liby
MULBERRY CL
HIGH ST
QUEEN ANNE'S CL
ST MARY'S AVE
THE HAVEN
MEADOW WAY
STOTFOLD
MILLWOOD
ALEXANDER RD
THE AVENUE
THE CROFTS

37

6

5

CRICKETERS RD
ST JOHN'S RD
PH
PRIMARY WAY
WESLEY CL
CHAPEL
DAVIS ROW
OLD SCHOOL
HINWICK
SG15
Arlesey
1 PRIMROSE CL
2 CHERRY TREE CL
3 LANTHONY CT
CROWN LODGE
Church Farm
WEST DR
PRIMROSE LA
STATION RD
ALBERT RD
HOSPITAL RD
PO
Ind Est
HITCHIN RD
Recn Gd
HITCHIN RD
ROE CL
PIX RD
HIGHBUSH RD
HYDE AVE
HOWARD CL
Brook End
SG5
A507

36

4

3

LAMB MDW
HOWBERRY GN
Green Farm
GEORGINA CT
NIGHTINGALE TERR
LONDON ROW
Hitchin Road Ind & Bsns Ctr
Portland Ind Est
Pig Development Unit
Pix Brook

35

2

JUBILEE CRES
LIMERICK GDNS
Sewage Works
Green Lagoon
HITCHIN RD
STOTFOLD RD
Sewage Works
LETCHWORTH
THE PARADE 1
MIDDLEFIELDS CT 2
MIDDLEFIELDS 3
GAUNTS WAY
CROSSLEYS
KIMBERLEY
BURLEY
Sch
NORTHFIELDS
WESTERN WAY
HEATHERMERE
CASLON WAY
NORMANS CL
SAXON CL

1

Cemy
Blue Lagoon
Lower Wilbury Farm
SG6
Stonehill JMI Sch
WESTERN CL
SAX HO
SOUTHERN WAY
SOUTHFIELDS
FIELDFARE
FIRECREST
LANGLEIGH
REYNOLDS
ORDELMERE
SAXON CL
KINGSWAY
PO
P

34

19 A 20 B C 20 D 21 E F

89 101

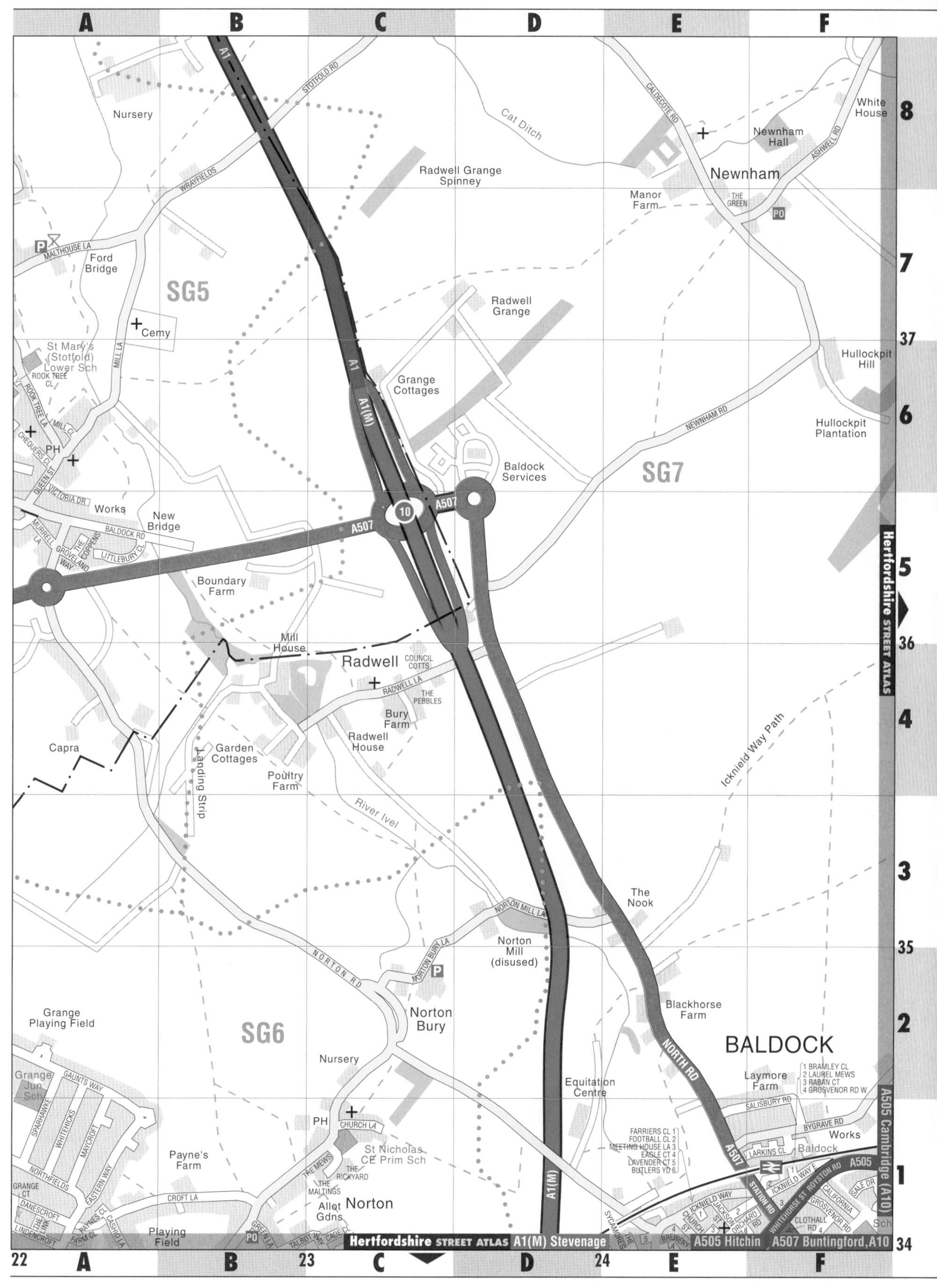
80
A
B
C
D
E
F
Nursery
STOTFOLD RD
Cat Ditch
CALDECOTE RD
White House
8
Newnham Hall
ASHWELL RD
Radwell Grange Spinney
Newnham
WRAYFIELDS
Manor Farm
THE GREEN
PO
MALTHOUSE LA
Ford Bridge
7
SG5
Radwell Grange
Cemy
37
St Mary's (Stotfold) Lower Sch
Hullockpit Hill
MILL LA
ROOK TREE CL
A1
Grange Cottages
A1(M)
6
NEWNHAM RD
Hullockpit Plantation
Baldock Services
SG7
PH
QUEEN ST
VICTORIA DR
Works
A507
10
New Bridge
BALDOCK RD
LITTLEBURY CL
Hertfordshire STREET ATLAS
5
Boundary Farm
36
Mill House
Radwell
COUNCIL COTTS
RADWELL LA
THE PEBBLES
4
Bury Farm
Radwell House
Icknield Way Path
Capra
Garden Cottages
Landing Strip
Poultry Farm
River Ivel
3
The Nook
NORTON MILL LA
Norton Mill (disused)
NORTON RD
NORTON BURY LA
35
Blackhorse Farm
Grange Playing Field
Norton Bury
2
SG6
NORTH RD
BALDOCK
Nursery
Laymore Farm
1 BRAMLEY CL
2 LAUREL MEWS
3 RABAN CT
4 GROSVENOR RD W
Grange Jun Sch
GAUNTS WAY
Equitation Centre
SALISBURY RD
A505 Cambridge (A10)
PH
CHURCH LA
BYGRAVE RD
Works
FARRIERS CL 1
FOOTBALL CL 2
MEETING HOUSE LA 3
EAGLE CT 4
LAVENDER CT 5
BUTLERS YD 6
Payne's Farm
St Nicholas CE Prim Sch
LARKINS CL
Baldock
A505
1
THE RICKYARD
THE MALTINGS
NORTHFIELDS
EASTERN WAY
CROFT LA
Allot Gdns
Norton
ICKNIELD WAY
STATION RD
ROYSTON RD
CALIFORNIA
GROSVENOR RD
CLOTHALL RD
Playing Field
PO
Hertfordshire STREET ATLAS
A1(M) Stevenage
A505 Hitchin
A507 Buntingford, A10
34
22
23
24

A B C D E F

A5 Milton Keynes

8

Longslade
Cottage

Birchmoor
Green

A5130 WOBURN RD

NEWPORT RD

A5130

CRAWLEY RD A4012

DRAKELOE
CL

ELEANOR CL

BEDFORD ST

Bell's
Copse

Tollhouse
Grove

Hundred's
Farm

Horsemoor
Farm

Dolton's
Farm

STAUNTON
HO

CASWELL'S

MARQUIS

Woburn

Woburn
Lower Sch
St Mary's
Church
(remains of)

TH

i

PO

A4012

GEORGE ST

7

MK17

33

Little Brickhill
Copse

Charle Wood

Landonhill
Plantation

Maryland Coll

MARKET
PL

HOWLAND
PL

BLOOMSBURY CL

LONDON END

DUKE LA

6

LEIGHTON ST

Pinfold
Pond

Wayn Close

TIMBER LA

Pumpkin Park

Pinfoldpond

Crowholt
Plantation

Milton Keynes Bdy Wlk

Job's Farm

Greensand Ridge Wlk

Utcoate
Grange

Lowe's Wood

5

32

Buttermilk
Farm

Apesfield Spring

Circuitt's
Covert

4

Buttermilk
Wood

Apesfield
Farm

3

Nun Wood

Sheeplane
Belt

31

A5

Rammamere
Farm

2

Sheeplane

Bushycommon
Wood

Hill Farm

1

Rammamere
Heath

Bragenham
Wood

PH

WOBURN RD

LU7

Arnold's
Cottages

LU7

30

A5

A B C D E F

A B C D E F

8

7

33

6

5

32

4

3

31

2

1

30

A4012

Cableway

Deer Paddock

Lower Drakeloe Pond

Redlodge Plantation

Safari Park

Wall Close

Star Lodge

Stump Cross

Froxfield

Upper Drakeloe Pond

PARK ST

Woburn Park

Whitnoe Orchard Pond

+

P

Hotel

Park Farm

Horse Pond

Charcoal Pond

Pipeswell Plantation

Cowhill Belt Pond

Shoulder of Mutton Pond

Deer Park

Duncombe's Breeches Pond

Stew Pond

Greensand Ridge Wlk

Purretts Hill

Basin Pond

Woburn Abbey

Speedwell Cottages

Basin Bridge

New Pond

Speedwell

Coldbath Clump

The Maze

Speedwell Farm

Lower Hopgarden Pond

MK17

Upper Hopgarden Pond

Cow Pasture Clump

Milton Wood

Speedwell Belt

Commons Clump

Grange Farm

LONDON RD

MEAD'S CL

Fourteen Acre Spinney

Old Farm

London Entrance Lodge

Church End

+

Cuckoopit Spinney

Milton Lodge

Leys Farm

BATTLESDEN AVE

Milton Bryan

The Manor House

South End

PH

Home Farm

Potsgrove

Grove Wood

A4012

M&GS LA

Fountaine's Farm

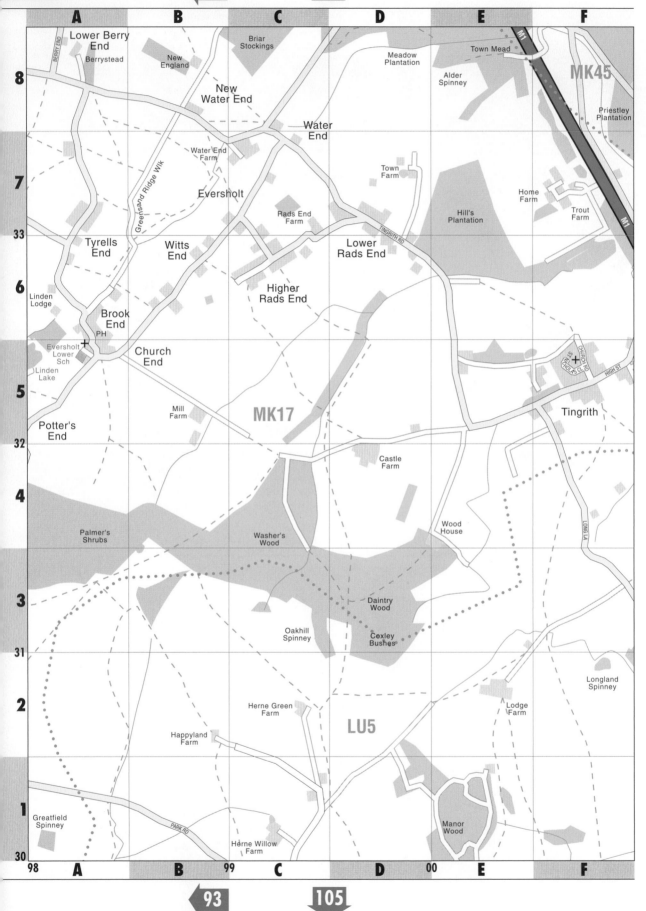

A **B** **C** **D** **E** **F**

Lower Berry End
Berrystead
New England
Briar Stockings
Meadow Plantation
Town Mead
Alder Spinney

8

MK45

New Water End

Water End

Water End Farm

7

Greensand Ridge Wlk

Eversholt

Town Farm

Rads End Farm

Home Farm

Trout Farm

33

Tingrith Rd

Tyrells End

Witts End

Lower Rads End

Hill's Plantation

6

Linden Lodge

Brook End
PH

Higher Rads End

5

Eversholt Lower Sch

Linden Lake

Church End

Mill Farm

MK17

St Nicholas Rd

Church Rd

High St

Tingrith

32

Potter's End

Castle Farm

Long La

4

Palmer's Shrubs

Washer's Wood

Wood House

3

Daintry Wood

Oakhill Spinney

Coxley Bushes

31

Longland Spinney

2

Herne Green Farm

Lodge Farm

LU5

Happyland Farm

1

Greatfield Spinney

Park Rd

Manor Wood

30

Herne Willow Farm

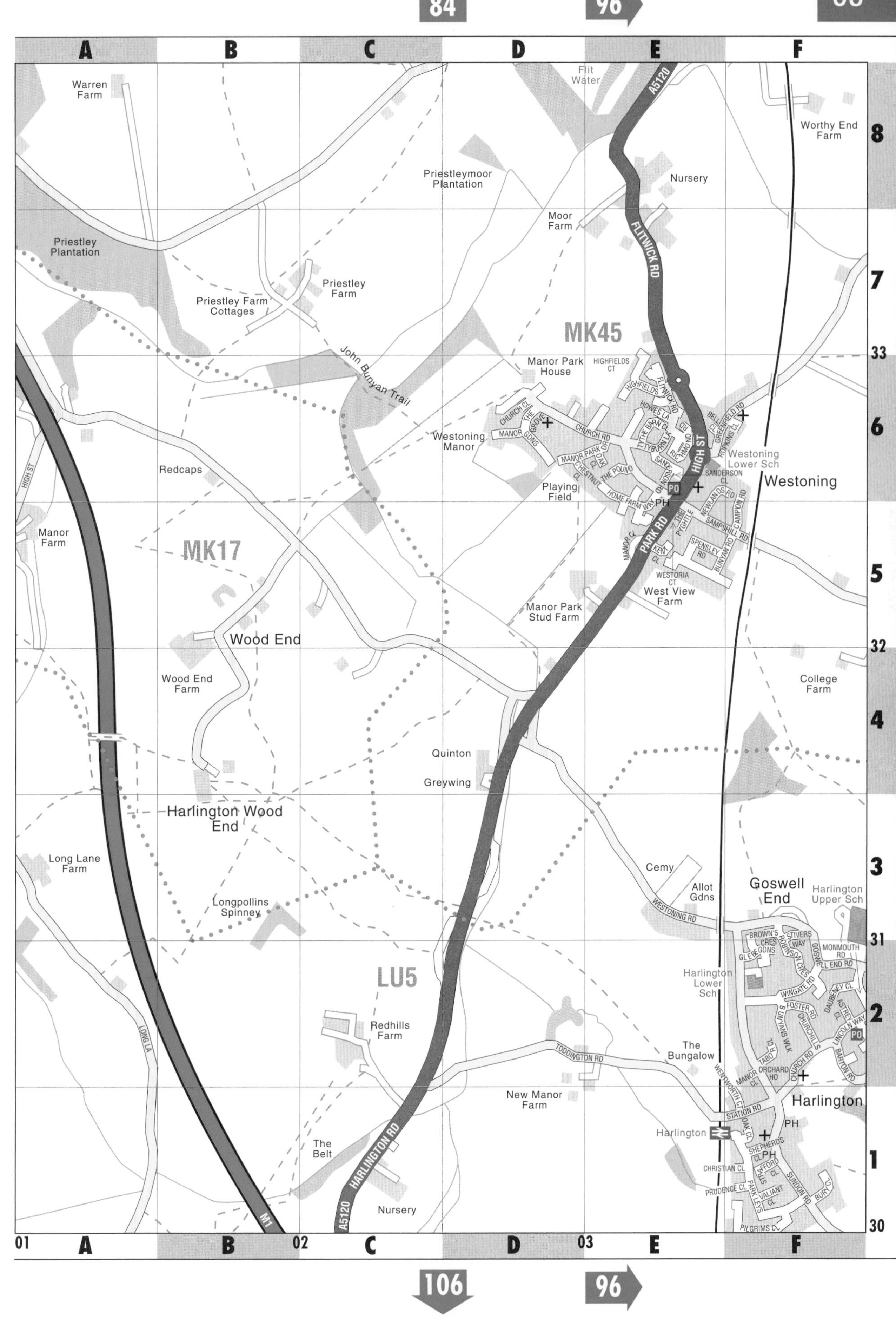
84
96
A
B
C
D
E
F
Warren Farm
Flit Water
A5120
Worthy End Farm
8
Priestleymoor Plantation
Nursery
Moor Farm
FLITWICK RD
Priestley Plantation
Priestley Farm
Priestley Farm Cottages
7
MK45
33
John Bunyan Trail
Manor Park House
HIGHFIELDS CT
Westoning Manor
CHURCH RD
HIGH ST
Westoning Lower Sch
Westoning
6
HIGH ST
Redcaps
Playing Field
SANDERSON CL
PARK RD
Manor Farm
MK17
5
WESTORIA CT
West View Farm
Manor Park Stud Farm
Wood End
32
Wood End Farm
College Farm
4
Quinton
Greywing
Harlington Wood End
Long Lane Farm
3
Cemy
Allot Gdns
Goswell End
Harlington Upper Sch
Longpollins Spinney
WESTONING RD
31
LU5
Harlington Lower Sch
2
Redhills Farm
LONG LA
TODDINGTON RD
The Bungalow
New Manor Farm
Harlington
Harlington
1
The Belt
HARLINGTON RD
CHRISTIAN CL
PRUDENCE CL
Nursery
M1
A5120
PILGRIMS CL
30
01
02
03

95
85

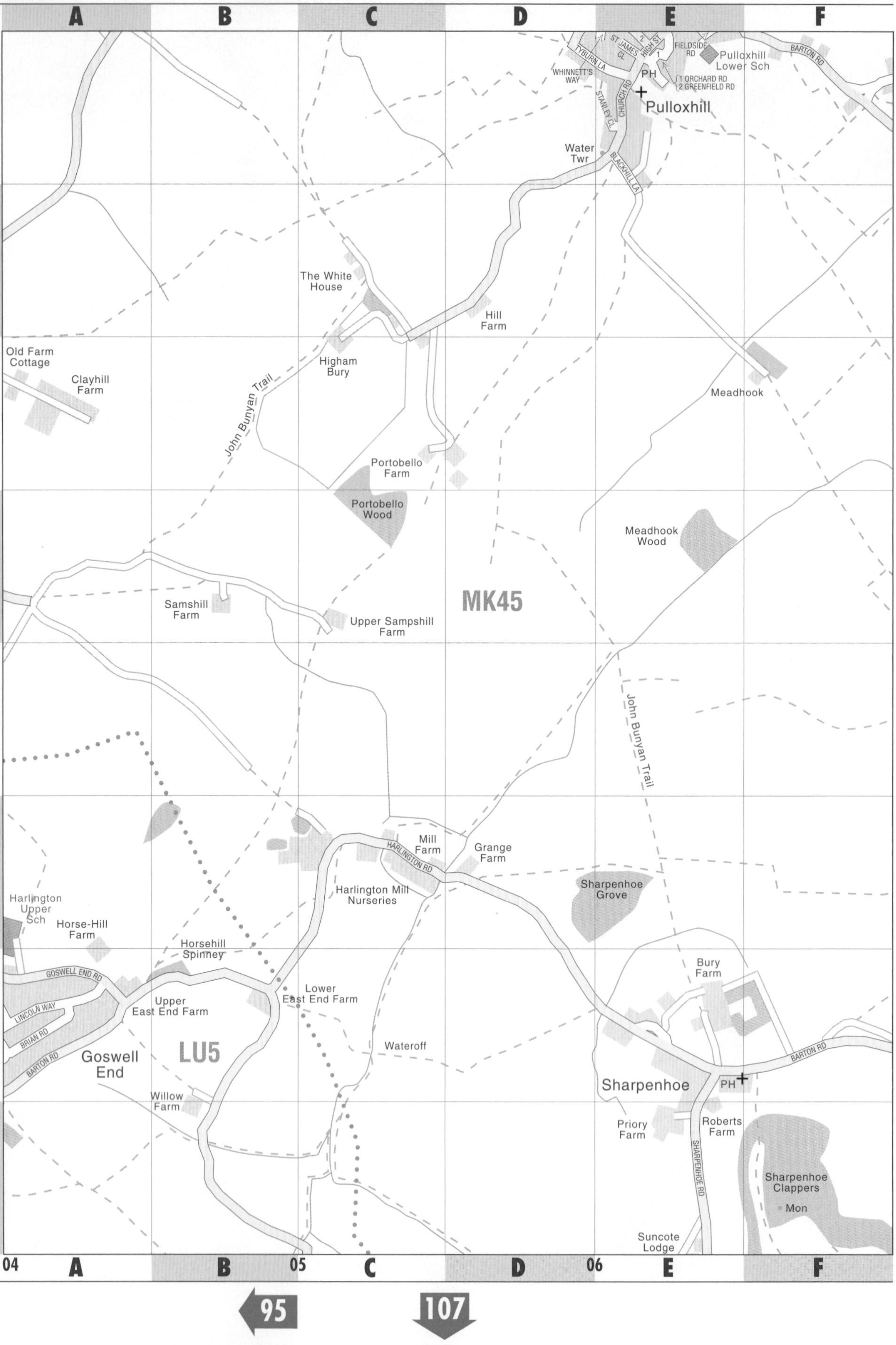

A B C D E F

8

7

33

6

5

32

4

3

31

2

1

30

04 A 05 B C 06 D E F

Old Farm Cottage

Clayhill Farm

John Bunyan Trail

The White House

Higham Bury

Hill Farm

Water Twr

ST JAMES CL
TYBURN LA
HIGH ST
WHINNETT'S WAY
FIELDSIDE RD
Pulloxhill Lower Sch
BARTON RD
PH
STANLEY CL
CHURCH RD
1 ORCHARD RD
2 GREENFIELD RD
BLACKHILL LA
Pulloxhill

Meadhook

Portobello Farm

Portobello Wood

Meadhook Wood

MK45

Samshill Farm

Upper Sampshill Farm

John Bunyan Trail

Mill Farm

Harlington Mill Nurseries

Grange Farm

Sharpenhoe Grove

HARLINGTON RD

Harlington Upper Sch

Horse-Hill Farm

Horsehill Spinney

Bury Farm

GOSWELL END RD

Upper East End Farm

Lower East End Farm

LINCOLN WAY

BRIAN RD

LU5

BARTON RD

Goswell End

Wateroff

BARTON RD

Sharpenhoe

PH

Willow Farm

Priory Farm

Roberts Farm

SHARPENHOE RD

Sharpenhoe Clappers

Mon

Suncote Lodge

95
107

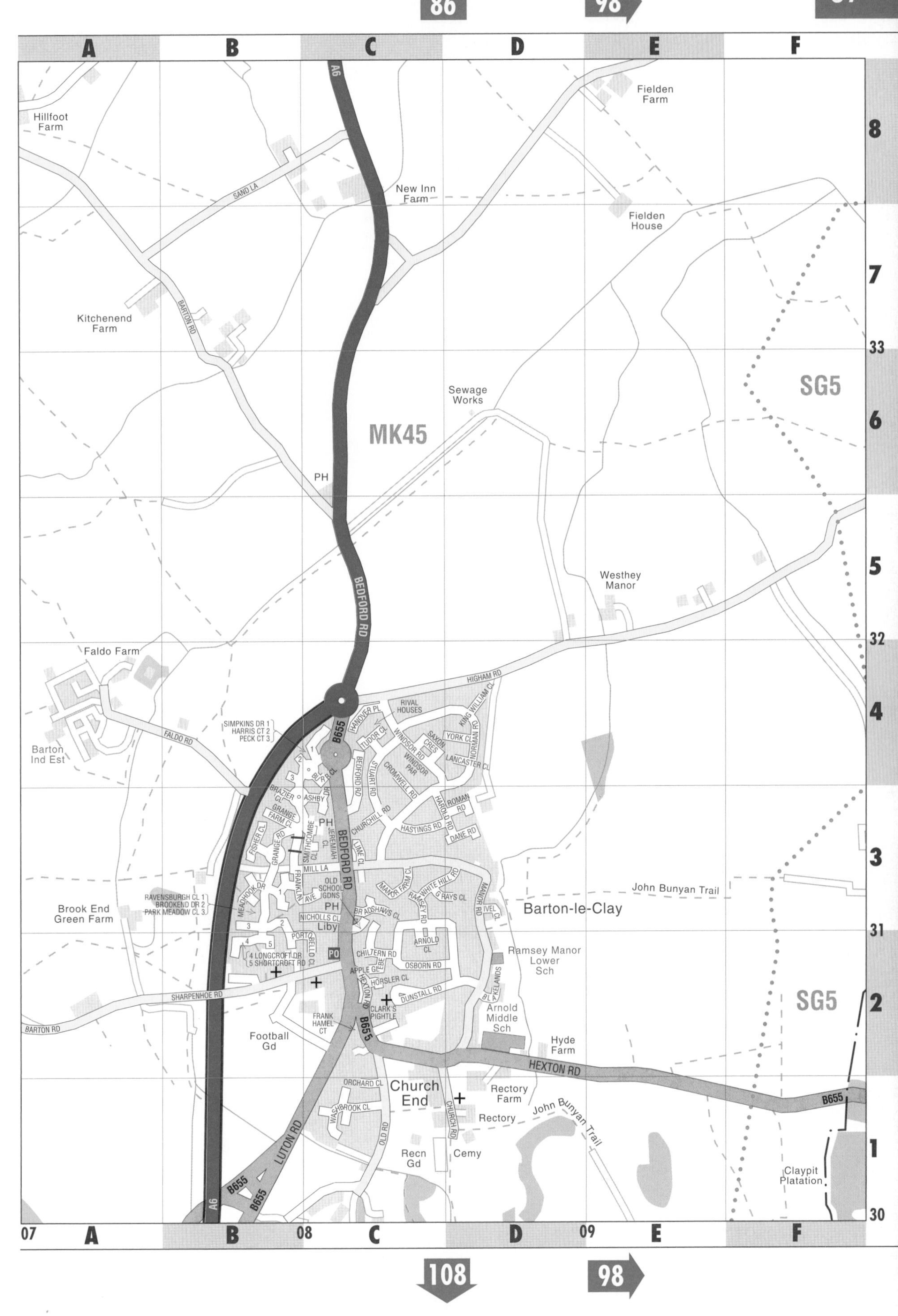
86
98
A
B
C
D
E
F
8
7
33
6
5
32
4
3
31
2
1
30
07
08
09
Hillfoot Farm
Fielden Farm
New Inn Farm
Fielden House
SAND LA
A6
Kitchenend Farm
BARTON RD
Sewage Works
MK45
SG5
PH
BEDFORD RD
Westhey Manor
Faldo Farm
Barton Ind Est
FALDO RD
HIGHAM RD
SIMPKINS DR 1
HARRIS CT 2
PECK CT 3
RIVAL HOUSES
HANOVER PL
KING WILLIAM CL
YORK CL
NORMAN RD
SAXON CRES
TUDOR CL
WINDSOR RD
WINDSOR PAR
LANCASTER CL
B655
BEDFORD RD
STUART RD
CROMWELL RD
BRAZIER CL
ASHBY DR
GRANGE FARM CL
CHURCHILL RD
ROMAN RD
HAROLD RD
HASTINGS RD
DANE RD
FISHER CL
GRANGE RD
SMITHCOMBE CL
JEREMIAH CL
LIME CL
MILL LA
OLD SCHOOL GDNS
FRANKLIN AVE
MANOR FARM CL
WHITE HILL RD
RAMSEY RD
GRAYS CL
MANOR RD
IVEL CL
John Bunyan Trail
Barton-le-Clay
RAVENSBURGH CL 1
BROOKEND DR 2
PARK MEADOW CL 3
MEADHOOK DR
NICHOLLS CL
BRADSHAWS CL
Brook End Green Farm
Liby
PORTOBELLO CL
ARNOLD CL
4 LONGCROFT DR
5 SHORTCROFT RD
PO
CHILTERN RD
GLEBE
OSBORN RD
Ramsey Manor Lower Sch
APPLE
HORSLER CL
SHARPENHOE RD
HEXTON RD
DUNSTALL RD
BLACKELANDS
BARTON RD
FRANK HAMEL CT
CLARK'S PIGHTLE
Arnold Middle Sch
Football Gd
Hyde Farm
HEXTON RD
ORCHARD CL
Church End
Rectory Farm
WASHBROOK CL
CHURCH RD
Rectory
John Bunyan Trail
LUTON RD
OLD RD
Recn Gd
Cemy
Claypit Platation
108
98

97
87

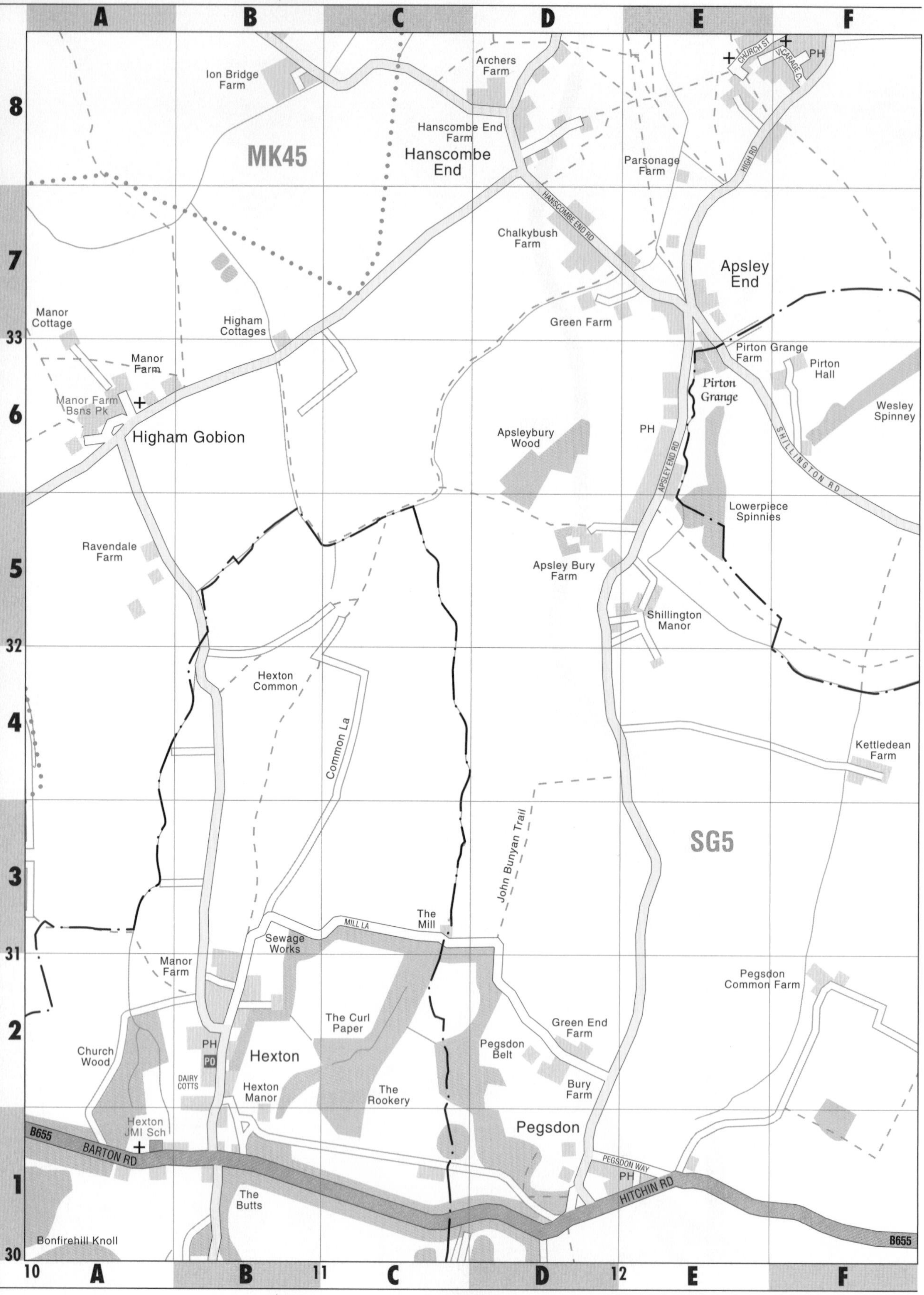

A B C D E F

8

MK45

Ion Bridge Farm

Archers Farm

Hanscombe End Farm

Hanscombe End

Parsonage Farm

CHURCH ST

VICARAGE CL

PH

HIGH RD

7

Chalkybush Farm

Apsley End

HANSCOMBE END RD

Manor Cottage

Higham Cottages

33

Green Farm

Pirton Grange Farm

Pirton Hall

Manor Farm

Pirton Grange

Wesley Spinney

6

Manor Farm Bsns Pk

Higham Gobion

Apsleybury Wood

PH

APSLEY END RD

SHILLINGTON RD

Lowerpiece Spinnies

Ravendale Farm

Apsley Bury Farm

5

Shillington Manor

32

Hexton Common

Common La

4

John Bunyan Trail

SG5

Kettledean Farm

3

31

MILL LA

The Mill

Sewage Works

Manor Farm

Pegsdon Common Farm

2

The Curl Paper

Hexton

Green End Farm

PH

Pegsdon Belt

PO

Church Wood

DAIRY COTTS

Hexton Manor

The Rookery

Bury Farm

Pegsdon

B655

BARTON RD

Hexton JMI Sch

Pegsdon Way

PH

1

The Butts

HITCHIN RD

30

Bonfirehill Knoll

B655

10 A B 11 C D 12 E F

88
100

A B C D E F
8 7 33 6 5 32 4 3 31 2 1 30
13 14 15
Rosehill Farm
SG16
New Wrights Farm
HOLWELL RD
Burge End Farm
Hammonds Farm
Burge End
West Lane Farm
BURGE END LA
SHILLINGTON RD
Rectory Farm
WEST LA
LITTLE LA
DAVIS CR
COLEMANS CL
FRANKLIN CL
BUNYAN CL
CROMWELL WAY
ROYAL OAK LA
PO
Pirton Sch
HIGH ST
ST MARY'S CL
Pirton
DOCKLANDS
CRAB TREE LA
POLLARDS WAY
HAMBRIDGE WAY
PRIORS HILL
DANEFIELD RD
Wr Twr
Hill Farm
Toot Hill
THREE CLOSES
GREAT GN
BURY END
WALNUT TREE RD
Hill Farm
MALTINGS ORCH
Icknield Way Path
Walnut Tree Farm
Icknield Way Path
Wood La
SG5
Knocking Knoll
HITCHIN RD
Highdown Farm
High Down House
Tingley Wood
Lower Plantation
Highdown Plantation
Hanginghill Plantation
Punch's Cross
Tingley Field Platation
Shrub Wood
B655

100

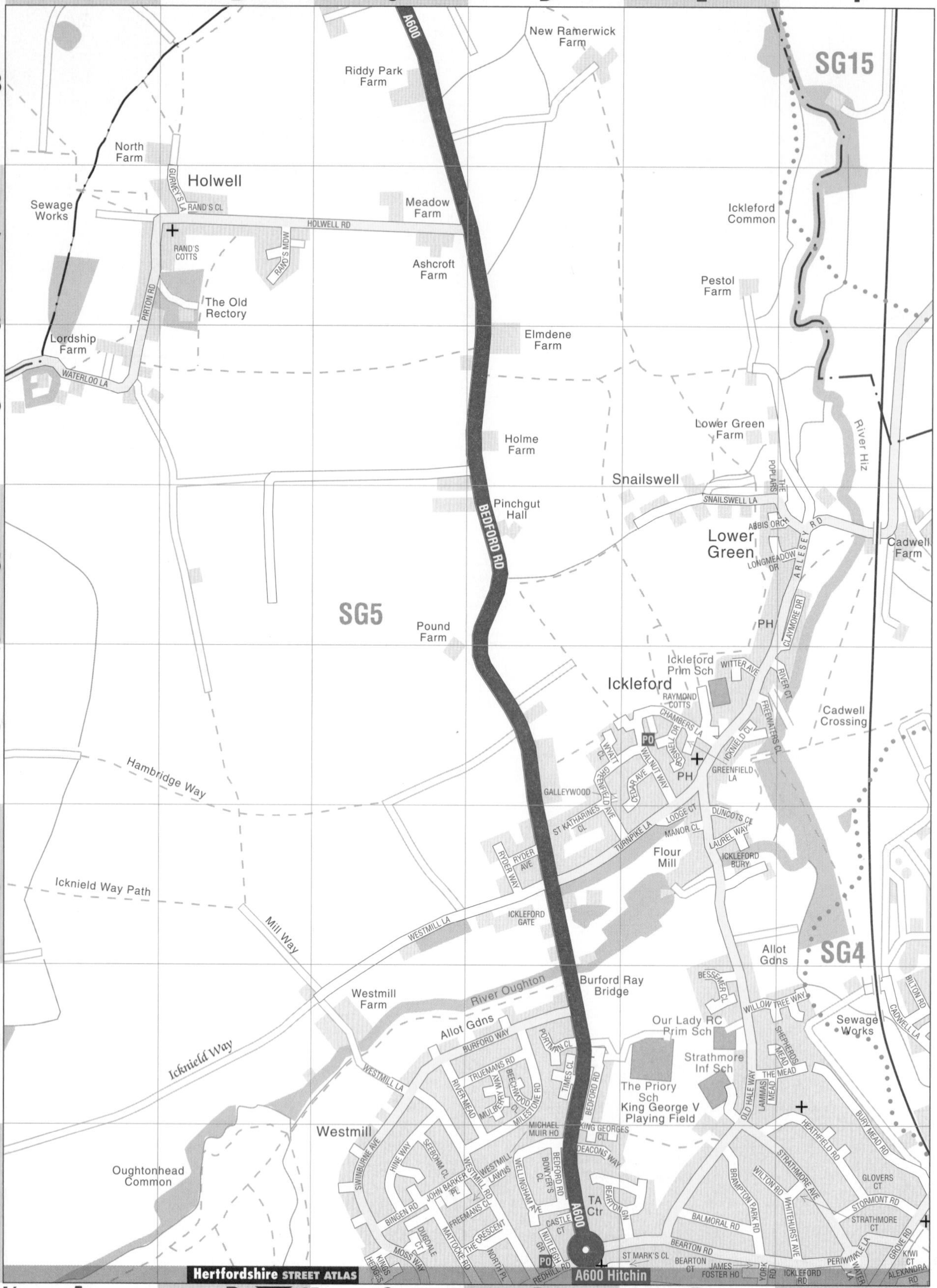

A B C D E F

8

SG15

New Ramerwick Farm

Riddy Park Farm

North Farm

Sewage Works

Holwell

GURNEY'S LA

RAND'S CL

7

HOLWELL RD

Meadow Farm

Ickleford Common

RAND'S COTTS

RAND'S MDW

Ashcroft Farm

Pestol Farm

The Old Rectory

PIRTON RD

33

Elmdene Farm

Lordship Farm

WATERLOO LA

6

Holme Farm

Lower Green Farm

River Hiz

Snailswell

Lower Green

THE POPLARS

SNAILSWELL LA

ABBIS ORCD

ARLSEY RD

CADWELL RD

5

SG5

Pinchgut Hall

LONGMEADOW DR

Cadwell Farm

BEDFORD RD

Pound Farm

GLAYMORE DR

PH

RIVER CT

32

Ickleford Prim Sch

WITTER AVE

Ickleford

Cadwell Crossing

RAYMOND COTTS

CHAMBERS LA

FREEWATERS CL

CADWELL LA

4

PO

ICKNIELD CL

GREENFIELD LA

Hambridge Way

PH

CEDAR AVE

WHARF

WALNUT WAY

GALLEYWOOD

ST KATHARINES CL

LODGE CT

DUNCOTS CL

LAUREL WAY

Flour Mill

ICKLEFORD BURY

3

Icknield Way Path

RYDER WAY

TURNPIKE LA

MANOR CL

RYDER AVE

Mill Way

WESTMILL LA

ICKLEFORD GATE

31

Westmill Farm

River Oughton

Burford Ray Bridge

Allot Gdns

SG4

BESSEMER CL

BILTON RD

WILLOW TREE WAY

Sewage Works

2

Icknield Way

WESTMILL LA

Allot Gdns

Burford Way

POTTON RD

Our Lady RC Prim Sch

SHEPHERDS

THE MEAD

TRUEMANS RD

AVON RD

TIMES CL

BEDFORD RD

Strathmore Inf Sch

OLD HALE WAY

HEATHFIELD RD

BURY MEAD RD

RIVER MEAD

BEECHWOOD RD

MILLSTONE CT

The Priory Sch

LAMMAS MEAD

MULBERRY CT

King George V Playing Field

Westmill

SWINBURNE AVE

HINE WAY

WESTMILL LAWNS

KING GEORGES WAY

STRATHMORE AVE

WILTON RD

WHITEHURST AVE

GLOVERS CT

1

Oughtonhead Common

SEEBOHM PL

JOHN BARKER PL

DEACONS WAY

BEARTON GN

BRAMPTON PARK RD

STORMONT RD

STRATHMORE CT

BINGEN RD

FREMANS RD

THE CRESCENT

WELLINGHAM AVE

BEDFORD RD

CASTLE CT

BOWYER'S RD

BEARTON RD

BALMORAL RD

PERIWINKLE LA

GROVE RD

KIWI CT

DURRANT

MATTOCKE RD

NORTH PL

MICHAEL MUIR HO

TA Ctr

ST MARK'S CL

JAMES FOSTER HO

ICKLEFORD RD

ALEXANDRA RD

KINGS HEDGES

MOSS WAY

REDHILL RD

PO

BEARTON CT

A600 Hitchin

30

90

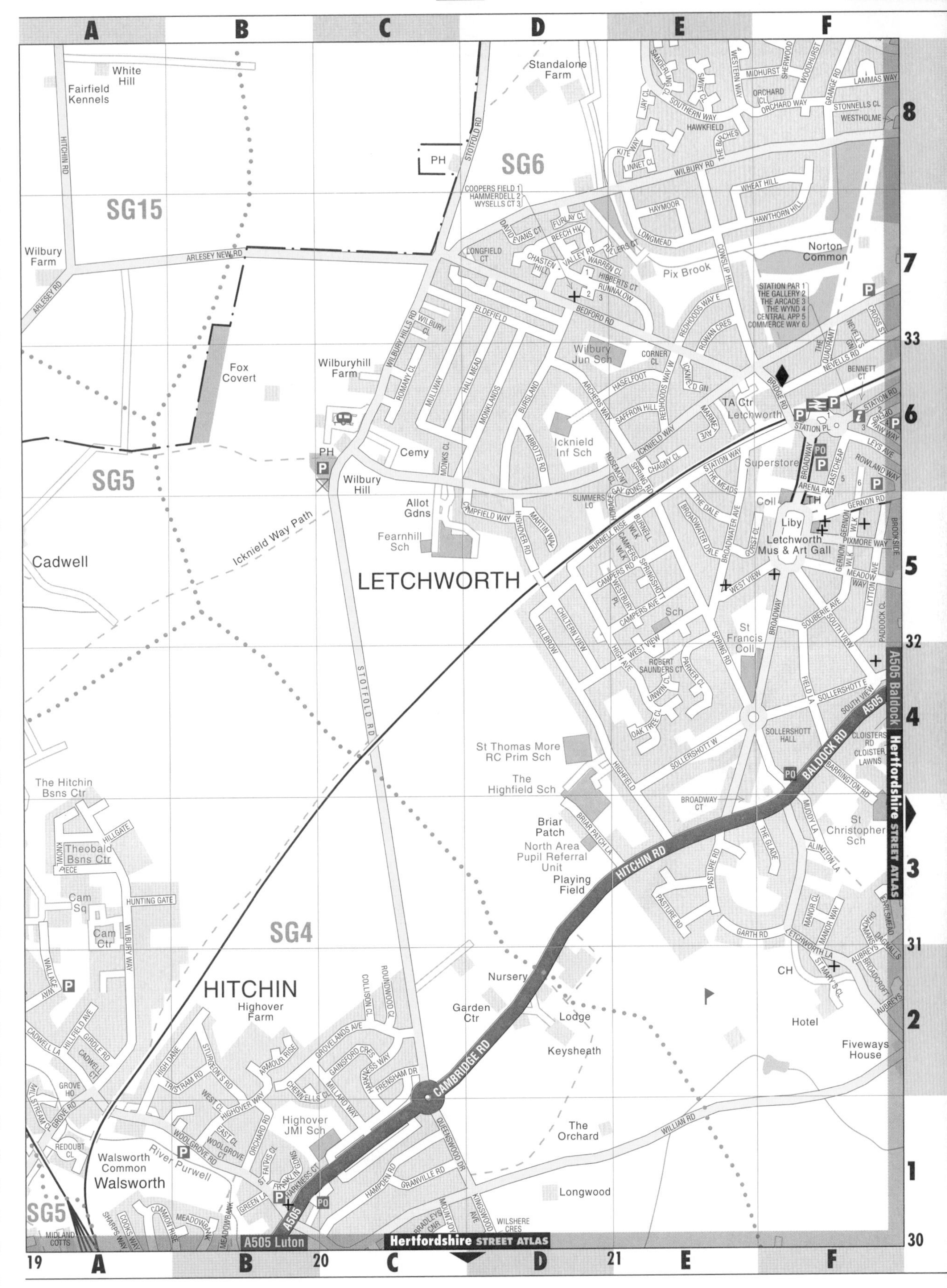

LETCHWORTH
HITCHIN
SG15
SG6
SG5
SG4
Walsworth
Cadwell
Fox Covert
Wilburyhill Farm
Wilbury Hill
Standalone Farm
White Hill
Fairfield Kennels
Wilbury Farm
Norton Common
Pix Brook
Icknield Way Path
St Thomas More RC Prim Sch
The Highfield Sch
Letchworth Mus & Art Gall
St Francis Coll
St Christopher Sch
Fiveways House
Keysheath
Longwood
The Orchard
Highover JMI Sch
Walsworth Common
River Purwell
The Hitchin Bsns Ctr
Theobald Bsns Ctr
HITCHIN RD
CAMBRIDGE RD
BALDOCK RD
STOTFOLD RD
WILBURY RD
ARLESEY NEW RD
WILLIAN RD
A505 Luton
A505 Baldock
Hertfordshire STREET ATLAS

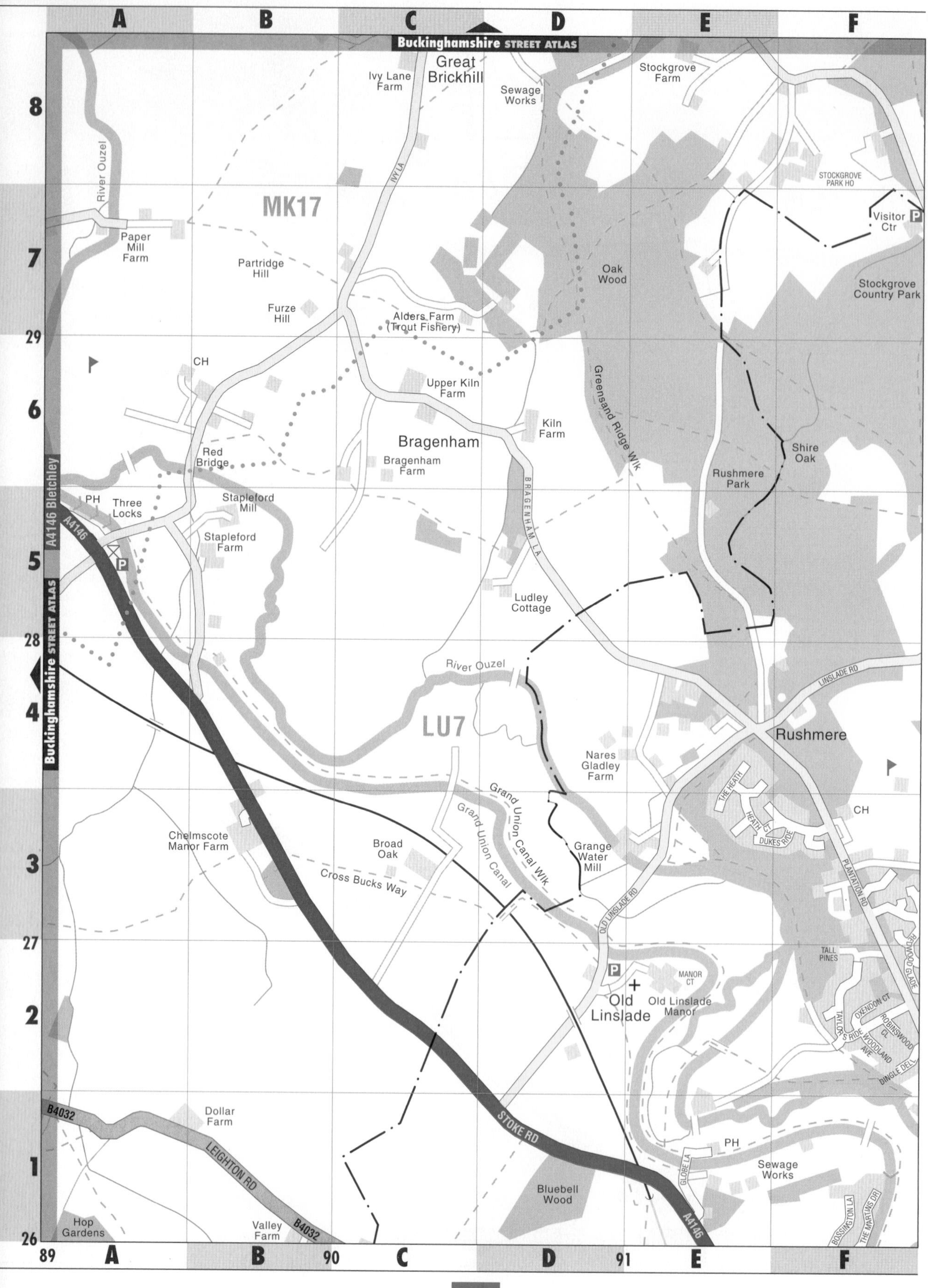

Great
Brickhill

Ivy Lane
Farm

Sewage
Works

Stockgrove
Farm

STOCKGROVE
PARK HO

Visitor
Ctr

River Ouzel

MK17

Paper
Mill
Farm

Partridge
Hill

Furze
Hill

Alders Farm
(Trout Fishery)

Oak
Wood

Stockgrove
Country Park

CH

Upper Kiln
Farm

Bragenham

Kiln
Farm

Greensand Ridge Wlk

Shire
Oak

Red
Bridge

Bragenham
Farm

Rushmere
Park

PH

Three
Locks

Stapleford
Mill

BRAGENHAM LA

Stapleford
Farm

P

Ludley
Cottage

River Ouzel

LINSLADE RD

Rushmere

LU7

CH

Chelmscote
Manor Farm

Broad
Oak

Cross Bucks Way

Grand Union Canal Wlk

Grand Union Canal

Nares
Gladley
Farm

Grange
Water
Mill

THE HEATH

HEATH CT

DUKES RIDE

PLANTATION RD

TALL
PINES

A4146 Bletchley

A4146

Buckinghamshire STREET ATLAS

Dollar
Farm

OLD LINSLADE RD

P

MANOR
CT

Old
Linslade

Old Linslade
Manor

OXENDON CT

ROBINSWOOD
CL

WOODLAND
AVE

DINGLE DELL

B4032

LEIGHTON RD

B4032

STOKE RD

Bluebell
Wood

GLOBE LA

PH

Sewage
Works

A4146

BOSSINGTON LA

THE MAGPIES DR

Hop
Gardens

Valley
Farm

89   A   B   90   C   D   91   E   F

92
104

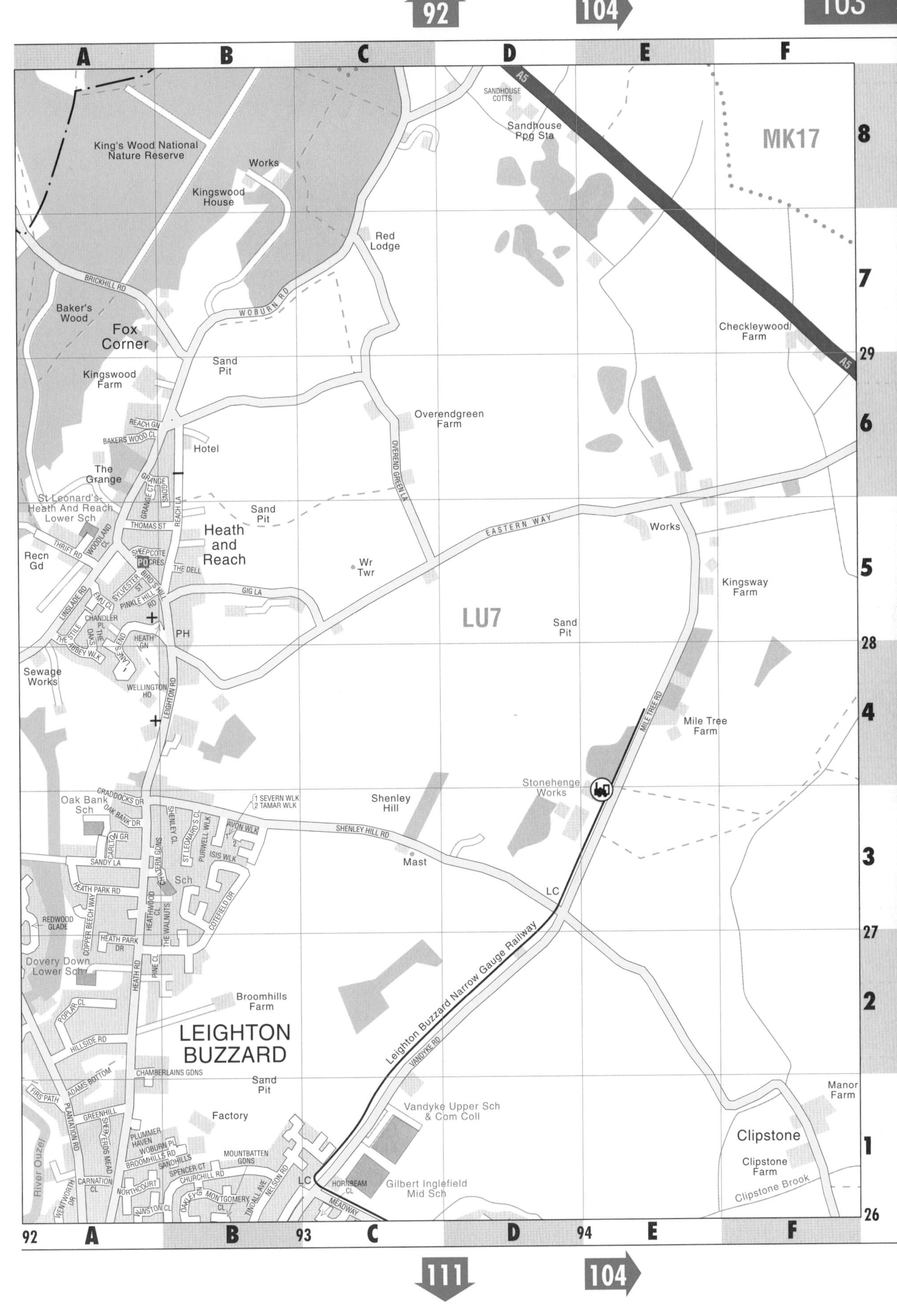
King's Wood National Nature Reserve
Works
Kingswood House
Red Lodge
Sandhouse Cotts
Sandhouse Ppg Sta
MK17
Baker's Wood
Fox Corner
Kingswood Farm
Sand Pit
Checkleywood Farm
Overendgreen Farm
Hotel
The Grange
St Leonard's Heath And Reach Lower Sch
Heath and Reach
Works
Recn Gd
Wr Twr
Kingsway Farm
LU7
Sand Pit
PH
Sewage Works
Mile Tree Farm
Stonehenge Works
Shenley Hill
Oak Bank Sch
Mast
Sch
LC
Dovery Down Lower Sch
Broomhills Farm
LEIGHTON BUZZARD
Leighton Buzzard Narrow Gauge Railway
Sand Pit
Manor Farm
Factory
Vandyke Upper Sch & Com Coll
Clipstone
Clipstone Farm
Clipstone Brook
Gilbert Inglefield Mid Sch
River Ouzel
A5
BRICKHILL RD
WOBURN RD
EASTERN WAY
GIG LA
OVEREND GREEN LA
LEIGHTON RD
MILE TREE RD
SHENLEY HILL RD
VANDYKE RD
HEATH RD
MEADWAY
A B C D E F
1 2 3 4 5 6 7 8
92 93 94
26 27 28 29

111
104

A   B   C   D   E   F

Manor Farm
The Old Rectory
+ Potsgrove

New Planting

Town Farm

8

BATTLESDEN AVE

Home Wood

Hungerhill Wood

LONDON RD

A4012

Battlesden House

Ford Spinney

7

MK17

29

Battlesden Park

Centre Farm

A5

6

EASTERN WAY

Mast

HOCKLIFFE RD

Fourne Hill Farm

Battlesden Lodge

Hill Farm

5

28

The Coops

Watergate Lodge

4

LU7

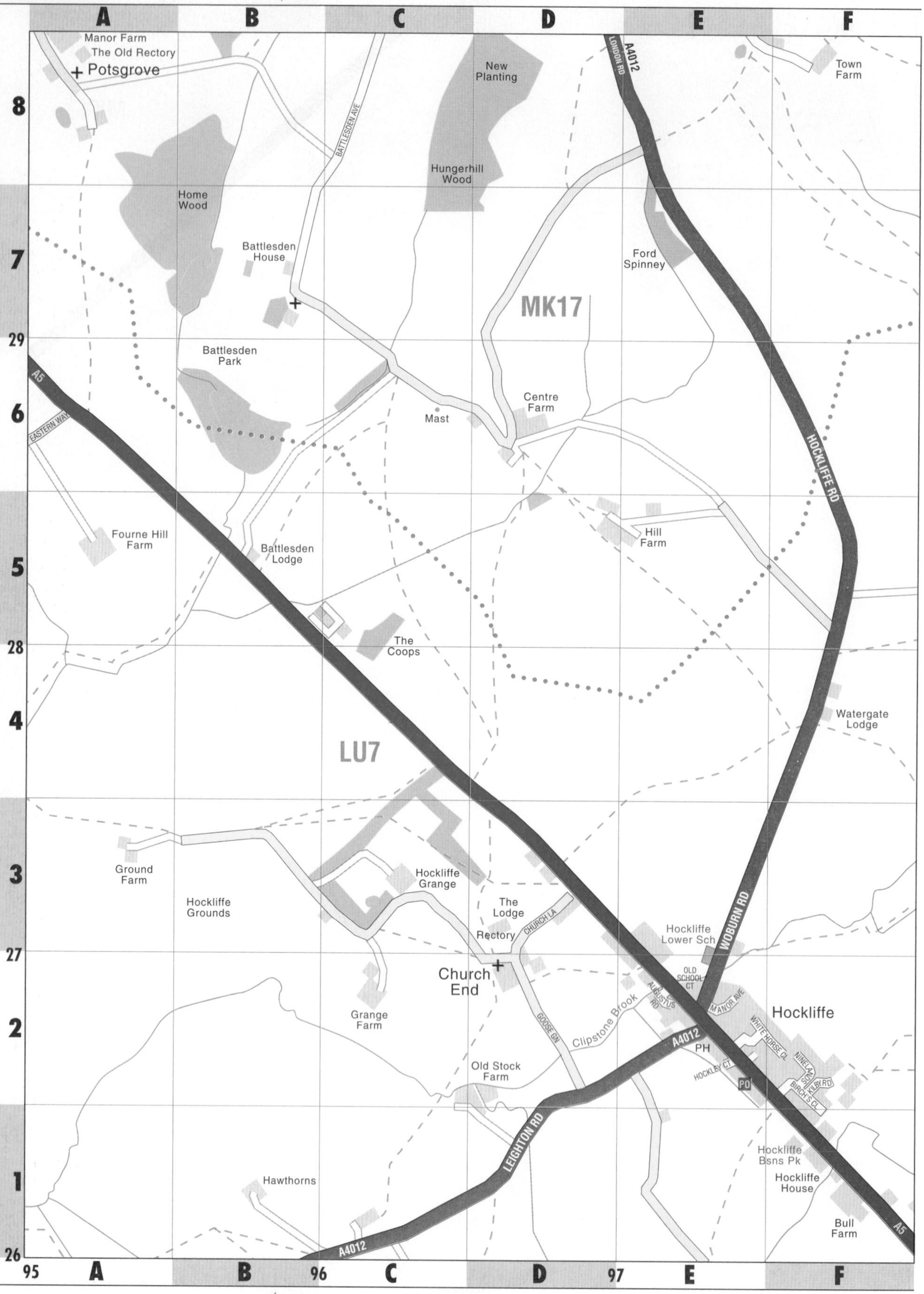

Ground Farm

Hockliffe Grange

Hockliffe Lower Sch

WOBURN RD

3

Hockliffe Grounds

The Lodge

Rectory

CHURCH LA

OLD SCHOOL CT

Hockliffe

27

Church End +

GORSE GN

CLIPSTONE BROOK

AUGUSTUS RD

MANOR AVE

WHITE HORSE CL

2

Grange Farm

Old Stock Farm

A4012

PH

HOCKLEY CT

NINE A...

BIRCH'S CL

PO

Hockliffe Bsns Pk

LEIGHTON RD

Hockliffe House

1

Hawthorns

Bull Farm

A5

26

95   A   B   96   C   D   97   E   F

A4012

A B C D E F

8

MK17

Toddington Manor

Toddington Park

Herne Manor Farm

The Lodge

Herne Farm

PARK RD

Manor Lodge

7

Herne Grange

WARREN CL
HERNE CL
WENTWORTH CL
Park Hill
PARK HILL

LONG LA

LU5

29

MONMOUTH AVE
BROUGHTON AVE
EXETER
ELM
STRATFORD GR
LEIGH CL
MANOR RD
CHENEY CL
Parkfields Mid Sch
GEORGE ST
LEWIN CRES
HIGH ST A5120
CHURCH SQ
PO
PH
Sch

Herne Poplar Farm

6

Alma Farm

ALMA FARM RD
MARLBOROUGH PL
CHAPEL
WALNUT ACRE
GRANGE RD
ORCHARD RD
LAKES
THE GRANGE
GRANGE GDNS
THE CRESCENT

Toddington

Warmark Farm

LEIGHTON RD
MEADOW RD
RUSSELL RD
2 1 3
CRESCENT CT 1
CRESCENT CL 2
DALE CL
BRYANT WAY
STOCKDALE
PRINCES ST
B579

5

Watergate Farm

HOLMFIELD CL 1
PEAR TREE CL 2
FRENCHMANS CL 3

Fairview Farm

ROSE WLK
WILLOW WAY
CLEAVERS
THE CLEAVERS

RANDALL DR

28

BRADFORD WAY 1
KIMBERWELL CL 2
DE MONTFORT CT 3
MOUNT PLEASANT CL 4
SHELTON CL 5
MOUNT PLEASANT AVE
3 4
SHELTON AVE
5

4

Dropsholt Farm

THE LANE

DUNSTABLE RD

3

Chalgrave

LU7

TODDINGTON RD

CHALGRAVE RD

College Farm

27

Icknield Way Path

2

PO PH
ST MARY'S CL
PARK FARM
PARKVIEW LA
WINGFIELD RD
Tebworth
WOODLANDS

Great Wood

Upper Tithe Farm

Rose Farm

THE MEADOWS
TEBWORTH RD
PH

Lords Hill Cottage

1

Hill Cottage

HOCKLIFE RD

HILL CL

A5120

LORD'S HILL

Wingfield

A5

TEBWORTH RD

26

105
95

A B C D E F

8

Graham Farm
Boastings Farm

Dunedin

M1

A5120

B530

HARLINGTON RD

Old Park Farm

Harlington Spinney

7

Briarmead Farm

Mill Farm

A5120 STATION RD

PH THE BUNGALOWS

29

Cemy

Crooked Oak Farm

Icknield Way Path

MARKET SQ

Conger Hill

CONGER LA

LU5

Liby

WENTWORTH GDNS

6

Toddington

Toddington Service Area

B579

FINN'S VILLAS

River Flit

Leyhill Lince

THE CRESCENT

THE PADDOCKS

Cowbridge Farm

B579

PRINCES ST

Hipsey Spinney

5

BUSH CL

Sewage Works

PRESTON RD

BRADFORD RD

28

Horse Hill Farm

White Hart Farm

B530

PH

Chalton Spinney

4

Crowbush Farm

Fancott

Feoffee Farm

LU3

Icknield Way Path

Chalgrave Manor

Manor Farm

LUTON RD

3

Sewage Works

27

Warrenmore Spinney

Common Farm

CH

Mast

2

Manor Farm

WATER END LA

FORD CL

PH LU4

New Barn

Chalton

Chalton Lower Sch

PO

Chalton Lower Sch

THE LANE

1

Grove Spinney

CHALTON HTS

Grove Farm

Chiltern Way

SUNDON RD

B579

M1

26

01 A 02 B C 02 D 03 E F

96
108

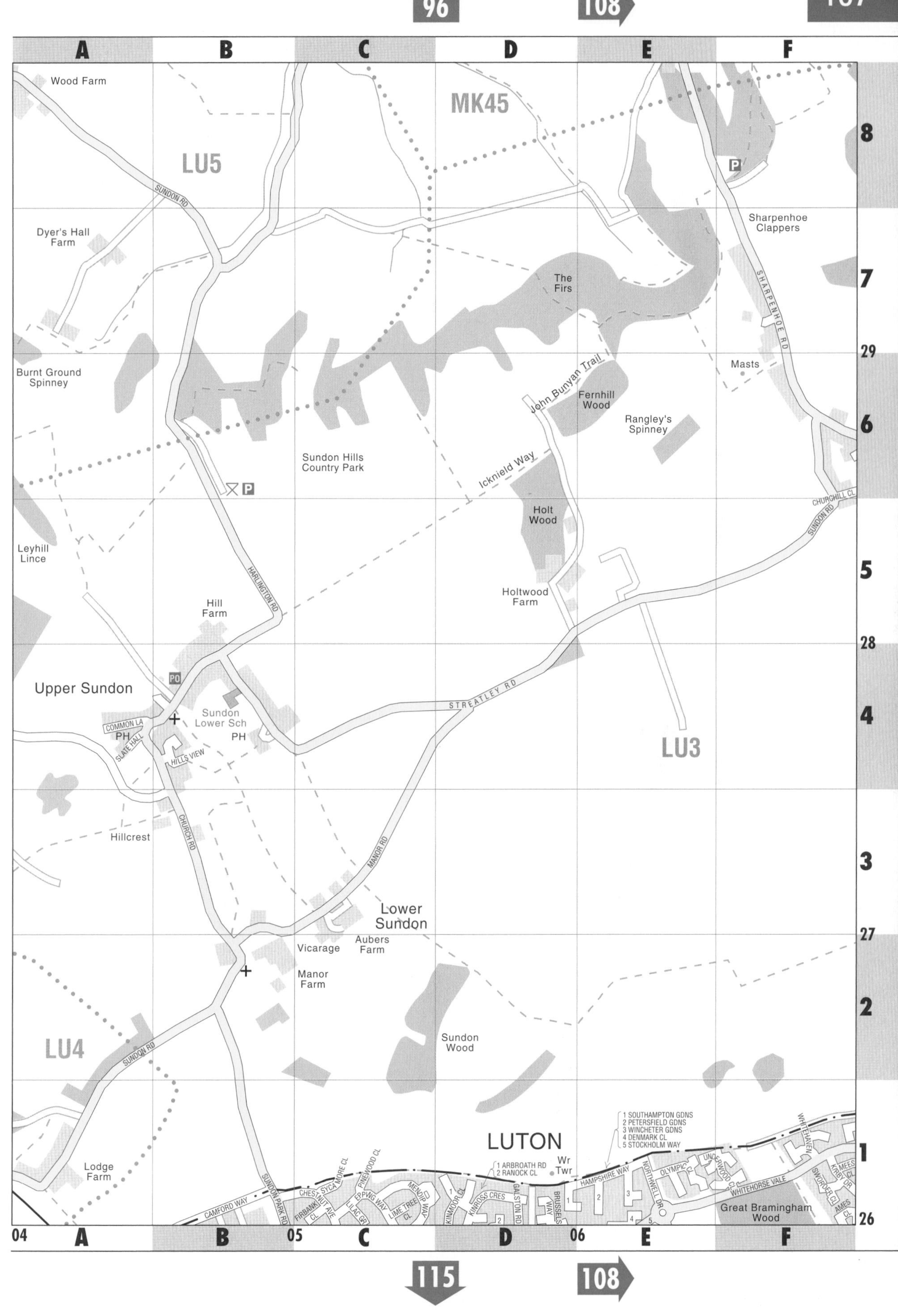
A
B
C
D
E
F
Wood Farm
MK45
LU5
SUNDON RD
Dyer's Hall Farm
Sharpenhoe Clappers
The Firs
SHARPENHOE RD
Burnt Ground Spinney
Masts
John Bunyan Trail
Fernhill Wood
Rangley's Spinney
Sundon Hills Country Park
Icknield Way
CHURCHILL CL
SUNDON RD
Holt Wood
Leyhill Lince
HARLINGTON RD
Holtwood Farm
Hill Farm
STREATLEY RD
Upper Sundon
PO
Sundon Lower Sch
COMMON LA
PH
SLATE HALL
HILLS VIEW
LU3
CHURCH RD
Hillcrest
MANOR RD
Lower Sundon
Vicarage
Aubers Farm
Manor Farm
LU4
SUNDON RD
Sundon Wood
1 SOUTHAMPTON GDNS
2 PETERSFIELD GDNS
3 WINCHETER GDNS
4 DENMARK CL
5 STOCKHOLM WAY
LUTON
Wr Twr
1 ARBROATH RD
2 RANOCK CL
Lodge Farm
HAMPSHIRE WAY
NORTHWELL DR
OLYMPIC CL
UNDERWOOD CL
WHITEHAVEN
WHITEHORSE VALE
CAMFORD WAY
SUNDON PARK RD
CHESTNUT AVE
SYCAMORE CL
PINEWOOD CL
EPPING WAY
LILAC GR
FIRBANK CL
MENDIP WAY
LIME TREE CL
KINMOOR CL
KINROSS CRES
GALSTON RD
BRUSSELS WAY
Great Bramingham Wood
SWORDER CL
KIRBY DR
MEES CL
AMES CL
8
7
29
6
5
28
4
3
27
2
1
26
04
05
06

115
108

107
97

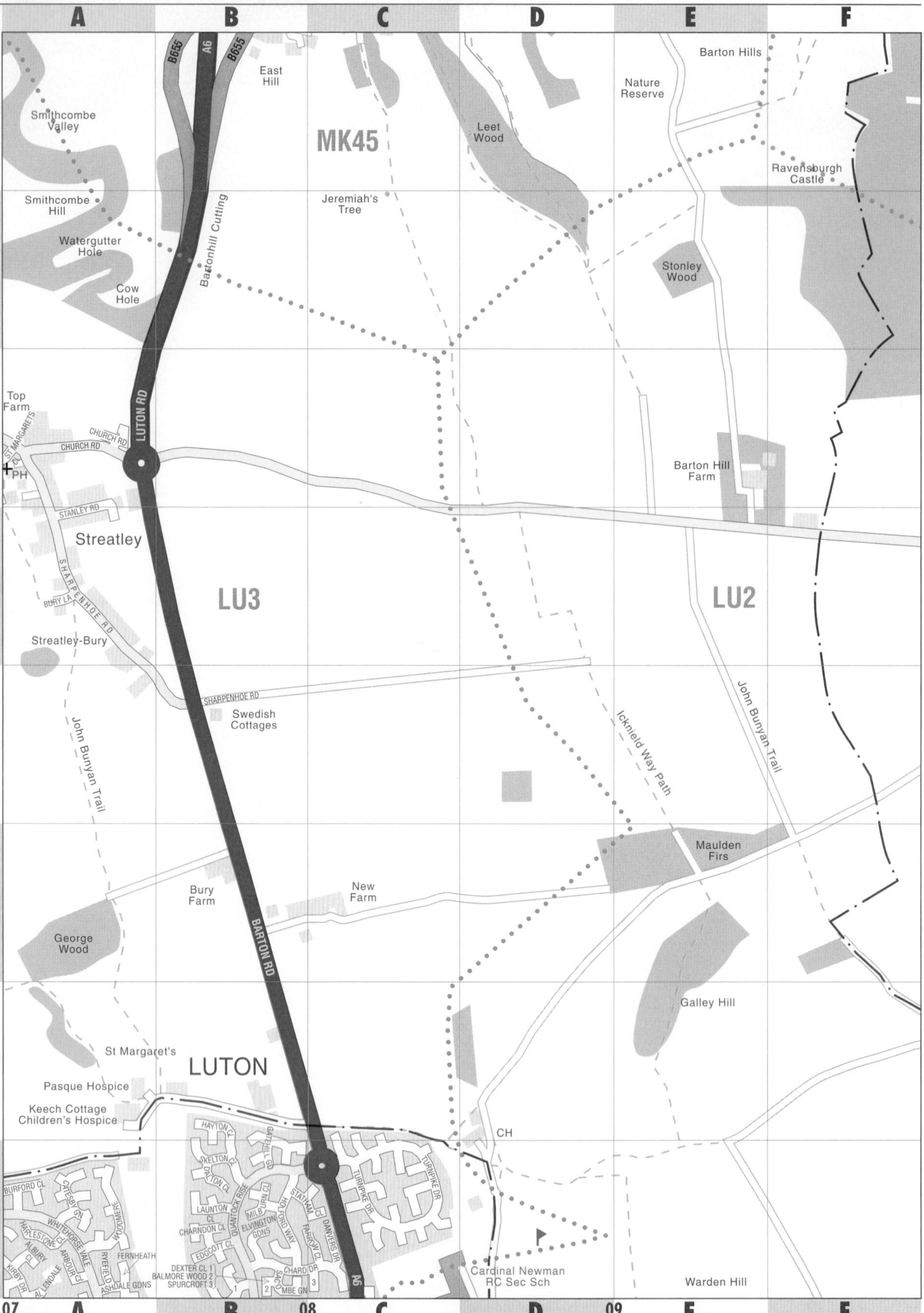

A B C D E F

8

Smithcombe Valley

East Hill

B655 A6 B655

MK45

Leet Wood

Barton Hills

Nature Reserve

Ravensburgh Castle

Smithcombe Hill

Jeremiah's Tree

7

Watergutter Hole

Bartonhill Cutting

Stonley Wood

Cow Hole

29

Top Farm

LUTON RD

6

St MARGARET'S CL

CHURCH RD

CHURCH RD

Barton Hill Farm

+ PH

STANLEY RD

Streatley

5

SHARPENHOE RD

BURY LA

LU3

LU2

John Bunyan Trail

Streatley-Bury

28

SHARPENHOE RD

Swedish Cottages

4

John Bunyan Trail

Icknield Way Path

John Bunyan Trail

Maulden Firs

3

Bury Farm

New Farm

George Wood

27

Galley Hill

BARTON RD

2

St Margaret's

LUTON

Pasque Hospice

Keech Cottage Children's Hospice

CH

1

BURFORD CL

CATSBY CL

HAYTON CL

AXELTON CL

AXELTON CL

CHILTON CL

DUANTOCK RISE

GREENFIELD RD

HOFORD WAY

STATHAM CL

FAIRWAY CL

DANVERGE DR

TURNPIKE DR

TURNPIKE DR

WHITEHORSE VALE

ALBURY CL

KINGS DR

ALESDALE DR

RYEFIELD GDNS

ASHDALE GDNS

FERNHEATH

LAUNTON CL

CHARNDON CL

EDSCOTT CL

BILL O FORD WAY

SECC

CHARD DR

MBE GN

ELVINGTON GDNS

Cardinal Newman RC Sec Sch

Warden Hill

DEXTER CL 1
BALMORE WOOD 2
SPURCROFT 3

A6

26

107
116

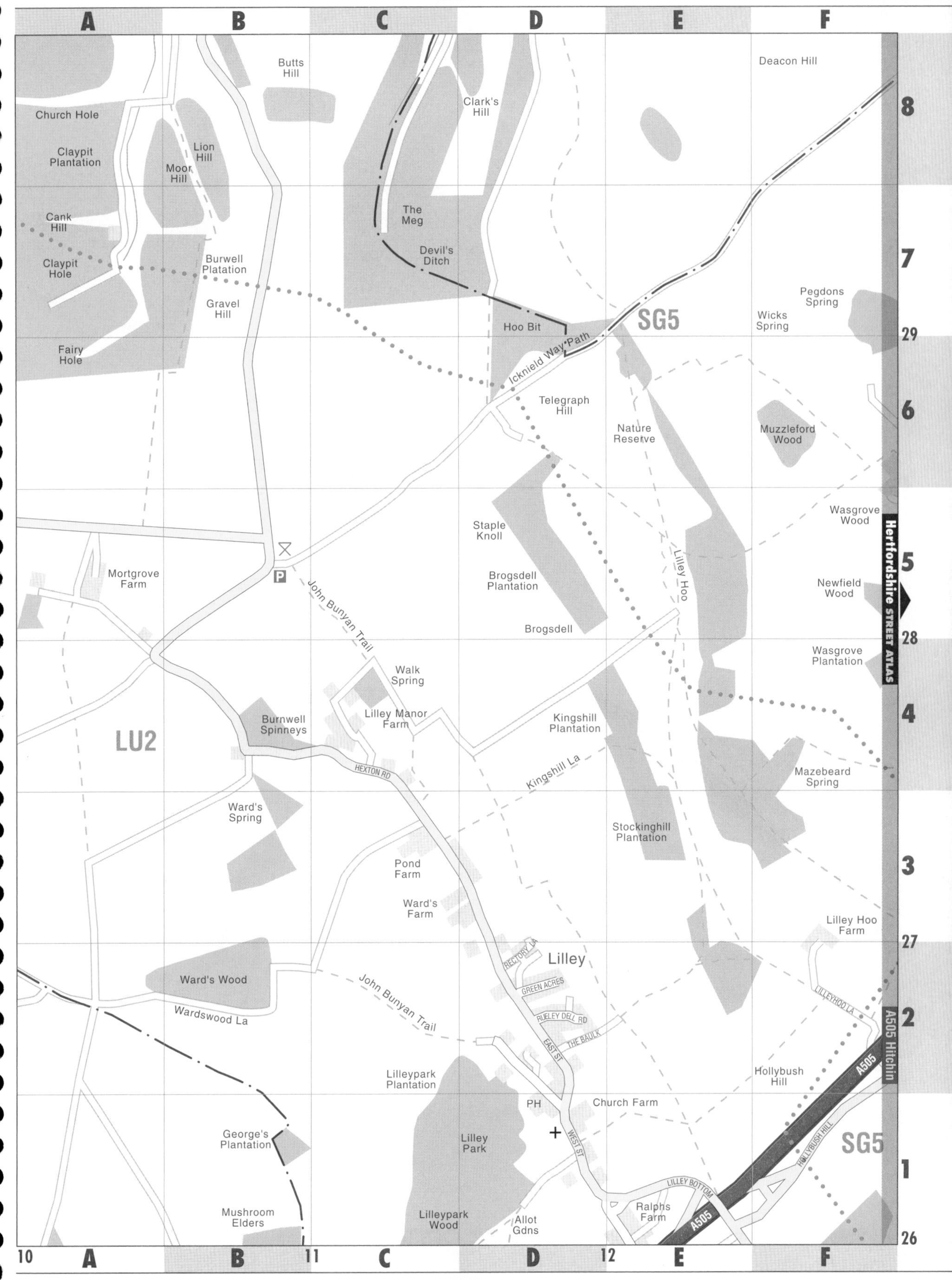

A B C D E F

8
Deacon Hill
Butts Hill
Clark's Hill
Church Hole
Lion Hill
Claypit Plantation
Moor Hill
7
The Meg
Cank Hill
Devil's Ditch
Burwell Platation
Claypit Hole
Pegdons Spring
Gravel Hill
Wicks Spring
Hoo Bit
29
Fairy Hole
SG5
Icknield Way Path
6
Telegraph Hill
Muzzleford Wood
Nature Reserve
Wasgrove Wood
Staple Knoll
5
Mortgrove Farm
Brogsdell Plantation
Newfield Wood
John Bunyan Trail
Lilley Hoo
28
Brogsdell
Wasgrove Plantation
4
Walk Spring
LU2
Burnwell Spinneys
Lilley Manor Farm
Kingshill Plantation
Mazebeard Spring
HEXTON RD
Ward's Spring
Kingshill La
3
Pond Farm
Stockinghill Plantation
Ward's Farm
27
Ward's Wood
Lilley
Lilley Hoo Farm
John Bunyan Trail
RECTORY LA
LILLEYHOO LA
Wardswood La
GREEN ACRES
2
RUELEY DELL RD
A505 Hitchin
Lilleypark Plantation
EAST ST
THE BAULK
Hollybush Hill
PH
Church Farm
George's Plantation
WEST ST
SG5
1
Lilley Park
LILLEY BOTTOM
A505
Ralphs Farm
HOLLYBUSH HILL
Mushroom Elders
Lilleypark Wood
Allot Gdns
A505
26
10 A 11 B C 12 D E F

Hertfordshire STREET ATLAS

102

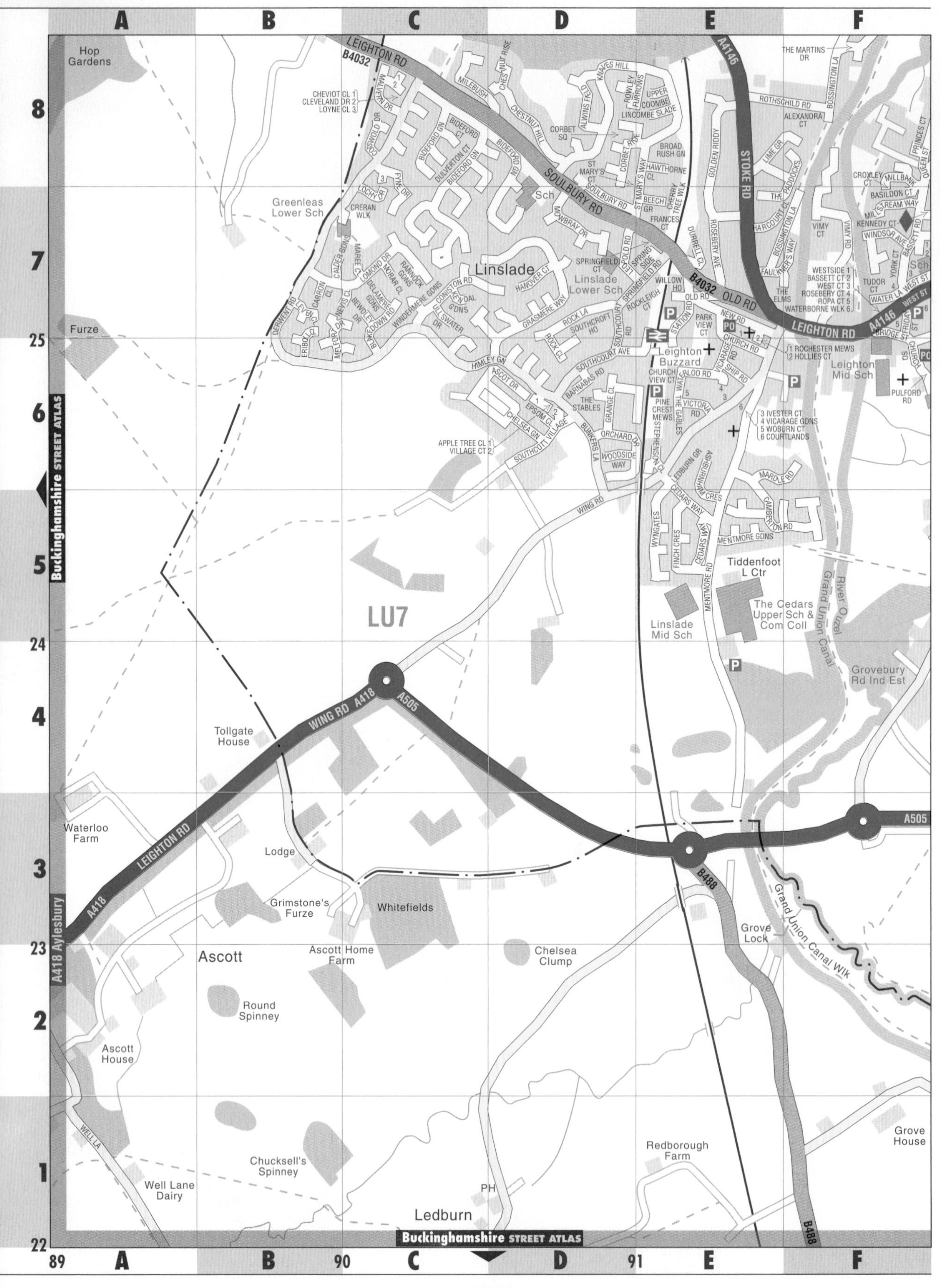
Hop Gardens
Greenleas Lower Sch
Furze
Linslade
Linslade Lower Sch
Leighton Buzzard
Leighton Mid Sch
LU7
Tiddenfoot L Ctr
The Cedars Upper Sch & Com Coll
Linslade Mid Sch
Grovebury Rd Ind Est
Tollgate House
Waterloo Farm
Lodge
Grimstone's Furze
Whitefields
Ascott
Ascott Home Farm
Chelsea Clump
Round Spinney
Ascott House
Grove Lock
Grand Union Canal
River Ouzel
Grand Union Canal Wlk
Grove House
Redborough Farm
Chucksell's Spinney
Well Lane Dairy
Ledburn
LEIGHTON RD
SOULBURY RD
WING RD
STOKE RD
OLD RD
A418
A505
A4146
B4032
B488
Buckinghamshire STREET ATLAS
A418 Aylesbury

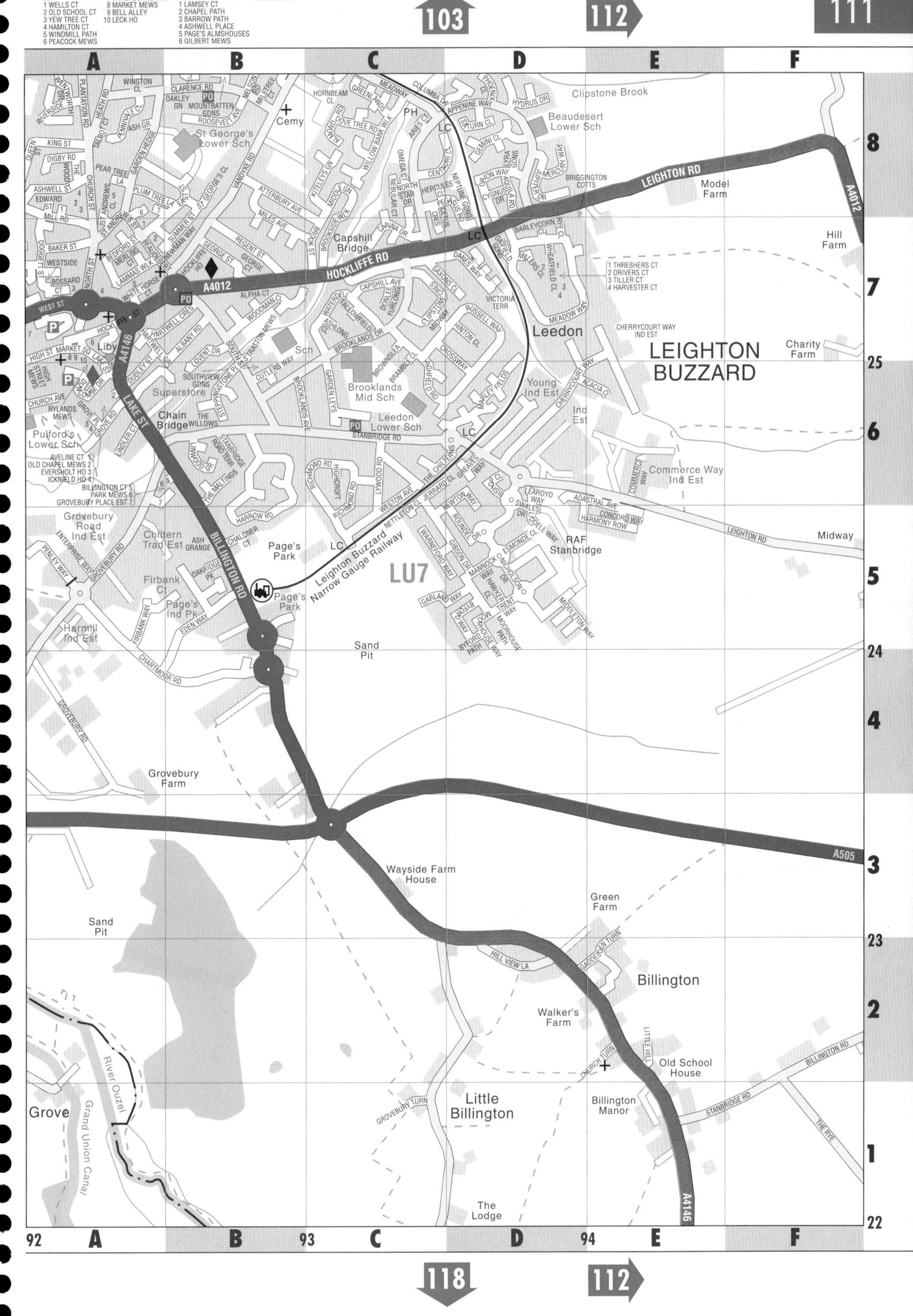

A
B
C
D
E
F
8
7
25
6
5
24
4
3
23
2
1
22
95
96
97
A4012
LEIGHTON RD
Hill Farm
Hill Farm
Eggington
Manor Farm
Eggington House
Claridge's Farm
CHURCH WLK
HIGH ST
PH
ORCHARD EST
Ppg Sta
LEIGHTON RD
MILL RD
Old Windmill
The Old Vicarage
HIGH BANKS
Stanbridge Lower Sch
KINGS WAY
Stanbridge
TILSWORTH RD
GREEN CL
ORCHARD WAY
LORDS CL
PH
BURY RISE
BLACKHILL
DUNSTABLE RD
PH
STANBRIDGE RD
Tilsworth
Tilsworth Manor
LU7
Mast
LEIGHTON RD
ST JOHNS CL
PH
BEACON VIEW
PEDDARS LA
Corner Farm
Bluegate Farm
Tullian Park
BILLINGTON RD
STATION RD
Stanbridge Wood
Greenacre Farm
Blackgrove Wood
A505
Deans Farm
STANBRIDGE CROSSING
Stanbridgeford
STANBRIDGE RD
A505
Mead Open Farm & Rare Breeds
BILLINGTON RD
Works
Sewage Works
STANBRIDGE RD
Allot Gdns
KNOLLS VIEW
Works
Lower End
LU6
THE RYE
EATON BRAY RD
CASTLE HILL RD
Manor Farm
Castle Hill

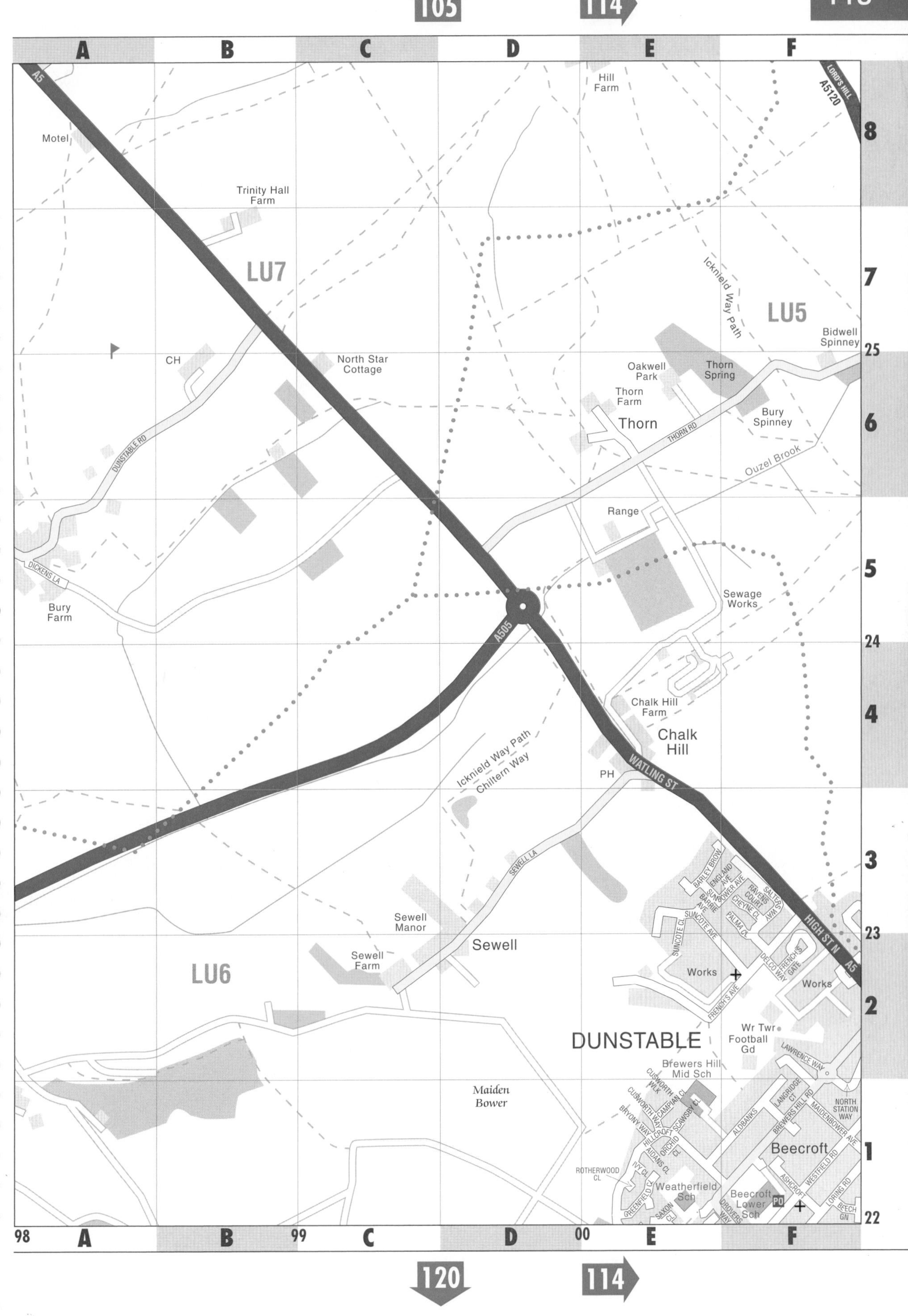

A   B   C   D   E   F

A5

LORD'S HILL
A5120

Motel

8

Hill
Farm

Trinity Hall
Farm

LU7

7

Icknield Way Path

LU5

CH

North Star
Cottage

Bidwell
Spinney

25

DUNSTABLE RD

Oakwell
Park

Thorn
Spring

Thorn
Farm

Bury
Spinney

6

Thorn

THORN RD

Ouzel Brook

DICKENS LA

Range

Sewage
Works

5

Bury
Farm

A505

24

Chalk Hill
Farm

4

Chalk
Hill

Icknield Way Path
Chiltern Way

PH

WATLING ST

SEWELL LA

3

BARLEY BROW
ENGLAND AVE
RACING
SALTISA
BADBIE
CHEYNE CL
SUNCOTE AVE
RABBURY
PALMA CL

HIGH ST N

23

Sewell
Manor

SUNCOTE CL

DALECO WAY

FRENCH'S GATE

Works

Works

A5

Sewell
Farm

Sewell

FRENCH'S AVE

2

LU6

Wr Twr
Football
Gd

DUNSTABLE

LAWRENCE WAY

Brewers Hill
Mid Sch

Maiden
Bower

CUSWORTH
WALK

CUSWORTH WAY
CAMPIAN CL
SEAWSBY CL

ALDBANKS

LANGRIDGE
CT RD
BREWERS HILL RD
MAUDSBOWER AVE

NORTH
STATION
WAY

Beecroft

1

BRYONY WAY
HILLFORD
ORCHID
ALDANS CL

GREENFIELD CL
IVY CL
SAXON CL

ROTHERWOOD
CL

Weatherfield
Sch

Beecroft
Lower
Sch

P.O.

ASHCROFT
WESTFIELD RD
LORING RD
BEECH
GN
DICKENS
WAY

22

98   A   B   99   C   D   00   E   F

A B C D E F

8
7
25
6
5
24
4
3
23
2
1
22

01 A B 02 C D 03 E F

HOUGHTON REGIS

DUNSTABLE
DVROCOBRIVIS

LU5
LU4
LU6

Grove Farm
Calcutt Lodge
The Orchard
Chiltern Way
Bidwell Farm
Bidwell
Victoria Cotts
Dunstablians Rugby Football Club
Tithe Farm
Tithe Farm Lower Sch
Thornhill Lower Sch
Osborne House
Chalton Cross Lodge
Chalton Cross Farm
Kings Houghton Mid Sch
Kingsland Com Coll
Houghton Park
Recn Gd
Sch
The Hyde
Hawthorn Park Lower Sch
Parkside
Longmeadow
Church End
Harrington Hts
Liby PO
The Green
Brookfield
Moore Cres
Houghton Hall
The Linden
Townsend Ind Est
Kensington Cl
Wheatfield Ct
Plough Ct
Liby
St Dominics Sq
Sch
Lewsey Farm
Woodside Park Ind Est
Nimbus Pk
Works
Apex Bsns Ctr
Centrus Ind Est
Woodside Ind Est
Mill Vale Mid Sch
Hadrian Lower Sch
Northfields Tech Coll
Mayer Way
Halyard High Sch
Dunstable Coll
White Lion Ret Pk (d/s)
Works
Hillcrest Sch
Ashton CE Mid Sch
Superstore
Liby
Dukeminster Trad Est
Superstore
The Maltings
TA Ctr
HPO

LUTON RD
BEDFORD RD
HIGH ST
HOUGHTON RD
HIGH ST N
A5120
A5
A505
M1
LUTON RD B579

SHORT PATH 1
BORDERS WAY 2
THE CLOISTERS 3
GRASMERE WLK 4
GABLE WAY 5
WILLOW WAY 6
ST DAVID'S WAY 7

1 THERFIELD WLK
2 ABBEY WLK
3 ASHWELL WLK
4 ROSE WLK
5 NEPTUNE CL
6 NEPTUNE SQ
7 LEASIDE

1 GAINSBOROUGH DR
2 WINDSOR PL

1 THE TOWNSEND CTR
2 CIRCLE BSNS CTR
3 ARIANNE BSNS CTR
4 IVINGHOE BSNS CTR

1 HIGH ST N
2 WATLING CT
3 HOUGHTON PAR

FREEMANS CL 1
TOWNSEND TERR 2

A1
1 THE PARADE
2 CROSS ST N
3 JUBILEE CT
4 STEWART CLARK CT
5 WATERLOW CHAPEL
6 LYNWOOD LODGE
7 BROOK CL

B4
1 WATLING CT
2 ROMAN CT

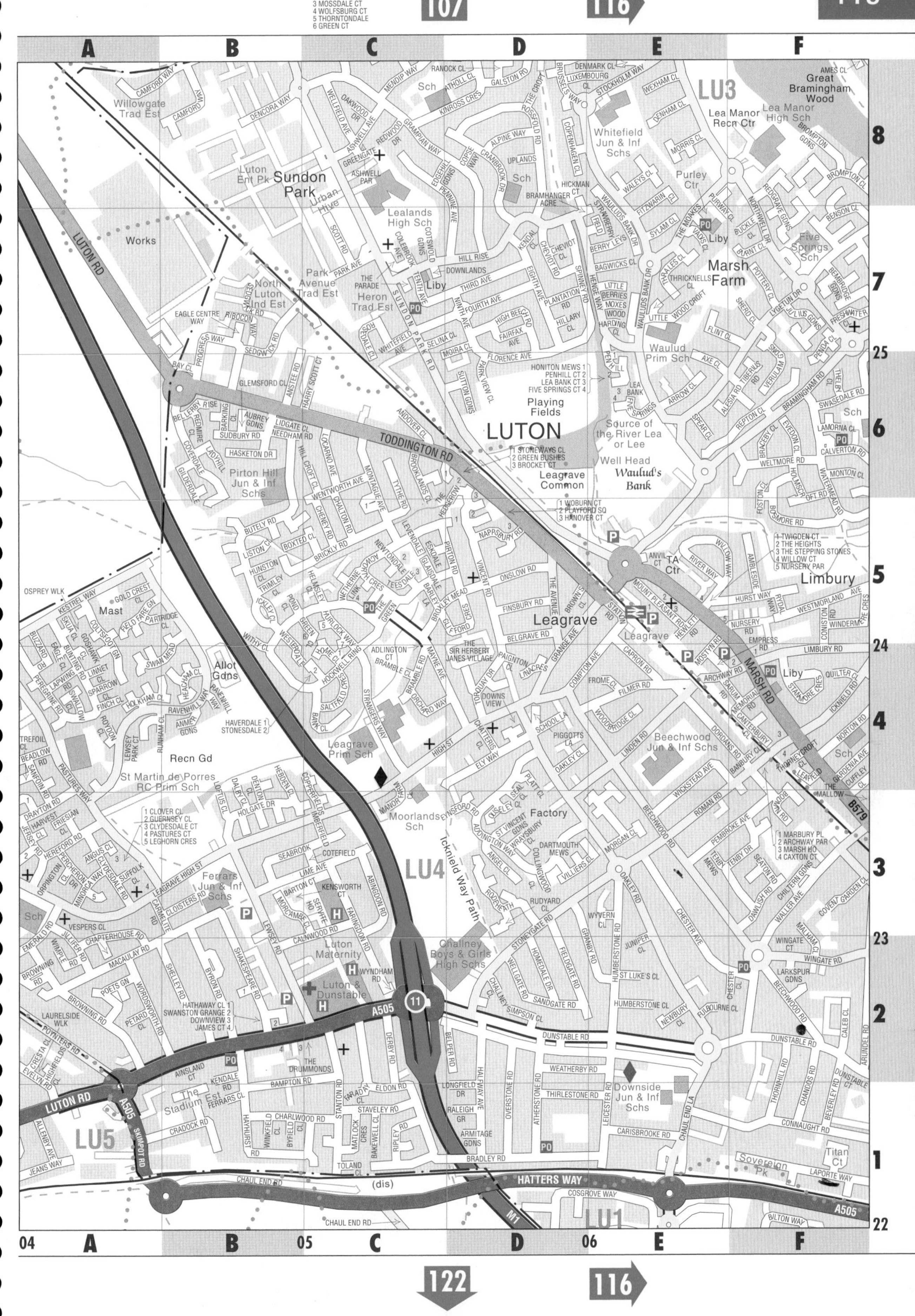
C5
1 CHAWORTH GN
2 ACWORTH CT
3 MOSSDALE CT
4 WOLFSBURG CT
5 THORNTONDALE
6 GREEN CT
7 WHARFDALE
107
116
A
B
C
D
E
F
8
7
25
6
5
24
4
3
23
2
1
22
04
05
06
122
116
Willowgate Trad Est
CAMFORD WAY
DENCORA WAY
MENDIP WAY
RANOCK CL
ATHOLL CL
GALSTON RD
KINROSS CRES
THE CROFT
ROSSFOLD RD
DENMARK CL
LUXEMBOURG CL
BRUSSELS WAY
STOCKHOLM WAY
WEXHAM CL
LU3
Great Bramingham Wood
AMES CL
Lea Manor Recn Ctr
Lea Manor High Sch
BROMPTON GDNS
Whitefield Jun & Inf Schs
COPENHAGEN CL
DENHAM CL
MORRIS CL
Purley Ctr
BROMPTON CL
Luton Ent Pk
Sundon Park
Urban Hive
Lealands High Sch
ASHWELL PAR
GREENGATE
GRAMPIAN WAY
ALPINE WAY
UPLANDS
CORSE WAY
CRANBROOK DR
Sch
HICKMAN CT
BRAMHANGER ACRE
WALEYS CL
FITZWARIN CL
SYLAM CL
THE MOXES
PURWAY CL
NORTHWELL DR
REDGRAVE GDNS
BENSON CL
Works
LUTON RD
SCOTT RD
PARK AVE
COLEBROOK AVE
COTSWOLD GDNS
HILL RISE
DOWNLANDS
Liby
Marsh Farm
Five Springs Sch
North Luton Ind Est
Park Avenue Trad Est
THE PARADE
Heron Trad Est
SUNDON PARK RD
THIRD AVE
FOURTH AVE
EIGHTH AVE
KENDAL CT
CHEVIOT CL
CHEVIOT RD
PLANTATION RD
HILLARY CL
SPINNEY RD
HENGE WAY
BERRY LEYS
BAGWICKS CL
LITTLE BERRIES
MOXES WOOD
HARDING CL
WAULUDS BANK DR
THRICKNELLS CL
LITTLE WOOD CROFT
FLINT CL
LYGETUN DR
JULIUS GDNS
FRESHWATER CL
EAGLE CENTRE WAY
RIBOCON WAY
PROGRESS WAY
SEDGWICK RD
WHITEFIELD AVE
ROSEDALE CL
SELINA CL
MOIRA CL
HIGH BEECH RD
FAIRFAX AVE
FLORENCE AVE
Waulud Prim Sch
AXE CL
VERULAM GDNS
PENDA CL
BAY CL
GLEMSFORD CL
ANSTEE RD
HARRY SCOTT CT
SUTTON GDNS
PARK VIEW CL
HONITON MEWS 1
PENHILL CT 2
LEA BANK CT 3
FIVE SPRINGS CT 4
Playing Fields
PEN HILL
LEA BANK
FIVE SPRINGS
ARROW CL
ALESIA RD
TIBERIUS SQ
BRAMINGHAM RD
SWASEDALE RD
THELBY CL
BELLERBY RISE
REDMIRE CL
BARKING CL
AUBREY GDNS
SUDBURY RD
LIDGATE CL
NEEDHAM RD
ANDOVER CL
TODDINGTON RD
LUTON
Source of the River Lea or Lee
SPEAR CL
REPTON CL
BRACEBY CL
EVEDON CL
LAMORNA CL
CALVERTON RD
COVERDALE
LADYHILL
HASKETON DR
Pirton Hill Jun & Inf Schs
GILDERDALE
HILL CROFT CL
LOCARNO AVE
MONTAGUE AVE
BROOKLANDS CL
1 STONEWAYS CL
2 GREEN BUSHES
3 BROCKET CT
Well Head
Waulud's Bank
Leagrave Common
WELTMORE RD
HOLMSCROFT RD
WATERMEAD RD
MONTON CL
WENTWORTH AVE
CHALTON RD
TYTHE RD
THE HEDGEROW
1 WOBURN CT
2 PLAYFORD SQ
3 HANOVER CT
FOSTON CL
BOSMORE RD
BUTELY RD
LISTON CL
BOXTED CL
CHENEY RD
BRICKLY RD
NEWTONDALE
LEVENDALE
ESKDALE
GLAISDALE
PIRTON RD
NAPPSBURY RD
1 TWIGDEN CT
2 THE HEIGHTS
3 THE STEPPING STONES
4 WILLOW CT
5 NURSERY PAR
AMBLESIDE
WILLOW WAY
RIVER WAY
ANVIL CT
TA Ctr
Limbury
HUNSTON CL
TRIMLEY CL
ICKLEY CL
HELMSLEY CL
POND CL
WETHERNE LINK
ROUNDWOOD
ACWORTH CRES
LEESDALE
BARLEY LA
BROXLEY MEAD
VINCENT RD
ONSLOW RD
THE AVENUE
BROWN'S CL
STATION RD
MOUNT PLEASANT RD
HURST WAY
RYDAL WAY
WESTMORLAND AVE
OSPREY WLK
KESTREL WAY
GOLD CREST CL
Mast
FIELD FARE GN
PARTRIDGE CL
COLTSFOOT GN
HURLOCK WAY
THE GREEN
CLIFFORD CRES
FINSBURY RD
Leagrave
HEWLETT RD
NURSERY CL
CONISTON RD
WINDERMERE CRES
BUZZARD RD
EAGLE CL
BUNTING RD
GOSHAWK CL
SWAN MEAD
WITHY CL
WESTERDALE
HOME CL
HOCKWELL RING
ADLINGTON CT
BRAMBLE CL
MAYNE AVE
THE SIR HERBERT JANES VILLAGE
BELGRAVE RD
PAIGNTON CL
LINACRES
GRANGE AVE
COMPTON AVE
CAPRON RD
MOSTYN RD
EMPRESS RD
LIMBURY RD
MARSH RD
LAPWING RD
LINNET CL
SPARROW CL
FINCH CL
HEACHAM CL
Allot Gdns
HOLKHAM CL
RAVENHILL WAY
RAVENHILL
ANMER GDNS
SALTFIELD CRES
BRAMBLE RD
ORCHARD WAY
TORQUAY DR
DOWNS VIEW
FROME CL
FILMER RD
ARCHWAY RD
SARUM RD
QUILTER CL
STANMORE CRES
ICKNIELD RD
PEREGRINE RD
SWALLOW CL
ROYDON CL
LEWSEY PARK CT
RUNHAM CL
HAVERDALE 1
STONESDALE 2
BANK CL
STRANGERS WAY
CHATTERIS CL
SCHOOL LA
WOODBRIDGE CL
Beechwood Jun & Inf Schs
DORDANS RD
MEMORIAL RD
CANTERBURY
NORTON RD
TREFOIL CL
BEADLOW RD
SAINFOIN RD
PASTURES WAY
Recn Gd
Leagrave Prim Sch
HIGH ST
ELY WAY
PIGGOTTS LA
OAKLEY CL
LINDEN RD
WICKSTEAD AVE
BANBURY CL
THORNEYCROFT
Sch
GARDENIA AVE
CUFFLEY CT
LEAFIELD
THE MALLOW
DRAYTON RD
HARVEST RD
FRIESIAN CL
St Martin de Porres RC Prim Sch
LOFTUS CL
DALBY CL
DENTON CL
HEBDEN CL
COPPERFIELDS
TIMBERFIELD
HOLGATE DR
MANOR FARM CL
Moorlands Sch
SEAL CL
PLATT CL
OUSELEY CL
Factory
ROMAN RD
BEECHWOOD RD
BOURNE RD
B579
JERSEY RD
HEREFORD RD
1 CLOVER CL
2 GUERNSEY CL
3 CLYDESDALE CT
4 PASTURES CT
5 LEGHORN CRES
ANGUS CL
PERCHERON DR
ORPINGTON CL
MINORCA WAY
SUFFOLK CL
CLYDESDALE RD
SEABROOK
COTEFIELD
LIME AVE
KENSWORTH CT
ABINGDON RD
LU4
Icknield Way Path
ADDINGTON WAY
ST VINCENT GDNS
WRAYSBURY CL
ANGEL CL
DARTMOUTH MEWS
COLLINGWOOD CL
VILLIERS CL
MORGAN CL
PEMBROKE AVE
TENBY MEWS
TENBY DR
SEATON RD
DAWLISH RD
1 MARBURY PL
2 ARCHWAY PAR
3 MARSH HO
4 CAXTON CT
CHILTERN GDNS
WALLER AVE
COVENT GARDEN CL
Sch
Ferrars Jun & Inf Schs
LEAGRAVE HIGH ST
CLOISTERS RD
CARMELITE RD
BARTON CT
SERPHI HO
MORCAMBE CL
FARINGDON RD
ROOKHEATH
RUDYARD CL
WYVERN CL
OAKLEY RD
CHESTER AVE
VESPERS CL
EMERALD RD
JILLIFER RD
WIMPLE RD
CHAPTERHOUSE RD
MACAULAY RD
SHELLEY RD
BYRON RD
SHAKESPEARE RD
LEWSEY RD
CALNWOOD RD
Luton Maternity
Challney Boys & Girls High Schs
STONEYGATE RD
HOMEDALE DR
FIELDGATE RD
GRANBY RD
HUMBERSTONE RD
JUNIPER CL
WINGATE CT
MALHAM CL
WINGATE RD
BROWNING CL
POETS GN
WORDSWORTH RD
WYNDHAM RD
Luton & Dunstable
11
WELLGATE RD
SANDGATE RD
ST LUKE'S CL
CHESTER CL
LARKSPUR GDNS
BEECHWOOD RD
BROWNING RD
PETARD CL
HATHAWAY CL 1
SWANSTON GRANGE 2
DOWNVIEW 3
JAMES CT 4
A505
CHALLNEY GDNS
SIMPSON CL
HUMBERSTONE CL
FULBOURNE CL
NEWBURY CL
LAURELSIDE WLK
POYNTERS RD
THE DRUMMONDS
DERBY RD
BELPER RD
DUNSTABLE RD
CALEB CL
ARUNDEL RD
CRESTA CL
EVELYN RD
HIGHFIELDS
AINSLAND CT
KENDALE RD
BAMPTON RD
FARADAY CL
ELDON RD
LONGFIELD DR
HALFWAY AVE
OVERSTONE RD
ATHERSTONE RD
WEATHERBY RD
THIRLESTONE RD
Downside Jun & Inf Schs
LEICESTER RD
THORNHILL RD
CHANDOS RD
BEVERLEY RD
DUNSTABLE CT
LUTON RD
The Stadium Est
FERRARS CL
CRADOCK RD
HAYHURST RD
WINKFIELD CL
CHARLWOOD RD
BYFIELD CL
STANTON RD
MATLOCK CRES
BAKEWELL CL
STAVELEY RD
RIPLEY RD
RALEIGH GR
ARMITAGE GDNS
CARISBROOKE RD
CHAUL END LA
CONNAUGHT RD
SKIMPOT RD
LU5
ALLENBY AVE
JEANS WAY
TOLAND CL
BRADLEY RD
Titan Ct
Sovereign Pk
LAPORTE WAY
CHAUL END RD
(dis)
HATTERS WAY
COSGROVE WAY
M1
LU1
A505
BILTON WAY
CHAUL END RD

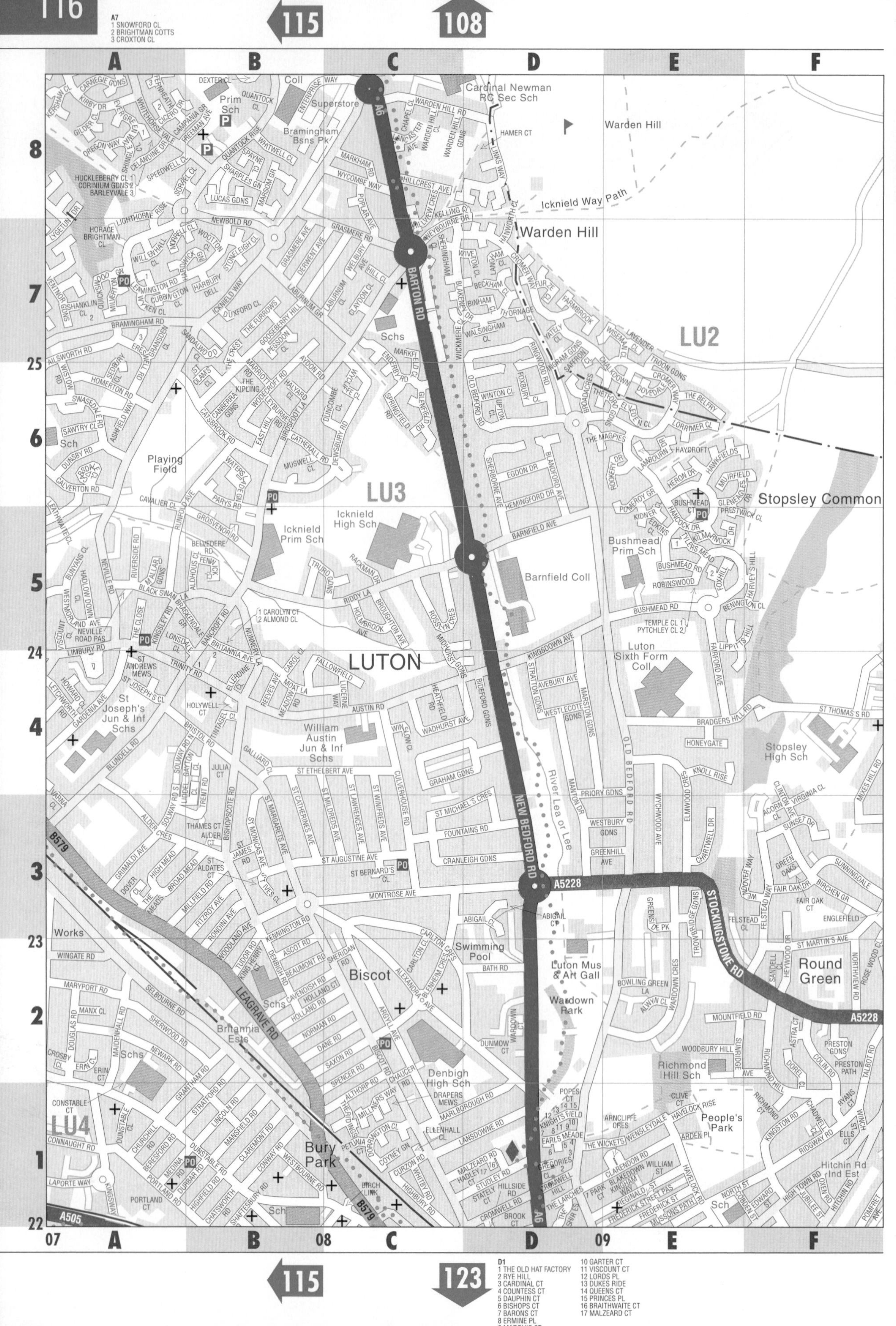
A7
1 SNOWFORD CL
2 BRIGHTMAN COTTS
3 CROXTON CL
115
108
A
B
C
D
E
F
8
7
25
6
5
24
4
3
23
2
1
22
07
08
09
Coll
Superstore
Bramingham Bsns Pk
Prim Sch
Cardinal Newman RC Sec Sch
Warden Hill
Icknield Way Path
Warden Hill
HUCKLEBERRY CL 1
CORINIUM GDNS 2
BARLEYVALE 3
HORACE BRIGHTMAN CL
BARTON RD
A6
Schs
LU2
LU3
Icknield High Sch
Icknield Prim Sch
Playing Field
Sch
Stopsley Common
Bushmead Prim Sch
Barnfield Coll
1 CAROLYN CT
2 ALMOND CL
TEMPLE CL 1
PYTCHLEY CL 2
LUTON
Luton Sixth Form Coll
St Joseph's Jun & Inf Schs
William Austin Jun & Inf Schs
Stopsley High Sch
NEW BEDFORD RD
River Lea or Lee
OLD BEDFORD RD
B579
A5228
STOCKINGSTONE RD
Works
Swimming Pool
Luton Mus & Art Gall
Wardown Park
Biscot
Round Green
LEAGRAVE RD
Britannia Ests
Schs
Denbigh High Sch
Richmond Hill Sch
People's Park
LU4
Bury Park
Hitchin Rd Ind Est
A505
115
123
D1
1 THE OLD HAT FACTORY
2 RYE HILL
3 CARDINAL CT
4 COUNTESS CT
5 DAUPHIN CT
6 BISHOPS CT
7 BARONS CT
8 ERMINE PL
9 MARQUIS CT
10 GARTER CT
11 VISCOUNT CT
12 LORDS PL
13 DUKES RIDE
14 QUEENS CT
15 PRINCES PL
16 BRAITHWAITE CT
17 MALZEARD CT

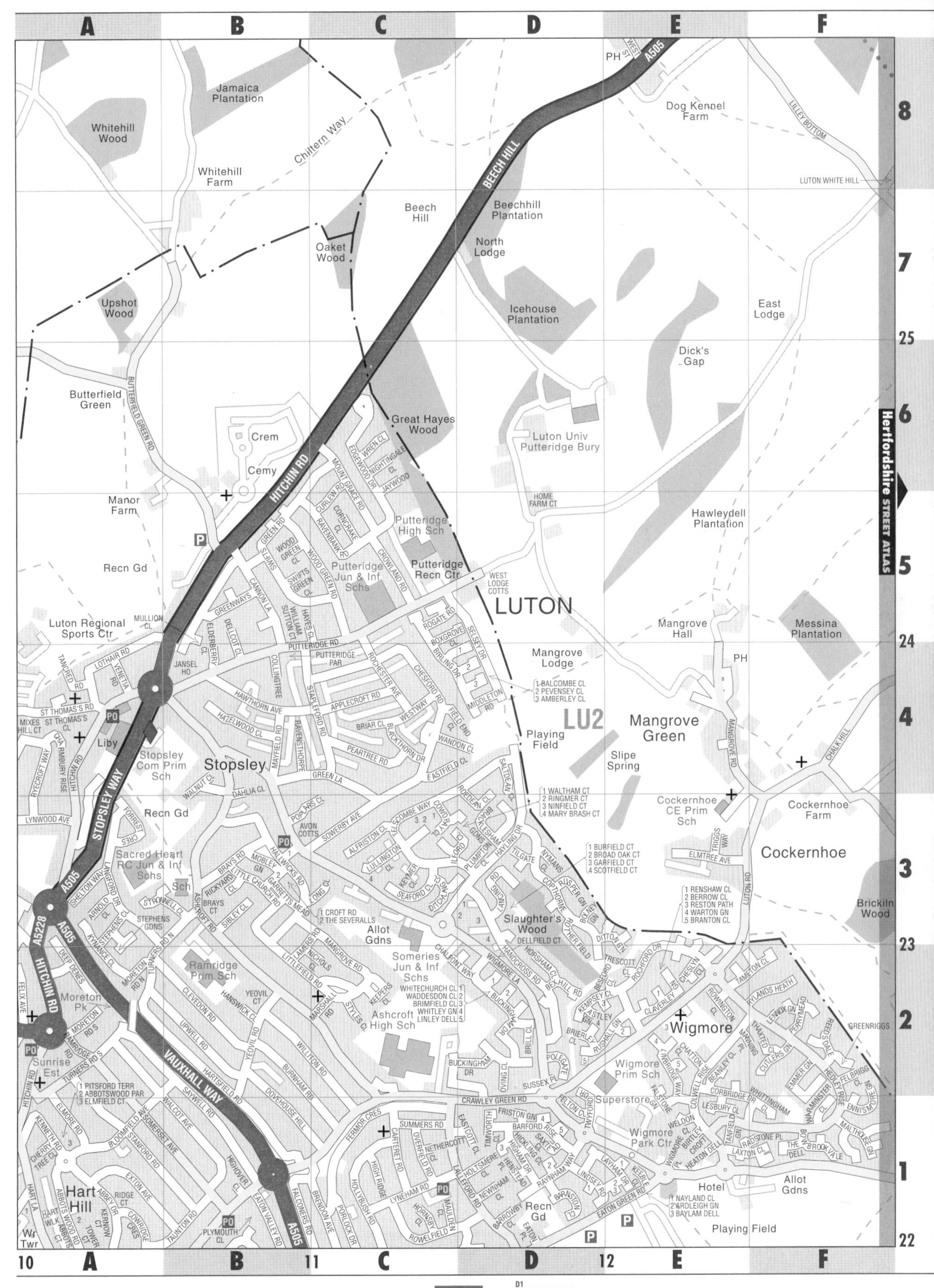

D1
1 CHELSWORTH CL
2 MUTFORD CROFT
3 MELFORD CL
4 PINFORD DELL
5 ALDERTON CL

111

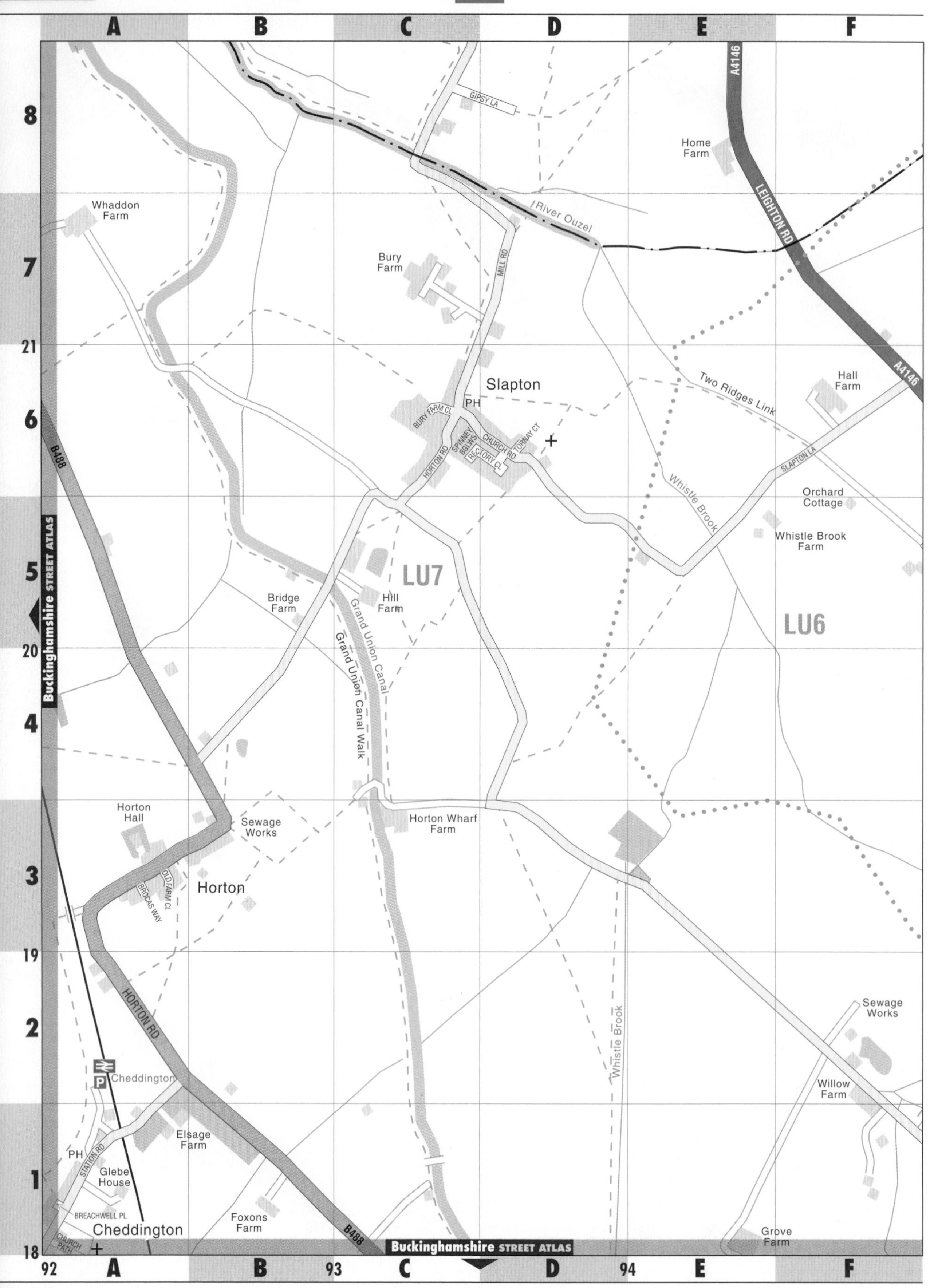
A
B
C
D
E
F
8
7
21
6
5
20
4
3
19
2
1
18
92
93
94
GIPSY LA
A4146
Home Farm
Whaddon Farm
River Ouzel
LEIGHTON RD
Bury Farm
MILL RD
Slapton
PH
Two Ridges Link
Hall Farm
BURY FARM CL
SPINNEY BGLWS
CHURCH RD
TORNAY CT
RECTORY CL
HORTON RD
SLAPTON LA
Whistle Brook
Orchard Cottage
Whistle Brook Farm
B488
LU7
LU6
Bridge Farm
Hill Farm
Grand Union Canal
Grand Union Canal Walk
Buckinghamshire STREET ATLAS
Horton Hall
Sewage Works
Horton Wharf Farm
OLDFARM CL
BROCAS WAY
Horton
HORTON RD
Cheddington
Elsage Farm
Sewage Works
Willow Farm
PH
STATION RD
Glebe House
BREACHWELL PL
Cheddington
CHURCH PATH
Foxons Farm
Grove Farm

Buckinghamshire STREET ATLAS

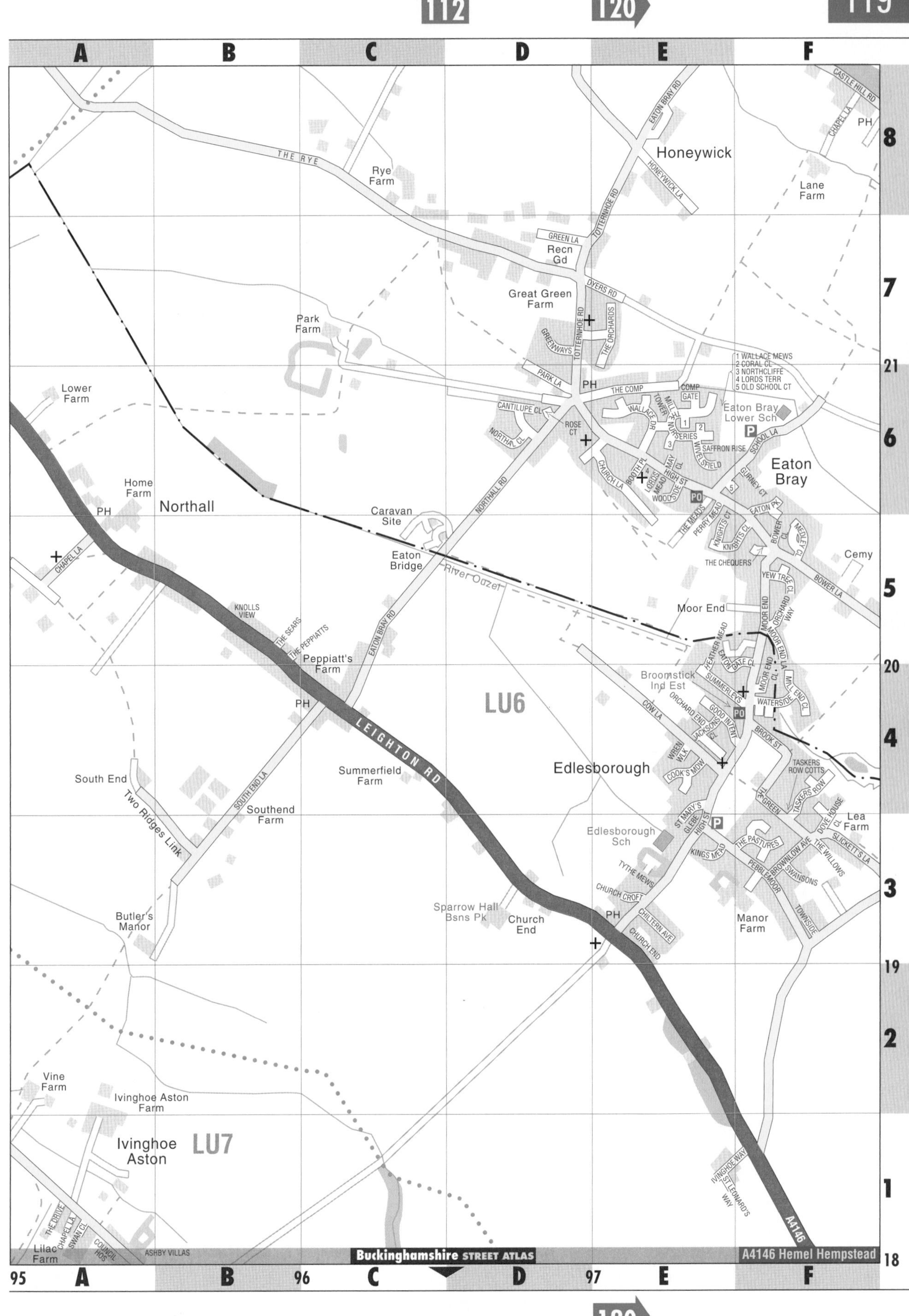
A
B
C
D
E
F
8
7
21
6
5
20
4
3
19
2
1
18
THE RYE
Rye Farm
Honeywick
EATON BRAY RD
HONEYWICK LA
TOTTERNHOE RD
CASTLE HILL RD
CHAPEL LA
PH
Lane Farm
GREEN LA
Recn Gd
DYERS RD
Great Green Farm
Park Farm
GREENWAYS
THE ORCHARDS
1 WALLACE MEWS
2 CORAL CL
3 NORTHCLIFFE
4 LORDS TERR
5 OLD SCHOOL CT
PARK LA
THE COMP
COMP GATE
Eaton Bray Lower Sch
CANTILUPE CL
ROSE CT
WALLACE DR
TOWER CL
MILL
NURSERIES
SAFFRON RISE
WIVELSFIELD
SCHOOL LA
Lower Farm
NORTHALL CL
CHURCH LA
BOTH PL
LORDS MEAD
MAY CL
HIGH ST
WOODSIDE
Eaton Bray
GURNEY CT
PO
Home Farm
PH
Northall
NORTHALL RD
Caravan Site
THE MEADS
PERRY MEAD
KNIGHTS CT
KNIGHTS CL
EATON PK
BOWER CL
MEDLEY CL
CHAPEL LA
Eaton Bridge
THE CHEQUERS
Cemy
River Ouzel
YEW TREE CL
BOWER LA
KNOLLS VIEW
THE SEARS
THE PEPPIATTS
Moor End
MOOR END
ORCHARD WAY
HEATHER MEAD
EATON GATE CL
EATON BRAY RD
Peppiatt's Farm
Broomstick Ind Est
MOOR END LA
MOOR END CL
MILL END CL
LU6
SUMMERLEYS
ORCHARD END
WATERSIDE
PH
COW LA
GOOD INTENT
JACKSONS CL
PO
BROOK ST
LEIGHTON RD
WREN WLK
COOK'S MDW
Edlesborough
TASKERS ROW COTTS
TASKERS ROW
South End
Summerfield Farm
SOUTH END LA
Two Ridges Link
Southend Farm
THE GREEN
DOVE HOUSE CL
Lea Farm
ST MARY'S GLEBE
HIGH ST
P
Edlesborough Sch
THE PASTURES
BROWNLOW AVE
THE WILLOWS
SLICKETT'S LA
KINGS MEAD
TYTHE MEWS
PEBBLEMOOR
SWANSONS
CHURCH CROFT
Butler's Manor
Sparrow Hall Bsns Pk
Church End
PH
CHILTERN AVE
CHURCH END
Manor Farm
TOWNSIDE
Vine Farm
Ivinghoe Aston Farm
Ivinghoe Aston
LU7
IVINGHOE WAY
ST LEONARD'S WAY
A4146
THE DRIVE
CHAPEL LA
SWAN CL
COUNCIL HOS
ASHBY VILLAS
Lilac Farm

119
113

A
B
C
D
E
F
8
7
21
6
5
20
4
3
19
2
1
18
98
99
00
Middle End
Totternhoe Knolls Nature Reserve
BROOKFIELD PK CVN PK
BROWNLOW RISE
CASTLE CL
Poplar Farm
CASTLE HILL RD
PARK AVE
LANCOTBURY CL
Recn Gd
Totternhoe
CHURCH END FARM
CHURCH GN
FURLONG LA
Allot Gdns
Church End
Totternhoe Lower Sch
PH
BRIGHTWELL AVE
ELLESMERE CL
The Vicarage
THE RIDE
CHURCH RD
WELL HEAD RD
DUNSTABLE RD
LU6
SAXON CL 1
REDFIELD CL 2
NORMAN WAY
WEATHERBY
GREEN LA
BUNHILL CL
COCKFIELD CL
AYNSCOMBE CL
LANSING RD
CROFT GN
PASCOMB RD
BEECROFT WAY
DROVERS WAY
WORTHINGTON RD
HAMBLING PL
FRANKLIN RD
Lancot Lower Sch
LANCOT PL
SPINNEY CRES
BADGERS GATE
LANCOT AVE
LANCOT DR
OAKWELL CL
BEECHWOOD CT
MEADWAY
TOTTERNHOE RD
B489
WESTDOWN GDNS
MEADWAY CT
HARVEY RD
GARDNER'S CL
MARINA DR
BEACON AVE
COOMBE DR
MELTON CT
B4541
WHIPSNADE RD
PIPERS CROFT
ROYCE CL
THE AVENUE
TRING RD
SPOONDELL
Five Knolls
Pillow Mounds
California
Pascomb Pit
Ware Hill Cottage
DUNSTABLE RD
Doolittle Mill (disused)
BOTTOM DR
MANTON RD
ICKNIELD WAY
SPRINGFIELD RD
Well Head
London Gliding Club
CH
BOWER LA
Rosebury Farm
Wellhead Farm
Visitor Ctr
ROBERTSON CNR
Bellows Mill
TRING RD
Shepherds Farm
HARLING RD
Norfolk House Farm
ICKNIELD WAY FARM COTTS
Patrick's Cottage
Harling House
SLICKETT'S LA
Dunstable Downs Ctry Pk
B4541
Icknield Way Farm
PH
Icknield Way Path
Edlesborough Mills (disused)
Edlesborough Hill
B4506
Mast
Sallowspring Wood
B4540
SALLOWSPRINGS
Chute Farm
Valance-end Farm
DAGNALL RD
ICKNIELD WAY
Tree Cathedral
B4506
Whipsnade
B4540
B489
Willow Farm

119
126

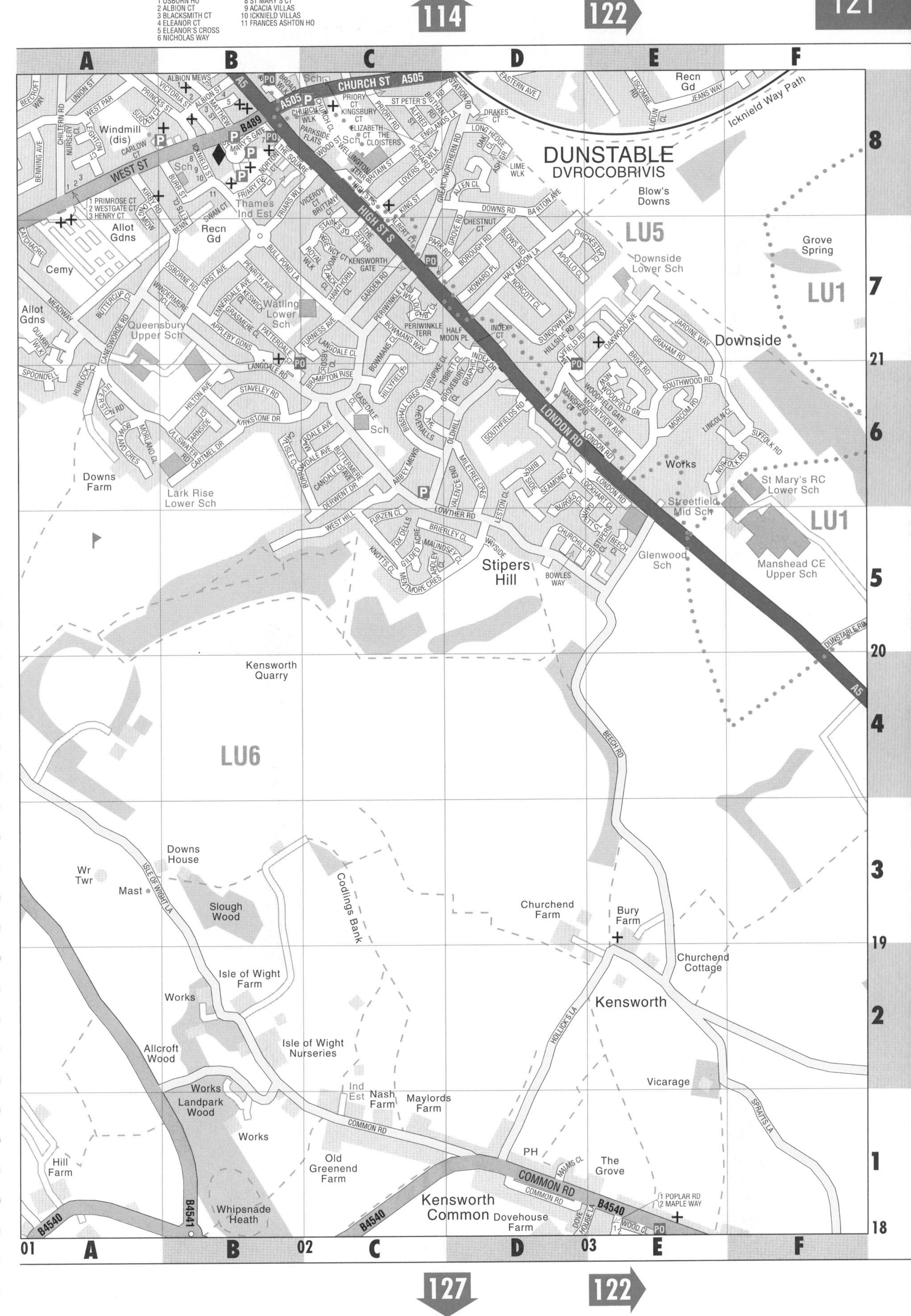
B8
1 OSBORN HO
2 ALBION CT
3 BLACKSMITH CT
4 ELEANOR CT
5 ELEANOR'S CROSS
6 NICHOLAS WAY
7 ASHTON SQ
8 ST MARY'S CT
9 ACACIA VILLAS
10 ICKNIELD VILLAS
11 FRANCES ASHTON HO
114
122
A
B
C
D
E
F
8
7
21
6
5
20
4
3
19
2
1
18
01
02
03
DUNSTABLE
DVROCOBRIVIS
Blow's Downs
LU5
LU1
LU6
Icknield Way Path
Recn Gd
Grove Spring
Downside
Downside Lower Sch
Windmill (dis)
Allot Gdns
Cemy
Thames Ind Est
Watling Lower Sch
Queensbury Upper Sch
Lark Rise Lower Sch
Downs Farm
Works
St Mary's RC Lower Sch
Streetfield Mid Sch
Glenwood Sch
Manshead CE Upper Sch
Stipers Hill
Kensworth Quarry
CHURCH ST
WEST ST
HIGH ST S
LONDON RD
A5
A505
B489
DUNSTABLE RD
BEECH RD
Downs House
Wr Twr
Mast
Slough Wood
Codlings Bank
Churchend Farm
Bury Farm
Churchend Cottage
Kensworth
Isle of Wight Farm
Isle of Wight Nurseries
Allcroft Wood
Landpark Wood
Works
Ind Est
Nash Farm
Maylords Farm
Vicarage
Old Greenend Farm
Hill Farm
Whipsnade Heath
Kensworth Common
Dovehouse Farm
PH
The Grove
COMMON RD
B4540
B4541
1 POPLAR RD
2 MAPLE WAY
HOLLICK'S LA
SPRATTS LA
ISLE OF WIGHT LA
127
122

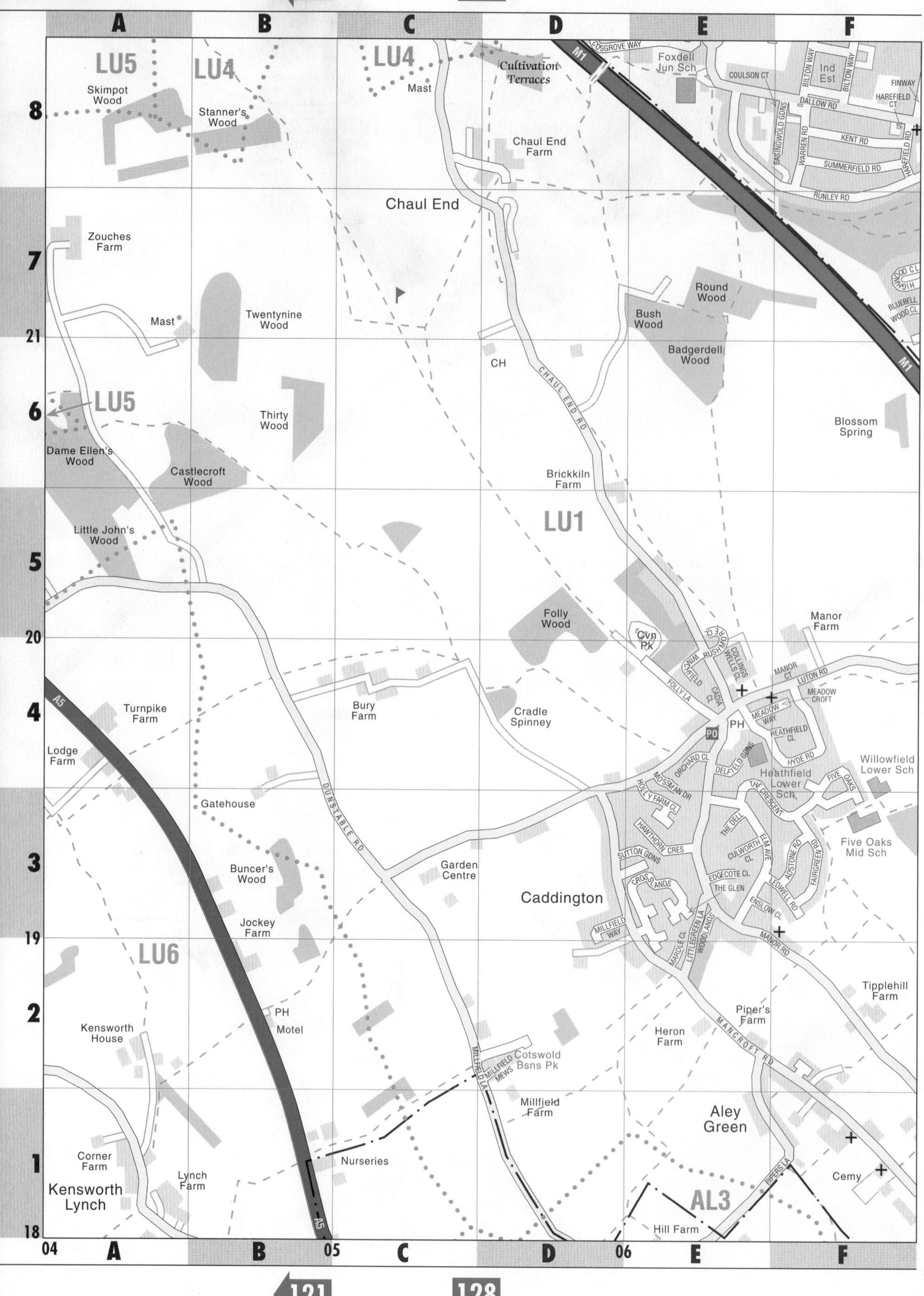

A B C D E F

8 LU5 Skimpot Wood | LU4 Stanner's Wood | LU4 Mast | Cultivation Terraces | M1 Losgrove Way | Foxdell Jun Sch | Ind Est COULSON CT | BILTON WAY BILTON WAY FINWAY HAREFIELD CT

DALLOW RD
KENT RD
SUMMERFIELD RD
RUNLEY RD

Chaul End Farm

Chaul End

7 Zouches Farm

Round Wood

Bush Wood

WOOD CL HIGH

BLUEBELL WOOD CL

21 Mast | Twentynine Wood

CH

Badgerdell Wood

M1

6 LU5 | Thirty Wood

Brickkiln Farm

Blossom Spring

Dame Ellen's Wood

Castlecroft Wood

LU1

CHAUL END RD

5 Little John's Wood

Manor Farm

Folly Wood

Cvn Pk

COLLINS NURS WELLS CL RUSHMEAD

20 Bury Farm

MANOR CT | Luton Rd
MEADOW CROFT

FOLLY LA | CADBA

4 A5 Turnpike Farm

Cradle Spinney

MEADOW WAY | HEATHFIELD CL | HYDE RD

PO PH

Lodge Farm

Gatehouse

ORCHARD CL | DELFIELD GDNS | Heathfield Lower Sch | FIVE OAKS

MOSSMAN DR | HOLLY FARM CL | THE DELL | THE CRESCENT | ELM AVE | KEYSTONE RD | FAIRGREEN

Willowfield Lower Sch

Five Oaks Mid Sch

3 Buncer's Wood

Garden Centre

Caddington

HAWTHORN CRES | SUTTON GDNS | CROSSLANDS | CULWORTH CL | EDGECOTE CL | LEDWELL RD | THE GLEN | ENSLOW CL

19 Jockey Farm

MILLFIELD WAY | MARDLE CL | LITTLEGREEN LA | WOODLANDS | MANOR RD

Tipplehill Farm

2 LU6 | Kensworth House | PH Motel

Heron Farm

Piper's Farm

MANCROFT RD

1 Corner Farm | Lynch Farm | Nurseries | Cotswold Bsns Pk | Millfield Mews | Millfield Farm | Aley Green | Cemy

MILLFIELD LA

Kensworth Lynch

AL3

PIPERS LA

Hill Farm

18

04 A B 05 C D 06 E F

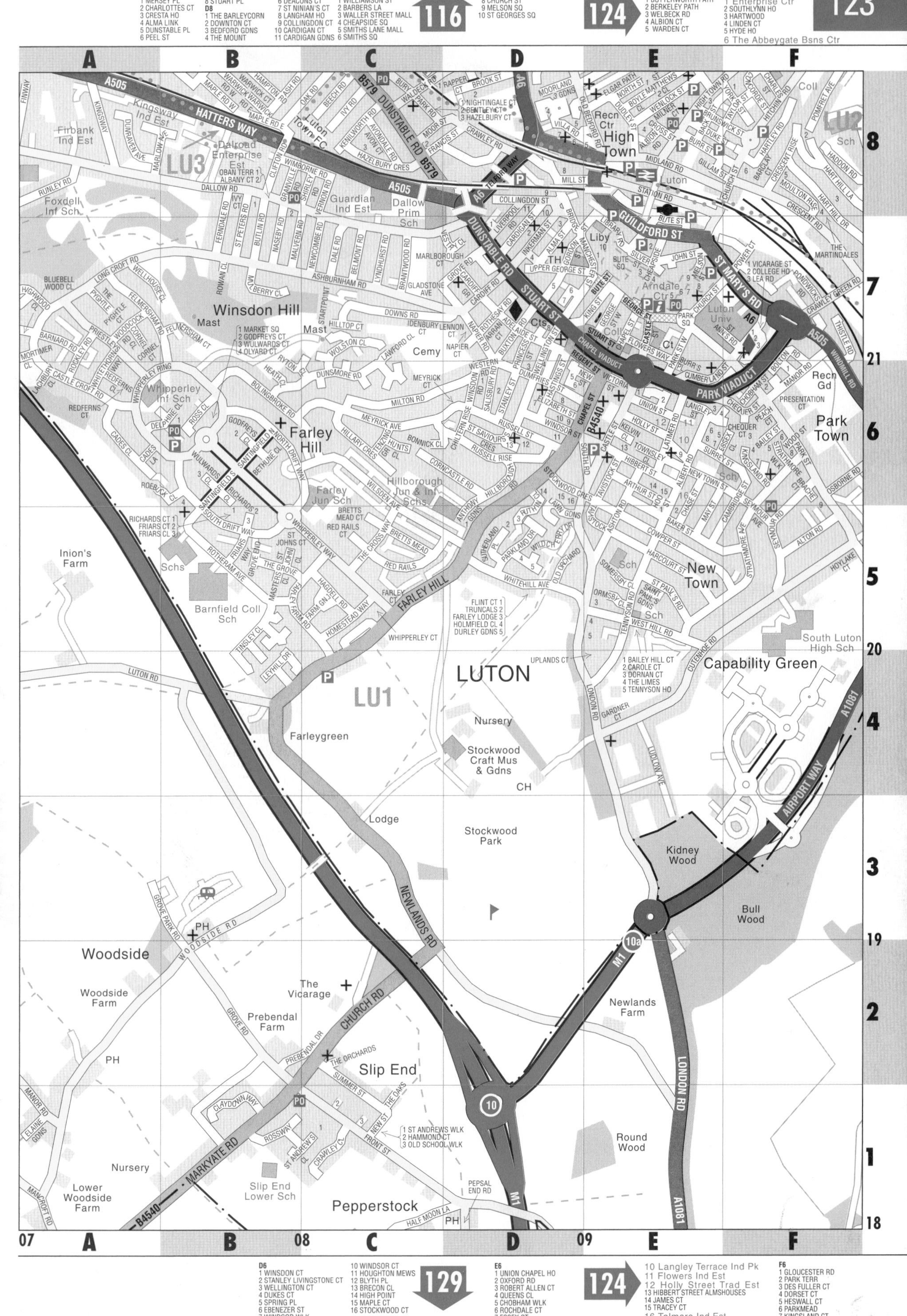
123
D7
1 MERSEY PL
2 CHARLOTTES CT
3 CRESTA HO
4 ALMA LINK
5 DUNSTABLE PL
6 PEEL ST
7 PEEL PL
8 STUART PL
D8
1 THE BARLEYCORN
2 DOWNTON CT
3 BEDFORD GDNS
4 THE MOUNT
5 VILLA CT
6 DEACONS CT
7 ST NINIAN'S CT
8 LANGHAM HO
9 COLLINGDON CT
10 CARDIGAN CT
11 CARDIGAN GDNS
E7
1 WILLIAMSON ST
2 BARBERS LA
3 WALLER STREET MALL
4 CHEAPSIDE SQ
5 SMITHS LANE MALL
6 SMITHS SQ
7 THE GALLERY
8 CHURCH ST
9 MELSON SQ
10 ST GEORGES SQ
116
124
E8
1 BUTTERWORTH PATH
2 BERKELEY PATH
3 WELBECK RD
4 ALBION CT
5 WARDEN CT
F8
1 Enterprise Ctr
2 SOUTHLYNN HO
3 HARTWOOD
4 LINDEN CT
5 HYDE HO
6 The Abbeygate Bsns Ctr
A B C D E F
8 7 21 6 5 20 4 3 19 2 1 18
07 08 09
A505
HATTERS WAY
Kingsway Ind Est
Firbank Ind Est
Dalroad Enterprise Est
LU3
Luton Town FC
DUNSTABLE RD
B579
Guardian Ind Est
Dallow Prim Sch
Foxdell Inf Sch
High Town
Recn Ctr
Luton
GUILDFORD ST
Liby
TH
Arndale Ctr
Coll
Luton Univ
ST MARY'S RD
A6
STUART ST
CHAPEL VIADUCT
PARK VIADUCT
Cts
Ct
LU2
Sch
Winsdon Hill
Mast
Cemy
Farley Hill
Whipperley Inf Sch
Farley Jun Sch
Hillborough Jun & Inf Schs
Schs
Barnfield Coll Sch
Inion's Farm
FARLEY HILL
B4540
Recn Gd
Park Town
New Town
Sch
South Luton High Sch
Capability Green
LUTON
LU1
Farleygreen
Nursery
Stockwood Craft Mus & Gdns
CH
Lodge
Stockwood Park
Kidney Wood
Bull Wood
AIRPORT WAY
A1081
M1
10a
NEWLANDS RD
LONDON RD
Woodside
Woodside Farm
PH
The Vicarage
Prebendal Farm
CHURCH RD
Slip End
Newlands Farm
10
Round Wood
Nursery
Lower Woodside Farm
Slip End Lower Sch
Pepperstock
MARKYATE RD
HALF MOON LA
PH
D6
1 WINSDON CT
2 STANLEY LIVINGSTONE CT
3 WELLINGTON CT
4 DUKES CT
5 SPRING PL
6 EBENEZER ST
7 WINDSOR WLK
8 DUMFRIES CT
9 ELIZABETH CT
10 WINDSOR CT
11 HOUGHTON MEWS
12 BLYTH PL
13 BRECON CL
14 HIGH POINT
15 MAPLE CT
16 STOCKWOOD CT
129
E6
1 UNION CHAPEL HO
2 OXFORD RD
3 ROBERT ALLEN CT
4 QUEENS CL
5 CHOBHAM WLK
6 ROCHDALE CT
7 ESSEX CT
8 KIRKDALE CT
9 NEW TOWN RD
124
10 Langley Terrace Ind Pk
11 Flowers Ind Est
12 Holly Street Trad Est
13 HIBBERT STREET ALMSHOUSES
14 JAMES CT
15 TRACEY CT
16 Telmere Ind Est
F6
1 GLOUCESTER RD
2 PARK TERR
3 DES FULLER CT
4 DORSET CT
5 HESWALL CT
6 PARKMEAD
7 KINGSLAND CT
8 GREEN DRAGON CT
9 OSBORNE CT

123
117

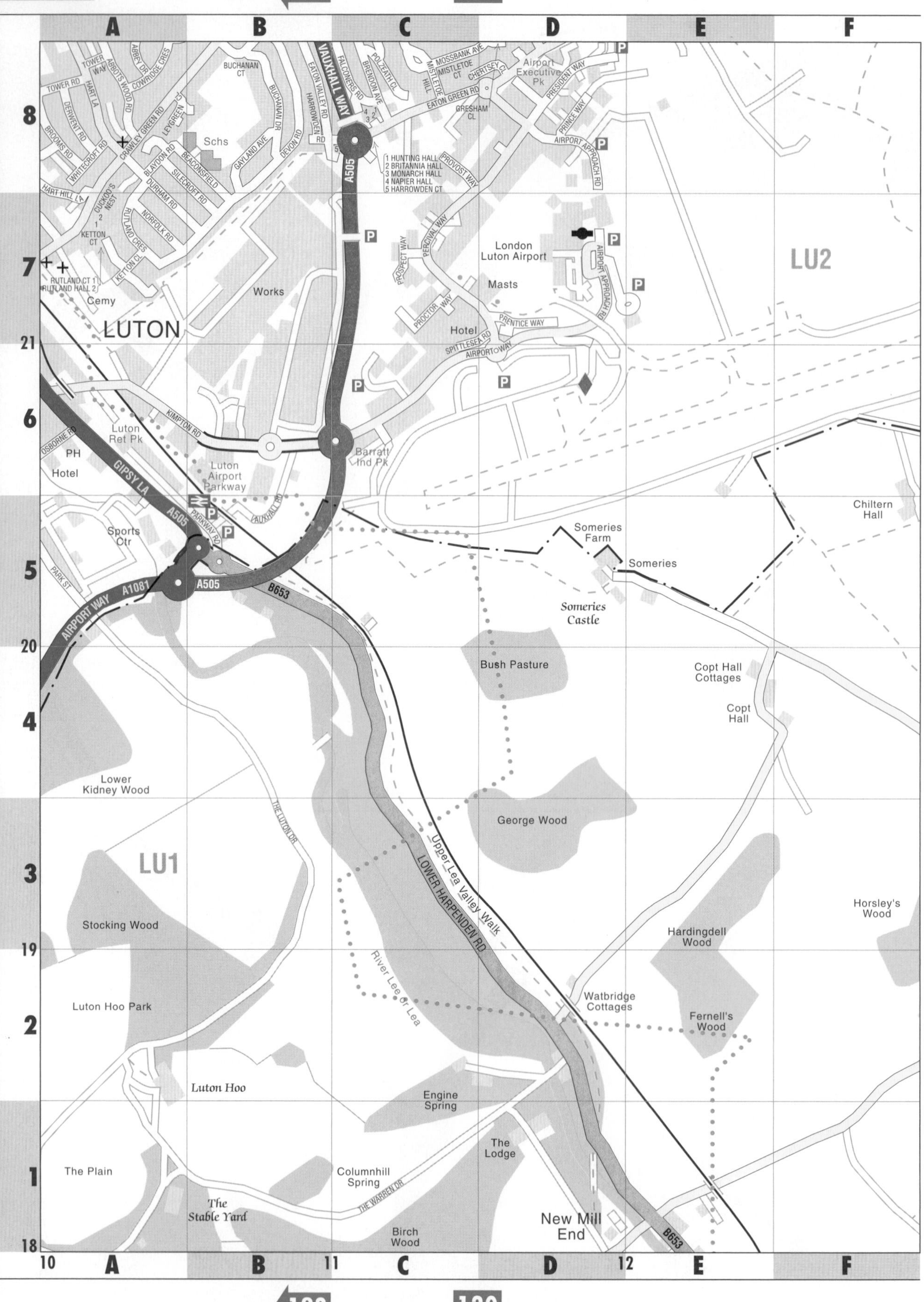
A
B
C
D
E
F
8
7
21
6
5
20
4
3
19
2
1
18
10
11
12
TOWER RD
TOWER WAY
ABBOTS WOOD RD
ABBEY DR
COWRIDGE CRES
HART LA
DERWENT RD
BROOMS RD
WHITECROFT RD
CRAWLEY GREEN RD
LEYGREEN
BUCHANAN CT
BUCHANAN DR
GAYLAND AVE
DEVON RD
Schs
BLAYDON RD
BEACONSFIELD
SILECROFT RD
DURHAM RD
NORFOLK RD
RUTLAND CRES
KETTON CL
KETTON CT
HART HILL LA
CUCKOO'S NEST
RUTLAND CT 1
RUTLAND HALL 2
Cemy
LUTON
Works
VAUXHALL WAY
EATON VALLEY RD
HARROWDEN RD
FALCONERS RD
BRENDON AVE
POLZEATH CL
MISTLETOE HILL
MOSSBANK AVE
MISTLETOE CT
EATON GREEN RD
CHERTSEY CL
GRESHAM CL
Airport Executive Pk
PRESIDENT WAY
PRINCE WAY
AIRPORT APPROACH RD
1 HUNTING HALL
2 BRITANNIA HALL
3 MONARCH HALL
4 NAPIER HALL
5 HARROWDEN CT
PROVOST WAY
A505
PERCIVAL WAY
PROSPECT WAY
London Luton Airport
Masts
LU2
PROCTOR WAY
PRENTICE WAY
Hotel
SPITTLESEA RD
AIRPORT WAY
KIMPTON RD
Luton Ret Pk
OSBORNE RD
PH
Hotel
GIPSY LA
Luton Airport Parkway
Barratt Ind Pk
PARKWAY RD
VAUXHALL RD
Sports Ctr
PARK ST
A1081
AIRPORT WAY
B653
Somerles Farm
Someries
Someries Castle
Chiltern Hall
Bush Pasture
Copt Hall Cottages
Copt Hall
Lower Kidney Wood
THE LUTON DR
George Wood
Upper Lea Valley Walk
LOWER HARPENDEN RD
LU1
Stocking Wood
River Lee or Lea
Horsley's Wood
Hardingdell Wood
Luton Hoo Park
Watbridge Cottages
Fernell's Wood
Luton Hoo
Engine Spring
The Lodge
The Plain
Columnhill Spring
THE WARREN DR
The Stable Yard
Birch Wood
New Mill End

123
130

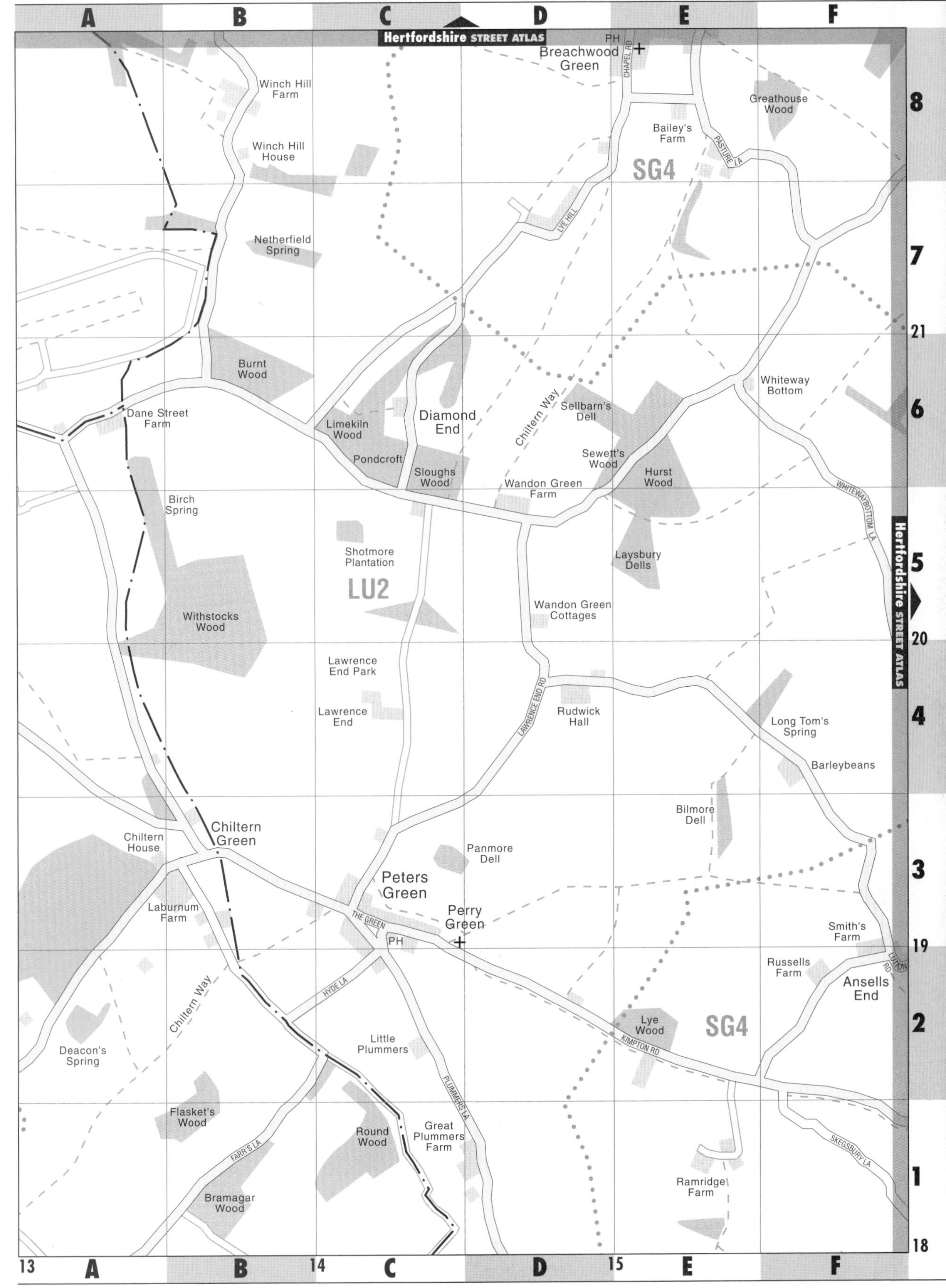

Breachwood
Green
PH +

Bailey's
Farm

Greathouse
Wood

SG4

Winch Hill
Farm

Winch Hill
House

LYE HILL

CHAPEL RD

PASTURE LA

8

7

21

Netherfield
Spring

Chiltern Way

Sellbarn's
Dell

Whiteway
Bottom

Burnt
Wood

Diamond
End

Sewett's
Wood

Hurst
Wood

WHITEWAY BOTTOM LA

6

Dane Street
Farm

Limekiln
Wood

Pondcroft

Sloughs
Wood

Wandon Green
Farm

Birch
Spring

Shotmore
Plantation

Laysbury
Dells

5

LU2

Withstocks
Wood

Wandon Green
Cottages

20

Lawrence
End Park

LAWRENCE END RD

Rudwick
Hall

Long Tom's
Spring

Barleybeans

4

Lawrence
End

Bilmore
Dell

Chiltern
House

Chiltern
Green

Panmore
Dell

Smith's
Farm

3

19

Laburnum
Farm

THE GREEN

Peters
Green

Perry
Green
PH +

Russells
Farm

KIMPTON RD

Ansells
End

SG4

Deacon's
Spring

Chiltern Way

HYDE LA

Little
Plummers

Lye
Wood

KIMPTON RD

2

Flasket's
Wood

FARR'S LA

Round
Wood

Great
Plummers
Farm

PLUMMERS LA

Ramridge
Farm

SKEGSBURY LA

1

Bramagar
Wood

18

13   14   15

A   B   C   D   E   F

A B C D E F

8
7
17
6
5
16
4
3
15
2
1
14

98 A B 99 C D 00 E F

B489
ICKNIELD WAY
A4146 Leighton Buzzard
Willow Farm
White Lion
B4506
B4540
Dukes Ave
Dell Farm
B4540
The Green
ESCARPMENT AVE
CENTRAL AVE
P
Whipsnade Wild Animal Park
MISSDOANS RIDE
Chiltern Farm
Mast
MAIN RD N
Collyers
DUNSTABLE RD
CUT THROAT AVE
VALLEY CL
SIR JOHN'S WAY
HUMPHREY TALBOT
P
Bethshan Farm
Dagnall
Lower Farm
Ickhield Way Path
HOG HALL LA
Icknield Way Path
PH
Dagnall Farm
HAMILTON CL
CASTLIN RD
B4506
BEANS MDW
HUNTSMANS CL
CHESTNUT CL
MALTING LA
Dagnall Sch
Highbury Farm
Ickhield Way Path
CH
Cross Keys Farm
Dagnallhall Farm
Hog Hall
HP4
STUDHAM LA
C06
Cha Reetaa
RINGSHALL RD
Well Farm
Sewage Works
MAIN RD S
Man's Grove
Ringshall Coppice
Oakley Wood
Meadow Farm
Goose Hill Farm
Levi Spring
Lamsey Farm
Hoo Wood
Milebarn Farm
Ashridge Farm
Hall Farm
TRUST COTTS
Ringshall
HEMEL HEMPSTEAD RD
A4146
P
BEACON RD
Ivanhoe Common
B4506
Gade Plas

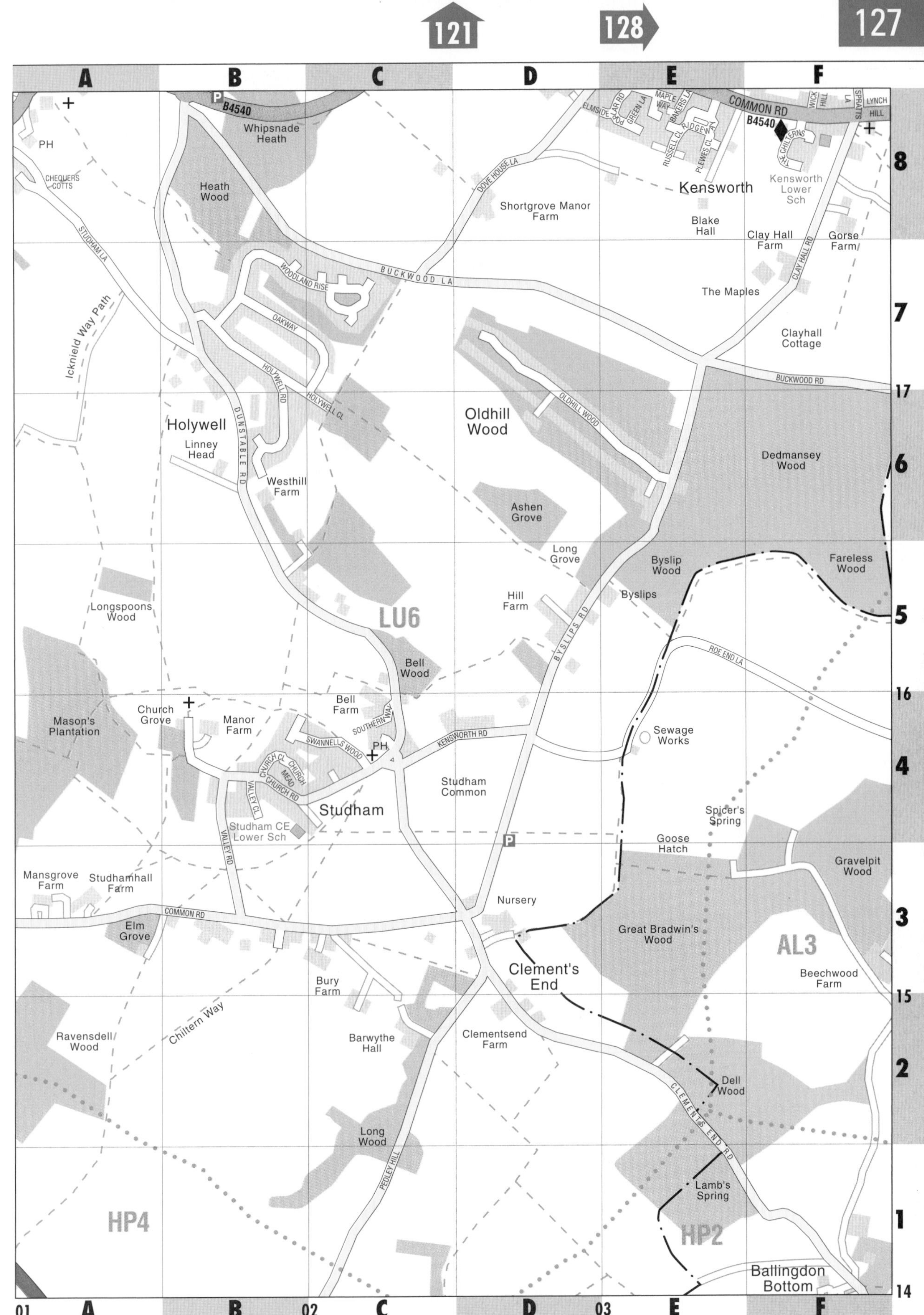

A   B   C   D   E   F

PH

CHEQUERS COTTS

STUDHAM LA

Icknield Way Path

P

B4540

Whipsnade Heath

Heath Wood

WOODLAND RISE

OAKWAY

BUCKWOOD LA

DOVE HOUSE LA

Shortgrove Manor Farm

ELMSIDE RD

GREEN LA

MAPLE WAY

RUSSELL CL

BAKERS LA

RIDGEWN

PLEWES CL

COMMON RD

B4540

WICK HILL

SPRATTS

LYNCH HILL

THE CHILTERNS

8

Kensworth

Kensworth Lower Sch

Blake Hall

Clay Hall Farm

CLAY HALL LA

Gorse Farm

The Maples

Clayhall Cottage

7

HOLYWELL RD

HOLYWELL CL

DUNSTABLE RD

Holywell

Linney Head

Westhill Farm

Oldhill Wood

OLDHILL WOOD

BUCKWOOD RD

17

Dedmansey Wood

6

Longspoons Wood

Ashen Grove

Long Grove

Byslip Wood

Byslips

Fareless Wood

LU6

Hill Farm

BYSLIPS RD

ROE END LA

5

16

Mason's Plantation

Church Grove

Manor Farm

SWANNELLS WOOD

Bell Farm

Bell Wood

SOUTHERN WAY

PH

KENSWORTH RD

Sewage Works

Spicer's Spring

Gravelpit Wood

4

CHURCH CL

CHURCH MEAD

CHURCH RD

VALLEY CL

Studham CE Lower Sch

Studham

Studham Common

Goose Hatch

Beechwood Farm

AL3

15

VALLEY RD

Mansgrove Farm

Studhamhall Farm

COMMON RD

Elm Grove

P

Nursery

Great Bradwin's Wood

3

Bury Farm

Clement's End

CLEMENTS END RD

Dell Wood

2

Ravensdell Wood

Chiltern Way

Barwythe Hall

Clementsend Farm

Lamb's Spring

HP4

Long Wood

PEDLEY HILL

HP2

Ballingdon Bottom

1

14

A   B   C   D   E   F

01   02   03

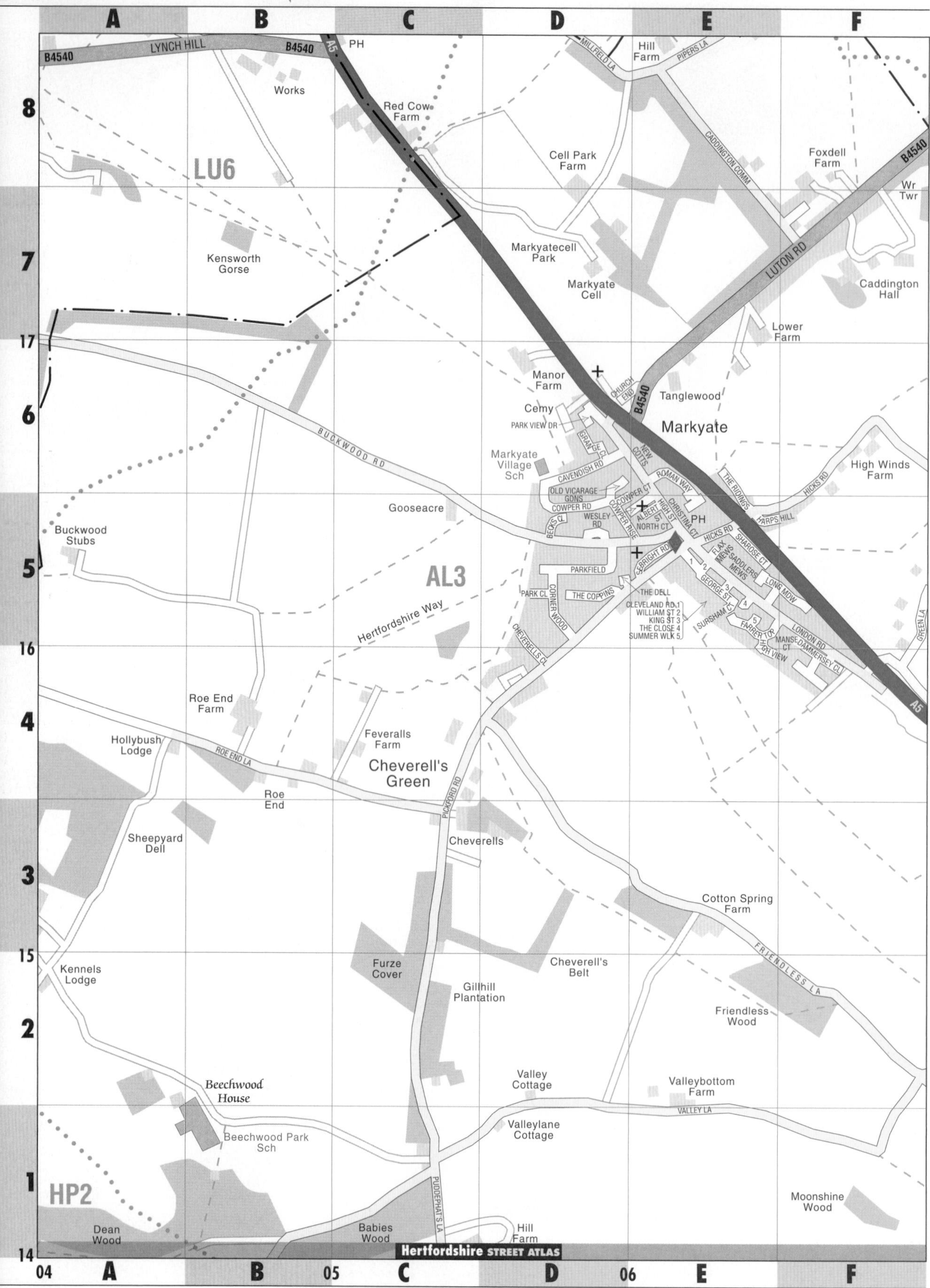

LU6

HP2

AL3

Markyate

Hertfordshire Way

Kensworth Gorse

Buckwood Stubs

Gooseacre

Roe End Farm

Hollybush Lodge

Roe End

Sheepyard Dell

Kennels Lodge

Cheverell's Green

Feveralls Farm

Cheverells

Furze Cover

Gillhill Plantation

Cheverell's Belt

Cotton Spring Farm

Friendless Wood

Beechwood House

Beechwood Park Sch

Valley Cottage

Valleylane Cottage

Valleybottom Farm

Moonshine Wood

Dean Wood

Babies Wood

Hill Farm

Cell Park Farm

Markyatecell Park

Markyate Cell

Hill Farm

Foxdell Farm

Caddington Hall

Lower Farm

Tanglewood

High Winds Farm

Manor Farm

Red Cow Farm

Works

LYNCH HILL

B4540

B4540

A5

PH

MILLFIELD LA

PIPERS LA

CADDINGTON COMM

LUTON RD

B4540

Wr Twr

BUCKWOOD RD

ROE END LA

PACKFORD RD

PUDDEPHAT'S LA

VALLEY LA

FRIENDLESS LA

CHEVERELL'S CL

CORNER WOOD

PARK CL

Parkfield

Cemy

PARK VIEW DR

GRANGE RD

CAVENDISH RD

OLD VICARAGE GDNS

COWPER RD

WESLEY RD

ALBERT ST

HIGH ST

NEW GOTTS

ROMAN WAY

CHRISTINA CT

COWPER CT

COWPER RING

NORTH CT

THE ROUNDS

HICKS RD

HRPS HILL

THE COPPINS

CORNER WOOD

BRIGHT RD

GEORGE ST

SURSHAM CT

FLAX MEWS

SADDLERS MEWS

SPAROSE CT

LONG MDW

FARRIER TOW

DRY VIEW

FAMEY VIEW

LONDON RD

MANSE CT

DAMMERSEY CL

GREEN LA

A5

THE DELL
CLEVELAND RD 1
WILLIAM ST 2
KING ST 3
THE CLOSE 4
SUMMER WLK 5

CHURCH END

Markyate Village Sch

PH

PH

Cheverells

MANGROT RD · B4540
L · MARKYATE RD · B4540

Woodside Farm and Wildfowl Park

Grove Farm

Limekiln Plantation

Top Spring

Middle Spring

Half Moon La

Stable Spring

Sewage Works

Broomhill Leys Wood

WINDMILL RD

Bonner's Farm

Ivy Farm

Doone Brae Farm

Smallgrove Farm

Cockrums

Rainbow Hall Farm

School House Farm

Hotel

Works

OLD WATLING ST

CHAD LA

Highfield Farm

Chad Lane Farm

River Hall

River Ver

HOLLYBUSH LA

Hertfordshire Way

Millfield Cottage

FRIENDLESS LA

MILL LA

PRIETLEY HILL

PRIORY RD

CHAPEL RD

TROWLEY BTS

RIVER HILL

HIGH ST

PO

Cemy

RCH RD

PIE CNR

VICARAGE GDNS

PARSON'S CL

TROWLEY HILL RD

Flamstead

Flamstead Sch

TRIS POND

CHEQUERS HILL

Singlets La

Sunny Ridge

Chiltern Way

DELMEREND LA

Delmerend Farm

Lower Sawpit Wood

Half Moon La

Birchin Grove

Pepsal End

PEPSAL END RD

LU1

Pepsalend Farm

M1

A1081

The New Lodge

Chalk Wood

Heavens Wood

LONDON RD

Gibraltar Cottages

Gibraltar Farm

A1081

Hogtrough Wood

Lady Bray Farm

AL5

Brickfield Farm

Eight Acre Spring

ANNABLES LA

White Walls

WATERY LA

Turner Hall Farm

Hill & Coles Farm

AL3

Friar's Wash

A5

9

Verlam End

Norringtonend

M1

REDDING LA

M1 Watford

Showground

DUNSTABLE RD

A5183

A5183 St Albans

A B C D E F

8

Luton Hoo
Home Farm

Birch
Wood

Hillside

Sewage
Works

East
Hydé

Saw Mill The Gables

B653

River Lea or Lee

VIADUCT COTTS

HAMBRO CL

LEA
BRIDGE
CNR

FARR'S LA

LOWER HARPENDEN RD

PH

SOUTHERNE RISE

7

FARM RD

Tumble
Grove

LU1

Graves
Wood

West
Hyde

Upper Lea Valley Walk

LU2

B653

17

A1081

LIMETREE AVE.

Lady Bute's
Lodge

Circus
Wood

Thrales
End

COOTERS END LA

6

LONDON RD

Thrales End
Farm

Cooters Hill
Farm

KENNEL LA

BEECH
RIDGE

5

PH

Kinsbourne
Green

+ + PO

PH

Thrales End
Farm

Cooters End
Farm

16

THE COMMON

SPRINGL

CHAMBERLAINES

ANNABLES LA

Long
Spring

Pollard's
Farm

LUTON RD

KINSBOURNE CRES

KLONDYKE

RIDGEWAY

Cooters Hill
Farm

AMBROSE LA

4

FERMVENT RD

TINTERN CL

CROSSPATHS

GREATFIELD CL

KINSBOURNE CL

THE CLOSE

HERDS WAY

VALE CL

FARM CL

TUFFNELLS WAY

CARPENDERS CL

FARM AVE

PENSHURST CL

MOLESCROFT

RIDGE AVE

WELLS CL

LUTON CL

Dove House
Farm

AL5

KENNESBOURNE
CT

WOOD END HILL

YEOMANS AVE

WOODLANDS

RICHMOND DR

HIGHBURY RD

RIDGEWOOD GDNS

MAXTED CL

HOMEDELL HO

Annables
Farm

Mast

Faulkners End
Farm

Wood End
JM Sch

ASHLEY GDNS

WOOD END RD

BLACKSDALE GR.

HAS.LINGDEN CL

APPLECROFT RD

How Field

FALCONERS FIELD

Harpenden Rise

OTTERTON CL

1 ROUNDWOOD CT
2 ST NICHOLAS CT
3 KINSBOURNE CT
4 BRAMBLE CL

REED
PL

BL.COOMBFIELD
PL

BEECH
CT

HILLSIDE RD

LAMBOURN
CT

BOND
CT

BRIDGE DT

HOLLYBUSH LA

OVERTREES

A1081

3

KINSBOURNE GREEN LA

Delgarth

ROUNDWOOD LA

PARK RISE

PARK RISE

THE SPINNEY

ROUNDWOOD GDNS

ROUNDWOOD RD

PARK MOUNT

HARPENDEN RISE

PARK HILL

MORETON END LA

MORETON
PL. Sch.

15

HARPENDEN

Roundwood
Park Sch

THE MEADOWS

MORETON AVE

NELSON RD

MANSTON RD

CHEPSTON

DOUGLAS RD

St Hilda's
Sch

THE
COPPICE

TIMBERS CT

2

Chiltern Way

Roundwood
Prim Sch

CLAYGATE AVE

POMMICK RD

ALDERS END LA

BROADFIELDS

TANGLEWOOD

SALISBURY AVE

ROSEBERY AVE

BARNS DENE

1

Chiltern Way

AL3

Northfield
Spring

Harpenden
Stables

Nicky Line

HARTWELL GDNS

TOWNSEND LA

TOWNSEND CL

PARK AVE N

ST ANDREW'S
AVE

LONGCROFT AVE

MAPLE RD

KIRKWICK
AVE

ROTHAMSTED AVE

ORCHARD AVE

AMENBURY LA.

PARK.

14

LUTON LA

BADINGHAM DR

10 A B 11 C D 12 E F

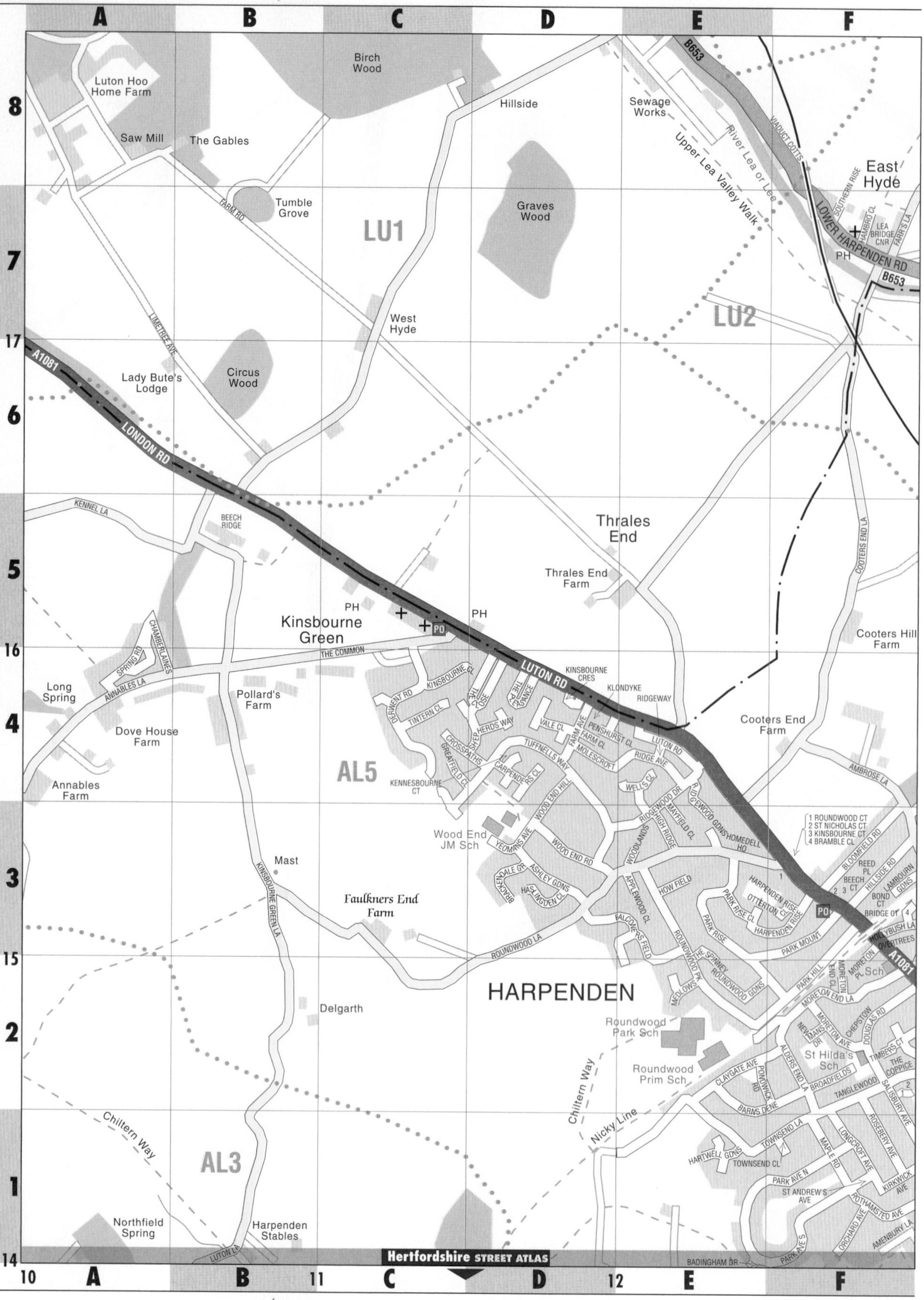

F2
1 THE BOURNE
2 THE BOURNE APTS

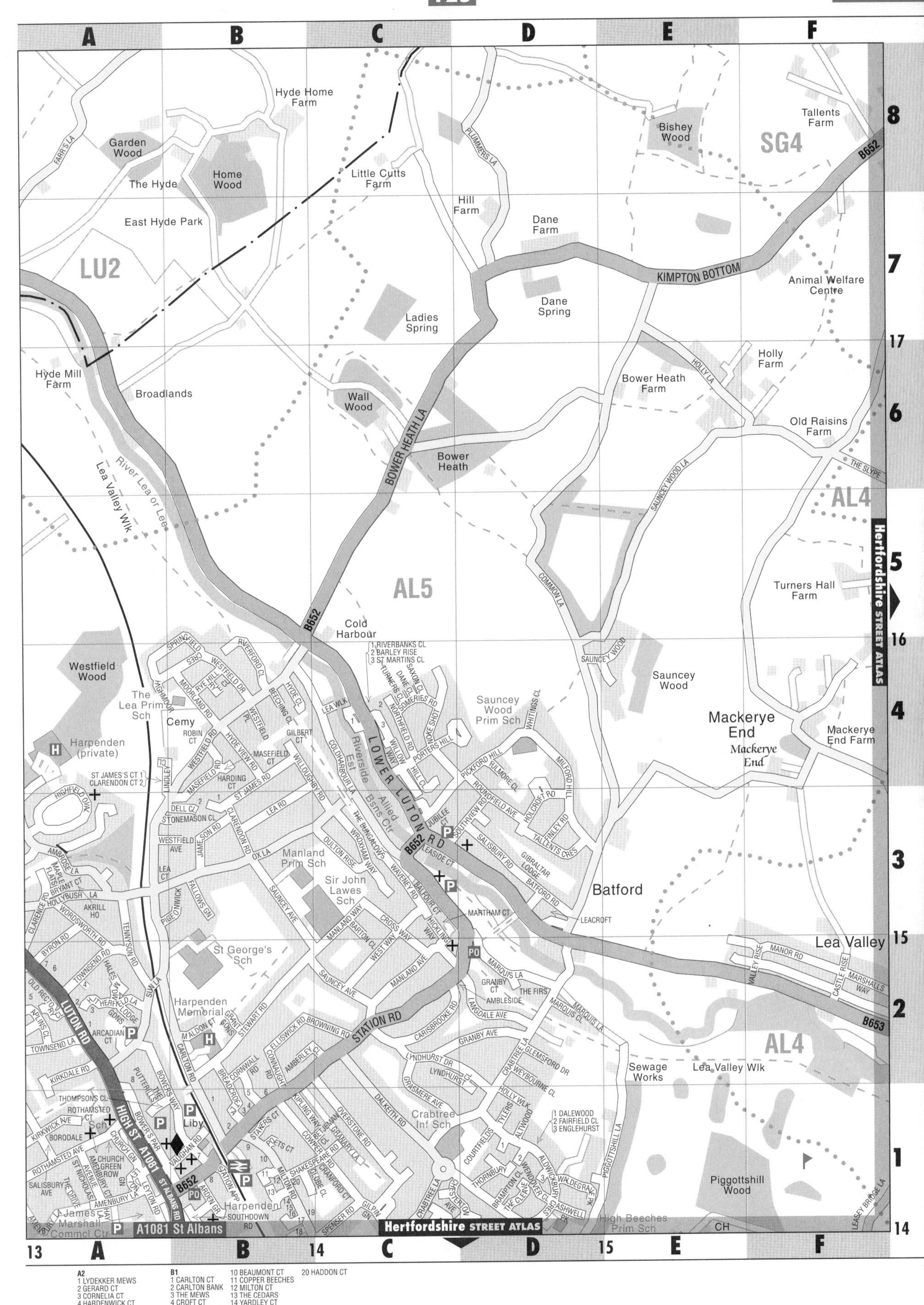

A2
1 LYDEKKER MEWS
2 GERARD CT
3 CORNELIA CT
4 HARDENWICK CT
5 SOUTHGATE CT
6 BERKELEY CT
7 FERNDALE
8 ANVIL HO

B1
1 CARLTON CT
2 CARLTON BANK
3 THE MEWS
4 CROFT CT
5 DEVONSHIRE RD
6 KINLOCH CT
7 VICTORIA RD
8 HARDING PAR
9 COLERIDGE CT

10 BEAUMONT CT
11 COPPER BEECHES
12 MILTON CT
13 THE CEDARS
14 YARDLEY CT
15 KEATS HO
16 SHELLEY CT
17 AVON CT
18 FURZEDOWN CT
19 CHILTERN CT

20 HADDON CT

127

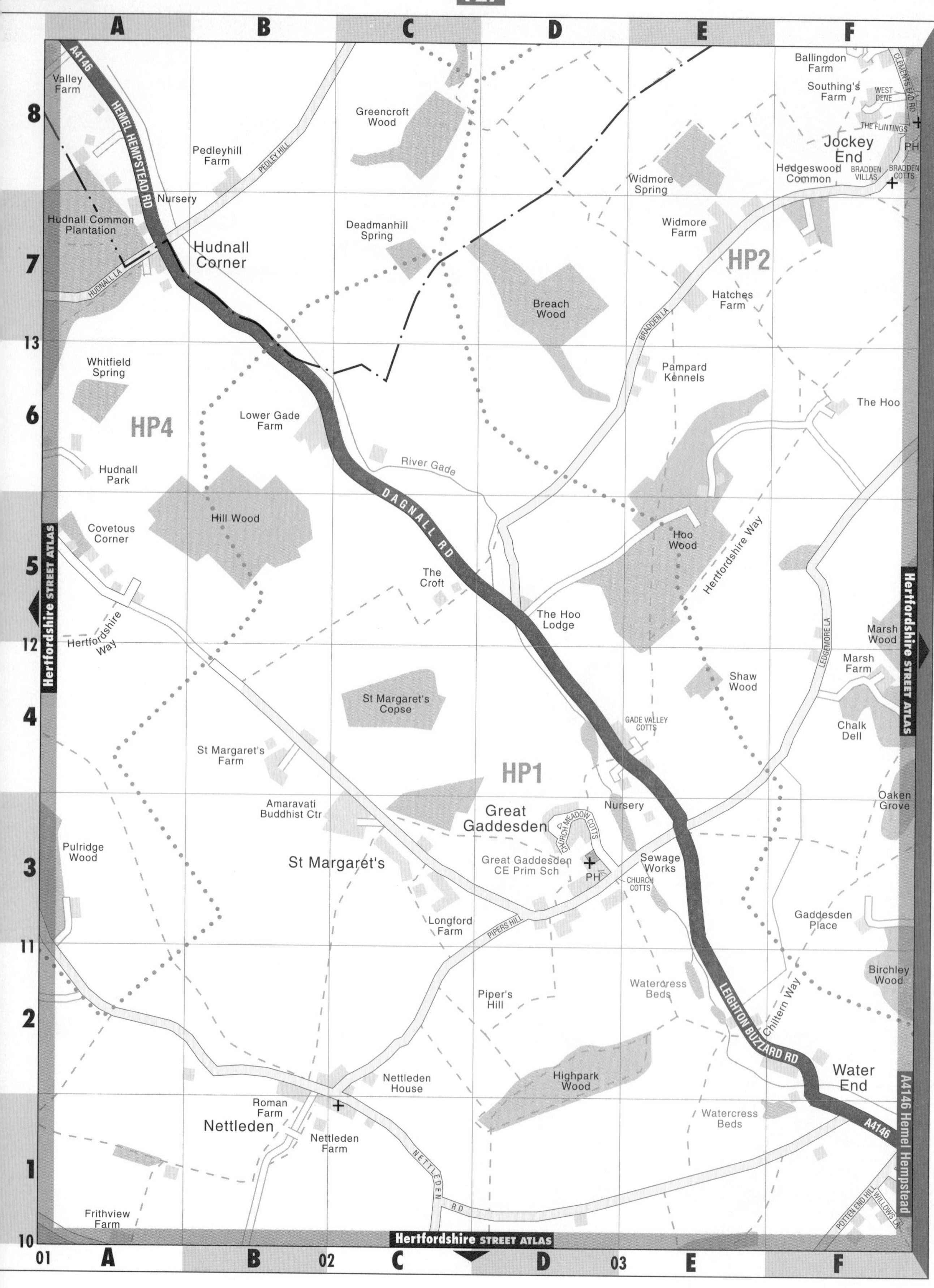
A
B
C
D
E
F
8
7
13
6
5
12
4
3
11
2
1
10
01
02
03
A4146
HEMEL HEMPSTEAD RD
Valley Farm
Greencroft Wood
Pedleyhill Farm
PEDLEY HILL
Nursery
Hudnall Common Plantation
Hudnall Corner
HUDNALL LA
Deadmanhill Spring
Ballingdon Farm
Southing's Farm
WEST DENE
CLEMENTS END RD
THE FLINTINGS
Jockey End
PH
Hedgeswood Common
BRADDEN VILLAS
BRADDEN COTTS
Widmore Spring
Widmore Farm
HP2
Hatches Farm
BRADDEN LA
Breach Wood
Whitfield Spring
Pampard Kennels
Lower Gade Farm
HP4
The Hoo
Hudnall Park
River Gade
DAGNALL RD
Hill Wood
Covetous Corner
Hoo Wood
Hertfordshire Way
The Croft
The Hoo Lodge
Marsh Wood
Marsh Farm
LEDGEMORE LA
Shaw Wood
St Margaret's Copse
GADE VALLEY COTTS
Chalk Dell
St Margaret's Farm
HP1
Oaken Grove
Amaravati Buddhist Ctr
Great Gaddesden
CHURCH MEADOW COTTS
Nursery
Pulridge Wood
St Margaret's
Great Gaddesden CE Prim Sch
PH
Sewage Works
CHURCH COTTS
Longford Farm
PIPERS HILL
Gaddesden Place
Watercress Beds
Birchley Wood
Piper's Hill
LEIGHTON BUZZARD RD
Chiltern Way
Water End
Highpark Wood
Nettleden House
Roman Farm
Nettleden
Nettleden Farm
Watercress Beds
NETTLEDEN RD
Frithview Farm
POTTEN END HILL
WILLOWS LA
Hertfordshire STREET ATLAS
A4146 Hemel Hempstead

Index

Church Rd **6** Beckenham BR2..........**53** C6

Place name
May be abbreviated on the map

Location number
Present when a number indicates the place's position in a crowded area of mapping

Locality, town or village
Shown when more than one place has the same name

Postcode district
District for the indexed place

Page and grid square
Page number and grid reference for the standard mapping

Public and commercial buildings are highlighted in magenta   **Places of interest** are highlighted in blue with a star★

Abbreviations used in the index

Acad	Academy	Comm	Common	Gd	Ground	L	Leisure	Prom	Prom
App	Approach	Cott	Cottage	Gdn	Garden	La	Lane	Rd	Road
Arc	Arcade	Cres	Crescent	Gn	Green	Liby	Library	Recn	Recreation
Ave	Avenue	Cswy	Causeway	Gr	Grove	Mdw	Meadow	Ret	Retail
Bglw	Bungalow	Ct	Court	H	Hall	Meml	Memorial	Sh	Shopping
Bldg	Building	Ctr	Centre	Ho	House	Mkt	Market	Sq	Square
Bsns, Bus	Business	Ctry	Country	Hospl	Hospital	Mus	Museum	St	Street
Bvd	Boulevard	Cty	County	HQ	Headquarters	Orch	Orchard	Sta	Station
Cath	Cathedral	Dr	Drive	Hts	Heights	Pal	Palace	Terr	Terrace
Cir	Circus	Dro	Drove	Ind	Industrial	Par	Parade	TH	Town Hall
Cl	Close	Ed	Education	Inst	Institute	Pas	Passage	Univ	University
Cnr	Corner	Emb	Embankment	Int	International	Pk	Park	Wk, Wlk	Walk
Coll	College	Est	Estate	Intc	Interchange	Pl	Place	Wr	Water
Com	Community	Ex	Exhibition	Junc	Junction	Prec	Precinct	Yd	Yard

Index of localities, towns and villages

Ampthill 84 E6
Arlesey 90 A4
Ascott 110 B2
Aspley Guise 81 F4
Astwick 79 E1
Astwood 47 A3
Baldock 91 F2
Barton-le-Clay 97 D3
Bedford 50 D7
Beeston 54 B4
Biddenham 37 C1
Biggleswade 67 C6
Billington 111 E2
Bletsoe 17 C1
Blunham 41 E3
Bolnhurst 19 D4
Breachwood Green . .125 D8
Brogborough 71 D1
Bromham 36 F3
Broom 66 C3
Caddington 122 D3
Campton 77 A1
Cardington 51 D4
Carlton 25 B4
Chalton 106 E1
Chawston 31 E5
Cheddington 118 A1
Chelveston 3 C8
Chicksands 76 E4
Church End 90 B7
Clapham 37 D7
Clifton 78 B3
Clophill 86 D8
Cockernhoe 117 D7
Cold Brayfield 34 B5
Colmworth 20 B2
Cople 52 A6
Cotton End 63 D7
Covington 2 D2
Cranfield 59 B1

Dagnall 126 C6
Dunstable 121 D8
Dunton 68 D5
East Hyde 130 F8
Eaton Bray 119 F6
Edlesborough 119 E4
Edworth 80 A6
Eggington 112 B7
Elstow 50 C2
Eversholt 94 B7
Everton 43 C3
Eyeworth 68 F8
Felmersham 26 C7
Flamstead 129 E1
Flitton 85 E4
Flitwick 84 C3
Gamlingay 44 E5
Gravenhurst 87 D5
Great Barford 40 F4
Great Gaddesden . .132 D3
Great Staughton 13 F6
Greenfield 85 C2
Guilden Morden 69 F4
Hardmead 46 D4
Hargrave 1 E2
Harlington 95 F1
Harpenden 130 D2
Harrold 24 F6
Harrowden 51 A3
Hatley St George . . .45 F3
Haynes 64 A1
Haynes Church End . .75 C7
Heath and Reach . .103 B5
Henlow 78 D1
Hexton 98 B2
Hinxworth 80 C5
Hitchin 101 B2
Hockliffe 104 F2
Holwell 100 B7
Honeydon 21 B2

Horton 118 B3
Houghton Conquest . .74 B7
Houghton Regis 114 B6
Hulcote 70 E2
Husborne Crawley . . .82 B4
Ickleford 100 E4
Ickwell 65 E7
Irchester 7 B7
Ivinghoe Aston 119 A1
Jockey End 132 F8
Kempston 49 C4
Kempston Hardwick . .61 D5
Kensworth 121 E2
Keysoe 12 B2
Kimbolton 6 F6
Knotting Green 9 F1
Langford 78 E6
Lavendon 34 A8
Lea valley 131 F2
Leighton Buzzard . . .111 E6
Letchworth 101 C5
Lidlington 72 B2
Lilley 109 D2
Little Barford 32 E6
Little Staughton 13 A2
Lower Caldecote 54 D2
Lower Dean 5 C7
Lower Stondon 88 F2
Lower Sundon 107 C3
Luton 123 D4
Markyate 128 E6
Marston Moretaine . .72 D8
Maulden 74 C1
Melchbourne 10 D8
Meppershall 88 B5
Millbrook 73 A2
Milton Bryan 93 E1
Milton Ernest 27 A5
Moggerhanger 53 C6
Nettleden 132 B1

Newnham 91 E8
Newton Blossomville . .34 A7
Newton Bromswold . . .9 D8
Northall 119 B6
North Crawley 58 A6
Northill 53 E8
Oakley 37 A7
Odell 25 C8
Old Warden 65 B4
Pavenham 26 B4
Pepperstock 123 C1
Pertenhall 12 C8
Peters Green 125 C3
Pirton 99 E4
Podington 7 E2
Potton 56 B7
Pulloxhill 96 E8
Radwell 26 E8
Ravensden 29 B1
Renhold 39 E6
Ridgmont 82 E5
Ringshall 126 B1
Riseley 11 A2
Roxton 31 F1
Rushden 8 D8
St Neots 22 B6
Salford 70 C3
Sandy 54 C6
Sharnbrook 16 B4
Sharpenhoe 96 E2
Shefford 77 D3
Shillington 87 F1
Shortstown 51 A2
Silsoe 86 B4
Slapton 118 D6
Slip End 123 C2
Souldrop 16 B8
Southill 77 E8
Stagsden 48 A7
Stanbridge 112 C5

Stanford 78 A7
Steppingley 84 A3
Stevington 36 B7
Stewartby 61 C1
Stotfold 90 E7
Streatley 108 A5
Studham 127 C4
Sutton 56 A3
Swineshead 11 D8
Tebworth 105 C2
Tempsford 42 B8
Thurleigh 18 C1
Tilbrook 6 B7
Tilsworth 112 F5
Tingrith 94 F5
Toddington 105 E6
Totternhoe 120 B7
Turvey 34 F6
Upper Caldecote . . .66 B7
Upper Dean 5 A4
Upper Stondon 88 D4
Upper Sundon 107 A4
Westoning 95 F6
Wharley End 58 D2
Whipsnade 120 F1
Wick End 48 B8
Wilden 29 F3
Willington 52 C8
Wilstead 62 F3
Wingfield 105 E1
Woburn 92 F7
Woburn Sands 81 A4
Wood End 6 D1
Woodside 123 A2
Wootton 61 A7
Workhouse End 40 A5
Wrestlingworth 57 C4
Wyboston 32 A5
Wymington 8 B5
Yelden 4 A2

A

Abbey Cl Ampthill MK45 84 F7
Elstow MK42 50 B3
Renhold MK41 39 B7
Abbey Dr LU2 117 A1
Abbey Gr SG19 54 C8
Abbey La MK45 85 A6
Abbey Mews LU6 121 C6
Abbey Mid Sch MK42 50 C3
Abbey Rd MK41 39 A2
Abbey Sq MK43 34 E5
Abbey Way NN10 8 A8
Abbey Wlk
Heath & Reach LU7 103 A4
Houghton Regis LU5 114 E6
Abbeyfields MK42 50 C3
Abbeygate Bsns Ctr The 6 LU2 123 F8
Abbis Orch SG5 100 E5
Abbot Cres MK42 49 D2
Abbots Ct LU2 117 A1
Abbots Wlk 4 SG18 67 A6
Abbots Wood Rd LU2 124 A8
Abbotswood Par LU2 117 A1
Abbotts Rd SG6 101 D6
Abercorn Rd LU4 114 F3
Abigail Cl LU3 116 D3
Abigail Ct LU3 116 D3
Abingdon Rd LU4 115 C3
Acacia Cl LU7 111 E6
Acacia Rd MK43 50 D6
Acacia Villas 9 LU6 121 B8
Ackerman Gdns PE19 22 C2
Ackerman St PE19 22 C2
Acorn Cl LU2 116 F3
Acorn Ctr 3 SG18 67 A6
Acorn Ho SG18 66 F7
Acorn Way MK42 50 D5
Acres The SG17 88 B5
Acworth Cres LU4 115 C5
Acworth Ct 2 LU4 115 C5
Adaern Cl 7 LU7 111 A8
Adams Bottom LU7 103 A1
Adams Cl Ampthill MK45 84 F7
Kempston MK42 49 E1
Adamson Ct MK42 49 D5
Adamson Wlk MK42 49 D5
Adastral Ave LU7 111 E6
Addington Cl
Bedford MK41 39 A1
Henlow SG16 78 D1
Addington Way LU4 115 D3
Addington Wlk PE19 22 C2
Addingtons Rd MK44 41 A5
Addison Cl MK42 49 F4
Adelaide Cl MK45 74 B8
Adelaide Sq MK40 38 B1
Adelaide St LU1 123 D7
Adlington Ct LU4 115 C4
Admiral Row MK45 84 E4
Admirals Way PE19 22 A2
Adstone Rd LU1 122 F3
Aelfric Ct MK41 38 C5
Aidans Cl LU6 113 E1
Ailesbury Rd MK45 84 F8
Ailsworth Rd LU3 116 A7
Ailwyns Acre MK43 71 B7
Ainsland Ct LU4 115 B2
Aintree Rd NN10 8 D8
Aire Wlk MK41 38 C7
Airedale Cl MK45 84 D4
Airport Approach Rd LU2 124 D8
Airport Executive Pk LU2 124 D8
Airport Way LU1, LU2 124 A5
Akrill Ho AL5 131 A3
Alameda Mid Sch MK45 84 E8
Alameda Rd MK45 84 E8
Alameda Wlk MK45 84 E8
Alamein Ave MK42 50 E6
Alamein Cl SG17 77 C1
Alamein Ct PE19 22 C5
Alban CE Mid Sch MK44 40 F5
Albany Ct LU1 123 B8
Albany Rd Bedford MK40 50 C8
Leighton Buzzard LU7 111 B7
Albermarle Cl LU4 114 F3
Albert Ct LU6 121 C7
Albert Pl Ampthill MK45 84 D6
Houghton Conquest MK45 74 B8
Albert Rd Arlesey SG15 90 A4
Luton LU1 123 E6
Albert St 10 Bedford MK40 38 B1
Markyate AL3 128 E5
Albion Ct
2 Dunstable LU6 121 B8
4 Luton LU2 123 E8
Albion Mews LU6 121 B8
Albion Rd LU2 123 E8
Albion St LU6 121 B8
Albone Way SG18 66 F4
Albone Way Ind Est SG18 66 F4
Alburgh Cl MK42 50 F5
Albury Cl LU3 108 A1
Aldbanks LU6 113 F1
Aldenham Cl
Bedford MK41 51 B8
Luton LU4 114 F3
Aldens Mead MK41 38 F4
Alder Cl PE19 22 B6
Alder Cres LU3 116 A3
Alder Ct LU3 116 B3
Alders End La AL5 130 F2
Alders The MK42 49 E3
Alderton Cl 5 LU2 117 D1
Aldgate Cl SG19 56 B7
Aldhous Cl LU3 116 B5
Aldwickbury Cres AL5 131 D1
Aldwyck Ct MK42 50 A6
Alesia Rd LU3 115 F6
Alexa Ct MK42 51 A5
Alexander Cl Clifton SG17 78 A2
Stewartby MK43 61 C1
Alexander Ct NN29 7 B8
Alexander Rd Stotfold SG5 90 F6
Wrestlingworth SG19 57 B4
Alexandra Ave LU3 116 C2
Alexandra Ct LU7 110 F8
Alexandra Pl 4 MK40 50 B8
Alexandra Rd
Bedford MK40 50 A8
Hitchin SG5 100 F1
Alfred Cope Rd SG19 54 C8
Alfred St Dunstable LU5 121 C8
Irchester NN29 7 A8
Alfriston Cl LU2 117 C3
Alington La SG6 101 F3
Alington Rd PE19 22 E1
All Saints CE Lower Sch SG17 78 B2
All Saints Rd
Bedford MK40 49 F8
Cople MK44 52 A7
Houghton Regis LU5 114 B5
All Saints Way SG19 54 B8
Allen Cl Bedford MK40 49 F8
Dunstable LU5 121 D8
Allen Ct MK43 60 E1
Allenby Ave LU5 115 A1
Allendale LU3 108 A1
Allhallows Bedford MK40 50 B8
Sandy SG19 54 B8
Allied Bsns Ctr AL5 131 C3
Allton Rd SG16 89 A4
Alma Farm Rd LU5 105 E6
Alma Link 4 LU1 123 D7
Alma St LU1 123 D7
Almer's Cl MK45 74 B8
Almond Cl LU3 116 B4
Almond Dr SG19 44 C5
Almond Rd
Leighton Buzzard LU7 111 C8
St Neots PE19 22 F6
Almonds The MK42 50 A3
Alnwick Cl SG19 54 C8
Alnwick Ct PE19 22 F2
Alpha Ct Kempston MK42 49 D3
Leighton Buzzard LU7 111 B7
Alpine Way LU3 115 D8
Alsop Cl LU5 114 B5
Althorp Cl MK45 84 F3
Althorp Rd LU3 116 C1
Althorpe St MK42 50 B6
Alton Rd LU1 123 F5
Altwood AL5 131 D1
Alwen Wlk MK41 38 C5
Alwins Field LU7 110 D8
Alwyn Cl LU2 116 E2
Amaravati Buddhist Ctr HP1 132 C3
Amberley Cl
Harpenden AL5 131 B2
Luton LU2 117 D4
Amberley Gdns MK40 38 D2
Ambleside
Harpenden AL5 131 D2
Luton LU3 115 F5
Ambrose La AL5 130 F4
Amenbury Ct AL5 131 A1
Amenbury La AL5 131 A1
Ames Cl LU3 107 F1
Amhurst Rd LU4 114 F3
Ampthill Ind Est & Bsns Pk MK45 84 C7
Ampthill Rd Bedford MK42 50 B5
Chicksands SG17 76 E2
Silsoe MK45 86 B5
Steppingley MK45 84 D5
Ampthill St MK42 50 C7
Andover Cl LU4 115 C6
Andrew Rd PE19 22 F2
Andrews Cl MK45 74 C1
Angel Cl LU4 115 D3
Angel View MK42 50 C5
Angels La LU5 114 B5
Angus Cl LU4 115 A3
Anmer Gdns LU4 115 B4
Annables La AL5 130 A4
Anne St SG18 67 A7
Annes Ct MK42 50 C7
Anson Pl PE19 22 A2
Anstee Rd LU4 115 B6
Anthony Gdns LU1 123 D6
Antonie Farm Cotts MK44 15 F4
Anvil Ct LU3 115 E5
Anvil Ho 8 AL5 131 A2
Apex Bsns Ctr LU5 114 C2
Aplins Cl AL5 131 A2
Apollo Cl LU5 121 D7
Appenine Way LU7 111 D8
Apple Glebe MK45 97 C2
Apple Gr PE19 22 C4
Apple Tree Cl
Biggleswade SG18 67 B5
Leighton Buzzard LU7 110 D6
Silsoe MK45 86 B5
Appleby Ct PE19 22 E6
Appleby Gdns LU6 121 B7
Applecroft SG16 89 B3
Applecroft Rd LU2 117 C4
Applecross Wlk MK41 39 B3
Applewood Cl AL5 130 E3
Apsley End Rd SG5 98 E6
Aquila Rd LU7 111 D8
Aragon Ct MK45 84 E8
Aragon Pl PE28 6 F5
Aragon Rd MK45 84 F7
Arbour Cl LU3 108 A1
Arbroath Rd LU3 107 D1
Arcade The
14 Bedford MK40 50 B8
Letchworth SG6 101 F6
Arcadian Ct AL5 131 A2
Archers Way SG6 101 D6
Archway Par LU3 115 F4
Archway Rd LU3 115 E4
Arden Gr AL5 131 B1
Arden Pl LU2 116 E1
Arden Wlk MK41 39 B3
Ardleigh Gn LU2 117 E1
Ardley Cl LU6 121 C5
Ardley Hill Lower Sch LU6 121 C6
Arena Par SG6 101 F6
Arenson Way LU5 114 C2
Argyll Ave LU3 116 C2
Argyll St MK40 38 B2
Arianne Bsns Ctr LU5 114 B3
Aries Ct LU7 111 C8
Arkwright Rd
Bedford MK42 51 A5
Irchester NN29 7 C7
Milton Ernest MK44 27 B5
Arkwright Road Ind Est MK42 51 A5
Arlesey Ho SG15 90 A8
Arlesey New Rd SG6, SG15 101 B7
Arlesey Rd
Church End SG16 89 E8
Henlow SG16 89 D8
Ickleford SG5 100 F5
Arlesey Sta SG15 90 A8
Arlington Ct 15 MK40 38 B1
Armitage Gdns LU4 115 D1
Armour Rise SG4 101 B2
Armstrong Cl MK45 62 F3
Armstrong Dr MK42 50 C6
Arnald Way LU5 114 A4
Arncliffe Cres LU2 116 E1
Arndale Ctr LU1 123 E7
Arnhem Cl PE19 22 C5
Arnhem Pl SG17 77 C2
Arnold Cl
Barton-le-C MK45 97 C2
Luton LU2 117 A3
Arnold Middle Sch MK45 97 D2
Arnolds La SG7 80 D6
Arran Cl SG19 54 B8
Arran Ct LU1 123 D7
Arrow Cl LU3 115 E6
Arrow Leys MK41 38 F4
Arthur St Ampthill MK45 84 E8
Luton, New Town LU1 123 E6
Arum Cl NN10 8 C7
Arun Cl MK41 38 D5
Arundel Cl MK45 84 D1
Arundel Cres PE19 22 E2
Arundel Ct NN10 8 A8
Arundel Dr MK41 39 A4
Arundel Rd Luton LU4 115 F2
Marston Moretaine MK43 72 C8
Ascot Dr LU7 110 D6
Ascot Rd Luton LU3 116 B2
Rushden NN10 8 D8
Ascott Ho★ LU7 110 A2
Asgard Dr MK41 39 D4
Ash Cl Beeston SG19 54 B6
Flitwick MK45 84 F2
Irchester NN29 7 A7
Ash Gr Biggleswade SG18 66 F8
Dunstable LU5 121 D8
Leighton Buzzard LU7 111 A8
Ash Grange LU7 111 B5
Ash Rd Biggleswade SG18 67 A7
Luton LU4 123 B8
Ash Tree Rd LU5 114 B6
Ash Well Wlk LU5 114 E6
Ash Wlk MK42 49 F3
Ashburnham Cres LU7 110 E6
Ashburnham Ct MK40 50 A8
Ashburnham Rd
Ampthill MK45 84 E7
Bedford MK40 50 A8
Luton LU1 123 C7
Ashby Ct SG18 78 F6
Ashby Dr Barton-le-C MK45 97 C3
Rushden NN10 8 A8
Upper Caldecote SG18 66 B8
Ashby Villas LU6 119 A1
Ashcraft Cl MK43 72 C7
Ashcroft LU6 113 F1
Ashcroft High Sch LU2 117 C2
Ashcroft Rd LU2 117 B3
Ashdale Ave MK42 49 F5
Ashdale Gdns LU3 108 A1
Ashdown SG6 90 F1
Ashdown Rd SG17 77 E3
Ashfield PE28 6 F5
Ashfield Way LU3 116 A6
Ashington Ct SG17 78 B2
Ashley Gdns
Biggleswade SG18 67 B7
Harpenden AL5 130 D3
Ashlong Cl LU7 111 C7
Ashridge Cl NN10 8 A8
Ashridge Dr MK41 39 C4
Ashton CE Mid Sch LU6 114 B1
Ashton Rd Dunstable LU6 114 B1
Luton LU1 123 E5
Ashton Sq 7 LU6 121 B8
Ashton St Peter CE Sch LU5 114 C1
Ashwell Ave LU3 115 C8
Ashwell Par LU3 115 C8
Ashwell Pk AL5 131 D1
Ashwell Pl 4 LU7 111 A8
Ashwell Rd
Guilden Morden SG8 69 F1
Hinxworth SG7 80 E5
Newnham SG7 91 F8
Ashwell St LU7 111 A8
Aspects L Ctr MK41 50 F7
Aspen Ave MK41 38 E4
Asplands Cl MK17 81 B4
Aspley Cl LU4 114 E3
Aspley Ct Bedford MK40 38 A1
Woburn Sands MK17 81 C3
Aspley Guise Lower Sch MK17 81 F4
Aspley Guise Sta MK17 81 D6
Aspley Hill MK17 81 C4
Aspley La MK17 81 E2
Aspley Rd MK42 50 B6
Astley Gn LU2 117 D2
Aston Rd MK42 51 A5
Astra Ct LU2 116 F2
Astral Cl SG16 89 B3
Astrey Cl LU5 95 F2
Astwick Rd SG5 79 F2
Astwood Cl SG19 56 A8
Astwood Dr MK45 84 D4
Astwood Rd MK43 59 C7
Atherstone Abbey MK41 51 B8
Atherstone Rd LU4 115 D1
Atholl Cl LU3 115 D8
Atholl Wlk MK41 39 B4
Attadale Wlk MK41 39 B4
Atterbury Ave LU7 111 B8
Aubrey Gdns LU4 115 B6
Aubreys SG6 101 F2
Auckland Rd SG18 67 B7
Augustus Rd LU7 104 E2
Austin Canons MK42 50 A6
Austin Cl NN29 7 C8
Austin Rd LU3 116 C4
Avebury Ave LU2 116 D4
Aveline Ct LU7 111 A6
Avenells Way SG19 44 D5
Avenue Rd Rushden NN10 8 F5
St Neots PE19 22 F6
Avenue St Nicholas AL5 131 A1
Avenue The Ampthill MK45 84 E7
Bedford MK40 50 A8
Biggleswade SG18 67 B6
Bletsoe MK44 17 C1
Blunham MK44 41 D2
Dunstable LU6 120 E7
Flitwick MK45 84 F3
Langford SG18 78 F6
Luton LU4 115 D5
Sandy SG19 54 B7
Stotfold SG5 90 F6
Aviary Wlk MK41 38 C5
Avoca Ho MK43 36 F3
Avocet SG6 90 E1
Avocet Cl
Biggleswade SG18 66 F4
Sandy SG19 42 B1
Avon Chase SG16 89 C4
Avon Cotts LU2 117 B3
Avon Ct
17 Harpenden AL5 131 B1
Luton LU1 123 C8
St Neots PE19 22 C3
Avon Dr MK41 38 C5
Avon Rd SG16 89 B4
Avon Rise MK45 84 D2
Avon Wlk LU7 103 B3
Avondale Rd LU1 123 C8
Axe Cl LU3 115 E6
Axis Way PE19 22 B5
Aydon Rd LU3 116 B6
Aylesbury Ct MK41 38 F1
Aylesbury Rd MK41 50 F8
Aylmerton Ct SG17 77 D2
Aylott Cl PE28 5 B4
Aynscombe Cl LU6 120 F8

B

Back La MK44 16 A8
Back St Biggleswade SG18 67 A6
Clophill MK45 75 C1
Luton LU2 123 E8
Badgers Cl MK45 84 E3
Badgers Gate LU6 120 E8
Badingham Dr AL5 130 E1
Bagwicks Cl LU3 115 E7
Bailey Hill Ct LU1 123 E5
Bailey St LU1 123 F6
Baileys Villas MK43 26 C8
Baker Ave SG19 56 A7
Baker St Ampthill MK45 84 E8
Leighton Buzzard LU7 111 A7
Luton LU1 123 E5
Baker's La SG19 42 B8
Bakers Cl MK43 34 D5
Bakers Cres NN29 7 A8
Bakers La LU6 127 E8
Bakers Wood Cl LU7 103 A6
Bakery Cl MK43 59 B1
Bakery The MK43 36 B7
Bakewell Cl LU4 115 C1
Balcombe Cl LU2 117 D4
Baldock Cl LU4 114 F3
Baldock Rd
Letchworth SG6 101 F4
Stotfold SG5 91 A5
Baldock Sta SG7 91 F1
Baldur Cl MK41 39 D3
Balfour Ct AL5 131 C3
Balham Cl NN10 7 F8
Ballinghall Cl MK41 39 A2
Balliol Lower Sch MK42 49 D3
Balliol Rd MK42 49 D3
Balls La MK44 52 B8
Balmoral Ave MK40 38 D2
Balmoral Cl Flitwick MK45 84 D1
Sandy SG19 42 B1
Balmoral Rd SG5 100 E1
Balmoral Way PE19 22 F2
Balmore Wood LU3 108 B1
Balsall St E 6 MK40 38 B1
Balsall St W MK40 38 B1
Bamburgh Dr MK41 39 A4
Bamford Rd MK42 50 F5
Bamfords La MK43 34 E6
Bamfords Yd MK43 34 E5
Bampton Rd LU4 115 B2
Banbury Cl LU4 115 F4
Bancroft Ave SG18 66 B2
Bancroft Rd LU3 116 B5
Bank Cl LU4 115 C4
Bank's Rd SG18 67 B7
Banks Cl MK43 72 C7
Banks Dr SG19 54 B7
Bankside Cl LU5 114 A5
Bar La SG19 45 E3
Barber End SG17 77 D3
Barbers La 2 LU1 123 E7
Barclay Ct LU2 123 F8
Barford Ave MK42 50 D6
Barford Rd Blunham MK44 41 C3
St Neots PE19 22 E2
Willington MK44 40 C7
Barford Rise LU2 117 D1
Barker's La MK41 51 A8
Barkers Cl MK45 84 E6
Barkers Piece MK43 60 D1
Barking Cl LU4 115 B6
Barley Brow LU6 113 E3
Barley Ct Rushden NN10 8 C8
St Neots PE19 22 D5
Barley La LU4 115 C5
Barley Rd PE19 22 C3
Barley Rise AL5 131 C4
Barley Way MK41 39 A3
Barleycorn Cl LU7 111 D7
Barleycorn The 1 LU3 123 D8
Barleyfield Way LU5 114 A4
Barleyvale LU3 116 A8
Barnabas Rd LU7 110 D6
Barnard Ave MK42 49 C3
Barnard Cl PE19 22 F1
Barnard Rd LU1 123 A7
Barncroft MK43 34 E6
Barndell Cl SG5 90 F6
Barnes Cl PE19 22 E6
Barnes Rd MK43 60 F6
Barnett Cl SG18 67 A6
Barnfield Ave LU2 116 D5
Barnfield Coll Luton LU2 116 D5
Luton LU2 123 F8
Luton LU3 116 B8
Barnfield Coll S LU1 123 B5
Barnhill MK41 39 A2
Barns Dene AL5 130 E2
Barns The Blunham MK44 41 D3
Riseley MK44 11 A2
Barnstaple Rd MK40 38 E2
Barnston Cl LU2 117 D1
Barnwell Dr NN10 8 A8
Baron Ct PE19 22 B4
Barons Ct 7 LU2 116 D1
Barratt Ind Pk LU2 124 C6
Barrie Ave LU6 113 E3
Barringer Way PE19 22 F7
Barrington Rd
Letchworth SG6 101 F4
Rushden NN10 8 C8
Barrow Path 3 LU7 111 A8
Barrowby Cl LU2 117 D1
Barton Ave LU5 121 D8
Barton Cl AL5 131 C3
Barton Ct LU4 115 B3
Barton Ind Est MK45 97 A4
Barton Rd
Barton-le-C MK45 97 B7
Bedford MK42 50 F5
Gravenhurst MK45 87 C4
Harlington LU5 96 A2
Hexton SG5 98 A1
Luton LU3 116 C7
Sharpenhoe MK45 96 F2
Silsoe MK45 86 C3
Bartram Cl MK42 49 C3
Bartram Ct MK42 49 C3
Basildon Ct LU7 110 F7
Bassett Ct LU7 110 F7
Bassett Rd LU7 110 F7
Bassie Cl MK42 50 C6
Batcheldor Gdns MK43 36 E1
Batford Rd AL5 131 D3
Bath Abbey MK41 51 B8
Bath Pl SG17 78 B3
Bath Rd LU3 116 D2
Battison St MK40 50 B8
Battle Abbey MK41 39 B1
Battlesden Ave MK17 104 C8
Baulk The Beeston SG19 54 B6

Baulk The *continued*
Biggleswade SG18 ...67 B6
Clapham MK41 ...37 F7
Lilley LU2 ...109 D2
Potton SG19 ...56 C6
Baxter Dr PE19 ...22 E2
Bay Cl LU4 ...115 B6
Bayham Cl MK42 ...50 D3
Baylam Dell LU2 ...117 E1
Beachampstead Rd PE19 13 F6
Beacon Ave LU6 ...120 E7
Beacon Rd HP4 ...126 A1
Beacon View LU7 ...112 D5
Beaconsfield LU2 ...124 B8
Beaconsfield St MK41 ...38 B2
Beadlow Rd LU4 ...114 F4
Beale St LU6 ...114 A1
Beancroft Rd MK43 ...60 B1
Beanley Cl LU2 ...117 E2
Bearton Ct SG5 ...100 E1
Bearton Gn SG5 ...100 D1
Bearton Rd SG5 ...100 E1
Beatrice St MK42 ...50 A5
Beatty Rd PE19 ...22 B2
Beauchamp Cl PE19 ...22 B3
Beauchamp Ct 9 MK40 ...38 A1
Beauchamp Mid Sch
MK41 ...38 C5
Beauchamp Rd MK43 ...61 A7
Beaudesert LU7 ...111 A7
Beaudesert Lower Sch
LU7 ...111 D8
Beaufort Way MK41 ...38 C6
Beaulieu Way MK41 ...38 E5
Beaumanor Pl SG17 ...76 E3
Beaumont Ct
Flitwick MK45 ...84 E3
10 Harpenden AL5 ...131 B1
Beaumont Gdns MK42 ...49 E3
Beaumont Ho MK40 ...37 F2
Beaumont Rd
Flitwick MK45 ...84 E3
Luton LU3 ...116 B2
Beaver Cl PE19 ...22 B5
Bec Rd PE19 ...22 E5
Becher Cl MK41 ...39 F5
Beckett Ct 3 MK40 ...50 B8
Beckett St MK40 ...50 B8
Becketts Cl MK45 ...74 B1
Beckham Cl LU2 ...116 D7
Becks Cl AL3 ...128 D5
Bedesman La MK42 ...50 C7
Bedford Ave MK45 ...86 C4
Bedford Bsns Ctr MK42 ...50 D4
Bedford Butterfly Pk*
MK44 ...29 F1
Bedford Cl SG5 ...87 E2
Bedford Coll MK42 ...50 B7
Bedford Ct LU5 ...114 B5
Bedford Gdns 3 LU2 ...123 D8
Bedford High Sch MK40 ...38 B1
Bedford Hospl (North Wing)
MK40 ...38 D1
Bedford Hospl (South Wing)
MK42 ...50 B6
Bedford Modern Sch
MK41 ...38 A3
Bedford Mus* MK40 ...50 C8
Bedford Rd
Aspley Guise MK17 ...81 F5
Barton-le-C MK45 ...97 C3
Brogborough MK43 ...82 C8
Cardington MK44 ...51 C5
Clapham MK41 ...37 F5
Clophill MK45 ...86 C8
Cold Brayfield MK46 ...34 B5
Cranfield MK43 ...59 C2
Cranfield MK43 ...60 A3
Great Barford SG18 ...40 E4
Haynes SG18 ...64 E5
Hitchin SG5 ...100 D2
Hitchin, Westmill SG5 ...100 D1
Houghton Conquest MK45 ...62 A1
Houghton Regis LU5 ...114 A6
Kempston MK42 ...49 E4
Kempston Hardwick MK45 ...61 F5
Letchworth SG6 ...101 D7
Lower Stondon SG16 ...89 B3
Marston Moretaine MK43 ...72 D8
Milton Ernest MK44 ...27 B3
Moggerhanger MK44 ...53 B7
Northill SG18 ...53 B2
Ravensden MK44 ...28 E1
Roxton MK44 ...31 E2
Rushden NN10 ...8 D5
Sandy SG19 ...54 B7
Shefford SG17 ...77 B4
Stagsden MK43 ...36 C1
Turvey MK43 ...35 B5
Wick End MK43 ...48 B8
Willington MK44 ...52 B7
Wilstead MK45 ...62 D5
Wilstead, Duck End MK45 ...62 C7
Wootton MK43 ...61 A8
Bedford Road Lower Sch
MK42 ...49 E4
Bedford Sch MK40 ...38 C1
Bedford Sq LU5 ...114 B5
Bedford St Ampthill MK45 ...73 E1
Leighton Buzzard LU7 ...111 A7
St Neots PE19 ...22 E6
Woburn MK17 ...92 F7
Bedford St Johns Halt
MK42 ...50 B7
Bedford Sta MK40 ...50 A8
Beeby Way MK43 ...25 A3
Beech Ave SG18 ...66 F8
Beech Cl Dunstable LU6 ...121 E5
Beech Cl *continued*
Greenfield MK45 ...85 D2
Beech Cres NN29 ...7 A7
Beech Ct 5 Bedford MK40 38 A1
Harpenden AL5 ...130 F3
Beech Gn LU6 ...114 A1
Beech Gr
Leighton Buzzard LU7 ...110 E7
St Neots PE19 ...22 F6
Beech Hill
Letchworth SG6 ...101 D7
Luton LU2 ...117 D8
Beech Hill Com Prim Sch
LU4 ...116 B1
Beech Ho PE19 ...22 F3
Beech Rd Dunstable LU6 ...121 E4
Flitwick MK45 ...84 F2
Luton LU1 ...123 C8
Beech Ridge AL5 ...130 B5
Beech Tree Way LU5 ...114 B5
Beech Wlk MK42 ...49 F3
Beechdale Rd MK42 ...50 C5
Beeches The MK45 ...86 C4
Beeching Cl AL5 ...131 B4
Beechside SG19 ...44 C6
Beechwood Cl SG5 ...100 D2
Beechwood Ct LU6 ...120 F7
Beechwood Inf Sch LU4 115 E4
Beechwood Jun Sch
LU4 ...115 E4
Beechwood Park Sch
AL3 ...128 B1
Beechwood Rd LU4 ...115 E3
Beechwood Rise SG17 ...77 D2
Beecroft Lower Sch
LU6 ...113 F1
Beecroft Way LU6 ...121 A8
Beeston Gn SG19 ...54 B5
Beezling Cl PE19 ...22 C6
Begwary Cl PE19 ...22 B5
Belam Way SG19 ...42 B1
Belfry Cl MK42 ...50 B4
Belfry Ct SG19 ...54 C7
Belfry The LU2 ...116 E6
Belgrave Rd LU4 ...115 D5
Bell Alley 9 LU7 ...111 A7
Bell Cl MK45 ...95 E6
Bell Foundry Cl SG19 ...44 D5
Bell La MK45 ...63 D7
Bell's Cl MK42 ...51 A3
Bellamy Cl PE19 ...22 E2
Bellamy Rd MK43 ...60 F6
Bellerby Rise LU4 ...115 B6
Bellevue Cl SG19 ...55 F7
Bellingham Pl SG18 ...67 B7
Bells Cl SG5 ...87 F1
Bellway MK17 ...81 A6
Belmont Rd LU1 ...123 C7
Belper Rd LU4 ...115 D2
Belsize Rd LU4 ...114 F3
Belvedere Rd LU3 ...116 B5
Belvoir Wlk MK41 ...39 A4
Bembridge Gdns LU3 ...115 F7
Benedict Cl NN10 ...7 F8
Benington Cl LU2 ...116 F5
Bennett Ct SG6 ...101 F6
Bennetts Cl Bletsoe MK44 ...17 C1
Dunstable LU6 ...121 B7
Benning Ave LU6 ...121 A8
Benson Cl LU3 ...115 F7
Bentley Cl SG18 ...78 F6
Bentley Ct LU1 ...123 C8
Bentley Mews SG17 ...77 B2
Bents Cl MK41 ...37 D7
Berberry Dr MK45 ...85 E4
Bereford Cl MK44 ...40 F5
Beresford Rd
Bedford MK40 ...50 E8
Luton LU4 ...116 A1
Berkeley Cl SG18 ...67 A4
Berkeley Ct 6 AL5 ...131 A2
Berkeley Path 2 LU2 ...123 E8
Berkeley Rd MK42 ...50 C4
Berkley Ct PE19 ...22 E4
Berkley St PE19 ...22 F4
Bernard Cl LU5 ...114 C1
Berrill St NN29 ...7 A7
Berrow Cl LU2 ...117 E2
Berry Dr MK43 ...36 E2
Berry End MK17 ...83 A1
Berry La MK17 ...81 F6
Berry Leys LU3 ...115 E7
Berwick Way SG19 ...54 C8
Besford Cl LU2 ...117 E2
Bessemer Cl SG5 ...100 E2
Bethune Cl LU1 ...123 B6
Betjeman Cl AL5 ...131 C1
Betony Wlk NN10 ...8 B8
Beverley Cres MK40 ...37 F1
Beverley Gdns MK45 ...86 C8
Beverley Gr MK40 ...37 E1
Beverley Rd LU4 ...115 F1
Bevery Cl MK43 ...37 A8
Bevington Way PE19 ...22 E2
Bewcastle Cl MK41 ...39 A5
Bewdley Dr LU7 ...110 C7
Bexhill Rd LU2 ...117 D2
Bibshall Cres LU6 ...121 C6
Bickerdikes Gdns SG19 ...54 B8
Biddenham Turn MK40 ...37 B2
Biddenham Upper Sch
MK40 ...49 D8
Bideford Ct LU7 ...110 C8
Bideford Gdns LU3 ...116 D4
Bideford Gn LU7 ...110 C8
Bidwell Hill LU5 ...114 B5
Bidwell Path LU5 ...114 B4
Biggleswade Hospl SG18 67 C8
Biggleswade Rd
Dunton SG18 ...68 B5
Sutton SG19 ...55 E4
Upper Caldecote SG18 ...66 C8
Biggleswade Sta SG18 ...67 A5
Bigthan Rd LU5 ...121 C8
Bilberry Cl PE19 ...22 C5
Bilberry Rd SG17 ...78 B3
Billington Cl MK45 ...84 D3
Billington Ct LU7 ...111 B6
Billington Rd
Billington LU7 ...112 A2
Stanbridge LU7 ...112 B4
Bilsdon Cl NN10 ...7 F8
Bilton Rd SG4 ...100 F2
Bilton Way LU1 ...115 F1
Binder Cl LU4 ...114 E4
Bindon Abbey MK41 ...51 A8
Bingen Rd SG5 ...100 C1
Binham Cl LU2 ...116 D7
Birbeck Cl MK41 ...37 C7
Birch Cl Broom SG18 ...66 C2
Clifton SG17 ...77 F2
Birch Gr SG19 ...54 B6
Birch Link LU4 ...116 C1
Birch Rd SG18 ...67 A7
Birch Side LU6 ...121 D6
Birch's Cl LU7 ...104 F2
Birchdale Ave MK42 ...49 F4
Birchen Gr LU2 ...116 F3
Birches The Flitwick MK45 84 D5
Letchworth SG6 ...101 E8
Birchfield Rd MK44 ...40 E7
Birchmead SG19 ...44 C6
Bird Ct MK45 ...62 E4
Bird's Hill LU7 ...103 A5
Birdsfoot La LU3 ...116 B6
Birkdale Rd MK41 ...38 E5
Birling Dr LU2 ...117 C4
Birse Gn MK41 ...39 B4
Birtley Croft LU2 ...117 E1
Biscot Rd LU3 ...116 C2
Bishop Cl LU7 ...111 D6
Bishops Ct 6 LU3 ...116 D1
Bishops Rd Bedford MK41 ...39 B1
St Neots PE19 ...22 F2
Bishops Wlk MK17 ...81 B3
Bishopscote Rd LU3 ...116 B3
Bishopstone Ct MK40 ...50 A8
Bittern Dr SG18 ...66 F5
Bittern Way SG6 ...90 E1
Black Hat Cl MK45 ...62 E4
Black Swan La LU3 ...116 A5
Black Thorn Rd LU5 ...114 C6
Blackbird Cl MK45 ...84 D2
Blackbird St SG19 ...56 A7
Blackburn Cl MK42 ...51 B2
Blackburn Rd LU5 ...114 B3
Blackfriars NN10 ...7 F8
Blackhill LU7 ...112 F5
Blackhill La MK45 ...96 E8
Blacksmith Cl
Everton SG19 ...43 C3
Stotfold SG5 ...90 F7
Blacksmith Ct 3 LU6 ...121 B8
Blackthorn Dr LU2 ...117 C4
Blackthorn Gr MK17 ...81 A4
Blackwood Rd PE19 ...22 B3
Blair Way PE19 ...22 E2
Blakedown LU2 ...116 E1
Blakedown Rd LU7 ...110 C7
Blakelands MK45 ...97 D2
Blakeney Dr LU2 ...116 C7
Blakes Way PE19 ...22 B2
Blandford Ave LU2 ...116 D6
Blaydon Rd Luton LU2 ...124 A8
Sandy SG19 ...42 C2
Blenheim Cl Rushden NN10 8 A8
St Neots PE19 ...22 C4
Blenheim Cres LU3 ...116 C2
Blenheim Link MK45 ...84 D1
Blenheim Rd MK42 ...51 A2
Bliss Ave Cranfield MK43 ...59 C2
Shefford SG17 ...77 D3
Bloomfield Ave LU2 ...117 A1
Bloomfield Dr SG17 ...77 B2
Bloomfield Rd AL5 ...130 F3
Bloomsbury Cl MK17 ...92 F6
Bloomsbury Gdns LU5 ...114 D5
Blows Rd LU5 ...121 D7
Blue Spruce Cl MK43 ...36 C4
Bluebell Cl Bedford MK42 ...50 F4
Biggleswade SG18 ...67 C4
Flitwick MK45 ...84 D3
Bluebell Rise NN10 ...8 B8
Bluebell Wood Cl LU1 ...123 A7
Blundell Pl MK42 ...50 C4
Blundell Rd LU3 ...116 A4
Blunham Rd
Biggleswade SG18 ...66 F5
Moggerhanger MK44 ...53 C8
Blyth Pl 12 LU1 ...123 D6
Blythe Way SG19 ...44 D5
Boddington Gdns SG18 ...67 C7
Boddington Ind Est SG18 67 B6
Bodiam Way PE19 ...22 F2
Bodmin Rd LU4 ...115 F3
Bolingbroke Rd LU1 ...123 B6
Bolney Gn LU2 ...117 D3
Bolton Rd LU1 ...123 F7
Bond Ct AL5 ...130 F3
Bonds La SG18 ...67 A5
Bonnick Cl LU1 ...123 C6
Boot La SG18 ...68 D5
Booth Pl LU6 ...119 E6
Boothey Cl SG18 ...67 A7
Borden La SG18 ...64 C5
Borders Way LU5 ...114 C6
Borodale AL5 ...131 A1
Borough Rd LU5 ...121 D7
Borrowdale Ave LU6 ...121 C6
Borton Ave SG16 ...89 B4
Boscombe Rd LU5 ...114 C2
Bosmore Rd LU3 ...115 F5
Bossard Ct LU7 ...111 A7
Bossington La
Leighton Buzzard LU7 ...110 F8
Leighton Buzzard, Linslade
LU7 ...110 F7
Boswell Ct 13 MK40 ...38 B1
Boswell Dr SG5 ...100 E4
Boswell Pl 8 MK40 ...38 B1
Boteler Gdns MK42 ...50 F5
Bothy The SG18 ...66 C2
Bottom Dr LU6 ...120 D5
Boughton Dr NN10 ...8 A8
Boughton End La MK43 ...72 B1
Boundary The MK41 ...39 A2
Bourne Apts The 2 AL5 130 F2
Bourne End La MK44 ...17 B4
Bourne End Rd
Cranfield MK43 ...59 C4
Kempston MK43 ...48 B1
Bourne Rd MK44 ...10 F2
Bourne The 1 AL5 ...130 F2
Bourneside MK41 ...38 D6
Bow Brickhill Rd MK17 ...81 A4
Bowbrook Vale LU2 ...117 F1
Bower Cl LU6 ...119 F5
Bower Heath La AL5 ...131 C6
Bower La LU6 ...119 F5
Bower St MK40 ...50 D8
Bower's Mill PE19 ...22 E5
Bower's Par AL5 ...131 A1
Bowers Cl MK44 ...11 B3
Bowers La MK44 ...11 B3
Bowers Way AL5 ...131 A1
Bowhill MK41 ...38 F3
Bowland Cres LU6 ...121 A6
Bowles Way LU6 ...121 D5
Bowling Green La LU2 ...116 E2
Bowling Green Rd MK43 ...59 C1
Bowmans Cl LU6 ...121 C7
Bowmans Way LU6 ...121 C7
Bowyer's Cl SG5 ...100 D1
Box End Rd MK43 ...48 F7
Boxgrove Cl LU2 ...117 C5
Boxgrove Priory MK41 ...39 B1
Boxted Cl LU4 ...115 C5
Boyde Gdns MK40 ...49 E7
Boyle Cl LU2 ...123 E8
Brabazon Cl MK42 ...51 A2
Brace St 16 MK40 ...50 B8
Braceby Cl LU3 ...115 F6
Brache Ct LU1 ...123 F6
Brache The MK45 ...74 C1
Bracken Pl MK41 ...39 B1
Brackendale Gr
Harpenden AL5 ...130 D3
Luton LU3 ...116 B5
Bracklesham Gdns LU2 117 D3
Brackley Rd MK42 ...50 C5
Bracknell Cl LU4 ...114 F3
Bradden Cotts HP2 ...132 F8
Bradden La HP1,HP2 ...132 E7
Bradden Villas HP2 ...132 F8
Bradford Rd LU5 ...106 A5
Bradford Way LU5 ...105 F5
Bradgate Rd MK40 ...38 D1
Bradgers Hill Rd LU2 ...116 E4
Bradley Rd LU4 ...115 D1
Bradleys Cnr SG4 ...101 C1
Bradshaws Cl MK45 ...97 C3
Braemar Ct MK40 ...50 A8
Braeside MK41 ...38 F4
Bragenham La LU7 ...102 D5
Braggs La SG19 ...57 C4
Braintree Cl LU4 ...114 F3
Braithwaite Ct 16 LU3 ...116 D1
Bramble Cl
Harpenden AL5 ...130 F3
Leighton Buzzard LU7 ...111 C7
Luton LU4 ...115 C4
Bramble Rd LU4 ...115 C4
Brambles MK45 ...62 F4
Brambling Cl SG19 ...42 C2
Bramhanger Acre LU3 ...115 D7
Bramingham Bsns Pk
LU3 ...116 B8
Bramingham Prim Sch
LU3 ...116 B8
Bramingham Rd LU3 ...115 F6
Bramley Cl Baldock SG7 ...91 F1
Shefford SG17 ...77 B2
Bramley Ct MK43 ...24 F6
Brampton Cl
Bedford MK42 ...50 F5
Harpenden AL5 ...131 D1
Brampton Park Rd SG5 ...100 E1
Brampton Rise LU6 ...121 C6
Brancaster Cl MK42 ...50 F4
Brancker Ave MK42 ...51 A2
Brandreth Ave LU5 ...114 E1
Brandreth Pl SG19 ...54 D6
Brangwyn Gdns MK41 ...38 B3
Branton Cl LU2 ...117 E2
Brantwood Rd LU1 ...123 C7
Braybrook SG19 ...54 A8
Braybrooks Dr SG19 ...56 A7
Brayes Manor SG5 ...90 F6
Brays Ct LU2 ...117 B3
Brays Rd LU2 ...117 B3
Brazier Cl MK45 ...97 B3
Breachwell Pl LU7 ...118 A1
Breadcroft La AL5 ...131 B1
Breamish Wlk MK41 ...38 C7
Brecon Cl 13 LU1 ...123 D6
Brecon Way MK41 ...38 E5
Brendon Ave
Bedford MK41 ...38 E3
Luton LU2 ...117 C1
Brentwood Cl LU5 ...114 D6
Brereton Rd MK40 ...50 B8
Brett Dr MK43 ...36 F1
Bretts Mead LU1 ...123 C5
Bretts Mead Ct LU1 ...123 C5
Brewers Hill Mid Sch
LU6 ...113 E1
Brewers Hill Rd LU6 ...113 F1
Brewery La Ampthill MK45 ...73 E1
Baldock SG7 ...91 E1
Brian May Gr MK45 ...86 B3
Brian Rd LU5 ...96 A2
Briar Bank Cvn Pk MK45 ...62 F2
Briar Cl Ampthill MK45 ...84 E8
Luton LU2 ...117 C4
Briar Patch La SG6 ...101 D3
Briars The MK42 ...49 F3
Brickfield Rd MK41 ...39 B6
Brickhill Cl Blunham MK44 41 E3
Sandy SG19 ...54 D8
Brickhill Dr MK41 ...38 C4
Brickhill Lower Sch
MK41 ...38 D5
Brickhill Rd
Heath & Reach LU7 ...103 A7
Sandy SG19 ...54 D7
Brickle Pl SG17 ...78 B2
Brickly Rd LU4 ...115 C5
Bridge Ct AL5 ...130 F3
Bridge Rd Bedford MK42 ...50 C6
Letchworth SG6 ...101 F6
Bridge St
Leighton Buzzard LU7 ...110 F7
Luton LU1 ...123 E8
Turvey MK43 ...34 D5
Bridge View MK40 ...50 D8
Bridgeman Dr LU5 ...114 D5
Bridgend MK43 ...25 B4
Bridle Dr MK41 ...37 C7
Brierley Cl
Dunstable LU6 ...121 D5
Luton LU2 ...117 D2
Briggington Cotts LU7 ...111 D8
Brigham Gdns SG18 ...67 A6
Brightman Cotts 2 LU3 116 A7
Brightmans Dr MK45 ...74 B1
Brightwell Ave LU6 ...120 C7
Brill Cl LU2 ...117 D2
Brimfield Cl LU2 ...117 D2
Brindley Cl SG19 ...42 B1
Brinsmade Rd MK45 ...73 F1
Bristol Rd LU3 ...116 B4
Britain St LU5 ...121 C8
Britannia Ave LU3 ...116 B4
Britannia Ests LU3 ...116 B2
Britannia Hall LU2 ...124 C8
Britannia Rd MK42 ...50 B6
Brittains Rise SG16 ...88 E2
Brittany Ct LU6 ...121 C8
Britten Cl NN9 ...3 C8
Britten Rd SG17 ...77 D3
Brittons Cl MK44 ...16 E3
Brittons La MK17 ...70 C3
Brive Rd LU5 ...121 E6
Brixham Cl MK40 ...38 E2
Broad Ave MK42 ...50 D4
Broad Mead LU3 ...116 A3
Broad Oak Ct LU2 ...117 D3
Broad Rush Gn LU7 ...110 E8
Broad St SG17 ...78 B2
Broad Wlk Clifton SG17 ...78 B2
Dunstable LU5 ...121 B8
Broad Wlk The PE19 ...22 E3
Broadacres LU2 ...116 D6
Broadcroft SG6 ...101 F2
Broadfields AL5 ...130 F2
Broadhurst Abbey MK41 ...51 A8
Broadmead SG18 ...67 B5
Broadmead Bsns Pk
MK43 ...61 C2
Broadmead Lower Sch
MK43 ...61 C2
Broadmead Rd MK43 ...61 C2
Broadmead Sch LU1 ...123 E5
Broadwater Ave SG6 ...101 E5
Broadwater Dale SG6 ...101 E5
Broadway
Houghton Conquest MK45 ...74 B8
Letchworth SG6 ...101 F5
Broadway Ct SG6 ...101 E3
Broadway The MK40 ...38 B1
Brocas Way LU7 ...118 A3
Brocket Ct LU4 ...115 D5
Brockwell MK43 ...37 A8
Brockwood Cl SG19 ...44 D6
Bromham CE Lower Sch
MK43 ...36 F3
Bromham Mill* MK43 ...37 A2
Bromham Rd
Biddenham MK40 ...37 D1
Bromham MK40 ...37 A2
Bromley Gdns LU5 ...114 D5
Brompton Cl LU3 ...115 F8
Brook Cl
7 Dunstable LU6 ...114 A1
Henlow SG16 ...78 D1
Upper Caldecote SG18 ...66 B8
Brook Ct LU3 ...116 D1
Brook Dr MK42 ...49 C3

Brook End
North Crawley MK16 ......58 A6
Potton SG19 ....56 A7
Brook Farm Cl NN10 ......8 B5
Brook La Flitton MK45 ....85 D4
Great Barford MK44 ......41 A5
Harrold MK43 ....24 F6
Newton Blossomville MK43 .34 B3
Renhold MK41 ....39 B6
Upper Dean PE28 ....5 B4
Brook Rd
Marston Moretaine MK43 ..72 C7
St Neots PE19 ....22 C4
Brook St Bedford MK42 ...50 D5
Edlesborough LU6 ....119 F4
Hargrave NN9 ....1 E3
Leighton Buzzard LU7 ....111 C7
Luton LU3 ....123 D8
St Neots PE19 ....22 E5
Stotfold SG5 ....90 E6
Brook Way MK43 ....36 E2
Brookend Dr MK45 ......97 B3
Brookes Rd MK45 ....84 F3
Brookfield Ave LU5 ....114 D5
Brookfield Pk LU5 .....114 C5
Brookfield Pk Cvn Pk
LU6 ....120 A8
Brookfield Rd MK41 .....38 F2
Brookfields
Pavenham MK43 ....26 C4
Potton SG19 ....56 B7
Brooklands MK42 ....49 E2
Brooklands Ave LU7 ....111 B6
Brooklands Cl LU4 .....115 C6
Brooklands Dr LU7 .....111 C7
Brooklands Mid Sch
LU7 ....111 C6
Brooklands Rd MK44 .....10 F1
Brookmead SG17 ....88 C6
Brookside Campton SG17 ..87 F8
Great Barford MK44 ......41 A5
Letchworth SG6 ....101 F5
Meppershall SG17 ....88 C6
Renhold MK41 ....39 B7
Shillington SG5 ....87 E1
Brookside Wlk LU7 ....111 C7
Brookvale SG16 ....88 E3
Broom Crossroads SG18 .66 A1
Broom Hall SG18 ....66 C2
Broomhills Rd LU7 .....103 A1
Brooms Rd LU2 ....124 A8
Broomstick Ind Est LU6 119 E4
Broughton Ave
Luton LU3 ....116 C5
Toddington LU5 ....105 E6
Broughton Rd MK17 .....70 C3
Brown's Cl LU4 ....115 D5
Brown's Cres LU5 ....95 F3
Brown's Sq PE19 ....22 F5
Browney Path MK41 .....38 C7
Browning Dr PE19 ....22 C6
Browning Rd
Harpenden AL5 ....131 C2
Luton LU4 ....115 A2
Brownlow Ave LU6 ......119 F3
Brownlow Rise LU6 .....120 A8
Browns Cl MK43 ....72 D7
Browns Ct MK40 ....50 C8
Browns La MK43 ....60 F6
Browns Way MK17 ....81 E5
Brownshill MK45 ....74 C1
Brownslea LU7 ....111 C7
Broxley Mead LU4 ......115 D5
Bruce Rd MK42 ....49 D3
Brunel Ct LU4 ....114 E3
Brunel Rd Bedford MK41 ..51 A8
Luton LU4 ....114 E3
Brunswick Cl SG18 ......67 A6
Brunswick St LU2 ......123 F8
Brunt's La SG18 ....66 F6
Brussels Way LU3 ......115 D8
Bruthwaite Gn MK41 .....39 C4
Bryans Cres MK16 ....58 A6
Bryant Ct AL5 ....131 A3
Bryant Way LU5 ....105 F5
Bryants Cl SG5 ....87 F2
Bryony Cl MK41 ....39 B1
Bryony Way LU6 ....113 E1
Buchanan Ct LU2 ....124 B8
Buchanan Dr LU2 ....124 B8
Buckfast Ave MK41 ......38 F5
Buckingham Dr LU2 .....117 D2
Buckingham Mews MK45 84 D1
Buckle Cl LU3 ....115 F7
Buckley Rd PE19 ....22 E4
Bucks Cl MK43 ....36 F2
Buckwood Ave LU5 ......114 F1
Buckwood La LU6 ....127 C7
Buckwood Rd AL3 ....128 C6
Budna Rd SG19 ....53 C4
Buff La SG19 ....45 F1
Bull Pond La LU6 ......121 B7
Bull St SG19 ....56 A7
Bungalows The
Harpenden AL5 ....131 C3
Toddington LU5 ....106 A7
Bunhill Cl LU6 ....120 F8
Bunkers Dr MK45 ....63 D7
Bunkers La LU7 ....110 D6
Bunting Rd LU4 ....115 A4
Buntings The
Bedford MK41 ....38 D4
Sandy SG19 ....42 C2
Bunyan Cl Clifton SG17 ...78 A2
Gamlingay SG19 ....44 D4
Bunyan Cl *continued*
Houghton Conquest MK45 ..74 A8
Pirton SG5 ....99 D4
Bunyan Ctr MK42 ....50 E4
Bunyan Meeting Ho & Mus★
MK40 ....50 C8
Bunyan Rd Bedford MK42 ..50 B5
Biggleswade SG18 ....67 A5
Kempston MK42 ....49 E3
Sandy SG19 ....42 B1
Westoning MK45 ....95 E5
Bunyans Cl LU3 ....116 A5
Bunyans Mead MK42 ......50 C3
Bunyans Wlk LU5 ....95 F2
Burdett's Ct SG19 ....56 A7
Bure Cl MK41 ....38 D6
Burfield Ct LU2 ....117 D3
Burford Cl LU3 ....108 A1
Burford Way SG5 ....100 D2
Burford Wlk LU5 ....114 E5
Burge End La SG5 ....99 C5
Burges Cl LU6 ....121 D6
Burgess Cl Haynes MK45 ..75 F8
Kempston MK42 ....49 D6
Burgess Way SG16 ....78 D3
Burghley Cl MK45 ....84 C1
Burgoyne Ct SG19 ....56 A8
Burgoyne Mid Sch SG19 .55 F7
Burleigh Pl MK43 ....37 A8
Burley SG6 ....90 F2
Burnaby Rd MK40 ....38 C1
Burnell Rise SG6 ....101 D5
Burnell Wlk SG6 ....101 E5
Burnett Ave SG16 ....89 B4
Burnham Rd LU2 ....117 B2
Burns Ct PE19 ....22 D5
Burnt Cl Luton LU3 .....115 F7
St Neots PE19 ....22 F3
Burr Cl MK45 ....97 C4
Burr St Dunstable LU6 ..121 B8
Luton LU2 ....123 E8
Burr's Pl LU1 ....123 E6
Burridge Cl MK43 ....72 D8
Burridge's Cl MK43 .....36 C7
Burrows Cl Clifton SG17 ..78 A2
Woburn Sands MK17 ......81 B5
Burrsholt MK44 ....52 A5
Bursland SG6 ....101 D6
Burwell Rd PE19 ....22 C6
Bury Cl LU5 ....95 F1
Bury Ct MK41 ....39 B2
Bury End SG5 ....99 D4
Bury Farm Cl LU7 ......118 C6
Bury Hill SG19 ....56 B7
Bury La LU3 ....108 A5
Bury Mead SG15 ....90 A7
Bury Mead Rd SG5 ......100 F1
Bury Park Rd LU1 ......123 C8
Bury Rd Shefford SG17 ...77 E3
Shillington SG5 ....87 E2
Bury Rise LU7 ....112 F5
Bury The MK43 ....26 C4
Bury Wlk MK41 ....39 B2
Bush Cl LU5 ....106 A5
Bushmead Ave MK40 ......50 D8
Bushmead Cross MK44 ....20 C5
Bushmead Ct LU2 ....116 E5
Bushmead Gdns PE19 .....22 B3
Bushmead Prim Sch
Luton LU2 ....116 E5
St Neots PE19 ....22 A3
Bushmead Priory★
MK44 ....20 D6
Bushmead Rd Luton LU2 116 E5
St Neots PE19 ....22 A3
Bustard Hill PE28 ....6 D8
Butcher's La SG19 ......57 B4
Bute Sq LU1 ....123 E7
Bute St LU1 ....123 E7
Butely Rd LU4 ....115 B5
Butler St MK44 ....28 F1
Butler Way MK42 ....49 E5
Butlers Yd SG7 ....91 E1
Butlin Rd LU1 ....123 B7
Buttercup Cl
Bedford MK42 ....50 F4
Dunstable LU6 ....121 A7
Buttercup Mead SG18 ....67 C5
Butterfield Green Rd
LU2 ....117 A6
Buttermere Ave LU6 .....121 C6
Buttermere Cl
Flitwick MK45 ....84 E2
Kempston MK42 ....49 D3
Buttermere Path SG18 ...67 A4
Butterworth Path 1
LU2 ....123 E8
Butts The Langford SG18 ..78 F6
Riseley MK44 ....10 E1
Buxton Cl SG17 ....88 C6
Buxton Rd LU1 ....123 D7
Buxtons La SG8 ....69 F3
Buzzard Rd LU4 ....115 A4
Byards Gn SG19 ....55 F8
Bye Rd MK43 ....72 B3
Byfield Cl Luton LU4 ...115 B1
Toddington LU5 ....105 E6
Byford Path LU7 ....111 D5
Byford Way LU7 ....111 D5
Bygrave Rd SG7 ....91 F1
Byng Cl PE19 ....22 B2
Byron Cl
Biggleswade SG18 ....67 A5
Upper Caldecote SG18 ....66 C8
Byron Cres Bedford MK40 .37 F2
Flitwick MK45 ....84 D3
Byron Pl PE19 ....22 C6
Byron Rd Harpenden AL5 .131 A2
Byron Rd *continued*
Luton LU4 ....115 B2
Byslips Rd LU6 ....127 D5

C

Caddington Comm AL3 .128 E8
Cade Cl SG6 ....91 C1
Cades Cl LU1 ....123 A6
Cades La LU1 ....123 A6
Cadia Cl LU1 ....122 E4
Cadwell Ct SG4 ....101 A2
Cadwell La SG4 ....101 A2
Caernarvon Rd PE19 .....22 F1
Cainhoe Rd MK45 ....86 C8
Caister Rd MK41 ....39 B4
Calcutt Cl LU5 ....114 F2
Caldecote Lower Sch
SG18 ....66 B8
Caldecote Rd
Ickwell SG18 ....65 E8
Newnham SG7 ....91 E8
St Neots PE19 ....22 E3
Caldecott Rd NN9 ....3 B7
Calder Gdns LU7 ....110 B7
Calder Rise MK41 ....38 D6
Caleb Cl LU4 ....115 F2
California SG7 ....91 F1
Calnwood Rd LU4 ....115 C3
Calshot Wlk MK41 ....39 A5
Calverton Rd LU3 ......116 A6
Cam Ctr SG4 ....101 A3
Cam Sq SG4 ....101 A3
Camberton Rd LU7 ......110 E5
Cambrian Way MK41 ......38 E3
Cambridge Cl SG18 ......78 F4
Cambridge Ct PE19 ......22 F5
Cambridge Gdns
Langford SG18 ....78 F5
St Neots PE19 ....22 F5
Cambridge Rd
Bedford MK42,MK44 ......51 A5
Cardington MK44 ....51 D6
Dunton SG18 ....68 D6
Hitchin SG4 ....101 C2
Langford SG18 ....78 F5
Sandy SG19 ....54 C7
Cambridge St Luton LU1 .123 F6
St Neots PE19 ....22 F5
Wymington NN10 ....8 A7
Cambridge Way SG18 .....78 F5
Camestone Lower Sch
MK42 ....49 F4
Camford Ct MK42 ....49 D4
Camford Way LU3 ....107 B1
Camp Dr LU5 ....114 B5
Campania Gr LU3 ....116 A8
Campbell Cl MK42 ....49 D3
Campbell Rd MK40 ....38 D1
Campers Ave SG6 ....101 E5
Campers Rd SG6 ....101 E5
Campers Wlk SG6 ....101 E5
Campfield Way SG6 .....101 D5
Campian Cl LU6 ....113 E1
Campin Ct MK43 ....60 E1
Campion Cl NN10 ....8 B8
Campion Rd MK45 ....95 F5
Campion Way MK45 ....84 D3
Campton Lower Sch
SG17 ....76 F1
Campton Rd
Gravenhurst MK45,SG17 ...87 D6
Meppershall SG17 ....87 F6
Shefford SG17 ....77 A2
Canberra Gdns LU3 .....116 B6
Canberra Rd MK42 ....50 F2
Candale Cl LU6 ....121 C6
Caneswordе Rd LU6 .....121 A7
Cannock Chase MK41 .....39 C4
Cannon La LU2 ....117 B5
Cannon's Cl SG8 ....69 F5
Canons Cl MK43 ....60 F8
Canterbury Cl
Kempston MK42 ....49 E6
Luton LU3 ....115 F4
Canterbury Rd MK45 .....84 E4
Cantilupe Cl LU6 ......119 D6
Canvin Way MK42 ....50 E5
Capron Ct LU5 ....114 A2
Capron Rd
Dunstable LU5 ....114 A2
Luton LU4 ....115 E4
Capshill Ave LU7 ......111 C7
Captains Cl MK44 ....17 C1
Capulet Cl PE19 ....22 C3
Cardiff Gr LU1 ....123 D7
Cardiff Rd LU1 ....123 D7
Cardigan Ct 10 LU1 ....123 D8
Cardigan Gdns 11 LU1 ..123 D8
Cardigan St LU1 ....123 D7
Cardinal Ct 3 LU2 .....116 D1
Cardinal Newman RC Sec Sch
LU2 ....108 C1
Cardington Ct MK42 .....50 F5
Cardington Rd MK42,
MK44 ....50 F6
Carfax Cl LU4 ....114 E3
Carina Dr LU7 ....111 C7
Carisbrooke Rd
Harpenden AL5 ....131 C2
Luton LU4 ....115 E1
Carisbrooke Way
Bedford MK41 ....39 A4
St Neots PE19 ....22 F2
Carlisle Cl Dunstable LU6 121 B6
Sandy SG19 ....54 C8
Carlisle Rd MK40 ....49 E7
Carlow Ct LU6 ....121 A8
Carlton Bank 2 AL5 ....131 B1
Carlton Cl Luton LU3 ...116 C2
Rushden NN10 ....8 A7
Carlton Cres LU3 ......116 C2
Carlton Ct 1 AL5 ......131 B1
Carlton Gdns MK41 ......38 D4
Carlton Gr LU7 ....103 A3
Carlton Lower Sch MK43 25 A4
Carlton Rd
Felmersham MK43 ....25 F7
Harpenden AL5 ....131 B2
Harrold MK43 ....25 B5
Turvey MK43 ....34 E7
Carmarthen Way NN10 ....8 C8
Carmelite Rd LU4 ......115 A3
Carnaby PE28 ....6 F4
Carnation Cl LU7 ......103 A1
Carnegie Gdns LU3 .....116 A8
Carnell Cl MK42 ....49 C2
Carnoustie Dr MK40 .....49 B7
Carol Cl LU3 ....116 B4
Carole Ct LU1 ....123 E5
Carolyn Ct LU3 ....116 B4
Carpenders Cl AL5 .....130 D4
Carrick Rd MK41 ....39 B4
Carriers Way MK43 ......25 B4
Carroll Dr MK42 ....50 C4
Carron Cl LU7 ....110 B7
Carron Rd MK41 ....38 C7
Carsdale Cl LU3 ....116 A6
Carter Cl MK42 ....50 E6
Carter St SG19 ....54 B8
Carteret Rd LU2 ....117 C1
Carters Cl SG15 ....90 A7
Carters La SG19 ....56 A7
Carters Way SG15 ....90 A7
Carters Wlk SG15 ....90 A7
Carterweys LU5 ....114 E2
Carthagena Rd SG19 .....55 E5
Cartmel Dr LU6 ....121 B6
Cartmel Priory MK41 ....51 B8
Cartwright Cl MK43 .....36 F1
Cashio La SG6 ....91 A1
Caslon Way SG6 ....90 F1
Castle Cl Totternhoe LU6 .120 A8
Wilstead MK45 ....62 F4
Castle Croft Rd LU1 ...123 A6
Castle Ct Hitchin SG5 ..100 D1
Rushden NN10 ....8 A8
Castle Gdns PE28 ....6 F4
Castle Hill Cl PE19 .....22 C2
Castle Hill Ct MK45 .....75 E1
Castle Hill Rd LU6 ....119 F8
Castle La MK40 ....50 C8
Castle Lower Sch MK40 .38 D1
Castle Rd Bedford MK40 ..50 D8
Lavendon MK46 ....23 F1
Castle Rise AL4 ....131 F2
Castle St
Luton, High Town LU1 ...123 E7
Luton, New Town LU1 ....123 E6
Castles Cl SG5 ....90 F8
Caswell La MK17 ....92 F7
Catchacre LU6 ....121 A7
Cater St MK42 ....49 E4
Catesby Gn LU3 ....108 A1
Catherall Rd LU3 ......116 B6
Catherine Rd MK45 ......84 E3
Catherines Cl SG19 .....56 A7
Catsbrook Rd LU3 ......116 B6
Cauldwell Ct
Bedford MK42 ....50 A6
Sandy SG19 ....54 C8
Cauldwell Lower Sch
MK42 ....50 B6
Cauldwell Pl MK42 ......50 B7
Cauldwell St MK42 ......50 B7
Cauldwell Wlk MK42 .....50 A6
Cause End Rd MK43 ......60 F7
Causeway PE19 ....13 F6
Causeway Cl PE19 ....13 F6
Causeway The
Carlton MK43 ....25 B3
Clophill MK45 ....86 D8
Cavalier Cl LU3 ....116 A5
Cave's Ct SG19 ....56 A7
Cave's La MK40 ....38 E2
Cavendish Ct
Bedford MK40 ....37 F2
6 Biggleswade SG18 .....67 A6
St Neots PE19 ....22 D5
Cavendish Rd Luton LU3 .116 B2
Markyate AL3 ....128 D6
Cavendish St MK40 ......38 B1
Cawdor Cl MK41 ....39 B4
Cawdor Pl PE19 ....22 F2
Caxton Ct LU3 ....115 F4
Caxton Pk MK41 ....39 C3
Caxton Rd MK41 ....39 D3
Cedar Ave
Biggleswade SG18 ....66 F7
Ickleford SG5 ....100 E4
Cedar Cl Ampthill MK45 ..84 F7
Irchester NN29 ....7 A7
Luton LU4 ....114 E3
Rushden NN10 ....8 A8
Shefford SG17 ....77 E2
Cedar Gdns SG19 ....54 B7
Cedar Rd MK42 ....50 D5
Cedars Ctyd MK45 ....84 E7
Cedars The Ampthill MK45 .84 E7
Dunstable LU6 ....121 C7
13 Harpenden AL5 ......131 B1
Wootton MK43 ....61 A8
Cedars Upper Sch & Com
Coll The LU7 ....110 E5
Cedars Way LU7 ....110 E5
Cedars Wlk MK45 ....84 E7
Celandine Cl NN10 ....8 C7
Celandine Dr LU3 ......116 A8
Cemetery Rd
Houghton Regis LU5 ....114 B3
Kempston MK43 ....49 B3
St Neots PE19 ....22 F5
Centauri Cl LU7 ....111 C8
Central App SG6 ....101 F6
Central Ave Henlow SG16 .89 B3
Shortstown MK42 ....51 A2
Wharley End MK43 ....58 E2
Whipsnade LU6 ....126 E8
Centrus Ind Est LU5 ...114 B2
Century Cl MK45 ....84 F2
Cetus Cres LU7 ....111 C7
Chad La AL3 ....129 C4
Chadwell Cl LU2 ....116 F1
Chadwick Cl LU6 ....114 A1
Chagford Cl MK40 ....38 E1
Chagny Cl SG6 ....101 E6
Chainbridge La PE28 ......2 F8
Chalfont Way LU2 ......117 D2
Chalgrave Rd LU5,LU7 ..105 D3
Chalk Hill LU2 ....117 F4
Chalkdown LU2 ....116 E6
Challney Boys High Sch
LU4 ....115 D2
Challney Cl LU4 ....115 D2
Challney Girls High Sch
LU4 ....115 D2
Chaloner Ct LU7 ....111 B5
Chalton Hts LU4 ....106 E1
Chalton Lower Sch LU4 106 E1
Chalton Rd LU4 ....115 C5
Chamberlain Way PE19 ...22 F7
Chamberlaines AL5 .....130 A5
Chamberlains Gdns
LU7 ....103 A2
Chambers La SG5 ....100 E4
Chambers Way SG18 ......67 C5
Chancellors SG15 ....90 B7
Chandler Path MK42 .....49 D5
Chandler Pl LU7 ....103 A5
Chandlers Cl MK43 ......72 C8
Chandlers Wharf PE19 ...22 E5
Chandos Ct 14 MK40 .....38 B1
Chandos Rd Ampthill MK45 84 E8
Luton LU4 ....115 F1
Chandos St MK40 ....38 B1
Channels End Rd MK44 ...30 C6
Chantry Ave MK42 ....49 F2
Chantry Cl MK17 ....81 A6
Chantry Piece SG18 .....53 E2
Chantry Prim Sch LU4 ..114 F4
Chantry Rd MK42 ....49 E3
Chaomans SG6 ....101 F3
Chapel Cl Bedford MK41 ..39 B1
Great Barford MK44 .....40 F5
Honeydon MK44 ....21 B2
Luton LU2 ....116 C8
Shefford SG17 ....77 F2
Toddington LU5 ....105 F6
Wrestlingworth SG19 ....57 B4
Chapel Ct SG18 ....78 F6
Chapel Dr SG15 ....90 A4
Chapel End Rd MK45 .....74 D8
Chapel Field
Gamlingay SG19 ....44 D4
Great Barford MK44 .....40 F5
Chapel Fields SG18 .....66 F6
Chapel Hill NN29 ....7 B8
Chapel La Ampthill MK45 ..73 E1
Cardington MK44 ....51 E5
Colmworth MK44 ....20 A1
Ivinghoe Aston LU7 ....119 A1
Northall LU6 ....119 A5
Souldrop MK44 ....16 A8
Totternhoe LU6 ....119 F8
Willington MK44 ....40 C1
Wilstead MK45 ....62 F4
Chapel Path
Houghton Regis LU5 ....114 B4
2 Leighton Buzzard LU7 .111 A8
Chapel Pl SG5 ....90 F6
Chapel Pound MK43 ......37 A8
Chapel Rd
Breachwood Green SG4 ..125 E8
Flamstead AL3 ....129 B2
Flitwick MK45 ....84 D3
Meppershall SG17 ....88 D6
Chapel St Dunton SG18 ...68 D5
Hinxworth SG7 ....80 D6
Luton, High Town LU1 ...123 E7
Luton, New Town LU1 ....123 E6
Potton SG19 ....56 A7
Woburn Sands MK17 ......81 B4
Chapel Viaduct LU1 ....123 E7
Chapel Way SG16 ....78 D1
Chapel Yd MK44 ....6 E1
Chapelfields MK44 ......18 D1
Chapman Cl
Kempston MK42 ....49 D6
Potton SG19 ....56 A7
Chapman Way PE19 ....22 E2
Chapmans Cl NN29 ....7 B8
Chapterhouse Rd LU4 ...115 A3
Chard Dr LU3 ....108 B1
Charlbury Ct MK40 ......38 D1
Charles St LU2 ....123 F8
Charles' St PE19 ....22 F5
Charlewood Ho MK17 .....81 B3
Charlottes Ct 2 LU1 ...123 D7
Charlwood Rd LU4 ......115 B1
Charmbury Rise LU2 ....117 A4
Charndon Cl LU3 ....108 B1
Charnocks Cl SG19 ......44 D5
Charnwood Ave MK41 .....39 B3

Chartmoor Rd LU7 . . . . .111 A4
Chartwell Dr LU2 . . . . .116 E3
Chase Cl SG15 . . . . .90 A8
Chase Hill Rd SG15 . . . . .90 A7
Chase St LU1 . . . . .123 E6
Chase The MK43 . . . . . . .49 A2
Chasten Hill SG6 . . . . . .101 D7
Chatsworth Rd LU4 . . . .116 B1
Chatteris Cl LU4 . . . . . .115 D4
Chatton Cl LU2 . . . . . . .117 E2
Chaucer Dr SG18 . . . . . . .67 A5
Chaucer Pl PE19 . . . . . . .22 D6
Chaucer Rd Bedford MK40 . 37 F1
  Flitwick MK45 . . . . .84 D3
  Luton LU3 . . . . .116 C2
Chaul End La LU4 . . . . . .115 E1
Chaul End Rd
  Caddington LU1,LU4 . . . .122 D6
  Luton LU4 . . . . .115 E1
Chauntry Cl MK45 . . . . . .84 E5
Chauntry Way MK45 . . . . .84 E5
Chaworth Gn 1 LU4 . . . . .115 C5
Chawston Cl PE19 . . . . . .22 C5
Cheapside LU1 . . . . .123 E7
Cheapside Sq 4 LU1 . . . .123 E7
Cheddington Sta LU7 . . . .118 A2
Chelmer Cl MK41 . . . . . . .38 D7
Chelsea Gdns LU5 . . . . .114 D5
Chelsea Gn LU7 . . . . . .110 D6
Chelsworth 1 LU2 . . . . .117 D1
Cheltenham Cl
  Bedford MK41 . . . . .39 B3
  Rushden NN10 . . . . .8 C8
Chelveston Base Cres
  NN9 . . . . .3 D5
Chelveston Rd NN9 . . . . . .3 A7
Cheney Cl LU5 . . . . .105 F6
Cheney Rd LU4 . . . . . . .115 C5
Chennells Cl SG4 . . . . . .101 B2
Chepstow AL5 . . . . .130 F2
Chepstow Gdns MK41 . . . .39 A4
Chequer Ct LU1 . . . . . . .123 F6
Chequer St LU1 . . . . . . .123 F6
Chequers
  Marston Moretaine MK43 . .60 D2
  Stotfold SG5 . . . . .91 A6
Chequers Cotts LU6 . . . .127 A8
Chequers Hill
  Flamstead AL3 . . . . . . .129 C2
  Wilden MK44 . . . . .30 A4
Chequers La MK16 . . . . . .58 B6
Chequers The LU6 . . . . .119 F5
Cherry Cl MK45 . . . . .74 B8
Cherry Gr SG19 . . . . .44 C5
Cherry Tree Cl
  Arlesey SG15 . . . . .90 A4
  Luton LU2 . . . . .117 A1
Cherry Tree Wlk
  Houghton Regis LU5 . . . .114 B6
  Leighton Buzzard LU7 . . .110 E7
Cherry Trees SG16 . . . . . .89 B3
Cherry Wlk MK42 . . . . . . .49 F3
Cherrycourt Way LU7 . . .111 D6
Cherrycourt Way Ind Est
  LU7 . . . . .111 E7
Cherrycroft SG19 . . . . . . .54 D7
Cherrytree Way MK45 . . . .85 A7
Chertsey Cl LU2 . . . . . . .124 D8
Cherwell Rd MK41 . . . . . .38 C5
Chesford Rd LU2 . . . . . .117 C4
Cheslyn Cl LU2 . . . . . . .117 E2
Chessington Cl MK41 . . . .51 B8
Chester Ave LU4 . . . . . .115 E3
Chester Cl LU4 . . . . . . .115 F2
Chester Rd MK40 . . . . . . .49 E7
Chesterfield Way PE19 . . .22 E2
Chesterton Ave AL5 . . . .131 D1
Chesterton Ct PE19 . . . . .22 E6
Chesterton Mews MK40 . . .37 F1
Chestnut Ave
  Bedford MK40 . . . . .49 E7
  Biggleswade SG18 . . . . . .67 A6
  Bromham MK43 . . . . .36 D3
  Henlow SG16 . . . . .89 C3
  Luton LU3 . . . . .107 C1
Chestnut Cl Ampthill MK45 84 F8
  Dagnall HP4 . . . . .126 C6
  Westoning MK45 . . . . . . .95 D6
  Wymington NN10 . . . . .8 B5
Chestnut Cres MK45 . . . . .85 B8
Chestnut Ct LU6 . . . . . .121 C7
Chestnut Farm SG16 . . . . .78 D1
Chestnut Gdns MK42 . . . . .49 E3
Chestnut Gr PE19 . . . . . .22 F4
Chestnut Hill LU6 . . . . . .110 D8
Chestnut Rise LU7 . . . . .110 D8
Chestnuts The PE28 . . . . . .6 F5
Chethams MK42 . . . . .50 C7
Cheveralls The LU6 . . . . .121 C6
Cheverells AL3 . . . . .128 D4
Cheviot Cl Bedford MK41 . .38 E3
  Flitwick MK45 . . . . .84 D2
  Leighton Buzzard LU7 . . .110 C8
  Luton LU3 . . . . .115 D7
Cheviot Rd LU3 . . . . . . .115 D7
Cheyne Cl LU6 . . . . .113 F3
Cheynes Inf Sch LU3 . . . .115 D8
Chicheley Rd MK16 . . . . . .58 A7
Chichester Cl LU5 . . . . . .121 E7
Chicksands Ave SG17 . . . .76 F2
Chillingham Gn MK41 . . . .39 B4
Chiltern Ave
  Bedford MK41 . . . . .38 E3
  Edlesborough LU6 . . . . . .119 E3
Chiltern Cl Ampthill MK45 .84 F8
  Flitwick MK45 . . . . .84 D2
  Lidlington MK43 . . . . . . .72 B2
Chiltern Ct 15 AL5 . . . . .131 B1

Chiltern Gdns
  Leighton Buzzard LU7 . . .103 A3
  Luton LU5 . . . . .115 F3
Chiltern Pk LU5 . . . . . . .114 D2
Chiltern Pl SG16 . . . . .78 C1
Chiltern Rd
  Barton-le-C MK45 . . . . . .97 C2
  Dunstable LU6 . . . . . . .114 A1
Chiltern Rise LU6 . . . . . .123 D6
Chiltern Trad Est LU7 . . .111 A5
Chiltern View SG6 . . . . . .101 D5
Chilterns The
  Kensworth LU6 . . . . . . .127 F8
  Leighton Buzzard LU7 . . .111 D6
Chinnor Cl MK41 . . . . . . .39 B1
Chobham St LU1 . . . . . . .123 F6
Chobham Wlk 5 LU1 . . . .123 E6
Christchurch Ct LU6 . . . .114 A1
Christian Cl LU5 . . . . .95 F1
Christie Rd MK42 . . . . . . .50 D6
Christina Ct AL3 . . . . . . .128 E5
Christy's Yd SG7 . . . . .80 D6
Chudleigh Cl MK40 . . . . . .38 E2
Church Ave Ampthill MK45 73 F1
  Leighton Buzzard LU7 . . .111 A6
Church Cl Bedford MK41 . . .39 B1
  Dunstable LU5 . . . . . . .121 C8
  Houghton Conquest MK45 . .74 A7
  Milton Ernest MK44 . . . . .27 A5
  Rushden NN10 . . . . .8 B5
  Studham LU6 . . . . .127 B4
  Westoning MK45 . . . . . . .95 D6
Church Cotts HP1 . . . . . .132 D3
Church Cres SG18 . . . . . . .78 F7
Church Croft LU6 . . . . . .119 E3
Church End Arlesey SG15 . .90 A8
  Biddenham MK40 . . . . . . .49 B8
  Edlesborough LU6 . . . . . .119 E5
  Elstow MK42 . . . . .50 B3
  Everton SG19 . . . . .43 C3
  Felmersham MK43 . . . . . .26 C8
  Gamlingay SG19 . . . . . . .44 E5
  Houghton Regis LU5 . . . .114 E5
  Markyate AL3 . . . . .128 D6
  Milton Bryan MK17 . . . . . .93 E2
  Ravensden MK44 . . . . . . .29 B1
  Renhold MK41 . . . . .39 D6
  Steppingley MK45 . . . . . .84 A3
  Willington MK44 . . . . . . .52 B8
Church End Farm LU6 . . .120 B7
Church End Lower Sch
  MK43 . . . . .72 D7
Church End Rd MK45 . . . . .75 C7
Church Farm Ave MK45 . . .62 E3
Church Farm Cl
  Langford SG18 . . . . .78 F7
  Sutton SG19 . . . . .55 F3
Church Gn
  Harpenden AL5 . . . . . . .131 A1
  Milton Ernest MK44 . . . . .27 B5
  Totternhoe LU6 . . . . . . .120 B7
Church Green Row AL5 . . .131 A1
Church Hill MK17 . . . . . . .81 E5
Church La Arlesey SG15 . . .90 A5
  Bedford MK41 . . . . .39 B3
  Bolnhurst MK44 . . . . . . .19 A4
  Cardington MK44 . . . . . . .51 D4
  Colmworth MK44 . . . . . . .19 D4
  Covington PE28 . . . . .2 C2
  Eaton Bray LU6 . . . . . . .119 E6
  Everton SG19 . . . . .43 C3
  Flitton MK45 . . . . .85 D4
  Gamlingay SG19 . . . . . . .44 E5
  Guilden Morden SG8 . . . . .69 F5
  Hockliffe LU7 . . . . .104 D3
  Letchworth SG6 . . . . . . .91 C1
  Lidlington MK43 . . . . . . .72 C2
  Little Staughton MK44 . . .13 B2
  Newton Bromswold NN10 . .9 D8
  Oakley MK43 . . . . .36 F6
  Odell MK43 . . . . .15 D1
  Pavenham MK43 . . . . . . .26 C4
  Riseley MK44 . . . . .10 F2
  Sharnbrook MK44 . . . . . .16 C4
  Stagsden MK43 . . . . .48 A7
  Tilbrook PE28 . . . . .6 B7
  Upper Dean PE28 . . . . . . .5 B4
  Wrestlingworth SG19 . . . .57 B3
  Wymington NN10 . . . . .8 B5
  Yelden MK44 . . . . .4 A3
Church Mdw PE19 . . . . . . .22 F5
Church Mead LU6 . . . . . .127 B4
Church Meadow Cotts
  HP1 . . . . .132 D3
Church Path
  Cheddington LU7 . . . . . .118 A1
  Sandy SG19 . . . . .54 B7
Church Row
  Barton-le-C MK45 . . . . . .97 D1
  Colmworth MK44 . . . . . . .20 B1
  Everton SG19 . . . . .43 C3
  Flamstead AL3 . . . . . . .129 B2
  Flitwick MK45 . . . . .84 D1
  Hargrave NN9 . . . . .1 F1
  Harlington LU5 . . . . .95 F2
  Henlow SG16 . . . . .78 D2
  Kempston MK43 . . . . . . .49 A4
  Keysoe MK44 . . . . .12 A1
  Leighton Buzzard LU7 . . .110 E6
  Maulden MK45 . . . . .85 D8
  Meppershall SG17 . . . . . .88 A5
  Pulloxhill MK45 . . . . .96 E8
  Silsoe MK45 . . . . .86 C4
  Slapton LU7 . . . . .118 D6
  Slip End LU1 . . . . .123 C2
  Steppingley MK45 . . . . . .84 A3
  Stevington MK43 . . . . . . .36 C7
  Stotfold SG5 . . . . .90 F6

Church Rd continued
  Streatley LU3 . . . . .108 A6
  Studham LU6 . . . . .127 B4
  Tingrith MK17 . . . . .94 F5
  Totternhoe LU6 . . . . . . .120 B6
  Upper Sundon LU3 . . . . .107 B3
  Westoning MK45 . . . . . . .95 E6
  Willington MK44 . . . . . . .52 B8
  Wilstead MK45 . . . . .62 E4
  Woburn Sands MK17 . . . .81 B3
  Wootton MK43 . . . . .60 F7
Church Row MK43 . . . . . . .60 E7
Church Sq
  Leighton Buzzard LU7 . . .110 F6
  Toddington LU5 . . . . . . .105 F6
Church St Ampthill MK45 . .73 F1
  Aspley Guise MK17 . . . . . .81 E5
  Baldock SG7 . . . . .91 E1
  5 Bedford MK40 . . . . . . .50 B8
  Biggleswade SG18 . . . . . .67 A6
  Clifton SG17 . . . . .78 B3
  Dunstable LU5 . . . . . . .121 C8
  Dunton SG18 . . . . .68 D5
  Gamlingay SG19 . . . . . . .44 D5
  Guilden Morden SG8 . . . . .69 F5
  Hargrave NN9 . . . . .1 E2
  Langford SG18 . . . . .78 F8
  Langford SG18 . . . . .78 F8
  Leighton Buzzard LU7 . . .111 A8
  Lidlington MK43 . . . . . . .72 C3
  8 Luton LU1 . . . . .123 E7
  Luton LU2 . . . . .123 E7
  Luton, High Town LU2 . . .123 F8
  Ridgmont MK43 . . . . .82 F5
  Shillington SG5 . . . . .98 E8
  St Neots PE19 . . . . .22 F5
  Tempsford SG19 . . . . . . .42 A6
Church Terr MK43 . . . . . . .34 F5
Church Turn LU7 . . . . . . .111 E2
Church View
  Ampthill MK45 . . . . .73 F1
  Clapham MK41 . . . . .37 F5
  St Neots PE19 . . . . .22 F5
Church View Ave SG5 . . . . .87 E1
Church View Ct LU7 . . . . .110 E6
Church Wlk
  Cranfield MK43 . . . . .71 A8
  Dunstable LU5 . . . . . . .121 C8
  Eggington LU7 . . . . .112 B7
  Harrold MK43 . . . . .25 A6
  Kempston MK42 . . . . . . .49 C3
  Marston Moretaine MK43 . .72 D7
  Newton Bromswold NN10 . .9 D8
  North Crawley MK16 . . . . .58 B6
  Shefford SG17 . . . . .77 C3
  6 St Neots PE19 . . . . . . .22 F5
Churchfield Rd LU5 . . . . .114 B5
Churchgate MK44 . . . . . . .41 A4
Churchill Cl
  Sharnbrook MK44 . . . . . .16 C3
  Stewartby MK43 . . . . . . .61 B1
  Streatley LU3 . . . . .107 F6
Churchill Dr SG17 . . . . . . .76 F4
Churchill Pl MK44 . . . . . . .40 B1
Churchill Rd
  Barton-le-C MK45 . . . . . .97 C3
  Dunstable LU6 . . . . . . .121 D5
  Leighton Buzzard LU7 . . .103 B1
  Luton LU4 . . . . .116 A1
  Marston Moretaine MK43 . .72 C8
Churchill Way
  Sandy SG19 . . . . .54 C8
  Shefford SG17 . . . . .77 C1
Churchills LU5 . . . . .95 F2
Churchville Rd MK42 . . . . .50 B5
Churnet Cl MK41 . . . . . . .38 D7
Cicero Dr LU3 . . . . .116 A8
Cinques Rd SG19 . . . . . . .44 C6
Cinques The SG19 . . . . . . .44 B6
Circle Bsns Ctr LU5 . . . . .114 B3
City La MK44 . . . . .20 C3
Clapham Rd MK41 . . . . . . .37 F4
Clare Ct SG19 . . . . .44 D5
Clare Ho SG18 . . . . .67 A6
Clare Rd MK41 . . . . .38 F5
Claremont Rd LU4 . . . . . .116 B1
Clarence Ct NN10 . . . . .8 A8
Clarence Rd
  Harpenden AL5 . . . . . . .131 A3
  Leighton Buzzard LU7 . . .111 B8
Clarendon Ct AL5 . . . . . .131 B3
Clarendon Rd
  Harpenden AL5 . . . . . . .131 B3
  Luton LU2 . . . . .116 E1
Clarendon St MK41 . . . . . .38 A2
Clark's Pightle MK45 . . . . .97 C2
Clarkes Way LU5 . . . . . . .114 C4
Claverley Gn LU2 . . . . . .117 E2
Clay Hall Rd LU6 . . . . . . .127 F7
Claydon Cl LU2 . . . . .116 C7
Claydon Ct MK40 . . . . . . .38 E2
Claydown Way LU1 . . . . .123 B1
Claygate Ave AL5 . . . . . .130 C4
Claymore Dr SG5 . . . . . . .100 F5
Cleat Hill MK41,MK44 . . . . .38 E7
Cleave The AL5 . . . . .131 D1
Cleavers The LU5 . . . . . .105 F5
Cleavers Wlk LU5 . . . . . .105 F5
Cleeve Abbey MK41 . . . . . .39 B1
Clements End Rd LU6,
  HP2 . . . . .127 E2
Clevedon Rd LU2 . . . . . . .117 E2
Cleveland Dr LU7 . . . . . .110 C8
Cleveland Rd AL3 . . . . . .128 E5
Cleveland St MK42 . . . . . .49 E4
Clifford Cres LU5 . . . . . . .115 D5
Clifton House Cl SG17 . . . .78 B3
Clifton Pk SG17 . . . . .78 A1

Clifton Rd Dunstable LU6 . 114 A1
  Henlow SG16 . . . . .78 C1
  Luton LU1 . . . . .123 B8
  Newton Blossomville MK43 .34 A4
  Shefford SG17 . . . . .77 D2
Clinton Ave LU2 . . . . . . .116 F3
Clipstone Brook Lower Sch
  LU7 . . . . .111 B7
Clipstone Cl MK43 . . . . . .39 B3
Clipstone Cres LU7 . . . . .111 C7
Clive Ct LU2 . . . . .116 E1
Cloches The SG19 . . . . . . .54 B5
Cloister Lawns SG6 . . . . .101 F4
Cloisters Rd
  Letchworth SG6 . . . . . . .101 F4
  Luton LU5 . . . . .115 B3
Cloisters The
  Ampthill MK45 . . . . .73 F1
  Bedford MK41 . . . . .39 B1
  Dunstable LU5 . . . . . . .121 C8
  Houghton Regis LU5 . . . .114 C6
Clophill Rd
  Gravenhurst MK45 . . . . . .87 B5
  Maulden MK45 . . . . .85 E8
Close Rd MK43 . . . . .26 E3
Close The
  Biggleswade SG18 . . . . . .66 F6
  Clapham MK41 . . . . .37 E5
  Great Barford MK44 . . . . .41 A5
  Hardmead MK16 . . . . . . .46 D4
  Harpenden AL5 . . . . . . .130 D4
  Hinxworth SG7 . . . . .80 D6
  Luton LU3 . . . . .116 A5
  Markyate AL3 . . . . .128 E5
  St Neots PE19 . . . . .22 F5
  Tempsford SG19 . . . . . . .42 C8
  Thurleigh MK44 . . . . . . .18 C2
  Woburn Sands MK17 . . . .81 B4
Clothall Rd SG7 . . . . .91 F1
Clovelly Way MK40 . . . . . .38 F1
Clover Ave MK41 . . . . . . .39 B1
Clover Cl
  Biggleswade SG18 . . . . . .67 C4
  Luton LU4 . . . . .115 A3
Clover Dr NN10 . . . . .8 C8
Clover Rd Flitwick MK45 . . .84 D3
  St Neots PE19 . . . . .22 C5
Cluny Way SG15 . . . . .90 A5
Clyde Cres MK41 . . . . . . .38 D5
Clydesdale Ct LU4 . . . . . .115 A3
Clydesdale Rd LU4 . . . . . .115 A3
Coach Rd SG16 . . . . .78 D1
Cobbett La MK45 . . . . . . .85 D4
Cobbitts Rd MK45 . . . . . . .74 C1
Cobblers La MK17 . . . . . . .83 C3
Cobden Sq 11 MK40 . . . . .38 B1
Cobden St LU2 . . . . .116 F1
Cockernhoe CE Prim Sch
  . . . . .117 E3
Codrington Cl PE19 . . . . .22 B3
Cody Rd MK41 . . . . .37 D6
Colchester Way MK41 . . . .39 A5
Coldharbour La AL5 . . . . .131 C4
Colebrook Ave LU3 . . . . .115 C7
Colemans Cl SG5 . . . . . . .99 D4
Colemoreham Ct SG18 . . . .65 E7
Coleridge Ct
  9 Harpenden AL5 . . . . .131 B1
  St Neots PE19 . . . . .22 C7
Coles Cl MK41 . . . . .39 A1
Colesden Rd
  Chawston MK44 . . . . . . .31 D5
  Wilden MK44 . . . . .30 C4
Colin Rd LU2 . . . . .116 F2
College Cl AL3 . . . . .129 B1
College Dr MK44 . . . . .10 F2
College Ho LU1 . . . . .123 F7
College Rd Bedford MK42 . .50 B5
  Sandy SG19 . . . . .42 C1
  Wharley End MK43 . . . . . .58 E2
College St MK42 . . . . .50 A5
Colley Rd MK44 . . . . .20 A1
Collie Rd MK43 . . . . .50 E6
Collingdon Ct 9 LU1 . . . .123 D8
Collingdon St LU1 . . . . . .123 D8
Collings Wells Cl LU1 . . . .122 F7
Collingtree LU7 . . . . .117 B4
Collingwood Cl LU7 . . . . .117 C4
Collingwood Rd PE19 . . . .22 B2
Collins Pl MK42 . . . . .50 F5
Collison Cl SG4 . . . . .101 C2
Colmworth Bsns Pk PE19 22 C1
Colmworth Gdns PE19 . . . .22 C2
Coltsfoot SG18 . . . . .67 C4
Coltsfoot Gn LU4 . . . . . . .115 A5
Coltsfoot Rd NN10 . . . . . . .8 C7
Columba Dr LU7 . . . . . . .111 C8
Columbine Cl MK41 . . . . . .39 C4
Colwell Rise LU2 . . . . . . .117 E2
Colworth Rd MK44 . . . . . .16 B4
Comet Dr MK42 . . . . .51 A2
Comfrey Cl NN10 . . . . .8 C7
Commerce Way
  Flitwick MK45 . . . . .85 A4
  Leighton Buzzard LU7 . . .111 E6
  Letchworth SG6 . . . . . . .101 F6
Commerce Way Ind Est
  . . . . .111 E6
Commercial Rd MK40 . . . . .50 B8
Common Farm La MK45 . . .84 D4
Common La
  Harpenden AL5 . . . . . . .131 D5
  Upper Sundon LU3 . . . . .107 A4
Common Rd
  Kensworth LU6 . . . . . . .121 D1
  Langford SG18 . . . . .78 E4
  Potton SG19 . . . . .56 A8
  Stotfold SG5 . . . . .90 F7

Common Rd continued
  Studham LU6 . . . . .127 B3
Common Rise SG4 . . . . . .101 A1
Common The AL5 . . . . . .130 C4
Comp Gate LU6 . . . . .119 E6
Comp The LU6 . . . . .119 E6
Compass Dr MK42 . . . . . .51 A3
Compton Ave LU4 . . . . . .115 D4
Compton Cl Flitwick MK45 .84 D1
  St Neots PE19 . . . . .22 E2
Concord Way LU7 . . . . . .111 E6
Concorde Cl MK42 . . . . . .51 A2
Concorde St LU2 . . . . . . .123 E8
Concra Pk MK17 . . . . .81 C4
Conduit Rd MK40 . . . . . . .50 A8
Coneygate SG17 . . . . .88 B5
Conger La LU5 . . . . .106 A6
Coniston Cl MK42 . . . . . . .49 E4
Coniston Rd Flitwick MK45 84 E2
  Leighton Buzzard LU7 . . .110 C2
  Luton LU3 . . . . .115 F5
Connaught Rd
  Harpenden AL5 . . . . . . .131 B2
  Luton LU4 . . . . .115 F1
Connaught Way MK41 . . . .38 D6
Conner's Cl SG8 . . . . .69 F4
Conquest Rd
  Bedford MK42 . . . . .50 C5
  Houghton Regis LU5 . . . .114 C5
Constable Ave PE19 . . . . .22 D5
Constable Cl LU5 . . . . . . .114 C6
Constable Ct LU4 . . . . . . .116 A1
Constable Hill MK41 . . . . .38 A2
Constables Leys PE28 . . . . .6 F5
Conway Cl
  Houghton Regis LU5 . . . .114 C5
  Rushden NN10 . . . . .8 A8
Conway Cres MK41 . . . . . .38 C5
Conway Dr MK43 . . . . . . .84 D1
Conway Pl PE19 . . . . .22 F2
Conway Rd LU4 . . . . .116 B1
Cook's Mdw LU6 . . . . . . .119 E4
Cookfield Cl LU6 . . . . . . .120 E8
Cooks Way SG4 . . . . .101 A1
Coombe Dr LU6 . . . . . . .120 E7
Coombs Cl MK42 . . . . . . .50 D6
Cooper Cl SG16 . . . . .88 E2
Coopers Cl
  Biddenham MK40 . . . . . . .49 C8
  Biggleswade SG18 . . . . . .67 B4
  Great Barford MK44 . . . . .40 F5
  Sandy SG19 . . . . .54 B6
Coopers Field SG6 . . . . . .101 F6
Coopers Way LU5 . . . . . .114 A4
Cooters End La AL5 . . . . .130 F5
Copeland Wlk MK41 . . . . .39 B3
Copenhagen Cl LU3 . . . . .115 D8
Cople Lower Sch MK44 . . .52 A6
Cople Rd MK44 . . . . .51 E5
Coplowe La MK44 . . . . . . .17 C1
Coppens The SG5 . . . . . . .91 A5
Copper Beech Way LU7 . . 103 A3
Copper Beeches 11 AL5 . .131 B1
Copperfields LU4 . . . . . . .115 C3
Copperfields Cl LU4 . . . . .114 D4
Coppice Mead
  Biggleswade SG18 . . . . . .67 B5
  Stotfold SG5 . . . . .90 E5
Coppice The AL5 . . . . . . .130 F2
Coppins The
  Ampthill MK45 . . . . .84 F8
  Markyate AL3 . . . . .128 D5
Copse The AL5 . . . . .39 B2
Copse Way LU3 . . . . .115 D8
Copthorne LU2 . . . . .117 D3
Copthorne Cl MK43 . . . . . .37 A8
Coral Cl LU6 . . . . .119 E6
Corbet Ride LU7 . . . . . . .110 D8
Corbet Sq LU7 . . . . .110 D8
Corbridge Dr LU2 . . . . . .117 E1
Corby Cl MK42 . . . . .50 D4
Corfe Pl PE19 . . . . .22 F2
Corfe Rd MK41 . . . . .39 A4
Corinium Gdns LU3 . . . . .116 A8
Corncastle Rd LU1 . . . . . .123 D6
Corncrake Cl LU2 . . . . . . .117 C5
Cornel Cl LU1 . . . . .123 A7
Cornel Ct LU1 . . . . .123 A7
Cornelia Ct 3 AL5 . . . . . .131 A2
Corner Cl
  Letchworth SG6 . . . . . . .101 E6
  Podington NN29 . . . . .7 E1
Corner Wood AL3 . . . . . .128 D5
Cornish Cl SG17 . . . . .77 C3
Cornland MK41 . . . . .39 A3
Cornwall Ct PE19 . . . . . . .22 C4
Cornwall Rd
  Ampthill MK45 . . . . .84 F8
  Bedford MK42 . . . . .38 D2
  Harpenden AL5 . . . . . . .131 B2
Cornwallis Cl MK43 . . . . . .36 E3
Cornwallis Dr PE19 . . . . . .22 A3
Coronation Rd MK43 . . . . .59 B1
Corunna Cl PE19 . . . . . . .22 C5
Cosgrove Way LU1 . . . . . .115 D1
Cosmic Ave LU3 . . . . .116 A8
Costin St MK40 . . . . .50 B8
Cotefield LU4 . . . . .115 C3
Cotefield Dr LU7 . . . . . . .103 B3
Cotman Cl MK41 . . . . . . .38 A2
Cotswold Bsns Pk LU1 . . .122 D2
Cotswold Cl MK41 . . . . . . .38 E7
Cotswold Dr LU7 . . . . . . .110 C8
Cotswold Gdns LU3 . . . . .115 C7
Cotswold Pl MK45 . . . . . . .84 D2

Cottage Rd SG19 ....42 B1
Cotton End Lower Sch
MK45 ....63 D8
Cotton End Rd MK45 ...63 B5
Cottril Way MK42 ......50 E6
Coulon Ct NN29 ....7 A7
Coulson Ct LU1 ....122 F8
Council Cotts
  Radwell SG7 ....91 C4
  Sharnbrook MK44 ......16 F4
Council Hos
  Ivinghoe Aston LU6 ...119 A1
  Podington NN29 ....7 E1
Countess Cl PE19 ....22 B3
Countess Ct 4 LU2 ...116 D1
Countess Gdns MK42 ...49 D3
Court Dr LU5 ....114 A6
Court La MK43 ....36 B7
Court Rd MK43 ....71 B8
Court The MK17 ....70 C3
Courtfields AL5 ....131 D1
Courtlands LU7 ....110 E6
Courtlands Dr SG18 ....67 C3
Covent Garden Cl LU4 .115 F3
Coventry Rd MK40 ......49 F8
Coverdale LU4 ....115 B6
Cow Cl SG18 ....67 A3
Cow La LU6 ....119 E4
Cowdray Cl LU2 ....117 C3
Cowper Cl AL3 ....128 D5
Cowper Rd Bedford MK40 .37 F2
  Harpenden AL5 ....131 C1
  Markyate AL3 ....128 D5
Cowper Rise AL3 ......128 D5
Cowper St LU1 ....123 E5
Cowpers Ct PE19 ....22 D6
Cowridge Cres LU2 ....124 A8
Cowslip Cl NN10 ....8 C8
Cowslip Hill SG6 .....101 E7
Cox's Cl Bedford MK40 ..49 F7
  Sharnbrook MK44 ......16 B4
Cox's Way SG15 ....90 A6
Coyney Gn LU3 ....116 C1
Crab Apple Way SG19 ..44 C5
Crab La SG18 ....67 A6
Crab Tree La SG5 ......99 D4
Crabtree Inf Sch AL5 .131 C1
Crabtree La
  Harpenden AL5 ....131 C1
  Harpenden AL5 ....131 D2
Crabtree Way LU6 .....114 B2
Crackle Hill Rd SG17 ..88 C6
Craddock St NN29 ....7 B8
Cradock Rd LU4 ....115 B1
Cranborne Cl MK41 ....39 B4
Cranbrook MK17 ....81 B5
Cranbrook Dr LU3 ....115 D8
Crancott Cl MK45 ......74 B8
Crane Way MK43 ....59 C2
Cranes Cl MK43 ....34 E5
Cranfield Lower Sch
  MK43 ....59 B1
Cranfield Rd
  Astwood MK16 ....47 B2
  Salford MK17 ....70 D5
  Woburn Sands MK17 ...81 B7
  Wootton MK43 ....60 E5
Cranfield Technology Pk
  MK43 ....70 D8
Cranfield Univ MK43 ...58 E2
Cranfield Univ Silsoe Coll
  MK45 ....86 C3
Cranford Ct AL5 ......131 C1
Cranleigh Gdns LU3 ..116 D3
Crawley Cl LU1 ....123 C5
Crawley Green Inf Sch
  LU2 ....124 B8
Crawley Green Rd
  Luton LU2 ....124 A8
  Luton, Wigmore LU2 .117 D1
Crawley Rd
  Cranfield MK43 ....59 C3
  Luton LU1 ....123 D8
  Woburn MK17 ....82 A1
Crayton Rd MK45 ......84 E8
Crecy Ct PE19 ....22 C5
Crediton Ct MK42 .....38 E2
Creran Wlk LU7 ......110 C7
Crescent Cl LU5 .....105 F5
Crescent Ct
  Lidlington MK43 ......72 B3
  Toddington LU5 .....105 F5
Crescent Rd LU2 .....123 F8
Crescent Rise LU2 ...123 F8
Crescent The
  Ampthill MK45 ....84 E7
  Bedford MK40 ....38 B1
  Beeston SG19 ....54 B5
  Caddington LU1 .....122 E3
  Cotton End MK45 ......63 D7
  Henlow SG16 ....89 C4
  Hitchin SG5 ....100 D1
  Moggerhanger MK44 ..53 C8
  Shortstown MK42 ......51 A3
  St Neots, PE19 ....22 F6
  St Neots, Eaton Socon PE19 22 C1
  Stanford SG18 ....78 A7
  Stewartby MK43 ....61 C1
  Toddington LU5 .....105 F5
  Wharley End MK43 ....58 E2
Cressener Terr 5 PE19 .22 F5
Crest The Dunstable LU5 .114 C5
  Luton LU3 ....116 B7
Cresta Cl LU5 ....115 A2

Cresta Ho 3 LU1 ......123 D7
Criccieth Way PE19 ....22 F1
Cricket Cl MK41 ....39 A2
Cricket La MK41 ....39 A2
Cricketer's Rd SG15 ...90 A4
Crocus Way NN10 ....8 B7
Croft Cl 4 AL5 ....131 B1
Croft Gn LU6 ....120 F8
Croft La SG6 ....91 B1
Croft Rd LU2 ....117 B3
Croft Stewart SG19 ....56 C6
Croft The Bedford MK41 .39 A2
  Flitwick MK45 ....84 E3
  Luton LU3 ....115 D8
Crofton Cl MK41 ....38 C4
Crofts The
  Sharnbrook MK44 ......16 E4
  Stotfold SG5 ....90 F6
Cromer Way
  Luton, Stopsley Common
  LU2 ....116 C6
  Luton, Warden Hill LU2 116 D7
Cromwell Ct
  Kempston MK42 ....49 E4
  St Neots PE19 ....22 F3
Cromwell Hill LU2 ....116 D1
Cromwell Rd
  Barton-le-C MK45 .....97 C3
  Bedford MK40 ....49 F7
  Luton LU3 ....116 D1
  St Neots PE19 ....22 F3
Cromwell Way SG5 .....99 D4
Crosby Cl Dunstable LU6 121 C6
  Luton LU4 ....116 A2
Cross End La MK44 .....18 E1
Cross End La MK44 .....18 E2
Cross Hall Rd PE19 ....22 D6
Cross Keys Mall 3 PE19 22 F5
Cross St Bedford MK40 .38 B1
  Covington PE28 ....2 D2
  Letchworth SG6 ......101 F7
  Luton LU2 ....123 E8
Cross St N 2 LU6 ....114 A1
Cross The SG19 ....44 D5
Cross Way AL5 ....131 C3
Cross Way The LU1 ...123 C5
Crosshall Inf Sch PE19 .22 C6
Crosshall Jun Sch PE19 22 C6
Crosslands LU1 ....122 E3
Crossleys SG6 ....90 F2
Crosspaths AL5 ....130 C4
Crossway LU7 ....111 D7
Crossways LU5 ....114 C5
Crossways SG16 ....78 D1
Crossways Pk SG15 ....89 F2
Crow La
  Husborne Crawley MK43 ...82 B4
  Woburn Sands MK17 ...81 B8
Crowland Rd LU2 .....117 C5
Crown La SG18 ....78 F6
Crown Lodge SG15 .....90 A4
Crown Pl MK42 ....50 B7
Crown Quay MK42 .....50 B7
Crown Wlk PE19 ....22 B4
Crowther Ct SG18 .....67 F7
Croxden Way MK42 ....50 D3
Croxley Ct LU7 ......110 F7
Croxton Cl 3 LU3 ....116 A7
Croyland Dr MK42 .....50 D3
Cryselco Cl MK42 .....49 D2
Cubbington Cl LU3 ...116 A4
Cuckoo Cl SG19 ....42 B2
Cuckoo's Nest LU2 ...124 A7
Cuffley Cl LU3 ....115 F4
Culloden Ct PE19 .....22 C5
Culver Ho MK40 ....38 A4
Culverhouse Rd LU3 ..116 C3
Culworth Ct LU1 .....122 E3
Cumberland St
  Houghton Regis LU5 .114 B4
  Luton LU1 ....123 E6
Cumberland Way PE19 ..22 F1
Cumbria Cl LU5 ......114 C5
Cunningham Way PE19 ..22 A2
Curlew Cl SG6 ....90 E1
Curlew Cres MK41 .....38 B4
Curlew Rd LU2 ....117 C5
Curzon Rd LU3 ....116 C1
Cusworth Way LU6 ...113 E1
Cusworth Wlk LU6 ...113 E1
Cut Throat Ave HP4,LU6 126 F7
Cut Throat La MK41 ...37 F2
Cutcliffe Gdns MK40 ..49 F8
Cutcliffe Gr MK40 ....49 F8
Cutcliffe Pl MK40 ....49 F8
Cutenhoe Rd LU1 ....123 E4
Cutlers Gn LU2 ......117 F2
Cutlers Way LU7 .....111 B6
Cygnus Dr LU7 ......111 D8
Cymbeline Ct 6 MK40 .38 A1
Cynthia Ct MK43 ......61 A6

D

Daffodil Dr NN10 ....8 B7
Dag La MK44 ....10 F2
Dagnall Rd
  Dunstable LU6 ....120 D2
  Great Gaddesden HP1 .132 C5
Dagnall Sch HP4 .....126 C5
Dagnalls SG6 ....101 F2
Dahl Cl MK42 ....50 C4
Dahlia Cl LU7 ....117 B4
Dairy Cotts SG5 ......98 B2
Dairy Ct PE19 ....22 F6
Daisy Croft NN10 ....8 C8
Dalby Cl LU4 ....115 B3

Dale Cl Bedford MK41 ..39 A3
  Dunstable LU5 ....114 F1
  Toddington LU5 .....105 F5
Dale Rd Dunstable LU5 .114 F1
  Luton LU1 ....123 C7
Dale The SG6 ....101 E5
Dalewood AL5 ....131 D1
Dalkeith Rd AL5 .....131 C1
Dallas Rd MK42 ....50 A6
Dalling Dr LU5 ......114 C5
Dallow Prim Sch LU1 .123 C8
Dallow Rd LU1 ....123 B8
Dalroad Ind Est LU1 .123 B8
Dalton Cl LU3 ....108 B1
Dame Alice Harpur Sch
  MK42 ....50 C7
Dame Alice St MK40 ...38 B1
Dammersey Cl AL3 ...128 F4
Dane Cl Harpenden AL5 .131 C4
  Stotfold SG5 ....90 F8
Dane La AL5 ....62 C5
Dane Rd Barton-le-C MK45 97 D3
  Luton LU3 ....116 C2
Dane St MK40 ....50 B8
Danefield Rd SG5 .....99 C4
Danes Way LU7 ....111 D7
Danesborough Dr MK17 .81 A2
Danescroft SG5 ....91 A1
Daneswood MK17 ......81 A1
Danvers Dr AL3 ......108 C1
Dapifer Dr SG19 ......54 C8
Dark La SG18 ....66 F6
Darlington Cl SG19 ...42 D1
Darlow Dr AL5 ....37 D1
Darrington Cl PE19 ...22 B3
Dart Rd MK41 ....38 C5
Dartmouth Mews LU4 .115 D3
Darwin Rd MK42 ......50 C5
Daubeney Cl LU5 ......95 F2
Daubeney Mid Sch MK42 49 F3
Dauphin Ct 5 LU2 ...116 D1
David Evans Ct SG6 ..101 D7
Davis Cl LU2 ....50 B5
Davis Cres SG5 ....99 D4
Davis' Row SG15 ......90 A4
Dawlish Dr MK40 ......38 E1
Dawlish Rd LU4 ......115 F3
Dawson Ct SG16 ....89 C5
Day's La MK41 ....37 D1
Daysfield MK45 ....74 B8
De Grey Mausoleum★
  MK45 ....85 D4
De Havilland Ave MK42 .51 B2
De Montfort Ct LU5 ..105 F4
De Montfort Univ MK41 .38 F1
De Montfort Univ
(Lansdowne Campus)
  MK40 ....38 A1
De Parys Ave MK40 ...38 C1
Deacon Ave MK42 .....49 C3
Deacon Mews MK43 ...72 C8
Deacons Ct 6 LU2 ...123 D8
Deacons Way SG5 ....100 D1
Deadman's Hill MK45 ..75 B2
Dean Cl NN10 ....8 A8
Dean St MK40 ....38 F1
Deans Mdw HP4 ......126 C5
Dearmans Cl MK45 ....75 C1
Dearne Villas MK40 ...50 A8
Dearne Wlk MK41 .....38 C5
Deep Denes LU2 ......117 A2
Deep Spinney MK43 ...37 C1
Deepdale Water Gdns★
  SG19 ....55 D7
Deeside MK17 ....81 B5
Deethe Cl MK17 ....81 B5
Degray Manor SG16 ...78 D2
Delamare Cl SG19 .....42 B1
Delamere Gdns LU7 ..110 C7
Delamere Wlk MK41 ...39 B3
Delco Way LU6 ....113 F2
Delfield Gdns LU1 ...122 E4
Dell Cl AL5 ....131 B3
Dell Rd LU5 ....114 B5
Dell The Caddington LU1 122 E3
  Heath & Reach LU7 ..103 B5
  Kempston MK42 ....49 B2
  Luton LU2 ....117 F1
  Markyate AL3 ....128 D5
Dellcot Cl LU2 ......117 B4
Dellfield Ct LU2 ....117 D2
Dellmont Rd LU5 ....114 B5
Dells La MK42 ....49 B2
Dells The SG18 ....67 A5
Delmerend La AL3 ...129 C1
Delphine Cl LU1 .....123 B6
Denbigh Cl MK43 .....72 D8
Denbigh High Sch LU3 116 C2
Denbigh Inf Sch LU3 .116 B2
Denbigh Jun Sch LU3 .116 B2
Denbigh Way MK41 ...39 A4
Dencora Way LU3 ....115 B8
Dene Cl MK17 ....81 C4
Dene Way SG18 ....66 B8
Denel Cl MK45 ....84 E4
Denham Cl LU3 ......115 E8
Denmark Cl   LU3 ....107 E1
Denmark St MK40 .....50 E8
Dennis Cl MK42 ......49 D2
Dennis Rd MK42 ......49 D2
Denny Cres SG18 .....78 F8
Denton Cl Irchester NN29 .7 B8
  Kempston MK42 ....49 D6
  Luton LU4 ....115 B3
Denton Dr MK43 ......72 C7
Dents Cl MK42 ....50 D5
Derby Pl MK40 ....38 B1

Derby Rd LU4 ....115 C2
Derwent Ave
  Biggleswade SG18 ....67 B4
  Luton LU3 ....116 B7
Derwent Cotts MK43 ..26 B3
Derwent Dr LU6 .....121 C6
Derwent Lower Sch
  SG16 ....89 B5
Derwent Pl MK42 .....50 B6
Derwent Rd
  Harpenden AL5 ......130 C4
  Henlow SG16 ....89 B4
  Leighton Buzzard LU7 110 B7
  Luton LU3 ....124 A8
Derwent Rise MK45 ...84 E2
Des Fuller Ct 3 LU1 .123 F6
Devizes Ave MK45 ....39 A5
Devon Rd Bedford MK40 .38 D2
  Luton LU4 ....124 B8
Devonshire Rd 5 MK45 131 B1
Dew Pond Rd MK45 ...84 D1
Dewlands MK43 ....36 F7
Dewsbury Rd LU3 ...116 C6
Dexter Cl LU3 ....108 B1
Dickens Cl MK43 ......24 F6
Dickens Ct SG18 .....67 A5
Dickens La LU3 ......113 A5
Dickens Ct LU3 ......84 C3
Dickerson Cl SG19 ...44 D6
Digby Cl PE19 ....22 B3
Digby Ct LU7 ....111 A8
Dimmock Rd MK43 ....60 F7
Dines Cl MK45 ....62 E4
Dingle Dell LU7 ....102 F2
Disbrowe Ct NN9 ......3 C7
Ditchling Cl LU2 ...117 C3
Ditmas Ave MK42 .....49 C2
Ditton Gn LU2 ......117 E3
Docklands SG5 ....99 D4
Dodds Cl MK41 ....11 B3
Dog Kennel Path LU6 114 B1
Doggett St LU7 .....111 A7
Dolphin Dr LU5 .....114 E6
Dolphins Way SG5 ....44 D6
Don Butler Cl MK45 ..86 B3
Donlee Furlong LU7 .111 C7
Donnelly Dr MK41 ....39 B1
Doolittle Mill MK45 ..84 D5
Dorchester Cl LU3 ..114 B1
Dorchester Way MK42 .50 C3
Dordans Rd LU4 .....115 C4
Dorel Cl LU2 ....116 F2
Dornan Ct LU1 ....123 E5
Dorrington Ct LU3 ..116 C1
Dorset Ct 4 LU1 ....123 F6
Dorsey Dr MK42 ......50 B5
Dothans Cl MK44 .....40 F5
Doug Harris Way MK45 .36 B3
Douglas Cres LU5 ...114 B2
Douglas Rd Bedford MK41 38 D6
  Harpenden AL5 ......130 F2
  Luton LU4 ....116 A2
Dove Cl SG19 ....42 C2
Dove House Cl LU6 ..119 F3
Dove House Dr SG16 ..78 D1
Dove House La LU6 ..127 D8
Dove La MK43 ....25 A6
Dove Rd MK41 ....38 D4
Dove Tree Rd LU7 ...111 C8
Dove Wlk MK45 ....84 E1
Dovedale LU2 ....116 E6
Dovehouse Cl
  Bromham MK43 ....36 F7
  St Neots PE19 ....22 F6
Dovehouse Hill LU2 .117 B1
Dover Cl LU3 ....116 A3
Dover Cres MK41 .....39 A5
Dovery Down Lower Sch
  LU7 ....103 A2
Downfield Way MK42 ..49 E5
Downham Rd MK17 ...81 C4
Downlands LU3 ......115 C7
Downs Rd Dunstable LU5 121 D8
  Luton LU1 ....123 C7
Downs View LU4 .....115 D4
Downside MK41 ....39 A3
Downside Gdns SG19 ..56 A8
Downside Inf Sch LU4 115 E1
Downside Jun Sch LU4 115 E1
Downside Lower Sch
  LU5 ....121 E7
Downton Ct 2 LU3 ..123 D8
Downview LU4 ....115 B2
Drake Rd PE19 ....22 B2
Drakeloe Cl MK17 ....92 F8
Drakes Ct LU5 ......121 D8
Drapers Mews LU3 ..116 C1
Drayton Cl PE19 .....22 B2
Drayton Rd
  Kempston MK42 ....49 D2
  Luton LU4 ....115 A3
Drewels La PE19 ......33 E4
Drive The Harpenden AL5 131 A1
  Ivinghoe Aston LU6 ..119 A1
  Oakley MK43 ....36 F7
  Sharnbrook MK44 .....16 C4
  Wharley End MK43 ....58 D2
Drivers Ct LU7 .....111 D7
Drove Rd
  Biggleswade SG18 ....67 B6
  Gamlingay SG19 ......44 B7
Drovers Way LU6 ....120 F8
Drummonds The LU4 .115 C2
Drury Cl LU5 ....114 C5
Drury La LU5 ....114 C5
Dryden Ct PE19 ......22 F5
Dubbs Knoll Rd SG8 ..69 F5
Duchess Ct PE19 .....22 A3

Duchess Ct LU5 .....114 C1
Duchess Rd MK42 .....50 F4
Duchy Cl NN9 ....3 B8
Duck End Cl MK45 ....62 A1
Duck End La
  Biddenham MK40 .....37 B1
  Maulden MK45 ....85 B8
  Wilstead MK45 ....62 E5
Duck La Shefford SG17 .77 C3
  St Neots PE19 ....22 F4
  Woburn MK17 ....92 F7
Duck Mill La MK42 ...50 C7
Duckmill Cres MK42 ..50 C7
Dudley Cl MK42 ......49 E3
Dudley St Bedford MK40 .50 E8
  Leighton Buzzard LU7 111 A6
  Luton LU2 ....123 E8
Dugdale Ct SG5 .....100 C1
Duke Dr MK43 ....37 D7
Duke St Aspley Guise MK17 81 D4
  Bedford MK40 ....50 C8
  Luton LU2 ....123 E8
Dukeminster Trad Est
  LU5 ....114 C1
Dukes Ave LU6 ......126 E8
Dukes Ct Flitwick MK45 .85 A2
  4 Luton LU1 ....123 D6
Dukes Ct Ampthill MK45 .84 F8
  St Neots PE19 ....22 B4
Dukes Ride
  Leighton Buzzard LU7 102 F3
  13 Luton LU2 ....116 D1
Dukes Row PE28 ....6 F5
Duloe Brook PE19 ....22 B4
Duloe Rd PE19 ....22 B5
Dulverton Ct LU7 ...110 C8
Dumfries Ct 8 LU1 ..123 D6
Dumfries St LU1 ....123 D6
Duncan Rd MK43 .....58 E2
Duncombe Cl LU3 ...116 C6
Duncombe Ct LU5 ...114 E2
Duncombe Dr
  Dunstable LU5 ......114 E2
  Leighton Buzzard LU7 111 A6
Duncombe St MK42 ...49 F4
Duncots Cl SG5 .....100 E3
Dunham Cl MK42 .....50 F5
Dunkirk Cl MK42 ....50 A5
Dunlin SG6 ....90 E1
Dunmow Ct LU3 .....116 D2
Dunraven Ave LU1 ..123 A8
Dunsby Rd LU3 .....116 A6
Dunsmore Rd LU2 ...123 C6
Dunstable Cl
  Flitwick MK45 ....84 E2
  Luton LU4 ....116 A1
Dunstable Coll LU5 .114 C1
Dunstable Ct LU4 ...115 F2
Dunstable Downs Ctry Pk★
  LU6 ....120 E3
Dunstable Pl 5 LU1 .123 D7
Dunstable Rd
  Caddington LU1 .....122 C3
  Dagnall HP4,LU6 ....126 C7
  Eaton Bray LU6 .....120 A5
  Flamstead AL3 ......129 F1
  Flitwick MK45 ....84 E1
  Houghton Regis LU5 .114 B3
  Luton LU4 ....116 B1
  Studham LU6 ....127 B6
  Tilsworth LU7 ......113 A6
  Toddington LU5 .....105 F5
  Totternhoe LU6 .....120 D7
Dunstable St MK45 ...84 E8
Dunstall Rd MK45 ....97 C2
Dunster Gdns MK41 ..39 B5
Dunster Way PE19 ....22 F2
Dunton La
  Biggleswade SG18 ....67 C4
  Biggleswade SG18 ....67 C5
  Dunton Lower Sch SG18 .68 D5
Dunvegan Way MK41 .38 F7
Dunville Rd MK40 ....49 F8
Durbar Rd LU4 ......116 B1
Durham Cl
  Biggleswade SG18 ....67 A4
  Flitwick MK45 ....84 E4
Durham Rd LU2 .....124 A7
Durler Ave MK42 .....49 C3
Durley Gdns LU1 ....123 D5
Durrell Cl LU7 .....110 C7
Dutter End SG19 .....44 C5
Duxford Cl LU3 .....116 B7
Dyers Rd LU6 ....119 E5
Dylan Ct LU5 ....114 C5
Dynes Pl MK44 ....53 C7
Dynevor Cl MK43 .....36 F2
Dynevor Rd MK40 ....38 A1

E

Eagle Centre Way LU4 .115 B7
Eagle Cl LU4 ....115 A4
Eagle Ct SG7 ....91 E1
Eagle Dr MK45 ....84 D2
Eagle Farm Rd SG18 ..67 B5
Eagle Gdns MK41 .....38 B3
Eagle Way MK43 .....24 F6
Earl Cl PE19 ....22 B4
Earls Ct LU5 ....114 C1
Earls Holme MK42 ...49 D6
Earls Meade LU2 ....116 D1
Earlsmead SG6 ......101 F3
Easby Abbey MK41 ...51 B8
Easedale Cl LU6 ....121 C6
Easingwold Gdns LU1 .122 F8

East Cl SG4 .... 101 B1
East Ct Bedford MK41 .... 39 A2
2 St Neots PE19 .... 22 F5
East End LU5 .... 114 C5
East End La MK44 .... 30 B3
East Hill LU3 .... 116 B6
East Hills MK43 .... 59 B1
East La SG19 .... 44 C6
East Lodge Sch SG17 .... 77 A2
East Rd Langford SG18 .... 78 F8
Sandy SG19 .... 54 B8
Wharley End MK43 .... 58 D2
East Side SG19 .... 54 C5
East Sq MK42 .... 51 A3
East St Irchester NN29 ..... 7 B8
Kimbolton PE28 .... 6 F4
Leighton Buzzard LU7 .... 111 B8
Lilley LU2 .... 109 D2
St Neots PE19 .... 22 F5
East Wlk SG18 .... 67 B7
Eastcheap SG6 .... 101 F6
Eastcote MK42 .... 51 A3
Eastcott Cl LU2 .... 117 D1
Eastcotts Rd MK42 .... 50 F5
Eastdale Cl MK42 .... 50 A4
Eastern Ave
Dunstable LU5 .... 121 D8
Henlow SG16 .... 89 C3
Eastern Way
Heath & Reach LU7 ..... 103 D5
Letchworth SG6 .... 91 A1
Eastfield Cl LU2 .... 117 C4
Easthill Rd LU5 .... 114 C5
Eastnor Gdns MK41 ...... 39 A4
Easton Cl MK45 .... 84 F3
Easton Rd MK45 .... 84 F3
Eastville Rd MK42 .... 50 B5
Eaton Bray Lower Sch
LU6 .... 119 F6
Eaton Bray Rd
Northall LU6 .... 119 C5
Totternhoe LU6 .... 119 E8
Eaton Ford Gn PE19 ..... 22 D5
Eaton Green Rd LU2 .... 124 D8
Eaton Pk LU6 .... 119 F6
Eaton Pl LU2 .... 117 D1
Eaton Rd MK42 .... 49 E2
Eaton Valley Rd LU2 .... 124 B8
Eatongate Cl LU6 .... 119 F4
Ebble Mead MK41 .... 38 D6
Ebenezer St 6 LU1 ..... 123 D6
Eddiwick Ave LU5 ...... 114 D7
Eden Way Bedford MK41 .. 38 D5
Leighton Buzzard LU7 ... 111 B5
Edens La MK43 .... 25 B2
Edgcott Cl LU3 .... 108 B1
Edgcumbe Ct SG19 ...... 54 C7
Edgecote Cl LU1 .... 122 E3
Edgehill Gdns LU3 ..... 115 C8
Edgewood Dr LU2 ...... 117 C6
Edinburgh Cl MK42 ..... 50 D5
Edinburgh Dr PE19 ..... 22 C4
Edison Rd MK41 .... 39 C3
Edith Cavell Lower Sch
MK41 .... 38 A2
Edkins Cl LU2 .... 116 E5
Edlesborough Sch LU6 .. 119 E3
Edward Arnold Ct MK42 .. 49 D5
Edward Peake Mid Sch
SG18 .... 67 C8
Edward Rd Bedford MK42 .. 50 A6
Biggleswade SG18 .... 67 B7
Irchester NN29 .... 7 B7
St Neots PE19 .... 22 F2
Edward St Dunstable LU6 114 B1
Leighton Buzzard LU7 ... 111 A8
Luton LU2 .... 116 F1
Edworth Rd SG18 .... 79 C5
Egdon Dr LU2 .... 116 D6
Egglestone Cl MK42 ..... 49 D4
Eighth Ave LU3 .... 115 D7
Eileen Wade Lower Sch
PE28 .... 5 B4
Eisenhower Pl SG17 ..... 76 E2
Eisenhower Rd SG17 .... 77 C1
Elaine Gdns LU1 .... 123 A1
Eldefield SG6 .... 101 D7
Elder Cl SG19 .... 54 B6
Elderberry Cl LU2 ..... 117 B4
Eldon Rd LU4 .... 115 C1
Eldon Way SG18 .... 67 A4
Eleanor Cl MK17 .... 92 F7
Eleanor Ct 4 LU6 ..... 121 B8
Eleanor Wlk MK17 ...... 92 F7
Eleanor's Cross 5 LU6 . 121 B8
Elgar Dr SG17 .... 77 D3
Elgar Path LU2 .... 123 E8
Elger Cl MK40 .... 37 D1
Elizabeth Ct
Dunstable LU5 .... 121 C8
Henlow SG16 .... 78 D1
9 Luton LU1 .... 123 D6
St Neots PE19 .... 22 C4
Elizabeth St LU1 ...... 123 D6
Elizabeth Way SG19 .... 44 C6
Ellenhall Cl LU3 ...... 116 C1
Ellenshaw Ct MK45 ..... 84 F4
Ellerdine Cl LU3 ...... 116 B4
Ellesmere Cl LU6 ...... 120 C6
Ellington Rd MK42 ..... 50 B5
Elliot Cres MK41 ...... 39 B3
Ellis Rd MK41 .... 38 D3
Elliswick Rd AL5 ...... 131 B2
Ells Ct LU2 .... 116 F1
Elm Ave LU1 .... 122 E3
Elm Cl Bedford MK41 .... 38 E4
Campton SG17 .... 76 F1
Hargrave NN9 .... 1 F2
Elm Cl *continued*
Henlow SG16 .... 78 D1
Elm Dr MK45 .... 86 B5
Elm Farm Cl SG17 ...... 78 B2
Elm Gr Toddington LU5 .. 105 F6
Woburn Sands MK17 ..... 81 B4
Elm Ho PE19 .... 22 F3
Elm Lodge PE19 .... 22 F3
Elm Park Cl LU5 ...... 114 D6
Elm Rd Biggleswade SG18 . 67 B5
Shefford SG17 .... 77 D2
Elm Tree Gr MK44 ...... 19 C7
Elmfield Ct LU2 ...... 117 A1
Elmhurst Gdns SG5 ..... 87 F1
Elmore Rd LU2 .... 117 A1
Elms Cl MK45 .... 84 F7
Elms Ind Est
Bedford, Elms Farm MK41 . 39 D3
Bedford, Goldington MK41 . 39 B2
Elms La MK45 .... 63 C4
Elms The Kempston MK42 . 49 E3
Leighton Buzzard LU7 ... 110 E7
Elmsdale Rd MK43 ...... 61 A8
Elmside LU6 .... 127 E8
Elmtree Ave LU2 ...... 117 E3
Elmtree Rd SG19 .... 54 B8
Elmwood MK43 .... 34 E6
Elmwood Cres
Flitwick MK45 .... 84 F2
Luton LU2 .... 116 E3
Elstow Lower Sch MK42 .. 50 B4
Elstow Moot Hall Mus*
MK42 .... 50 B4
Elstow Rd Bedford MK42 .. 50 C5
Kempston MK42 .... 49 F4
Elveden Cl LU2 .... 116 E6
Elvington Gdns LU3 ... 108 B1
Ely Cl MK45 .... 84 E4
Ely Croft SG18 .... 67 A4
Ely Way Kempston MK42 .. 49 E6
Luton LU4 .... 115 D4
Embankment The MK40 .. 50 D8
Emerald Rd LU4 .... 115 A3
Emerton Way MK43 ..... 60 F8
Emery Pl PE19 .... 22 F7
Emmer Gn LU2 .... 117 F2
Emmerton Rd MK42 ..... 49 D5
Empire Cl SG18 .... 66 F5
Empress Rd LU3 .... 115 E4
Emu Cl LU7 .... 103 A5
Enderby Rd LU3 ...... 116 C6
Endsleigh Rd MK42 .... 50 B6
Enfield Cl LU5 .... 114 D6
Engayne Ave SG19 ..... 42 B1
England Ave LU6 ...... 113 F3
Englands La LU5 ...... 121 C8
Englefield LU2 .... 116 F3
Englehurst AL5 .... 131 D1
Ennerdale Ave LU6 .... 121 B7
Ennerdale Cl MK42 .... 49 D3
Ennismore Gn LU2 .... 117 F1
Enslow Cl LU1 .... 122 E3
Enterprise Ctr 1 LU2 . 123 F8
Enterprise Way
Flitwick MK45 .... 84 F3
Leighton Buzzard LU7 .. 111 A5
Luton LU3 .... 116 B8
Epping Way LU3 ...... 107 C1
Epping Wlk MK41 ...... 39 B3
Epsom Cl
Leighton Buzzard LU7 .. 110 D6
Rushden NN10 .... 8 D8
Ereswell Rd LU3 ...... 116 A7
Eriboll Cl LU7 .... 110 B6
Erin Cl LU4 .... 116 A2
Erin Ct LU4 .... 116 A2
Ermine Pl 8 LU2 ..... 116 D1
Ernulf Com Sch PE19 .... 22 E2
Escarpment Ave HP4,
LU6 .... 126 D8
Eskdale LU4 .... 115 C5
Esmonde Cl LU7 ...... 111 D5
Essex Cl LU1 .... 123 F6
Essex Ct 7 LU1 ...... 123 E6
Essex Gdns MK42 ...... 50 D5
Eton Ct MK40 .... 38 D2
Etonbury Mid Sch SG15 . 90 C7
Ettrick Dr MK41 ...... 39 C4
Eugster Ave MK42 ..... 49 C3
Evans Cl LU5 .... 114 E4
Evedon Cl LU3 .... 115 F6
Evelyn Rd LU5 .... 114 F2
Evelyn Way NN29 .... 7 C7
Everard Rd MK41 ...... 38 F2
Everest Cl SG15 ...... 90 B5
Evergreen Way LU3 .... 116 A8
Eversholt Ho LU7 ..... 111 A6
Eversholt Lower Sch
MK17 .... 94 A5
Eversholt Rd
Ridgmont MK43 .... 82 F4
Steppingley MK45 ...... 83 F3
Everton Hill SG19 ..... 43 B3
Everton Lower Sch SG19 43 C3
Everton Rd Everton SG19 . 43 E3
Potton SG19 .... 55 F8
Sandy SG19 .... 55 A8
Eves Field MK45 ...... 85 D3
Evesham Abbey MK41 ... 51 A8
Evesham Ct MK41 ...... 38 C5
Exeter Cl SG18 .... 67 A4
Exeter Wlk MK41 ...... 39 A5
Exton Ave LU2 .... 117 A1
Exton Cl MK45 .... 85 A8
Eyeworth Rd SG19 ..... 57 B2
Eyncourt Rd LU5 ..... 114 D2
Eynesbury CE Prim Sch
PE19 .... 22 E4
Eynesbury Gn PE19 ..... 22 F4
Eynsford Rd LU4 ..... 115 D3

F

Fair Oak Ct LU2 ...... 116 F3
Fair Oak Dr LU2 ...... 116 F3
Fair Way MK44 .... 40 F5
Fairfax Ave LU3 ..... 115 D7
Fairfax Cl SG17 ...... 78 A2
Fairfax Ct PE19 ...... 22 F3
Fairfax Rd MK40 ...... 49 F7
Fairfield SG19 .... 44 D5
Fairfield Cl
Dunstable LU5 .... 114 F1
Harpenden AL5 .... 131 D1
Fairfield Rd
Biggleswade SG18 ...... 66 F7
Dunstable LU5 .... 114 E1
Fairford Ave LU2 .... 116 E4
Fairgreen Rd LU1 .... 122 F3
Fairground Way SG17 .. 78 B2
Fairholme Bedford MK41 .. 38 F3
Biggleswade SG18 ...... 66 F7
Fairlands SG18 .... 66 F7
Fairmead Cres NN10 ..... 7 F8
Fairway The MK41 ..... 39 A2
Fairways The MK45 .... 86 C4
Fakeswell La SG16 .... 88 E2
Falcon Ave MK41 ...... 38 C5
Falcon Cl Dunstable LU6 . 114 B1
Sandy SG19 .... 42 B1
Falcon Cres MK45 ..... 84 E1
Falconers Field AL5 . 130 E3
Falconers Rd LU2 .... 117 B1
Faldo Rd Barton-le-C MK45 97 B4
Bedford MK42 .... 50 D6
Fallow Dr PE19 .... 22 B5
Fallowfield Ampthill MK45 . 84 E7
Leighton Buzzard LU7 .. 111 C7
Luton LU3 .... 116 C4
Fallows Gn AL5 ...... 131 B3
Falstaff Rd PE19 ..... 22 C3
Falstone Gn LU2 ..... 117 E1
Faraday Cl LU4 ...... 115 C1
Faraday Rd MK42 ...... 50 C5
Faraday Sq MK42 ...... 50 C5
Farcet Cl PE19 .... 22 C6
Fareham Way LU5 ..... 114 E5
Faringdon Rd LU4 .... 115 C3
Farley Ct LU1 .... 123 C5
Farley Farm Rd LU1 .. 123 B5
Farley Hill LU1 ..... 123 C5
Farley Jun Sch LU1 .. 123 C6
Farley Lodge LU1 .... 123 D5
Farley Way MK43 ...... 36 C7
Farm Ave AL5 .... 130 D4
Farm Cl Ampthill MK45 .. 84 D7
Houghton Regis LU5 ... 114 C5
Letchworth SG6 .... 91 A1
Wyboston MK44 .... 31 F6
Farm Gn LU1 .... 123 C5
Farm Rd LU1 .... 130 B7
Farmbrook LU2 ...... 116 D7
Farndish Rd NN29 ...... 7 B7
Farnham Dr NN10 .... 7 F8
Farnham Way MK41 ..... 39 A5
Farr's La LU2 ...... 125 B1
Farrell Rd MK43 ...... 60 F7
Farrer St MK42 .... 49 E4
Farrer Top AL3 ..... 128 E5
Farriers Cl SG7 ...... 91 E1
Farrow Cl LU3 ...... 108 C1
Farsands MK43 .... 36 F8
Faulkner's Way LU7 . 110 E7
Faynes Ct SG19 ...... 54 C7
Fearnhill Sch SG6 .. 101 C5
Fearnley Cres MK42 .... 50 A4
Fedden Ho MK43 ...... 58 D3
Felbrigg Cl LU2 .... 117 F2
Felix Ave LU2 ...... 117 A2
Felmersham Ct LU1 .. 123 B7
Felmersham Gravel Pits
Nature Reserve* MK43 . 16 C1
Felmersham Rd
Carlton MK43 .... 25 C5
Luton LU1 .... 123 A7
Radwell MK43 .... 26 E7
Felstead Cl LU2 ... 116 F3
Felstead Way LU2 ... 116 F3
Felton Cl LU2 ..... 117 D1
Fen End SG5 .... 90 F8
Fenlake Rd MK42 ..... 50 D6
Fensome Dr LU5 .... 114 E5
Fenwick Cl LU3 .... 116 B5
Fenwick Rd LU5 .... 114 E5
Feoffee Almshouses
MK45 .... 73 F1
Fermor Cres LU2 ... 117 C1
Fern Gdns MK45 ...... 84 E3
Ferndale 7 AL5 .... 131 A2
Ferndale Rd LU1 ... 123 B7
Fernheath LU3 ..... 108 A1
Fernlea Cl MK40 ..... 49 E7
Fernwood Sch MK17 .... 81 B2
Ferrars Ave PE19 .... 22 E4
Ferrars Cl LU4 .... 115 B1
Ferrars Inf Sch LU4 . 115 B3
Ferrars Jun Sch LU4 . 115 B3
Festival Rd SG19 ..... 55 F7
Fetlock Cl MK41 ..... 37 D7
Field Cottage Rd PE19 .. 22 C3
Field End Cl LU2 .. 117 C4
Field Fare Gn LU4 . 115 A5
Field La SG6 ...... 101 F4
Fieldfare Letchworth SG6 .. 90 E1
Sandy SG19 .... 42 C2
Fieldgate Rd LU4 .. 115 D2
Fielding Ct PE19 .... 22 C7
Fields Rd MK43 ...... 61 A6
Fields The SG18 ..... 66 F1
Fieldside MK41 ...... 39 B3
Fieldside Rd MK45 ... 85 E1
Fildyke Cl SG17 ..... 88 C5
Fildyke Rd SG17 ..... 88 C5
Filland Ct SG19 ..... 54 B6
Filmer Rd LU4 ..... 115 E4
Finch Cl LU4 ...... 115 A4
Finch Cres LU7 .... 110 E5
Finch Wlk MK45 ...... 84 E1
Finchale Priory MK41 .. 51 B8
Finches The
Bedford MK40 .... 38 A1
Sandy SG19 .... 42 C2
Finley Rd AL5 ..... 131 D3
Finn's Villas LU5 . 106 A6
Finsbury Rd LU4 ... 115 D5
Finway LU1 .... 123 A8
Fir Tree Cl MK45 .... 84 E1
Fir Tree Rd MK45 .... 86 B4
Firbank Cl LU3 ... 107 C1
Firbank Ct LU7 ... 111 B5
Firbank Ind Est LU1 . 123 A8
Firbank Rd MK42 .... 50 C6
Firbank Way LU7 .. 111 A5
Firecrest SG6 ...... 90 E1
Firs Lower Sch The
MK45 .... 84 E8
Firs Path LU7 .... 103 A1
Firs The Harpenden AL5 . 131 D2
Kempston MK42 .... 49 F3
First Ave LU6 .... 121 B7
Fisher Cl MK45 ..... 97 B3
Fishers Cl
Gravenhurst MK45 ..... 87 C4
Great Barford MK44 ... 40 E6
Fishers Yd PE19 .... 22 E5
Fitzgerald Cl MK42 .. 50 C6
Fitzroy Ave LU3 .. 116 B3
Fitzwarin Cl LU3 . 115 E8
Five Oaks LU1 .... 122 F4
Five Oaks Mid Sch LU1 . 122 F3
Five Springs LU3 . 115 E6
Five Springs Ct LU3 . 115 E6
Five Springs Sch LU3 . 115 F7
Flamstead Sch AL3 . 129 B1
Flanders Cl MK42 ... 50 A5
Flawn Way PE19 ..... 22 E2
Flax Mews AL3 .... 128 E5
Fleming Cl MK40 .... 37 C1
Flexmore Way SG18 .. 78 F5
Flight Path SG16 ... 89 B3
Flint Cl LU3 ..... 115 E7
Flint Ct Dunstable LU6 . 114 A1
Luton LU1 .... 123 D5
Flint Way Bedford MK41 . 39 B5
Bedford, Woodside MK41 . 39 A4
St Neots PE19 ...... 22 E2
Flintings The HP2 . 132 F8
Flintwick Rd MK45 .. 84 A3
Flitton Hill MK45 .. 85 E5
Flitton Rd
Greenfield MK45 ..... 85 D3
Pulloxhill MK45 ..... 85 E1
Flitwick Lower Sch MK45 84 E2
Flitwick Rd Ampthill MK45 . 84 E6
Flitwick MK45 .... 95 E7
Maulden MK45 .... 85 B7
Steppingley MK45 .... 84 B3
Westoning MK45 ...... 95 E6
Flitwick Sta MK45 .. 84 E2
Florence Ave LU3 . 115 D6
Flowerdale Wlk MK41 . 39 B4
Flowers Ind Est 11 LU1 . 123 E6
Flowers Way LU1 .. 123 E7
Folly Farm MK43 .... 71 A8
Folly La Caddington LU1 . 122 E4
North Crawley MK16 .. 58 B5
Fontwell Cl MK40 ... 38 D1
Foot La NN9 .... 3 C8
Football Cl SG7 .... 91 E1
Ford Cl PE19 .... 22 D5
Ford End Rd MK40 ... 49 F7
Ford La MK44 .... 31 E1
Ford The MK41 ...... 37 E5
Fordfield Rd MK45 .. 84 B6
Forest Ctr The* MK43 .. 72 E8
Foresters' Cl MK45 . 64 A1
Forge Cl Chalton LU4 . 106 E2
St Neots PE19 .... 22 B2
Forge Gdns MK44 ...... 4 A3
Forrest Cres LU2 . 117 A3
Forty Foot La MK44 ... 9 A1
Foster Ave LU5 .. 114 C3
Foster Gr SG19 ..... 54 C6
Foster Hill Rd MK40 . 38 B1
Foster Pl MK42 ..... 49 E4
Foster Rd Harlington LU5 . 95 F2
Kempston MK42 .... 49 E5
Wootton MK43 .... 60 F8
Foster St MK40 ..... 38 B1
Foster Way MK43 .... 60 F8
Foston Cl LU3 ... 115 F6
Foundry La SG18 .... 67 A5
Foundry Way PE19 ... 22 B1
Fountain Gr MK42 ... 49 D5
Fountaine Ct MK45 .. 73 D1
Fountains Rd
Bedford MK41 .... 38 F5
Luton LU3 .... 116 D3
Fourth Ave LU3 .. 115 D7
Fowler Cl MK42 ..... 49 D5
Fowlers Dr SG17 .... 88 B6
Fox Brook Ct PE19 .. 22 F5
Fox Cl Clapham MK41 . 37 C7
Fox Cl *continued*
Dunton SG18 .... 68 D5
Fox Cnr SG8 .... 69 F5
Fox Dells LU6 ... 121 C5
Fox Hill SG8 .... 69 F5
Fox Hill Rd SG8 .... 69 F5
Foxbrook MK43 ..... 36 C7
Foxbury Cl LU2 .. 116 D6
Foxdell Inf Sch LU1 . 123 A8
Foxdell Jun Sch LU1 . 122 E8
Foxglove Cl Rushden NN10 . 8 C8
St Neots PE19 .... 22 C5
Foxglove Dr SG18 .... 67 C4
Foxglove Way MK42 ... 50 E4
Foxhill LU2 ..... 116 E5
Foxlease MK41 ...... 38 D5
Frampton Ct MK41 ... 38 C5
Frances Ashton Ho 11
LU6 .... 121 B8
Frances Ct LU7 .. 110 E7
Francis Cl SG5 ..... 90 E6
Francis Groves Cl MK41 . 38 D4
Francis Rd SG7 ..... 80 C6
Francis St LU1 .. 123 D8
Franciscan Cl NN10 ... 7 F8
Frank Hamel Ct MK45 . 97 C2
Franklin Ave MK45 .. 97 B3
Franklin Cl
Marston Moretaine MK43 . 60 D2
Pirton SG5 .... 99 D4
Franklin Gdns SG4 . 101 B1
Franklin Rd
Biggleswade SG18 .... 66 F5
Dunstable LU6 .... 120 F8
Franklyn Gdns MK40 . 37 C1
Franks Cl SG16 ..... 89 B5
Fraser Rd MK44 ..... 51 C6
Frederick St LU2 . 116 E1
Frederick Street Pas
LU2 .... 116 E1
Freeman Ave LU3 . 116 B8
Freemans Cl Hitchin SG5 100 D1
Houghton Regis LU5 . 114 A4
Freemantle Ct PE19 .. 22 B3
Freewaters Cl SG5 . 100 E4
French's Ave LU6 . 113 E2
French's Gate LU6 . 113 F2
Frenchmans Cl LU5 . 105 E5
Frensham Dr SG4 .. 101 C2
Freshwater Cl LU3 . 115 F7
Friars Cl LU1 ... 123 B5
Friars Ct LU1 ... 123 B5
Friars Way LU1 .. 123 B5
Friars Wlk Dunstable LU6 121 B8
Sandy SG19 .... 54 D8
Friary Field LU6 . 121 B8
Friday St LU7 ... 110 F7
Friendless La AL3 . 128 F2
Friesian Cl LU4 . 115 A3
Frinton Cl NN10 ...... 7 F8
Friston Gn LU2 .. 117 D1
Froghall Rd MK45 ... 84 C5
Frome Cl Bedford MK41 . 38 C5
Luton LU4 .... 115 E4
Front St LU1 .... 123 C1
Fuchsia Way NN10 ..... 8 B7
Fulbourne Cl LU4 . 115 E2
Fulbrook Mid Sch MK17 . 81 B5
Fullers Ct SG6 .. 101 E7
Fulmar Rd MK41 ..... 38 D4
Fulmore Cl AL5 .. 131 D4
Furlay Cl SG6 ... 101 D7
Furlong La LU6 .. 120 C7
Furlong The MK41 ... 38 F4
Furness Ave LU6 . 121 C7
Furness Cl MK41 .... 38 F5
Furrows The LU3 . 116 B7
Furze Cl LU2 ... 116 D7
Furzedown Ct 13 AL5 . 131 B1
Furzefield MK41 .... 38 F3
Furzen Cl LU6 .. 121 C5
Furzenhall Rd SG18 . 55 A1
Fyne Dr LU7 .... 110 C8

G

Gable Way LU5 ... 114 C6
Gables The LU7 .. 110 E6
Gaddesden Turn LU7 . 111 E2
Gade Valley Cotts HP1 . 132 E4
Gadsby St MK40 ..... 50 C8
Gadsden Cl MK43 .... 59 D2
Gainsborough Ave PE19 . 22 D5
Gainsborough Dr LU5 . 114 D5
Gainsborough Rise MK41 38 B3
Gainsford Cres SG4 . 101 C2
Gallery The
Letchworth SG6 .... 101 F6
7 Luton LU1 ..... 123 E7
Galleywood SG5 .. 100 D4
Galliard Cl LU3 . 116 B4
Galloway Cl MK42 ... 49 C3
Galston Rd LU3 .. 115 D8
Gamblingay Village Coll
SG19 .... 44 E5
Gamligay Fst Sch SG19 . 44 D5
Gamlingay Rd
Gamlingay SG19 ..... 44 D8
Potton SG19 .... 44 C1
Garden Cl MK42 ..... 49 D5
Garden Fields SG19 .. 55 F8
Garden Fields Ct NN29 .. 7 C8
Garden Hedge LU7 . 111 A8
Garden Leys LU7 .. 111 C6

Garden Rd LU6 ....121 C7
Gardener Pl MK40 ......37 C1
Gardeners Cl MK45 .....85 A3
Gardenia Ave LU3 ......116 A4
Gardens The
Henlow SG16 ....89 D8
Stotfold SG5 ....90 E6
Gardner Ct LU1 ....123 E4
Gardner's Cl LU6 ....120 E7
Garfield Ct LU2 ....117 D3
Garfield St MK41 ....38 B2
Garland Way LU7 ......111 D5
Garner Cl SG18 ....53 E2
Garnith Cl MK42 ....49 F4
Garrett Cl LU6 ....121 E5
Garretts Mead LU2 .....117 B3
Garter Ct 10 LU2 ....116 D1
Garth Rd SG6 ....101 E3
Gatehill Gdns LU3 .....108 B1
Gateshead Cl SG19 ......42 C1
Gaunts Way SG6 ....91 A2
Gayland Ave LU2 ....124 B8
Gayton Cl LU3 ....116 B4
Gazelle Cl PE19 ....22 B5
Gelding Cl LU4 ....114 F5
Geldonia Ct MK40 ....38 D2
Gelt The MK41 ....38 C7
Gemini Cl LU7 ....111 D8
Gentian Cl NN10 ....8 C8
George Ct
Biggleswade SG18 ....67 A5
Leighton Buzzard LU7 ....111 B7
George Pl PE19 ....22 F2
George St Bedford MK40 ..50 E8
Clapham MK41 ....37 D6
Dunstable LU6 ....114 B1
Leighton Buzzard LU7 ....111 B7
Luton LU1 ....123 E7
Markyate AL3 ....128 E5
Maulden MK45 ....74 C1
Shefford SG17 ....77 C2
Woburn MK17 ....92 F6
George St W LU1 ......123 E7
Georgetown SG19 ....42 A2
Georgetown Rd SG19 ....42 A1
Georgina Ct SG15 ....90 A3
Gerald Ct MK40 ....37 F1
Gerard Ct 2 AL5 ....131 A2
Gernon Rd SG6 ....101 F5
Gernon Wlk SG6 ....101 F5
Gery Ct PE19 ....22 C5
Gibbons Rd MK40 ....50 A8
Gibraltar Lodge AL5 ....131 D3
Gibson Dr LU7 ....111 D5
Gifford Rd MK42 ....50 D6
Gig La LU7 ....103 B5
Gilbert Cl MK42 ....49 D6
Gilbert Ct AL5 ....131 B4
Gilbert Inglefield Mid Sch
LU7 ....103 C1
Gilbert Mews 6 LU7 ...111 A8
Gilded Acre LU6 ....121 C5
Gilder Cl LU3 ....116 A8
Gilderdale LU4 ....115 B6
Gillam St LU2 ....123 E8
Gillan Way LU5 ....114 E5
Gillespie Cl MK42 ....50 C6
Gilpin Cl
Houghton Regis LU5 .....114 D5
Stanford SG18 ....78 A7
Gilpin Gn AL5 ....131 C1
Gilpin St LU6 ....114 A2
Gilwell Cl MK41 ....38 E5
Gipping Cl MK41 ....38 D7
Gipsy La Luton LU1 .....124 A6
Slapton LU7 ....118 D8
Girdle Rd SG4 ....101 A2
Girtford Cres SG19 ......54 B7
Glade The Bromham MK43 .36 C3
Letchworth SG6 ....101 F3
Gladstone Ave LU1 .....123 C7
Gladstone Cl SG18 ....67 A6
Gladstone St MK41 ......38 B2
Glaisdale LU4 ....115 C5
Glamis Ct PE19 ....22 E2
Glamis Wlk MK41 ....39 A4
Glastonbury Abbey MK41 51 B8
Glebe Ave Arlesey SG15 ..90 A7
Flitwick MK45 ....84 E2
Glebe Cl Sandy SG19 .....54 B8
Thurleigh MK44 ....18 C2
Glebe Gdns LU5 ....95 F2
Glebe Ho MK40 ....38 C2
Glebe Rd Ampthill MK45 ..84 E7
Bedford MK40 ....38 C1
Biggleswade SG18 ....67 B7
Sandy SG19 ....54 C8
Glebe Rise MK44 ....16 C4
Glebe The Campton SG17 ..76 F1
Clapham MK41 ....37 C7
Gravenhurst MK45 ....87 C5
Lavendon MK46 ....34 A8
Glebe Way MK45 ....74 A7
Glemsford Cl LU4 ......115 B6
Glemsford Dr AL5 ......131 D2
Glen The Caddington LU1 .122 E3
Kempston MK42 ....49 D3
Glenariff PE19 ....22 E4
Glenavon Rd MK41 ......39 C4
Gleneagles Dr LU2 ......116 E6
Glenfield Rd LU3 ....116 C6
Glenrose Ave MK41 ......38 E6
Glenwood Sch LU6 ......121 E5
Globe Cl AL5 ....131 B1
Globe La LU7 ....102 E1
Glossop Way SG15 ......90 B7
Gloucester Ct MK45 .....84 E8
Gloucester Rd
Bedford MK42 ....50 C5
1 Luton LU1 ....123 F6
Glovers Ct SG5 ....100 F1
Godfrey La MK44 ....16 E4
Godfreys Cl LU1 ....123 B6
Godfreys Ct LU1 ....123 B6
Godso Cl MK41 ....38 F4
Godwin Cl MK43 ....36 F2
Godwin Way MK43 ......36 F2
Gold Crest Cl LU4 ......115 A5
Gold La MK40 ....37 B1
Gold St Podington NN29 ....7 E2
Riseley MK44 ....10 F2
Goldcrest Way MK41 ....38 B4
Golden Riddy LU7 ......110 E8
Goldington Ave MK40 ....38 D1
Goldington Gn MK41 ....39 A2
Goldington Green Lower Sch
MK41 ....39 B1
Goldington Mid Sch
MK41 ....38 F2
Goldington Rd MK41 ....39 A1
Goldstone Cres LU5 ....114 E2
Good Intent LU6 ....119 E4
Goodhall Cres MK45 ....86 C8
Goodman Rd MK42 ......50 B5
Goodmayes Cl MK42 .....50 F6
Goodrich Ave MK41 .....39 B4
Goodwins Yd MK44 ......41 A5
Goodwood Cl MK45 .....86 C8
Goose Gn LU7 ....104 D2
Gooseberry Hill LU3 ....116 B7
Gordon St LU1 ....123 D7
Gorham Pl PE19 ....22 D4
Gorham Way LU5 ....114 F2
Gorst Cl SG6 ....101 E5
Gosforth Cl SG19 ....42 C2
Goshawk Cl LU4 ....115 A4
Gostwick Pl MK44 ....52 C8
Gostwick Rd MK42 ......50 C4
Goswell End Rd LU5 .....95 F2
Gothic Mede Lower Sch
SG15 ....90 A5
Gothic Way SG15 ....90 B5
Gower Dr MK40 ....37 C1
Graces Cl MK43 ....59 C3
Grafton Rd MK40 ....50 A8
Graham Gdns LU3 ......116 C4
Graham Rd LU5 ....121 E7
Grampian Way LU3 .....115 C8
Granary La AL5 ....131 C1
Granby Ave AL5 ....131 D2
Granby Ct AL5 ....131 D2
Granby Rd LU4 ....115 E2
Granet Cl MK40 ....37 F1
Grange Ave LU4 ....115 D4
Grange Cl
Houghton Conquest MK45 ..74 A7
Irchester NN29 ....7 B7
Leighton Buzzard LU7 ....110 D6
Markyate AL3 ....128 D6
Oakley MK43 ....37 A8
Grange Ct Bromham MK43 36 E3
Heath & Reach LU7 .....103 A6
Letchworth SG6 ....91 A1
Grange Dr SG5 ....90 F5
Grange Farm Cl MK45 ...97 B3
Grange Gdns
Beeston SG19 ....54 B5
Campton SG17 ....76 F1
Heath & Reach LU7 .....103 B6
Sharnbrook MK44 ....16 C4
Toddington LU5 ....105 F5
Grange Jun Sch SG6 ....91 A2
Grange La Bromham MK43 36 F3
Cople MK44 ....52 A5
Grange Rd Ampthill MK45 .84 E7
Barton-le-C MK45 ....97 B3
Bedford MK41 ....39 A1
Blunham MK44 ....41 E5
Felmersham MK43 ....26 C8
Letchworth SG6 ....101 F8
Toddington LU5 ....105 F6
Grange Specl Sch MK42 .49 E5
Grange St SG17 ....78 A3
Grange The
Lower Caldecote SG18 ....54 D2
Toddington LU5 ....105 E6
Grange Way Irchester NN29 7 B7
Willington MK44 ....52 C8
Grangeway
Houghton Regis LU5 .....114 E6
Rushden NN10 ....8 A8
Gransden Cl LU3 ....116 A7
Grant Gdns AL5 ....131 B2
Grantham Rd LU4 ......116 B1
Granville Rd Hitchin SG4 101 C1
Luton LU1 ....123 B8
Granville St MK42 ....50 A6
Graphic Cl LU6 ....121 D6
Grasmere Ave
Harpenden AL5 ....131 C1
Luton LU3 ....116 B7
Grasmere Cl
Dunstable LU6 ....121 B7
Flitwick MK45 ....84 E2
Kempston MK42 ....49 E3
Grasmere Rd
Biggleswade SG18 ....67 A4
Luton LU3 ....116 C7
Grasmere Way LU7 .....110 D7
Grasmere Wlk LU5 .....114 C6
Grass Yd PE28 ....6 F4
Gratton Rd MK40 ....49 F8
Gravel Pit Rd MK45 .....84 F2
Gravenhurst Lower Sch
MK45 ....87 C4
Gravenhurst Rd
Campton SG17 ....87 F8
Shillington SG5 ....87 E4
Gray St NN29 ....7 A7
Gray's Rd SG19 ....44 D6
Graylings The MK41 .....38 F4
Grays Cl MK45 ....97 C3
Grays Gr MK44 ....13 B2
Graze Hill MK44 ....28 C2
Great Aldens MK41 .....38 F4
Great Barford Lower Sch
MK44 ....40 F5
Great Farm Cl MK43 .....72 C3
Great Gaddesden CE Prim
Sch HP1 ....132 D3
Great Gn SG5 ....99 D4
Great Hill SG17 ....77 C4
Great La MK45 ....75 D4
Great North Rd
St Neots PE19 ....22 B2
Wyboston MK44 ....32 A6
Great Northern Rd LU5 .121 D8
Great Portway MK40 ....49 B6
Great Staughton Prim Sch
PE19 ....13 F6
Greatfield Cl AL5 ......130 C4
Greaves Way LU7 ......111 D6
Grebe Cl MK45 ....84 D2
Green Acres
Gamlingay SG19 ....44 C5
Lilley LU2 ....109 D2
Green Bushes LU4 .....115 D6
Green Cl Luton LU4 ....115 C5
Stanbridge LU7 ....112 D5
Green Ct 6 LU4 ....115 C5
Green Dragon Ct 8
LU1 ....123 F6
Green End
Gamlingay SG19 ....44 C5
Little Staughton MK44 .....13 A3
Workhouse End MK41 .....40 A5
Green End Rd
Great Barford MK44 ......40 E6
Kempston MK43 ....49 A4
Green Gables PE19 ......22 D4
Green La
Aspley Guise MK17 ....81 E4
Clapham MK41 ....37 F6
Dunstable LU6 ....120 E8
Eaton Bray LU6 ....119 D7
Everton SG19 ....43 C3
Great Staughton PE19 .....13 F6
Hitchin SG4 ....101 B1
Kensworth LU6 ....127 E8
Letchworth SG6 ....91 B1
Luton LU2 ....117 C4
Markyate AL3 ....128 F5
Renhold MK41 ....39 B6
Swineshead MK44 ....11 C8
Green Milverton LU3 ...116 A7
Green Oaks LU2 ....116 F3
Green The Bromham MK43 .36 F3
Cardington MK44 ....51 D4
Chelveston NN9 ....3 C8
Edlesborough LU6 ......119 F4
Great Staughton PE19 .....13 F7
Harrold MK43 ....25 A6
Houghton Regis LU5 .....114 C4
Luton LU4 ....115 C5
Marston Moretaine MK43 ..72 D7
Newnham SG7 ....91 E7
Peters Green LU2 ....125 C3
Stotfold SG5 ....90 F7
Turvey MK43 ....34 E5
Wharley End MK43 ....58 E2
Greenacre Dr
Rushden NN10 ....8 B7
Rushden NN10 ....8 B8
Greenacres MK41 ....38 E4
Greenfield Ave SG5 ....100 D4
Greenfield CE Lower Sch
MK45 ....85 D2
Greenfield Cl LU6 ......113 E1
Greenfield La SG5 .....100 E4
Greenfield Rd
Flitton MK45 ....85 D3
Flitwick MK45 ....85 A2
Pulloxhill MK45 ....85 D1
Westoning MK45 ....95 F6
Greenfield Way SG18 ....68 D5
Greenfields SG5 ....87 E1
Greengate LU3 ....115 C8
Greenhill LU7 ....103 A1
Greenhill Ave LU2 .....116 E3
Greenhill St 12 MK40 ....50 B8
Greenlands LU7 ....111 C8
Greenleas Lower Sch
LU7 ....110 C7
Greenriggs LU2 ....117 F2
Greens Cl SG19 ....54 C7
Greensand Ridge MK43 ..72 B2
Greenshields Rd MK40 ...50 E8
Greenside Pk LU2 ......116 E3
Greenview Cl MK42 .....49 C3
Greenway SG17 ....77 A1
Greenways
Eaton Bray LU6 ....119 D7
Flitwick MK45 ....84 F3
Luton LU2 ....117 B5
Gregories Cl LU3 ......116 D1
Gregory Cl SG17 ....88 B5
Greig Cl SG17 ....77 D3
Grenidge Way MK43 ....36 F8
Grenville Way PE19 .....22 B2
Gresham Cl LU2 ....124 D8
Gresham Ct MK40 ....38 D2
Gresham Way SG17 .....77 C4
Greskine Cl MK41 ....39 C4
Greycote MK42 ....51 A2
Greyfriars MK40 ....50 B8
Greys Education Ctr
MK42 ....49 D4
Greystoke Wlk MK41 ....38 F4
Grimaldi Ave LU3 ......116 A3
Grisedale Ct MK42 ......49 E2
Groat La SG19 ....44 D8
Grosvenor Gdns
Biggleswade SG18 ....67 B6
St Neots PE19 ....22 E6
Grosvenor Rd Baldock SG7 91 F1
Luton LU3 ....116 B5
Grosvenor Rd W SG7 ....91 F1
Grosvenor St MK42 ......50 C6
Grove Ct Arlesey SG15 ...90 A8
Turvey MK43 ....34 E6
Grove End LU1 ....123 B5
Grove Ho SG4 ....101 A2
Grove Park Rd LU1 .....123 B3
Grove Pl 2 Bedford MK40 .50 C8
Leighton Buzzard LU7 ....111 A6
Grove Rd Dunstable LU5 .121 D7
Hitchin SG4 ....100 F1
Houghton Regis LU5 .....114 C7
Leighton Buzzard LU7 ....111 A6
Luton LU1 ....123 D7
Slip End LU1 ....123 B2
Turvey MK43 ....34 E6
Grove The Bedford MK40 ..38 C1
Biggleswade SG18 ....67 B5
Houghton Conquest MK45 ..74 A7
Lidlington MK43 ....72 C3
Luton LU1 ....123 B5
Silsoe MK45 ....86 B5
St Neots PE19 ....22 E6
Westoning MK45 ....95 D6
Woburn Sands MK17 ......81 B5
Grovebury Cl LU6 ......121 D6
Grovebury Ct MK43 .....60 F7
Grovebury Place Ct
LU7 ....111 A6
Grovebury Rd
Leighton Buzzard LU7 ....111 A4
Leighton Buzzard LU7 ....111 A5
Grovebury Road Ind Est
LU7 ....111 A5
Grovebury Turn LU7 ....111 C1
Groveland Way SG5 .....91 A5
Grovelands Ave SG4 ...101 C2
Groveside SG16 ....78 D2
Guardian Ind Est LU1 ..123 C8
Guernsey Cl LU4 ....115 A3
Guilden Morden CE Prim Sch
SG8 ....69 F5
Guildford St LU1 ....123 E7
Guinness Pl MK41 ....51 A8
Guise Ct MK17 ....81 F4
Gulliver Cl MK42 ....49 D5
Gunnersbury Pk MK41 ...39 B1
Gurney Ct LU6 ....119 F6
Gurney's La SG5 ....100 B7
Gwyn Ct 2 MK40 ....50 B8
Gwyn St 5 MK40 ....38 B1
Gypsy La
Aspley Guise MK17 ....81 F3
Biggleswade SG18 ....66 D5

H

Hackett Pl MK16 ....58 A6
Haddon Cl NN10 ....8 A8
Haddon Ct 20 AL5 .....131 B1
Haddon Rd LU2 ....123 F8
Haden Cl MK41 ....38 A3
Hadfield Ct MK42 ....50 B6
Hadleigh Cl MK41 ....39 A4
Hadley Ct LU3 ....116 D1
Hadlow Down Cl LU3 ..116 A5
Hadrian Ave LU5 ......114 E2
Hadrian Lower Sch LU5 114 E2
Hagdell Rd LU1 ....123 C5
Hailes Cl MK41 ....38 E5
Hale Lodge MK40 ....38 C2
Halegate MK43 ....60 F8
Hales Mdw AL5 ....131 A2
Halesowen Dr MK42 .....50 D3
Half Moon La
Dunstable LU5 ....121 D7
Pepperstock LU1 ....129 C8
Half Moon Pl LU6 ......121 D7
Halfway Ave LU4 ......115 D1
Halifax Rd MK42 ....51 A2
Hall Ave NN10 ....8 A8
Hall Cl Harrold MK43 .....25 A6
Sharnbrook MK44 ....16 C4
Hall End Cl MK45 ....86 B8
Hall End Rd MK43 ....60 E7
Hall La PE28 ....6 C8
Hall Mead SG6 ....101 D6
Hall Rd PE19 ....22 E3
Hall Way MK45 ....63 D7
Hallards The PE19 ....22 C6
Halley's Way LU5 ......114 D4
Hallside SG18 ....68 C5
Hallwicks Rd LU2 ......117 B3
Hallworth Dr SG5 ....90 E6
Hallworth Ho SG5 ....90 E6
Halsey Rd MK42 ....49 E5
Halyard Cl LU3 ....116 B6
Halyard High Sch LU4 ..114 F3
Hamble Rd MK41 ....38 D7
Hambling Pl LU6 ....120 F8
Hambridge Way SG5 ....99 D4
Hambro Cl LU2 ....130 F7
Hamer Ct LU2 ....116 D8
Hamilton Cl HP4 ....126 C5
Hamilton Ct 4 LU7 ....111 A7
Hammerdell SG6 ....101 D7
Hammersmith Cl LU5 ..114 C5
Hammersmith Gdns
LU5 ....114 C5
Hammond Ct LU1 ......123 C1
Hammond Rd MK41 .....39 D4
Hampden Cl MK45 ......84 E1
Hampden Ct MK40 ......37 B1
Hampden Rd
Flitwick MK45 ....84 E1
Hitchin SG4 ....101 C1
Hampshire Way LU3 ....107 E1
Hampton Cl MK45 ....62 F4
Hampton Rd LU4 ....123 B8
Hamsterley Cl MK41 ....39 B4
Hancock Dr LU2 ....116 E5
Handcross Rd LU2 .....117 D2
Handley Page Cl MK43 ..58 E2
Hanover Cl PE19 ....22 D5
Hanover Ct
Leighton Buzzard LU7 ....110 D7
Luton LU4 ....115 D5
Wootton MK43 ....60 F8
Hanover Pl MK45 ....97 C4
Hanscombe End Rd SG5 .98 D7
Hanswick Cl LU2 ....117 B2
Hanworth Cl LU2 ......116 D7
Harbrook La SG17 ....78 A2
Harbury Dell LU3 ......116 B7
Harcourt Cl LU7 ....110 E7
Harcourt St LU1 ....123 E5
Hardenwick Ct 4 AL5 ..131 A2
Harding Cl Bedford MK42 .50 E6
Luton LU3 ....115 E7
Harding Ct AL5 ....131 B4
Harding Par 8 AL5 .....131 B1
Hardmead Rd MK43 .....34 A3
Hardwick Cl SG17 ....77 C3
Hardwick Gn LU3 ......116 B7
Hardwick Hill MK45 .....61 F7
Hardwick Mews MK17 ...81 B3
Hardwick Pl MK17 ......81 B4
Hardwick Rd
Bedford MK42 ....50 C6
St Neots PE19 ....22 E3
Woburn Sands MK17 ......81 B4
Hardy Pl PE19 ....22 D6
Harefield Ave MK42 .....50 A4
Harefield Ct LU1 ....122 F8
Harefield Rd LU1 ......122 F8
Harepark Terr SG16 .....88 E3
Harewood Rd MK42 .....50 C4
Hargood Ct PE19 ....22 B3
Hargreaves Ct MK42 ....50 C4
Harkness Ct SG4 ....101 B1
Harkness Way SG4 .....101 C2
Harland Rd PE19 ....22 F6
Harlech Ct PE19 ....22 F2
Harlech Rd MK41 ....38 F4
Harlestone Cl LU3 .....108 A1
Harling Rd LU6 ....120 B4
Harlington Lower Sch
LU5 ....95 F2
Harlington Rd
Sharpenhoe MK45 ....96 C3
Toddington LU5 ....106 B7
Upper Sundon LU3 ......107 B5
Harlington Sta LU5 .....95 E1
Harlington Upper Sch
LU5 ....95 F3
Harmill Ind Est LU7 ....111 A5
Harmony Row LU7 .....111 E5
Harold Rd MK45 ....97 C3
Harpenden Cl MK41 .....39 A1
Harpenden Hospl (private)
AL5 ....131 A4
Harpenden Meml Hospl
AL5 ....131 B2
Harpenden Prep Sch
AL5 ....130 F2
Harpenden Rise AL5 ...130 F3
Harpenden Sta AL5 ....131 B1
Harps Hill AL3 ....128 E5
Harpur Ctr 8 MK40 .....50 B8
Harpur Sq 15 MK40 .....50 B8
Harpur St MK40 ....50 B8
Harrier Cl SG18 ....66 F4
Harrier Way MK42 ......49 E2
Harriers The SG19 ......42 B1
Harrington Dr MK41 ....38 E4
Harrington Hts LU5 ....114 A5
Harris Cl MK42 ....49 E4
Harris Ct MK45 ....97 B4
Harrold Lower Sch MK43 24 F6
Harrold Odell Ctry Pk*
MK43 ....25 B7
Harrold Priory MK41 ....39 B1
Harrold Priory Mid Sch
MK43 ....24 F6
Harrold Rd MK46 ....24 C1
Harrold-Odell Visitor Ctr*
MK43 ....25 B6
Harrow Piece MK45 .....85 C8
Harrow Rd LU7 ....111 B5
Harrowden Ct LU2 .....124 C8
Harrowden La
Bedford MK42 ....50 E4
Harrowden MK42,MK44 ...51 B4
Harrowden Mid Sch
MK42 ....50 E5
Harrowden Rd
Bedford MK42 ....50 F4
Luton LU2 ....124 C8
Harry Scott Ct LU4 .....115 C6
Hart Hill Dr LU2 ....123 F8

Hart Hill La LU2 123 F8
Hart Hill Prim Sch LU2 123 F8
Hart La LU2 124 A8
Hart Wlk LU2 117 A1
Harter Ave MK43 71 B7
Harter Rd MK42 49 D2
Hartington St MK41 38 B2
Hartland Ave MK40 38 E1
Hartley Rd LU2 123 F8
Hartop Cl MK41 38 F4
Hartsfield JMI Sch SG7 91 F1
Hartsfield Rd LU2 117 B2
Hartshill MK41 38 E3
Hartwell Cres LU7 111 B7
Hartwell Dr MK42 49 E6
Hartwell Gdns AL5 130 E1
Hartwell Gr LU7 111 A7
Hartwood 3 LU2 123 F8
Harvest Cl LU4 115 A3
Harvester Ct LU7 111 D7
Harvey Cl SG18 66 C8
Harvey Rd Bedford MK41 39 A2
Dunstable LU6 120 D7
Rushden NN10 8 B7
Harvey St PE19 22 E4
Harvey's Hill LU2 116 F5
Haselfoot SG6 101 E6
Hasketon Dr LU4 115 B6
Haslingden Cl AL5 130 D3
Hassett St MK40 50 B8
Hastingbury Upper Sch & Com Coll MK42 49 C2
Hastings Rd
Barton-le-C MK45 97 C3
Kempston MK42 49 D2
Hastings St LU1 123 D6
Hatch Comm SG19 53 F4
Hatch La MK44 19 A6
Hatfield Ave MK43 71 B7
Hatfield Cl MK45 84 F3
Hatfield Cres
Bedford MK41 38 F1
Flitwick MK45 84 F3
Hatfield Rd MK45 84 F3
Hathaway Cl Luton LU4 115 B2
St Neots PE19 22 C3
Hatley Rd Gamlingay SG19 45 B4
Potton SG19 56 E7
Hatters Way LU1 123 B8
Havelock Cl
Gamlingay SG19 44 C5
Sandy SG19 42 B1
Havelock Rd
Biggleswade SG18 67 A7
Luton LU2 116 E1
Havelock Rise LU2 116 E1
Havelock St MK40 50 A7
Haven The SG5 90 F6
Haverdale LU4 115 C4
Hawes Cl MK45 84 E3
Hawesmere Cl SG18 67 A4
Hawk Cl MK45 84 D2
Hawk Dr Bedford MK41 38 B6
Sandy SG19 42 B2
Hawker Cl LU7 111 D5
Hawkesford Way PE19 22 F7
Hawkfield SG6 101 E8
Hawkfields LU2 116 E6
Hawkins Rd MK42 50 C5
Hawthorn Ave LU2 117 B4
Hawthorn Cl
Ampthill MK45 84 F7
Biggleswade SG18 66 F8
Dunstable LU6 121 C7
Turvey MK43 34 E6
Hawthorn Cres LU1 122 E3
Hawthorn End SG19 44 C5
Hawthorn Hill SG6 101 F7
Hawthorn Park Lower Sch LU5 114 D6
Hawthorn Rd PE19 22 E6
Hawthorn Way
Lower Stondon SG16 88 F2
Silsoe MK45 86 B4
Hawthorne Ave MK40 49 F7
Hawthorne Cl LU7 110 E8
Hawthorne Ct MK45 75 E1
Hawthorns The
Cranfield MK43 59 B1
Henlow SG16 78 D3
Hay Cl NN10 8 B8
Hay La AL5 131 A1
Haycroft Luton LU2 116 E6
Wootton MK43 61 A6
Hayes Cl LU2 117 C5
Hayhurst Rd LU4 115 B1
Haylands Way MK41 38 F2
Hayley Ct LU5 114 C6
Hayling Dr LU2 117 D3
Haylock Cl MK42 49 D2
Haymarket Rd LU4 114 E4
Haymoor SG6 101 E7
Haynes Lower Sch MK45 64 A1
Haynes Rd MK42 50 C5
Hayton Cl LU3 108 B2
Hazel Cl SG17 77 B2
Hazel Gr SG5 90 E5
Hazel Wlk SG18 66 F8
Hazelbury Cres LU1 123 C8
Hazelbury Ct LU1 123 C8
Hazeldene Lower Sch MK41 38 E3
Hazelwood Cl LU2 117 B4
Hazelwood La MK45 73 E3
Hazelwood Rd MK42 50 D5
Heacham Cl LU4 115 B4
Heath Cl Luton LU1 123 B6
Woburn Sands MK17 81 C3
Heath Ct LU7 102 F3
Heath Gn LU7 103 A5
Heath La MK17 81 A2
Heath Park Dr LU7 103 A2
Heath Park Rd LU7 103 A3
Heath Rd Gamlingay SG19 44 B4
Leighton Buzzard LU7 103 A2
Heath The LU7 102 E4
Heather Dr SG18 67 C4
Heather Gdns MK41 39 B1
Heather Mead LU6 119 E4
Heathermere SG6 90 F1
Heathfield MK41 39 A3
Heathfield Cl LU1 122 F4
Heathfield Lower Sch LU1 122 E4
Heathfield Rd
Hitchin SG5 100 F1
Luton LU3 116 C4
Heathwood Cl LU7 103 A3
Heathwood Lower Sch LU7 103 B3
Heaton Dell LU2 117 E1
Hebden Cl LU4 115 B4
Hedgerow The LU4 115 D6
Hedley Rise LU2 117 F2
Hedley Way MK45 86 B8
Heights The LU3 115 E5
Helen Ho MK42 50 B6
Helford Cl MK41 38 D6
Helmsley Ave MK41 39 A5
Helmsley Cl LU4 115 C5
Hemel Hempstead Rd HP4 126 F1
Hemingford Dr LU2 116 D6
Hempsals PE19 22 C6
Hen Brook PE19 22 F4
Henderson Way MK42 49 F4
Henge Way LU3 115 E7
Henley Cl LU5 114 E5
Henlow Ind Est SG16 89 B4
Henlow Mid Sch SG16 78 D1
Henry Ct LU6 121 A8
Henson Cl MK43 58 E2
Henstead Pl LU2 117 D1
Herbrand Rd MK42 51 A4
Hercules Cl LU7 111 C8
Hereford Gr SG18 67 A4
Hereford Rd
Bedford MK42 50 E4
Luton LU4 115 A3
Hermitage Gdns MK45 63 D7
Hermitage The SG15 90 B8
Herne Cl LU5 105 F7
Heron Cl
Biggleswade SG18 66 F4
Sandy SG19 54 B6
Shefford SG17 77 C2
Heron Dr LU2 116 E6
Heron Hts MK41 39 A2
Heron Quay MK40 50 B8
Heron Rd MK45 84 E1
Heron Trad Est LU3 115 C7
Heron Way SG5 90 E6
Herons Mead MK43 36 F2
Heronscroft MK41 38 F2
Heswall Ct 5 LU1 123 F6
Hever Cl NN10 8 C8
Hewlett Rd LU3 115 E5
Hexton JMI Sch SG5 98 A1
Hexton Rd
Barton-le-C MK45 97 C2
Barton-le-C, Church End MK45 97 D2
Lilley LU2 109 C4
Heywood Dr LU2 116 F2
Hibbert St LU1 123 E6
Hibbert Street Almshouses 13 LU1 123 E6
Hibberts Ct SG6 101 E7
Hickling Cl Bedford MK40 49 E7
Luton LU2 117 D1
Hickling Way AL5 131 C3
Hickman Ct LU3 115 D8
Hicks Rd AL3 128 F6
High Ave SG6 101 E4
High Banks LU7 112 C5
High Beech Rd LU3 115 D7
High Beeches Prim Sch AL5 131 D1
High Dane SG4 101 A2
High Elms MK43 25 A1
High Mead LU3 116 A3
High Point 14 LU1 123 D6
High Rd Beeston SG19 54 B5
Broom SG18 66 D3
Cotton End MK45 63 D5
Shillington SG5 98 E8
High Rd The
Felmersham MK43 26 C8
Harrowden MK42 51 A4
High Ridge
Harpenden AL5 130 E3
Luton LU2 117 C1
High St Arlesey SG15 90 A5
Bedford MK40 50 C8
Biggleswade SG15 67 A6
Blunham MK44 41 E3
Broom SG18 66 C3
Carlton MK43 25 A3
Chelveston NN9 3 C8
Clophill MK45 75 D1
Cranfield MK43 59 B2
Dunton SG18 68 D5
Eaton Bray LU6 119 E6
Edlesborough LU6 119 E3
Eggington LU7 112 B7
Elstow MK42 50 B4
High St *continued*
Eyeworth SG19 68 F8
Flamstead AL3 129 B2
Flitton MK45 85 D4
Flitwick MK45 84 E3
Gravenhurst MK45 87 C4
Great Barford MK44 41 A4
Greenfield MK45 85 C2
Guilden Morden SG8 69 F4
Guilden Morden, Eyeworth SG19 69 A8
Harpenden AL5 131 A1
Harrold MK43 24 F6
Henlow SG16 78 D2
Hinxworth SG7 80 D6
Houghton Conquest MK45 74 B8
Houghton Regis LU5 114 B4
Irchester NN29 7 B8
Kempston MK42 49 C3
Kimbolton PE28 6 F4
Langford SG18 78 F6
Leighton Buzzard LU7 111 A7
Lidlington MK43 72 C2
Little Staughton MK44 13 B1
Lower Dean PE28 5 C7
Luton LU4 115 C4
Markyate AL3 128 E5
Meppershall SG17 88 B5
North Crawley MK16 58 B6
Oakley MK43 36 F8
Odell MK43 25 C8
Pavenham MK43 26 B3
Pirton SG5 99 D4
Podington NN29 7 E2
Pulloxhill MK45 85 E1
Ridgmont MK43 82 F5
Riseley MK44 11 A2
Roxton MK44 31 E2
Sandy SG19 54 C7
Sharnbrook MK44 16 D4
Shefford SG17 77 C3
Silsoe MK45 86 C4
Souldrop MK44 16 B8
St Neots PE19 22 B8
St Neots, Eynesbury PE19 22 E5
Stagsden MK43 48 A6
Stotfold SG5 90 F6
Sutton SG19 56 A3
Swineshead MK44 11 D8
Thurleigh MK44 18 C2
Tilbrook PE28 6 B6
Tingrith MK17 94 F5
Toddington LU5 105 F6
Turvey MK43 34 E5
Upper Dean PE28 5 B4
Westoning MK45 95 E6
Wilden MK44 29 F3
Woburn Sands MK17 81 B4
Wrestlingworth SG19 57 B3
Wymington NN10 8 B5
Yelden MK44 4 A2
High St N LU6 114 A1
High St S LU6 121 C7
High Street Mews LU7 111 A6
High Top Barns MK44 4 A2
High Town Rd LU2 116 F1
High View Bedford MK41 39 A3
Markyate AL3 128 E5
High Wood Cl LU1 122 F7
Higham Dr LU2 117 D1
Higham Park Rd NN10 9 A5
Higham Rd
Barton-le-C MK45 97 D4
Chelveston NN9 3 B7
Highbury Gr MK41 37 E6
Highbury Rd LU3 116 C1
Highbush Rd SG5 90 E5
Highcroft LU7 111 C6
Highfield Bedford MK41 38 C5
Letchworth SG6 101 E4
Highfield Cres MK43 71 C1
Highfield Oval AL5 131 A4
Highfield Parc MK43 27 B1
Highfield Rd Flitton MK45 85 E4
Kempston MK42 49 E3
Leighton Buzzard LU7 111 C6
Luton LU4 116 B1
Oakley MK43 27 B1
Highfield Sch The SG6 101 D4
Highfields MK45 95 E6
Highfields Cl LU5 115 A2
Highfields Ct MK45 95 E6
Highlands MK45 84 E3
Highlands Lodge Art Ctr SG17 87 D7
Highmoor AL5 131 A4
Highover Cl LU2 117 B1
Highover JMI Sch SG4 101 C1
Highover Rd SG6 101 D5
Highover Way SG4 101 B1
Highway The MK42 51 A3
Hill Cl Harpenden AL5 131 C4
Luton LU3 116 C7
Wingfield LU7 105 E1
Hill Cres MK43 71 C1
Hill Croft Cl LU4 115 C6
Hill End House La MK43 72 B2
Hill La Biggleswade SG18 66 F7
Ickwell SG18 65 F6
Upper Caldecote SG18 66 C7
Hill Milford AL5 131 D3
Hill Pickford AL5 131 D4
Hill Rise Bedford MK41 38 B2
Kempston MK42 49 B2
Luton LU3 115 D7
Hill The MK44 41 E3
Hill View SG19 54 C5
Hill View La LU7 111 D2
Hillary Cl LU3 115 D7
Hillary Cres LU1 123 C6
Hillary Rise SG15 90 B5
Hillborough Cres LU5 114 C7
Hillborough Inf Sch LU1 123 C6
Hillborough Jun Sch LU1 123 C6
Hillborough Rd LU1 123 D6
Hillbrow SG6 101 D5
Hillcrest MK43 59 C2
Hillcrest Ave LU2 116 C8
Hillcrest Sch LU5 114 E1
Hillcroft LU6 113 E1
Hillesden Ave MK42 50 B4
Hillfield Ave SG4 101 A2
Hillfoot Rd SG5 87 E1
Hillgate SG4 101 A3
Hillgrounds Rd MK42 49 D6
Hills Cl MK44 31 E1
Hills Lower Sch The MK41 38 E3
Hills View LU3 107 B4
Hillside Chelveston NN9 3 B8
Houghton Regis LU5 114 B5
Hillside Cl SG5 87 E1
Hillside Rd
Dunstable LU5 121 D7
Harpenden AL5 130 F3
Leighton Buzzard LU7 103 A2
Luton LU3 116 D1
Shillington SG5 87 E1
Upper Stondon SG16 88 E3
Hillson Cl MK43 72 D8
Hilltop Ct LU1 123 C7
Hilltop View SG17 88 B6
Hillview Cres LU2 116 C8
Hillway MK17 81 A6
Hillyfields LU6 121 C6
Hilton Ave LU6 121 B6
Himley Gn LU7 110 D6
Hindburn Cl MK41 38 D6
Hine Way SG5 100 C1
Hinksley Rd MK45 84 F3
Hinton Cl LU7 111 D7
Hinton Wlk LU5 114 E6
Hinwick Cl SG15 90 B7
Hinwick Hall Coll of F Ed NN29 7 C1
Hinwick Rd NN29 7 A2
Hinxworth Rd
Hinxworth SG7 80 C3
Hinxworth SG7 80 F4
Hitchin Bsns Ctr The SG4 101 A3
Hitchin La SG17 78 B2
Hitchin Rd Arlesey SG15 90 A2
Henlow SG16 89 C6
Hexton SG5 98 E1
Letchworth SG6 101 E3
Luton LU2 117 A4
Pirton SG5 99 E2
Shefford SG17 77 E1
Stotfold SG5 90 E5
Upper Caldecote SG18 66 B7
Hitchin Road Ind & Bsns Ctr SG15 90 A3
Hitchin Road Ind Est LU2 116 F1
Hitchin St SG18 66 F5
Hitchmead Rd SG18 67 B6
Hitchmead Spec Sch SG18 67 C6
Hitherfield La AL5 131 A2
Hives The PE19 22 D4
Hockley Ct Hockliffe LU7 104 E2
Marston Moretaine MK43 72 D8
Hockliffe Bsns Pk LU7 104 F1
Hockliffe Ho LU7 111 B7
Hockliffe Lower Sch LU7 104 E3
Hockliffe Rd
Bedford MK42 50 D6
Hockliffe LU7,MK17 104 F6
Leighton Buzzard LU7 111 C7
Tebworth LU7 105 B1
Hockliffe St LU7 111 A7
Hockwell Ring LU4 115 C4
Hodder Rd MK41 38 C7
Hog Hall La HP4 126 A5
Hogarth Cl MK41 38 B2
Hogarth Pl PE19 22 D5
Holcroft Rd AL5 131 D3
Holden Cl MK40 37 C1
Holford Way LU3 108 B1
Holgate Dr LU4 115 B3
Holkham Cl LU4 115 A4
Holland Ct LU3 116 C2
Holland Rd Ampthill MK45 84 E7
Luton LU3 116 B2
Hollick's La LU6 121 D2
Hollies Ct LU7 110 E7
Hollies The
Kempston MK42 49 F3
Shefford SG17 77 C3
Hollies Wlk MK43 60 F8
Hollis La MK44 29 F2
Holliwick Rd LU5 114 E2
Holly Cl SG18 67 A8
Holly Farm Cl LU1 122 E3
Holly La AL5 131 E6
Holly St LU1 123 E6
Holly Street Trad Est 12 LU1 123 E6
Holly Wlk Harpenden AL5 131 D1
Silsoe MK45 86 B4
Woburn Sands MK17 81 B2
Hollybush Hill SG5 109 F1
Hollybush La
Flamstead AL3 129 B3
Harpenden AL5 131 A3
Hollybush Rd
Flitwick MK45 84 F2
Luton LU2 117 C1
Holm Oak Gn MK44 51 D4
Holmbrook Ave LU3 116 C5
Holme Cl MK43 72 D8
Holme Court Ave SG18 67 B3
Holme Cres SG18 67 A5
Holme St MK42 50 B7
Holmemead Mid Sch SG18 67 B4
Holmewood Rd MK45 85 D2
Holmfield Cl Luton LU1 123 D5
Toddington LU5 105 E5
Holmscroft Rd LU3 115 F6
Holmwood Cl LU5 114 D2
Holt Row MK42 50 B7
Holts Ct LU6 114 B1
Holtsmere Cl LU2 117 D1
Holwell Rd Holwell SG5 100 C7
Pirton SG5 99 E6
Holywell CE Mid Sch MK43 59 B1
Holywell Cl LU6 127 C6
Holywell Ct LU3 116 B4
Holywell Rd LU6 127 B6
Home Cl
Houghton Conquest MK45 74 A8
Luton LU4 115 C4
Renhold MK41 39 B6
Sharnbrook MK44 16 D3
Stotfold SG5 90 F7
Wilstead MK45 62 E3
Home Farm Cl SG19 42 B8
Home Farm Ct LU2 117 D5
Home Farm Way MK45 95 E5
Home Rd MK43 48 F3
Homebrook Ho MK42 50 C7
Homedale Dr LU4 115 D2
Homedell Ho AL5 130 E3
Homefield SG7 80 D6
Homefield Rd MK44 31 E5
Homerton Rd LU3 116 A6
Homestead Way LU1 123 C5
Honey Hill SG19 44 D4
Honey Hill Gdns MK40 49 E7
Honey Hill Rd MK40 49 E7
Honeydon Ave PE19 22 C5
Honeydon Rd MK44 20 C2
Honeygate LU2 116 E4
Honeysuckle Cl SG18 67 C4
Honeysuckle Way MK41 39 B1
Honeywick La LU6 119 E8
Honiton Mews LU3 115 E6
Honiton Way MK40 38 E2
Hoo Cl MK43 60 F8
Hoo La MK43 60 E3
Hoo Rd SG17 88 D6
Hoo St LU1 123 E5
Hoo The MK42 49 B2
Hooked La MK45 63 A5
Hookhams La MK41 39 B6
Hooper Cl MK42 49 C2
Hoover Pl SG17 76 E2
Hope Rd MK42 50 B4
Horace Brightman Cl LU3 116 A7
Horace Gay Gdns SG6 101 E6
Hornbeam Cl
Leighton Buzzard LU7 111 C8
Podington NN29 7 E2
Hornbeams The MK42 49 F4
Horne La Bedford MK40 50 B8
Potton SG19 56 A7
Hornes End Rd MK45 84 E1
Hornsby Cl LU2 117 C1
Horsefair La MK43 25 C8
Horsepool La MK43 82 A3
Horseshoe Cl
Dunton SG18 68 D5
Marston Moretaine MK43 60 E1
Horseshoe Ct MK42 49 D3
Horseshoe The MK42 50 B7
Horsham Cl LU2 117 D2
Horsler Cl MK45 97 C2
Horslow St SG19 56 A7
Horton Rd Horton LU7 118 A2
Slapton LU7 118 C6
Hospital Rd SG15 90 A4
Hotch Croft MK43 59 C3
Houghton Cl MK45 84 E7
Houghton Conquest Lower Sch MK45 74 B8
Houghton House (rems of)* MK45 73 F4
Houghton Mews 11 LU1 123 D6
Houghton Par LU6 114 A2
Houghton Park Rd LU5 114 E6
Houghton Rd
Bedford MK42 50 B6
Houghton Regis LU5 114 A3
Houghton Regis Lower Sch LU5 114 A4
House La SG15 90 A7
How End Rd MK45 73 E5
How Field AL5 130 E3
Howard Ave MK40 49 F8
Howard Cl
Cardington MK44 51 E4
Haynes MK45 63 F1
Luton LU3 116 A4

Howard Cl *continued*
Stotfold SG5 .... 90 E5
Wilstead MK45 .... 62 E3
Howard Ct MK45 .... 84 E1
Howard Ctr 7 MK40 .... 50 B8
Howard Pl Bedford MK40 .. 49 F8
Dunstable LU5 .... 121 D7
Howard Rd PE19 .... 22 C1
Howard Road Ind Est PE19 .... 22 C1
Howard St Bedford MK40 .50 C8
Kempston MK42 .... 49 F4
Howard's Cl SG18 .... 65 F1
Howards Mews MK45 .... 86 C8
Howberry Gn SG15 .... 90 A3
Howbury St MK40 .... 50 D8
Howden Gdns MK40 .... 37 C1
Howes Dr MK43 .... 72 C7
Howes La MK45 .... 95 E6
Howitt's Gdns PE19 .... 22 F2
Howitt's La PE19 .... 22 F3
Howland Pl MK17 .... 92 F7
Hoylake Ct LU1 .... 123 F5
Hubbard Cl MK45 .... 84 E1
Huckleberry Cl LU3 .... 116 A8
Huddleston Way MK41 ... 51 A8
Hudnall Rd HP4 .... 132 A7
Hudson Cl MK43 .... 72 B3
Hudson Rd MK41 .... 39 C3
Hulme Cl Clapham MK41 .. 37 C7
Kempston MK42 .... 49 E4
Humber Ave MK41 .... 38 D5
Humberley Cl PE19 .... 22 F3
Humberstone Cl LU4 ... 115 E2
Humberstone Rd LU4 ... 115 E2
Humphrey Talbot Ave LU6 .... 126 F7
Humphrys Rd LU5 .... 114 E3
Hunston Cl LU4 .... 115 B5
Hunter Cl MK42 .... 51 A2
Hunter's Cl MK41 .... 37 C6
Hunters Cl SG5 .... 90 E6
Hunters Way PE28 .... 6 F5
Hunters Yd MK44 .... 11 B3
Hunting Gate SG4 .... 101 A3
Hunting Hall LU2 .... 124 C8
Huntingdon Rd
Kempston MK42 .... 49 D3
St Neots PE19 .... 22 F7
Huntingdon St PE19 .... 22 F6
Huntingdonshire Regional Coll (St Neots Ctr) PE19 22 F6
Hunts Cl LU1 .... 123 C6
Hunts Field MK44 .... 40 F5
Hunts La MK43 .... 26 B8
Hunts Path MK43 .... 37 A8
Huntsmans Cl HP4 .... 126 C5
Huntsmans Way MK44 .... 27 B5
Hurlock Cl LU6 .... 121 A6
Hurlock Way LU4 .... 115 C5
Hurst Gr Bedford MK40 ... 49 F8
Lidlington MK43 .... 72 B3
Hurst Way LU3 .... 115 F5
Husborne Crawley Lower Sch MK43 .... 82 B4
Hutton Way MK17 .... 81 B5
Hyacinth Way NN10 .... 8 B7
Hyde Ave SG5 .... 90 E5
Hyde Cl AL5 .... 131 B4
Hyde Ho 5 LU2 .... 123 F8
Hyde La LU2 .... 125 C2
Hyde Rd LU1 .... 122 F4
Hyde The LU5 .... 114 C6
Hyde View Rd AL5 .... 131 B4
Hydrus Dr LU7 .... 111 D8

I

Ibbett Cl MK43 .... 49 A2
Ibbetts Yd 4 PE19 .... 22 E5
Ickleford Bury SG5 .... 100 E3
Ickleford Gate SG5 .... 100 D3
Ickleford Prim Sch SG5 100 E4
Ickleford Rd SG5 .... 100 F1
Ickley Cl LU4 .... 115 B5
Icknield Cl SG5 .... 100 E4
Icknield Gn SG6 .... 101 E6
Icknield High Sch LU3 .116 C5
Icknield Ho LU7 .... 111 A6
Icknield Inf Sch SG6 .... 101 D6
Icknield Lower Sch LU6 121 B8
Icknield Prim Sch LU3 .116 B5
Icknield Rd LU3 .... 115 F4
Icknield St LU6 .... 121 B8
Icknield Villas 10 LU6 ... 121 B8
Icknield Way Baldock SG7 .91 E1
Dunstable LU6 .... 120 B1
Dunstable, Well Head LU6 120 D5
Letchworth SG6 .... 101 E6
Luton LU3 .... 116 B7
Icknield Way E SG7 .... 91 F1
Icknield Way Farm Cotts LU6 .... 120 D3
Ickwell Rd Northill SG18 ... 53 D1
Upper Caldecote SG18 .... 66 A8
Iddesleigh Rd MK40 .... 49 F7
Idenbury Ct LU1 .... 123 C7
Ilford Cl LU2 .... 117 D3
Imberfield LU4 .... 115 C3
Index Ct LU6 .... 121 D7
Index Dr LU6 .... 121 D7
Ingles Ct PE19 .... 22 F6
Ingram Cl MK43 .... 72 C8
Ingram Gdns LU2 .... 116 D7
Inkerman Rise PE19 .... 22 C5
Inkerman St LU1 .... 123 D7
Inns La MK45 .... 86 B3
Instow Ct MK40 .... 38 E2
Interchange Ret Pk MK42 49 F2
Irchester Jun & Inf Schs NN29 .... 7 A8
Irchester Rd NN29 .... 7 B4
Ireton Cl PE19 .... 22 F3
Irthing Cl MK41 .... 38 D6
Irvine Ct MK41 .... 38 D5
Irwin Rd MK40 .... 38 E1
Isis Rd MK41 .... 38 C5
Isis Wlk LU7 .... 103 B3
Isle Of Wight La LU6 ... 121 A3
Ison Cl MK40 .... 49 D8
Itchen Cl MK41 .... 38 C5
Ivel Cl Barton-le-C MK45 .. 97 D3
Bedford MK41 .... 38 D6
Langford SG18 .... 78 E5
Shefford SG17 .... 77 D2
St Neots PE19 .... 22 C4
Ivel Cotts SG18 .... 66 F1
Ivel Gdns SG18 .... 66 F6
Ivel Rd Sandy SG19 .... 54 C6
Shefford SG17 .... 77 D2
Ivel View SG19 .... 54 D6
Ivel Way Flitwick MK45 .... 85 A3
Stotfold SG5 .... 90 F8
Iveldale Dr SG17 .... 77 D3
Ivester Ct LU7 .... 110 E6
Ivinghoe Bsns Ctr LU5 .. 114 B3
Ivinghoe Way LU6 .... 119 E1
Ivy Cl Dunstable LU6 .... 113 E1
Tempsford SG19 .... 42 B8
Ivy Ct LU1 .... 123 B8
Ivy La
Heath & Reach MK17 .... 102 C8
Wilstead MK45 .... 63 A4
Ivy Rd Bedford MK42 .... 50 D6
Luton LU1 .... 123 C8

J

J F Kennedy Dr SG17 .... 76 E2
Jacey Ct MK42 .... 49 D6
Jack's La MK43 .... 34 F5
Jackman Cl MK43 .... 36 F1
Jackson Pl SG17 .... 76 E2
Jackson St SG7 .... 91 E1
Jacksons Cl LU6 .... 119 E4
Jacobs Cl SG19 .... 56 A8
Jacques La MK45 .... 75 E1
James Ct Luton LU4 .... 115 B2
14 Luton, New Town LU1 .. 123 E6
St Neots PE19 .... 22 F2
James Foster Ho SG5 .. 100 E1
James Marshall Commercial Ctr AL5 .... 131 A1
James St 9 Bedford MK40 50 B8
Irchester NN29 .... 7 B7
Jameson Rd AL5 .... 131 B3
Jansel Ho LU2 .... 117 B4
Jardine Way LU5 .... 121 E7
Jasmine Cl Bedford MK41 .39 C4
Biggleswade SG18 .... 67 C4
Jasmine Ct SG5 .... 90 F7
Jasmine Gdns NN10 .... 8 B7
Jay Cl SG6 .... 101 E8
Jays The SG19 .... 42 C2
Jaywood LU2 .... 117 C6
Jeans Way LU5 .... 114 F1
Jellicoe Pl PE19 .... 22 A2
Jenkins Cl PE19 .... 22 B2
Jenkyn Rd MK43 .... 60 E6
Jennings Ave PE19 .... 22 E2
Jennings Cl SG19 .... 55 F8
Jeremiah Cl MK45 .... 97 C3
Jerrard Cl LU7 .... 111 C6
Jersey Rd LU4 .... 115 A3
Jillifer Rd LU4 .... 115 A2
Joes Cl MK45 .... 85 C2
John Barker Pl SG5 .... 100 C1
John Bunyan Cl MK45 .... 85 B8
John Bunyan Upper Sch & Com Coll MK42 .... 50 E4
John Donne CE Lower Sch MK44 .... 41 E3
John Howland Cl SG16 .. 78 D1
John St LU1 .... 123 E7
Johnson Cl
Biddenham MK40 .... 37 C1
Marston Moretaine MK43 .. 72 C8
Johnson Ct LU5 .... 114 D5
Joint The SG17 .... 78 B2
Jordan Cl SG16 .... 78 D2
Jowitt Ave MK42 .... 49 F4
Jubilee Cl Clifton SG17 .... 78 B2
Lower Stondon SG16 .... 89 B3
St Neots PE19 .... 22 E4
Jubilee Cotts MK43 .... 72 D6
Jubilee Cres SG15 .... 90 A2
Jubilee Ct
3 Dunstable LU6 .... 114 A1
Harpenden AL5 .... 131 C3
Jubilee Gdns SG18 .... 67 B7
Jubilee La SG18 .... 78 F6
Jubilee Pl SG17 .... 77 C4
Jubilee St LU2 .... 116 F1
Judith Gdns
Kempston MK42 .... 49 D3
Potton SG19 .... 56 B8
Julia Ct LU3 .... 116 B4
Julius Gdns LU3 .... 115 F7
Juniper Cl Luton LU4 .... 115 E2
Silsoe MK45 .... 86 C4
Juniper Wlk MK42 .... 49 F2
Jupiter Dr LU7 .... 111 D8
Jutland Rise PE19 .... 22 C5

K

Karen Ho SG16 .... 89 A4
Katherine Dr LU5 .... 114 F2
Katherine's Ct MK45 ... 84 E8
Katherine's Gdn MK45 ... 84 E8
Kathie Rd MK42 .... 50 D5
Kayser Ct SG18 .... 66 F4
Keaton Cl LU5 .... 114 D5
Keats Cl MK40 .... 37 F2
Keats Ct PE19 .... 22 C6
Keats Ho 15 AL5 .... 131 B1
Keats Rd MK45 .... 84 D3
Keeble Cl LU2 .... 117 E1
Keeley Farm Ct MK43 .... 48 F1
Keeley La MK43 .... 48 E1
Keepers Cl LU2 .... 117 C2
Kelling Cl LU2 .... 116 C8
Kelvin Ave MK42 .... 50 C5
Kelvin Cl LU1 .... 123 E6
Kempsey Cl LU2 .... 117 D2
Kempston Ct MK43 .... 61 E5
Kempston Hardwick Gypsy Site MK45 .... 61 F5
Kempston Hardwick Sta MK43 .... 61 D6
Kempston Rd MK42 .... 50 A6
Kempston Rural Lower Sch MK43 .... 49 B4
Kendal Cl LU3 .... 115 D7
Kendal Dr MK45 .... 84 E2
Kendal Gdns LU7 .... 110 C7
Kendale Rd LU4 .... 115 B2
Kendall Dr SG17 .... 76 F3
Kendall Rd MK42 .... 49 D3
Kenilworth Cl PE19 .... 22 C3
Kenilworth Rd LU1 .... 123 C8
Kenilworth Wlk MK41 ... 39 A4
Kennedy Ct LU7 .... 110 F7
Kennedy Rd MK42 .... 50 C5
Kennel La AL5 .... 130 A5
Kennell Hill MK44 .... 16 D3
Kennesbourne Ct AL5 .. 130 D4
Kennet Rise MK41 .... 38 C6
Kenneth Rd LU2 .... 117 A1
Kenneth Way MK45 .... 62 B6
Kennington Rd LU3 .... 116 B3
Kensington Cl LU5 .... 114 E4
Kensworth Ct LU4 .... 115 B3
Kensworth Gate LU6 .... 121 C7
Kensworth Lower Sch LU6 .... 127 F8
Kensworth Rd LU6 .... 127 D4
Kent Ave MK42 .... 50 C5
Kent Cl MK45 .... 95 E5
Kent Rd
Houghton Regis LU5 .... 114 D7
Luton LU1 .... 122 F8
Kentmere Cl MK42 .... 49 D3
Kentwick Sq LU5 .... 114 D7
Kenworth Ct MK41 .... 38 B2
Kernow Ct LU2 .... 117 A1
Kershaw Cl LU3 .... 116 A8
Kershope Cl MK41 .... 39 A3
Kestrel Rd Bedford MK41 .38 C4
Flitwick MK45 .... 84 D1
Kestrel Way Luton LU4 .... 115 A5
Sandy SG19 .... 42 B2
Keswick Cl LU6 .... 121 B7
Ketton Cl LU2 .... 124 A7
Ketton Ct LU2 .... 124 A7
Keymer Cl LU2 .... 117 C3
Keysoe Rd Riseley MK44 ... 11 B1
Thurleigh MK44 .... 18 D3
Keysoe Row E MK44 .... 19 D8
Keysoe Row W MK44 .... 19 D7
Keyston Rd PE28 .... 2 D2
Kidner Cl LU2 .... 116 E5
Kielder Path MK41 .... 39 B4
Kilby Rd LU7 .... 104 F2
Kilmarnock Dr LU2 .... 116 E5
Kiln La MK45 .... 75 D2
Kilpin Cl MK42 .... 50 D6
Kilpin Gn MK16 .... 58 B6
Kimberley SG6 .... 90 F2
Kimberley Cl LU4 .... 114 E3
Kimberwell Cl LU5 .... 105 F4
Kimble Dr MK41 .... 51 A8
Kimbolton Ave MK40 .... 38 D2
Kimbolton Cl MK41 .... 38 E3
Kimbolton Ct MK40 .... 38 D2
Kimbolton Overhills Cty Prim Sch PE28 .... 6 F5
Kimbolton Rd
Bedford MK40,MK41 .... 38 D4
Chelveston NN9 .... 3 D8
Pertenhall MK44 .... 12 D7
St Neots PE19 .... 22 A8
Wilden MK44 .... 19 D4
Kimbolton Sch
Kimbolton PE28 .... 6 E5
Kimbolton PE28 .... 6 F4
Kimpton Bottom AL5, SG4 .... 131 E7
Kimpton Rd
Luton LU1, LU2 .... 124 A6
Peters Green LU2,SG4 ... 125 E2
King Cup Cl NN10 .... 8 C7
King Edward Rd MK41 .... 39 A1
King George Cl SG18 .... 78 F7
King Georges Cl SG5 ... 100 D1
King Henry Ct LU3 .... 116 B2
King St Clapham MK41 .... 37 D6
Dunstable LU5 .... 121 C8
King St *continued*
Houghton Regis LU5 .... 114 B4
Kempston MK42 .... 49 E4
Leighton Buzzard LU7 .... 111 A8
Luton LU1 .... 123 E7
Markyate AL3 .... 128 E5
Potton SG19 .... 56 A7
King William Cl
Barton-le-C MK45 .... 97 D4
Kempston MK42 .... 49 D4
King William Rd MK42 ... 49 C4
King's Pl MK42 .... 50 B6
King's Rd Broom SG18 .... 66 C3
Flitwick MK45 .... 84 F2
Sandy SG19 .... 54 C7
St Neots PE19 .... 22 F6
King's Wood National Nature Reserve* LU7 .... 103 A8
Kingfisher Cl
Bedford MK41 .... 38 D3
Biggleswade SG18 .... 66 F5
Sandy SG19 .... 42 C2
Kingfisher Rd
Flitwick MK45 .... 84 D1
Shefford SG17 .... 77 C2
Kinghamway LU2 .... 116 E1
Kings Cl MK44 .... 10 F2
Kings Ct Dunstable LU5 .. 114 C1
Flitwick MK45 .... 84 F2
Kings Hedges SG5 .... 100 C1
Kings Houghton Mid Sch LU5 .... 114 D7
Kings Mead LU6 .... 119 E3
Kings Pond Cl SG18 .... 68 D5
Kings Rd Maulden MK45 .. 74 C1
St Neots PE19 .... 22 B3
Kings Way LU7 .... 112 D5
Kingsbrook Rd MK42 .... 50 C7
Kingsbury Ave LU5 .... 114 E1
Kingsbury Ct LU5 .... 121 C8
Kingsbury Gdns LU5 ... 114 F1
Kingscroft Ave LU5 .... 114 C1
Kingsdown Ave LU2 .... 116 D5
Kingsland Cl LU4 .... 114 E4
Kingsland Com Coll LU5 114 E6
Kingsland Ct 7 LU1 .... 123 F6
Kingsland Rd LU1 .... 123 F6
Kingsley Ct SG19 .... 54 B8
Kingsley Rd Bedford MK40 50 E8
Luton LU3 .... 116 A5
Kingsmead Pk Mobile Home Pk NN10 .... 8 C7
Kingsmede SG17 .... 77 C3
Kingsmoor Cl MK45 .... 84 F3
Kingsmoor Lower Sch MK45 .... 84 F3
Kingston Cl MK42 .... 49 E6
Kingston Ct MK42 .... 50 A6
Kingston Rd LU2 .... 116 F1
Kingsway Bedford MK42 .. 50 C7
Dunstable LU5 .... 114 C1
Luton LU4 .... 116 A1
Stotfold SG5 .... 90 F7
Kingsway Gdns SG5 .... 90 F7
Kingsway Ind Est LU1 .. 123 A8
Kingswood Ave SG4 .... 101 D1
Kingswood Cl MK45 .... 74 B7
Kingswood Way MK40 ... 49 B6
Kinloch Ct 6 AL5 .... 131 B1
Kinmoor Cl LU3 .... 107 D1
Kinross Cres LU3 .... 115 D8
Kinsbourne Cl AL5 .... 130 C4
Kinsbourne Cres AL5 .. 130 D4
Kinsbourne Ct AL5 .... 130 F3
Kinsbourne Green La AL5 .... 130 B3
Kipling Pl PE19 .... 22 D5
Kipling The LU3 .... 116 B6
Kipling Way AL5 .... 131 B1
Kirby Dr LU3 .... 116 A8
Kirby Rd LU6 .... 121 A8
Kirkdale Ct 8 LU1 .... 123 E6
Kirkdale Rd AL5 .... 131 A2
Kirkman Cl MK42 .... 50 D6
Kirkstall Cl MK42 .... 50 C3
Kirkstone Dr LU6 .... 121 B6
Kirkwick Ave AL5 .... 131 A1
Kirkwood Rd LU4 .... 114 F3
Kirton Way LU5 .... 114 E6
Kitchener Pl MK43 .... 61 D1
Kite Way SG6 .... 101 E8
Kitelands Rd SG18 .... 67 C4
Kiteleys Gn LU7 .... 111 C8
Kittiwake Cl SG18 .... 66 F4
Kiwi Ct SG5 .... 100 F1
Klondyke AL5 .... 130 D4
Knaresborough Ct PE19 .22 F1
Knarsdale Wlk MK41 .... 39 B4
Knaves Hill LU7 .... 110 D8
Kneller Cl MK41 .... 38 A2
Knights Ave MK41 .... 37 D7
Knights Cl
Eaton Bray LU6 .... 119 F5
St Neots PE19 .... 22 B4
Knights Ct LU6 .... 119 E5
Knights Field LU2 .... 116 D1
Knoll Rise LU2 .... 116 E4
Knoll The Maulden MK45 .. 85 D8
Woburn Sands MK17 .... 81 A1
Knolls The SG19 .... 54 B5
Knolls View Northall LU6 .119 B5
Totternhoe LU6 .... 112 F1
Knolls Way SG17 .... 77 F2
Knotting La MK44 .... 10 C1
Knotting Rd MK44 .... 10 C7
Knotts Cl LU6 .... 121 C5
Knowl Piece SG4 .... 101 A3
Kym Rd PE19 .... 22 C4
Kymbrook Lower Sch MK44 .... 19 C7
Kynance Cl LU2 .... 117 A2

L

Laburnam Rd SG18 .... 67 B7
Laburnum Ave MK40 .... 49 F7
Laburnum Cl LU3 .... 116 C7
Laburnum Gr LU3 .... 116 B7
Laburnum Lower Sch SG19 .... 54 B7
Laburnum Rd SG19 .... 54 B7
Lachbury Cl LU1 .... 123 A6
Lady Way PE19 .... 22 B4
Lady Zia Wernher Sch LU2 .... 117 B3
Ladybridge Terr MK43 ... 34 E5
Ladyhill LU4 .... 115 B6
Lake St LU7 .... 111 A6
Lakefield Ave LU5 .... 105 F5
Lakes Cl SG18 .... 78 E5
Lakeview MK43 .... 60 E1
Lalleford Rd LU2 .... 117 D1
Lamb Mdw SG15 .... 90 A3
Lambourn Dr LU2 .... 116 E6
Lambourn Gdns AL5 .... 130 F3
Lambourn Way MK41 .... 38 D6
Lambs Cl LU5 .... 114 F1
Lamers Rd LU2 .... 117 B2
Lammas Mead SG5 .... 100 E2
Lammas Way
Ampthill MK45 .... 84 E6
Letchworth SG6 .... 101 F8
St Neots PE19 .... 22 E6
Lammas Wlk LU7 .... 111 A7
Lamorna Cl LU3 .... 115 F6
Lamsey Ct 1 LU7 .... 111 A8
Lancaster Ave
Bedford MK42 .... 50 C5
Luton LU2 .... 116 C8
Lancaster Cl MK45 .... 97 D4
Lancaster Pl SG17 .... 77 C1
Lancaster Rd MK42 .... 51 A2
Lanchester Cl MK41 .... 37 E6
Lanchester Rd MK43 .... 58 D2
Lancing Rd LU2 .... 117 D3
Lancot Ave LU6 .... 120 F8
Lancot Dr LU6 .... 120 F8
Lancot Lower Sch LU6 .120 E8
Lancot Pl LU6 .... 120 E8
Lancotbury Cl LU6 .... 120 C7
Landrace Rd LU4 .... 114 E4
Landseer Wlk MK41 .... 38 A2
Lane The Chalton LU4 .... 106 E1
Tebworth LU7 .... 105 B3
Wyboston MK44 .... 31 F6
Lane's End LU7 .... 103 A4
Langdale MK41 .... 38 E3
Langdale Ave AL5 .... 131 D2
Langdale Cl LU6 .... 121 C7
Langdale Rd LU6 .... 121 B6
Langford Dr LU2 .... 117 A3
Langford Lower Sch SG18 .... 78 F7
Langford Mill SG18 .... 78 E7
Langford Rd
Biggleswade SG18 .... 66 F2
Henlow SG16 .... 78 D4
Langham Cl LU2 .... 116 D7
Langham Ho 8 LU1 .... 123 D8
Langleigh SG6 .... 90 F1
Langley St LU1 .... 123 E6
Langley Terrace Ind Pk 10 LU1 .... 123 E6
Langridge Ct LU6 .... 113 F1
Langwood Cl PE19 .... 22 C6
Lansbury Cl PE19 .... 22 E4
Lansdowne Rd
Bedford MK40 .... 38 A1
Luton LU3 .... 116 D1
Lansdowne Terr 7 MK40 38 A1
Lanthony Ct SG15 .... 90 A4
Laporte Way LU4 .... 115 F1
Lapwing Rd LU4 .... 115 A4
Larch Cl NN29 .... 7 A7
Larches The
Kempston MK42 .... 49 F3
Luton LU2 .... 116 D1
Lark Rise Lower Sch LU6 .... 121 B6
Larkins Cl SG7 .... 91 F1
Larks Rise SG19 .... 42 C2
Larkspur Gdns LU4 .... 115 F2
Larkway Bedford MK41 ... 38 D4
Flitwick MK45 .... 84 D2
Latimer Rd LU1 .... 123 E6
Launton Cl LU3 .... 108 B1
Laurel Cl PE19 .... 22 F4
Laurel Mews SG7 .... 91 F1
Laurel View 2 SG18 .... 67 A6
Laurel Way SG5 .... 100 E3
Laurel Wlk MK42 .... 50 A3
Laurelside Wlk LU5 .... 115 A2
Lavender Cl LU2 .... 116 E7
Lavender Ct
Ampthill MK45 .... 84 E7
Baldock SG7 .... 91 E1
Lavender Way
Biggleswade SG18 .... 67 C5
Rushden NN10 .... 8 C8
Lavenham Dr MK40 .... 37 C1
Lawford Cl LU1 .... 123 C7
Lawn Gdns LU1 .... 123 D6
Lawns The SG19 .... 43 C3
Lawnside SG18 .... 67 B6

Lawnside Lower Sch
SG18 .....67 B6
Lawrence End Rd LU2 ..125 D4
Lawrence Rd
Biggleswade SG18 .....67 A6
St Neots PE19 .....22 C5
Lawrence St MK40 .....49 F7
Lawrence Way LU6 .....113 F2
Laws Cl MK43 .....34 E6
Laxton Cl Luton LU2 .....117 E1
St Neots PE19 .....22 C4
Laycock Abbey MK41 .....51 B8
Layham Dr LU2 .....117 E1
Lea Bank LU3 .....115 E6
Lea Bank Ct LU3 .....115 E6
Lea Ct AL5 .....131 A3
Lea Manor High Sch
LU3 .....115 F8
Lea Manor Recn Ctr
LU3 .....115 F8
Lea Prim Sch The AL5 ..131 B4
Lea Rd Ampthill MK45 .....84 F8
Harpenden AL5 .....131 B3
Luton LU1 .....123 F7
Lea Wlk AL5 .....131 C4
Leacroft AL5 .....131 D3
Leaf Rd LU5 .....114 B6
Leafield LU3 .....115 F4
Leafield Ct MK45 .....84 E8
Leafields LU5 .....114 C5
Leagrave High St LU4 ..115 B3
Leagrave Prim Sch LU4 115 C4
Leagrave Rd LU4 .....116 B2
Leagrave Sta LU4 .....115 E5
Lealands High Sch LU3 .115 C8
Leamington Rd LU3 .....116 A7
Learoyd Way LU7 .....111 D6
Leasey Bridge La AL4,
AL5 .....131 F1
Leaside LU5 .....114 E6
Leaside Ct AL5 .....131 C3
Leasway MK41 .....38 F3
Leathwaite Cl LU3 .....116 A6
Leck Ho 10 LU7 .....111 A7
Ledburn Gr LU7 .....110 E6
Ledgemore La HP2 .....132 F5
Ledwell Rd LU1 .....122 F3
Lee Bridge Cnr LU2 .....130 F7
Lee Cl MK40 .....37 C1
Lee Ct PE19 .....22 E5
Lee Farm Cotts MK44 .....15 E6
Leedon Lower Sch LU7 .111 C6
Leeds Smith Dr SG19 .....54 C8
Lees Cl SG18 .....68 D5
Leghorn Cres LU4 .....115 A3
Leicester Rd LU4 .....115 E1
Leigh Cl LU5 .....105 F6
Leigh Ct MK40 .....38 B1
Leighfield Cl MK41 .....39 C3
Leighton Buzzard Narrow
Gauge Rly★ LU7 .....103 C1
Leighton Buzzard Rd
HP1 .....132 E2
Leighton Buzzard Sta
LU7 .....110 E6
Leighton Ct Bedford MK41 38 C5
Dunstable LU6 .....121 A8
Leighton Mid Sch LU7 ..110 F6
Leighton Rd Ascott LU7 .110 A3
Eggington LU7 .....112 A7
Heath & Reach LU7 .....103 B4
Leighton Buzzard LU7 .....102 B1
Leighton Buzzard LU7 .....110 F7
Leighton Buzzard,Eggington
LU7 .....112 B8
Northall LU6 .....119 C4
Stanbridge LU7 .....112 B5
Toddington LU5 .....105 E5
Leighton St MK17 .....92 E6
Leith Rd MK42 .....50 F5
Lely Cl MK41 .....38 A3
Lennon Ct LU1 .....123 D7
Lennox Gn LU2 .....117 F2
Leopold Rd LU7 .....110 D7
Lesbury Cl LU2 .....117 E1
Leston Cl LU6 .....121 D5
Letchworth La SG6 .....101 F3
Letchworth Mus & Art Gall★
SG6 .....101 F5
Letchworth Rd LU3 .....116 A4
Letchworth Sta SG6 .....101 F6
Levellers La PE19 .....22 F3
Leven Cl LU7 .....110 B7
Leven Wlk MK41 .....38 C7
Levendale LU4 .....115 C5
Lewens Croft MK16 .....47 A3
Lewes Gdns MK41 .....39 A5
Lewis La SG15 .....90 A6
Lewsey Park Ct LU4 .....115 A4
Lewsey Rd LU4 .....115 B2
Ley Side MK43 .....36 F2
Leyburne Rd LU3 .....116 B6
Leydene Pl SG17 .....76 F3
Leygreen Cl LU2 .....124 A8
Leyhill Dr LU1 .....123 B4
Leys Ave SG6 .....101 F6
Leys Rd PE19 .....22 E6
Leys The Ampthill MK45 ...84 F7
Langford SG18 .....78 F6
Woburn Sands MK17 .....81 A4
Leyton Gn AL5 .....131 A1
Leyton Rd AL5 .....131 A1
Library Rd LU1 .....123 E7
Library Wlk MK41 .....38 F4
Lichfield SG18 .....67 A4
Lichfield Cl MK42 .....49 E5
Liddel Cl LU3 .....116 B3
Liddell Way LU7 .....111 D5
Lidgate Cl LU4 .....115 B6
Lidlington Sta MK43 .....72 B3
Life Cl LU4 .....114 F4
Lighthorne Rise LU3 ..116 A7
Lilac Gr Biggleswade SG18 67 C5
Luton LU3 .....107 C1
Rushden NN10 .....8 B7
Lilac Wlk MK42 .....49 F3
Lilleshall Dr MK42 .....50 C3
Lilley Bottom LU2 .....117 F8
Lilleyhoo La LU2,SG5 ...109 F2
Lily Cl MK42 .....50 F4
Limbersey La MK45 .....74 D3
Limbury Rd LU3 .....115 F4
Lime Ave Beeston SG19 ...54 B6
Luton LU4 .....115 C3
Lime Cl Barton-le-C MK45 .97 C3
Bromham MK43 .....36 E1
Flitwick MK45 .....84 F2
Lime Gr
Leighton Buzzard LU7 .....110 E8
St Neots PE19 .....22 F6
Woburn Sands MK17 .....81 B4
Lime St MK40 .....50 B8
Lime Tree Cl LU3 .....107 C1
Lime Tree Rd SG17 .....78 A3
Lime Tree Wlk SG18 .....67 A7
Lime Wlk Dunstable LU5 .121 D8
Henlow SG16 .....78 D2
Limes The Arlesey SG15 ..90 A8
Luton LU1 .....123 E5
Limetree Ave LU1 .....130 A7
Linacres LU4 .....115 D4
Linbridge Way LU2 .....117 E2
Linclare Pl PE19 .....22 C4
Lincoln Cl Dunstable LU5 121 F6
Flitwick MK45 .....84 E4
Lincoln Cres SG18 .....67 A4
Lincoln Ct MK40 .....50 E8
Lincoln Rd
Kempston MK42 .....49 D2
Luton LU4 .....116 B1
Shortstown MK42 .....51 A2
Lincoln Way LU5 .....96 A2
Lincombe Slade LU7 ...110 E8
Lincroft Cranfield MK43 ..59 B1
Oakley MK43 .....37 A7
Lincroft Mid Sch MK43 ..37 A7
Linden Cl LU5 .....114 F1
Linden Ct Bedford MK40 ..38 A2
4 Luton LU2 .....123 F8
Linden Rd Bedford MK40 ..38 A1
Dunstable LU5 .....114 F2
Luton LU4 .....115 E4
Lindencroft SG6 .....91 A1
Lindens The LU5 .....114 B4
Lindisfarne Cl Sandy SG19 54 C8
St Neots PE19 .....22 F1
Lindisfarne Priory MK41 .51 B8
Lindler Ct LU7 .....111 A6
Lindley Cl AL5 .....131 A4
Lindsell Cres SG18 .....67 A7
Lindsey Rd LU2 .....117 D1
Link Rd NN10 .....8 B7
Link The
Houghton Regis LU5 .....114 B5
Letchworth SG6 .....91 A1
Link Way SG17 .....78 A2
Links The MK42 .....49 E3
Links Way LU2 .....116 D8
Linkway MK41 .....39 A2
Linley Dell LU2 .....117 D2
Linley Rd PE19 .....22 E3
Linmere Wlk LU5 .....114 E6
Linnet Cl Letchworth SG6 101 E8
Luton LU4 .....115 A4
Sandy SG19 .....42 C2
Linnet Way MK41 .....38 C4
Linnins Pond AL3 .....129 B1
Linslade Lower Sch
LU7 .....110 D7
Linslade Mid Sch LU7 ..110 E5
Linslade Rd LU7 .....102 F4
Linwood Gr LU7 .....111 B6
Lippitts Hill LU2 .....116 E5
Lipscombe Dr MK45 .....84 E1
Liscombe Rd LU5 .....121 E8
Liston Cl LU4 .....115 B5
Litchfield MK44 .....11 A2
Little Beeches SG18 .....66 F7
Little Berries LU3 .....115 E7
Little Church Rd LU2 ...117 B3
Little End Rd PE19 .....22 B2
Little End Road Ind Est
PE19 .....22 B2
Little Grove Pl MK40 .....50 C8
Little Headlands MK41 ...38 F4
Little Heath SG19 .....44 C4
Little Hill LU7 .....111 E2
Little La Clophill MK45 ...75 D1
Pirton SG5 .....99 D5
Little Portway MK40 .....49 B6
Little Spinney MK43 .....59 C3
Little Staughton Airfield
MK44 .....20 D8
Little Staughton Rd
MK44 .....20 C3
Little Townsend Cl MK42 .50 B4
Little Wood Croft LU3 ..115 E7
Littlebury Cl SG5 .....91 A5
Littledale St MK42 .....49 F5
Littlefield Rd LU2 .....117 B2
Littlegreen La LU1 .....122 E3
Liverpool Rd LU1 .....123 D7
Livingstone Lower Sch
MK41 .....38 A2
Loake Cl MK41 .....37 C7
Locarno Ave LU4 .....115 C6
Lochy Dr LU7 .....110 C7
Lockhart Cl LU6 .....121 E6
Lockington Cres LU5 ...114 F2
Lodge Ave MK42 .....49 C3
Lodge Cl MK44 .....16 C4
Lodge Ct SG5 .....100 E3
Lodge Gdns AL5 .....131 A2
Lodge Rd Cranfield MK43 .71 A7
Rushden NN10 .....8 A8
Sharnbrook MK44 .....16 C4
Lodge The MK41 .....37 D6
Lodge The Nature Reserve★
SG19 .....54 F4
Loftus Cl LU4 .....115 B3
Lollard Cl LU4 .....114 E3
Lombard St MK43 .....72 C3
Lombardy Cl MK41 .....38 E4
Lomond Dr LU7 .....110 C7
London End Irchester NN29 7 B8
Milton Ernest MK44 .....27 B4
Woburn MK17 .....92 F6
London La
Houghton Conquest MK45 ..74 D6
Riseley MK44 .....10 F1
London Luton Airport
LU2 .....124 D7
London Rd Astwick SG18 ..79 E7
Bedford MK42 .....50 D6
Biggleswade SG18 .....67 C4
Dunstable LU6 .....121 D6
Luton LU1 .....129 F7
Luton, New Town LU1 ...123 E4
Markyate AL3 .....128 F5
Sandy SG19 .....54 B7
Woburn MK17 .....93 B3
London Road Ind Est
SG19 .....42 A1
London Road Trad Est
SG18 .....67 C3
London Row SG15 .....90 A3
Long Acre SG17 .....88 B5
Long Cl
Lower Stondon SG16 .....88 E2
Luton LU2 .....117 C3
Long Croft Rd LU1 .....123 A7
Long Dr MK45 .....76 A5
Long Hedge LU5 .....121 D8
Long La Gamlingay SG19 ..45 B6
Tingrith LU5 .....95 A2
Long Mdw Dunstable LU6 121 A8
Markyate AL3 .....128 F5
Long Mead LU5 .....114 B6
Long Wlk SG17 .....76 D3
Longborns MK43 .....59 C2
Longbrooke LU5 .....114 D4
Longcroft Ave AL5 .....130 F1
Longcroft Rd MK45 .....97 B2
Longden Cl MK45 .....64 A1
Longfellow Ave PE19 ....22 D5
Longfield Ct SG6 .....101 D7
Longfield Dr LU4 .....115 D1
Longfield Rd SG19 .....54 B8
Longholme Way MK40,
MK41, MK42 .....50 E7
Longleat MK41 .....39 B1
Longleat Cl MK45 .....84 D1
Longmead SG6 .....101 E7
Longmeadow LU5 .....114 E5
Longmeadow Dr
Ickleford SG5 .....100 F5
Wilstead MK45 .....62 E2
Lonsdale Cl LU3 .....116 B5
Lord's Hill LU5 .....105 F1
Lords Cl LU7 .....112 E5
Lords Mead LU6 .....119 E6
Lords Pl 12 LU2 .....116 D1
Lords Terr LU6 .....119 E6
Lordsmead MK43 .....59 C2
Loring Rd Dunstable LU6 .113 F1
Sharnbrook MK44 .....16 B4
Lorraine Ct MK41 .....39 A1
Lorraine Rd MK43 .....60 F8
Lorrimer Cl LU2 .....116 E6
Loseby Cl NN10 .....8 A8
Lothair Rd LU2 .....117 A4
Lottings Way PE19 .....22 C6
Lovat Wlk MK42 .....49 E3
Lovell Meml Homes
MK43 .....37 B6
Lovell Rd Bedford MK42 ..50 F5
Oakley MK43 .....37 B6
Lovent Dr LU7 .....111 B7
Loveridge Ave MK42 .....49 D6
Lovers' Wlk LU5 .....121 C8
Lovet Rd MK45 .....84 E1
Lovett Way LU5 .....114 D3
Lower End Rd MK17 .....81 A8
Lower Farm Cotts SG18 ..80 B7
Lower Farm Rd MK43 ....37 C4
Lower Harpenden Rd
LU1, LU2 .....124 C3
Lower Luton Rd AL5 ...131 C3
Lower Shelton Rd MK43 .60 D2
Lowry Dr LU5 .....114 D5
Lowry Rd PE19 .....22 C6
Lowther Rd Bedford MK41 38 E5
Dunstable LU6 .....121 D5
Loyne Cl LU7 .....110 C8
Lucas Ct MK40 .....37 C1
Lucas Gdns LU3 .....116 B8
Lucas Way SG17 .....77 C4
Lucerne Way LU3 .....116 C4
Ludlow Ave LU1 .....123 E4
Ludlow Wlk MK41 .....39 A4
Ludun Cl LU5 .....121 E8
Luffenham Pl SG17 .....76 D3
Luke Pl MK42 .....50 C4
Luke St PE19 .....22 E4
Lullington Cl LU2 .....117 C3
Lune Wlk MK41 .....38 C5
Lunedale Cl MK42 .....49 E3
Lurke St MK40 .....50 C8
Luton & Dunstable Hospl
LU4 .....115 C2
Luton & Dunstable Hospl
(Faringdon Wing) LU4 115 C3
Luton Airport Parkway Sta
LU1 .....124 B5
Luton Dr The LU1 .....124 B3
Luton Ent Pk LU3 .....115 B8
Luton Ind Coll LU1 .....123 E7
Luton La AL3 .....130 B1
Luton Maternity Hospl
LU4 .....115 C2
Luton Mus & Art Gall★
LU3 .....116 D2
Luton Rd Barton-le-C MK45 97 B1
Caddington LU1 .....123 A4
Chalton LU4,LU5 .....106 C3
Cockernhoe LU2 .....117 E3
Dunstable LU5 .....114 E1
Harpenden AL5 .....130 D4
Luton LU4 .....115 A7
Markyate AL3 .....128 F7
Peters Green SG4 .....125 F2
Streatley LU3 .....108 A6
Wilstead MK45 .....62 E3
Luton Regional Sports Ctr
LU2 .....117 A5
Luton Ret Pk LU1 .....124 A6
Luton Sixth Form Coll
LU2 .....116 E4
Luton Sta LU2 .....123 E8
Luton Town FC LU1 .....123 C8
Luton Univ LU1 .....123 F7
Luton Univ,Putteridge Bury
LU2 .....117 D6
Luton White Hill LU2 ...117 F8
Luxembourg Cl LU3 .....115 D8
Lyall Cl MK45 .....84 F2
Lyall Ct MK45 .....85 A4
Lychmead SG17 .....78 B3
Lydds Hill MK43 .....82 E5
Lydekker Mews 1 AL5 .131 A2
Lydford Cl MK40 .....38 E1
Lye Hill SG4 .....125 D7
Lygetun Dr LU3 .....115 F7
Lymans Rd SG15 .....90 A6
Lyme Rd MK45 .....84 E8
Lymington Gdns MK41 ...39 C4
Lynch Hill LU6 .....128 A8
Lyndhurst Cl AL5 .....131 C2
Lyndhurst Dr AL5 .....131 C2
Lyndhurst Rd LU1 .....123 C7
Lyneford Way NN10 .....7 F8
Lyneham Rd LU2 .....117 C1
Lynn Cl MK42 .....50 C2
Lynton Ave SG15 .....90 A5
Lynton Gr MK42 .....50 B4
Lynwood Ave LU2 .....117 A3
Lynwood Lodge 6 LU6 .114 A1
Lyon Cl MK42 .....49 E2
Lyra Gdns LU7 .....111 D8
Lytham Pl MK40 .....49 B6
Lytton Ave SG6 .....101 F5
Lywood Rd LU7 .....111 C6

M

Mabel Rd MK42 .....50 B5
Macaulay Rd LU4 .....115 A2
Maddison Ho PE19 .....22 E6
Magdalene Cl SG18 .....68 D5
Magnolia Cl MK42 .....49 F2
Magnolia Dr NN10 .....8 B7
Magnolia Pl SG18 .....67 C4
Magpies The Luton LU2 ..116 E6
Maulden MK45 .....74 C1
Mags La MK17 .....93 E1
Mahew Ct MK42 .....49 D5
Maidenbower Ave LU6 .113 F1
Maidenhall Inf Sch LU4 116 A2
Maidenhall Jun Sch
LU4 .....116 A2
Maidenhall Rd LU4 .....116 A2
Main Rd Astwood MK16 ...47 A3
Biddenham MK40 .....49 C8
Main Rd N HP4 .....126 A6
Main Rd S HP4 .....126 D4
Main St SG19 .....45 F3
Maitland St MK40 .....50 B8
Malakand Rd MK42 .....50 A5
Malaunay Pl SG19 .....54 C7
Malcote Cl MK40 .....37 C1
Malden Ho PE19 .....22 E6
Maldon Ct AL5 .....131 B2
Malham Cl Flitwick MK45 .84 E2
Luton LU4 .....115 F2
Mall The LU5 .....114 C1
Mallard Cl SG17 .....77 C2
Mallard Gdns LU3 .....116 A5
Mallard Hill MK41 .....38 C4
Mallard La PE19 .....22 F4
Mallow The LU3 .....115 F3
Malmesbury Abbey MK41 51 A8
Malms Cl LU6 .....121 D1
Malthouse Gn LU2 .....117 F1
Malthouse La SG5 .....91 A7
Malting La HP4 .....126 C5
Maltings Cl MK43 .....59 A1
Maltings Orch SG5 .....99 D3
Maltings Pl SG19 .....44 D5
Maltings The
Ampthill MK45 .....73 E1
Dunstable LU6 .....114 A1
Maltings The *continued*
Henlow SG16 .....78 D1
Leighton Buzzard LU7 ....111 B6
Letchworth SG6 .....91 C1
Shefford SG17 .....77 C3
St Neots PE19 .....22 C5
Maltings Way MK44 .....41 A5
Malvern Ave MK41 .....38 F2
Malvern Cl MK45 .....84 D2
Malvern Dr LU7 .....110 C8
Malvern Rd LU1 .....123 B7
Malzeard Ct 17 LU3 .....116 D1
Malzeard Rd LU3 .....116 D1
Manchester Pl LU5 .....114 B1
Manchester St LU1 .....123 E7
Mancroft Rd LU1 .....122 E2
Mander Cl LU5 .....105 F6
Mangrove Rd
Cockernhoe LU2 .....117 E4
Luton LU2 .....117 C2
Manland Ave AL5 .....131 C2
Manland Prim Sch AL5 .131 B3
Manland Way AL5 .....131 C3
Manning Ct LU5 .....114 C5
Manning Pl LU2 .....117 E2
Mannock Way LU7 .....111 D5
Manor Ave LU7 .....104 E2
Manor Cl Bromham MK43 .37 A4
Carlton MK43 .....25 A3
Clifton SG17 .....78 A3
Great Staughton PE19 .....13 F6
Harlington LU5 .....95 F2
Ickleford SG5 .....100 E3
Irchester NN29 .....7 B8
Kempston MK42 .....49 D4
Langford SG18 .....78 F6
Letchworth SG6 .....101 F3
Salford MK17 .....70 D3
Westoning MK45 .....95 E5
Wilden MK44 .....29 F3
Manor Ct Caddington LU1 122 F4
Leighton Buzzard LU7 .....102 E2
Marston Moretaine MK43 ..72 C7
Rushden NN10 .....8 C8
Manor Dr MK42 .....49 D4
Manor Farm Bsns Pk
SG5 .....98 A6
Manor Farm Cl
Barton-le-C MK45 .....97 C3
Luton LU4 .....115 C3
Manor Farm Way MK44 ..16 C3
Manor Gdns MK45 .....95 D6
Manor Hospl MK40 .....49 B8
Manor House Cl PE19 ...22 C2
Manor La NN10 .....8 A5
Manor Lodge MK42 .....49 D4
Manor Park Dr MK45 ....95 D6
Manor Pk LU5 .....114 C4
Manor Pl SG18 .....66 B8
Manor Rd
Barton-le-C MK45 .....97 D3
Bedford MK41 .....39 A2
Biddenham MK40 .....49 B8
Caddington LU1 .....122 F2
Gamlingay SG19 .....44 D6
Henlow SG16 .....78 C1
Kempston Hardwick MK43 .61 D6
Lea valley AL4 .....131 F2
Lower Sundon LU3 .....107 C3
Luton LU1 .....123 F6
Marston Moretaine MK43 ..72 C7
Rushden NN10 .....8 B8
Sandy SG19 .....54 B8
Toddington LU5 .....105 F6
Wootton MK43 .....61 A7
Manor The SG19 .....56 B8
Manor Way
Cotton End MK45 .....63 D7
Flitwick MK45 .....84 D2
Letchworth SG6 .....101 F3
Potton SG19 .....56 B8
Manorbier Rd MK41 .....38 F5
Manse Ct AL3 .....128 F5
Mansfield Rd LU4 .....116 B1
Manshead CE Upper Sch
LU1 .....121 F5
Manshead Ct LU5 .....121 D6
Mansion La MK43 .....24 F6
Manton Cl MK45 .....84 F8
Manton Ctr The MK41 ...38 A3
Manton Dr LU2 .....116 D3
Manton La MK41 .....38 A3
Manton Rd LU6 .....120 D5
Manx Cl LU4 .....116 A2
Maple Cl
Biggleswade SG18 .....67 A7
Clifton SG17 .....77 F2
Greenfield MK45 .....85 D2
Lower Stondon SG16 .....88 E2
Maple Ct Gamlingay SG19 .44 C5
15 Luton LU1 .....123 D6
Maple Dr SG17 .....77 E2
Maple Flats AL5 .....131 A3
Maple Gdns MK44 .....11 A3
Maple Gr MK17 .....81 B4
Maple Rd Harpenden AL5 130 F1
Sandy SG19 .....42 C1
Maple Rd E LU4 .....123 B8
Maple Rd W LU4 .....123 B8
Maple Tree Lower Sch
SG19 .....42 B2
Maple Way Cranfield MK43 71 A8
Kensworth LU6 .....127 E8
Maple Wood NN10 .....8 B7

Maples The
Kempston MK42 ....49 E3
Silsoe MK45 ....86 B4
Marbury Pl LU3 ....115 F4
Marchioness Way PE19 ..22 B4
Mardale Ave LU6 .....121 C6
Mardale Cl LU6 ....49 E4
Mardle Rd LU6 ....110 E6
Maree Cl LU7 ....110 C7
Maresfield Ave SG17 ...76 F2
Mareth Rd MK42 ....50 E6
Margaret Beaufort Mid Sch
MK44 ....11 B3
Margetts Rd MK42 .....49 F4
Marigold Way MK42 ....50 F4
Marina Ct MK42 ......50 A6
Marina Dr LU6 ....120 E7
Mark Rutherford Rd
MK42 ....50 D6
Mark Rutherford Upper Sch
& Com Coll MK41 ....39 A5
Market Mews 8 LU7 ...111 A7
Market Pl Ampthill MK45 ..73 E7
Woburn MK17 ....92 F7
Market Sq Bedford MK40 ..50 B8
Biggleswade SG18 .....67 A6
Leighton Buzzard LU7 ..111 A7
Luton LU1 ....123 B6
Potton SG19 ....56 A7
Sandy SG19 ....54 C7
St Neots PE19 ....22 E5
Toddington LU5 ......105 F6
Markfield Cl LU3 .....116 C7
Markham Cres LU5 ....114 F2
Markham Rd LU3 ......116 C8
Markyate Rd LU1 .....123 B1
Markyate Village Sch
AL3 ....128 C6
Marlborough Ct LU1 ...123 C7
Marlborough Lower Sch
MK40 ....49 F8
Marlborough Pk MK42 ..49 F6
Marlborough Pl LU5 ...105 F6
Marlborough Rd
Bedford MK40 ....49 F8
Luton LU3 ....116 D1
Marley Fields LU7 ....111 D6
Marlin Cl LU4 ....114 E4
Marlin Rd LU4 ....114 E3
Marlow Ave LU1 ......123 A8
Marlowe Ct PE19 .....22 D6
Marlow Way MK41 .....38 C6
Marmet Ave SG6 .....101 C4
Marne St MK42 ....50 A5
Marquis Cl
Harpenden AL5 ......131 D2
St Neots PE19 ....22 B4
Marquis Ct 9 Luton LU2 116 D1
Woburn MK17 ....92 F7
Marquis Hill SG5 .....88 A1
Marquis La AL5 ......131 D2
Marriott Rd LU3 .....116 B6
Marriotts Cl MK43 ....26 B8
Marschefield SG5 ....90 E6
Marsh Ho LU3 ....115 F4
Marsh La MK44 ....27 B5
Marsh Leys Ind Est MK43 61 D8
Marsh Rd LU3 ....115 F4
Marsh The MK43 ......25 A3
Marshall Cl MK42 ....49 D5
Marshall Ct MK41 ....39 A1
Marshall Rd Luton LU2 ..117 C2
St Neots PE19 ....22 F5
Marshalls Ave SG5 ...87 F1
Marshalls Way AL4 ...131 F2
Marsom Gr LU3 ......116 B8
Marston Gdns LU2 ....116 D4
Marston Hill MK43 ....59 F2
Marston Rd MK43 .....72 C3
Marston Thrift (Nature
Reserve)★ MK43 .....71 E8
Marston Vale Mid Sch
MK43 ....61 C1
Marston Vale Millennium
Country Pk★ MK43 ...72 E7
Marston Vale Millennium
Ctry Pk★ MK43 ......60 F1
Martham Ct MK40 .....49 D7
Martham Ct AL5 ......131 C3
Martin Cl MK41 ......38 D4
Martin Rd MK45 ......84 D1
Martin Way SG6 .....101 D5
Martindales The LU2 ..123 F7
Martins Dr The LU7 ...102 F1
Mary Bassett Lower Sch
LU7 ....110 F7
Mary Brash Ct LU2 ...117 C3
Maryland Coll MK17 ...92 E6
Maryport Rd LU4 .....116 A2
Maryville Rd MK42 ....50 B5
Marywells SG6 ....88 B5
Masefield Ave PE19 ...22 C6
Masefield Cl AL5 .....131 B4
Masefield Rd AL5 ....131 B4
Massey Cl MK42 .....49 E4
Masters Cl LU1 ......123 B5
Matlock Cres LU4 ....115 C1
Matthew St LU1 ......121 B8
Mattocke Rd SG5 ....100 C1
Maulden Cl LU2 ......117 C1
Maulden Lower Sch
MK45 ....85 D8
Maulden Rd MK45 ....85 A4

Maulden Road Ind Est
MK45 ....85 A4
Maule Cl PE19 ....22 E1
Maundsey Cl LU6 ....121 D5
Maurice Ct PE28 .....6 F5
May Cl Eaton Bray LU6 ..119 E6
Rushden NN10 ....8 C7
May Rd MK43 ....34 E6
May St LU1 ....123 E5
Maycroft SG6 ....91 A1
Mayer Way LU5 ......114 A3
Mayes Ct MK44 ......29 F2
Mayfield Cl
Harpenden AL5 ......130 E3
Kempston MK42 ......49 E5
Mayfield Cres SG16 ...88 E2
Mayfield Ct SG19 ....54 B7
Mayfield Rd
Dunstable LU5 ......121 D7
Luton LU2 ....117 B4
Mayfields SG17 ......77 D3
Mayhew Rd MK43 .....36 E1
Maynards The SG18 ...66 C3
Mayne Ave LU4 ......115 C4
Mead End SG18 ......67 B5
Mead Open Farm & Rare
Breeds★ LU7 ....112 A2
Mead The SG5 ....100 F2
Mead's Cl MK17 ......93 E2
Meadhook Dr MK45 ...97 B3
Meadow Cl Beeston SG19 54 B5
St Neots PE19 ....22 F5
Meadow Croft LU1 ....122 E4
Meadow La Bedford MK44 51 D7
Gamlingay SG19 .....44 D3
Houghton Regis LU5 ..114 B5
Meadow Piece MK45 ..76 A8
Meadow Rd Luton LU3 ..116 B4
Toddington LU5 ......105 F5
Meadow Sweet Rd NN10 ..14 B7
Meadow View MK17 ...81 D6
Meadow Way
Ampthill MK45 ......84 D7
Caddington LU1 .....122 E4
Leighton Buzzard LU7 ..111 D7
Letchworth SG6 .....101 F5
Stotfold SG5 ....90 F6
Meadow Wlk SG16 ....78 D1
Meadowbank SG4 ....101 B1
Meadows The
Flitwick MK45 ....84 D5
Stewartby MK43 .....61 C1
Wingfield LU7 ....105 E1
Meadowsweet
Lower Stondon SG16 ..88 F2
St Neots PE19 ....22 E5
Meadowsweet Dr MK42 ..50 E4
Meadowview Rd MK42 ..49 C3
Meads Cl LU5 ....114 C5
Meads Prim Sch The
LU2 ....116 A6
Meads The
Eaton Bray LU6 .....119 E5
Letchworth SG6 .....101 E6
Luton LU1 ....116 A3
Meadway Bedford MK41 ..39 A2
Dunstable LU5 ......121 A7
Harrold MK43 ....25 A7
Leighton Buzzard LU7 ..111 C8
Meadway Ct LU6 .....120 F7
Medallion Ct 4 PE19 ..22 F5
Medbury La MK42 ....50 C2
Medina Rd LU4 ......116 A1
Medley Cl LU6 ......119 F5
Medlows AL5 ....130 E2
Medmenham Ave SG17 ..76 F2
Medusa Way SG19 ....42 B1
Medway Cl MK45 .....84 D2
Medway Ct MK41 .....38 D5
Mees Cl LU3 ....107 F1
Meeting Cl MK45 .....63 D7
Meeting House La SG7 ..91 E1
Meeting La SG19 .....56 F1
Melbourn Cl SG5 ....90 F6
Melbourne St MK42 ...50 B7
Melchbourne Rd MK44 ..9 F4
Melford Cl 3 LU2 ....117 D1
Melfort Dr LU7 ......110 B6
Melrose Dr MK42 ....50 C3
Melson Sq 9 LU1 ....123 E7
Melson St LU1 ......123 E7
Melton Ct LU6 ......120 F7
Melton Wlk LU5 .....114 E6
Memorial La
Bletsoe MK44 ....17 C1
Felmersham MK43 ...26 C8
Memorial Rd LU3 ....115 F4
Mendham Way MK45 ..86 C8
Mendip Cl MK45 .....84 D2
Mendip Cres MK41 ...38 F3
Mendip Way LU3 .....107 C1
Mentmore Cl MK40 ...49 B6
Mentmore Cres LU6 ..121 C5
Mentmore Gdns LU7 ..110 E5
Mentmore Rd LU7 ....110 E5
Mentone Ave MK17 ...81 D4
Mepham Rd MK43 ....36 F2
Meppershall CE Lower Sch
SG17 ....88 B5
Meppershall Rd
Meppershall SG17,SG5 ..88 A3
Upper Stondon SG16 ..88 D4
Merchant La
Cranfield MK43 ......59 A1
Wharley End MK43 ...58 F2
Mercury Pl SG17 .....76 D3
Mercury Way LU7 ....111 D8
Merlin Dr SG19 ......42 B2

Merlin Gdns MK41 ....38 C4
Merlins Ct LU7 ......111 A7
Mersey Cl MK41 .....84 D2
Mersey Pl 1 LU1 ....123 D7
Mersey Way MK41 ....38 C5
Merton Ho MK40 .....38 B1
Merton Rd MK40 .....38 D2
Mews The
3 Harpenden AL5 ...131 B1
Letchworth SG6 .....91 C1
Meyrick Ave LU1 .....123 C6
Meyrick Ct LU1 ......123 D6
Mickle Hill PE28 .....2 D7
Middle Gn LU1 ......111 C8
Middlefield Com Prim Sch
PE19 ....22 F2
Middlefield Ind Est SG19 54 D8
Middlefield La SG16 ..89 C7
Middlefields SG6 ....90 F1
Middlefields Ct SG6 ..90 F1
Middleham Cl LU4 ...54 C8
Middlesex Univ (Bedford)
MK40 ....38 A1
Middleton Rd LU2 ...117 D4
Middleton Way LU7 ..111 D5
Midhurst SG6 ....101 F8
Midhurst Gdns LU3 ..116 C4
Midland Cl SG17 .....77 C2
Midland Cotts SG4 ...101 A1
Midland Rd Bedford MK40 50 B8
Luton LU2 ....123 E8
Sandy SG19 ....54 C8
Midway LU1 ....111 C7
Milburn Cl LU3 ......108 E1
Milburn Rd MK41 ....39 B4
Mile Rd MK42 ....50 D4
Mile Tree Rd LU7 ....103 E4
Milebush LU7 ....110 C8
Miles Ave LU7 ......111 B7
Miles Dr SG17 ......78 B2
Milestone Rd SG5 ...100 D2
Miletree Cres LU6 ...121 D6
Miletree Ct LU7 .....111 B8
Milford Hill AL5 .....131 D4
Mill Cl Biggleswade SG18 ..66 F5
Henlow SG16 ....78 D3
Stotfold SG5 ....91 A6
Mill End Cl LU6 .....119 F4
Mill Est NN10 ....8 B7
Mill Hill Keysoe MK44 ..12 B2
Thurleigh MK44 .....18 B1
Mill Hill Rd PE19 ....22 C2
Mill La Arlesey SG15 ...89 F4
Astwick SG5 ....79 F1
Barton-le-C MK45 ...97 C3
Biggleswade SG18 ...66 F5
Campton SG17 ......88 A8
Clophill MK45 ......75 C1
Everton SG19 ....43 D1
Flamstead AL3 ......129 A1
Greenfield MK45 ....85 C3
Hexton SG5 ....98 C3
Houghton Conquest MK45 62 B1
Hulcote MK17 ....70 E1
Kempston MK45 .....49 C4
Keysoe MK44 ....12 B2
Langford SG18 ......78 E7
Odell MK43 ....25 D8
Pavenham MK43 ....26 B3
Potton SG19 ....55 F8
Salford MK17 ....70 C3
Sandy SG19 ....54 B6
St Neots PE19 ......22 F8
Stotfold SG5 ....91 A6
Tempsford SG19 ....42 A7
Turvey MK43 ....34 D5
Woburn Sands MK17 ..81 C5
Mill Mdw SG18 ......78 E7
Mill Rd Colmworth MK44 ..30 C7
Cranfield MK43 .....59 C2
Houghton Regis LU5 ..114 A4
Husborne Crawley MK43 ..82 D5
Leighton Buzzard LU7 ..111 A8
Sharnbrook MK44 ...16 F3
Slapton LU7 ....118 D7
Stanbridge LU7 .....112 C6
Stanford SG18 ......78 B7
Thurleigh MK44 .....28 B7
Mill Rise MK43 ......34 D5
Mill St Bedford MK40 ..50 C8
Gamlingay SG19 ....44 D5
Luton LU1 ....123 D8
Mill Twr LU7 ....119 E6
Mill Vale Mid Sch LU5 114 E2
Mill View Ct PE19 ....22 C2
Mill Way MK17 ......81 D5
Millard Way SG4 ....101 C1
Millards Cl Cranfield MK43 59 B2
Flitwick MK45 ....84 D3
Millbank Bedford MK40 ..50 D8
Leighton Buzzard LU7 ..110 F8
Millbrook Rd MK42 ...50 B6
Millbrook Sta MK45 ..72 F6
Miller Rd MK42 .....50 B5
Millers Ct LU7 ......111 D7
Millers Cl SG18 .....66 F5
Millers Lay LU5 .....114 F2
Millers Way LU5 .....114 A4
Millfield MK43 ......36 F2
Millfield Cl Cranfield MK43 59 B2
Flitwick MK45 ....85 A2
Millfield La AL3,LU1 ..122 D2
Millfield Mews LU1 ..122 D2
Millfield Rd LU3 .....116 B3
Millfield Way LU1 ...122 D3
Milliners Way LU3 ...116 C1
Mills Wlk SG19 ......54 C8
Millstream Cl SG4 ...101 A1

Millstream Ct SG17 ..77 D3
Millstream Way LU7 ..110 F7
Millwood Ct SG5 ....90 F6
Millwright Way MK45 ..84 D4
Milne Row MK40 .....37 F1
Milner Ct LU2 ......123 E8
Milton Ave PE19 .....22 D6
Milton Ct 12 AL5 ....131 B1
Milton Ernest Lower Sch
MK44 ....27 B5
Milton Rd Bedford MK40 ..37 F1
Clapham MK41 ......37 C7
Flitwick MK45 ....84 D3
Harpenden AL5 .....131 B1
Luton LU1 ....123 C6
Milton Way LU5 .....114 D4
Milton Wlk LU5 .....114 D4
Milverton Gn LU3 ...116 A7
Minden Cl MK45 .....84 E4
Minden Ct PE19 .....22 C5
Minorca Way LU4 ....115 A3
Miss Joans Ride HP4,
LU6 ....126 E7
Mistletoe Ct LU2 ....124 C8
Mistletoe Gdns LU7 ..124 C8
Mistletoe Hill LU2 ...124 C8
Mitchell Ct MK42 ....51 A3
Mitchell Rd MK43 ...58 E2
Mitford Cl MK41 .....39 A4
Mitre Cl MK41 ......39 B1
Mixes Hill Ct LU2 ...117 A4
Mixes Hill Rd LU2 ...116 F4
Mixies The SG5 .....90 F7
Moakes The LU3 ....115 E7
Moat Farm Cl
Greenfield MK45 ....85 B2
Marston Moretaine MK43 ..72 C7
Moat La LU3 ....116 B4
Mobbs Cl MK42 .....49 D5
Mobley Gn LU2 .....117 B3
Moggerhanger Lower Sch
MK44 ....53 C7
Moira Cl LU3 ....115 D7
Molescroft AL5 ......130 E4
Molivers La MK43 ...36 F3
Molly Moore Ave MK42 ..49 D3
Monarch Hall LU2 ...124 C8
Monarch Rd PE19 ...22 B4
Monklands SG6 .....101 D6
Monks Cl Dunstable LU5 ..114 C1
Letchworth SG6 ....101 C6
Monks Row MK43 ...26 B3
Monkshill MK41 .....39 A3
Monmouth Cl
Bedford MK42 ......50 D5
Toddington LU5 .....105 C4
Monmouth Rd LU5 ..95 F2
Monoux Pl SG19 ....54 C7
Monoux Rd MK43 ...61 A6
Montagu Ct PE19 ...22 E4
Montagu Gdns PE28 ..6 F1
Montagu Ho PE19 ...22 E4
Montagu Sq PE19 ...22 E4
Montagu St PE19 ...22 E4
Montague Ave LU4 ...115 C4
Montgomery Ave SG17 ..77 C1
Montgomery
Leighton Buzzard LU7 ..103 B1
Stewartby MK43 .....61 C1
Montgomery Ct MK42 ..50 A5
Montgomery Way SG18 ..67 D3
Monton Cl LU3 ......115 F6
Montrose Ave LU3 ...116 C3
Moor End LU6 ......119 F5
Moor End Cl LU6 ....119 F4
Moor End La
Eaton Bray LU6 .....119 F5
Felmersham MK43 ...16 F1
Moor End Rd MK43 ...26 F8
Moor La Bedford MK42 ..50 D4
Flitwick MK45 ....85 A2
Moor Pond Piece MK45 ..73 D1
Moor Rd PE19 ......13 E1
Moor St LU1 ....123 C8
Moor The MK43 .....25 A4
Moore Cres LU5 .....114 C4
Moore's Cl MK45 ....86 C3
Moores Wlk 7 PE19 ..22 E5
Moorhouse Path LU7 ..111 D5
Moorhouse Way LU7 ..111 D5
Moorland Gdns LU2 ..123 D8
Moorland Rd AL5 ...131 B4
Moorlands Sch LU4 ..115 C3
Morar LU2 ....110 C7
Morcambe Cl LU4 ...115 B3
Morcom Rd LU5 ....121 E6
Mordaunt Cl MK43 ..34 E6
Moreteyne Rd MK43 ..72 E8
Moreton Ave AL5 ...130 F2
Moreton End Cl AL5 ..130 F2
Moreton End La AL5 ..130 F2
Moreton Pk LU2 ....117 A2
Moreton Pl AL5 .....130 F3
Moreton Rd N LU2 ..117 A2
Moreton Rd S LU2 ..117 A2
Morgan Cl LU4 .....115 E3
Morgans Cl MK45 ...62 F3
Moriston Rd MK41 ...38 C6
Morland Cl LU6 ....121 A6
Morland Way MK41 ..38 B2
Morrell Cl LU3 .....116 A7
Morris Cl Henlow SG16 ..89 C5
Luton LU3 ....115 D6
Morris Gdns MK42 ...84 D7
Morris Wlk MK44 ...31 F6
Mortimer Cl LU1 ....123 A7
Mortimer Rd MK42 ..49 D6
Moss La MK42 ......50 C1

Moss Way SG5 ......100 C1
Mossbank Ave LU2 ..124 C8
Mossdale Ct 8 LU4 ..115 C5
Mossman Dr LU1 ....122 E4
Mostyn Rd LU3 .....115 E4
Moulton Ave MK42 ...50 E6
Moulton Rise LU2 ...123 F8
Mount Dr MK41 .....39 A3
Mount Grace Rd LU2 ..117 C6
Mount Pleasant
Aspley Guise MK17 ...81 F4
Ridgmont MK43 .....82 F5
Mount Pleasant Ave
LU5 ....105 F4
Mount Pleasant Cl LU5 105 F4
Mount Pleasant Rd
Clapham MK41 ......37 D6
Luton LU3 ....115 E5
Mount The
Aspley Guise MK17 ...81 D4
4 Luton LU2 ......123 D8
Mountbatten Ct PE19 ..22 C4
Mountbatten Dr SG18 ..67 B7
Mountbatten Gdns LU7 ..123 C8
Mountbatten Pl MK41 ..39 B1
Mountbatten Way SG17 ..76 E4
Mountfield Rd LU2 ...116 C6
Mountfort Cl PE19 ...22 F3
Mountjoy SG4 ......101 C1
Mountview Ave LU5 ..121 E6
Mowbray Cl MK43 ...36 E3
Mowbray Cres SG5 ...90 F7
Mowbray Dr LU7 ....110 D7
Mowbray Pl MK44 ...40 C1
Mowbray Rd MK42 ...50 C4
Mowhills MK43 ......24 F6
Moxes Wood LU3 ...115 E7
Muddy La SG6 ......101 F3
Muirfield Biddenham MK40 49 B6
Luton LU2 ....116 E6
Mulberry Cl
Biggleswade SG18 ..66 F8
Luton LU1 ....123 B7
Stotfold SG5 ....90 F5
Mulberry Way SG5 ..100 D2
Mulberry Wlk MK42 ..49 F3
Mullein Cl PE19 .....22 C5
Mullion Cl LU3 .....117 B5
Mullway SG6 ....101 C6
Muntjac Cl PE19 ....22 B5
Murdock Rd MK41 ...38 A4
Murfitt Way SG19 ...44 D6
Murrell Cl PE19 ....22 F7
Murrell Ct PE19 ....22 F7
Murrell La SG5 .....91 A5
Musgrave Way 6 PE19 ..22 E5
Mussons Path LU2 ..116 E1
Muswell Cl LU3 .....116 B6
Muswell Rd MK42 ...50 B5
Mutford Croft 2 LU2 ..117 D1
Myers Rd SG19 .....56 A4
Myrtle Rd MK42 .....50 D5

N

Nags Head La NN9 ....1 F2
Nagshead La MK44 ...32 A5
Napier Ct LU1 ......123 D7
Napier Hall LU2 .....124 C8
Napier Rd Bedford MK41 ..39 D3
Luton LU1 ....123 D7
Nappsbury Rd LU4 ...115 D5
Narrow Path MK17 ...81 B3
Naseby Pl MK45 .....84 E4
Naseby Rd LU1 .....123 B7
Nash Cl LU5 ....114 D5
Nash Rd MK42 ......50 E6
Navigation Wharf PE19 ..22 E5
Nayland Cl LU2 .....117 C1
Naylor Ave MK42 ...49 E2
Neale Rd MK43 .....60 F8
Neale Way MK43 ....60 F8
Neath Abbey MK41 ..51 B8
Nebular Ct LU7 .....111 C8
Needham Rd LU4 ...115 B6
Needwood Rd MK41 ..39 C3
Nelson Rd
Chicksands SG17 ...76 E4
Dagnall HP4 ....126 C5
Leighton Buzzard LU7 ..103 B1
St Neots PE19 ....22 B2
Nelson St MK40 .....49 F7
Nene Rd Flitwick MK45 ..84 D2
Henlow SG16 ....89 B4
St Neots PE19 ....22 C4
Neotsbury Ct MK45 ..84 F8
Neotsbury Rd MK45 ..84 F8
Neptune Cl LU5 .....114 E6
Neptune Gdns LU7 ..111 D8
Neptune Sq LU5 ....114 E6
Nethercott Cl LU2 ...117 C1
Netherstones SG5 ...90 F7
Nettle Cl LU4 ....114 E4
Nettleden Rd HP1 ...132 C1
Nettleton Cl LU7 ....111 C6
Nevell's Gn SG6 ....101 F6
Nevells Rd SG6 ....101 F6
Nevern Gdns MK40 ..37 C1
Neville Cl MK43 .....36 E2
Neville Cres MK43 ..36 F2
Neville Rd LU3 .....116 A5
Neville Road Pas LU3 ..116 A5
Nevis Cl LU7 ....110 C7
New Bedford Rd LU3 ..116 D3
New Cl MK44 ....28 F1
New Cotts AL3 .....128 E6
New Inn Rd SG7 ....80 D5

New Rd Bromham MK43 ... 36 E1
Clifton SG17 ... 78 A1
Colmworth MK44 ... 29 F8
Great Barford MK44 ... 41 B5
Harrold MK43 ... 24 E6
Leighton Buzzard LU7 ... 110 E7
Maulden MK45 ... 85 C6
Sandy SG19 ... 54 D5
New St Irchester NN29 ... 7 B8
Luton LU1 ... 123 E6
Shefford SG17 ... 77 C2
Slip End LU1 ... 123 C1
St Neots PE19 ... 22 E5
New Street Ct NN29 ... 7 B8
New Town Rd 9 LU1 ... 123 E6
New Town St LU1 ... 123 E6
New Wlk Shillington SG5 ... 87 E1
Shillington SG5 ... 87 F1
New Woodfield Gn LU5 ... 121 E6
Newark Ave MK41 ... 39 A5
Newark Rd LU4 ... 116 A2
Newbold Rd LU3 ... 116 B7
Newbury Cl
Kempston MK42 ... 49 D4
Luton LU4 ... 115 E2
Silsoe MK45 ... 86 B5
Newbury Ct MK45 ... 86 B5
Newbury Ho MK40 ... 38 D2
Newbury La MK45 ... 86 B5
Newbury Rd LU5 ... 114 E6
Newcombe Rd LU1 ... 123 C7
Newis Cres SG17 ... 78 B2
Newlands Rd Luton LU1 ... 123 C3
Westoning MK45 ... 95 E6
Newman Way LU7 ... 111 B7
Newmans Dr AL5 ... 130 F2
Newnham Ave MK41 ... 50 F8
Newnham Cl LU2 ... 117 D1
Newnham Mid Sch MK41 ... 38 E2
Newnham Rd
Bedford MK40 ... 50 C8
Newnham SG7 ... 91 E6
Newnham St MK40 ... 50 C8
Newport Pagnell Rd
MK43 ... 47 D5
Newport Rd
Hardmead MK16 ... 46 C2
Woburn MK17 ... 92 F8
Woburn Sands MK17 ... 81 A6
Newstead Way MK41 ... 38 F5
Newton Blossomville CE First
Sch MK43 ... 34 B4
Newton Rd Bedford MK42 ... 50 C5
Chelveston NN10 ... 3 B3
Rushden NN10 ... 8 F8
Turvey MK43 ... 34 E5
Newton Way
Leighton Buzzard LU7 ... 111 D6
Sandy SG19 ... 54 C8
Newtondale LU4 ... 115 C5
Newtown Henlow SG16 ... 78 D3
Kimbolton PE28 ... 6 F5
Potton SG19 ... 55 F7
St Neots PE19 ... 22 B8
Newtown Ct SG18 ... 67 B7
Newtown La PE28 ... 6 F5
Nicholas Way 6 LU5 ... 121 B8
Nicholls Cl
Barton-le-C MK45 ... 97 C3
Marston Moretaine MK43 ... 72 C8
Nicholls Rd MK42 ... 50 D6
Nichols Cl LU2 ... 117 C2
Nicholson Dr LU7 ... 111 D5
Nightingale Ave MK41 ... 38 C5
Nightingale Cl LU2 ... 117 C6
Nightingale Ct LU3 ... 123 C8
Nightingale Mews SG17 ... 77 C2
Nightingale Terr SG15 ... 90 A3
Nimbus Pk LU5 ... 114 C3
Nimrod Dr SG17 ... 76 E4
Ninelands LU7 ... 104 F2
Ninfield Ct LU2 ... 117 C3
Ninth Ave LU3 ... 115 D7
Nith Wlk MK41 ... 38 C7
Nodders Way MK40 ... 37 C1
Noke Shot AL5 ... 131 C4
Norcott Cl LU5 ... 121 D7
Norfolk Cl MK41 ... 38 D6
Norfolk Rd
Dunstable LU5 ... 121 F6
Luton LU2 ... 124 A7
Turvey MK43 ... 34 E6
Norman Cl MK44 ... 40 F5
Norman Rd
Barton-le-C MK45 ... 97 D4
Luton LU3 ... 116 B2
Sharnbrook MK44 ... 16 D3
Norman Way
Dunstable LU6 ... 120 E8
Irchester NN29 ... 7 C8
Normandy Cl MK42 ... 50 A5
Normandy La SG18 ... 67 D3
Normans Cl SG6 ... 90 F1
Norse Rd MK41 ... 39 D4
North Area Pupil Referral
Unit SG6 ... 101 D3
North Crawley CE Fst Sch
MK16 ... 58 B6
North Ct AL3 ... 128 E5
North Dr MK42 ... 51 A3
North Drift Way LU1 ... 123 B6
North End MK42 ... 51 A3
North Hertfordshire Coll
SG6 ... 101 F5
North La Gamlingay SG19 ... 44 B6
Haynes MK45 ... 63 F1
North Luton Ind Est LU4 ... 115 B7
North Par 2 MK40 ... 38 B1
North Pl SG5 ... 100 D1
North Rd SG7 ... 91 E2
North St
Leighton Buzzard LU7 ... 111 A7
Luton LU2 ... 116 E1
Luton, High Town LU2 ... 123 E8
North Star Dr LU7 ... 111 C8
North Station Way LU6 ... 114 A2
Northall Cl LU6 ... 119 D6
Northall Rd LU6 ... 119 D6
Northampton Rd
Bromham MK43 ... 36 B3
Bromham MK43 ... 36 E3
Northbridge St SG17 ... 77 C3
Northbridge Wharf SG17 ... 77 C3
Northcliffe LU6 ... 119 E6
Northcote MK41 ... 39 A3
Northcourt LU7 ... 103 A1
Northcroft SG19 ... 54 C7
Northdale Cl MK42 ... 50 A4
Northern Ave SG16 ... 89 C3
Northfield Cl
Gamlingay SG19 ... 44 D6
Henlow SG16 ... 78 D2
Northfield Rd
Guilden Morden SG7 ... 69 C2
Harpenden AL5 ... 131 C4
Wyboston MK44 ... 21 F1
Northfields
Biggleswade SG18 ... 67 A7
Dunstable LU5 ... 114 A3
Letchworth SG6 ... 90 F1
Northfields Inf Sch SG6 ... 90 F1
Northfields Tech Coll
LU5 ... 114 A3
Northill CE Lower Sch
SG18 ... 53 D2
Northill Rd Cople MK44 ... 52 D3
Ickwell SG18 ... 65 D8
Northview Rd
Houghton Regis LU5 ... 114 A2
Luton LU2 ... 116 F2
Northway Ct MK42 ... 50 D6
Northwell Dr LU3 ... 115 F7
Northwood End Rd MK45 ... 76 B7
Northwood La MK45 ... 63 A4
Norton Bury La SG6 ... 91 C2
Norton Ct LU6 ... 121 B8
Norton Mill La SG6 ... 91 D3
Norton Rd Letchworth SG6 ... 91 C2
Luton LU3 ... 115 F4
Stotfold SG5 ... 91 A4
Norton Road Prim Sch
LU3 ... 115 F4
Nunnery La LU3 ... 116 B5
Nurseries The LU6 ... 119 E6
Nursery Cl
Biggleswade SG18 ... 67 B8
Clophill MK45 ... 86 B8
Dunstable LU6 ... 121 A8
Potton SG19 ... 55 E7
Nursery Dr SG19 ... 54 A8
Nursery Gdns MK41 ... 38 D4
Nursery Par LU3 ... 115 E5
Nursery Rd Luton LU3 ... 115 F5
St Neots PE19 ... 22 F4
Nutleigh Gr SG5 ... 100 D1
Nutwood Cl MK41 ... 39 C3
Nymans Cl LU2 ... 117 D3

O

Oak Bank Dr LU7 ... 103 A3
Oak Bank Sch LU7 ... 103 A3
Oak Cl Dunstable LU5 ... 121 D8
Harlington LU5 ... 95 F1
Irchester NN29 ... 7 A7
Sandy SG19 ... 54 B8
Westoning MK45 ... 95 E6
Wootton MK43 ... 61 A8
Oak Cres
Biggleswade SG18 ... 67 B4
Potton SG19 ... 55 F7
Upper Caldecote SG18 ... 66 B8
Oak Dr Greenfield MK45 ... 85 D2
Henlow SG16 ... 78 D1
Oak Gdns MK43 ... 72 C2
Oak Rd Bedford MK42 ... 50 E5
Flitwick MK45 ... 84 F2
Luton LU4 ... 123 C8
Oak Tree Cl SG6 ... 101 E4
Oakcroft MK43 ... 48 A6
Oakham Cl NN10 ... 8 A8
Oaklands Rd MK40 ... 38 D2
Oakley Cl LU4 ... 115 D4
Oakley Gn LU7 ... 103 B1
Oakley Lower Sch MK43 ... 37 A7
Oakley Rd Bromham MK43 ... 37 A4
Clapham MK41 ... 37 C6
Luton LU4 ... 115 E3
Oakridge Pk LU7 ... 111 B5
Oaks The
Heath & Reach LU7 ... 103 A5
Silsoe MK45 ... 86 C4
Slip End LU1 ... 123 C1
Oaktree Rd MK45 ... 84 F7
Oakway LU6 ... 127 B7
Oakwell Cl LU6 ... 120 F7
Oakwood Ave LU5 ... 121 E7
Oakwood Dr LU3 ... 115 C8
Oakwood Rd SG17 ... 77 D2
Oatfield Cl LU4 ... 114 F4
Oatfield Gdns LU7 ... 111 D7
Oban Terr LU1 ... 123 B8
Oberon Ct MK40 ... 38 A1
Ockendon Ct PE19 ... 22 B3
Odell Cl MK42 ... 49 D6
Odell Rd Odell MK43 ... 25 A8
Sharnbrook MK44 ... 16 B2
Odin Cl MK41 ... 39 D4
Offa Rd MK42 ... 50 B5
Old Allotments The
MK44 ... 13 A2
Old Bakery Yd SG18 ... 68 D5
Old Barn Cl SG16 ... 78 D2
Old Barns The MK40 ... 49 B8
Old Bedford Rd
Luton LU2 ... 116 D6
Luton LU2 ... 116 E4
Potton SG19 ... 55 F7
Old Brewery Cl SG5 ... 90 F7
Old Bridge Ct SG17 ... 77 C2
Old Bridge Way SG17 ... 77 C2
Old Chapel Mews LU7 ... 111 A6
Old Chapel The PE19 ... 22 B2
Old Church Path MK45 ... 75 E1
Old Dairy Cl LU5 ... 114 F2
Old Farm Cl LU7 ... 118 A3
Old Ford End Rd MK40 ... 49 E7
Old Hale Way SG5 ... 100 E2
Old Harrowden Rd MK42 ... 51 A3
Old Hat Factory The 1
LU2 ... 116 D1
Old Kiln La MK45 ... 75 C2
Old Linslade Rd LU7 ... 102 D3
Old Main Rd MK45 ... 75 A6
Old Market Ct PE19 ... 22 E5
Old Mews MK41 ... 38 A2
Old Mill Cl SG18 ... 78 E7
Old Mill La MK45 ... 87 D4
Old Milton Rd MK44 ... 28 A8
Old Oak Cl SG15 ... 90 A8
Old Orch LU1 ... 123 D5
Old Orchard The SG18 ... 67 B6
Old Rd Barton-le-C MK45 ... 97 C1
Leighton Buzzard LU7 ... 110 E7
Old Rd The MK43 ... 16 D1
Old Rectory Cl AL5 ... 131 A2
Old School Ct
Clifton SG17 ... 78 B2
Eaton Bray LU6 ... 119 E6
Hockliffe LU7 ... 104 E2
2 Leighton Buzzard LU7 ... 111 A7
Old School Gdns
Barton-le-C MK45 ... 97 C3
St Neots PE19 ... 22 C2
Wootton MK43 ... 60 F7
Old School La SG18 ... 78 A7
Old School Wlk
Arlesey SG15 ... 90 A4
Slip End LU1 ... 123 C1
Old School Yd PE19 ... 22 F4
Old Silsoe Rd MK45 ... 86 C8
Old Station Ct MK44 ... 41 D2
Old Station Way SG17 ... 77 C3
Old Vicarage Gdns
Henlow SG16 ... 78 D2
Markyate AL3 ... 128 D6
Old Watling St AL3 ... 129 B3
Old Way MK44 ... 17 C1
Oldfield Farm Rd
Henlow SG16 ... 89 B4
Henlow SG16 ... 89 C4
Oldfield Rd MK40 ... 49 E8
Oldhill LU6 ... 121 D6
Oldhill Wood LU6 ... 127 D6
Oldways Rd MK44 ... 28 F1
Oliver Ct MK40 ... 38 B1
Oliver St MK45 ... 84 F7
Oliver's La SG5 ... 90 F7
Olivier Way SG17 ... 78 B2
Olma Rd LU5 ... 114 A2
Olyard Ct LU1 ... 123 B6
Olympic Cl LU3 ... 107 E1
Olympus Rd SG16 ... 89 B4
Ombersley Rd MK42 ... 50 B6
Omega Ct LU7 ... 111 C8
Omega Ctr The SG18 ... 67 D3
Onley Ct SG19 ... 54 D6
Onslow Rd LU4 ... 115 D5
Openshaw Way SG6 ... 101 F6
Orchard Ave AL5 ... 130 F1
Orchard Cl
Barton-le-C MK45 ... 97 C1
Bedford MK41 ... 38 E3
Biggleswade SG18 ... 67 B6
Bromham MK43 ... 37 A4
Caddington LU1 ... 122 E4
Cranfield MK43 ... 59 A1
Gravenhurst MK45 ... 87 C4
Houghton Regis LU5 ... 114 B3
Letchworth SG6 ... 101 F8
Meppershall SG17 ... 88 C6
Potton SG19 ... 56 A7
St Neots PE19 ... 22 C4
Toddington LU5 ... 105 F6
Orchard Dr
Chicksands SG17 ... 76 F2
Leighton Buzzard LU7 ... 110 D6
Orchard End LU6 ... 119 E4
Orchard Est LU7 ... 112 A7
Orchard Ho LU5 ... 95 F2
Orchard La MK43 ... 24 F7
Orchard Pl NN29 ... 7 A8
Orchard Rd Baldock SG7 ... 91 E1
Beeston SG19 ... 54 C5
Hitchin SG4 ... 101 B1
Pulloxhill MK45 ... 96 E8
St Neots PE19 ... 22 C4
Orchard St MK42 ... 49 F3
Orchard The MK44 ... 10 F2
Orchard Way
Cranfield MK43 ... 59 A1
Eaton Bray LU6 ... 119 F5
Flitwick MK45 ... 84 F2
Orchard Way *continued*
Great Barford MK44 ... 41 A4
Letchworth SG6 ... 101 F8
Lower Stondon SG16 ... 89 B3
Luton LU4 ... 115 C4
North Crawley MK16 ... 58 A6
Stanbridge LU7 ... 112 D5
Orchards The
Eaton Bray LU6 ... 119 E7
Silsoe MK45 ... 86 C4
Slip End LU1 ... 123 C2
Orchid Cl Dunstable LU6 ... 113 E1
St Neots PE19 ... 22 C6
Ordelmere SG6 ... 90 F1
Oregon Way LU3 ... 116 A8
Orion Way LU7 ... 111 D8
Ormesby Way MK40 ... 49 E7
Ormsby Cl LU1 ... 123 E5
Orpington Cl LU4 ... 115 A3
Orwell Cl MK41 ... 38 C5
Osborn Cres SG17 ... 77 C2
Osborn Ho 1 LU6 ... 121 B8
Osborn Rd MK45 ... 97 C2
Osborne Ave SG17 ... 76 E2
Osborne Ct 9 LU1 ... 123 F6
Osborne Rd
Dunstable LU6 ... 121 B7
Luton LU1 ... 123 F6
Osier Ct PE19 ... 22 C6
Osier Link MK45 ... 84 F7
Osprey Cl Kempston MK42 ... 49 E2
Sandy SG19 ... 42 B2
Osprey Rd
Biggleswade SG18 ... 66 F5
Flitwick MK45 ... 84 E2
Osprey Wlk LU4 ... 115 A5
Ossory Pl MK45 ... 84 E8
Ossory Way MK42 ... 50 B6
Othello Ct MK40 ... 37 F2
Otter Way PE19 ... 22 B5
Otter Wlk MK41 ... 38 C5
Otterton Cl AL5 ... 130 F3
Oulton Rise AL5 ... 131 C3
Our Lady RC Prim Sch
SG5 ... 100 E2
Ouse Rd Bedford MK41 ... 39 A2
St Neots PE19 ... 22 C4
Ouseland Rd MK40 ... 49 E7
Ouseley Cl LU4 ... 115 D3
Oval The SG16 ... 89 C3
Overdale MK41 ... 39 A3
Overend Green La LU7 ... 103 C6
Overfield Rd LU2 ... 117 C1
Overlord Cl SG17 ... 77 C1
Overstone Rd
Harpenden AL5 ... 131 C1
Luton LU4 ... 115 D1
Overtrees AL5 ... 130 F3
Oving Cl LU2 ... 117 D2
Owen Cl Kempston MK42 ... 49 D3
Marston Moretaine MK43 ... 72 C8
Owen Jones Cl SG16 ... 89 C5
Ox La AL5 ... 131 B3
Oxen Rd LU2 ... 116 F1
Oxendon Ct LU7 ... 102 F2
Oxford Rd 2 LU1 ... 123 E6
Oxford St NN10 ... 8 A7

P

Padbury Ho 4 MK40 ... 38 A1
Paddlers Ct MK40 ... 49 E7
Paddock Cl
Clapham MK41 ... 37 D7
Letchworth SG6 ... 101 F5
Luton LU4 ... 114 F5
Paddock The
Biddenham MK40 ... 49 D8
Lidlington MK43 ... 72 C2
St Neots PE19 ... 22 D5
Paddocks The
Bromham MK43 ... 36 F1
Flitwick MK45 ... 84 D5
Leighton Buzzard LU7 ... 110 F8
Potton SG19 ... 55 F7
Toddington LU5 ... 106 A5
Page's Almshouses 5
LU7 ... 111 A8
Page's Ind Pk LU7 ... 111 B5
Paignton Cl LU4 ... 115 D4
Paines Mill PE19 ... 22 E6
Palace St SG18 ... 67 A5
Palma Cl LU6 ... 113 F3
Palmer Cl SG17 ... 77 C3
Palmerston St MK41 ... 38 B2
Parade The
1 Dunstable LU6 ... 114 A1
Letchworth SG6 ... 90 F1
Luton LU3 ... 115 C7
Paradine Rd MK42 ... 50 D6
Park Ave Bedford MK40 ... 38 C2
Houghton Regis LU5 ... 114 C5
Luton LU3 ... 115 C7
Totternhoe LU6 ... 120 B8
Park Ave N AL5 ... 130 F1
Park Ave S AL5 ... 130 F1
Park Avenue Trad Est
LU3 ... 115 C7
Park Cl Markyate AL3 ... 128 D5
Moggerhanger MK44 ... 53 B6
Park Cres MK43 ... 61 C1
Park Ct Luton LU2 ... 116 D1
Sandy SG19 ... 54 C6
Park Farm LU7 ... 105 B2
Park Farm Cl SG16 ... 89 D8
Park Farm Ct MK41 ... 37 F6
Park Hill Ampthill MK45 ... 73 E1
Park Hill *continued*
Harpenden AL5 ... 130 F2
Toddington LU5 ... 105 F7
Park La Blunham MK44 ... 41 E3
Eaton Bray LU6 ... 119 D6
Gamlingay SG19 ... 44 C5
Henlow SG16 ... 78 D1
Kimbolton MK44,PE19 ... 6 F2
Sharnbrook MK44 ... 16 E5
Park Lane Cres SG16 ... 78 D2
Park Leys LU5 ... 95 F1
Park Meadow Cl MK45 ... 97 B3
Park Mews
Leighton Buzzard LU7 ... 111 A6
Sandy SG19 ... 54 C7
Park Mount AL5 ... 130 F3
Park Palings Wlk MK45 ... 75 F8
Park Rd Dunstable LU5 ... 121 C7
Kempston MK42 ... 49 F5
Melchbourne MK44 ... 10 D8
Moggerhanger MK44 ... 53 B7
Roxton MK44 ... 31 E2
Sandy SG19 ... 54 C7
St Neots PE19 ... 22 F7
Stevington MK43 ... 36 D6
Toddington LU5 ... 105 D7
Westoning MK45 ... 95 E5
Park Rd N Bedford MK41 ... 38 B2
Houghton Regis LU5 ... 114 D4
Park Rd W MK41 ... 38 B2
Park Rise AL5 ... 130 E3
Park Rise Cl AL5 ... 130 E3
Park Sq LU1 ... 123 E7
Park St Ampthill MK45 ... 73 E1
Dunstable LU6 ... 114 A1
Luton LU1 ... 123 F6
Woburn MK17 ... 93 A7
Park St W LU1 ... 123 E7
Park Terr 2 LU1 ... 123 F6
Park Viaduct LU1 ... 123 F6
Park View MK44 ... 41 D3
Park View Cl LU3 ... 115 D6
Park View Ct
Leighton Buzzard LU7 ... 110 E7
St Neots PE19 ... 22 D5
Park View Dr AL3 ... 128 D6
Park Way PE19 ... 22 F7
Parker Cl Letchworth SG6 ... 101 E4
St Neots PE19 ... 22 E2
Parkers La SG7 ... 80 D5
Parkfield AL3 ... 128 D5
Parkfields Mid Sch LU5 ... 105 F7
Parkland MK43 ... 36 D3
Parkland Dr LU1 ... 123 D5
Parklands MK41 ... 38 F2
Parkmead 6 LU1 ... 123 F6
Parkside
Gravenhurst MK45 ... 87 B4
Milton Ernest MK44 ... 27 B5
Parkside Cl LU5 ... 114 D5
Parkside Dr LU5 ... 114 D6
Parkside Flats LU6 ... 121 C8
Parkstone Cl MK41 ... 38 E6
Parkview La LU7 ... 105 C2
Parkway
Houghton Regis LU5 ... 114 E6
Woburn Sands MK17 ... 81 A6
Parkway Rd LU1 ... 116 B5
Parmiter Way MK45 ... 84 D7
Parrish Cl MK43 ... 72 B8
Parrot Cl LU5 ... 114 E1
Parson's Cl AL3 ... 129 B1
Parsonage Cl MK43 ... 37 A7
Parsons Rd NN29 ... 7 B8
Partridge Cl LU4 ... 115 A5
Partridge La MK43 ... 36 D1
Partridge Piece
Cranfield MK43 ... 59 C3
Sandy SG19 ... 42 B2
Parys Rd LU3 ... 116 B6
Pascomb Rd LU6 ... 120 F8
Pashley Ct PE19 ... 22 E2
Pasture La SG4 ... 125 E8
Pasture Rd SG6 ... 101 E3
Pastures Ct LU4 ... 115 A3
Pastures The
Edlesborough LU6 ... 119 F3
Lower Stondon SG16 ... 88 E3
Stewartby MK43 ... 61 C1
Upper Caldecote SG18 ... 66 C8
Pastures Way LU4 ... 115 A4
Pathway The MK45 ... 74 B1
Patterdale Cl LU6 ... 121 B7
Patteshull Ct 1 MK40 ... 50 B8
Paul Waller Ave MK42 ... 51 B3
Paula Radcliffe Way
MK41,MK43 ... 37 C5
Paulsons Cl MK44 ... 11 A2
Pavenham Rd
Felmersham MK43 ... 26 C7
Pavenham MK43 ... 26 F3
Stevington MK43 ... 25 D4
Pax Hill MK41 ... 38 E4
Payne Rd MK43 ... 60 F7
Paynes Cl SG6 ... 91 A1
Peach Ct LU1 ... 123 F6
Peach's Cl MK43 ... 25 A6
Peacock Mews 6 LU7 ... 111 A7
Peakes End MK45 ... 84 A3
Pear Tree Cl
Bromham MK43 ... 36 D1
Lower Stondon SG16 ... 89 B3
Pear Tree La LU7 ... 111 A8
Pear Tree View MK42 ... 50 C2
Pearcey Rd MK42 ... 50 C5

Pearmain Cl MK41 38 F1
Pearson Cl PE19 22 E2
Peartree Cl Shefford SG17 77 E2
Toddington LU5 105 E5
Peartree Rd LU2 117 C4
Peashill La MK44 40 F6
Pebblemoor LU6 119 F3
Pebbles The SG7 91 C4
Peck Ct MK45 97 B4
Peckworth Ind Est SG16 89 A4
Peddars La LU7 112 D4
Pedley Hill HP4,LU6 127 C1
Pedley La SG17 77 F3
Peel Pl 7 LU1 123 D7
Peel St 7 Bedford MK40 38 B1
Houghton Regis LU5 114 B5
6 Luton LU1 123 D7
Peel's Pl SG19 54 D7
Peer Rd PE19 22 B4
Peers Dr MK17 81 E3
Pegasus Ct SG18 66 F7
Pegasus Dr SG18 67 D3
Pegasus Rd LU7 111 D8
Pegsdon Cl LU3 116 B7
Pegsdon Way SG5 98 E1
Pelican Way SG6 90 F1
Pemberley Ave MK40 38 C2
Pemberley La MK40 38 C1
Pembroke Ave
Luton LU4 115 F3
St Neots PE19 22 F2
Pembroke Cl MK43 72 D8
Pembroke Rd MK45 74 B7
Pembroke St MK40 50 D8
Penda Cl LU3 115 F7
Pendennis Rd MK41 39 A4
Penfold Cl SG17 77 A2
Penhill LU3 115 E6
Penhill Ct LU3 115 E6
Penlee Cl MK41 38 F1
Penley Way LU7 111 A5
Pennine Ave LU3 115 D8
Pennine Rd MK41 38 E3
Pennine Rise MK45 84 D2
Pennivale Cl LU7 111 A8
Pennyfarthers Cl MK45 86 B8
Penrith Ave LU6 121 B7
Penrwyn Ct PE19 22 F1
Penshurst Cl AL5 130 D4
Pentelowes The PE28 2 D2
Pentland Cl SG19 54 B8
Pentland Rise MK41 38 E3
Penwright Cl MK42 49 D5
Penwrights La MK44 40 F5
Peppercorns La PE19 22 C2
Peppiatts The LU6 119 B5
Pepsal End Rd LU1 129 C7
Percheron Dr LU4 115 A3
Percival Way LU2 124 C7
Peregrine Rd LU4 115 A4
Periwinkle La
Dunstable LU6 121 C7
Hitchin SG5 100 F1
Periwinkle Terr LU6 121 C7
Perkins Rd MK41 39 C2
Perring Cl MK44 16 C4
Perry Mead LU6 119 E6
Perrymead LU2 117 F2
Pershore Cl MK41 38 E5
Pertenhall Rd MK44 12 B4
Petard Cl LU4 115 A2
Petersfield Gdns LU3 107 E1
Petley Cl MK45 84 E1
Petteril Wlk MK41 38 C7
Petunia Ct LU3 116 C1
Pevensey Cl LU2 117 D4
Pevensey Gr MK45 84 C1
Pevensey Rd MK41 39 A3
Pheasant Wlk MK45 84 D2
Philip Gdns PE19 22 F2
Philip Larkin Ho MK40 50 A8
Phillips Mdws MK44 4 A3
Phillpotts Ave MK40 38 E1
Phipps Cl MK45 62 F3
Phoenix Cl LU7 111 D8
Phoenix Sq PE19 22 E6
Pickering Cl SG19 54 C8
Pickford Hill AL5 131 C3
Pickford Rd AL3 128 C3
Pie Cnr AL3 129 B1
Pie Gdn AL3 129 C1
Pietley Hill AL3 129 A1
Pigeonwick AL5 131 B3
Piggotts La LU4 115 D4
Piggottshill La AL5 131 E1
Pilcroft St MK42 50 C7
Pilgrim Ctr MK41 38 D3
Pilgrims Cl Bedford MK42 50 C4
Flitwick MK45 84 E3
Harlington LU5 95 F1
Pilgrims Pre-Prep Sch
MK41 38 C3
Pilgrims Way MK42 50 C4
Pillinge Rd MK43 61 C1
Pinchmill Cl MK44 16 C3
Pinchmill Lower Sch
MK43 26 C8
Pinchmill Way MK44 16 C3
Pine Cl Biggleswade SG18 67 A7
Irchester NN29 7 A7
Leighton Buzzard LU7 103 A2
Rushden NN10 8 A8
Pine Crest Mews LU7 110 E6
Pine Gr MK17 81 A4
Pine View Pk MK45 86 B7
Pinemead SG17 77 E2
Pines The Ampthill MK45 84 E8
Kempston MK42 49 F3
Pinewood Cl LU3 107 C1
Pinford Dell 4 LU2 117 D1
Pinkle Hill Rd LU7 103 A5
Pinsent Ave MK43 36 E1
Pioneer Pk MK42 50 B5
Pipers Croft LU6 120 F7
Pipers Hill HP1 132 D3
Pipers La AL3,LU1 122 F1
Pipit Cl MK45 84 E2
Pipit Gr SG19 42 B2
Pipit Rise MK41 38 D4
Pirton Hill Inf Sch LU4 115 B6
Pirton Hill Jun Sch LU4 115 B6
Pirton Rd Holwell SG5 100 A7
Luton LU4 115 D5
Pirton Sch SG5 99 D4
Pitsdean Rd PE19 33 F3
Pitsford Terr LU2 117 A1
Pix Ct SG15 90 A8
Pix Rd SG5 90 E5
Pixmore Way SG6 101 F5
Plaiters Cl MK43 26 B3
Plaiters Way LU5 114 A5
Plane Tree Cl SG19 44 C6
Planes The MK42 49 E3
Plantation Rd
Leighton Buzzard LU7 102 F3
Luton LU3 115 D7
Platt Cl LU4 115 D4
Platz Ho LU5 114 D5
Playfield Cl SG18 67 B5
Playford Sq LU4 115 D5
Pleasance The AL5 130 D4
Pleasent Pl SG19 54 C7
Plewes Cl LU6 127 E8
Plough Cl Cranfield MK43 71 A8
Luton LU4 114 E4
Plough Ct LU4 114 E4
Plover Way MK41 38 B4
Plum Tree La LU7 111 A8
Plum Tree Rd SG16 89 B2
Plummer Haven LU7 103 A1
Plummers La
Haynes MK45 75 F8
Peters Green LU2 125 C2
Plumpton Cl LU2 117 D3
Plymouth Cl LU2 117 B1
Podington Prim Sch NN29 7 E1
Podington Rd NN10 8 A4
Poets Ct AL5 131 B1
Poets Gn LU4 115 A2
Pokas Cotts NN9 3 C8
Polam Sch MK40 38 A1
Polegate LU2 117 D2
Polhill Ave MK40,MK41 38 E2
Pollards Cl MK45 62 E3
Pollards Way SG5 99 D4
Polo Field Way MK42 50 A2
Polzeath Cl LU2 124 C8
Pomeroy Gr LU2 116 E6
Pomfret Ave LU2 116 F1
Pond Cl LU4 115 B5
Pondwick Rd AL5 130 E2
Pondwicks Rd LU1 123 F7
Pope Cl MK45 84 E1
Pope Rd PE19 22 E4
Popes Ct LU2 116 D1
Popes Way MK43 60 E7
Popham Cl PE19 22 A3
Poplar Ave Bedford MK41 38 E4
Luton LU3 116 C8
Poplar Cl
Biggleswade SG18 67 A8
Irchester NN29 7 A7
Leighton Buzzard LU7 103 A2
Roxton MK44 31 E1
Rushden NN10 8 A8
Silsoe MK45 86 C4
Poplar Dr SG5 90 F7
Poplar Gr SG19 54 B7
Poplar Rd LU6 127 E8
Poplars Cl LU2 117 B3
Poplars The Arlesey SG15 90 A8
Flitwick MK45 84 E3
Ickleford SG5 100 F5
Poppy Cl NN10 8 C8
Poppy Field SG18 67 C5
Poppyfields MK41 39 C4
Porlock Dr LU2 117 C1
Porters Hill AL5 131 C4
Portland Cl Bedford MK41 39 A2
Houghton Regis LU5 114 B4
Portland Ct LU4 116 A1
Portland Ind Est SG15 90 A3
Portland Rd LU4 116 A1
Portland Ride LU5 114 B2
Portman Cl SG5 100 D2
Portnall Pl MK43 59 B1
Portobello Cl MK45 97 C2
Porz Ave LU5 114 D3
Postley Rd MK42 49 E2
Potten End Hill HP1 132 F1
Potter Way MK42 50 C4
Potters Cross MK43 61 A8
Pottery Cl LU3 115 F7
Potton Lower Sch SG19 55 F7
Potton Rd
Biggleswade SG18 67 A7
Biggleswade SG18 67 B8
Everton SG19 43 D2
Gamlingay SG19 44 D3
Guilden Morden SG8 69 F6
Potton SG19 43 F3
Sandy SG19 55 B6
St Neots PE19 22 F2
Potton Rd *continued*
Wrestlingworth SG19 57 B4
Poulter Cl 6 MK40 50 B8
Pound Cl Blunham MK44 41 E4
Langford SG18 78 F7
Upper Caldecote SG18 54 B1
Pound Gn SG8 69 F5
Pound La Kimbolton PE28 6 F4
North Crawley MK16 58 B7
Pound The MK45 95 E6
Pounds Cl MK43 59 B1
Powells Rd SG17 77 C3
Power Ct LU1 123 F7
Powers Cl SG19 42 B1
Powis Mews MK45 84 D1
Powis Pl PE19 22 F1
Powis Rd MK41 39 B4
Poynters Rd LU4 114 E3
Prebend St MK40 50 B7
Prebendal Dr LU1 123 B2
Prentice Gdns MK42 49 F6
Prentice Way LU2 124 D7
Presentation Ct LU1 123 F6
Preservine Wlk MK41 37 E5
President Way LU2 124 D8
Preslent Cl SG5 87 F1
Preston Cl MK45 84 E8
Preston Gdns LU2 116 F2
Preston Path LU2 116 F2
Preston Rd Bedford MK40 49 F8
Toddington LU5 106 A5
Prestwick Cl LU2 116 E5
Prestwick Rd MK40 49 B8
Priestleys LU1 123 A7
Primary Way SG15 90 A4
Primrose Cl Arlesey SG15 90 A4
Biggleswade SG18 67 C4
Flitwick MK45 84 D2
Marston Moretaine MK43 72 C7
Primrose Ct LU6 121 A8
Primrose La SG15 90 A4
Prince Cl PE19 22 B5
Prince Philip Ave MK43 58 D2
Prince Way LU2 124 D8
Prince's St SG5 90 F7
Princes Ct Dunstable LU5 114 C1
Leighton Buzzard LU7 110 F8
Princes Pl 15 LU2 116 D1
Princes Rd MK43 36 E2
Princes St
9 Bedford MK40 38 B1
Dunstable LU6 121 A8
Toddington LU5 106 A5
Princess St Clapham MK41 37 D6
Luton LU1 123 D7
Prinknash Rd MK41 38 E5
Printers Ct MK45 73 F1
Printers Way LU6 114 B1
Priors Cl NN10 7 F8
Priors Hill SG5 99 C4
Priory Bsns Pk MK44 51 C6
Priory Cl Harrold MK43 25 A6
Turvey MK43 35 B5
Priory Ct 1 Bedford MK40 38 B1
Dunstable LU5 121 C8
Priory Ctry Pk★ MK41 51 A7
Priory Gate SG17 77 A2
Priory Gdns LU2 116 D4
Priory La PE19 22 E5
Priory Lower Sch MK40 50 A8
Priory Mall 2 PE19 22 E5
Priory Mews PE19 22 E6
Priory Mid Sch LU5 121 C8
Priory Orch AL3 129 B2
Priory Park Inf Sch PE19 22 F6
Priory Rd Campton SG17 76 F1
Dunstable LU5 121 C8
St Neots PE19 22 E6
Priory Sch The SG5 100 E2
Priory St MK40 50 B8
Priory Terr 4 MK40 38 B1
Priory The PE19 22 E5
Proctor Cl MK42 49 D5
Proctor Way LU2 124 C7
Progress Pk MK42 50 A2
Progress Way
Elstow MK42 50 B4
Luton LU4 115 B7
Prospect Ave NN29 7 A7
Prospect Rd SG18 78 F8
Prospect Row 3 PE19 22 F5
Prospect Way LU2 124 C7
Provost Way LU2 124 C8
Prudden Cl MK42 50 B4
Prudence Cl LU5 95 F1
Puddephat's La AL3 128 C1
Pulford Rd LU7 110 F6
Pulford's Lower Sch
LU7 111 A6
Pulloxhill Bsns Pk MK45 85 D2
Pulloxhill Lower Sch
MK45 96 E8
Pulloxhill Rd MK45 85 D2
Purbeck Cl MK41 39 A2
Purcell Rd LU4 114 F3
Purcell Way SG17 77 E3
Purley Ctr LU3 115 E7
Purway Cl LU3 115 E7
Purwell Wlk LU7 103 B3
Putnoe Hts MK41 38 F4
Putnoe La MK41 38 E4
Putnoe Lower Sch MK41 39 A3
Putnoe St MK41 39 A4
Putteridge High Sch
LU2 117 C5
Putteridge Jun & Inf Sch
LU2 117 C5
Putteridge Par LU2 117 B4
Putteridge Rd LU2 117 C4
Putteridge Recn Ctr
LU2 117 C5
Putterills The AL5 131 A1
Pyghtle Ct LU1 123 A7
Pyghtle The Luton LU1 123 A7
Turvey MK43 34 E6
Westoning MK45 95 E5
Pym's Way SG19 42 B1
Pyms Cl MK44 40 F5
Pynders La LU5 114 E2
Pytchley Cl LU2 116 E5

Q

Quadrant The
Houghton Regis LU5 114 C5
Letchworth SG6 101 F6
Quantock Cl
Bedford MK41 38 E2
Luton LU3 116 B8
Quantock Rise LU3 108 B1
Quantocks The MK45 84 D2
Quantrelle Ct MK42 51 A3
Quarry Wlk LU6 121 A7
Queen Alexandra Rd
MK41 39 A1
Queen Anne's Cl SG5 90 F5
Queen Elizabeth Cl SG17 77 D2
Queen St Bedford MK40 38 B1
Houghton Regis LU5 114 B4
Leighton Buzzard LU7 110 F8
Stotfold SG5 91 A6
Queen's Cl MK40 37 D1
Queen's Cres MK41 38 F3
Queen's Ct 12 MK40 38 B1
Queen's Dr MK41 38 F3
Queen's Rd SG19 54 B7
Queen's Way SG18 78 F8
Queens Cl Flitwick MK45 84 F2
4 Luton LU1 123 E6
Northill SG18 53 E1
Oakley MK43 36 F8
Queens Cres MK41 37 D7
Queens Ct Dunstable LU5 114 C1
14 Luton LU2 116 D1
Shefford SG17 77 D2
St Neots PE19 22 B3
Queens Gdns PE19 22 B4
Queens Park Lower Sch
MK40 49 F8
Queens Rd Ampthill MK45 84 F8
Colmworth MK44 20 B2
Queensbury Cl MK40 49 F8
Queensbury Upper Sch
LU6 121 B7
Queensway
Dunstable LU5 114 B1
St Neots PE19 22 F7
Queenswood Dr SG4 101 C1
Quenby Way MK43 36 F1
Quickswood LU3 116 A7
Quilter Cl LU3 115 F4

R

Raban Ct SG7 91 F1
Race Meadows Way
MK42 49 F2
Rackman Dr LU3 116 C5
Radburn Ct LU6 114 A1
Radnor Rd LU4 114 F4
Radnor Wlk MK41 39 B3
Radstone Pl LU2 117 E1
Radwell La SG7 91 C4
Radwell Rd
Felmersham MK43 26 D8
Milton Ernest MK43,MK44 26 F6
Raglan Cl LU4 114 F3
Raglan Gn MK41 39 A4
Railton Rd MK42 49 D1
Railway Cotts
Kempston Hardwick MK45 61 F4
Oakley MK43 37 A8
Railway View 1 SG18 67 A6
Rainbow Sch MK43 36 D3
Raleigh Cl PE19 22 A2
Raleigh Gr LU4 115 D1
Raleigh St MK40 49 F7
Rally The SG15 90 A7
Ram Yd MK40 50 C8
Ramerick Gdns SG15 90 A2
Ramillies Cl MK42 49 F5
Ramridge Prim Sch
LU2 117 B2
Ramridge Rd LU2 117 A2
Ramsay Cl MK41 38 B3
Ramsey Cl
Kempston MK42 49 D2
Luton LU4 114 F3
Ramsey Ct LU4 114 F3
Ramsey Manor Lower Sch
MK45 97 D2
Ramsey Rd MK45 97 C3
Rand's Cl SG5 100 B7
Rand's Cotts SG5 100 B7
Rand's Mdw SG5 100 B7
Randall Dr LU5 105 F5
Randalls Cl MK43 36 F2
Rannock Gdns LU7 110 C7
Ranock Cl LU3 115 D8
Ranworth Wlk MK40 49 D7
Rapper Ct LU3 123 D8
Raunds Rd NN9 3 C8
Raven Wlk MK45 84 E2
Ravenbank Rd LU2 117 C5
Ravenhill Way LU4 115 B4
Ravensburgh Cl MK45 97 B3
Ravenscourt LU6 113 F3
Ravensden CE Lower Sch
MK44 29 B1
Ravensden Rd
Renhold MK41 39 B7
Wilden MK44 29 D3
Ravensthorpe LU2 117 B4
Ray's Cl MK42 50 C7
Raymond Cotts SG5 100 E4
Raynham Way LU2 117 D1
Raynsford Lower Sch
SG16 78 D1
Reach Gn LU7 103 A6
Reach La LU7 103 B5
Readers Cl LU6 114 B2
Readshill MK45 86 C8
Ream Cl PE19 22 E2
Reaper Cl LU4 114 E4
Recreation Rd LU5 114 C6
Recreation Rise MK45 87 C4
Rectory Cl Carlton MK43 25 A4
Clifton SG17 78 B3
Slapton LU7 118 D6
Rectory Ct SG19 54 D7
Rectory Farm Bsns Pk
SG16 88 D4
Rectory La Ampthill MK45 73 F1
Cranfield MK43 71 B8
Houghton Conquest MK45 74 A7
Lilley LU2 109 D2
Rectory Rd Campton SG17 76 F1
Meppershall SG17 88 B5
Steppingley MK45 83 F3
Red Cedar Rd MK43 36 C4
Red Lion Cl MK43 59 B1
Red Oak Cl MK43 36 C4
Red Rails LU1 123 C5
Red Rails Ct LU1 123 C5
Redborne Upper Sch & Com
Coll MK45 84 E6
Reddall Cl MK42 50 F5
Redding Cl NN10 8 A7
Reddings La AL3 129 F1
Rede Cl MK41 38 C6
Redferns Cl LU1 123 A6
Redferns Ct LU1 123 A6
Redfield Cl LU6 120 E8
Redgrave Gdns LU3 115 F7
Redhill Rd SG5 100 D1
Redhoods Way E SG6 101 E7
Redhoods Way W SG6 101 E6
Redman Gdns SG18 67 A7
Redmire Cl LU4 115 B6
Redoubt Cl SG4 101 A1
Redwald Cl MK42 49 E4
Redwood Cl NN29 7 A7
Redwood Dr LU3 115 C8
Redwood Glade LU7 103 A3
Redwood Gr MK42 50 C6
Reed Pl AL5 130 F3
Reedsdale LU2 117 F2
Reeves Ave LU3 116 B4
Regency Court Park Homes
SG16 88 E2
Regency Ct LU6 121 C7
Regent Cl Bedford MK41 38 C6
St Neots PE19 22 B4
Regent Ct
1 Bedford MK40 38 A1
Stotfold SG5 90 F7
Regent St Dunstable LU6 114 B1
Leighton Buzzard LU7 111 B7
Luton LU1 123 E7
Stotfold SG5 90 F7
Regents Mews MK40 49 C8
Reginald St LU2 116 E1
Regis Rd LU4 114 E4
Rendlesham Wlk MK41 39 C3
Renhold Lower Sch
MK41 39 D6
Renhold Rd MK44 29 E1
Renshaw Cl LU2 117 E2
Repton Cl Bedford MK41 38 F4
Luton LU3 115 F6
Repton Rd SG17 76 E4
Reston Path LU2 117 E2
Restormel Cl MK41 38 F5
Retreat The LU5 114 F1
Reynes Cl MK43 72 D7
Reynes Dr MK43 37 A8
Reynolds SG6 90 F1
Reynolds Cl Bedford MK41 38 A2
Biggleswade SG18 67 A7
Wharley End MK43 58 E2
Reynolds Ct PE19 22 D6
Rhineland Way MK41 38 D6
Ribble Way MK41 38 C6
Ribocon Way LU4 115 B7
Richard St LU5 121 C8
Richard's Cres SG18 65 A4
Richards Cl LU1 123 B6
Richards Ct LU1 123 B5
Richbell Ct MK40 38 B1
Richmond Cl PE19 22 F1
Richmond Ct LU2 116 F1
Richmond Hill LU2 116 F2
Richmond Hill Sch LU2 116 E2
Richmond Rd
Bedford MK40 38 D1
Leighton Buzzard LU7 111 C6
Westoning MK45 95 E6
Rickyard Cl LU2 117 B3
Rickyard The SG6 91 C1
Riddy La LU3 116 C5
Ride The LU6 120 B6
Ridge Ave AL5 130 E4

Ridge Ct LU2 ....117 A1
Ridge Rd MK42 ....49 B2
Ridgeway Harpenden AL5 130 E4
  Kensworth LU6 ....127 E8
  St Neots PE19 ....22 F3
Ridgeway Ave LU5 ....114 D2
Ridgeway Bsns Pk The
  SG19 ....53 E8
Ridgeway Dr LU5 .....114 E1
Ridgeway Sch MK42 ..49 C2
Ridgeway The
  Bedford MK41 ......39 A4
  Blunham MK44 .....53 E8
  Flitwick MK45 .....84 E4
  Potton SG19 ....56 A7
Ridgewood Dr AL5 ...130 E4
Ridgewood Gdns AL5 130 E4
Ridgmont Lower Sch
  MK43 ....82 F4
Ridgmont Rd MK43 ...82 D4
Ridgmont Sta MK43 ..82 C7
Ridgmount St MK42 ..50 B6
Ridgway MK17 ....81 B6
Ridgway Rd
  Brogborough MK43 ..71 C1
  Luton LU2 ....116 F1
Ridings The Luton LU3 116 C1
  Markyate AL3 ......128 E6
Ringmer Ct LU2 ......117 C3
Ringshall Rd HP4 ....126 B3
Ringwood Cl MK42 ...49 F4
Ringwood Rd LU2 ....116 D7
Ripley Rd LU4 ....115 C1
Ripon Cl MK42 ....49 E6
Ripon Ct SG18 ....67 A4
Risborough Cl MK41 ..38 F1
Risborough Rd MK41 .38 F1
Riseley CE Lower Sch
  MK44 ....10 F2
Riseley Rd MK44 .....12 A3
Risings The MK44 ....39 A3
Rival Houses MK45 ..97 C4
River Ct SG5 ....100 F4
River Hill AL3 ......129 B2
River La MK44 ....27 B4
River Mead SG5 .....100 C2
River Rd PE19 ....22 C4
River Row MK43 .....26 B3
River St MK40 ....50 B8
River Terr St Neots PE19 22 E4
  St Neots, Eynesbury PE19 ..22 E4
River Way LU3 ....115 E5
Riverbanks Cl AL5 ...131 C4
Riverfield Dr MK41 ..39 B1
Riverford Cl AL5 ....131 B4
Riverhead Gdns SG19 .54 B6
Rivermead St SG18 ..78 E5
Riverside
  Leighton Buzzard LU7 .111 A8
  Shefford SG17 .....77 C1
Riverside Cl MK42 ...50 A4
Riverside Est AL5 ...131 C4
Riverside Gdns SG18 .78 E5
Riverside Rd LU3 ...116 A5
Riverside View MK44 .27 A5
Rivermead PE19 .....22 E6
Riverview Way MK42 .49 C4
Robert Allen Ct **3** LU2 123 E6
Robert Bloomfield Mid Sch
  SG17 ....77 B2
Robert Bruce Mid Sch
  MK42 ....49 D4
Robert Hunt Gdns SG19 54 B7
Robert Peel Lower Sch
  SG19 ....54 C8
Robert Saunders Ct
  SG6 ....101 E4
Roberts Ct PE19 .....22 B2
Roberts Dr MK43 ....60 E2
Robertson Cnr LU6 ..120 F4
Robin Cl Flitwick MK45 84 B1
  Sandy SG19 ....42 B1
Robin Ct AL5 ....131 B4
Robin Hill MK41 ....38 C4
Robins Folly MK44 ..28 E4
Robins Cres LU5 ....95 F2
Robinson Ct SG19 ...44 D6
Robinswood LU2 ....116 E5
Robinswood Cl LU2 ..102 F2
Rochdale Ct **6** LU1 .123 E6
Rochester Ave LU2 ..117 C4
Rochester Mews LU7 110 E7
Rochford Dr LU2 ....117 C2
Rock Cl LU7 ....110 D6
Rock La LU7 ....110 D7
Rockbeck Ct MK42 ..49 E4
Rockingham Ct NN10 .8 A8
Rockingham Wlk MK41 39 B3
Rockleigh Ct LU7 ....110 E7
Rockley Rd LU1 .....123 A7
Rodean Ct MK40 ....38 D2
Rodeheath LU4 .....115 D3
Rodney Cl LU4 ......114 F3
Roe Cl SG5 ....90 E5
Roe End La AL3 .....128 B4
Roe Gn PE19 ....22 B5
Roebuck Cl LU1 .....123 B6
Roecroft Lower Sch SG5 90 F6
Roedean Cl LU2 .....117 C4
Roff Ave MK42 ......38 B2
Rogate Rd LU2 ......117 C5
Roise Ct **3** MK40 ...38 B1
Roise St MK40 ......38 B1
Roman Ct **2** LU5 ...114 B4
Roman Gdns LU5 ...114 B4
Roman Rd
  Barton-le-C MK45 ..97 D3
  Luton LU4 ....115 E3

Roman View SG19 ....54 D6
Roman Way Flitwick MK45 .84 F4
  Irchester NN29 .....7 B7
  Markyate AL3 ......128 E6
Romany Cl SG6 .....101 C6
Romney Ct PE19 ....22 C5
Romney Wlk MK41 ..38 B3
Romsey Way MK42 ..50 C3
Ronald Cl MK42 .....49 E2
Rondini Ave LU3 ....116 B3
Rook Tree Cl SG5 ...91 A6
Rook Tree La SG5 ...91 A6
Rookery Dr LU2 .....116 E6
Rookery Rd MK44 ...31 F8
Rookery The LU5 ....42 C2
Rookery Wlk SG17 ..78 B2
Rooksmead MK44 ...38 C4
Rooktree Way MK45 .64 A1
Roosevelt Ave
  Leighton Buzzard LU7 .111 B8
  Shefford SG17 .....77 C1
Ropa Ct LU7 ....110 F7
Rope Wlk MK42 .....50 C7
Ropkins Cl MK45 ....95 F6
Rosamond Rd MK40 .38 E1
Rosata La SG17 .....76 E4
Rose Cotts SG15 ....90 A6
Rose Ct Eaton Bray LU6 .119 D6
  Irchester NN29 .....7 B8
  St Neots PE19 .....22 C4
Rose La SG18 ....67 A6
Rose Wlk Ampthill MK45 .73 E1
  Houghton Regis LU5 114 E6
  Toddington LU5 ...105 F5
Rose Wood Cl LU2 ..116 F3
Rosebay Cl MK45 ...84 D3
Rosebery Ave
  Harpenden AL5 .....130 F1
  Leighton Buzzard LU7 110 E7
Rosebery Ct LU7 ...110 F7
Roseby Way MK41 ..51 A8
Rosedale LU5 ....114 E5
Rosedale Cl LU3 ....115 C7
Rosedale Way MK42 .49 E4
Rosemary Dr MK43 ..36 F2
Rosemont Cl SG6 ...101 E6
Roslyn Way LU5 ....114 A5
Ross Cl LU1 ....123 B6
Rossendale Wlk MK41 39 B4
Rossfold Rd LU3 ...115 D8
Rosslyn Cres LU3 ..116 C5
Rossway LU1 ....123 B1
Rothamsted Ave AL5 131 A1
Rothamsted Ct AL5 .131 A1
Rothbury Cl SG19 ...42 C3
Rothbury Ct MK41 ..39 B4
Rother Cl MK41 .....38 D5
Rother Field LU2 ...117 D3
Rotheram Ave LU1 .123 B5
Rotherwood Cl LU6 113 C1
Rothesay Rd LU1 ...123 D7
Rothsay Gdns MK40 .38 D5
Rothsay Pl MK40 ...50 D8
Rothsay Rd MK40 ..50 D8
Rothschild Rd LU7 .110 E8
Rotten Row MK44 ...10 F2
Roundel Dr LU7 ....111 D5
Roundfield Ave AL5 131 D3
Roundmead MK41 ..39 A4
Roundwood Cl SG4 .101 C6
Roundwood Ct AL5 .130 F3
Roundwood Gdns AL5 130 F3
Roundwood La MK43 130 D3
Roundwood Park Sch
  AL5 ....130 E2
Roundwood Pk AL5 130 E3
Roundwood Prim Sch
  AL5 ....130 E2
Rousbury Rd MK43 ..61 C1
Rowallan Dr MK41 ..38 E5
Rowan Cl LU1 ......123 B7
Rowan Cres
  Biggleswade SG18 ..67 B7
  Letchworth SG6 ...101 E7
Rowan Ct SG19 ....54 B8
Rowan Gdns SG19 ..44 C5
Rowan Way MK43 ..71 A8
Rowans The
  Kempston MK42 ...49 F3
  Silsoe MK45 ......86 C4
Rowelfield LU2 .....117 C1
Rowington Ct LU2 ..117 E2
Rowland Way SG6 ..101 F6
Rowlands The LU6 ..67 C4
Rowlandson Way MK41 .38 A3
Rowley Furrows LU7 110 E8
Rowney Forest Wlk★
  SG17 ....76 F5
Roxhill Rd MK43 ....59 F3
Roxton CE Lower Sch
  MK44 ....31 E2
Roxton Rd
  Great Barford MK44 .41 B7
  Roxton MK44 ......31 F4
Royal Ct PE19 ......22 B4
Royal Oak Cl SG18 ..66 F7
Royal Oak La SG5 ..99 D4
Royal Wlk LU6 .....121 C7
Royce Ct LU4 ......115 A4
Royce Ct PE19 .....22 D5
Royce Rd MK43 ....58 D7
Roydon Cl LU4 .....115 A4
Royle Gdns MK42 ..50 F5
Royston Ct SG19 ...56 A7
Royston Rd SG7 ...91 F1
Royston St SG19 ...56 A7
Rtow MK45 ....63 C7
Rudyard Cl LU4 ....115 D3

Rueley Dell Rd LU2 109 D2
Ruffs Furze MK43 ...36 F7
Runfold Ave LU4 ...116 A5
Runham Cl LU4 ....115 A4
Runley Rd LU1 .....122 F7
Runnalow SG6 .....101 E7
Rush Ct MK40 ......38 C1
Rushall Gn LU2 ....117 E2
Rushbrook Cl MK45 .73 F1
Rushden Hospl NN10 .8 B8
Rushden
  Milton Ernest MK44 .27 B5
  Newton Bromswold NN10 .9 A4
  Wymington NN10 ...8 A6
Rushmoor Cl MK40 ..37 F2
Rushmore Cl LU1 ..122 E4
Rusper Gn LU2 ....117 D3
Russel Ctr MK45 ...84 E2
Russell Ave MK40 ..50 E8
Russell Cl LU6 .....127 E8
Russell Cres MK45 ..85 D8
Russell Dr Ampthill MK45 84 F7
  Willington MK44 ...40 C1
Russell Gr MK45 ...73 B2
Russell Lower Sch MK45 84 F8
Russell Rd LU5 ....105 C5
Russell Rise LU1 ..123 D6
Russell St Luton LU1 123 D6
  St Neots PE19 ....22 E6
  Woburn Sands MK17 81 C4
Russell Way
  Leighton Buzzard LU7 .111 D7
  Wootton MK43 ....60 F6
Russet Cl MK43 ....61 B1
Russett Cl MK45 ...73 E1
Ruthin Cl LU1 ......123 D5
Rutland Cres LU2 ..124 A7
Rutland Ct LU2 ....124 A7
Rutland Gdns LU2 ..54 D7
Rutland Hall LU2 ..124 A7
Rutland Rd MK40 ..50 A8
Ryans Ct LU2 ......116 F1
Rycroft Ave PE19 ..22 F6
Rydal Cres SG18 ...67 A4
Rydal Way LU3 ....115 F5
Ryder Ave SG5 ....100 D3
Ryder Way SG5 ....100 D3
Rye Cl Harpenden AL5 .131 B4
  Leighton Buzzard LU7 .111 D7
  Rushden NN10 .....8 C8
Rye Cres MK44 ....52 A6
Rye Hill Harpenden AL5 131 B4
  2 Luton LU2 ....116 D1
Rye The LU6 ......119 C8
Ryecroft Way LU2 ..117 A4
Ryefield LU3 ....108 A1
Rylands Heath LU2 117 F2
Rylands Mews LU7 111 A6
Ryley Cl LU3 ....89 B5
Ryswick Rd MK42 ..50 A5
Ryton Cl Bedford MK41 .38 C6
  Luton LU1 ....123 B6

S

Sabel Cl SG18 ......67 C3
Sacombe Gn LU3 ..108 A7
Sacred Heart Jun & Inf Schs
  LU2 ....117 A3
Saddle Cl MK41 ....37 C7
Saddlers Mews AL3 128 E6
Sadleirs Gn MK41 ..81 B5
Saffron Cl Arlesey SG15 90 A7
  10 Bedford MK40 ..50 B8
Saffron Ct SG18 ....67 C3
Saffron Hill SG6 ...101 E6
Saffron Rd LU5 ....67 A5
Saffron Rise LU6 ..119 E6
Saint Paul's Gdns LU1 123 E6
St Alban Rd MK40 ..38 D2
St Albans Cl MK45 .84 E4
St Albans Rd AL5 ..131 B1
St Aldates LU2 .....116 D7
St Andrew's Ave AL5 130 F1
St Andrew's Cl
  Ampthill MK45 .....73 F1
  Slip End LU1 ......123 B1
St Andrew's Sch MK40 .38 C2
St Andrew's St
  Biggleswade SG18 ..66 F6
  Leighton Buzzard LU7 .111 A8
St Andrew's Way SG18 78 F8
St Andrews CE Lower Sch
  SG18 ....66 F6
St Andrews Cl
  Biggleswade SG18 ..66 F5
  Flitwick MK45 .....84 E4
  Leighton Buzzard LU7 .111 A7
St Andrews Ct SG18 66 F6
St Andrews La
  Houghton Regis LU5 114 C5
  Kimbolton PE28 ....6 F1
St Andrews Mews LU3 116 A4
St Andrews Rd MK40 38 C2
St Andrews Wlk LU1 123 C1
St Ann's Rd LU1 ...123 F7
St Anselm Pl PE19 ..22 E6
St Augustine Ave LU3 116 C3
St Augustine's Rd MK40 38 D2
St Bede's RC Mid Sch
  MK40 ....38 A1
St Bernard's Cl LU3 116 C3
St Catherines Ave LU3 116 B3
St Christopher Sch SG6 101 F3

St Christopher's Cl LU5 114 F1
St Christopher's Lower Sch
  LU5 ....114 F1
St Cuthbert's St **1** MK40 50 C8
St Cuthberts Ct **3** MK40 50 C8
St David's Way LU5 ..114 D6
St Dominics Sq LU4 114 F4
St Edmond Rd MK40 38 D2
St Ethelbert Ave LU3 116 C4
St Faiths Cl SG4 ...101 B1
St Francis Coll SG6 101 E4
St Francis Ct SG17 ..77 C3
St Francis Way SG17 77 C2
St George's Cl
  Leighton Buzzard LU7 111 B8
  Toddington LU5 ...105 F6
St George's Lower Sch
  LU7 ....111 B8
St George's Rd MK40 38 C2
St George's Sch AL5 131 B2
St Georges Twr SG19 45 F3
St Gregory's RC Mid Sch
  MK40 ....37 E1
St Helena Rd MK40 50 D5
St Helenas Gdn MK42 50 B4
St Hilda's Cl AL5 ..130 F2
St Ives Cl LU3 .....116 B3
St James CE Lower Sch
  MK40 ....37 C1
St James Cl
  Houghton Regis LU5 114 E4
  Pulloxhill MK45 ....96 E8
St James St MK40 ..38 C2
St James Rd AL5 ..131 B4
St James' Rd LU3 ..116 B3
St James's Ct AL5 .131 B3
St John LU1 ....123 B5
St John Rigby RC Lower Sch
  MK41 ....38 C2
St John's Ave LU2 .124 A7
St John's Homes MK42 49 D4
St John's Rd Arlesey SG15 90 A4
  Moggerhanger MK44 53 C7
  Sandy MK44 ......49 F6
St John's St Bedford MK42 50 C7
  Biggleswade SG18 ..67 A7
  Kempston MK42 ...49 D3
St John's Terr MK42 50 C7
St John's Wlk MK42 49 D3
St Johns Cl LU7 ...112 C5
St Johns Cl LU1 ...123 B5
St Johns Ctr MK42 50 C7
St Joseph's Cl LU3 116 A4
St Joseph's RC Inf Sch
  LU3 ....116 A4
St Joseph's RC Jun Sch
  LU3 ....116 A4
St Joseph's RC Lower Sch
  MK40 ....49 E8
St Katharines Cl SG5 100 D3
St Kilda Rd LU4 ...114 F4
St Lawrence Lower Sch
  NN10 ....8 B5
St Lawrence Wlk LU3 116 B5
St Lawrences Ave LU3 116 C3
St Leonard's Cl LU7 103 E3
St Leonard's St MK42 50 C6
St Leonard's Way LU6 119 E1
St Leonard's-Heath & Reach
  Lower Sch LU7 ...103 A5
St Leonards Ct MK42 50 B6
St Loyes St **17** MK40 50 B8
St Luke's Cl LU5 ...115 C4
St Margaret of Scotland RC
  Inf Sch LU1 ......123 C1
St Margaret of Scotland RC
  Jun Sch LU1 .....123 B1
St Margarets Ave LU3 116 B3
St Margarets Cl
  Lidlington MK43 ...72 C3
  Streatley LU3 .....89 D5
St Margarets Gdns SG18 67 C4
St Mark's Cl SG5 ..100 D1
St Marks Cl MK45 ..84 E4
St Martin de Porres RC Prim
  Sch LU4 ....115 A4
St Martin's Ave LU2 116 F2
St Martins Bsns Ctr
  MK42 ....51 B5
St Martins Cl AL5 ..131 C4
St Martins Way MK42 51 A5
St Mary's SG19 ....44 E5
St Mary's (Clophill) Lower
  Sch MK45 ....75 D1
St Mary's (Stotfold) Lower
  Sch SG5 ....91 A6
St Mary's Ave SG5 ..90 D4
St Mary's Cl
  Felmersham MK43 ..26 C8
  Letchworth SG6 ...101 F2
  Pirton SG5 ....99 D4
  Tebworth LU5 .....105 C2
St Mary's Ct
  8 Dunstable LU6 121 D8
  Leighton Buzzard LU7 110 D8
  St Neots PE19 ....22 E4
St Mary's Gate LU6 121 B8
St Mary's Glebe LU6 119 E4
St Mary's Pl SG17 ..88 D5
St Mary's RC Lower Sch
  LU1 ....121 F6
St Mary's Rd LU1 ..123 F7
St Mary's St Bedford MK42 50 C7
  St Neots PE19 ....22 E4
St Mary's Way LU7 110 E8
St Mary's Wlk SG19 43 C3
St Marys Cl Bletsoe MK44 17 C1

St Marys Cl continued
  Elstow MK42 ......50 B3
  Marston Moretaine MK43 72 D7
St Marys Ct PE19 ..22 C3
St Marys Rd MK43 ..60 F7
St Mathews Cl MK42 49 D3
St Matthew's Inf Sch
  LU2 ....116 E1
St Matthews Cl LU2 123 E8
St Mellion Dr MK40 49 B7
St Michael's Cres LU3 116 D3
St Michael's Rd MK40 38 D2
St Michael's Cts MK40 38 D2
St Michaels Ave LU3 114 B4
St Mildreds Ave LU3 116 C3
St Minver Rd MK40 38 D2
St Monicas Ave LU3 116 B3
St Neots Mus★ PE19 22 E5
St Neots Rd Bedford MK41 40 B3
  Bolnhurst MK44 ....19 E4
  Little Barford PE19 33 F7
  Sandy SG19 ......54 B8
  St Neots PE19 ....22 D4
St Nicholas CE Prim Sch
  Harpenden AL5 ....131 A1
  Letchworth SG6 ...91 C1
St Nicholas Cl MK17 94 B3
St Nicholas Ct AL5 130 F3
St Ninian's Ct **7** LU2 123 D8
St Olam's Cl LU3 ..116 B6
St Olives SG5 ......90 E6
St Paul's Rd Bedford MK40 49 F7
  Luton LU1 ....123 E5
St Paul's Sq MK40 ..50 B8
St Pauls Cl MK45 ..84 F3
St Peter's Ave SG15 90 A7
St Peter's Ct MK44 16 C4
St Peter's Rd LU5 .121 C8
St Peter's St MK40 38 C1
St Peters Cl MK45 ..84 F4
St Peters Ct SG19 ..56 A8
St Peters Rd LU1 ..123 B7
St Saviours's Cres LU1 123 D6
St Swithun's Way SG19 54 D7
St Swithuns Lower Sch
  SG19 ....54 C7
St Thomas More RC Prim Sch
  SG6 ....101 D4
St Thomas More RC Sch
  MK41 ....38 C6
St Thomas's Cl LU2 117 A4
St Thomas's Rd LU2 117 A4
St Vincent Gdns LU4 115 D3
St Vincent's RC Lower Sch
  LU5 ....114 C5
St Vincents MK17 ..81 C4
St Winifreds Ave LU3 116 C3
Salcombe Cl MK40 ..38 E1
Sale Dr SG7 ....91 F1
Salford Rd
  Aspley Guise MK17 81 D7
  Brogborough MK43 82 B8
Salisbury Ave AL5 ..131 A1
Salisbury Ho **8** MK40 38 A1
Salisbury Rd Baldock SG7 91 F1
  Flitwick MK45 .....84 E4
  Harpenden AL5 ....131 B1
  Luton LU1 ....123 D6
Salisbury St MK41 ..38 B2
Sallowsprings LU6 120 F2
Saltash Cl LU3 .....38 E2
Saltdean Cl LU2 ...117 D4
Salters Way LU6 ..113 F3
Saltfield Cres LU4 115 C4
Sambar Cl PE19 ....22 B5
Sampshill Rd MK45 95 E5
Samuel Whitbread Com Coll
  SG17 ....77 C3
San Remo Rd LU7 ..81 F4
Sand La Barton-le-C MK45 97 B8
  Biggleswade SG18 ..67 A6
  Northill SG18 .....53 E1
  Sandy SG19 ......54 E7
Sand Rd MK45 .....85 E3
Sandalwood Cl LU3 116 E5
Sandell Cl LU2 .....116 F2
Sanderling Cl SG6 101 E8
Sanders Cl MK42 ..49 D6
Sanders Way MK43 60 F8
Sanderson Cl MK45 95 E6
Sanderson Rd MK45 95 E6
Sandfields Rd PE19 22 F5
Sandford Rise SG19 54 A7
Sandgate Rd LU4 ..115 D2
Sandhill Cl MK45 ...73 A1
Sandhills LU7 ....103 B1
Sandhouse Cotts LU7 103 D8
Sandhurst Pl MK42 50 B6
Sandhurst Rd MK42 50 B6
Sandland Cl LU6 ...114 A1
Sandleford Dr MK42 50 C7
Sandon Cl SG19 ...54 C8
Sandpiper Cl SG18 66 F5
Sandringham Dr LU5 114 E4
Sandringham Rd MK45 84 D1
Sandy Acres MK45 .74 B1
Sandy Bsns Pk SG19 42 C2
Sandy La Chicksands SG17 76 E5
  Husborne Crawley MK17 82 D3
  Leighton Buzzard LU7 103 A3
  Tilbrook PE28 .....6 C6
  Woburn Sands MK17 81 B2
Sandy Rd Bedford MK41 39 A1
  Everton SG19 .....43 B2
  Potton SG19 ......55 E7

Sandy Rd continued
Willington MK44 ....52 E8
Sandy Sta SG19 ....54 D6
Sandy Upper Sch & Com Coll
SG19 ....42 A1
Sandy View SG18 ....67 B8
Sandye La MK44 ....11 D8
Sandye Place Mid Sch
SG19 ....54 C6
Sanfoin Rd LU4 ....115 A4
Santa Pod Raceway
NN29 ....15 C6
Santingford N LU1 ....123 B6
Santingford S LU1 ....123 B6
Sarum Rd LU3 ....115 F4
Saturn Cl LU7 ....111 D8
Sauncey Ave
Harpenden AL5 ....131 B3
Harpenden AL5 ....131 C2
Sauncey Wood AL5 ....131 E4
Sauncey Wood La AL5 .131 E6
Sauncey Wood Prim Sch
AL5 ....131 D4
Saunders Gdns MK40 ....49 E7
Saunders Piece MK45 ....84 F8
Savannah Cl MK42 ....49 F5
Savernake Wlk MK41 ....39 B3
Savile's Cl PE19 ....22 D7
Saville Ct MK44 ....41 A5
Sawtry Cl LU4 ....116 A6
Sawyers Cres NN9 ....3 B8
Sax Ho SG6 ....90 E1
Saxon Ave SG6 ....90 F8
Saxon Cl Dunstable LU6 ..120 C8
Flitwick MK45 ....84 F4
Harpenden AL5 ....131 C4
Letchworth SG6 ....90 F1
Roxton MK44 ....31 C1
Saxon Cres MK45 ....97 C4
Saxon Ctr MK42 ....49 E4
Saxon Pl PE19 ....22 F4
Saxon Pool & L Ctr SG18 .67 C5
Saxon Rd LU3 ....116 C2
Saxon Rise NN29 ....7 C8
Saxons Cl LU7 ....111 C7
Saxtead Ct LU2 ....117 D1
Saywell Rd LU2 ....117 B1
Scawsby Cl LU6 ....113 E1
School Cl SG19 ....44 D5
School Hill NN29 ....7 B8
School House Mews
MK45 ....86 C4
School La Carlton MK43 ....25 A2
Colmworth MK44 ....20 A2
Eaton Bray LU6 ....119 F6
Great Barford MK44 ....41 A5
Greenfield MK45 ....85 C2
Husborne Crawley MK43 ..82 B4
Irchester NN29 ....7 A8
Luton LU4 ....115 D4
Roxton MK44 ....31 F2
Shefford SG17 ....77 B2
Southill SG18 ....65 D1
St Neots PE19 ....22 C2
St Neots, Eynesbury PE19 .22 E4
Stewartby MK43 ....61 C1
Wootton MK43 ....60 F7
School Rd NN29 ....7 A8
Scotchbrook Rd MK43 ..72 D7
Scotfield Ct LU2 ....117 D3
Scott Ave MK42 ....51 A4
Scott Ct LU5 ....114 C1
Scott Lower Sch MK41 ..38 C5
Scott Rd LU3 ....115 C7
Seabrook LU4 ....115 B3
Seaford Cl LU2 ....117 C3
Seal Cl LU4 ....115 D3
Seamons Cl LU6 ....121 D6
Sears Cl SG17 ....78 B3
Sears The LU6 ....119 B5
Seaton Dr MK40 ....38 E2
Seaton Rd LU4 ....115 F3
Sebright Rd AL3 ....128 E5
Sedbury Cl LU3 ....116 A6
Sedgwick Rd LU4 ....115 B7
Seebohm Cl SG5 ....100 C1
Segenhoe Cl MK43 ....82 F5
Selbourne Rd LU4 ....116 A2
Selina Cl LU3 ....115 C7
Selsey Dr LU2 ....117 D4
Selsey Way MK41 ....38 E2
Sergeants Way MK41 ....39 C2
Servite Ho LU4 ....115 C3
Setchel PE19 ....22 B3
Severalls The LU2 ....117 B3
Severn Cl MK45 ....84 D2
Severn Way MK41 ....38 C5
Severn Wlk LU7 ....103 B3
Sewell La LU6 ....113 D3
Sexton Ave MK42 ....50 A4
Seymour Ave LU1 ....123 F5
Seymour Rd LU1 ....123 F5
Shackleton Lower Sch
MK42 ....50 C5
Shady Wlk PE19 ....22 F5
Shaftesbury Ave
Bedford MK40 ....50 E8
St Neots PE19 ....22 F5
Shaftesbury Rd LU4 ..116 B1
Shakespeare Dr SG18 ..66 C8
Shakespeare Rd
Bedford MK40 ....38 A1
Harpenden AL5 ....131 C1
Luton LU4 ....115 B2
St Neots PE19 ....22 C3

Shaldon Ct MK40 ....38 E2
Shanklin Cl LU3 ....116 A7
Shannon Cl
Lower Stondon SG16 ....88 F2
Sandy SG19 ....42 B1
Shannon Ct SG19 ....54 C7
Shannon Pl SG19 ....55 F7
Sharnbrook Ct MK44 ....16 D3
Sharnbrook John Gibbard
Lower Sch MK44 ....16 C4
Sharnbrook Rd MK44 ....16 B7
Sharnbrook Upper Sch &
Com Coll MK44 ....16 B3
Sharnside MK44 ....16 D4
Sharose Ct AL3 ....128 E5
Sharp Cl MK45 ....86 B7
Sharpenhoe Clappers★
.........107 F7
Sharpenhoe Rd
Barton-le-C MK45 ....97 B2
Streatley LU3 ....107 F7
Sharples Gn LU3 ....116 B8
Sharps Way SG4 ....101 A1
Shay La PE28 ....5 B4
Shearley Cl MK40 ....49 F7
Sheepcote Cres LU7 ....103 A5
Sheepfold Hill MK45 ....84 F3
Sheeplands MK41 ....39 B3
Sheeptick End MK43 ....72 B3
Sheepwalk Cl SG19 ....56 B6
Sheffield Cl SG19 ....56 A6
Shefford Bsns Pk SG17 ..77 D3
Shefford Ind Pk SG17 ....77 C2
Shefford Lower Sch
SG17 ....77 B2
Shefford Rd Clifton SG17 .78 F2
Clophill MK45 ....76 A2
Meppershall SG17 ....88 C7
Sheldon Ct MK17 ....81 B4
Shelford La MK44 ....20 B3
Shelley Ct 16 AL5 ....131 B1
Shelley Pl PE19 ....22 D6
Shelley Rd LU4 ....115 B2
Shelton Ave LU5 ....105 F4
Shelton Cl LU5 ....105 F4
Shelton Ct MK44 ....40 F5
Shelton Lower Sch MK43 .60 C3
Shelton Rd Hargrave NN9 .1 A3
Upper Dean PE28 ....5 A5
Shelton Way LU2 ....117 A3
Shenley Cl LU7 ....103 B3
Shenley Hill Rd LU7 ....103 C3
Shepherd La LU4 ....114 F4
Shepherds Cl LU5 ....95 F1
Shepherds Mead
Hitchin SG5 ....100 F2
Leighton Buzzard LU7 ....103 A1
Shepherds Way AL5 ....130 D4
Sherborne Ave LU2 ....116 D6
Sherbourne Way MK41 ..38 F5
Sherd Cl LU3 ....115 F7
Sheridan Rd LU3 ....116 C2
Sheriden Cl LU6 ....114 B1
Sheringham Cl LU2 ....116 C7
Sherwood SG6 ....101 F8
Sherwood Rd LU4 ....116 A3
Sherwood Terr NN29 ....7 B8
Sherwood Wlk MK41 ....39 B3
Shillington Lower Sch
SG5 ....87 E1
Shillington Rd
Gravenhurst MK45 ....87 D4
Lower Stondon SG5 ....88 C2
Meppershall SG17 ....88 B4
Pirton SG5 ....99 B5
Shingle Cl LU3 ....116 A8
Ship Rd LU7 ....110 E6
Shirdley Rd PE19 ....22 F4
Shire La MK16 ....58 E4
Shires The LU2 ....116 D1
Shirley Rd LU1 ....123 C8
Short Path LU5 ....114 C6
Short St MK40 ....49 F7
Shortcroft Ct MK45 ....97 B2
Shortmead St SG18 ....66 F6
Shorts Ave MK42 ....51 A2
Shortstown Lower Sch
MK42 ....50 F2
Shrubbery La MK44 ....29 C4
Shuttleworth Coll SG18 ..65 D5
Shuttleworth Collection Mus
The★ SG18 ....65 D6
Shuttleworth Ct SG18 ..67 A6
Shuttleworth Ct Bsns Pk
MK41 ....39 C3
Shuttleworth Rd MK41 ..39 C2
Sibley Cl LU2 ....117 B3
Sibton Abbey MK41 ....51 B8
Sidings The MK42 ....50 C6
Sidmouth Cl MK40 ....38 E2
Sidney Rd Ampthill MK45 ..84 E7
Bedford MK40 ....37 F1
Signal Cl SG16 ....89 B3
Silbury Cl LU1 ....123 C8
Silecroft Rd LU2 ....124 B8
Silsoe Lower Sch MK45 .86 C4
Silsoe Rd Flitton MK45 ..85 E3
Maulden MK45 ....85 E7
Silver Birches The MK42 .49 F4
Silver End Rd MK45 ....63 F1
Silver St Bedford MK40 ....50 B8
Great Barford MK44 ....40 F5
Guilden Morden SG8 ....69 F4
Luton LU1 ....123 E7
St Neots PE19 ....22 F4
Stevington MK43 ....36 B7
Silverbirch Ave SG5 ....90 F8
Silverbirches La MK17 ..81 B2

Silverdale St MK42 ....49 F4
Silverweed PE19 ....22 C5
Simdims MK43 ....59 A1
Simpkin Cl PE19 ....22 C2
Simpkins Dr MK45 ....97 C4
Simpson Cl LU4 ....115 D2
Singer Ct MK42 ....49 D2
Singer Way MK42 ....49 D2
Singlets La AL3 ....129 C2
Sir Herbert Janes Village The
LU4 ....115 D4
Sir John Lawes Sch
AL5 ....131 C3
Sir Malcolm Stewart Homes
MK43 ....73 C8
Sir Peter's Way HP4 ....126 E6
Skegsbury La SG4 ....125 F1
Skelton Cl LU3 ....108 B1
Skerne Pas MK41 ....38 C7
Skimpot Rd LU4 ....115 A1
Skipton Cl SG19 ....54 C8
Skua Cl LU4 ....115 A5
Slade The Clapham MK41 .37 E6
Clophill MK45 ....75 C1
Wrestlingworth SG19 ....57 B3
Slapton La LU6 ....118 F6
Slate Hall LU3 ....107 A4
Slate Row MK44 ....16 A8
Slater Cl MK42 ....49 D5
Slickett's La LU6 ....119 F3
Slip End Lower Sch LU1 123 B1
Slip The LU3 ....26 C7
Slype The AL5 ....131 F6
Smithcombe Cl MK45 ....97 C3
Smiths Lane Mall 5
LU1 ....123 E7
Smiths Sq 6 LU1 ....123 E7
Snagge Ct MK45 ....60 E1
Snailswell La SG5 ....100 E5
Snow Hill MK45 ....74 B1
Snowdrop Wlk SG18 ....67 C5
Snowford Cl 1 LU3 ....116 A7
Sollershott E SG6 ....101 F4
Sollershott Hall SG6 ....101 F4
Sollershott W SG6 ....101 E4
Solway Rd N LU3 ....116 A4
Solway Rd S LU3 ....116 A3
Someries Jun & Inf Sch
LU2 ....117 C3
Someries Rd AL5 ....131 C4
Somersby Cl LU1 ....123 E5
Somerset Ave LU2 ....117 A1
Somerton Cl MK41 ....39 A5
Sopwith Way MK42 ....51 A2
Sorrel Cl LU3 ....116 B8
Souberie Ave SG6 ....101 F5
Soulbury Rd LU7 ....110 D7
Souldrop Rd MK44 ....16 C5
South Ave MK42 ....50 C1
South Dr MK42 ....51 A2
South Drift Way LU1 ....123 B5
South End Jun & Inf Schs
NN10 ....8 B8
South End La LU6 ....119 B4
South Gr NN10 ....8 B5
South Luton High Sch
LU1 ....123 D6
South Rd Luton LU1 ....123 D6
Sandy SG19 ....54 B7
South St
Leighton Buzzard LU7 ....111 B7
St Neots PE19 ....22 E5
South View
Biggleswade SG18 ....67 A5
Letchworth SG6 ....101 F5
South Wlk SG18 ....67 B7
Southampton Gdns LU3 107 D1
Southbridge St SG17 ....77 C3
Southcott Lower Sch
LU7 ....110 D7
Southcott Village LU7 ....110 D6
Southcourt Ave LU7 ....110 D6
Southcourt Rd LU7 ....110 D7
Southcroft Ho LU7 ....110 D7
Southdown Rd AL5 ....131 B1
Southern Ave SG16 ....89 C3
Southern Rise LU2 ....130 F7
Southern Way
Letchworth SG6 ....101 E8
Studham LU6 ....127 C4
Southfield Jun & Inf Schs
LU4 ....114 F4
Southfields
Letchworth SG6 ....90 F1
Roxton MK44 ....31 C1
Shefford SG17 ....77 E2
Southfields Ct SG17 ....77 E2
Southfields Rd
Dunstable LU6 ....121 D6
Kempston MK42 ....50 A3
Southgate Ct 5 AL5 ....131 A2
Southill Lower Sch SG18 65 D1
Southill Rd Broom SG18 ..66 B2
Cardington MK44 ....51 C2
Southland Rise SG18 ....78 F5
Southlands Lower Sch
SG18 ....67 B4
Southlynn Ho 2 LU2 ....123 F8
Southview MK44 ....40 F5
Southview Gdns MK44 ....111 B6
Southview Rd AL5 ....131 D3
Southville Rd MK45 ....50 B5
Southway MK42 ....50 E5
Southwood Rd LU5 ....121 E6
Sovereign Pk LU4 ....115 F1
Sovereigns Quay MK40 ....50 B8
Sowerby Ave LU2 ....117 C3
Spa Ho PE19 ....22 F5

Sparhawke SG6 ....91 A1
Sparksfield SG16 ....78 D2
Sparrow Cl LU4 ....115 A4
Sparrow Hall Bsns Pk
LU6 ....119 D3
Spayne Cl LU3 ....116 B8
Spear Cl LU3 ....115 E6
Speedwell Cl LU3 ....116 A8
Spencer Cl Potton SG19 ..56 A8
St Neots PE19 ....22 D6
Spencer Ct LU7 ....103 B1
Spencer Ho SG5 ....90 F6
Spencer Rd Luton LU3 ..116 C2
Sandy SG19 ....54 D6
Spencers The MK44 ....41 A5
Spenser Ct MK40 ....37 F1
Spenser Rd Bedford MK40 .37 F1
Harpenden AL5 ....131 C1
Spensley Rd MK45 ....95 E5
Spinney Bglws LU7 ....118 C5
Spinney Cres LU6 ....120 F8
Spinney La MK17 ....81 F4
Spinney Rd
Chawston MK44 ....31 E4
Luton LU3 ....115 D7
Spinney The
Bedford MK41 ....39 B3
Harpenden AL5 ....130 E3
Spitfire Rd LU7 ....77 C1
Spittlesea Rd LU2 ....124 C7
Spoondell LU6 ....121 A6
Spratts La LU6 ....121 F1
Spreckley Cl SG16 ....89 B5
Spriggs Cl MK41 ....37 C1
Spring Cl Ampthill MK45 .84 F7
Biggleswade SG18 ....67 B6
Spring Gdns MK42 ....50 A4
Spring Gr Sandy SG19 ....54 B7
Woburn Sands MK17 ....81 B5
Spring Hill MK45 ....13 A3
Spring La Stagsden MK43 .48 C5
Yelden MK44 ....4 A3
Spring Pl 5 LU1 ....123 D6
Spring Rd Clifton SG17 .78 A2
Harpenden AL5 ....130 A4
Kempston MK42 ....50 A4
Letchworth SG6 ....101 E4
Letchworth SG6 ....101 E4
Springbrook PE19 ....22 F4
Springfield SG18 ....68 C5
Springfield Ave MK42 ....49 E4
Springfield Cres AL5 ....131 B5
Springfield Ct LU7 ....110 E7
Springfield Ctr MK42 ....49 F3
Springfield Dr MK43 ....36 E3
Springfield Lower Sch
MK42 ....49 E3
Springfield Rd
Dunstable LU6 ....120 D5
Leighton Buzzard LU7 ....110 E7
Luton LU3 ....116 C6
Rushden NN10 ....8 D8
Springfield Way MK43 ....59 C2
Springshott SG6 ....101 E5
Springside LU7 ....110 E7
Spruce Wlk MK42 ....49 F3
Spurcroft LU3 ....108 C1
Square The
Aspley Guise MK17 ....81 E4
Dunstable LU6 ....121 B8
Wilstead MK45 ....62 E4
Squires Cl SG17 ....77 E2
Squires Ct PE19 ....22 C4
Squires Pl LU5 ....105 F6
Squires Rd
Marston Moretaine MK43 ..72 D7
Wootton MK43 ....60 F6
Stables The Ampthill MK45 84 F7
Leighton Buzzard LU7 ....110 D6
Stadium Est The LU4 ....115 B1
Stafford Rd MK42 ....50 A6
Stagsden Rd MK43 ....36 E2
Staines Sq LU6 ....121 C7
Stainmore Rd MK41 ....39 C4
Stakers Cl AL5 ....131 B1
Stanbridge Crossing
LU7 ....112 B3
Stanbridge Lower Sch
LU7 ....112 D5
Stanbridge Rd
Billington LU7 ....111 F1
Leighton Buzzard LU7 ....111 C4
Tilsworth LU7 ....112 F5
Totternhoe,Lower End LU6 112 E2
Totternhoe,Stanbridgeford
LU7 ....112 E3
Stanbridge Road Terr
LU7 ....111 B6
Stanbridge Way MK45 ....74 B8
Stanbrook Way MK44 .....4 A3
Stancliffe Rd MK42 ....38 E3
Standalone Farm★ SG6 101 D7
Standalone Warren
MK45 ....76 C7
Stanford La SG17 ....78 A3
Stanford Rd
Clifton SG17,SG18 ....78 A5
Luton LU2 ....117 A1
Shefford SG17 ....77 D3
Southill SG18 ....77 F8
Stanhope Rd MK41 ....38 E4
Stanley Cl MK45 ....96 E8
Stanley Livingstone Ct 2
LU1 ....123 D6
Stanley St Bedford MK41 .38 B2
Kempston MK42 ....49 F4
Luton LU1 ....123 D6

Stanmore Cres LU3 ....115 F4
Stannard Way MK44 ....51 C6
Stanton Rd
Kempston MK42 ....49 D5
Luton LU4 ....115 C1
Stapleford Rd LU2 ....117 C4
Stapleton Rd MK42 ....50 D4
Staploe Rd MK44 ....21 D2
Starey Cl MK44 ....27 B5
Starling Cl SG19 ....42 B1
Starling Way MK41 ....38 C4
Startpoint LU1 ....123 C7
Stately Ct LU3 ....116 D1
Statham Cl LU3 ....108 B1
Station App AL5 ....131 B1
Station Cres MK43 ....72 B3
Station Ct SG19 ....55 F7
Station Par SG6 ....101 F6
Station Pl SG6 ....101 F6
Station Rd Ampthill MK45 .84 C7
Ampthill MK45 ....84 D7
Arlesey SG15 ....90 A4
Baldock SG7 ....91 F1
Bedford MK42 ....50 C7
Biggleswade SG18 ....67 A5
Blunham MK44 ....41 D2
Cheddington LU7 ....118 A1
Dunstable LU5 ....121 D8
Flitwick MK45 ....84 F2
Gamlingay SG19 ....44 F4
Hargrave NN9 ....1 D7
Harlington LU5 ....95 F1
Harpenden AL5 ....131 C2
Irchester NN29 ....7 C8
Langford SG18 ....78 F6
Leighton Buzzard LU7 ....110 F7
Letchworth SG6 ....101 F6
Lidlington MK43 ....72 B3
Lower Stondon SG16 ....88 F3
Luton, High Town LU1 ....123 E8
Luton, Leagrave LU4 ....115 E5
Marston Moretaine MK43 ..72 D6
Oakley MK43 ....37 A8
Potton SG19 ....55 F7
Ridgmont MK43 ....82 D6
Sandy SG19 ....54 D6
Sharnbrook MK44 ....16 E4
Stanbridge LU7 ....112 D4
Tempsford SG19 ....42 C8
Tilbrook PE28 ....6 C7
Toddington LU5 ....106 A7
Turvey MK43 ....35 B5
Willington MK44 ....52 C8
Woburn Sands MK17 ....81 B5
Station Sq MK45 ....84 E2
Station Way SG6 ....101 E6
Staughton Pl PE19 ....22 C4
Staughton Rd MK44 ....12 D5
Staunton Ho MK17 ....92 F7
Staveley Rd
Dunstable LU6 ....121 B6
Luton LU4 ....115 C1
Stephens Gdns LU2 ....117 A3
Stephenson Cl LU7 ....110 E6
Stephenson Lower Sch
MK42 ....50 E5
Stepping Stones The
LU3 ....115 E5
Steppingley Hospl MK45 .84 C4
Steppingley Rd MK45 ...84 D3
Steppingley Road Trad Est
MK45 ....84 E3
Steppingstone Pl LU7 .111 B6
Stevenson Ct PE19 ....22 D6
Stevington Windmill★
MK43 ....36 C6
Stewart Cl MK43 ....37 A4
Stewart Clark Ct 4 LU6 114 A1
Stewart Ct MK43 ....61 A6
Stewart Rd AL5 ....131 B2
Stewartby Sta MK43 ....61 B1
Stewartby Way MK43 ....61 C1
Stile The LU7 ....103 A5
Stileman Way MK44 ....16 C4
Stipers Cl LU5 ....121 E5
Stirling Cl SG19 ....42 B1
Stirling Rd MK42 ....51 A2
Stivers Way LU5 ....95 F3
Stockbridge Rd SG17 ....78 C3
Stockdale LU5 ....105 F5
Stocker Way PE19 ....22 F5
Stockgrove Ctry Pk★
LU7 ....102 F7
Stockgrove Park Ho
LU7 ....102 F8
Stockholm Way LU3 ....115 E8
Stockingstone Rd LU2 ..116 E3
Stocks La SG19 ....44 D5
Stockton End SG19 ....54 D6
Stockwood Craft Mus &
Gdns★ LU1 ....123 D4
Stockwood Cres LU1 ....123 D6
Stockwood Cl 16 LU1 ....123 D6
Stockwood Pk★ LU1 ....123 D3
Stoke Albany Mews 3
MK40 ....38 A1
Stoke Rd LU7 ....102 D1
Stokesay Cl MK41 ....39 A4
Stondon Lower Sch SG16 88 E3
Stondon Rd SG17 ....88 C4
Stondon Transport Mus★
SG16 ....88 F3
Stone Cl MK40 ....49 B6
Stone Pine Rd MK43 ...36 D3
Stonecroft SG19 ....54 D7
Stonedale Rd MK42 ....50 A4
Stonehenge Works Sta★
LU7 ....103 E3

Stonehill JMI Sch SG6 90 E1
Stoneland Ave SG18 67 A7
Stoneleigh Cl LU3 116 B7
Stoneley SG6 90 F1
Stonemason Cl AL5 131 A3
Stonesdale LU4 115 C4
Stoneways Cl LU4 115 C6
Stoneygate Rd LU4 115 D3
Stonnells Cl SG6 101 F8
Stopsley Com Prim Sch LU2 117 A4
Stopsley High Sch LU2 116 F4
Stopsley Way LU2 117 A3
Stormont Rd SG5 100 F1
Stotfold Ho SG5 90 F6
Stotfold Rd Arlesey SG15 90 C7
Hinxworth SG7 80 C1
Letchworth SG4,SG6 101 C4
Letchworth SG6 90 D1
Stour Way MK41 38 C5
Stow Rd PE28 6 F5
Strafford Cl LU5 95 F1
Strand The MK45 75 C1
Strangers Way LU4 115 C4
Stratford Cl LU5 105 E6
Stratford Ct MK40 38 A2
Stratford Pl PE19 22 C3
Stratford Rd Luton LU4 116 B1
Sandy SG19 54 E5
Stratford Way MK43 60 D2
Strathconon Rd MK41 39 C4
Strathmore Ave
Hitchin SG5 100 F1
Luton LU1 123 F5
Strathmore Ct SG5 100 F1
Strathmore Inf Sch SG5 100 E2
Strathmore Wlk LU1 123 F6
Stratton Bsns Pk SG18 67 D3
Stratton Ct 7 SG18 67 A6
Stratton Gdns LU2 116 D4
Stratton Mews LU7 111 B7
Stratton Pk SG18 67 D4
Stratton Upper Sch & Com Coll SG18 67 C6
Stratton Way
Bedford MK41 39 D3
Biggleswade SG18 67 B7
Straw Plait SG15 89 F4
Strawberry Field LU3 115 E7
Strawberry Hill Cotts MK44 9 F2
Streatley Rd LU3 107 D4
Street Cl MK43 25 A3
Streetfield Mid Sch LU5 121 F6
Stringfellow Cl MK43 58 E2
Stronnell Cl LU2 117 B3
Stuart Rd
Barton-le-C MK45 97 C4
Kempston MK42 49 E4
Stuart St Dunstable LU6 114 A1
Luton LU1 123 D7
Stubbs Cl LU5 114 D5
Studham CE Lower Sch LU6 127 B4
Studham La Dagnall HP4 126 D4
Whipsnade LU6 127 A7
Studio Ho MK40 50 A8
Studley Rd Luton LU3 116 D1
Wootton MK43 60 E7
Sturgeon's Rd SG4 101 B2
Styles Cl LU2 117 C2
Sudbury Rd LU4 115 B6
Sudeley Wlk MK41 39 B4
Suffield Ho 1 PE19 22 F5
Suffolk Cl LU4 115 A3
Suffolk Rd LU5 121 F6
Sugden Ct LU6 121 A8
Sullivan Cl SG17 77 D3
Summer St
Leighton Buzzard LU7 111 B7
Slip End LU1 123 C1
Summer Wlk AL3 128 E5
Summerfield Dr MK43 60 F6
Summerfield Rd LU1 122 F8
Summerleys LU6 119 E4
Summers Lo SG6 101 D5
Summers Rd LU2 117 C1
Sun La AL5 131 A2
Sun St Biggleswade SG18 66 F7
Potton SG19 56 A7
Sunbeam Rd MK42 49 D1
Sunbower Ave LU6 113 F3
Suncote Ave LU6 113 E3
Suncote Cl LU6 113 E3
Sunderland Cl MK44 28 F1
Sunderland Hill MK44 29 A4
Sunderland Pl MK42 51 A2
Sunderland Rd SG19 54 D8
Sundew Cl Bedford MK42 50 F4
St Neots PE19 22 B6
Sundon Hills Ctry Pk* LU3 107 C6
Sundon La LU5 114 C5
Sundon Lower Sch LU3 107 B4
Sundon Park Jun Sch LU3 115 C8
Sundon Park Rd LU3 115 C7
Sundon Rd Chalton LU4 107 A2
Harlington LU5 107 B8
Houghton Regis LU5 114 D7
Streatley LU3 107 F5
Sundown Ave LU5 121 D7
Sunningdale LU2 116 F3
Sunningdale Dr NN10 8 D8
Sunningdale Wlk MK41 38 E5
Sunnyside Special Sch SG18 67 A6
Sunridge Ave LU2 116 E2
Sunrise Est LU2 117 A2
Sunset Dr LU2 116 F3
Surrey St LU1 123 E6
Surrey Street Prim Sch LU1 123 F6
Sursham Ct AL3 128 E5
Sussex Cl LU4 114 F4
Sussex Pl LU2 117 D2
Sutherland Pl LU1 123 D5
Sutton Ave SG18 67 B6
Sutton CE Lower Sch SG19 56 A3
Sutton Cross Roads SG19 55 E4
Sutton Gdns
Caddington LU1 122 D3
Luton LU3 115 D6
Sutton Mill Rd SG19 55 F6
Sutton Rd Eyeworth SG18 68 F8
Potton SG19 56 C7
Sutton SG19 56 B3
Swaden SG19 54 E6
Swaffield Cl MK45 73 E1
Swale Path MK41 38 C7
Swales Dr LU7 111 D6
Swallow Cl Flitwick MK45 84 D2
Luton LU4 115 A4
Shefford SG17 77 C2
Swallowfield
Upper Caldecote SG18 66 D8
Wyboston MK44 31 F6
Swallowfield Lower Sch MK17 81 B5
Swamsholme Garden Ct SG19 54 C7
Swan Cl LU7 119 A1
Swan Ct Dunstable LU6 121 B8
Milton Ernest MK44 27 B5
Swan La
Guilden Morden SG8 69 F4
Sandy SG19 54 B7
Swan Mead LU4 115 B4
Swanbourne Cl SG18 67 B5
Swannells Wood LU6 127 C4
Swansholme MK43 26 D8
Swansholme Gdns SG19 54 C6
Swansons LU6 119 F3
Swanston Grange LU4 115 B2
Swasedale Rd LU3 116 A6
Swift Cl Bedford MK41 38 B4
Flitwick MK45 84 D2
Letchworth SG6 101 E8
Sandy SG19 42 C2
Swifts Green Cl LU2 117 B5
Swifts Green Rd LU2 117 B5
Swinburne Ave SG5 100 C1
Swindale MK41 38 D6
Swiss Garden The* SG18 65 D6
Sworder Cl LU3 107 F1
Sybil's Way MK45 74 A7
Sycamore Cl
Biggleswade SG18 67 A8
Flitwick MK45 84 F2
Luton LU3 107 C1
Sycamore Rd LU5 114 C6
Sycamores The
Baldock SG7 91 E1
Kempston MK42 49 F3
Silsoe MK45 86 B5
St Neots PE19 22 F6
Sylam Cl LU3 115 E7
Sylmond Gdns NN10 8 A7
Sylvester St LU7 103 A5
Symonds Cl MK43 36 F1
Syon Path MK45 84 D1

T

Tabor Cl LU5 95 F2
Taddy Cl SG18 66 B8
Tadlow Rd SG19 57 C3
Taft Pl SG17 76 E2
Talbot Ct LU7 111 A8
Talbot Rd Bedford MK40 38 E1
Luton LU2 116 F2
Talbot Way SG6 91 B1
Talisman Cl SG19 42 B1
Tall Pines LU7 102 F2
Tallents Cres AL5 131 D3
Tamar Rd MK41 38 D5
Tamar Wlk LU7 103 B3
Tameton Cl LU2 117 F2
Tamworth Rd MK41 39 A5
Tan Yd PE19 22 E5
Tancred Rd LU2 117 A4
Tandys Cl Pavenham MK43 26 C4
Turvey MK43 34 E5
Tanfield Gn LU2 117 E1
Tanglewood AL5 130 F2
Tannery La MK43 15 D1
Tanqueray Ave MK45 86 C8
Tansur Ct PE19 22 F8
Tansy Cl Bedford MK42 50 F4
St Neots PE19 22 B5
Tarnside Cl LU6 121 B6
Taskers Row LU6 119 F4
Taskers Row Cotts LU6 119 F4
Taunton Cl MK41 39 A5
Taunton Rd LU2 117 B1
Tavistock Ave MK45 84 D6
Tavistock Cl MK17 81 B6
Tavistock Cres LU1 123 E5
Tavistock Ct PE19 22 E6
Tavistock Pl MK40 38 B1
Tavistock St
Bedford MK40 38 B1
Tavistock St *continued*
Dunstable LU6 114 A2
Luton LU1 123 E6
Taylor St LU2 123 F8
Taylor's Rd SG5 80 A1
Taylor's Ride LU7 102 F2
Taylors Cl SG17 88 B5
Taylors End MK45 74 B1
Teal Rd SG18 66 F5
Teasel Cl Rushden NN10 8 C7
St Neots PE19 22 C5
Tebbutts Rd PE19 22 E5
Tebworth Rd
Tebworth LU7 105 A1
Wingfield LU5,LU7 105 E1
Tedder Ave SG16 89 B5
Teesdale LU4 115 C5
Telford Way
Bedford MK42 51 B5
Luton LU1 123 D8
Telmere Ind Est 16 LU1 123 E6
Telscombe Way LU2 117 C3
Templars Way MK44 16 E4
Temple Cl LU2 116 E5
Temple Way MK45 84 E2
Templefield Lower Sch MK45 84 E3
Templer Way SG17 76 F3
Tempsford Rd
Everton SG19 42 E5
Sandy SG19 42 A3
Sutton SG19 43 C3
Tempsford SG19 41 F5
Tempsford St MK42 49 E4
Tenby Dr LU4 115 F3
Tenby Mews LU4 115 E3
Tenby Way PE19 22 F1
Tennyson Ave
Biggleswade SG18 67 A5
Houghton Regis LU5 114 D4
Tennyson Ho LU1 123 E5
Tennyson Pl PE19 22 D6
Tennyson Rd
Bedford MK40 50 E8
Flitwick MK45 84 D3
Harpenden AL5 131 A2
Luton LU1 123 E5
Tennyson Road Prim Sch LU1 123 E5
Tenth Ave LU3 115 C7
Tenzing Gr LU1 123 C6
Terrace The MK17 81 E5
Test Cl MK41 38 D7
Tetworth Hill SG19 44 A8
Teversham Way PE19 22 C6
Tewkesbury Dr NN10 8 D8
Tewkesbury Rd MK42 50 D3
Thames Cl MK45 84 D2
Thames Ct LU3 116 B3
Thames Ind Est LU6 121 B8
Thatch Cl LU4 114 F4
Thaxted Cl LU2 117 F2
Thelby Cl LU3 115 F6
Theobald Bsns Ctr SG4 101 A3
Therfield Wlk LU5 114 E6
Thetford Cl MK42 49 F4
Thetford Gdns LU2 116 E6
Theydon Ave MK17 81 B4
Thickthorn La MK45 62 A3
Thinnings The MK45 84 E3
Third Ave LU3 115 D7
Thirlestone Rd LU4 115 D1
Thirlmere Cl SG18 67 B4
Thirlmere Gdns MK45 84 E2
Thirlmere Rd MK42 49 E3
Thistle Rd LU1 123 F7
Thistley La MK43 36 E1
Thomas Johnson Lower Sch MK43 72 B3
Thomas St LU7 103 A5
Thomas Whitehead CE Sch LU5 114 B5
Thompsons Cl AL5 131 A1
Thompsons Mdw SG8 69 F4
Thomson Ave MK42 51 A2
Thor Dr MK41 39 D3
Thorn Rd LU5 113 E6
Thorn View Rd LU5 114 B5
Thornage Cl LU2 116 D7
Thornbridge Cl NN10 8 A8
Thornbury Dunstable LU5 114 F2
Harpenden AL5 131 D1
Thornbury Ct LU5 114 C7
Thorncote Rd SG18,SG19 53 E4
Thorneycroft Cl LU3 115 F4
Thornhill Cl LU5 114 D7
Thornhill Lower Sch LU5 114 D7
Thornhill Rd LU4 115 F2
Thornton St MK42 49 F5
Thorntondale 5 LU4 115 C5
Thorpe Cl MK40 37 B1
Thorpe Way MK43 60 F8
Thrales Cl LU3 115 E7
Thrapston Rd PE28 6 F5
Threave Cl MK41 38 F5
Three Closes SG5 99 C4
Thresher Cl LU4 114 F4
Threshers Ct LU7 111 D7
Thricknells Cl LU3 115 E7
Thrift Rd LU7 103 A5
Thrift St NN29 7 A7
Thrift View MK43 59 C2
Thrupp End MK43 72 B3
Thurleigh Airfield Bsns Pk MK44 18 B5
Thurleigh Lower Sch MK44 18 C2
Thurleigh Rd
Bolnhurst MK44 19 C2
Milton Ernest MK44 27 D5
Ravensden MK44 28 E2
Thurlestone Cl MK40 38 F1
Thurlow Cl LU4 114 F4
Thurlow St 11 MK40 50 B8
Thurne Way MK41 38 D7
Tibbett Cl LU6 121 D7
Tiberius Rd LU3 115 F6
Tidbury Cl MK17 81 A4
Tiddenfoot L Ctr LU7 110 E5
Tilbrook Rd PE28 6 D6
Tilgate LU2 117 D3
Tiller Ct LU7 111 D7
Tilsworth Rd LU7 112 D5
Timber La MK17 92 F7
Timbers Ct AL5 130 F2
Times Cl SG5 100 D2
Timworth Cl LU2 117 D1
Tindall Ave LU7 103 B1
Tingey's Cnr SG18 54 E1
Tingrith Rd MK17 94 D6
Tinker's Cnr MK43 48 E1
Tinkers Hill MK42 51 A3
Tinsley Cl Clapham MK41 37 C7
Luton LU1 123 B5
Tintagel Cl LU3 116 B4
Tintagel Ct PE19 22 F2
Tintagel Wlk MK41 39 B5
Tintern Abbey MK41 51 A8
Tintern Cl AL5 130 C4
Tipcat Cl MK42 50 B4
Tippett Dr SG17 77 D3
Titan Ct LU4 115 F1
Titchfield Dr MK42 50 C3
Tithe Barn MK43 26 C8
Tithe Barn Rd MK43 60 F7
Tithe Farm Cl SG18 78 F7
Tithe Farm Lower Sch LU5 114 B6
Tithe Farm Rd LU5 114 B6
Tithe Rd MK43 48 E4
Tithe The MK43 26 C8
Tiverton Rd MK40 38 E2
Toddington Manor* LU5 105 E8
Toddington Rd
Harlington LU5 95 D2
Luton LU4 115 C6
Tebworth LU7 105 C3
Toddington St George Lower Sch LU5 105 F6
Toland Cl LU4 115 C1
Tollers Mews PE19 22 E5
Tollfield PE28 6 F4
Tollgate Cl MK43 36 E1
Tomlinson Ave LU4 114 F4
Tompions End SG18 65 E8
Top End MK41 39 F6
Top Row MK44 17 C1
Topham Ct PE19 22 F7
Tornay Ct LU7 118 D6
Torquay Dr LU4 115 D4
Torre Abbey MK41 51 B8
Torridge Rise MK41 38 C5
Torrington Cl SG19 55 F8
Totnes Cl MK40 38 E1
Totternhoe Knolls Nature Reserve* LU6 120 B8
Totternhoe Lower Sch LU6 120 B7
Totternhoe Rd
Dunstable LU6 120 E7
Eaton Bray LU6 119 D7
Tower Ct LU2 117 A1
Tower Rd LU2 124 A8
Tower Way LU2 124 A8
Town Cl MK45 62 E4
Town Farm Cl SG8 69 F4
Town Farm Ct SG16 78 D1
Town Lot La MK43 26 B8
Town Meadow Dr SG17 77 C3
Town Shott MK45 75 F1
Town The PE19 13 E6
Townfield Rd MK45 84 F1
Towns End Rd MK44 16 C4
Townsend Cl
Cranfield MK43 71 A8
Harpenden AL5 130 F1
Townsend Ctr The LU5 114 B3
Townsend Farm Rd LU5 114 B3
Townsend Ind Est LU5 114 B4
Townsend La AL5 130 F1
Townsend Rd AL5 131 A2
Townsend Terr LU5 114 A4
Townside LU6 119 F3
Townsley Cl LU1 123 E6
Townwell La NN29 7 B8
Tracey Ct 15 LU1 123 E6
Trafalgar Dr MK45 84 E4
Trafalgar Rd PE19 22 C5
Trailly Cl MK44 4 A3
Trefoil Cl Luton LU4 114 F4
Rushden NN10 8 C7
Trenchard Ave SG17 76 D4
Trenchard La SG17 76 E4
Trent Ave MK45 84 D2
Trent Rd Bedford MK41 38 D5
Luton LU3 116 B4
Trent Way LU7 111 D5
Trescott Cl LU2 117 E2
Trevor Dr MK43 36 E2
Trevor St MK40 38 A1
Trident Dr LU5 114 E6
Triggs Way LU2 117 E3
Trilley Fields MK45 86 B8
Trimley Cl LU4 115 B5
Tring Rd Dunstable LU6 120 C4
Dunstable LU6 120 E7
Trinity Cl
Biggleswade SG18 66 F6
Felmersham MK43 26 C8
Roxton MK44 31 E2
Trinity Rd Bedford MK40 49 F7
Luton LU3 116 A4
Stotfold SG5 90 F7
Tristram Rd SG4 101 B2
Triumph Way MK42 49 E2
Troon Cl MK41 38 E5
Troon Gdns LU2 116 E7
Trowbridge Gdns LU2 116 E3
Trowley Hill Rd AL3 129 B1
Trowley Hts AL3 129 B2
Truemans Rd SG5 100 D2
Truman Pl SG17 76 E2
Truncals LU1 123 D5
Trunk Furlong Est MK17 81 D6
Truro Gdns Flitwick MK45 84 E4
Luton LU3 116 C5
Trust Cotts HP4 126 A1
Tudor Cl Barton-le-C MK45 97 C4
Bedford MK40 38 A1
Bromham MK43 36 F3
Tudor Ct Dunstable LU6 114 A2
Kimbolton PE28 6 F5
Leighton Buzzard LU7 110 F7
Tudor Dr LU5 114 E4
Tudor Rd LU3 116 B2
Tudors The MK44 20 B2
Tuffnells Way AL5 130 D4
Tulip Cl SG18 67 C5
Tulip Dr NN10 8 B7
Tulip Tree Cl MK43 36 C3
Tunstall Wlk MK41 39 C3
Turnberry Wlk MK41 38 E5
Turner Cl LU5 114 D5
Turner Rd PE19 22 C6
Turner Way MK41 38 A2
Turners Cl AL5 131 C4
Turners Rd N LU2 117 A2
Turners Rd S LU2 117 A2
Turnpike Cl LU6 121 C6
Turnpike Ct MK17 81 A5
Turnpike Dr LU3 108 C1
Turnpike La SG5 100 E3
Turnpike Rd MK43 82 B3
Turnpike Way MK41 39 B3
Turvey Lower Sch MK43 34 E6
Turvey Mill MK43 34 D5
Turvey Rd Astwood MK16 46 F6
Carlton MK43 24 E2
Tweedsmuir Rd MK41 38 F4
Twigden Ct LU3 115 E5
Twinwood Rd MK41 37 C7
Twyford Dr LU2 117 D1
Tyburn La Pulloxhill MK45 96 D8
Westoning MK45 95 E6
Tylecote Cl MK43 72 C7
Tylers AL5 131 D1
Tylers Mead LU2 116 E5
Tyne Cl MK45 84 D2
Tyne Cres MK41 38 C6
Tyne Rd SG19 42 C2
Tythe Barn Cl MK45 95 E6
Tythe Cl Flitwick MK45 85 A2
Sharnbrook MK44 16 E3
Tythe Mews LU6 119 E3
Tythe Rd LU4 115 C6

U

Ullswater Cl
Biggleswade SG18 67 B4
Flitwick MK45 84 D2
Kempston MK42 49 E3
Ullswater Ct MK42 49 E3
Ullswater Dr LU7 110 C7
Ullswater Rd LU6 121 B6
Ulverston Rd LU6 121 A6
Underwood Cl LU3 107 F1
Union Chapel Ho 1 LU1 123 E6
Union St Bedford MK40 38 A1
Dunstable LU6 114 A1
Luton LU1 123 E6
University Way MK43 58 D1
Unwin Cl SG6 101 E4
Uplands Bedford MK41 38 F4
Luton LU3 115 D8
Uplands Ct LU1 123 E4
Upper Coombe LU7 110 E8
Upper George St LU1 123 D7
Upper Shelton Rd MK43 60 C3
Upperstone Cl SG5 90 F6
Upton Cl LU2 116 D6
Upton Ct MK41 38 C5
Upton End Rd SG5 87 F2
Upwell Rd LU2 117 B2
Urban Hive LU3 115 C7
Urban Way SG18 67 A7
Ursula Taylor Lower Sch MK41 37 E5
Ursula Taylor Wlk MK41 37 E5

V

Vadis Cl LU3 115 E7
Valarian Cl PE19 22 C6
Vale Cl AL5 130 D4
Vale Ct MK43 59 D2

Valence End LU6 121 D6
Valentine Gdns PE28 6 F5
Valiant Cl LU5 95 F1
Valley Cl Studham LU6 127 B4
Whipsnade HP4 126 E7
Valley La AL3 128 E1
Valley Rd
Letchworth SG6 101 D7
Studham LU6 127 B3
Valley Rise AL4 131 F2
Vanbrugh Dr LU5 114 D5
Vandyke Cl MK17 81 B6
Vandyke Rd LU7 103 C2
Vandyke Upper Sch & Com Coll LU7 103 C1
Vanguard Cl MK42 49 D6
Varna Cl LU3 116 A3
Vaughan Rd
Harpenden AL5 131 B1
Stotfold SG5 90 E7
Vauxhall Rd LU1, LU2 124 B5
Vauxhall Way LU2 117 B1
Venetia Rd LU2 117 A4
Ventnor Gdns LU3 116 A7
Verey Rd LU5 114 C2
Verne Dr MK45 84 F8
Vernon Pl LU5 114 B1
Vernon Rd LU1 123 C8
Verulam Gdns LU3 115 F6
Vespers Cl LU4 115 A2
Vestry Cl LU1 123 D7
Viaduct Cotts LU1 130 F8
Vicarage Cl Arlesey SG15 90 A8
Langford SG18 78 F8
Ravensden MK44 29 B1
Shillington SG5 98 F8
Vicarage Gdns
Flamstead AL3 129 B1
Leighton Buzzard LU7 110 E6
Vicarage Gn MK44 18 C1
Vicarage Hill MK45 84 E1
Vicarage La MK45 62 E3
Vicarage Rd
Houghton Regis LU5 114 B5
Leighton Buzzard LU7 110 E6
Silsoe MK45 86 C4
Vicarage St Luton LU1 123 F7
Woburn Sands MK17 81 C4
Vicarage Wlk PE19 13 F6
Vicars Cl MK40 49 C8
Vicars Wlk MK41 39 B2
Viceroy Cl PE19 22 A3
Viceroy Ct LU6 121 C8
Victor Cl MK42 51 A2
Victoria Cl Langford SG18 78 E6
Wrestlingworth SG19 57 B4
Victoria Cotts LU5 114 A6
Victoria Ct 5 SG18 67 A6
Victoria Dr
Houghton Conquest MK45 74 A8
Stotfold SG5 91 A5
Victoria Pl SG18 67 A6
Victoria Rd Bedford MK42 50 B6
7 Harpenden AL5 131 B1
Leighton Buzzard LU7 110 E6
Shefford SG17 77 D2
Victoria St
Dunstable LU6 114 A1
Luton LU1 123 E6
Victoria Terr LU7 111 D7
Viking Gr MK42 49 D6
Viking Ind Est MK41 39 D4
Villa Ct 5 LU2 123 D8
Villa Park (Mobile Home Pk) MK43 70 F7
Villa Rd LU2 123 D8
Village Ct LU7 110 D6
Village Rd MK43 36 F3
Villiers Cl LU4 115 D3
Vimy Ct LU7 110 F7
Vimy Rd LU7 110 F7
Vincent Rd LU4 115 D5
Vinegar Hill SG19 54 A3
Vines The SG5 90 E6
Vineyard Way MK42 49 E5
Violet Cl Bedford MK42 50 F4
Biggleswade SG18 67 C4
Violets Cl MK16 58 B6
Virginia Cl LU2 116 F3
Viscount Cl LU3 116 A5
Viscount Ct
11 Luton LU2 116 D1
St Neots PE19 22 B4
Voyce Way MK42 50 D6
Vulcan St MK42 50 C6
Vulcan Way PE19 22 B1
Vyne Cl MK42 49 D5

W

Waddesdon Cl LU2 117 D2
Wadhurst Ave LU3 116 C4
Wagstaffe Cl MK41 38 E6
Walcot Ave LU2 117 B1
Walcourt Rd MK42 50 A5
Waldeck Rd LU3 123 C8
Waldegrave Pk AL5 131 D1
Waleys Cl LU3 115 E8
Walgrave Rd LU5 114 F2
Walk House Cl MK43 59 B1
Walkley Rd LU5 114 B4
Wallace Dr LU6 119 E6
Wallace Mews LU6 119 E6
Wallace Way SG4 101 A2
Waller Ave LU4 115 F3
Waller Street Mall 3 LU1 123 E7
Walmsley House Sch MK40 38 D2
Walnut Acre LU5 105 F6
Walnut Cl
Biggleswade SG18 66 F8
Blunham MK44 41 D3
Bromham MK43 36 D1
Luton LU2 117 B4
Pavenham MK43 26 B3
Stotfold SG5 90 F6
Walnut Gr MK43 72 B3
Walnut Tree Rd SG5 99 D3
Walnut Way SG5 100 E4
Walnut Wlk MK42 49 F3
Walnuts The LU7 103 B2
Walsingham Cl LU2 116 D7
Waltham Cl MK41 38 F5
Waltham Ct LU2 117 C3
Waltham Dr MK42 50 D3
Walton Cl SG17 77 E3
Wandon Cl LU2 117 C4
Wansbeck Rd MK41 38 C5
Wantage Pl NN29 7 B8
Wantage Rd NN29 7 B8
Warden Abbey MK41 39 B1
Warden Ct 5 LU1 123 E8
Warden Hill SG19 43 C3
Warden Hill Cl LU2 116 C8
Warden Hill Gdns LU2 116 C8
Warden Hill Inf Sch LU3 116 C7
Warden Hill Jun Sch LU3 116 C7
Warden Hill Rd LU2 116 C8
Warden Rd SG18 65 D7
Wardhedges Rd MK45 85 E4
Wardown Cres LU2 116 E2
Wardown Ct LU3 116 D2
Ware Rd PE19 22 E6
Waresley Rd SG19 44 D7
Warkworth Cl SG19 54 C8
Warminster Cl LU2 117 F1
Warneford Way LU7 111 C5
Warren Cl
Biggleswade SG18 67 A7
Irchester NN29 7 C7
Letchworth SG6 101 D7
Toddington LU5 105 F7
Warren Dr The LU1 124 C1
Warren Rd Ampthill MK45 84 F7
Luton LU1 122 F8
Warren The MK41 37 E5
Warton Gn LU2 117 E2
Warwick Ave MK40 38 A1
Warwick Cl MK45 84 D1
Warwick Ct Luton LU4 123 B8
St Neots PE19 22 C3
Warwick Ho MK40 38 A2
Warwick Rd E LU4 123 B8
Warwick Rd W LU4 123 B8
Washbank Rd PE19 22 E4
Washbrook Cl MK45 97 C1
Washburn Cl MK41 38 D6
Washingleys MK43 59 C2
Washington Ave SG17 76 F2
Water End Cople MK44 52 B4
Workhouse End MK41 40 A4
Wrestlingworth SG19 57 B3
Water End La LU4 106 E2
Water End Rd MK45 85 F7
Water La Chelveston NN9 3 B8
Flitwick MK45 85 A2
Hitchin SG5 100 F1
Kempston MK42 49 C3
Leighton Buzzard LU7 110 F7
Waterborne Wlk 7 LU7 111 A7
Waterdell LU7 111 C7
Waterloo Cl MK45 84 E4
Waterloo Dr PE19 22 F3
Waterloo La SG5 100 A6
Waterloo Rd
Bedford MK40 50 D8
Leighton Buzzard LU7 110 E6
Waterlow Chapel 5 LU6 114 A1
Waterlow Rd LU6 114 A1
Watermead Rd LU3 115 F6
Waters End SG5 90 E6
Waterside LU6 119 F4
Waterslade Gn LU3 116 B6
Watery La AL3 129 E3
Watkin Wlk SG18 66 F7
Watling Ct
Dunstable LU6 114 A2
1 Houghton Regis LU5 114 B4
Watling Lower Sch LU6 121 C7
Watling Pl LU5 114 B4
Watling St LU6 113 E4
Watson Rd MK45 62 C6
Waulud Prim Sch LU3 115 E7
Wauluds Bank Dr LU3 115 E7
Wavell Cl MK43 61 D1
Wavendon Ho MK17 81 A8
Wavendon House Dr MK17 81 B8
Wavendon Rd MK17 70 C2
Waveney Ave MK41 38 D5
Waveney Rd AL5 131 C3
Waverly Ave SG19 42 B1
Waverly Pre-Prep Sch MK45 84 E3
Wayside LU6 121 D5
Wear The MK41 38 C7
Weatherby LU6 120 E8
Weatherby Rd LU4 115 D2
Weathercock Cl MK17 81 B5
Weathercock La MK17 81 C4
Weatherfield Sch LU6 113 E1
Weaver Cl MK41 38 D6
Weavers Gn SG19 42 C2
Weavers La MK43 26 C4
Weavers Orch SG15 90 A4
Webber Cl SG17 77 D3
Webbs Cl MK43 36 F2
Wedgewood Rd LU4 114 F4
Wedgwood Rd MK41 38 B3
Weedon Cl SG16 89 C5
Welbeck Gdns MK41 38 F5
Welbeck Rd 3 LU2 123 E8
Welbourne Gdns MK42 50 F5
Welbury Ave LU3 116 C7
Weldon Cl LU2 117 E1
Well Head Rd LU6 120 C6
Well La LU7 110 A1
Welland Ct Bedford MK41 38 D5
St Neots PE19 22 C4
Wellfield Ave LU3 115 C8
Wellgate Rd LU4 115 D2
Wellhouse Cl LU1 123 A7
Wellingham Ave SG5 100 D1
Wellington Ct 3 LU1 123 D8
Wellington Dr SG17 76 F3
Wellington Ho LU7 103 A4
Wellington Rd MK42 50 F2
Wellington St
Bedford MK40 38 B1
Luton LU1 123 D7
Wellington Terr LU5 121 C8
Wellpond Cl MK44 16 D3
Wells Cl Harpenden AL5 130 E4
Kempston MK42 49 E6
Wells Ct 1 LU7 111 A7
Wells Rd MK44 10 F2
Wellsfield MK44 41 E3
Weltmore Rd LU3 115 F6
Wendover Cl AL5 131 D1
Wendover Ct MK41 38 F1
Wendover Dr MK41 39 A1
Wendover Way LU2 116 F3
Wenlock CE Jun Sch LU2 124 B8
Wenlock Rd MK42 49 C3
Wenlock St LU2 123 E8
Wensleydale LU2 116 E1
Wentworth Ave LU4 115 C6
Wentworth Cl LU5 105 F7
Wentworth Ct LU5 95 F1
Wentworth Dr
Bedford MK41 38 F5
Leighton Buzzard LU7 111 A8
Wentworth Gdns LU5 106 A6
Werth Dr MK17 81 B2
Wesley Cl SG15 90 A4
Wesley Rd Markyate AL3 128 E5
Sandy SG19 42 C1
West Arc 13 MK40 50 B8
West Cl SG4 101 B1
West Ct Bedford MK41 39 A2
Leighton Buzzard LU7 110 F7
West Dene HP2 132 F8
West Dr SG15 90 B4
West End Elstow MK42 50 B3
Stevington MK43 36 A8
West End La SG19 56 A8
West End Rd
Kempston MK43 48 D5
Silsoe MK45 86 B3
West Gr MK40 49 F8
West Hill
Aspley Guise MK17 81 D4
Dunstable LU6 121 C5
West Hill Rd LU1 123 E5
West La SG5 99 D5
West Lodge Cotts LU2 117 D5
West Par LU6 121 A8
West Rd Gamlingay SG19 44 C4
Sandy SG19 54 B8
Wharley End MK43 58 D2
Woburn Sands MK17 81 B5
West St Dunstable LU6 121 A8
Leighton Buzzard LU7 110 F7
Lilley LU2 109 D1
St Neots PE19 22 E5
West View Beeston SG19 54 B5
Langford SG18 78 F6
Letchworth SG6 101 E4
Letchworth SG6 101 E5
West Way
Harpenden AL5 131 C2
Moggerhanger MK44 53 C7
West Wlk SG18 67 B7
Westbourne Rd
Bedford MK40 49 F7
Luton LU4 116 B1
Westbury Cl LU5 114 B3
Westbury Ct
Ampthill MK45 84 F8
Bedford MK41 38 C5
Westbury Gdns LU2 116 E3
Westbury Pl SG6 101 E5
Westbury Prim Sch SG6 101 E5
Westdale Wlk MK42 49 F4
Westdown Gdns LU6 120 F7
Westerdale LU4 115 B5
Western Ave SG16 89 B3
Western Cl SG6 90 E1
Western Rd LU1 123 D6
Western St MK40 50 B8
Western Way
Dunstable LU6 114 E1
Letchworth SG6 90 E1
Sandy SG19 54 B8
Westfield Ave AL5 131 A3
Westfield Dr AL5 131 B4
Westfield Gdns SG19 54 B8
Westfield Mid Sch MK40 49 E8
Westfield Pl AL5 131 B4
Westfield Rd
Bedford MK40 49 F8
Dunstable LU6 113 F1
Harpenden AL5 131 B4
Henlow SG16 78 C1
Oakley MK43 36 E8
Wyboston MK44 31 F8
Westgate Ct LU6 121 A8
Westholme SG6 101 F8
Westlecote Gdns LU2 116 D4
Westmill La Hitchin SG5 100 C2
Ickleford SG5 100 C3
Westmill Lawns SG5 100 D1
Westmill Rd SG5 100 D1
Westminster Gdns
Houghton Regis LU5 114 D6
Kempston MK42 49 E5
Westmorland Ave LU3 115 F5
Weston Ave LU7 111 C6
Weston Ct PE19 22 C4
Westoning Lower Sch MK45 95 E6
Westoning Rd
Greenfield MK45 85 B1
Harlington LU5 95 E3
Westoria Ct MK45 95 E5
Westrope Way MK41 38 D7
Westside
Leighton Buzzard LU7 110 F7
Leighton Buzzard LU7 111 A7
Westway LU2 117 C4
Westwood Cl MK42 51 A2
Wetherne Link LU4 115 C5
Wexham Cl LU3 115 E8
Weybourne Cl AL5 131 D2
Weybourne Dr LU2 116 C7
Wharf Mews SG18 66 F6
Wharfdale 7 LU4 115 C5
Wharfe The MK41 38 C6
Wheat Hill SG6 101 F8
Wheatfield Cl LU7 111 D7
Wheatfield Ct LU4 114 E4
Wheatfield Rd LU4 114 E4
Wheathouse Cl MK41 38 F4
Wheatlands Cl MK45 85 E8
Wheatsheaf Rd PE19 22 C3
Wheel Wright Cl SG5 87 F1
Whinnett's Way MK45 85 E1
Whipperley Ct LU1 123 C5
Whipperley Inf Sch LU1 123 A6
Whipperley Ring LU1 123 A6
Whipperley Way LU1 123 C5
Whipsnade Rd LU6 120 F7
Whipsnade Tree Cathedral★ LU6 120 F1
Whipsnade Wild Animal Pk★ LU6 126 E7
Whistler Rd PE19 22 C5
Whiston Cres SG17 78 B3
Whitbread Ave MK42 50 A6
Whitby Rd LU3 116 C1
Whitby Way MK42 50 C3
White Beam Cl MK42 49 F2
White Crofts SG5 90 F6
White Hill Rd MK45 97 C3
White Ho PE19 22 C4
White Horse Cl LU7 104 E2
White Horse Ct LU7 111 A7
White Lion Ret Pk LU5 114 C1
White Lodge Cl MK42 49 C3
Whitechurch Cl LU2 117 D2
Whitecroft Rd LU2 124 A8
Whitefield Ave LU3 115 C7
Whitefield Inf Sch LU3 115 E8
Whitefield Jun Sch LU3 115 E8
Whitefriars NN10 7 F8
Whitefriars Jun & Inf Schs NN10 7 F8
Whitehall MK43 72 B2
Whitehall Wlk PE19 22 F4
Whitehaven LU3 107 F1
Whitehicks SG6 91 A1
Whitehill Ave LU1 123 D5
Whitehorse St SG7 91 F1
Whitehorse Vale LU3 107 F1
Whitehouse Cl LU5 114 B4
Whitehurst Ave SG5 100 F1
Whiteman Cl SG18 78 F5
Whitethorn Way LU1 123 A6
Whitewaybottom La SG4 125 F5
Whitings MK40 49 B6
Whitings Cl AL5 131 D4
Whitley Gn LU2 117 D2
Whitley Rd MK42 51 A3
Whittingham Cl LU2 117 F1
Whittingstall Ave MK42 50 A4
Whittle Cl SG16 89 B4
Whitwell Cl LU3 116 B8
Whitworth Ct
Kempston MK42 49 E4
Shefford SG17 77 C3
Whitworth Jones Ave SG16 89 C5
Whitworth Way MK45 62 F3
Wick Hill LU6 127 F8
Wickets The LU2 116 E1
Wickmere Cl LU2 116 C7
Wickstead Ave LU4 115 E4
Widecombe Cl MK40 38 E2
Wigmore La LU2 117 D2
Wigmore Park Ctr LU2 117 E1
Wigmore Pl LU2 117 E1
Wigmore Prim Sch LU2 117 E2
Wigram Cl MK42 50 B4
Wilbury Cl SG6 101 C7
Wilbury Dr LU5 114 E3
Wilbury Hills Rd SG6 101 C7
Wilbury Jun Sch SG6 101 D6
Wilbury Rd SG6 101 E8
Wilbury Way SG4 101 A3
Wild Cherry Dr LU1 123 D5
Wildber Cl PE19 22 F4
Wilden CE Lower Sch MK44 29 F3
Wilden Rd
Colmworth MK44 30 A6
Renhold MK41 39 C7
Wildflower Way MK42 50 F4
Wilhamstead Lower Sch MK45 62 F4
Wilkinson Cl PE19 22 B3
Willenhall Cl LU3 116 A7
William Austin Inf Sch LU3 116 C4
William Austin Jun Sch LU3 116 C4
William Dr PE19 22 F1
William St Luton LU2 116 E1
Markyate AL3 128 E5
William Sutton Ct
Bedford MK40 50 A8
Luton LU2 117 B5
Williams Way MK45 84 D4
Williamson Ct MK42 49 C2
Williamson Rd MK42 49 D2
Williamson St 1 LU1 123 E7
Willian Rd SG4,SG6 101 E1
Willington Lower Sch MK44 40 C1
Willington Rd MK44 52 A6
Williton Rd LU2 117 C2
Willmers Cl MK41 38 E4
Willoughby Cl
Dunstable LU6 121 C7
Great Barford MK44 40 F5
Willoughby Rd AL5 131 B4
Willow Bank Wlk LU7 111 C8
Willow Cl Bromham MK43 36 F3
St Neots PE19 22 F3
Willow Ct LU3 115 E5
Willow Herb Cl NN10 8 C7
Willow Ho LU7 110 E7
Willow Rd Bedford MK42 50 D5
Potton SG19 56 A7
Shefford SG17 77 D2
Willow Rise SG19 54 D6
Willow Springs MK43 71 A8
Willow Tree Way SG5 100 F2
Willow Views 1 PE19 22 E5
Willow Way Ampthill MK45 84 F7
Flitwick MK45 84 F1
Harpenden AL5 131 C4
Houghton Regis LU5 114 D6
Luton LU3 115 E5
Toddington LU5 105 F5
Willowfield Lower Sch LU1 122 F4
Willowgate Trad Est LU3 115 A8
Willows La HP1 132 F1
Willows The
Edlesborough LU6 119 F3
Flitwick MK45 84 E3
Leighton Buzzard LU7 111 B6
Wootton MK43 61 A8
Willsheres Rd SG18 67 A7
Wilman Ct SG18 78 E5
Wilsden Ave LU1 123 C6
Wilshere Cres SG4 101 D1
Wilson Ct MK45 62 F4
Wilstead Hill MK45 74 F7
Wilstead Ind Est MK45 62 C6
Wilstead Rd Elstow MK42 50 C2
Elstow MK42 62 C8
Wilstead MK45 63 C5
Wilton Rd SG5 100 E1
Wimborne Rd LU1 123 C8
Wimple Rd LU4 115 A2
Winch St LU2 116 E1
Winchester Gdns LU3 107 E1
Winchester Rd
Bedford MK42 50 F4
Sandy SG19 54 C8
Winchfield LU1 122 E4
Windermere Cl
Dunstable LU6 121 B7
Flitwick MK45 84 E2
Windermere Cres LU3 115 F5
Windermere Dr SG18 67 A4
Windermere Gdns LU7 110 C7
Windermere The MK42 49 D3
Windmill Cl MK41 39 B3
Windmill Ct MK44 16 D3
Windmill Hill MK40 37 D2
Windmill Path 5 LU7 111 A7
Windmill Rd
Flamstead AL3 129 B6
Flitwick MK45 84 D4
Luton LU1 123 F6
Windmill Row 5 PE19 22 E5
Windmill Way MK43 59 C3
Windrush Ave MK41 38 C5
Windrush Cl MK45 84 D2
Windsor Ave LU7 110 F7
Windsor Cl Flitwick MK45 84 D1
St Neots PE19 22 F2
Windsor Ct 10 LU1 123 D6
Windsor Dr LU5 114 D4
Windsor Gdns MK40 38 D2
Windsor Par MK45 97 C4
Windsor Pl LU5 114 D5

Windsor Rd
Barton-le-C MK45 ....**97** C4
Bedford MK42 ....**50** D4
Windsor St LU1 ....**123** D6
Windsor Way
Langford SG18 ....**78** F6
Sandy SG19 ....**54** C7
Windsor Wlk 7 LU1 ...**123** D6
Winfield St LU6 ....**114** B1
Wing Rd Ascott LU7 .....**110** B4
Leighton Buzzard LU7 ...**110** D5
Wingate Ct LU4 ....**115** F2
Wingate Dr MK45 ......**85** A8
Wingate Rd
Dunstable LU5 ....**114** F1
Harlington LU5 ....**95** F2
Luton LU4 ....**115** F2
Wingfield Ave MK45 ....**74** C1
Wingfield Cl MK40 ......**49** E7
Wingfield Ct MK45 ......**84** F8
Wingfield Dr SG19 ......**56** A8
Wingfield Rd
Bromham MK43 ....**36** F4
Tebworth LU7 ....**105** C2
Winhills Prim Sch PE19 ..**22** F4
Winifred Rd MK40 ....**49** F8
Winkfield Cl LU4 ....**115** B1
Winsdon Ct 1 LU1 .....**123** D6
Winsdon Rd LU1 ....**123** D6
Winslow Cl LU3 ....**116** C4
Winston Cl LU7 ....**103** A1
Winston Cres SG18 ......**67** A7
Winton Cl LU2 ....**116** D6
Wintringham Rd 7 PE19 ..**22** F5
Wiseman Cl NN10 ....**8** B7
Wisteria Cl NN10 ....**8** B7
Wistow Ct PE19 ....**22** C6
Wistow Rd LU3 ....**116** A6
Witham Cl MK41 ....**38** D7
Withy Cl LU4 ....**115** B4
Withybrook MK45 ....**84** E3
Witter Ave SG5 ....**100** E4
Wivelsfield LU6 ....**119** E6
Wiveton Cl LU2 ....**116** D7
Woburn Abbey★ MK17 ..**93** D6
Woburn Cl MK45 ....**84** C1
Woburn Ct
Kempston MK42 ....**49** D3
Leighton Buzzard LU7 ...**110** E6
Luton LU4 ....**115** D5

Woburn La MK17 ....**81** E4
Woburn Lower Sch MK17 **92** F7
Woburn Pl LU7 ....**103** A1
Woburn Rd Bedford MK40 **.50** A8
Heath & Reach LU7 .....**103** B7
Hockliffe LU7 ....**104** E3
Kempston MK42 ....**49** D2
Kempston MK43 ....**61** C8
Marston Moretaine MK43 .**72** C7
Millbrook MK45 ....**73** B1
Woburn Sands MK17 .....**81** C1
Woburn Road Ind Est
MK42 ....**49** D1
Woburn Safari Pk★
MK17,MK43 ....**82** D1
Woburn Sands Sta MK17 .**81** A5
Woburn St MK45 ....**73** D1
Wodecroft Rd LU3 .....**116** B6
Wolfsburg Ct 4 LU4 ...**115** C5
Wollaston Rd NN29 ......**.7** A8
Wolseley Bsns Pk MK42 .**49** D1
Wolseley Ct MK42 ......**49** E1
Wolseley Rd MK42 ......**49** E1
Wolston Cl LU1 ....**123** C7
Wood Cl Biddenham MK40 .**37** C1
Kensworth LU6 ....**121** E1
Wood End Hill AL5 .....**130** D4
Wood End JM Sch AL5 .**130** D3
Wood End La MK43 .....**48** F2
Wood End Rd
Cranfield MK43 ....**71** B7
Harpenden AL5 ....**130** D3
Kempston MK43 ....**48** D2
Wood Green Cl LU2 ....**117** B5
Wood Green Rd LU2 ...**117** C5
Wood La
Aspley Guise MK17 ....**81** D4
Cotton End MK45 ....**63** D7
Renhold MK41 ....**39** E6
Willington MK44 ....**52** D7
Wood Rd MK43 ....**24** F7
Wood St Dunstable LU6 .**121** C8
Luton LU1 ....**123** F6
Woburn Sands MK17 .....**81** B4
Wood The LU7 ....**111** A8
Woodbridge Cl LU4 ....**115** E4
Woodbury Hill LU2 .....**116** E2
Woodcock Cl SG19 .....**42** B2
Woodcock Rd LU1 .....**123** A7
Woodcock Wlk MK45 ...**84** D1

Woodcote MK41 ....**39** A3
Woodend La MK44 .....**31** C2
Woodfield Gate LU5 ...**121** E6
Woodfield La MK41 .....**40** A6
Woodford Rd LU5 .....**114** E1
Woodhurst SG6 ....**101** F8
Woodland Ave
Leighton Buzzard LU7 ...**102** F2
Luton LU3 ....**116** B2
Woodland Cl
Heath & Reach LU7 .....**103** A5
Potton SG19 ....**56** A8
Woodland Dr MK43 .....**36** F4
Woodland Mid Sch MK45 **84** D2
Woodland Rise LU6 ....**127** B7
Woodland Way MK17 ...**81** B4
Woodlands Bedford MK41 .**38** B6
Caddington LU1 ....**122** E3
Harpenden AL5 ....**130** E3
Tebworth LU7 ....**105** C2
Woodlands Ave LU5 ....**114** C4
Woodlands Cl MK44 .....**52** A5
Woodlands Rd LU3 .....**116** A3
Woodlands The SG18 ....**66** C3
Woodman Cl LU7 ......**111** B7
Woodmer Cl SG5 ....**87** E2
Woodmere Bedford MK41 .**38** F3
Luton LU3 ....**108** A1
Woodpecker Way SG19 ..**42** B2
Woodside
Aspley Guise MK17 ....**81** D3
Eaton Bray LU6 ....**119** E6
Woodside Farm & Wildfowl
Pk★ LU1 ....**129** A8
Woodside Ind Est LU5 ..**114** D3
Woodside Mid Sch MK41 **39** B4
Woodside Park Ind Est
LU5 ....**114** C3
Woodside Rd LU1 .....**123** B3
Woodside Way LU7 ...**110** D6
Woodstock Rd MK40 ....**49** F7
Woodville Dr MK40 .....**49** B6
Woolfield SG19 ....**54** D6
Woolgrove Ct SG4 .....**101** B1
Woolgrove Rd SG4 ....**101** B1
Woolpack Cl LU6 ......**121** C7
Wooton Field SG19 .....**44** D4
Wootton Cl LU3 ....**116** B7
Wootton Lower Sch
MK43 ....**60** F7

Wootton Rd MK43 ....**49** A1
Wootton Upper Sch
MK43 ....**60** E7
Worboys Ct SG8 ....**69** F5
Worcester Rd MK42 .....**50** F4
Wordsworth Ave PE19 ..**22** D5
Wordsworth Cl SG18 ...**66** C8
Wordsworth Ct MK40 ...**37** E2
Wordsworth Rd
Harpenden AL5 ....**131** A3
Luton LU4 ....**115** A2
Worthington Rd LU6 ...**120** F8
Wrayfields SG5 ....**91** B8
Wraysbury Cl LU4 .....**115** D3
Wren Cl Flitwick MK45 ...**84** D1
Luton LU2 ....**117** C6
Wren Wlk LU6 ....**119** E4
Wrest Park Gdns★ MK45 **86** E3
Wrestlingworth CE Lower
Sch SG19 ....**57** B3
Wrestlingworth Rd SG19 **56** C6
Wroxham Way
Bedford MK40 ....**49** D7
Harpenden AL5 ....**131** D5
Wulwards Cl LU1 ......**123** B6
Wulwards Ct LU1 ......**123** B6
Wyatt Cl SG5 ....**100** D4
Wyatt Rd MK42 ....**49** D3
Wyboston Ct PE19 ......**22** C4
Wyboston L Pk★ MK44 ..**32** C7
Wybridge MK44 ....**12** B1
Wybridge Cl MK44 ......**12** B2
Wychwood Ave LU2 ...**116** E3
Wychwood Rd MK41 .....**39** B4
Wycklond Cl SG5 ....**90** E6
Wycliffe Cl LU3 ....**116** C6
Wycombe Way LU3 ....**116** C8
Wye Cl MK41 ....**38** D5
Wyken Cl LU3 ....**116** A7
Wymington Rd
Podington NN29 ....**.7** E3
Rushden NN10 ....**.8** B8
Wynchwood La SG17 ....**77** B2
Wynd The SG6 ....**101** F6
Wyndham Rd LU4 ......**115** C2
Wyngates LU7 ....**110** E5
Wynnefield Wlk SG19 ...**54** C8
Wysells Ct SG6 ....**101** D7
Wyton Ct SG17 ....**76** F2

Wyvern Cl LU4 ....**115** E3

Y

Yardley Ct 14 AL5 .....**131** B1
Yarrow Cl NN10 ....**.8** C7
Yately Cl LU2 ....**116** D7
Yelnow La MK44 ....**16** A3
Yeomans Ave AL5 .....**130** D3
Yeomans Gate MK44 ...**51** D4
Yeovil Ct LU2 ....**117** B2
Yeovil Rd LU2 ....**117** B2
Yew St LU5 ....**114** D7
Yew Tree Cl
Eaton Bray LU6 ....**119** F5
Silsoe MK45 ....**86** C3
Yew Tree Ct 3 LU7 ....**111** A7
Yew Tree Wlk SG17 .....**78** B2
York Cl Barton-le-C MK45 .**97** D4
Biggleswade SG18 ....**67** B5
York Ct LU7 ....**110** F7
York Rd SG5 ....**100** E1
York St Bedford MK40 ...**50** E8
Luton LU2 ....**123** F8
Young Ind Est LU7 .....**111** D6

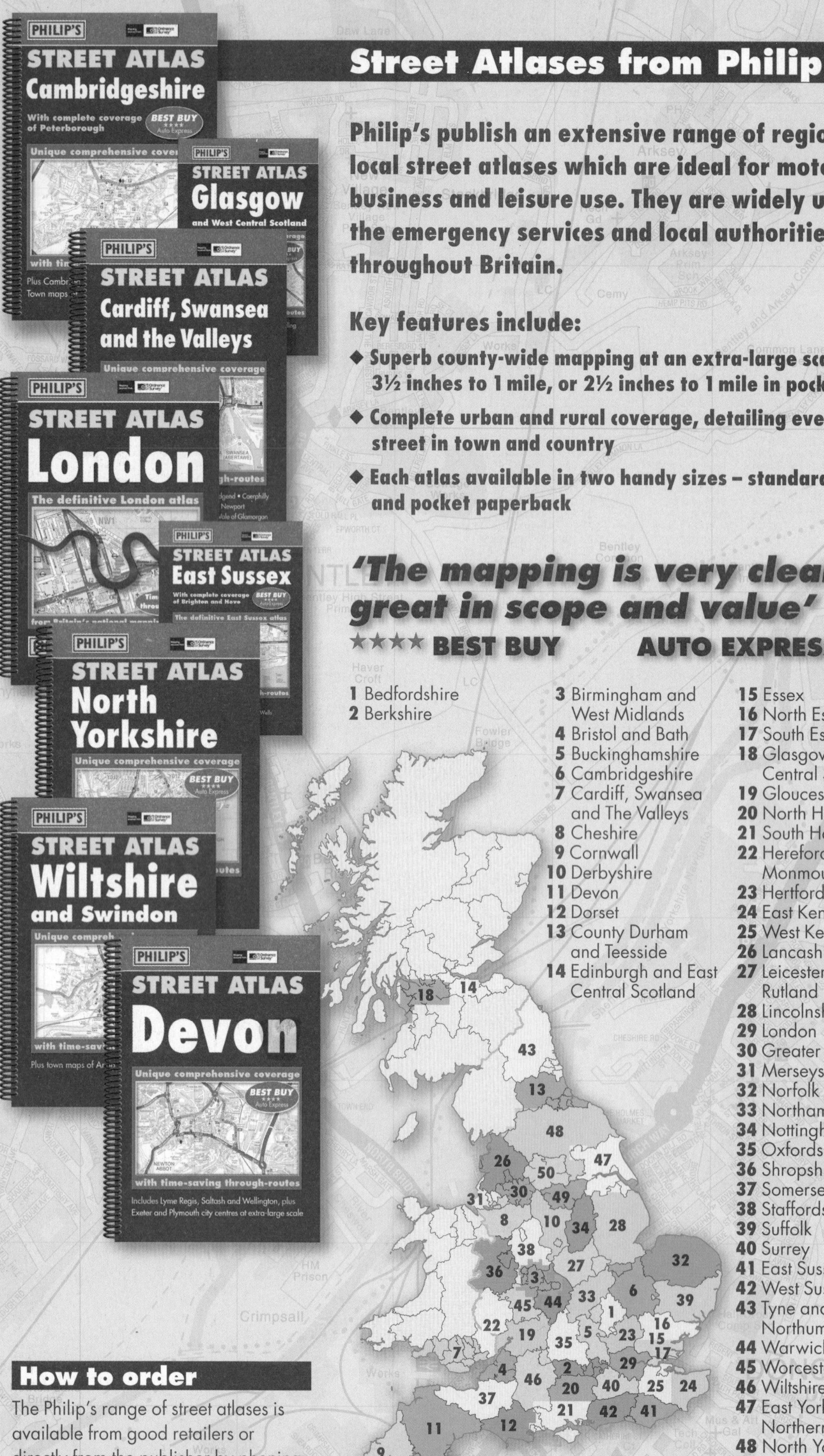